JURISPRUDENCE

A Book of Readings

Selected & Edited

by

JOHN WARWICK MONTGOMERY
M. Phil. (Essex), Ph.D. (Chicago), D. Théol. (Strasbourg)
of the Middle Temple and Lincoln's Inn, Barrister-at-Law
Member of the Bar of the Supreme Court of the United States

Principal Lecturer in Law
Luton College of Higher Education
England

INTERNATIONAL SCHOLARLY PUBLISHERS

I.S.P. 2, rue de Rome
67000 Strasbourg, France I.S.P.

Second Printing, 1980
Third Printing, 1987
Fourth Printing (with corrections), 1992

Printed in Hungary

For

W. HOWARD HOFFMAN, M. D.

The vision is his . . .
and "where there is no vision
the people perish: but he
that keepeth the law, happy is he."

(Proverbs 29:18)

CONTENTS

CONTENTS

PREFACE

The selections comprising this Reader appear without editorial notes or commentary. In the rable casebook tradition, the student is expected to derive inductively a perspective whose impact be all the more powerful for having been discovered rather than didactically imposed.

But a word concerning the overall aim of the book is warranted at the outset. The selections have chosen to introduce first-year law students to the great issues of jurisprudence, in line with the viction of the editor and of his law faculty that the meaning and significance of the law ought to nd all study of legal particulars. Only thus can legal education rise above the level of the iisticated trade school, law graduates become true professionals rather than mere technicians, and profession itself regain the stature it held when the word attorney made one think of the Inns of rt rather than Watergate.

Some years ago, as chairman of the Department of History of a Canadian university, the editor pared a volume introducing first-year college students to the philosophy of history.[1] The aims of t work were similar to those motivating the present production: to deal with larger issues from the y onset of study in the discipline itself. There I quoted George Williams' provocative book, *Some of Best Friends Are Professors,* and his comment applies as fully to the field of law as it does to torical study:

> Courses in the History Department are, as a rule, the university's most perfect type of the fact-loaded, idea-absent, academic exercise. Here the wood is everywhere lost among the trees; and it is the rare professor who can show the student any thing but a close-clustered thicket of details. . . . Cannot history be taught so as to have a meaningful relationship to law, literature, philosophy, religion, art, architecture; and a meaningful relationship to the fundamental motives, habits, aspirations, psychological peculiarities, self-deceptions, hypocrisies, and grandeurs of human nature; and a meaningful relationship to the present?[2]

A recognition of the need to reintroduce jurisprudence as the vital *point de départ* for all legal truction is steadily gaining ground. The most recent number of the *Journal of Legal Education* ries a stimulating paper by Professor Brendan F. Brown, editor of the widely used *Natural Law*

The Shape of the Past (Ann Arbor, Michigan: Edwards Brothers, 1963).

George Williams, *Some of My Best Friends Are Professors: A Critical Commentary on Higher Education* (New York and London: Abelard-Schuman, 1958), p. 226.

Reader,[3] on the theme, "Recent Trends in United States Legal Education." Trend numbe according to Brown: "Legal education is moving in the direction of the jurisprudential." His re are worth pondering here, since they well express the *raison d'être* of the present anthology:

> By the jurisprudentializing of legal education, I mean placing more emphasis upon the concept of *jus* law, as distinguished from that of law as a body of precepts and rules, deriving their authority from the will of a political sovereign, and detached from such orders as the historical, philosophical, and sociological. . . .
>
> In my opinion, the trend toward jurisprudential legal education is commendable. It is a return to the approach used in the first stage of legal education in the United States, characterized by the apprentice system. Then, the Anglo-American legal system was studied as a jurisprudential science made up of principles. Their application as an art was learned in the law office. The most influential text used was the *Commentaries* of Blackstone, originally delivered as lectures at All Souls College, Oxford, in the middle of the eighteenth century. Recognition of the jurisprudential nature of legal education in the first stage was evidenced by the fact that man-made law was presented as an implementation in some way of a higher law. This concept of the positive law was advocated by Blackstone in the first book of his *Commentaries* and dominated the whole work.
>
> But in the second stage of American legal education, beginning at the end of the nineteenth century, the jurisprudential approach to the study of law was abandoned. Law began to be studied merely as a body of legalistic precepts or a melange of abstractions, separated from morals and the idea of means-ends purpose for improving the common good of society. Lawyers were to be concerned only with positive or man-made law. The legal order had no connection with other orders, such as the social. This was the point of view introduced into the Harvard Law School by Dean Langdell. . . .
>
> I commend the present movement toward more jurisprudential legal education. . . . It enhances the learning of the legal profession. It prepares lawyers to perform services beyond the scope of their narrow legal practice. It presents a true picture of the Anglo-American legal system and the forces which shaped it. It communicates the teleological purpose of the legal order to achieve justice both individually and socially. . . .
>
> Certainly, professional responsibility can have no fixed genuine meaning if it is based only on manners or customs, or on an activity or skill constituting the essence of clinical legal education, or a vague humanitarianism.
>
> As the legal order is further detached from the objective moral order, witness the "shocker" of the abortion decision, and as more and more professional irresponsibility is found to exist in the high places of state and society, witness the events of recent months, I predict that public opinion will demand a new approach to legal education . . . That approach . . .will consider the graduation of ministers of justice, whatever their future life work may be, as the most important objective of legal education.[4]

---

3. Brendan F. Brown (ed.), *The Natural Law Reader* ("Docket Series," 13; New York: Oceana, 1960).
4. Brendan F. Brown, "Recent Trends in United States Legal Education," 26 *Journal of Legal Education* 283.

a detailed comment on Brown's article, John E. Murray, Jr., editor of the *Journal of Legal ation,* rightly notes: "There can be little doubt that the modern law student begins to thirst for preciation of the nature of law in society even in his first year." Hopefully this selection of ngs will help to slake that thirst.

*   *   *

ly debt to the ancient and modern authors of the materials here anthologized is evident. In every an effort has been made to acknowledge the sources employed.

JOHN WARWICK MONTGOMERY

Church, Virginia,
eptember, 1974

PART ONE

THE NATURE OF LAW

A. What Is Law?

H. Auden, "Law Like Love" (from *The Collected Poetry of W. H. Auden).*

o Dialogues in English, between a Doctor of Divinity, and a Student in the Laws of England, Of the Grounds of the said Laws, and of Conscience (rev. ed.; London, 1709), pp. 1-14.*

F. Roemer [Ph.D., Prof. of Philosophy, Notre Dame], "Jurisprudence and Legal Institutions": *American Law and Procedure,* Lecture 51 (Chicago: LaSalle Extension University, 1953), pp. 3-38.

*"Before Blackstone began to deliver his lectures on the law in Oxford, and to publish them, the books available for students were few in number and poor in quality. The best of them was called by the summary title of *Doctor and Student,* but its full title is *A Dialogue between a Doctor of Divinity and a Student of the Laws of England.* It was published in Latin first, apparently, in 1523, its author being Christopher St. Germain, who was a member of the Inner Temple. It remained the leading textbook right down to the middle eighteenth century. What purports to be the eighteenth edition was published as recently as 1815."—A. Edward Newton, *Newton on Blackstone* (Philadelphia: University of Pennsylvania Press, 1937), p. 20.

W. H. Auden

:

LAW LIKE LOVE

Law, say the gardeners, is the sun,
Law is the one
All gardeners obey
Tomorrow, yesterday, today.

Law is the wisdom of the old
The impotent grandfathers shrilly scold;
The grandchildren put out a treble tongue,
Law is the senses of the young.

Law, says the priest with a priestly look,
Expounding to an unpriestly people,
Law is the words in my priestly book,
Law is my pulpit and my steeple.

Law, says the judge as he looks down his nose,
Speaking clearly and most severely,
Law is as I've told you before,
Law is as you know I suppose,
Law is but let me explain it once more,
Law is The Law.

Yet law-abiding scholars write;
Law is neither wrong nor right,

Law is only crimes
Punished by places and by times,
Law is the clothes men wear
Anytime, anywhere,
Law is Good-morning and Good-night.

Others say, Law is our Fate;
Others say, Law is our State;
Others say, others say
Law is no more
Law has gone away.

And always the loud angry crowd
Very angry and very loud
Law is We,
And always the soft idiot softly Me.

If we, dear, know we know no more
Than they about the law,
If I no more than you
Know what we should and should not do
Except that all agree
Gladly or miserably
That the law is
And that all know this,
If therefore thinking it absurd
To identify Law with some other word,
Unlike so many men
I cannot say Law is again,
No more than they can we suppress
The universal wish to guess
Or slip out of our own position
Into an unconcerned condition.
Although I can at least confine
Your vanity and mine
To stating timidly
A timid similarity,
We shall boast anyway:
Like love I say.

Like love we don't know where or why
Like love we can't compel or fly
Like love we often weep
Like love we seldom keep.

TWO DIALOGUES IN ENGLISH,

Between

A Doctor of Divinity,

AND

A Student in the Laws of ENGLAND,

OF

The Grounds of the ſaid LAWS,

And of

CONSCIENCE.

Newly Reviſed and Re-printed.

LONDON,

Printed by the Aſſigns of *Richard* and *Edward Atkins* Eſquires. 1709.

THE FIRST DIALOGUE.

¶ *The Introduction.*

A Doctor of Divinity, that was of great acquaintance and familiarity with a Student in the Laws of *England*, said thus unto him; I have had great desire of long time to know whereupon the Law of *England* is grounded: But because the most part of the Law of *England* is written in the *French* Tongue, therefore I cannot, through mine own study, attain to the knowledge thereof; for in that Tongue I am nothing expert. And because I have found thee a faithful Friend to me in all my business, therefore I am bold to come to thee before any other, to know thy mind, what be the very Grounds of the Law of *England*, as thou thinkest.

Stud. That would ask a great leisure, and it is also above my cunning to do it: Nevertheless, that thou shalt not think that I would wilfully refuse to fulfil thy desire, I shall with good will do that in me is to satisfie thy mind. But I pray thee that thou wilt first shew me somewhat of other Laws that pertain most to this Matter, and that Doctors treat of,

A 2 how

how Laws have begun; and then I will gladly ſhew thee, as methinketh, what be the Grounds of the Law of *England*.

Doct. I will with good will do as thou ſayeſt. Wherefore thou ſhalt underſtand, that Doctors treat of four Laws, the which (as me ſeemeth) pertain moſt to this Matter. The firſt is the *Law Eternal*. The ſecond is the *Law of Nature* of Reaſonable Creatures, the which, as I have heard ſay, is called by them that be learned in the Law of *England*, the *Law of Reaſon*. The third is the *Law of God*. The fourth is the *Law of Man*. And therefore I will firſt treat of the *Law Eternal*.

CHAP. I.

Of the *Law Eternal*.

Like as there is in every Artificer a Reaſon of ſuch-like things as are to be made by his Craft: ſo likewiſe it behoveth that in every Governor there be Reaſon and a Foreſight in the governing of ſuch things as ſhall be ordered and done by him to them that he hath the Governance of. And foraſmuch as Almighty God is the Creator and Maker of all Creatures, to the which he is compared as a Workman to his Works, and is alſo the Governor of all Deeds and Movings that be found in any Creature: therefore as the reaſon of the Wiſdom of God (inaſmuch as Creatures be created by him) is the reaſon and foreſight of all crafts and works that have been or ſhall be; ſo the reaſon of the Wiſdom of God, moving all

all things by Wisdom made to a good end, obtaineth the name and reason of a Law, and that is called the Law Eternal

And this Law Eternal is called the first Law: and it is well called the first, for it was before all other Laws, and all other Laws be derived of it. Whereupon St. Augustine saith, in his 1 Book of Free Arbitrement, that in Temporal Laws nothing is righteous ne lawful, but that the People have derived to them out of the Law Eternal. Wherefore every Man hath right and title to have that he hath righteously, of the rightwise judgment of the first Reason, which is the Law Eternal.

Stud. But how may this Law Eternal be known? for, as the Apostle writeth in the second Chapter of his First Epistle to the Corinthians, Quæ sunt Dei nemo scit, nisi Spiritus Dei; that is to say, No Man knoweth what is in God but the Spirit of God: wherefore it seemeth that he openeth his mouth against Heaven, that attempteth to know it.

Doct. This Law Eternal no Man may know as it is in it self, but only blessed Souls that see God face to face. But Almighty God of his goodness sheweth of it as much to his Creatures as is necessary for them, for else God should bind his Creatures to a thing impossible: which may in no wise be thought in him. Therefore it is to be understood, that three manner of ways Almighty God maketh this Law Eternal known to his Creatures reasonable. First, by the light of Natural Reason; Secondly, by Heavenly Revelation; Thirdly, by the order of a Prince or any other secundary Governor that hath power to bind his Subjects to a Law.

A 2 And

And when the Law Eternal or the Will of God is known to his Creatures reasonable by the light of natural understanding or by the light of natural Reason, that is called the Law of Reason: and when it is shewed by heavenly Revelation in such manner as hereafter shall appear, then it is called the Law of God: and when it is shewed unto him by the order of a Prince, or of any other secundary Governor that hath a power to set a Law upon his Subjects, then it is called the Law of Man, though originally it be made of God. For Laws made by Man that hath received thereto power of God, be made by God. Therefore the said three Laws, that is to say, the Law of Reason, the Law of God, and the Law of Man, the which have several names after the manner as they be shewed to Man, be called in God one Law Eternal.

And this is the Law of which it is written Proverbiorum octavo, where it is said, Per me reges regnant, & Legum conditores justa discernunt; that is to say, By me Kings reign, and Makers of Laws discern the truth. And this sufficeth for this time for the Law Eternal.

CHAP. II.

¶ Of the *Law of Reason*, the which by Doctors is call'd the *Law of Nature* of reasonable Creatures.

FIrst it is to be understood, that the Law of Nature may be considered in two manners, that is to say, generally and specially. When it is considered generally, then it is referred to all Creatures, as well reasonable as unreasonable: for

for all unreasonable creatures live under a certain Rule to them given by Nature, necessary for them to the consideration of their being. But of this Law it is not our intent to treat at this time. The Law of Nature specially considered, which is also called the Law of Reason, pertaineth only to Creatures reasonable, that is, Man, which is created to the Image of God.

And this Law ought to be kept as well among Jews and Gentils, as among Christian Men: and this Law is alway good and righteous, stiring and inclining a Man to good, and abhorring evil. And as to the ordering of the deeds of Man, it is preferred before the Law of God and it is written in the Heart of every Man, teaching him what is to be done, and what is to be fled: and because it is written in the Heart, therefore it may not be put away, ne it is never changeable by no diversity of place, ne time: and therefore against this Law, Prescription, Statute nor Custom may not prevail: and if any be brought in against it, they be not Prescriptions, Statutes nor Customs, but things void and against Justice. And all other Laws, as well the Laws of God as to the Acts of Men, as other, be grounded thereupon.

Stud. Sith the Law of Reason is written in the Heart of every Man, as thou hast said before, teaching him what is to be done, and what is to be fled, and the which thou sayest may never be put out of their Heart, what needeth it then to have any other Law brought in to order the acts and deeds of the People?

A 4 Doct.

Doct. Though the Law of Reason may not be changed, nor wholly put away; nevertheless before the Law written, it was greatly lett and blinded by evil Customs, and by many Sins of the People, beside our Original Sin; insomuch that it might hardly be discerned what was righteous, and what unrighteous, and what was good, and what evil. Wherefore it is necessary, for the good order of the People, to have many things added to the Law of Reason, as well by the Church as by Secular Princes, according to the manners of the Country and of the People where such Additions should be exercised. And this Law of Reason differeth from the Law of God in two manners. For the Law of God is given by Revelation of God; and this Law is given by a natural light of Understanding. And also the Law of God ordereth a Man of it self, by a nigh way, to the Felicity that ever shall endure; and the Law of Reason ordereth a Man to the Felicity of this Life.

Stud. But what be the things that the Law of Reason teacheth to be done, and what to be fled? I pray thee shew me.

Doct. The Law of Reason teacheth, that good is to be loved, and evil is to be fled: also that thou shalt do to another, that thou wouldest another should do to thee; and that we may do nothing against truth; and that a Man must live peacefully with others: that Justice is to be done to every Man; and also, that wrong is not to be done to any Man; and that also a Trespasser is worthy to be punished; and such other. Of the which follow divers other secundary Commandments, the which be as necessary Conclusions

ons derived of the first. As of that Commandment, that good is to be beloved; it followeth, that a Man shall love his Benefactor: for a Benefactor, in that he is a Benefactor, includeth in him a reason of Goodness, for else he ought not to be called a Benefactor, that is to say, a good Doer, but an evil Doer. And so in that he is a Benefactor, he is to be beloved in all times, and in all places. And this Law also suffereth many things to be done: as that it is lawful to put away Force with Force; and that it is lawful for every Man to defend himself and his goods against an unlawful Power. And this Law runneth with every Man's Law, and also with the Law of God, as to the deeds of Man, and must be always kept and observed, and shall alway declare what ought to follow upon the general Rules of the Law of Man, and shall restrain them if they be any thing contrary unto it.

And here it is to be understood, that after some Men, the Law whereby all things were in common, was never of the Law of Reason, but only in the time of extreme necessity. For they say, that the Law of Reason may not be changed; but they say, it is evident, that the Law whereby all things should be in common, is changed: wherefore they conclude, that was never the Law of Reason.

CHAP.

CHAP. III.

¶ Of the *Law of God.*

THE Law of God is a certain Law given by Revelation to a Reasonable Creature, shewing him the Will of God, willing that Creatures reasonable be bound to do a thing, or not to do it, for obtaining of the Felicity Eternal. And it is said, for the obtaining of the Felicity Eternal, to exclude the Laws shewed by revelation of God for the Political Rule of the People, the which be called Judicials. For a Law is not properly called the Law of God, because it was shewed by revelation of God, but also because it directed a Man by the nearest way to the Felicity Eternal, as been the Laws of the Old Testament, that been called Morals, and the Laws of the Evangelists, the which were shewed in much more excellent manner than the Law of the Old Testament was: for that was shewed by the mediation of an Angel; but the Law of the Evangelists was shewed by the mediation of our Lord Jesus Christ, God and Man. And the Law of God is alway righteous and just, for it is made and given after the Will of God. And therefore all acts and deeds of Man be called righteous and just, when they be done according to the Law of God, and be conformable to it. Also sometime a Law made by Man, is called the Law of God. As when a Law taketh his principal ground upon the Law of God, and is made for the declaration or conservation of the Faith,

Faith, and to put away Heresies, as divers Laws Canon, and also divers Laws made by the common people, sometime do; the which therefore are rather to be called the Law of God, than the Law of Man. Yet neverthe-less all the Laws Canon be not the Laws of God: for many of them be made only for the Political rule and conservation of the People. Whereupon John Gerson, in the Treatise of the Spiritual life of the Soul, the second Lesson, and the third Corolary, saith thus; All the Canons of Bishops nor their Decrees be not the Law of God: for many of them be made only for the Political conservation of the People. And if any Man will say, Be not all the goods of the Church Spiritual, for they belong unto the Spirituality, and lead to the Spirituality? We answer, That in the whole Political conservation of the People there be some specially deputed and dedicated to the service of God, the which most specially (as by an excellency) are called Spiritual Men, as Religious Men are. And other, though they walk in the way of God, yet nevertheless, because their Office is most specially to be occupied about such things as pertain to the Common-wealth and to the good order of the People, they be therefore called Secular-men or Lay-men. Nevertheless, the Goods of the first may no more be called Spiritual than the Goods of the other, for they be things mere Temporal, and keeping the body, as they do in the other. And by like reason, Laws made for the Political order of the Church be called many times Spiritual, or the Laws of God; nevertheless it it is but unproperly: and other be called Civil, or the Laws of Man. And in this point many be oft-times deceived, and also deceive other, the which judge the things to be spiritual, the which all Men know be things temporal and carnal. These be the words of John Gerson in the place alledged before. Farthermore, beside the Law of Reason and the Law of Man, it was necessary to have the Law of God, for four reasons.

The first, because Man is ordained to the end of the eternal Felicity, the which exceedeth the proportion and faculty of Mans power. Therefore it was necessary that beside the Law of Reason and the Law of Man, he should be directed to his end by a Law of God.

Secondly, forasmuch as for the uncertainty of Mans judgment, specially of things peculiar and seldom falling, it happened oft-times to follow divers Judgments of divers Men, and diversities of Laws; therefore, to the intent that a Man without any doubt may know what he should do, and what he should not do, it was necessary that he should be directed in all his deeds by a Law heavenly given by God, the which is so apparent, that no Man may swerve from it, as is the Law of God.

Thirdly, Man may only make a Law of such things as he may judge upon, and the judgement of Man may not be of inward things, but only of outward things; and nevertheless it belongeth to perfection that a Man be well ordered in both, that is to say, as well inward as outward. Therefore it was necessary to have

have the Law of God, the which should order a Man as well of inward things as of outward things.

The fourth is, because, as St. Augustine saith in his first Book of Free Arbitrement, the Law of Man may not punish all offences: for if all offences should be punished, the Common-wealth should be hurt, as is of Contracts: for it cannot be avoided, but that as long as Contracts be suffered, many offences shall follow thereby, and yet they be suffered for the Common-wealth. And therefore that no evil should be unpunished, it was necessary to have the Law of God that should leave no evil unpunished.

CHAp. IV.

¶ Of the *Law of Man.*

THE Law of Man (the which sometime is called the Law positive) is derived by Reason, as a thing which is necessary, and probably following of the Law of Reason, and of the Law of God. And that is called probable, in that it appeareth to many, and especially to wise Men, to be true. And therefore in every Law positive well made is somewhat of the Law of Reason, and of the Law of God: and to discern the Law of God and the Law of Reason from the Law positive, is very hard. And though it be hard, yet it is much necessary in every moral Doctrine, and in all Laws made for the Common-wealth. And that the Law of Man be just and rightwise, two things be be necessary, that is to say, Wisdom and Authority. Wisdom that he may judge after Reason, what is to be done for the Communalty, and what is expedient for a peaceable conversation and necessary sustentation of them, Authority, that he have Authority to make Laws. For the Law is derived of Ligare, that is to say, to bind. But the Sentence of a wise Man doth not bind the Communalty, if he have no Rule over them, Also to every good Law be required these Properties; that is to say, that it be honest, rightwise, possible in it self, and after the Custom of the Country, convenient for the place and time, necessary, profitable, and also manifest, that it be not captious by any dark sentences, ne mixt with any private wealth, but all made for the Commonwealth. And after St. Bridget, in the 4 Book, in the hundred twenty nine Chapter, Every good Law is ordained to the health of the Soul, and to the fulfilling of the Laws of God, and to induce the people to fly evil desires, and to do good works. Also the Cardinal of Cambrey writeth, whatsoever is righteous in the Law of Man, is righteous in the Law of God. For every Man's Law must be consonant to the Law of God. And therefore the Laws of Princes, the Commandments of Prelates, the Statutes of Communalties, ne yet the Ordinance of the Church is not righteous nor obligatory, but it be consonant to the Law of God.

And of such a Law of Man that is consonant to the Law of God, it appeareth who hath right to Lands and Goods, and who not: For

For whatsoevur a Man hath by such Laws of Man, he hath righteously ; and whatsoever he hath against such Laws, is unrighteously had.

For Laws of Man not contrary to the Law of God, nor to the Law of Reason, must be observed in the Law of the Soul : and he that despiseth them, despiseth God, and resisteth God. And furthermore, as Gratian saith, because evil Men fear to offend for fear of pain ; therefore it was necessary that divers pains should be ordained for divers Offences, as Physitians ordained divers Remedies for several Diseases. And such pains be ordained by the makers of Laws, after the necessity of the time, and after the disposition of the people. And though that Law that ordained such pains hath thereby a conformity to the Law of God, (for the Law of God commandeth that the people shall take away evil from amongst themselves ;) yet they belong not so much to the Law of God, but that other pains (standing the first Principles) might be ordained and appointed therefore. That is the Law that is called most properly the Law positive, and the Law of Man.

And the Philosopher said in the third Book of his Ethicks, that the intent of a Maker of a Law is to make the People good. and to bring them to Vertue. And although I have somewhat in general shewed thee whereupon the Law of England is grounded, (for of necessity it must be grounded of the said Laws, that is to say, of the Law Eternal, of the Law of Reason, and of the Law of God :) nevertheless I pray thee shew me more specially whereupon it is grounded.

ed, as thou thinkest, as thou before hast promised to do.

Stud. I will with good will do therein that lieth in me, for thou hast shewed me a right, plain, and straight way thereto. Therefore thou shalt understand, that the Law of England is grounded upon six principal Grounds. First, it is grounded on the Law of Reason. Secondly, on the Law of God. Thirdly on divers general Customs of the Realm. Fourthly, on divers Principles that be called Maximes. Fifthly, on divers particular Customs. Sixthly, on divers Statutes made in Parliaments by the King, and by the Common Counsel of the Realm. Of which Grounds I shall speak in order as they be rehearsed before. And first of the Law of Reason.

We presume that you are intensely interested in law, not only because in a business way you will be able to profitably apply your knowledge of the positive law of your state, but also because of the opportunity which a study of the science of law will afford you to become a well-informed judge of the social and political values which new and improved law will bring to your community. A high percentage of the leaders who have brought American civilization to its present level were jurists, and their example no doubt is going to stimulate you to bend every effort to know what progress in law is possible, what law *ought to be,* and what it can be despite the many conflicting conditions that oppose its development.

In speaking of the qualities which, to his way of thinking, the nine outstanding American judges have had in common, Mr. Roscoe Pound, former Dean of the Harvard Law School, says of them:

> "First of all, they were great lawyers, masters of their craft, masters of the authoritative materials in which judges in the English-speaking world are expected, as a duty of their office, to find the grounds of decision, and masters of the technique of applying those materials to the decision of cases.
>
> "Secondly, six of them, namely, Marshall, Kent, Story, Gibson, Shaw, and Ruffin, sat on the bench of courts of the first influence in the formative era of our law before the Civil War. They played controlling parts in shaping the received English legal materials to the needs of the New World. The other three, Cooley, Doe, and Holmes, had the like fortune of sitting on the bench where and when important bodies of law were formative. Cooley as a writer, teacher, and judge was one of the pioneers in the nineteenth-century development of due process of law. Afterwards he

was a pioneer in what led to our twentieth-century development of administrative tribunals and administrative law. Doe was a pioneer of modern procedure in the United States, forecasting the spirit which governs the procedure of today, where the reformers of the middle of the nineteenth century were concerned rather with rules. Holmes was the leader in twentieth-century interpretation and application of the bill of rights.

"Thirdly, they were great judges, great not merely in knowing the law, but in expounding, interpreting, and applying it. They knew the law for more than an aggregate of rules. They knew where rules applied and where recourse was to be had to principles and conceptions and standards. They appreciated what rules and principles and conceptions and standards are, and the extent to which a judge's task is one of knowing the instruments in the judicial tool box, what instrument to make use of in the particular case and how to use it. They had sound judgment in choosing starting points for legal reasoning from among competing analogies. They had a clear grasp of the received ideals of the legal order and ability to systematize and criticize them with reference to the ends of law. Along with these things they had the sound administrative discretion required for the application of legal standards.

"Fourthly, they were scholars, many of them legal scholars in an eminent degree. Kent, Story, Cooley, and Holmes were law judges. Kent's *Commentaries* stand with Blackstone's as the classical institutional books of the law of the English-speaking world."①

The history of the development of law is of practical interest to the average lawyer, but it is of supreme interest to the jurist, who is expected to be equipped with standards that will enable him to compare past aspects of law with its future possibilities. The lesson of the past is invaluable to one who is to be a judge and a statesman. A look at the ever-changing social conditions in Asia, Europe, and America will help us to appreciate the need of progress toward a better approximation of enacted law to right norms; and hence, there is always a need of sound statesmanship and legal scholarship. In order to

① In foreword to *Mr. Justice Cardozo*, by Joseph P. Pollard, The Yorktown Press, New York, 1935.

qualify ourselves for greater service to the state, having learned a great deal about English and American law and procedure, we shall now probe into the deeper principles which test the validity of all law, and which concern the relation of law to the other social sciences and to the several branches of philosophy.

It may appear rather audacious for anyone to attempt categorical generalizations regarding past and future developments of law. Nevertheless, it will be interesting, to say the least, to follow the subtle reasoning of Blackstone, Kent, Story, and other men of equal genius, who have given jurisprudence the most serious attention. They were philosophers who were not satisfied with theory and hypothesis. They sought proved truth, and since truth is one and not self-contradictory, they realized that what is true in one science cannot be false in another.

To the jurists—that is, to the lawyers who are judges and philosophers—is left the task of looking upon all known law as a totality, and in this unified perspective to find a rational co-ordination of law with all the other sciences. Into the findings of legal science, into a life study of philosophy, into truth as deep as the sea, jurisprudence will introduce you, but you will not lack a compass and a chart.

The Nature of a Science

Before seeking a detailed definition of jurisprudence, or the philosophic science of law, it is important for us to make sure that we grasp the difference between the sciences and ordinary knowledge.

A science, in general, is systematized knowledge of the many things which come under a common category, together with the explanation or causes of these things. Thus, we have many particular sciences. The science of Chemistry, for instance, comprises a systematic investigation into the nature and properties or activities of chemical elements and their compounds. In a similar way, logic is an important mental science which investigates the laws that guide men in reasoning to truth.

A science is not concerned solely with individual things or isolated facts, nor merely with the way that men are accustomed to act in relation to these facts. Taking an example from everyday life, it is not scientific knowledge of telephonic or radio communication that is had by the typical telephone switchboard operator. She does not need to know the causes of the phenomena which she has learned, in piece-meal fashion, in order to succeed in the purely utilitarian pursuit of everyday service and life.

Scientific knowledge is first of all unified and orderly, proceeding in a definite direction toward a goal; and the scientist is determined, moreover, to find the causes of the systematized facts within his subject matter. The scientist studies one or more correlated classes of things that are found to have the same nature or essence. By the essence of a thing as belonging to a class we mean the sum of qualities in which it is precisely like and identical specifically with every other member of its class. For example, every human being belongs to the same species —man—since each has the same rational and animal nature, even though every man differs accidentally from his neighbors.

There are two kinds of systematized knowledge, or science: one type investigates the *proximate causes* of things, the other studies *ultimate causes*. The first kind of science is usually simply called science, while the second kind is called philosophical science or philosophy.

Philosophy seeks to interpret the results which have been obtained in the various sciences by making clear the relationships which they have to each other and to the universe as a whole. Philosophy, for example, seeks the ultimate or first cause of the law and order which, after a comparison of the findings of various sciences, are found to be dominant in the universe. To do this, the philosopher must examine the assumptions with which the different sciences begin, to see if they all are consistent with each other and all valid. Ultimate causes, therefore, may be studied by the philosopher even though he does not possess a perfect and complete knowledge of all the minor relations and proximate causes so intriguing to the natural scientist.

The Methods of Science

The arrangement of study processes in a series with reference to a definite end is called "method." There are two methods that are used in both (natural) science and philosophy: the analytical or inductive, and the synthetic or deductive.

In what is known as the deductive method, thought processes "descend" from more general principles of being or action to particular truths.

In the analytical or inductive method, thought is expended first on the findings of observation (through the senses or by most guarded introspection), and then "ascends" to the recognition of laws that explain the facts of experience.

The inductive method. Examples from physical science will show better than definition how the analytical method is used, and how dependent this method is upon the deductive method. It sometimes happens that when chemists derive an "element" from different compounds, the atomic weight of the resultants exhibits unaccountable variations. Thus, "Lord Rayleigh noticed that a certain volume of nitrogen obtained from the air weighed 2.3102 grams, whereas the same volume of nitrogen obtained from other sources weighed 2.2990 grams. This discrepancy led to the hypothesis that the nitrogen of the air is combined with another substance; and laborious search for the unknown cause of the residual weight was rewarded by the isolation of argon.[2]"

In this case, the exact observation of a fact was repeated for the sake of utmost accuracy. The fact was then analyzed—taken apart—and the hypothesis tentatively adopted: that, very likely, some other chemical agent was combined with the nitrogen which was found in the air. Here the deductive method came into play, for on the assumption that something other than nitrogen was responsible for the greater weight of the nitrogen in air, it would be possible to isolate the hitherto unknown agent. Accordingly, the attempt was made and it was successful in the discovery of argon.

Let us see how the analytical method is followed in the case method used quite extensively in the study of law. You are given a set of facts and told to analyze them. You set out accurately to find the parties, the subject matter, the cause of action, and the object of action so that you may find judicial authorities and the law which will apply to the case in hand. Let us review one of these cases. In *Boren* v. *Bartelson,* 39 Illinois 43, the facts were the following: defendant had used insulting language to the plaintiff; the plaintiff struck the defendant in the breast; the defendant drew a revolver, snapped it at the plaintiff, and, while the plaintiff was in the act of retreating, struck him over the head with it, inflicting a severe wound. In the suit for assault and battery, it was found that the defendant had used more force than was necessary in defending himself. The plaintiff was retreating and therefore the defendant's act was not done in self-defense.

The court found that this set of facts, when properly

[2] Crumley, Thomas, *Logic*, The Macmillan Co., N. Y., p. 416.

analyzed, was, if not identical, at least essentially the same as many other situations in which judicial authority had found defendants guilty of assault and battery, a tortious act prohibited by law. As soon as the conclusion which placed the action in the common category of assault and battery was arrived at analytically, it was easy to deduce the decision and award damages. The more difficult part of the practicing attorney's work with clients is the analysis of facts and the ascertainment of cases deserving of a trial in court.

The deductive method. The second method used in science, the deductive, is more fruitful and more adaptable to philosophy. Here we find that "first philosophy" or metaphysics, pondering the attribute of "being" as universally predicated of every single thing in existence and experience, recognizes it to be the first and the simplest of all concepts. From the study of being is evolved a notion of necessary being—God—and contingent being—created being. For philosophers, like the natural scientists, assume the principle of causality as axiomatic, fundamental, and useful. On the basis of this principle, it is easy to see that there must have been some one Being which originated all others and which existed by itself necessarily, since an endless series of beings, one originating from another without any first cause or source, is illogical, unthinkable, and contradictory.

Basic Truths of Jurisprudence

In American law, the accepted philosophy upon which the Constitution of the United States rests as its ultimate bed-rock is theistic, assuming the existence of a supreme first cause or Deity. This truth is the first postulate in our study of jurisprudence. If you have not accepted this as truth, you should investigate the grounds upon which this philosophical conclusion rests, so that you may grasp the full import of English and American legal institutions. This postulate of God's existence, as a personal and intelligent Creator of the universe, who is the Supreme Lawgiver by title of ownership over men and their property, was incorporated as evident truth into the foundation of our Federal Constitution. It was briefly expressed in the second paragraph of the Declaration of Independence, which enunciated the right of Americans to form a new political state.

Theistic philosophy, which contains rational proof of the existence of a necessary self-existent Being, has had the most profound influence upon civilization. An atheistic philosophy, which denies a personal God and assumes that the material universe had no cause, springing into existence out of nothing, is a contradiction in itself: for "nothing" cannot be conceived as having given birth to anything. Atheism can find no alternative basis outside of God for a social order with a real sanction of authority. A few men may not rightfully dominate a multitude who possess co-equal human nature, unless they receive authority from some valid source.

It is worth our while to observe that in the state constitutions adopted during the American Revolution, we find ample contemporary interpretation of the generally accepted theistic philosophy.

A second postulate in English and American law, and in theistic Philosophical Jurisprudence, is the valid assumption that man has a free will. This truth does not deny that sometimes men can be influenced by practically ungovernable impulses.

A third postulate in this Philosophical Jurisprudence is the valid assumption that man is social by nature. By this is meant that man has natural fitness, natural inclination, and natural need for civil society and hence is impelled to seek co-operatively the very valuable ends of society, which can be obtained only through the organization of a state.

These, then, are the three postulates which are taken for granted in Philosophical Jurisprudence as truths validly proved elsewhere in sound philosophy. From this starting point we take our departure into the realm of Philosophical Jurisprudence.

Definition of Jurisprudence

In the detailed study of the definition of jurisprudence, we shall find sufficient reference to truths that are sources of our information. Hence, you should reflect long upon the meaning of every part of this definition, retaining the definition in memory: *"Jurisprudence is the practical science which investigates the nature, origin, and development of law."*

The definition will be explained in this lecture with emphasis upon the philosophic content of its meaning. When you are equipped with a summary of the principles involved in Philosophical Jurisprudence, you will find it easier to understand studies in historical, sociological, and analytical jurisprudence. The scope of these other phases of the subject is not quite as broad as that of Philosophical Jurisprudence, since in this primary and fundamental department of the science we include the investigation into the most generic and essential concepts of law and into the ultimate source of its obligatory character.

Philosophical Jurisprudence, being grounded on true metaphysical principles, directs our minds into deeper channels than those of human law alone; whereas the subsidiary studies mentioned above begin with a recital of human customs and man-made laws. All phases of the subject, however, offer advantages which the student of law does well not to overlook.

Philosophical Jurisprudence is chiefly concerned with ethical concepts, for Ethics is the practical science, based on reason, which determines the principles by which conduct ought to be regulated. In fact, the field of Philosophical Jurisprudence can correctly be said to lie within the domain of Ethics, which, however, extends beyond our present field to cover all acts of men which are deliberately and freely chosen. Consequently, we shall discover that Philosophical Jurisprudence is regulative of the actions of those law-makers who bring law into being; it is regulative of the content of the laws passed.[3]

Philosophical Jurisprudence is concerned with politics, because the latter is a practical science which treats of the nature, organization, and administration of the state. The fields of Jurisprudence and Politics overlap, since the jurist, in studying the fundamental character of law, must analyze the nature of the political state for whose benefit civil law is constituted.

Nature of Law

The definition and purpose of jurisprudence demands a definition of law understood, not merely in a collective sense, but precisely in a generic sense as well as a specific sense. Hence, it is defined specifically in relation to man as a *"rule of action, mandatory in form, established and promulgated by competent authority for the common good."*

Examining this broad notion of law, we see first of all that it is not confined in application to law in the purely legal sense, which is made by men politically organized. Notice that this wider definition of law fits into the pattern of every justly constituted legal enactment as "a

[3] Cf. Le Buffe, *Pure Jurisprudence*, page 8, Fordham University Press, N. Y., 1924. Kent, *Commentaries*, p. 342. Pound, Roscoe, *The Spirit of the Common Law*, Marshall-Jones Co., Boston, pp. 150-151.

rule of action, imposed by some being, possessing authority, upon some other being." The generic use of the term "law" fits perfectly into the correct meaning of the term "physical law," as used either particularly (for example, the law of gravity) or collectively (for example, the physical law of nature). For any law of physics is a rule of action impressed by God on those material and non-free agents that are compelled to act under suitable conditions in a uniform way by an intrinsic compulsion of their nature.[4]

A graphic illustration of the perfect order and law observed in the movements of the astronomical bodies, the planets, the sun, and the stars, can be obtained in a modern planetarium. The regularity and beautiful timing of the physical forces which are known to the science of astronomy furnish a clue to the existence of God and to the intelligent direction of matter by the Supreme Architect and Lawgiver of the universe.

Moral law. The generic use of the term "law" given in the preceding paragraph fits into the specific meaning of the term "moral law." The rules of moral action are placed on free creatures—on man—because the Supreme, Intelligent Lawgiver demands regularity of the proper kind in the free and deliberate actions peculiar to man's nature. The customs arising out of man's habitual and regular way of doing things are called his "mores," from which we derive the word "moral." While man is not physically bound to act in agreement with the will of his Creator, he is nevertheless *morally* bound or *obligated* to keep within the bounds or limits of duty under the rules which God has revealed to him.

In jurisprudence, special emphasis is laid upon the truth that the "moral law" is not completely divorced

---

[4] Cf. Blackstone, *Commentaries*, Sec. 2.

from "the law of the state," although the distinction between the nature of one and that of the other becomes clear upon reflection that God alone is the author of the moral law.[5]

It should be noticed that the term "law" is improperly used in such phrases as "the laws of polite society," "the laws of etiquette," etc., where the term "law" is used merely because of the analogy between purely social customs and those legal customs which have the force of law because prescribed by the mandate of competent authority.

The essentials of a law. A law is a guiding "rule of action," directing the inferior to a goal with proper caution or restraint. Notice how the laws known to physics, to chemistry, to astronomy, to physiology, etc., guide non-free agents to their proper end and function. Observe also how the legitimate laws of a state guide the citizens toward the goal of a common good.

By "mandatory in form" is meant that the rule of action prescribed is not merely directive or advisory of certain procedure, but that it is obligatory, laid upon the conscience as a duty under the circumstances.

The requirement that a law must be reasonably conceived by the lawmaker and freely determined upon as a proper course of action, is enunciated in the generic definition of law by the word "established."

"Promulgated" means published externally, so that subjects may become aware of the law.

The term "competent authority" implies that only those who have been duly entrusted with the affairs of government may lay down rules of statutory law or render judicial decisions that bind the subjects of a certain political society. We have seen that in many forms of government, judges of courts are clothed with au-

[5] Cf. Pound, *Law and Morals*, and *The Spirit of the Common Law*, passim.

thority to interpret law and to decide "what the law is in given cases."

"For the common good" indicates the very purpose and end of society. A law, in order that it may be law, must be directed so as to enable men to reach the perfection for which they are by nature fitted, toward which they are impelled by nature, and to which they are reasonably obliged. The common good is synonymous with "general welfare" in a political society. It may be defined as "the aggregate of those conditions which must exist so that all members of the state can provide for their physical and moral needs." Among these needs may be enumerated: life, health, home, property, truth, good name, liberty, government, education, and religion. These goods and needs may be summed up under the three headings: life (i.e., not only existence, but rational life with the economic value that attaches to an industrious work-a-day life), liberty, and the pursuit of happiness.

From this analysis of law, generically understood, we see the basic reason why "class legislation" is juridically and ethically banned as a voidance of the very purpose of civil society, which is the common good of the members of the state.

In political government, however, it is very difficult for the representatives of the people to eliminate class legislation for the simple reason that legislators are often insufficiently prepared by a knowledge of social science and find themselves at a loss to prescribe for the proper balancing of needs on the part of various interests clamoring for their rights. For example, banking interests, industrial interests, trade-union interests, etc., must all be given consideration and satisfactory protection in legislation, so that an equilibrium of forces working for the common good may be maintained.

Obligation and Sanction

The most easily neglected concept, and the most important in law and jurisprudence, is that implied by the term "mandatory." By law as applied to free agents (men), is meant a moral "ligation" or bond, forged from true ethical reasons, which links human conscience to the Supreme Lawmaker, whose reason and will *must* be obeyed. This *ought* or *must* is not merely hypothetical, as are the rules adopted in the training of athletes and the rules for the conduct of games such as golf, football, or bridge. In the latter cases, the rules are to be followed *if* the participants wish to achieve the purpose of the game or sport, which goal is not a necessary end demanded by man's nature or the nature of society.

The nature of obligation. The source of obligation lies first in the *right* of the superior, who is properly entitled to exercise this right, to exact the obedience of inferiors to his ruling; secondly, in the *fact* that the superior has actually exercised that right by placing a command or law on the subject or citizen; and, thirdly, in the fact that the subject is in position to know the command or law, thus becoming conscious of the obligations binding his (moral) freedom. This pressure is said to be unique in its kind, that man, being rational, is able to perceive the relation of the necessary means to the attainment of his ultimate end, i.e., the ultimate purpose of his existence.

Wherever obligation is present, it will be found, upon further analysis, that "there is some connection between the thing to which I am obliged and my ultimate end. The superior's right ultimately comes from God."[5]

What constitutes sanction. By "the sanction of law" is

[5] LeBuffe, *Pure Jurisprudence*, p. 25.

meant those rewards and punishments which are deemed practically necessary by the reasonable lawmaker in order to persuade the subjects or citizens to do their duty in obeying the law. Thus, physical power, "might," is enlisted as a sanction of the law, for it is only reasonable to accept such police power as an adjunct or subsidiary right legitimately conjoined with the law.

It is true that *might* does not constitute right or law. It is found to be equally true that human nature, with all its impulses, its accumulated evil habits, and selfishness, demands a sanction for every law. Nevertheless, the right to use force in applying legal rules to subjects springs from the essential nature of law, and not vice versa.[7]

Most of the analytical jurists, such as Austin and his followers, miss the most essential idea in the concept of "obligation" when they describe it as "liability to evil in the event of disobedience" to law. Austin confuses a property of law with an essential element of law—to use the terminology of the science of Logic. By *property* is meant an attribute which is found to be present whenever the generic or specific attributes of a certain nature are present, but which does not precisely enter into the essence of either genus or species.

An example from mathematics may be of help here. We all know what it is that makes a right triangle, namely, the genus triangle and the specific determination of right angularity. Yet Pythagoras discovered, as one of the properties of every right-angled triangle, that the square on the hypotenuse is equal in area to the sum of the squares constructed on the other two sides of the triangle. The latter attribute of the right triangle, as a property, accompanies the nature of every individual of

[7] Austin, *Jurisprudence*, Vol. I. Lect. XXII. No. 650.

its species but does not enter into the definition of the species.

Confusing a property with the nature or essence of any class of things is an error which often occasions very serious damaging results in a science. So it is in this particular case, when Austin fails to observe that the sanction of law is not of the essential nature of law.

The question whether sanction is of the essence of law or a "property" of law has been solved by philosophical jurisprudence in its clear exposition of the connection between human law and the moral law, from which the former gets its driving power.[8]

Even should this distinction between essence and property be overlooked, one should never make the mistake of substituting physical power or might for the essential basis of law or right. It is this very reversal of principle which is responsible for the most atrocious political disorders, national, and international. Witness the historical struggles within European countries, between nationalities and between economic classes; but especially, those between groups of allied governments in bitter conflict, seeking now to maintain, and then to upset, the balance of power.

The purpose of sanction. The purpose of sanction is to assure the observance of the law by re-enforcing the will to obey duly constituted authority with motives of self-advancement and self-protection from the disgrace and pain of punishment. The purpose of sanction is not vindictive but vindicative, by readjustment of the objective right order; it is also deterrent, by warning others who might contemplate illegal conduct. In the apportionment of sanctions for civil laws, the pragmatic effects of prison life should not be allowed to debase, but should

---

[8] Cf. Pollock, Sir Fred., *First Book of Jurisprudence*, 4th Ed., London: Macmillan and Co., 1918, ch. 1, pp. 22-26.

tend toward the uplifting of, the offending citizen. This social problem is receiving some attention in American institutions today.

Stability in Law

A relative permanence or stability is implied in law, for rules of conduct devised for a large number of subjects could not successfully accomplish their end and purpose if they were subject to change under the influence of fluctuating circumstance and the caprice of legislators, without being thoroughly tried. A statute may be passed, and yet the intent of the legislators, because of intentionally poor administration, may be deliberately frustrated. The end of law, the common good of peace and prosperity of the people, cannot be achieved except by the observance of well-co-ordinated long-range means, calculated to obtain the desired results.

What confusion would result were the laws of contract, such as that which obtains regarding consideration, nullified by statute one day and then shortly reinstated! Business would be paralyzed for very fear of the governmental agency, which would thus be defeating its own purpose.

It is equally evident that now and again new situations arise demanding, but seldom receiving, modification in the details of legal regulation. New mechanical inventions revolutionize customary processes. The automobile, airplane, radio, cotton-pickers, improvements in chemistry, and changes in agricultural conditions inject critical problems into the economy of a nation and of international trade. Surely, social and legal rules for the protection of labor and capital alike must keep pace with the times. Unemployment often results from sloth on the part of the legislators to provide courageously for profitable and regular opportunity to laboring men, without damaging legitimate capital.

The Natural Law

In giving you the definition of law in the strictly legal sense, as distinguished from the strictly moral content of its meaning, your course afforded you, at the beginning, the opportunity to study law analytically. This was good pedagogical strategy, for you know that we find it comparatively easy to grasp concrete facts before studying the abstract nature of these facts; and from the universalized facts, we pass readily unto an understanding of the abstract relations which one class of beings bears to another. In jurisprudence, our first study is that of the nature of law. We have already analyzed the concept of law and have learned that the essential element in all law is the element of mandatory regulation of conduct imposed by a superior upon inferiors for the common good.

It is logical to inquire further into the character of those superiors who are capable and qualified to make law. Assuming the existence of God, proved antecedently in philosophy to be the cause of all other beings, including man, we look about the world and the universe for one who may challenge His legitimate right to rule, unrivalled, the creatures which He has made. Since we find none equal to the one unique God who is infinitely perfect, we grant that His intelligence is unquestioned. Being supremely intelligent, He acts with plan and for an end. His plan, then, surely has place for the regulation, not only of non-free agents, but of free agents.

Hence, God planned certain ends and means for man to attain thereby the end of his creation—rules to guide man in his active relations with God, with his neighbor, and with himself, i.e., within his own mind and soul. This plan, directing in advance the universe by the Great Architect, is fittingly called the Eternal Law.

That part of this law which directs man's actions is called the Moral Law or the Natural Law, and its rules are promulgated to all mentally mature human minds by their natural power of reason, discerning what human acts are in accord with their nature, adequately considered, and what acts are not in accord with their rational nature. Put into a brief definition: the "Natural Law is the aggregate of those rules of actions, mandatory in form, which reason itself reveals as establishcd and promulgated by the Author of nature and imposed upon all men."

The term "laws of nature" is often used to include only the "physical laws of nature"—those which govern the non-free agents of the mineral, the vegetable, and the brute-animal kingdom. In jurisprudence, we are confining our attention to the Natural Law which regulates men, whose actions are deliberately and willingly guided by motives arising, not merely from instinct, but from the intellectual power called "reason."

We shall see that this conception of the Natural Law is objective and not purely subjective or relative to each individual's opinion and partial view of reality. For man's reason, studying human nature with the same industry which it exercises in searching the half-secrets of physics and chemistry, can and does arrive at true conclusions regarding the ordinary actions of men; certain acts being, by their very nature, perfective of the three basic relations of man, mentioned in a preceding paragraph. For example, since man, in relation to God, is ever a creature, his attitude to God is ever that of a subject; and, for man, blasphemy is therefore intrinsically evil. Since man's rational faculties, reason and will, specifically differentiate him from the brute-animal (which is governed by predetermined instinct), wanton drunkenness is intrinsically evil.[9]

Objective Ethical Basis for Law

The science of Philosophical Jurisprudence has sought and found the foundation for a set of fundamental, universally valid principles for civil and international law. The question whether there is an objective ethical basis for law is answered in the affirmative. In the essential relations of man to God, to other men, and to himself (which relations do not change, for abstract essences do not change), we have the unchanging, stable element which will be required in law wherever law is "made."

Law is not precisely made, then, in its entirety; for the stable element is found in the moral law of God, which is identified with, although not identical with, human law. This is what is meant by saying that law is found, not made. The element that is drawn from the natural law is found, and the positive element is "made" and suited to the transitory circumstances of social and political life in the passing day and the immediate future by human lawgivers.

Consequently, no man or group of men can disregard the Maker of men and God's law in the formation of regulations for his fellowmen, lest they step out of the bounds set by the higher Natural Law. No man may make himself the absolute dictator over his countrymen, so as to direct every detail of their conduct. No man is an absolute law unto himself, although a great latitude in indifferent matters, and in the choice of means, remains within the sphere of his freedom.

Using the language of philosophy, we find proof of the Natural Law in several sources, among them meta-

[9] Cf. Robinson, W. C., *Elements of American Jurisprudence*, Bryce, Jas., *Studies in History and Jurisprudence*, Little, Brown and Co., Boston, 1900, n. 5. Oxford University Press, N. Y.

physical premises, truths drawn from comparative psychology, and truths drawn from history in general, and legal history in particular. The metaphysical argument utilized by Philosophical Jurisprudence is based squarely on the ground that the all-wise Creator could not be conceived to be indifferent as to whether His creatures did or did not attain the end for which He designed them in His Eternal Plan. For such an indifference would imply a lack of intelligence and capricious folly in God, which is a contradiction of Divinity.

Once having constituted man a free-agent by endowing him with the faculty of choice between rationally known alternatives of conduct, God would direct and manage man only by moral law, which binds his nature with a moral obligation. Man is physically free to disregard law, to commit murder, suicide, and blasphemy; but he is morally bound to live according to the rules of Divine law, which his reason discovers to be clearly in accord with the triple essential relations which human nature bears to God, his fellow-men, and to himself. Thus, man comes to participate in the promulgation of God's law by the exercise of his reason, forming his conscience in specific and individual cases so as to conform to the objective standard as far as he knows it.

The history of philosophy should be open to the student of law and the jurist. More than any other student, the lawyer should concern himself with the history of this guiding conception of the Natural Law, without which ethical basis of all human law nothing but barbarism and anarchism can eventually supplant the civilization and culture to which man is directed by his rational nature.[18]

---

[18] Cf. Holaind, R., *Natural Law and Legal Practice*, Benzinger Bros., N. Y., 1899, Lect. II. Also, Wilson, Jas., *Works*, Ed. by J. DeWitt Andrews, Callaghan and Co., Chicago, Vol. I. Ch. III.

Origin of Law

Having studied the "nature of law," we turn to the second part of jurisprudence—the investigation into the "origin of law." Here there is no further question as to the origin of the Natural Law, for that Law has been seen to originate directly in the Divine Intelligence and Will of God. When the jurist speaks of the origin of law, he is inquiring into the origin of human positive law, i.e., law legitimately established by men with competency and authority to regulate the conduct of the members of an independent community.

When we use the term "law" in the strictly legal sense, we are thinking not of the Natural Law, which is promulgated by reason alone, but of law that has been either promulgated in positive verbal form or law established by judicial decisions that have received virtual ratification by the supreme authority of civil society—in the United States by the universal consent of the people.

Positive law. By "divine positive law" is meant the aggregate of those rules of action, mandatory in form, freely established and promulgated by God for mankind. The Ten Commandments of God, given to the Hebrews of the Old Testament, were Divine Positive Laws, confirming in most part the rules that might readily be known by reason as dictated by the Natural Law. By the term "positive law," unqualified by the word "divine," is meant any law freely put by any human superior or superiors having supreme authority in political society. Thus, John Austin defines positive law: "Every positive law or every law simply and strictly so called is set by a sovereign person, or a sovereign body of persons, to a member or members of the independent political society, wherein that person or body is sovereign or supreme."

By "sovereign" is meant that person or persons who

possess supreme power in legitimate title, and who have the duty to use that power for the end of the political society in which they are sovereign. "Human positive law" may be defined briefly as "a rule of action, mandatory in form, freely established and promulgated by competent human authority for the common good."[11]

Necessity for positive law. The Natural Law in its primary dictates is clear to every mature human mind; for example, it is evident that we are obligated to do good and avoid evil; and even though many so-called backward peoples have mistaken notions with regard to what constitutes right conduct under certain conditions, human reason does develop in all men well-defined principles regulative of conscience, which they acknowledge to bind them morally. Nevertheless, the dictates of right reason may be obscure under many circumstances; and so men in general need positive guidance by divine positive law and by human positive law, so that they may make that progress individually and collectively, which is in keeping with their nature and that of the state. As Sir Frederick Pollock puts it, "Natural justice has no means of fixing any rule to terms defined in number or measure, nor of choosing one practical solution out of two or more which are in themselves equally plausible."

Relation of civil law to natural law. Civil law is human positive law established by a civil society or state. Some state laws are nothing more than confirmations or promulgations declarative of the natural law. The state makes natural laws prohibiting murder, rape, etc., its own laws. Such laws are said to be declarative of the natural law.

Other laws are made to fill in, to make concrete, and to determine how the general abstract requirements of the

[11] Cf. De Wulf, Maurice, *Philosophy and Civilization in the Middle Ages*, Princeton University Press.

natural law shall be applied. For example, a gross-income tax law is freely chosen by the legislators of a state in preference to a proposed sales tax. By selecting this type of tax, the legislature determines the method of exercising the power conferred by the natural law, which declares that states once constituted may make provision for their necessary governmental expenses by taxation. All civil laws consist in the acceptance or application of natural law in one or other of these ways, and logically they are regarded as having been derived from the Natural Law.

Genetic origin of law. It is not everyone's privilege to issue law; for civil law, in order to share in the sanctity of natural law, must be issued by competent authority. Here comes another important question: How does the state and government acquire its authority? The answer leads us to inquire into the genesis of the state and its organ, the government. The state is generically a society (or "enduring union of two or more for a common good attainable by co-operative activity") and specifically "an enduring union of men for the common good of *public peace and prosperity,* attainable by co-operative activity."[9]

Civil authority—or the right of the civil ruler to direct effectively subjects of a state to promote, by the co-operative efforts of their external actions, "the public peace and prosperity"—consists in the moral power to *obligate* through law.

Leaving aside, for the moment, the various ways in which a civil ruler may be chosen or "consented to" by the members of a state, we direct our attention to the abstract problem of the origin of civil authority which can be vested in the supreme civil ruler. This problem is the ethical phase of the very practical study of sov-

[9] Cf. Haas, Francis J., *Man and Society*, The Century Co., N. Y., ch. IX.

ereignty, or the "right of the supreme civil ruler to direct effectively subjects of a state to promote, by the co-operative efforts of their external actions, the public peace and prosperity."[9]

Civil society is natural to man, since man is social by nature: his faculties of intelligent speech and hearing indicate that he was meant to communicate his knowledge and his thought to his fellows, and so to accomplish social ends, beneficial to himself and his neighbors. He has a natural inclination to live in this social companionship, to render assistance to, and to be helped by, others. He has a natural need for civil society, for so many of his needs can be satisfied only by social and civil life. Therefore, nature, i.e., the Author of Nature, designed man for civil society; and in so doing, He must have intended him to use the means for the proper conduct of civil society. The obvious means necessary for achieving the ends of civil society lie in the use of authority, which gives civil society quasi-organic functions. Only civil authority can make the state function. Law is the only way by which authority can guide the members of the state to the ends of peace and prosperity. Thus, we have clear evidence of the truth that civil authority comes from God.

Juridical origin of law. The question "Why must I obey the civil law?" finds an answer in the relation it bears to the Natural Law. A law established by competent authority in a state, directed to the common good of the community or state—since it does not conflict with the principles of Natural Law, even though it be not the best possible law—is in conformity with abstract standards of justice inherent in the triple essential relations in which man finds himself with respect to God, to his fellowmen, and to himself. The juridical origin of all justly enacted law is

---

[9] Burlamaqui, *The Principles of Natural and Politic Law*, Cambridge University Press, 1907, Vol. II, Pt. I, Ch. VI, Sect. VIII.

traced to its ultimate source in God's Intelligence and Will. Civil law, as long as it is not patently unjust, must be obeyed because "God wills it."

Some laws are categorically imperative, inasmuch as they are intended by the lawgiver to be obeyed by all without exception; and these laws bind the conscience of citizens. When, in exceptional cases, a law is established by a legislature with the sole intention of imposing a penalty upon the violation of some technical point of order without the intention of imposing a strict obligation upon the conscience of all citizens, the law so promulgated is only hypothetically imperative. Such an enactment may be styled a purely penal law, and the obligation to pay the penalty arises when an officer of the law detects one in the violation of the technicality. If a citizen is objectively certain that the lawmakers did *not* intend to bind his conscience to compliance with *both* the letter of the law and to the acceptance of the penalty when detection by an officer is had, the law may be regarded as purely penal.

Requisites for a Just Law

It is readily understood that very extensive latitude is left to the discretion of the lawmakers in their choice of legal regulations. Parliaments and Congresses, given the task and responsibility of accomplishing something of national betterment by virtue of constructive social engineering, must needs have a fairly free hand in planning. The needed locomotive structure which will carry the citizenry to the final ends of society must be continually remodeled to keep it up-to-date.

This thought is well expressed by Dean Roscoe Pound in his *Interpretations of Legal History.* Mr. Justice Benjamin Cardozo, in reviewing this volume of Mr. Pound's, says: "Juristic philosophy today is concerning itself more with ends than with beginnings. The anxiety to know how a principle or a rule 'derives' is less than the anxiety to consider how it functions. Pedigree is yielding to performance. 'Let us think of jurisprudence,' says our author, 'as a science of social engineering.' Engineering is 'a process, an activity,' not merely 'a body of knowledge' or 'a fixed order of construction.' It is a doing of things, not a serving as passive instruments through which mathematical formulas and mechanical laws realize themselves in the eternally appointed way. The engineer is judged by what he does. His work is judged by the adequacy to the purpose for which it is done, not by its conformity to some ideal form of a traditional plan."

The citizenry of a democratic state consider themselves justified in judging their laws today principally upon a pragmatic basis, and most of the people are willing to assume that their representatives have planned laws with architecturally correct measure and moral rectitude. It is painful and disappointing for the better-informed citizens to observe that there are representatives in legislative chambers who are not possessed of deep insight into the primary principles of jurisprudence. Wherefore, it is not surprising that, at times, particularly well-qualified experts in law, politics, and ethics will judge the values of a legislative program in a truly objective way, detecting errors in the fundamental structure of a particular law. It is reasonable to grant that the objective evidence of moral values in a law occasionally will be apparent and illuminating to careful students of morals. The justice of a legal rule is not always so deeply hidden that it cannot be fairly easily discerned by disinterested classes. To doubt this is to deny reason and conscience to intellectually mature men and women, and that would be absurd.

Hence, it follows that the lawmakers, wherever and whoever they may be, are bound to attend to the justice of legal and judicial enactments. This justice can be known in the abstract, and its application relative to subject matter may be and must be studied and understood. With regard to its subject matter, a law must neither prescribe what is obviously immoral, nor must it demand from the citizens what is practically impossible, both according to physical nature and according to the firmly established custom of the country. For example, a civil law prohibiting the use of meat in times of plenty, or one prescribing the exclusive use of publicly owned streetcars, instead of private automobiles, in an American city in times of peace, would be an unjust law.

Public Acceptance of a Law

It would be the grossest fallacy, leading to anarchy and the disruption of law, for a citizen to argue that if he thinks that a particular law is not in accord with his conception of the natural law or with his conception of what is right, that he can on that account disregard it and avoid the moral and civil penalties. Such an appeal to individual interpretations of natural law, to right and justice, is clearly abortive, false, and disastrous. On the contrary, since the citizens of a state owe respect and obedience to the authority of the government, individuals and minorities have the duty to obey laws that appear unjust, in order that the law may have a chance to effect the purpose of the lawmakers; for its practical achievement may eventually fit very well into the complex sum of conditions which will spell the "general welfare." Public policy demands the relinquishment of uncertain private opinion; and good example demands such a submission to the law.

Apropos of this point, Dean Roscoe Pound, in *Law and*

Morals, scores the insidious fallacy of private interpretation in matters of law. "This notion," he says, "that there is an appeal from legislation to common right and reason as to the law of nature and that courts are bound to give effect to the latter as against positive law in conflict therewith, formerly had no little vogue and still appears in occasional dicta, sometimes as an absolute dogma, sometimes as a mere rule of moral obligation, and sometimes in its true place as a rule of interpretation. In practice we admit two propositions only:

"(a) As between a man and his conscience, he may under some circumstances be justified morally in disobeying a law. He may appeal to his reason and conscience for internal justification, but the courts can and will look only to the law.

"(b) There are certain points of contact between law and morals where the courts look primarily to general principles of right and justice for guidance. These are three: discretion, judicial lawmaking, and interpretation."

The rule of objective evidence is the final arbiter in legal and philosophical questions of justice. The injustice of a judicial decision, or of a misguided legislative enactment, may on rare occasions become so apparent to the intelligence of the citizenry that a fairly universal consensus of judgment may describe it as unjust. Under such circumstances, the citizenry owe a duty to their state to endeavor to obtain from the legislative authority a modification or abrogation of the unjust law.

When the Supreme Court of the United States (1792) decided that the Federal Constitution contained no provision which would prevent the state of Georgia from being sued without its consent, public opinion spontaneously rejected their judgment. The interpretation of the

Court doubtless was legally valid; but the people were of the opinion that if the law had been correctly interpreted, the law itself would work injustice, and so they promptly set about to modify the Constitution. In the language of the majority opinion delivered in a case arising after the eleventh amendment was passed:

"The decision made in the case of *Chisholm* v. *Georgia* created such a shock of surprise through the country that, at the first meeting of Congress thereafter, the eleventh amendment to the Constitution was almost unanimously proposed and was in due course adopted by the legislatures of the states. This amendment, expressing the (mind as well as the) will of the people, who are the ultimate sovereignty of the whole country, superior to all legislatures and all courts, actually reversed the decision of the Supreme Court."[14]

In a democratic form of government, custom may in rare instances reflect the well-considered objective evidence that a law is unjust and hence unsuited to the long-term interests of a citizenry. The nullification of "laws" against public meetings on Sunday may serve as an instance in which the saner and larger element of a state has gradually corrected the error of their own government.

Precedent and Judicial Interpretation

In the legal system of some states, such as the United States, Canada, and Australia, the national constitution is the supreme positive law, and the congress or parliament is legally restrained from making any laws which conflict with the constitutional law; and the supreme court may find such congressional enactments null and void. In these countries, the governments are said to

---

[14] Cf. *Chisholm* v. *Georgia*, 2 Dall. 419, 1 L. Ed. 440 and *Hans* v. *Louisiana*, 134 U. S. 1, 33 L. Ed. 842.

be a matter of law, rather than a matter of men. In some countries, for example in France and Switzerland, even though there is a written constitution, it is not regarded as strictly supreme and fundamental law, enforceable in the courts against either government or individual. For, in France as in Switzerland, the constitution is held to be merely a set of political restraints upon the legislative body, so that if they are violated by the Chamber of Deputies and Senate, only political action can furnish the remedy.

Where courts have the legal right to interpret a national constitution, which is accepted as the fundamental and supreme law of the land, the power of judicial interpretation is a vital force in the development or retardation of law. Here the law is quite often said to be what the supreme court says it is, and the philosophy of the majority of the court prevails for the nonce. Mr. Justice Holmes, in his opinion in *Missouri* v. *Holland,* 252 U.S. 416, says, with respect to the growth of Constitutional Law through judicial interpretation:

"When we are dealing with words that also are a constituent act like the Constitution of the United States, we must realize that they have called into life a being the development of which could not have been foreseen completely by the most gifted of its begetters. It was enough for them to realize or to hope that they had created an organism; it has taken a century and has cost their successors much sweat and blood to prove that they created a nation. The case before us must be considered in the light of our whole experience and not merely in that of what was said a hundred years ago."

Has not the American judiciary, like that of England, adopted and put into practice the principle of following precedent? They have indeed adopted the principle of following precedent in deciding cases that are similar in character to cases previously decided. In new types of cases, where precedent is lacking, new principles have been evolved by the judges; and here both philosophy and experience have combined their light to guide the judiciary.

Chief Justice Walter Clark of the Supreme Court of North Carolina[19] well states: "There is no superstitious sanctity attaching to a precedent. It is proper that precedents should not be lightly changed, or without sufficient cause. But they should not be adhered to when an opinion has clearly misconstrued a statute or is otherwise palpably erroneous. This court has never held that it was infallible, nor has any other court. We have repeatedly overruled our own decisions, and a large pamphlet was issued some years ago, containing a list of such cases, and a similar compilation now would be two or three times as large. The same is true of the United States Supreme Court and all other courts. Men and nations may 'Rise on steppingstones of their dead selves to higher things.' Courts can only maintain their authority by correcting their errors to accord with justice and the advance and progress of each age. They must slough off that which is obsolete, and correct whatever is erroneous or contrary to the enlightenment and sense of justice of the age and to the spirit of new legislation."

If judges are not always limited by precedent, they are limited to the interpretation of the supreme law and to the interpretation of the laws made by the legislatures.

Mr. Justice Marshall in *Osborn* v. *Bank of the United States*[20] expressed this thought when he stated that judicial power is never exercised for effecting the will of the judges, but it is always exercised for the purpose of giving effect to the judgment and will of the legislature, and hence to the "will of the law."

---

[19] *State* v. *Falkner*, 108 Southeastern Reporter 756.
[20] 9 Wheaton 738.

A very practical study in applied jurisprudence may be made by following the Supreme Court's interpretations of the clause in the Constitution of the United States which confers on Congress the "right to regulate commerce among the several states."[®]

In your study of Constitutional Law, you have observed a gradual judicial expansion of the commerce clause. By inclusion of more and more subject matter within the scope of "commerce," the Supreme Court has been instrumental in expanding the control of Congress over interstate commerce. It would seem that the wisdom of the court has kept it aware of the changes taking place in American life; changes have made commerce among the several states more complex and more extensive than it was in the close of the eighteenth and in the beginning of the nineteenth century, and the court has recognized these changes and the consequent enlargement of the field of Congressional regulation. Many observing students think that the Supreme Court has not allowed the power of Congress in recent years to maintain its original control over commerce and industry. They say that "commerce and industry have been reorganized since the middle eighties on a national scale," and they argue that the Supreme Court should not hamper the Congress in its attempt to regulate interstate business relationships which have expanded so enormously. The decisions of the Court, upholding the National Labor Relations Act, particularly the opinion of Chief Justice Hughes in the Jones and Laughlin Steel Company case, decided in April, 1937, announce broad principles with respect to the power of Congress under the commerce clause, which apparently leave Congress free to make whatever regulations may be required to meet the needs of the expanded field.

® Corwin, Edward, "*The Commerce Power vs. States Rights*," Princeton University Press, 1936.

In all the struggles by legislative and judicial bodies to make and interpret law to suit the essential common good of the citizenry, we discover the dual necessity of stability and change in law. The problems of law are today more than ever complicated because of the complexities of modern life. They are problems that can be solved only by educated and well-informed legislatures and jurists. This subject, which is the particular province of sociological jurisprudence, will be studied in the textbook, Volume 13 of *American Law and Procedure.*

The importance of the subject is well expressed in the words of Mr. Pound:

"The chief problem to which legal thinkers have addressed themselves has been how to reconcile the idea of a fixed body of law, affording no scope for individual wilfulness, with the idea of changes and growth and making of new law; how to unify the theory of law with the theory of making law and to unify the system of legal justice with the facts of administration of justice by magistrates.

"For, put more concretely, the problem of compromise between the need of stability and the need of change becomes in one aspect a problem of adjustment between rule and discretion, between administering justice according to settled rule, or at most by rigid deduction from narrowly fixed premises, and administration of justice according to the more or less trained intuition of experienced magistrates. In one way or another, almost all of the vexed questions of the science of law prove to be phases of this same problem."[18]

Forms of Government

Civil society originates by the consent of the people, who find themselves drawn by nature to live in society.

[18] *Interpretations of Legal History*, p. 1

When a number of families attempt to gain a livelihood in the same community, they come to realize that the urge to exercise their faculties for mutual betterment can best be satisfied by co-operative activity. The incorporation of the community may not at times have taken the same form in one locality as in another far-removed spot. Varieties of organization would be likely with primitive and uneducated aspirants to political unity. Their consent may not be in written contract or social compact of a formal sort. Again, the later form of governmental agency by which people wish to be guided may be one of many types, such as that of monarchy, democracy, or aristocracy.

Some people, having been born into circumstances in which, for instance, a monarchy has proved very well suited to their needs, wisely and justly cling to that form of government, consenting to the authority of their rulers in the belief that they can best attain their destiny under the machinery of monarchical government. They reason to the conclusion that radical attempts to remodel and reform governments lead to anarchy and chaos, and that it is good policy to seek perfection through improved law within the already-established framework of monarchy. Such a policy is just and wise in any form of government, because legitimate authority, once constituted and given a fair chance to accomplish its ends, must be respected by the people as having every right to make and enforce law.

It is only when agents of government misuse their powers—tyrannize over their citizens to the extent of usurping their natural personal rights so as to render life under that government intolerable—that a revolution can be justified; and even then reason demands that the leaders of the revolt must foresee that a successful outcome of the revolution can be accomplished without losing

more values to the people than those they have been asked to sacrifice.

B. Law and History

J. Friedrich [Harvard], "Law and History," 14 *Vanderbilt Law Review* 1027, and reprinted as Appendix I in the author's *Philosophy of Law in Historical Perspective* (2d ed.; Chicago: University of Chicago Press, 1963).

*Law and History**

Law is frozen history. In an elementary sense, everything we study when we study law is the report of an event in history, and all history consists of such records or reports. It therefore cannot be my task to develop a sermon on the importance of historical records for the understanding of the law; the tie is too intimate and too obvious to need laboring.

"The work of Professor Maine on 'Ancient Law,' " wrote Professor T. W. Dwight in his Introduction to that book in the sixties of the last century, "is almost the only one in the English language in which general jurisprudence is regarded from the historical point of view."[1] This is an astonishing statement, considering the strikingly historical pattern of the common law. It is possibly correct, if taken *very precisely*. But was not the work of Blackstone or the work of Coke general jurisprudence from the historical point of view? Was it not their preoccupation with history, with the past, which aroused Jeremy Bentham against the jurisprudence of Blackstone and his predecessors? Law cannot of course be identified with "general jurisprudence" in any case; but leaving that issue aside, English and American law appear in fact to be "frozen history"; the institutions by which they are constituted are the outgrowth of that process which in Burke's memorable phrase links the dead of the past with the generations yet unborn.

But what of history? Is history conceivable without law? Certainly not the history of our Western world, though there are civilizations, such as the Chinese during most of its existence, which have not placed law into such a central position. It is patent that

* From the *Vanderbilt Law Review*, XIV (October, 1961), 1027–48.

1 Introduction by T. W. Dwight to H. J. S. Maine's *Ancient Law* (3d American ed.; 1864), p. ix.

neither medieval nor modern history can be written or understood without careful attention to legal institutions. From feudalism to capitalism, from Magna Carta to the constitutions of contemporary Europe, the historian encounters law at every turn as a decisive factor.

It would seem, then, that any reconsideration of "law and history" is apt to be a string of commonplaces or the beating of a dead horse. Names such as Maine and Savigny, Maitland and Gierke, McIlwain and Olivier-Martin—not to mention Holmes, as the last in a succession of historically minded judges—clearly seem to settle the question of history's importance for law; it would not be difficult to match them with others signalizing the importance of law for history.

Such encounter between history and law is especially frequent in the history of political thought. One has only to open one of the books on the subject in order to discover that such a history is at least half a history of jurisprudence. From the Sophists and Plato to Hegel and Marx, the philosophy of law in historical perspective is inseparably intertwined with the history of political ideas. "The prevalent moral and political theories" were fully recognized by Oliver Wendell Holmes to be the key to the understanding of the law. It is equally true that the living law is one of the focal points of all political theory; in it is crystallized what men in their time consider just, and there can be no understanding of the political order without a grasp of the common coin of such values, interests, and beliefs as the idea of justice embodies at various stages of historical development. Political thought and legal thought are two sides of the same common coin.

The history of political thought and theory is itself not free from formidable difficulties, however. Unless we are to assume that words mean the same at all times or at least over long periods, virtually all the positions which it deals with are highly controversial. Plato and Aristotle, Cicero and St. Augustine, St. Thomas Aquinas and Machiavelli, Hobbes and Locke, Montesquieu, Rousseau and Kant—each and all have been the subject of extended learned controversy over what they *really* said. It may be true, and probably is, that "to know someone else's activity of thinking is possible only on the assumption that this same activity can be re-enacted in one's own mind."[2] But it cannot be "proven" that this condition can be fulfilled, that such re-enactment is possible. Similarly, it may well be that the task of "discovering 'what Plato thought' without inquiring 'whether it is true' " is "self-contradictory,"[3] but it is equally likely that the question whether what Plato thought be true is meaningless unless we first know what it was that he thought. This implies that "an act of thought, in addition to actually happening, is capable of sustaining itself and being revived and repeated without loss of its identity."[4] Such an implication is surely a self-evident proposition. If every thought, like all other acts, happens in context, is "an organic part of the thinker's life," then as the context changes the thought will necessarily also change. If then there is to be any continuity of thought it must be possible to relate degree of stability in context to degree of self-identity in thought. Hence the more abstract the thought, in the sense of being abstracted from specific detail in the context within and to which it applies, the more stable it presumably will be.[5] Here is the key dilemma of all historical effort at dealing with products of the mind which constitute creative responses to concrete problematic situations. Legal history shares it, as does political theory. By referring one to the other, we are possibly inviting the blind to lead the blind.

[2] R. G. Collingwood, *The Idea of History* (1946), Part V, para. 4. I do not share Collingwood's "idealist" premises, but I do find many of his formulations on history good. Cf. M. T. Swabey, *The Judgment of History* (1954), for a sounder position.

[3] Collingwood, *op. cit.*, p. 300.

[4] *Ibid.*

[5] Collingwood observes in this connection that "the mere fact that someone has expressed his thoughts in writing, and that we possess his works, does not enable us to understand his thoughts. In order that we may do so, we must come to the reading of them prepared with an *experience* sufficiently like his own to make those thoughts organic to it." Is it really probable that any man today will be able to share the experience of a fifth-century Athenian sufficiently to think Plato's thoughts on politics? I should say that, as best, only the most general features of such thought may be comprehended.

Neither a reference to the presupposed identity of experience, nor to the constancy in the environment so experienced resolves it.

In our age of doubt and scepticism, the problem cannot be so easily disposed of. "The life of the law" may not be "logic, but experience," as Holmes is ever again quoted as saying (though this view has a hoary ancestory). The wonderful passage which follows that famous generalization provides in a sense the theme for any discussion of law and history which is undertaken in light of the common law.

> The felt necessities of the time, the prevalent moral and political theories, intuitions of public policy, avowed or unconscious, even the prejudices which judges share with their fellowmen, have had a good deal more to do than the syllogism in determining the rules by which men should be governed. The law embodies the story of a nation's development through many centuries, and it cannot be dealt with as if it contained only the axioms and corollaries of a book of mathematics. In order to know what it is, we must know what it has been, and what it tends to become.[6]

The experience, then, is historical experience. This means that without history there cannot be, ther would not be, any law or jurisprudence. History is here conceived simply as the record of human experience. Yet, both "What is law?" and "What is history?" are questions which have not ceased to trouble the reflective student of both fields. It is not my intention to enter upon the task of seeking definitive answers to either of these never ending queries, though I will deal with both again later; rather, I intend to point out that neither question can be answered except within the context of a philosophical appraisal of law or history. And that means inescapably that he would discourse upon "law and history" would have to state first of all the philosophical context within which he is prepared to discuss either "in general." Such an undertaking might be of some interest, especially if the philosophy were novel. For if we stayed with established philosophical positions, such as those of Hegel or Dewey or Jaspers, all we would need to do would be to report what these eminent

[6] Oliver Wendell Holmes, *The Common Law* (1881), p. 1.

thinkers have had to say about our two fields and to match their positions as best we can. Thus Hegel concludes his remarkable but much misunderstood and misquoted *Philosophy of Right and Law* with a brief summary of his philosophy of history. This summary states with admirable succinctness his view of their relationship: Law is the embodiment of the ethical idea emanating from the state; as such it is embedded in history which consists in the unfolding of the world spirit's idea of freedom by way of the states which progressively realize it.[7] And if it were objected that such a view is hardly relevant today, we might reply that its Marxian variant in *Diamat* is still very much with us and indeed perhaps our major plague. But I am not a Hegelian and hence am merely giving his notions as an illustration of a thinker who clearly and explicitly argued the philosophical relation of law and history *in his terms*.[8]

The philosophy of history has moved a long way from Hegel. But it is very much alive. In our day, the skeptical view of Becker for whom every man was his own historian, the biological view of Spengler for whom history was embodied in cultural or civilizational wholes each of which was a law unto itself, its variant in Toynbee who believes in an ascent[9]—these and many lesser (though not less interesting) conceptions testify to the fascination which a view of the whole of man's existence on this globe exerts at present. Indeed, the extension of this view beyond the confines

[7] Georg Wilhelm Friedrich Hegel, *Grundlinien der Philosophie des Rechts* ("The Philosophy of Right," ed. J. Hoffmeister (1955), secs. 341–60. This most recent critical edition omits the additions (*Zusaetze*) which Hegel's editors had inserted on the basis of lecture notes, as well as the subtitle *Naturrecht und Staatswissenschaft* ("Natural Right and Political Science in Outline"). The latter omision is regrettable, since the subtitle better describes the content of the book.

[8] For a brief sketch of Hegel's philosophy of law, see chap. xv above. See the more detailed discusion in Huntington Cairns, *Legal Philosophy from Plato to Hegel* (1949), chap. xiv.

[9] Oswald Spengler, *The Decline of the West* (1926); Arnold Toynbee, *A Study of History* (1934–54). Among the many critical evaluations I especially found myself in accord with H. Stuart Hughes, *Oswald Spengler—A Critical Estimate* (1952), and Pieter Geyl, *Debates with Historians* (1955), chap. viii ("Toynbee the Prophet").

of written records to prehistory and the "endless journey"[10] which precedes it has added both poignancy and a certain weariness to the task, as ever more "cultures" have knocked at the gate to be admitted to "history" as well as to the United Nations. All such endeavors are somehow bound up with the convictions that history is something more than "making sense out of nonsense."[11] To the unsophisticated, history is "of course" that which happened, the concrete actions and events in all their specificity and effervescence. Indeed, many historians continue their arduous labors with something of this sort in mind. They are "looking" for history as it really happened—"*wie es wirklich gewesen.*" This memorable and simple phrase belongs of course to the great Ranke, himself a striking illustration of how far the great historian's achievement is from merely recounting how it really happened.[12] But the perplexing paradox of all historical work is that what actually happened can never be recaptured, although historical research would lose its point without a belief that more of it can be recaptured than is presently known. It is certainly true that each generation rewrites history in terms of its own values, interests, and beliefs, up to a point at least; it is also certainly true that discoveries of new material may from time to time alter important images of past events and personalities. But the quest is never complete, except in regard to such elementary data as the names and dates of particular tidbits. The happenings of history as contrasted with the reports about these happenings, the

[10] Loren Eisely, *The Immense Journey* (1946). Cf. Pierre Teilhard de Chardin, *The Phenomenon of Man* (1959); W. E. Le Gros Clarke, *The Antecedents of Man* (1959).

[11] T. Lessing, *Geschichte als Sinngebung des Sinnlosen* (1915); Carl Becker, *Every Man His Own Historian* (1935), which contains the essay by that name. For contrast, see Reinhold Niebuhr, *Faith and History* (1949).

[12] Fritz Wagner, *Geschichtswissenschaft* (1951), chap. ii, which gives many pertinent citations. The entire work is a most useful compendium of the "theories" of history from the beginning to Max Weber; it is, of course, written from the German perspective. The implicit idealism of Ranke which contradicts his oft- and above-quoted saying can be seen in such statements as "Alles Leben traegt sein Ideal in sich: der innerste Trieb des geistigen Lebens ist die Bewegung nach der Idee, nach einer groosseren Vortreffichkeit . . ." (quoted in Wagner, *op. cit.*, p. 194).

Geschehen in contrast to the *Geschichte*,[13] are devoured by time as soon as they happen. As we go through our days, they vanish into oblivion.

If, then, all history is a gloss upon the happenings, in the form of reports and interpretations of reports—such interpretations relating them to other reports and to thoughts upon them—the intellectual standing of such a gloss becomes a problem. And here the real issue of the relation of law to history is joined. As I see it, the reports of cases which occurred and are made part of the body of the law are related to other such reports in terms of the particular legal concept or rule which they demonstrate as an occurrence in time. Anyone opening a case book in any of the fields of law can see this clearly enough. And a good case book of the older type sought to illuminate the evolution of a concept and the rules it gave rise to by a succession of such cases. Well-known case books, such as Bigelow's or Wigmore's on torts or Williston's on contracts, are essentially histories of the particular legal institution with which they deal. Open any of them and an instance of the proposition just stated suggests itself. Thus in Scott and Simpson's *Judicial Remedies*[14] the first case is Slade's.[15] It is a case from the Court of Queen's Bench, and the report begins as follows:

> Be it remembered that heretofore, that is to say, in the term of St. Michael last past, before the lady the Queen at Westminster, came John Slade, by Nich. Weare his attorney, and brought here into the Court of the said lady the Queen, then there, his certain bill against Humphrey Morley, in custody of the Marshal, etc. of a plea of trespass upon the case. . . .

It then proceeds to tell how Morley defrauded John Slade by not paying him for some wheat that he had harvested and promised to pay for, the wheat growing on land which belonged to John Slade.

[13] The nicety of the contrast is not quite caught by the English words "happenings" and "history"; *Geschehen* carries the connotation of "bygones"—what *has* happened and is now accomplished fact. "Occurrences" suffers from the same defect.

[14] Austin W. Scott and Sidney P. Simpson, *Cases on Judicial Remedies* (1938), p. 23.

[15] 4 Co. Rep. 91a, 76 Eng. Rep. 1072 (K.B. 1602).

But what matters to the writers of this text is the form of pleadings in appellate review in an instance of actions at law. Alongside is placed a case from the Court of Appeals of the State of New York.[16] The vast differences between the England of Queen Elizabeth I and twentieth century America are of no significance to the point at issue which is stated by the text writers as follows: "After final judgment is rendered, the losing party can ordinarily carry the case to a higher court."[17] This statement presents a general principle of the law, deeply involved in the tradition of the "rule of law," a concept which has characterized adjudication over the centuries which have elapsed between the reign of Elizabeth and our time. The stress is on what is and has remained the same rather than on what has changed and evolved. The view is dogmatic rather than historical.

This instance illustrates, as would thousands of others, that the jurist is not concerned with the same dimension of interpretation as is the historian. For to the historian, the key question about the case would be: What does it tell us about the time of Queen Elizabeth? Is there anything here which sheds new light on Elizabeth or on the economic or social relations or any other of a number of possible individual historical features including the law *of her time?* And since the case as reported does not seem to do anything of the sort, it might well be considered irrelevant and trifling to the historian of Queen Elizabeth I's reign. Needless to say, the books on her reign and on the economic and social history of her reign do not make mention of this case. Nor do the legal histories, in fact. If we look up some of the leading texts on English legal history, such as Holdsworth or Pound, we do not find this case;[18] instead we find the rise of the Court of Chancery, from

[16] *Palsgraf* v. *Long Island R.R.*, 248 N.Y. 339, 162 N.E. 99 (1928).

[17] Interesting further points could be made regarding the fact that a "record" of a particular kind, defined at law, goes to the appeals court, embodying a report of what happened which excludes many events. In the days of Queen Elizabeth the record usually contained only the pleadings, the verdict, and the judgment; nowadays it also contains some of the proceedings at the trial.

[18] The case is actually cited by Holdsworth several times but in connection with another matter.

which this case is *not* taken, to be the key feature of the history of English law in this period. By the way, the rise of this court and of its equity jurisdiction has been described by a great legal historian as "an exceedingly curious episode." He added that "the whole nation seems to enter into one large conspiracy to evade its own laws, to evade laws which it has not the courage to reform."[19] The rise of this equity jurisdiction, in modification of the common law, was a matter of "stumbling into a scheme for the reconciliation of permanence with progress." Such a statement suggests that there is no effort made here to relate a decisive development in the history of the law of England with any of the other changing elements in the pattern of English life and politics. I am not going to indicate here what might be some of the correlations that suggest themselves but will merely remark that a deeper probing of the historical setting might well reveal connections which a strictly doctrinal approach tends to overlook.

But I wish to go a step further now and to advance the argument that the specific task of the student of law, of the jurist, is antithetical to that of the historian. By the very nature of his enterprise he is drawn into an ahistorical position.

In a challenging inaugural lecture, Frederic W. Maitland in 1888 discussed the question why the history of English law is not written.[20] He asserted at the outset that "English legal memory" went back to the year 1189 and no further, indeed to September 3, 1189.

> Glanvill had just finished the first text-book that would become a permanent classic for English lawyers; some clerk was just going to write the earliest plea-roll that would come to our hands; in a superb series of such rolls law was beginning to have a continuous written memory, a memory that we can still take in our hands and handle.[21]

Soon these records were to swell to a mighty chorus and "the practical limit set to our knowledge is not set by any lack of evidence,

[19] Frederic W. Maitland and Francis C. Montague, *A Sketch of English Legal History* (1915), p. 123.

[20] Frederic W. Maitland, *Collected Papers* (1911), ed. H. A. L. Fisher, pp. 480–97.

[21] *Ibid.*, p. 481.

it is the limit of our leisure, our strength, our studiousness, our curiosity."[22] It was obvious to Maitland that no one man could possibly hope to read the records even of one such reign as that of Edward I; how could the history of English law ever be written? "Seven hundred years of judicial records, six hundred years of law reports; think how long a time seven centuries would be in the history of Roman Law."[23] Centralization and the good fortune of England's insular position gave her "a series of records which for continuity, catholicity, minute detail and authoritative value has . . . no equal, no rival, in the world."[24] But it is the very fullness of this record which has been a major obstacle to legal history. Yet there are others, the most important being the isolation of English law and the conceit common to the guild that English law is something unique. "History," Maitland observed, "involves comparison and the English lawyer who knew nothing and cared nothing for any system but his own hardly came in sight of legal history."[25] And again: "[A]n isolated system cannot explain itself, still less explain its history."[26] Blackstone could write his remarkable volumes because he had an image of the feudal system, full of holes, in our modern perspective, but still an image that enabled him "to paint his great picture . . . the first picture ever painted"[27] of the history of English land law. So much for Maitland. There can be little doubt that the pursuit of legal history on the Continent was greatly stimulated by the confrontation of the local with the Roman law. The conflict between the two had profound political importance in the bargain; while the Roman law served ecclesiastical authorities at first, the "discovery" of its "true meaning" was a powerful weapon in the hands of the partisans of emperor and king. And eventually both were buried by the ivory tower learning of the great humanist jurists who insisted upon the historical record—Cujas, Doneau, and the rest. The work of these remarkable scholars serves at the same time to bring to light another aspect of the conflict between law and history, namely, that historical learning can kill the value of the

[22] *Ibid.*
[23] *Ibid.*
[24] *Ibid.*, p. 482.
[25] *Ibid.*, p. 488.
[26] *Ibid.*, p. 489.
[27] *Ibid.*

legal doctrine because it removes it from its contemporary application back to its original setting and thereby deprives it of authority and validity. The Roman law, which had been a live source of legal thought in the hands of the great glossators and post-glossators who used it for solving the problems of their changing society, was in danger of becoming dead and lifeless once the humanists had fully established its meaning in terms of a society long gone, the pagan world of ancient Rome.[28] However, the much argued "reception" of the Roman law into the German law in the course of the sixteenth and seventeenth centuries, though much lamented by romantics and "Germanists" such as Eichhorn and Gierke, gave it a new lease on life; it also continued in considerable vigor in the south of France until the great codification (see below). This can be vividly seen in Savigny's famous study on possession which makes a startling companion to Holmes's chapter in his *Common Law*. After reviewing the positions of Hegel and Kant which he thinks are related to the positions of the Roman law, Holmes remarks that Savigny did not follow them and quotes him as thinking that "every act of violence is unlawful" and as considering "protection of possession a branch of protection to the person."[29] He puts the matter as if this were a similarly philosophical opinion of Savigny's. But a reading of the adduced paragraph 6 shows that Savigny was arguing from the Roman law itself, was therefore insisting that the right of possession was part of the law of obligations rather than of the law of "things" (*Sachenrecht*). He sees the reason in the *historical* fact that the Romans classified according to the procedural considerations, exploring the distinction between *jus in rem* and *jus ad rem*. He noted that *possessio* had always been a thorn in the side of systematic jurists. All attempts to interpret possession not as a distinct right but as "provisional ownership" are in error. Savigny thinks; he adduces for authority a general principle of the Roman code: "*Nihil commune habet proprietas cum possessione.*" Having thus pointed

[28] Myron P. Gilmore, *Argument from Roman Law in Political Thought, 1200–1600* (1941).

[29] Holmes, *op. cit.*, p. 207.

out the basic *historical* position, Savigny proceeds to explore the linguistic usage of the Roman jurists to fortify his position, distinguishing between *possessio civilis* and *possessio naturalis.*[30] But I have already lingered too long over this fascinating issue. Suffice it to add that Savigny was well aware of the fact that the pristine Roman notions had undergone a basic development in the course of history. The modifications which occurred are clearly seen as the result of *historical* forces.

By the constitution of the Christian Church and of the European states rights have been created and have been linked to the possession and usufruct of the *soil* which the Romans partly did not know, and partly were far from recognizing as rights belonging to an individual. Thus the exercise of episcopal power depends upon the possession (*Besitz*) of the church and its possessions. . . .[31]

But a close examination leads Savigny to the conclusion that the notion of possession in Roman law has "not been changed, but has been very consistently developed." Roman law, then, can be seen here as alive and still providing answers to concrete problems of the "living law," albeit at times rather formal ones. Holmes, in commenting upon Savigny's historically argued position (in terms of authority and precedent), allows himself to be too much influenced by the philosophical generalizations of Kant and his followers. It was not these generalizations but the dead hand of the past that persuaded Savigny to take the position which Holmes criticizes in terms of the common law's view of possession. But I am not sure that he states Savigny's position correctly. I do not read him the way Holmes does;[32] it is clear in any case that he does not enter upon the *historical* argument but treats the discussion dogmatically.

30 Friedrich Karl von Savigny, *Das Recht des Besitzes* (1st ed., 1803). The paragraphs relevant here and referred to by Holmes are 6 and 7. To these should be added para. 48, in which the concept is discussed.

31 *Ibid.*, p. 481.

32 Holmes, *op. cit.*, p. 236. I find nothing in Savigny's careful historical analysis to support the sentence that Savigny "thinks that there must be always the same *animus* as at the moment of acquisition, and a constant power to reproduce at will the original physical relations to the object." See also *ibid.*, p. 238.

Maitland was fully aware of this conflict, but when considering the history of English law, he put it down as hindering the writing of English legal history because of the dogmatic preoccupation of the English lawyer. English lawyers were dealing with medieval law materials as lawyers, not as historians. "What is really required of the practising lawyer is not, save in the rarest cases, a knowledge of medieval law as it was in the middle ages, but rather a knowledge of medieval law as interpreted by modern courts to suit modern facts."[33] Thus a case is the more valuable the more recent it is; "what the lawyer wants is authority and the newer the better; what the historian wants is evidence and the older the better."[34] This point is of crucial importance for the right perspective on our problem. For the lawyer, Coke is better authority than Bracton, but for the historian seeking to interpret the law in the reign of Henry III "Bracton's lightest word is infinitely more valuable than all the tomes of Coke,"[35] not to mention more recent commentary. There is a basic conflict here which bedevils the task of legal history. We cannot say that Maitland has fully escaped it; for he proceeds to expound the notion that "any one who aspires to study legal history should begin by studying modern law."[36] Is it not like saying that anyone aspiring to study the history of philosophy or of art had better first study the contemporary practice of these subjects? No one will deny that such knowledge might be helpful, but is it essential? What then of the study of legal history where it extends to systems of law which no longer are alive? Can they not be studied at all? Indeed, such practical contemporary knowledge might be harmful, if not very carefully controlled, because it might cause the kind of "anachronism" which is so typically ahistorical in the work of, say, Sir Edward Coke. He knew the words and what use they could be made of in seventeenth-century England; he often did not know the meaning these words possessed at the time they were uttered. A medieval historian, fully alert to the conditions of the particular period and region in which

[33] Maitland, *Collected Papers*, I, 490.

[34] *Ibid.*, p. 491. [35] *Ibid.* [36] *Ibid.*, p. 494.

he had become an expert, would presumably be able to interpret more adequately the tenor of the phrases of the period; for law is not something separate and apart throughout the ages. It is part and parcel of the culture which it helps to organize and to define.

Thus legal history is seen as part of cultural history. Yet the term law does not even turn up in the index to Toynbee's magistral tomes—a scandal of sorts, if one remembers that Toynbee is an Englishman. How can culture, or at least Western culture, be imagined without laws? All of man's everyday activities, his government, and his economy are regularized and given form by law. In innumerable ways the history of certain cultures, and more especially Greco-Roman and Western cultures, is the history of the laws governing the communities which compose them. We need not go as far as Sir Henry Maine, who in one extraordinary passage attributed the difference between Roman (Western?) and Indian civilizations to the fact that the Romans had their Twelve Tables. These he saw as "merely an enunciation in words of the existing customs of the Roman people."[37] But he also saw a law that "usage which is reasonable generates usage which is unreasonable."[38] Stressing the common Indo-Germanic ancestry, which the ethnology of his time thought it could show, and acknowledging a "substratum of forethought and sound judgment"[39] in the Hindu jurisprudence, he yet imagined that the lack of an early code had thwarted the development of Hindu society; their law had been drawn up "after the mischief had been done."[40] The civilization of these unfortunate Hindus he saw as "feeble and perverted," while the Romans "*with* their code . . . were exempt from . . . so unhappy a destiny."[41] The foolishness of these comments, in our perspective of comparative cultural history, ought not to be allowed to hide the greater truth dimly perceived by the great Henry Maine, namely that a culture may be shaped, and often has been shaped, by its law.

There is an extraordinary passage in a later chapter (iv) of his work which I now wish to quote *in extenso*, because it pushes this

[37] Maine, *op. cit.*, p. 17.
[38] *Ibid.*, p. 18.
[39] *Ibid.*, p. 19.
[40] *Ibid.*
[41] *Ibid.*

issue further in a direction which seems to me crucial.[42] It ties in directly to what has just been discussed. And it raises a number of issues vital to our main theme. Among these the most crucial is that of the interaction between law and other aspects or components of culture. There are, Maine wrote,

two special dangers to which law and society which is *held together by law*, appear to be liable in their infancy. One of them is that law may be too rapidly developed. This occurred with the codes of the more progressive Greek communities, which disembarrassed themselves with astonishing facility from cumbrous forms of procedure and needless terms of art. . . . The Greek intellect, with all its nobility and elasticity, was quite unable to confine itself within the straight waistcoat of a legal formula; . . . the Greek tribunals exhibited the strongest tendency to confound law and fact. . . . No durable system of jurisprudence could be produced in this way. . . . Such jurisprudence would contain no framework to which the more advanced conceptions of subsequent ages could be fitted.[43]

If I understand him correctly, Maine wishes here to say that a society which fails to develop a suitably firm skeleton of law is in danger of falling to pieces because there is nothing to hold it together. He did not think that this danger threatened many peoples. Actually one wonders whether the proposition can be maintained in this generality. Certainly the Chinese civilization was built upon a similar confounding of "law and fact"; but the li of the Confucian bureaucracy provided as firm a framework for that society as did law for the West. The legal solution to the problem of political and social order was explicitly rejected in the struggle over the so-called legists.[44] But let us look for the other "danger," especially as Maine thought that "few national societies have had their jurisprudence menaced by this peculiar

[42] This passage was especially drawn to my attention in a discussion by Lon Fuller.

[43] Maine, *op. cit.*, pp. 72–73 (italics added).

[44] See William T. De Bary, Jr., "Chinese Despotism and the Confucian Ideal: A Seventeenth-Century View," in *Chinese Thought and Institutions* (1957), ed. John K. Fairbanks, pp. 163–203, for a recent reappraisal. The "totalitarian" interpretation of Chinese despotism in Karl A. Wittfogel, *Oriental Despotism* (1957), does not convince me.

danger of precocious maturity and untimely disintegration."[45] For the other danger is much more common and it has "prevented or arrested the progress of far the greater part of mankind."[46] It is the danger that "the rigidity of primitive law, arising chiefly from its early association and identification with religion, has chained down the mass of the human race to those views of life and conduct which they entertained at the time when their usages were first consolidated into a systematic form."[47] And "over the larger part of the world, the perfection of law has always been considered as consisting in adherence to the ground plan supposed to have been marked out by the original legislator."[48] What allowed the Romans to escape from this other danger was their theory of natural law. Now in point of fact, modern scholarship has greatly reduced the importance of natural law in the development of Roman jurisprudence[49] and has correspondingly emphasized the traditional, especially the religious, elements—in other words, precisely those elements which Maine saw as the second "danger." But leaving aside the Romans and Maine's questionable interpretation of their theory of natural law as a parallel to Bentham's doctrine,[50] I wish to stress here that Maine insisted that law can seriously affect cultural development, either by giving it too much or too little of a skeleton, framework, stability, rigidity, and so forth. This is, it seems to me, a major insight, and it is grounded in the paradox, the dialectic of the relation of

[45] Maine, *op. cit.*, p. 73.

[46] *Ibid.*, p. 74.

[47] *Ibid.*

[48] *Ibid.*, pp. 74–75.

[49] F. Schultz, *History of Roman Legal Science* (1946); E. F. Bruck, *Ueber roemisches Recht im Rahmen der Kulturgeschichte* (1954). In the latter, the natural law is not treated at all, and Cicero's position is correspondingly reduced to the point where Professor Bruck even says: "Jurist war er schwerlich."

[50] Maine is, of course, aware of the fact that philosophically the two doctrines are far apart; natural law is not "an anticipation of Bentham's principles." Still he considers it "not an altogether fanciful comparison if we call the assumptions [of natural law] the ancient counterpart of Benthamism." The reason is that they both gave the nation and the profession "a distinct object to aim at in the pursuit of improvement." Bentham gave England a "clear rule of reform." In short "law of nature" and "the general good of the community" fulfilled the same *function* in the reshaping of the law. For a sketch of the natural law doctrine, see chap. iv above.

jurisprudence and historical understanding. To put it hortatively: the dogmatic and conceptual foundation of the law needs the softening impact of an inquiry into the past in order to free itself for the future. But such historical "softening" must not be carried too far, or the legal fabric is dissolved and with it the society which it sustains. This twofold danger is by no means restricted to the infancy of human society; it persists to the very present.

In order to illuminate this aspect of the relation of law and history further, the mooted question of codification deserves treatment here. For the issue of codification has helped to precipitate the argument about jurisprudence and history, the argument over whether history and more especially the history of law matters to jurisprudence at all. Savigny's famous essay on behalf of the historical school of jurisprudence[51] was written in response to the proposal made at the time, and in a spirit of patriotism, that the Germans codify their law. Savigny cited Bacon for the opinion that the age in which a code is brought into being must excel the preceding ages in legal understanding, and he drew the inference that, therefore, some ages which might be highly cultured in other respects do not possess the requisite "calling" for making a code.[52] He insisted that Germany was in that position. He built his argument upon a general proposition in line with our analysis here that "a two-fold understanding is indispensable to a jurist: the historical, in order that he may grasp the peculiar [nature]

[51] Friedrich Karl von Savigny, *Vom Beruf unserer Zeit fuer Gesetzgebung und Rechtswissenschaft* (1814). I used the third edition, which contains two appendixes concerned with the matter. Savigny's views have been restudied in the past generation; there is the detailed scholarly biography of Adolf Stoll, *Friedrich Karl von Savigny* (1927), in three volumes; the brilliant essay of Erik Wolf, *Grosse Rechtsdenker der deutschen Geistesgeschichte* (1939), chap. xii; and the penetrating analytic essay by Franz Zwilgmeyer, *Der Rechtslehre Savignys* (1929). All three agree that behind Savigny's historicism there is to be found a dogmatic judgment in favor of the Roman law as the standard of what constitutes high achievement. This non-relative aspect of Savigny is crucial for an understanding of his position on the question of codification.

[52] Bacon's well-known proposals were made to King James and are entitled "A Proposition to His Majesty . . . Touching the Compiling and Amendment of the Laws of England" and "An Offer to King James of a Digest To Be Made of the Laws of England." They are found in Francis Bacon, *Works* (Philadelphia, 1852), II, 229–36.

of each age and of each legal form, and the systematic one, in order that he perceive each concept and each rule [principle] in living connection and interaction with the whole [of the law]. . . ."[53] Savigny felt that the German jurists of the eighteenth century did not possess this equipment, that they were shallow rationalists, and that the new beginning which had been made had not yet progressed far enough, though there was hope. To fix the law at such a point, he felt, was not only useless; it was dangerous, because it clothed with authority an unsatisfactory state of the law, and he reminded his readers of the Code of Theodoric in this connection. He also urged that the German language had not yet developed an adequate legal vocabulary. He then proceeded to analyze the codes that had come into being, more especially the Code Civil or Code Napoléon.[54] His very sharp criticism is primarily directed at the ignorance of the four men who drafted the code, since the *Conseil d'Etat* contained so many (in his view) juristically incompetent persons. How relatively irrelevant this sort of criticism was, has been pointed out.[55] For Savigny was inclined to gainsay the true historical functions of the Code Civil which lay in the cementing of national unity and to belittle the great principles underlying it, namely (1) freedom of the person and of contract, as well as equal right to engage in professions and to possess property; (2) suppression of all the old privileges, equality of all Frenchmen regardless of status, sex, or social condition; and (3) freedom of civil society from all ecclesiastical control. These were of course at the heart of the French Revolution, and for this revolution Savigny had little use.

[53] Savigny, *op. cit.*

[54] For this and what follows, see *The Code Napoléon and the Common Law World* (1956), ed. Bernard Schwartz, especially my essay, "The Ideological and Philosophical Background" (pp. 1–18), and A. P. Sereni's essay, "The Code and Case Law" (pp. 55–79). In a number of other essays, S. D. Elliott, A. von Mehren, Max Rheinstein, and others show how the code has been transformed by legislative and judicial interpretation.

[55] Thus, the renowned René Cassin remarked that "on the technical level, proponents of the historical school could criticize the codification for having ossified the rules of civil law and prevented certain necessary development" ("Codification and National Unity," in Schwartz, *op. cit.*, p. 49).

For him, as for so many other historicist thinkers, the rationalist ingredient of the revolutionary credo was anathema. Yet, the Code contained many notions deeply embedded in the old customary law, or *coutumes,* and it is truly surprising to note to how large an extent Savigny could overlook this element. "The Germanic, conservative and popular content [of the Code] Savigny did not recognize."[56] The "errors" which Savigny charged the drafters with were mistakes about the Roman law which he knew so well; that their great achievement lay in the skilful use of Pothier by Pourtalis he did not acknowledge.

It has been rightly said that "the promulgation of the Civil Code in the year 1804 is, historically, the legislative response to a desire expressed during many centuries by the French people."[57] The Code was not the hiatus in French legal development which Savigny's criticism implied. In the perspective of a century and a half, it is quite plain to see that the Code was a culmination and a starting point. If we approach the Code as historians, the codification can be seen as part of that ebb and flow of ideas by which the law is molded as it evolves. The seamless web of history appears then as not torn apart by a Code but as merely reinforced by such a "digest." Actually, the Code had become an inescapable necessity through the very work of the revolution which *threatened* to disrupt the legal continuity. This threat was averted and the continuity preserved with the help of the code which, in terms of Hegel's dialectic phrase, suspended, superseded, and preserved the old law. At this point, a distinction needs to be drawn between the different kinds of codes.

The idea of a code and a codification appears in at least three distinguishable forms. The Justinian Code represents a first type; one might call it the digest type. It tries to bring together and "digest" a body of existing law, clarifying it, eliminating possible contradictions, but not intending to alter it in any significant way. The work of the American Law Institute has been essentially of this character. Bacon, in the above cited memoranda, spoke as if

[56] Wolf, *op. cit.*, p. 476.

[57] A. Tunc, "The Grand Outlines of the Code," in Schwartz, *op. cit.*, p. 19.

such a digest were what he had in mind. "The work which I propound, tendeth to the pruning and grafting the law, and not to the ploughing up and planting it again; for such a remove I hold indeed for a perilous innovation. . . ."[58] But he actually aimed at the second type. This sort of code seeks to codify the law in terms of natural law or other general principles which would provide a pattern for systematization. These general principles are philosophical and political in nature and serve as a yardstick for the evaluation of existing law; that is to say, such a code seeks the clarification and reformation of the law in whole or in part. General philosophical reason is here assigned a distinctive role. Such were the codes the enlightened despots favored and enacted, the Prussian Common Code and the Austrian Civil Law Code, as well as the more limited codes made under Louis XIV with the help of Colbert. Such a code was in the mind of Bacon, who flattered the king about his knowledge of "justice and judicature" which enabled him to be a "lawgiver"; he proclaimed that "as the common law is more worthy than the statute law, so the law of nature is more worthy than them both."[59] Such codes were in line with the thinking of enlightened despotism. The *philosophes* were the authors of the general principles; the jurists, of the detailed application.

But there was implicit in this kind of thinking a yet more radical position enunciated by the greatest of the *philosophes,* Voltaire, when he exclaimed: "Do you want good laws? Burn yours and make new ones!" Voltaire's dramatic demand symbolizes the revolutionary attitude that underlay the insistent demand for a code of laws during the revolution. The original French revolutionary codes were of this type of "rationality." The draft code of 1793 was revolutionary in both intent and content. It was meant to change everything at once; it was "the fruit of liberty." The drafters told the assembly that "the nation will receive it as the guarantee of its happiness, and it will offer it one day to all the peoples. . . ." There was only one truth, and that was the revolutionary

[58] Bacon, *op. cit.,* II, 231.

[59] *Ibid.,* p. 169. Roscoe Pound, *The Development of Constitutional Guarantees of Liberty* (1957), p. 43, stresses Bacon's favoring absolute monarchy.

ideology which they had embodied in their draft code. A still more radical code was presented the following year; it was, in the words of one eminent French legal scholar, "much more a manual of practical morals than a code of civil law." Neither was adopted. The codifications of the USSR (and subsequently of the Communist states) are really the best examples of this type of code.[60] Thus the problem of codification shows dramatically the range of continuity and change that law in its historical dimension can exhibit.

It is clear that the two-fold danger of which Maine had warned is at the heart of the argument over the problem of codification: that is, does it make the law too rigid, or does it help to give it that tensile strength which it requires for fulfilling its societal functions? As has been often remarked, law in a certain sense is an organon, an organic whole extending over centuries. Being embedded in the history of nations, it must be seen in the perspective of their over-all significance. We may have come a long way from the romantic notions of a Gierke, who would interpret all history in terms of the struggle of the Romanist principle of *Herrschaft* with the Germanic principle of *Genossenschaft;* we may have left far behind the equally romantic notion of a Savigny, who would interpret the Roman law in terms of the folk spirit of the Roman people; we may have outdistanced Maine's utilitarian enthusiasm for the progress from status to contrast as the key to all legal development. But we cannot escape from the need of identifying our own philosophy of history, if we are to see the historical phenomena of law-in-the-making in the perspective of truth claims, whether scientific or humanist.[61]

[60] See H. J. Berman, *Justice in Russia* (1950); Boris A. Konstantinovsky, *Soviet Law in Action* (1953), ed. H. J. Berman, concerned with the codification problem; cf. also Andrei Vyshinsky, *The Law of the Soviet State* (1948), for an ex cathedra exposition.

[61] Besides Collingwood and the writers cited in the next few footnotes, the following deserve mention as significant contributions to the recent discussion: Raymond Aron, *Introduction à la Philosophie de l'Histoire* (1948); Isaiah Berlin, *Historical Inevitability* (1954); Marjorie L. Burke, *Origin of History as Metaphysic* (1950); Theodor Litt, *Wege und Irrwege geschichtlichen Denkens* (1947); Henri Marrou, *De la Connaissance Historique* (1954); U. A. Padovani, *Filosofia e Teologia della Storia* (1953).

Any attempt to answer the question, What is history? involves a philosophy of history in the sense of "general thoughts upon history." We have postponed this question until now, but we can avoid it no longer. Our time has produced a rich variety of answers and rejoinders to answers. Lord Acton, one of the great minds working in that field in the recent past, thought it "the office of historical science to maintain morality as the sole impartial criterion of men and things." Others, from St. Augustine to Hegel, have seen history as the theodicy in which God and the march of spirit were revealed in the world of man.[62] "Historicism," if not of the Augustinian, then certainly of the Hegelian and Marxian, variety, has been flailed again and again from different viewpoints. In a perspective somewhat akin to that of Lord Acton, one contemporary philosopher has juxtaposed a doctrine of natural right with all such historicism, which he has called "self-contradictory or absurd."[63] Another, noting the "poverty of historicism," argues on the contrary that historicism, "an antique and tottering philosophy," proclaims

> social science is nothing but history, not however history in the traditional sense of a mere chronicle of historical facts . . . but . . . of the laws of social development. . . . [I]t could be described as historical theory or as theoretical history, since the only universally valid social laws have been identified as historical laws.[64]

[62] For these, see Karl Loewith, *Meaning in History* (1949), who examines a baker's dozen writers from Burckhardt to Orosius.

[63] Leo Strauss, *Natural Right and History* (1953), p. 25. See *ibid.*, chap. i. Strauss states the position of "radical historicism" as follows: "All understanding, all knowledge, however limited and 'scientific,' presupposes a frame of reference; it presupposes a horizon, a comprehensive view within which understanding and knowing take place. Only such a comprehensive vision makes possible any seeing, any observation, any orientation. The comprehensive view of the whole cannot be validated by reasoning, since it is the basis of all reasoning. Accordingly, there is a variety of such comprehensive views, each as legitimate as any other: we have to choose such a view without any rational guidance" (*ibid.*, pp. 26–27).

[64] Karl Popper, *The Poverty of Historicism* (1957), p. 45. Popper, the philosopher of science, is impressed with the passive, contemplative aspect of historicism, its "quietism"; he notes that "the historical can only *interpret* social development and aid it in various ways; . . . *nobody can change it*" (*ibid.*, p. 52).

In writing thus, he emphasizes the exact opposite of the preceding critic, namely the doctrinaire, dogmatic aspect of historicism as contrasted with its relativist notions. Crucially conclusive against such a view is, in this critic's opinion, the fact that "we cannot predict, by rational or scientific methods, the future growth of our scientific knowledge," and "if there is such a thing as growing human knowledge, then we cannot anticipate to-day what we shall know only to-morrow."[65] The trouble with historicism (and with certain kinds of sociology derived from it) is that it believes it can predict confidently. But neither can you so predict on the basis of some kind of unchanging "human nature," as the other critic with his faith in natural right believed.

The contradiction in the two ways of seeing "historicism" is embedded in the phenomenon itself, as well as in the outlook of the critics. Of these the first hopes to return to an "unchanging world," such as was believed in before the historicists took over; the second wants to transcend the "fear of change" which has driven the historicist into believing in an "unchanging law" which governs the changing world.[66] To both it might be objected that the particular view of history which they reject is the only view worthy of respect as "philosophy of history."[67] For only when history is seen as a whole, is seen as world history with a meaning, can we in this perspective speak of a "philosophy of history." Now it has been asserted that if seen thus, philosophy of history is "entirely dependent upon theology," that is to say, upon the "theological interpretation of history as salvation."[68] Whether this be true or not, it is certainly a fact that such philosophies of history have been a peculiar and distinctive feature of the West, with definite roots in

[65] Popper, *op. cit.*, p. x. The last quoted passage is given by Popper in italics.

[66] Popper, *op. cit.*, p. 161.

[67] This appears to be the tendency of Loewith, who in his discriminating study, cited in n. 62, would not credit "every opinion about history" as a philosophy of history, but only "the systematic interpretation of world history on the basis of a principle" (Loewith, *op. cit.*, p. 11).

[68] *Ibid.* Loewith speaks of *Heilsgeschehen*, that is to say, literally, "the happening of salvation," and the title of the German edition of his book has therefore been changed into *Weltgeschichte als Heilsgeschehen* (1953).

the Bible, more especially the Old Testament. The theological roots may have something to do with the political function which such philosophies have had.

The great syntheses of these philosophies of history are closely related to the unique importance of historical thought for the West. For through them the *self* achieves the relatedness which he seeks as a cultural being. It provides the frame within which it becomes possible to say what needs to be said about the meaning and destiny of this particular human being, as well of man.[69] At the same time, such a projection of the self of man and his culture *expresses* and gives verisimilitude to a sense of superiority—cultural, spiritual, religious. Philosophies of history are, in this perspective, expressions of an intellectual or spiritual imperialism such as has characterized the West until recently and is now being transformed and reincarnated in the Soviet Union. This equality is inherent in such syntheses because they presuppose a universal goal or end of history which can only be asserted on the basis of faith. Thus philosophies of history are expressions of a will to power, a will to conquest even. They correspond to other forms of ideological aggression and the will (or at any rate the desire) to subjugate mankind in terms of its own good. Such destiny is apt to be described as manifest and well calculated to heal the ills of the world, in one form or another. It is evident that all such philosophies are variants upon the theme of the "chosen people."[70] Legal history, though rarely involved in the broad universalism of such philosophies, has tended to partake of the valuational aggressiveness. The well-known conceit of the common law lawyers is readily matched by the "Germanism" of a Gierke or the "Romanism" of a Savigny. That is to say, legal history is frequently infused by a preconceived notion of what constitutes valid law.

As against such extravagances, a more sober view of history, a more skeptical philosophy, might provide a possible antidote. The

[69] Reinhold Niebuhr, *The Nature and Destiny of Man* (1949), II, 299–321 ("Human Destiny"), esp. 299 ff.

[70] For further detail, see my article, "Die Philosophie der Geschichte als Form der Ueberlagerung," in *Wirtschaft und Kultursystem* (1955), ed. Gottfried Eisermann, p. 199, and the literature there cited.

great Burckhardt, in his *Reflections on World History,* clearly indicated his lack of interest in broad constructions. History, he thought, was not a science of objective, "neutral" facts, but a "report about such facts as one age finds remarkable in another." Only by thus selecting and interpreting the reports about past events can we determine which facts are noteworthy, important, of real significance. He noted that "Thucydides may mention a fact the importance of which will only be recognized in a hundred years." Such a view of history is eminently suited to the pursuit of legal history in the best sense. For is it not typical of the work of jurists that they reassess the law of past decisions—judicial, legislative, administrative—in the light of present concerns and preoccupations? But is it enough? Do we not need some kind of notion of an inner development, of an unfolding of the potentialities of the body that is law? In the work of the greatest historians of the law, some such idea seems to have been alive and a major motivating force of their work. Before considering this notion of "intrinsic" development in the Aristotelian sense of a *telos* that is embedded in the seed, let us consider yet another approach.

One of the best-known students of these problems believed that the idea of history could be circumscribed in four basic propositions, to wit, that "history should be (a) a science, or an answering of questions; (b) concerned with human actions in the past; (c) pursued by interpretation of evidence; and (d) for the sake of human self-knowledge."[71] In light of such a characterization, which the author believed to be generally held among historians, he asked the question: Of what can there be historical knowledge? And he answered: of that which can be re-enacted in the historian's mind. Such an answer is obviously favorable to the historical exploration of past events that belong to the realm of the mind, and law is certainly one of these. It reinforces the notion, considered by us earlier, that one should have a knowledge of the law to be a legal historian; it would certainly facilitate the "re-enacting." But is there not a fatal difficulty present also, the difficulty of

[71] Collingwood, *op. cit.,* Introduction. See n. 2 above and accompanying text.

re-enacting anything? Heraclitus' famous proposition that you cannot step into the same river twice, that all is in flux, applies to the subtle matters of the spirit more poignantly than to the "simple" passions felt by all men—love, hatred, ambition, and the rest of which so much ordinary human history is compounded. But can we ever again recapture the way men reasoned about justice in the days of Bracton or even of Coke? It seems most improbable. And when we read the detailed essays of renowned scholars in the field of legal history, it is usually clear enough what has been their concern. Think of the debunking of Magna Carta[72] and the corresponding work on the Declaration of Independence.[73] These two venerable documents of legal history can now be said to represent striking instances of myth-making and myth-destroying. As scholars have succeeded in "re-enacting," they have also succeeded in depriving of genuine legal value these and other records of the past. Is it too much to say that the more fully a particular historical event is understood, the more remote it becomes from present concerns? J. B. Ames recounts a rather touching anecdote of the young Langdell in his memorial article on that great scholar. It takes us back to the days when Langdell was studying and assisting at the Harvard Law School. When a fellow student, the later Judge Charles E. Phelps, surprised him among his books in the alcoves of Dane Hall, studying a black letter folio, Langdell exclaimed, "in a tone of mingled exhilaration and regret, and with an emphatic gesture: 'Oh, if only I could have lived in the time of the Plantagenets!' " To have lived at the time of the Plantagenets—this is indeed the problem, and the more nearly you succeed, the less you have to offer to the twentieth century.[74]

It is then clear (or at any rate suggested) that the continuity of legal thought processes is to a very considerable extent a fiction.

[72] See William S. McKechnie, *Magna Carta* (2d ed.; 1913).

[73] See Carl Becker, *The Declaration of Independence* (1922).

[74] Cf. James Barr Ames, *Lectures on Legal History* (1913), p. 471. It might be remarked in passing that Ames states the subject of his lectures to be "the origin and development of the ideas of crime, tort, contract, property and equity." The next sentence claims that "the common law is essentially of Teutonic origin." It is not fashionable to put it that way today.

No matter how history is conceived philosophically, the cases that are cited over and over produce in line with *stare decisis* a façade of historical support which any close inspection would reveal as largely untenable. At the same time it must be admitted that this fiction is of the greatest legal, that is, dogmatic, importance.

> In this country [England] and in the whole common-law world, the place of the systematic fiction is taken to a considerable extent by the fiction of historical continuity. Every decision appears in the cloak of a mere application or adaptation of pre-existing "principles" laid down in earlier judicial pronouncements. Where historical continuity and systematic consistency are in conflict, it is the former which prevails. . . .[75]

In the light of what can properly be called scientific history in the sense previously defined, this continuity is a fact only through its being a fiction; for if the historical appreciation were truly scientific, that is, if it were actually based upon the search and discovery of historical truth, it would forthwith cease to be operative as a fiction; for the cases in the past would cease to have any application to the problems of today.

This is my conclusion, then, but it is less skeptical than it sounds. History in the sense of past happenings is not the "meaningless" to which meaning is arbitrarily assigned. When these happenings are products of the mind, such as legal decisions, statutes, and opinions of jurists, they presumably had a meaning to those who brought them into being. In searching for this meaning, this historian will be sitting in judgment upon the rational content, both in terms of means and ends. Thus "the judicial role appears to fit the historian's activity better than that of the scientist checking hypotheses, the politician promoting his party's cause, or the artist fashioning a work of art."[76] This "judgment" which the historian is called upon to render provides the intellectual bridge between him and the jurist. It is not an arbitrary judgment, such as is often assumed to have been implied in Hegel's famous quote from Schiller's *Die Resignation,* but rather the resigned judgment of the

[75] O. Kahn-Freund, Introduction to Karl Renner's *The Institutions of Private Law and Their Social Functions* (1949), pp. 9–10.

[76] Swabey, *op. cit.*, p. 238.

truth-seeker who knows that he will never know all of it. Why should a past decision provide authority for a present one? Because there is a fair chance that the solution it offered related sound reasoning in terms of justice to that feature of a problematic situation which is persisting in the one now confronting the jurist. It may be fiction, and the farther removed in time, the more likely this is. But "life is but a dream," and even fictions have their place in the economy of the mind, especially the legal mind. The potential antagonism between the historian who may destroy a cherished illusion and the jurist who is called upon to provide reasoned solutions to the problems of injustice that are facing us here and now may be resolved time and again by the re-enforcement of a sharpened critical insight into the true "precedents" which a history of the law can provide.

C. Biblical Law

i. B. Clark [Law Editor], *Biblical Law* (2d ed.; Portland, Ore.: Binfords & Mort, 1944), pp. 1-49.

Biblical Law

BEING A TEXT OF THE STATUTES, ORDINANCES, AND JUDGMENTS ESTABLISHED IN THE HOLY BIBLE— WITH MANY ALLUSIONS TO SECULAR LAWS: ANCIENT, MEDIEVAL AND MODERN—DOCUMENTED TO THE SCRIPTURES, JUDICIAL DECISIONS AND LEGAL LITERATURE

By
H. B. CLARK
LAW EDITOR

SECOND EDITION

Published by BINFORDS & MORT
PORTLAND, OREGON
1944

PART I

INTRODUCTION AND GENERAL PRINCIPLES

CHAPTER 1

DEFINITIONS AND SOURCES OF LAW

[§1] The Bible is a book of principles rather than definitions. Though it abounds in legal doctrine, it may be searched in vain for a definition of law. But the term has often been defined by secular writers. Blackstone[1] described it as a rule of human action or conduct.[2] Holmes[3] considered it as a prediction or prophecy of what a court or officer would do to a man if he did or omitted to do certain things.[4] In this book law means a rule or a body of rules for the government of human life,[5] prescribing rights and duties and regulating conduct.[6] Law embraces custom, and includes expressions of attitudes or policies of the law-maker.[6a] And while the standards of the law are usually external,[6b] Biblical law also contains some rules pertaining to thought or emotion as distinguished from purely physical action or conduct.

[§2] The question may arise as to whether Biblical doctrines actually are law, for it has been said that a law must be prescribed by an authority that citizens or subjects are bound to obey, and that there must be a court or officer to administer and enforce it.[7] But these sayings are not necessarily true.[8] For though law rests in large measure upon com-

1 Sir Wm. Blackstone (1723-1780) English jurist, author of "Commentaries on the Laws of England"

2 1 Bl. Com. 38, 39

3 Oliver Wendell Holmes (1841-1935) American jurist, Associate Justice US Supreme Court 1902-1932

4 Holmes' Collected Legal Papers (1920) Path of the Law

"Law is a statement of the circumstances in which the public force will be brought to bear upon men through the courts." American Banana Co. v United Fruit Co. (1908) 213 US 347, 53 L ed 826, 832 (Holmes,J)

5 27 ABA Journal (1941) No. 2, 78

6 "In general, laws are meant to regulate and direct the acts and rights of citizens." United States v Hoar (1821) 2 Mason 311, 314, Fed.Cas.No.15373 (Story,Cir.J)

6a See, for example, §188, infra, showing the Scriptural attitude as to marriage.

6b Aikens v Wisconsin (1904) 195 US 194, 204, 49 L ed 154, 159 (Holmes,J)

"Law is concerned with external behavior and not with the inner life of man." Board of Education (W.Va.) v Barnette (1943) 319 US 624, 87 L ed adv opns 1171, 1187 (Frankfurter,J, dissenting)

7 Dickinson v Dickinson (1819) 7 NC 327; 30 Harv.LR (1917) 284

8 It is not always the case that enforcement in courts is necessary to make a rule law. See 28 Yale LJ (1918-19) 842

pulsion,[8a] nevertheless rules prescribed by an authority that persons ought to obey may properly be considered as law.[9] A rule may also be established by common consent or agreement of the people that it shall be binding upon them in their dealings among themselves. A law does not lose its legal character because violations are punished mildly or, in practice, are not punished at all, nor even though there is no physical means by which obedience can be presently enforced.[10]

[§3] Law is found in statutes and judgments,[11] and in custom. Statutes—or ordinances, as they are sometimes called[12]—are expressions of a law-maker, usually commanding or forbidding that certain things be done. Judgments are decisions of judges which expound or apply rules of law in settling disputes.[13] The ruling of a judge or court may become a general law, as in the case of the Daughters of Zelophehad.[14] And custom consists in rules arising out of common usages and practices of the people—for which the law has great regard.[15]

[§4] Custom is a fruitful source of law.[16] Error is not to be sanctioned because it has once got a footing.[17] But when a custom is not evil in itself nor in contravention of any law, it is accepted as a certain kind of law,[18] upon the theory that the law-making power commanded what it permitted over a long period of time.[18a] Ordinarily a custom must be common

8a Board of Education (W.Va.) v Barnette (1943) 319 US 624, 87 L ed adv opns 1171, 1187 (Frankfurter,J, dissenting)

9 "This is Law, to which all men ought to yield obedience for many reasons." Demosthenes, Adv. Aristogeiton I § 774

10 The Prometheus (1906) 2 Hongkong 207; and see infra §127, n 27

11 Ezek. 20:11

12 Ex. 15:25; Eph. 2:15

According to modern usage, "ordinances" are local laws or bylaws of cities or counties.

13 "From the decisions rules are drawn." Carpenters & Joiners Union v Ritter's Cafe (1942) 315 US 722, 86 L ed 1143 (Reed,J, dissenting)

"Decisions are but evidences of the law and not the law itself." Barnette v Board of Education (1942) 47 F Supp (W.Va.) 251, 253 (Parker, Cir J)

14 See infra §139

15 Carson v Blazer (1810) 2 Binney (Pa.) 475, 487 (Yeates,J), observing further that "the law itself" is "nothing else but common usage, with which it complies, and alters with the exigency of affairs"

16 Dewey, Philosophy of Law (1941) 78

17 Brown v Phoenix Ins. Co. (1812) 4 Binney (Pa.) 445, 478 (Brackenridge, J)

Age does not hallow error. In re Halcomb (1942) 21 Cal. 2d 126, 130 P 2d 384 (Traynor,J, dissenting)

Mere custom or usage cannot make lawful conduct that is actually unlawful. Milton v Motor Coach Co. (1942) 53 Cal.App. 2d 566, 570, 128 P 2d 178 (Shinn,J) saying that custom cannot make due care out of conduct that is in fact negligence.

Nor does long indulgence of a practice create a right to its continuance. Changing conditions have begotten modification of many practices once deemed a part of the individual's liberty. Martin v Struthers (1943) 319 US 141, 87 L ed adv opns 861, 869 (Reed,J, dissenting)

18 Gratian, Decretum, Canons 4, 5

18a Or in accordance with the maxim that "He who does not forbid when he can forbid, commands." Baillarge v Clark (1904) 145 Cal. 589, 104 ASR 75, 79 P 268 and well established before it has the binding effect of law. But "all Scripture . . . is profitable for doctrine, for reproof, for correction, for instruction in righteousness,"[19] and the recording of an act without comment on the part of a Biblical writer may therefore be taken, in a proper case, as an indication that it accords with the law or conformed with the custom of the time.[20]

CHAPTER 2

KINDS OF LAW

5 Various classes of law 6 Divine or revealed law 7 Moral law 8 Natural law 9 Human or secular law

[§5] The field of law has been called a seamless whole,[21] meaning that any particular rule ought to be read in connection with the whole body of the law. Yet some division is necessary for purposes of investigation or study. Law may be classified on the one hand as divine or revealed, on the other as human or secular. From other standpoints it is international or municipal, public or private, general or special, civil or criminal, statutory or judicial; and mandatory, permissive or declaratory. International law governs the relations between nations; municipal law, the domestic or internal affairs of a nation, state or city. Public or general law consists of rules of general application; private or special law, rules applicable to particular persons, things or localities. Civil law pertains to civil rights and their enforcement; criminal law, to crimes and their punishments. Statutory law is that which is enacted by legislators; judicial law, that which is formulated by judges in the decision of controversies. Law is mandatory, permissive or declaratory, when it either commands or permits a thing to be done or left undone or when it declares or defines a right, duty or policy.

[§6] Divine or revealed law is that which, according to the Scriptures, God gave directly to man.[22] As Blackstone said:

> "Divine Providence . . . hath been pleased at sundry times and in divers manners to discover and enforce its laws by an immediate and direct revelation. The doctrines thus discovered we call the 'revealed' or 'divine' law, and they are to be found only in the Holy Scriptures."[23]

19 2 Tim. 3:16

20 13 Gr.B. (1901) 38 (Amram)

21 1 Street's Foundations (1906) xxviii

22 1 Bl. Com. 41

23 1 Bl. Com. 42

Much of the revealed law of the Old Testament appears to have been "spoken" by the Lord or Jehovah, and some of the law of the New Testament is contained in the teachings of Jesus. Many other provisions of revealed law are found in the sayings, writings and acts of human authorities, both ecclesiastical and civil, such as prophets, disciples, apostles, kings, judges and governors.

The law was revealed in several ways:

1 By commandments to do or not to do certain things;
2 By judgments pronounced in particular cases;
3 By statements commending or reproving certain conduct; and
4 By the absence of comment upon conduct seeming to merit commendation or reproval.

But in the sense that "all scripture is given by inspiration of God,"[24] all law contained in the Bible is to be regarded as divine or revealed, regardless of the particular manner or circumstances of its revelation.

"It is . . . a fault of presumption, either to reject any of those things that are written, or to bring in any of those things that are not written."[25]

Nothing is to be allowed or considered "against the law of God, but what is prohibited in holy writ."[26]

[§7] Moral law consists in a body of ethical or moral rules for the conduct of man, "to secure him the greatest happiness in harmony with the conditions of his existence"[27]—rules once regarded as "eternally and universally binding upon mankind."[28] Judge Dillon,[29] in his commentary on the Laws and Jurisprudence of England and America, says:

"Not less wondrous than the revelations of the starry heavens, and much more important, and to no class of men more so than lawyers, is the moral law which Kant found within himself, and which is likewise found within, and is consciously recognized by, every man. This moral law holds its dominion by divine ordination over us all, from which escape or evasion is impossible. This moral law is the eternal and indestructible sense of justice and right written by God on the living tablets of the human heart and revealed in his Holy Word."[30]

24 2 Tim. 3:16

25 Preface to King James' Version (1611) "The Translators to the Reader," quoting S.Basil
"The Scriptures were from Moses' time to the time of the apostles and evangelists, in whose ages . . . the book of Scriptures was shut and closed, so as not to receive any new additions, and . . . the church hath no power after the Scriptures to teach and command anything contrary to the written Word." Bacon

26 Anderson v Winston (1736) Jefferson's (Va.) Reports, 27, citing 1 Hawk. 245

27 Moore v Strickling (1899) 46 W.Va. 515, 33 SE 274, 50 LRA 279 282 (Dent,P)

28 Anderson v Winston (1736) Jefferson's (Va.) Reports, 24

29 John F. Dillon (1831-1914) American jurist and author

30 Moore v Stricklin, ante

Many of the precepts of the moral law relate to mankind as members of an organized society and impose duties upon individuals which are of the same kind as those imposed by the human authority of the state. Others relate only to mankind as individuals, prescribing duties toward each other and toward God which human law does not and cannot recognize or enforce. The divine law as expounded in the Scriptures has, by some writers, been characterized as the moral law,[31] and it has been said:

"If our reason were always, as in our first ancestor before his transgression, clear and perfect, unruffled by passions, unclouded by prejudice, unimpaired by disease or intemperance, . . . we should need no other guide. . . . But every man now finds the contrary in his own experience—that his reason is corrupt and his understanding full of ignorance and error."[32]

[§8] Natural law is a moral system supposedly conformable to nature[33] that has been framed by ethical writers.[34] It is said to be inherent in man,[35] in that, according to St. Paul, the Lord has put it in the minds and written it into the hearts of men.[36] Its precepts "are not to be rummaged for among old parchments or musty records. They are written with a sunbeam, in the whole volume of human nature by the hand of divinity itself, and can never be erased or obscured by mortal power."[37]

"Things required by natural law are marriage, succession, bringing up of children, one common security for all, one liberty for all, and the right to acquire those things which are capable of possession in air, earth and sea."[38]

[§9] Human or secular law is that which has been made by human legislators or judges. "It is formed and perfected in the mind and will of man" and therefore is "a law of man and not of God Himself."[39] Yet it has often been considered as a development or reflection of divine law. So it has been said that human law is the offspring of divine law,[40] and that the municipal laws of nations and of communities are, in their origin and intrinsic force, no other than the rules of being given us by God.[41] Human law should doubtless be just, moral

31 1 Pomeroy's Eq.Jur. (1881) 5th ed. (1941) §§63, 64

32 Moore v Strickling, ante, quoting Blackstone

33 Cicero

34 1 Bl. Com. 39

35 22 Geo.LJ (1934) 420

36 Heb. 8:10, 10:16

37 1 Hamilton's Works, Lodge ed. (1903) 113

38 St.Isadore, Etymologies, v 4

39 22 Geo.LJ (1934) 419

40 See Equitable Life Assur. Soc. v Weightman (1916), 61 Okla. 106, 160 P 629, LRA 1917B 1210

41 10 West.Jur. (1876) 89
But not when they conflict with Biblical law. See infra §27, n 27

and righteous, conforming to the "eternal" and to the "design in nature."[42] And so it is, when founded, as it should be, on sound reason—"natural, moral or political."[42a] But in practice it does not, and perhaps cannot, in all respects satisfy the morality of a Christian community.

CHAPTER 3

DIVISIONS OF BIBLICAL LAW

[§10] Law is not a manufacture, but a growth.[43]—a "progressive science."[43a] In other words, it does not spring up instantaneously like Minerva is said to have sprung from the forehead of Jove, but is developed through years of human experience—by trial and error—according to the needs of the people and the wisdom of their law-makers.[44] This was doubtless true of Biblical law, which first appeared in the ancient world and continued its development to a time near the end of the first century after Christ. Historically, the law of the Bible is of three parts: Primitive, Mosiac, and Christian.

[§11] Primitive law preceded history. It arose in the very mists of antiquity, extending from the time of the First Chapter of the Book of Genesis to that of the beginnings of Mosaic law as recorded in the Book of Exodus, or presumably

42 22 Geo.LJ (1934) 419
"Every law is a discovery and gift of God." Demosthenes, Adv.Aristogeiton, I, §774

42a 5 Binney (1812) 244 (Brackenridge, J)
But according to Hitler, law or right consists in whatever is of expediency to the national socialist state.

43 4 Harv.LR (1890-91) 365

43a Norvell-Wilder Hardware Co. v McCamey (1926) 290 SW (Tex.Civ.App.) 772 (Pannill,CJ)

44 "The body of the law is like a great river, ever moving—sometimes swiftly and sometimes it appears very slow." 13 Miss.LJ (1941) 668
The development of Anglo-American law "has gone on for nearly a thousand years, like the development of a plant, each generation taking the inevitable next step, mind, like matter, simply obeying a law of spontaneous growth." Holmes' Collected Legal Papers (1920) "Path of the Law"
New rules are evolved (or borrowed) to meet new situations. Kerby v Hal Roach Studios (1942) Cal.App. 2d 207, 127 P 2d 577 Shaw, J pro tem, discussing the recently developed law of privavy)

about the year 1490 B.C.[45] Like other ancient law, this law was unwritten and consisted for the most part in traditional usages and forms which had the force of law. Nearly all of our information concerning it is found in Genesis, which contains "traditions hoary with age, reflecting conditions of law and society remotely anterior to the legislation found in the Pentateuch, and to the condition of society described in the Books of the Kings."[46] But Primitive law was not so much concerned with individuals as with the independent family groups of ancient society, each of which was ruled by its own head or patriarch. Having been supplemented by the commands of the heads of households, Primitive law did not develop a complete system of rules.[47]

[§12] Mosaic law comprises the greater part of the law of the Old Testament. According to the Scriptural record it was promulgated by Moses,[48] who is said to have commanded,[49] given[50] or written[51] the law, and to have "delivered it unto the priests . . . and unto all the elders of Israel."[52] It is chiefly found in the second to the fifth books of the Pentateuch or Five Books of Moses, and is called Mosaic law, not because it differs so much from Primitive law or Christian law, but to distinguish it from the law of other periods.[53] This is the ancient and divine authority[54] to which later writers—including those of the New Testament—usually refer when they speak of the law.[1]

45 Primitive law has existed for a much longer period than either Mosaic or Christian law. It continued to have force in some respects long after Moses.

46 13 Gr.B. (1901) 37

47 See Maine's Anc. L., pp 122, 147, 250

48 In his Panorama of World's Legal Systems, Library ed. (1936) p 107, Wigmore says that modern research tells us that these texts of the Pentateuch were only gradually built up during some eight centuries of development. Others think, and not without much reason, that Moses only codified for the newly organized nation of Israel the laws which had long been known. In Genesis, 26:5, it appears that the Lord said of Abraham that he "kept my charge, my commandments, my statutes, and my laws." Thus it is seen that there were "laws" more than four centuries before Moses.

49 Deut. 33:4

50 John 1:17, 7:19

51 Deut. 31:9

52 Deut. 31:9; and see Heb. 7:11, saying that the people received the law under the Levitical priesthood.

53 See Wigmore's Panorama, p 103 et seq.
Chapters 20 to 23 of Exodus presumably date from the 15th century, B.C. But the law found in Deuteronomy probably was not promulgated until the reign of King Josiah of Judah, about 624 B.C.

54 Hart v Geysel (1930) 159 Wash. 632, 294 P 570, 573 (Holcomb.J., dissenting)

1 In the writings of St.Paul frequent references are made to "the law," meaning the law of Moses.

[§13] —— The Ten Commandments are the basis of Mosaic law—the constitution of the Mosaic dispensation.[2] They have been called the greatest short moral code ever formulated[3] and the idealized model of all law,[4] and it has been argued that the whole of natural law may be deduced from them.[5]

"These commandments, which, like a collection of diamonds, bear testimony to their own intrinsic worth, in themselves appeal to us as coming from a superhuman or divine source, and no conscientious or reasonable man has yet been able to find a flaw in them. Absolutely flawless, negative in terms, but positive in meaning, they easily stand at the head of our whole moral system, and no nation or people can long continue a happy existence in open violation of them."[6]

[§14] —— —— The Scriptures contain two versions of the Ten Commandments, one in Exodus (chap. 20, verses 3-17) and the other in Deuteronomy (chap. 5, verses 7-21). The preferred version in Exodus reads thus:

I Thou shalt have no other gods before me.

II Thou shalt not make unto thee any graven image, or any likeness of any thing that is in heaven above, or that is in the earth beneath, or that is in the water under the earth: thou shalt not bow down thyself to them, nor serve them.

III Thou shalt not take the name of the Lord thy God in vain.

IV Remember the sabbath day, to keep it holy. Six days shalt thou labour, and do all thy work: but the seventh day is the sabbath of the Lord thy God: in it thou shalt not do any work, thou, nor thy son, nor thy daughter, thy manservant, nor thy maidservant, nor thy cattle, nor thy stranger that is within thy gates.

V Honour thy father and thy mother.

VI Thou shalt not kill.

VII Thou shalt not commit adultery.

VIII Thou shalt not steal.

IX Thou shalt not bear false witness against thy neighbour.

X Thou shalt not covet thy neighbour's house, thou shalt not covet thy neighbour's wife, nor his manservant, nor his maidservant, nor his ox, nor his ass, nor any thing that is thy neighbour's.

2 3 Ala.LJ (1928) 258

The oldest code of laws in the world, of which we are aware, was promulgated by king Hammurabi of Babylon, B.C. 2285-2242, and was discovered in 1902. Hughes v Medical Examiners (1926) 162 Ga. 246, 134 SE 42, 49 (Hill, J)

"The likeness of Hammurabi's Code to the Old Testament legislation in general is striking." Wardle, Israel and Babylon (3d ed, 1925) 272

The earliest code of Roman law was known as the "Twelve Tables," of which mere fragments have been preserved. The text of the tables probably did not survive the sixth century, A.D. They were the local law for Rome and its citizens. School boys were required to commit them to memory, so that each citizen might know the laws of his country. At the end of the Roman Republic. the Roman civil law had taken the place of the Twelve Tables. See 14 Ill.LR (1919-1920) 243

3 Wigmore's Panorama, p 105

"The laws of spiritual life, of civil life, and of moral life are all set forth in the ten commandments." 42 Wash. LR (1914) 770

4 10 Or.LR (1934-35) 91

5 27 Harv. LR (1915) 612, saying Melanchthon so argued.

6 Moore v Strickling (1899) 46 W.Va. 515, 33 SE 274, 50 LRA 279, 282

[§15] —— The Talmud is the body of Jewish civil and canonical law.

"Mosiac law was studied carefully for generations. Extensions and refinements in that law were made by scholars and orally transmitted to their students. This process continued until 189 A.D., when the oral law was set down in writing and called the Mishnah. Later scholars commented and elaborated upon the Mishnah and orally handed down their opinions to their students. In 500 A.D., these oral commentaries were compiled in a new work called the Gemara. The Mishnah and the Gemara together comprise the Talmud. It treats of civil and religious law, history, mathematics, astronomy, medicine, metaphysics, and theosophy. It passes from law to myth, from jest to earnest. It is replete with chaste diction, legendary illustration, touches of pathos, bursts of genuine eloquence, finished rhetoric, and flashes of wit and sarcasm. It has been justly called 'a microcosm embracing heaven and earth.'"[7]

[§16] —— The Mosaic concept or interpretation of law has been said to be founded "on absolute justice between man and man."

"It is made necessary by the bold assumption that every man belongs to himself, and has the right to do as he pleases with himself, so long as he accords the same right to others, and does nothing hurtful to interfere with their enjoyment thereof. In short, that he does not do unto others what he would not have them do unto him. If he does so, he is guilty of immorality, which may be slight or gross, according to circumstances. This interpretation demands 'life for life, eye for eye, tooth for tooth, hand for hand, foot for foot, burning for burning, wound for wound, stripe for stripe.'"[8]

[§17] Christian law is found in the New Testament, and mainly in the Gospels of Matthew, Mark, Luke and John, and and in the Epistles of St. Paul. After the New Testament, the oldest repository of Christian law which has come down to us is "The Tract on the Two Ways" from the "Doctrine of the Twelve Apostles," written in Greek by an unknown author near the beginning of the second Christian century.[9]

Strictly speaking, Christian law consists in the legal teaching of Jesus and his Disciples and Apostles.[10] But the New

7 38 Case & Comment (1932) No. 2, p 2
"The Talmud was finally closed in A.D. 490 by Rabbina Albina, the last of the Amoiram. . . . The Jews were taught to care more for it and to devote more continued study to its masses of casuistry and extravagance than to the divine beauty of the Psalms and the noble moral teaching of the Prophets." Farrar, History of Interpretation, 82, 94

8 Moore v Strickling, ante, quoting Exodus 21:23-25
See also Ruse v Williams (1913) 14 Ariz. 445, 130 P 887, 45 LRANS 923, 926 (Franklin, CJ) saying that "Among the Anglo-Saxon race the idea strongly prevails that each man is an individual by himself, and is to be dealt with as such; that the individual is the social unit."

9 See Appendix, p 309

10 "Where can the purest principles of morality be learned so clearly or so perfectly as from the New Testament? Where are benevolence, love of truth, sobriety, and industry, so powerfully and irresistibly inculcated as in the sacred volume?" Vidal v Girard's Executors (1844) 2 Howard (US) 127, 200, 11 L ed 205, 235 (Story,J)
Jesus was not so called during his earthly lifetime, but is said to have been known by the Hebrew name of Joshua.

Testament also reaffirms and emphasizes much of the law laid down in the Old,[11] and that law, though made originally for Israelites only, has therefore been adopted and followed by Christians throughout the world, thus becoming a law to them as a result of custom.[12] However, Jesus repudiated provisions of the old law pertaining to divorce, the emancipation of children, and oaths; and other provisions relating to religion were discarded by the early church.[13]

[§18] —— Love of one's brother or neighbor is the fundamental rule of Christian law. In the teachings of Jesus —also those of John the Baptist[14]—"brotherly" or "neighbourly" love[15] is made a duty, to be fulfilled by charity,[16] forgiveness,[17] mercy,[18] non-resistance to personal wrongs,[19] patience,[20] and practice of the Golden Rule. Yet this commandment that we love one another is one that "we had from the beginning."[21] Mosaic law had commanded that "thou shalt love thy neighbour as thyself;"[22] and charity and mercy had been commended or lack thereof denounced in numerous passages of the Old Testament.[23] But the concept of "love" seems not to have been understood nor fully appreciated until the time of Jesus. Nor has the law of Christ, in respect of love of neighbor, been generally accepted, as a matter of practice, to this day.[23a]

[§19] —— It is recognized in the New Testament that "the law made nothing perfect,"[24] also that without observ-

11 State v District School Board of Edgerton (1890) 76 Wis. 177, 20 ASR 41, 49 (Lyon, J) saying that "The New Testament . . . reaffirms and emphasizes the moral obligations laid down in the Ten Commandments."

12 Even today, in some quarters, the moral or non-ceremonial law of the Old Testament, as modified by the New, is recognized as in force. 22 Geo.LJ (1934) 501

13 See infra §39

14 See Luke 16:16, saying that "The law and the prophets were until John: since that time the kingdom of God is preached."

15 Heb. 13:1

16 See Matt. 5:42; Luke 6:30; Acts 20:35; 1 Cor. 13:13; Col. 3:14; Heb. 13:3
"The very essence" of religion is "that charity that suffereth long and is kind, which vaunteth not itself, doth not behave unseemly, is not easily provoked, and not only believeth and hopeth, but beareth and endureth all things." Poor v Poor (1836) 8 NH 207, 29 AD 664, 668 (Richardson,CJ)

17 See Matt. 18:35; Luke 6:37, 23:34

18 See Matt. 23:23; Luke 6:36

19 Matt. 5:38,39; Luke 6:28,29; see also Two Ways 1:4

20 See 1 Thess. 5:14
"If when ye do well and suffer for it, ye take it patiently, this is acceptable with God, says the Bible." Poor v Poor, ante, n 16

21 2 John v 5

22 Lev. 19:17,18; and see Tobit 4:13 ("love thy brethren"); Ecclesiaticus 10:6 ("Bear not hatred to thy neighbour for every wrong"), 27:17 ("Love thy friend, and be faithful unto him"), 28:2 ("Forgive thy neighbour the hurt that he hath done unto thee"), 28:7 ("Bear no malice to thy neighbour")

23 See, for example, Prov. 25:21; Isa. 58:7-10; Jer. 22:16; Zech. 7:9; Tobit, 4:7,8,16 and 14:9; Ecclesiasticus 4:5

23a See Appendix, p 315

24 Heb. 7:19

ance of the commandment of "love" the law as a whole failed of its purpose, and that, on the other hand, by its observance all the law would be fulfilled in one word.[25] And Jesus, avowedly desiring to fulfill rather than destroy the law,[26] repeated the commandment that "Thou shalt love thy neighbour as thyself,"[27] calling it the second "of all the commandments,"[28] and one of two "on which hang all the law and the prophets."[29] St. Paul also observed that "Love worketh no ill to his neighbour: therefore love is the fulfilling of the law."[30] The meaning of the Christian teaching seems unmistakable. The commandment of "love" was given as a basic law—or, more properly speaking, as a higher law—to be taught to the people and to be observed by each individual in his dealings with his fellows. Two thousand years of human experience in disregard of this commandment have shown the inadequacy of law without love.

[§20] —— Christian law recognizes the truth of the ancient proverb that "As he (a man) thinks in his heart, so is he"[30a]—in other words, that transgressions arise, not out of the environment in which one finds himself, but out of the human mind or heart.[31] In respect of this doctrine, Jesus said that

"... from within, out of the heart of men, proceed evil thoughts, adulteries, fornications, murders, thefts, covetousness, wickedness, deceit, lasciviousness, an evil eye, blasphemy, pride, foolishness. All these evil things come from within, and defile the man."[32]

Therefore the law is concerned with respect to the mental and spiritual condition of the individual who, as the blind Pharisee, should "cleanse first that which is within ... that the outside ... may be clean also."[33]

25 Gal. 5:14; and see Rom. 13:8, "he that loveth another hath fulfilled the law."

26 Matt. 5:17

27 Matt. 19:19, 22:39; Mark 12:31; Luke 6:27 ("love your enemies, do good to them which hate you"); John 15:12 ("love one another, as I have loved you"); Rom. 13:9; James 2:8; see also Two Ways 1:2

28 Matt. 22:39; Mark 12:31
As to "the first and great commandment," see infra §322

29 Matt. 22:40; and see Rom. 13:9, noting that the various commandments are "briefly comprehended in this saying, namely, Thou shalt love thy neighbour as thyself."

30 Rom. 13:10

30a Prov. 23:7; Kay v Board of Higher Education (1940) 173 Misc (NY) 943, 18 NYS 2d 821, 831 (McGeehan,J)

31 See Matt. 5:22.28
According to this doctrine, unless corrupted by lax discipline or law enforcement or otherwise misled, the "underprivileged" or those who live under "substandard conditions" are no more likely to become criminals than those enjoying a more comfortable position in society. See infra §335.

32 Mark 7:21-23; and see Matt. 15:19

33 Matt. 23:26

[§21] —— The "Law of Liberty" is mentioned in the Epistle of James,[34] and from the context of the Epistle it appears that this law is the commandment to "love thy neighbour as thyself,"[35] which James called the "royal law according to the Scripture."[36]

The doctrine of the law of liberty is that "what things soever the law saith, it saith to them who are under the law,"[37] and that "whoso looketh unto the perfect law of liberty, and continueth therein, he being not a forgetful hearer, but a doer of the word,"[38] has ceased to be "under" the numerous rules against wrong-doing. Doubtless one who loves his fellow man will not purposely harm or wrong him and it may be said of one who observes this higher and affirmative law that as to him the object of all other law is attained and the necessity therefor has ceased.[39]

[§22] —— A similar doctrine is that a righteous man who knows and keeps the law or who, though not knowing the law, observes its requirements by nature, is not under the law but walks at liberty. The notion is not peculiar to the New Testament, for it is said in Psalms:

> "So shall I keep thy law continually for ever and ever. And I will walk at liberty: for I seek thy precepts."[40]

St. Paul recognized this principle when he declared that "if ye be led of the spirit, ye are not under the law,"[41] that "where the Spirit of the Lord is, there is liberty,"[42] and that the law "was not made for a righteous man, but for the lawless and disobedient."[43] It is reflected also in St. Paul's statement that

> ". . . when the Gentiles, which have not the law, do by nature the things contained in the law, these, having not the law are a law unto themselves:
>
> "Which shew the work of the law written in their hearts, their conscience also bearing witness, and their thoughts the mean while accusing or else excusing one another."[44]

34 James 1:25, 2:12 ("So speak ye, and so do, as they that shall be judged by the law of liberty")

35 See supra §§18, 19

36 James 2:8

37 Rom. 3:19

38 James 1:25

39 When the object of a rule is attained, the necessity for the rule ceases. Watkins v Roth (1941) 47 Cal. App. 2d 693, 118 P2d 850

Also, "when the reason of the law ceases, the law ceases." Holmes v Inhabitants of Paris (1884) 75 Me. 559 (Peters,CJ)

40 Ps. 119:44,45

41 Gal. 5:18

42 1 Cor. 3:17

43 1 Tim. 1:9

44 Rom. 2:14,15

[§23] —— The Golden Rule has been called the most perfect expression of the moral law,[45] and it has been said that there is no principle of wider application and of higher wisdom.[46] This commandment, in its popular form, is to "Do unto others as you would have others do unto you."[47] As found in Matthew, it is thus expressed:

". . . all things whatsoever ye would that men should do to you, do ye even so to them: for this is the law and the prophets."[48]

The rule logically follows the commandment to "love thy neighbour as thyself,"[49] in which all other rules are said to be "briefly comprehended."[50]

It is required of one who would observe the "Golden Rule" that he do to others as he would be done by, but not that he accede to every demand made upon him, for the rule does not say that one shall do to others as they would have him do. And while it has been intimated that damages are imposed against a wrongdoer for the purpose of teaching him to do in the future as he would be done by, the rule can hardly be made effective by the force of the law,[51] any more than the duty of one to love his neighbour can be enforced. Nor does it justify an argument by an attorney to a jury that they should put themselves in the situation of his client and do by him as they would be done by. Such an argument is fallacious since it does not say, "Do unto me as you would have me do unto you," but rather, "Do to my opponent for me as you would like me to do to him for you if you were in my place."[1]

[§24] —— The Christian interpretation of law according to Judge Dent in the celebrated case of Moore v Strickling—

"is founded on the broad fundamental principle that no man belongs to himself, or has the right to do as he pleases with himself, but that he holds his body, mind, soul, and property of every description, by divine grant, in trust for the benefit of his fellowman. It requires the doing of good at all times, the love of enemies, the giving to him that asketh, the loaning to anyone that would borrow without the expectation of any

45 Furst-Edwards & Co. v St.Louis Southwestern R.Co. (1912) 146 SW (Tex. Civ.App.) 1025, 1028 (Jenkins,J)

46 Donahoe v Richards (1854) 38 Me. 379, 69 AD 256,275 (Appleton,J)

47 Mack v Shafer (1901) 135 Cal. 113, 67 P 40 (Cooper,C)

48 Matt. 7:12 ". . . as ye would that men should do to you, do ye also to them likewise." Luke 6:31

In the Tract on the Two Ways, the Golden Rule is given in negative form: Two Ways 1:2

49 See supra §§18,19

50 Rom. 13:9

51 4 Jn. Marshall LQ (1939) 482, quoting Atty.Gen. Marshall that "The Golden Rule cannot be made effective by United States marshals."

1 Leonard Bros. v Newton (1934) 71 SW 2d (Tex.Civ.App.) 613 (Lattimore,J); Fambrough v Wagley (1943) 140 Tex. 577, 169 SW 2d 478 (Critz,J)

return, and the complete devotion of self to the commonweal of humanity and the establishment of a kingdom of perfect righteousness. It condemns resistance to evil. War under any plea, even for humanity's sake, it does not justify, but condemns in unmistakable terms.[1a] It goes still further, enters the human heart as the foundation of all evil, and denounces the very conception thereof without overt act. It destroys all distinction between morality and religion. It makes the laws of morality concur fully with the laws of religion. According to it, he who serves man best worships God best, and he who worships God best serves man best. All other religion it denounces as pure hypocrisy. Because of their incapacity to understand it, through inability to live it, men deny it or wrest its meaning to suit their living, of whom it is said:

> 'Ye are they which justify yourselves before men, but God knoweth your hearts; for that which is highly esteemed among men is an abomination in the sight of God.'[2]

Its ostensible purpose is to make men perfect in all their conduct as their Creator is perfect. Man's environment, including his heritage and hereditary traits of character, customs, laws, business relations, and acquired necessities, is to an almost immeasureable degree directly opposed thereto. Hence they are immoral, not being in conformity with the will of God, and render man immoral. Thus have mankind woven around themselves, thread by thread, an invisible web, which they are powerless to break. Nor does this interpretation admit of degrees of morality; for all disobedience is equally heinous in the sight of God, and all immorality gross immorality.

> 'Why callest thou me good? There is none good, but one; that is God. But, if thou wilt enter into life, keep the commandments.'[3]

To accept it, we are compelled to admit at once that all mankind, either consciously or unconsciously, are guilty of gross immorality. Hence, most men reject it; for they would rather be blind, and leaders of the blind and perish in the same pit, than sit in condemnation of their own lives. To live in accordance with it in the present condition of the world's affairs requires a complete surrender of self, the giving up of worldly pleasures and enjoyments, the repression of all lustful passions and ambitions, and an entire devotion of time, service. and energies to the elevation of mankind, in regaining for them that greater liberty which must follow when the knowledge of truth fills the earth as the waters cover the sea. This interpretation . . . has never been accepted as, or become a part of, the law of the land. If such were the case we would have no need of prosecuting attorney, judge or court."[4]

1a But see infra §115 et seq.

2 Luke 16:15

3 Matt. 19:17

4 Moore v Strickling (1899) 46 W.Va. 515, 33 SE 274, 50 LRA 279, 282
"If we open our eyes, and if we will honestly acknowledge to ourselves what we discover, we shall be compelled to confess that all the life and efforts of the civilized people of our times are founded on a view of the world which is directly opposed to the view of the world which Jesus had." Ruse v Williams (1913) 14 Ariz. 445, 130 P 887, 45 LRA NS 923, 926 (Franklin, CJ) quoting Strauss, der Alter und der Neue Glaube, p 74

CHAPTER 4

BURDEN, GOODNESS AND OBJECTS OF THE LAW

[§25] Nature has not made men slaves, but free, with an intrinsic right to liberty[5] when they infringe not the equal freedom of others.[6] Not only so, but liberty is a divine principle,[7] recognized in Scripture.[8] So the Psalmist declared, "I will walk at liberty: for I seek thy precepts,"[9] and Jesus taught that it is lawful for a man to do what he wills with his own,[10] when he thereby commits no wrong to others.[11]

But the historic course of liberty has been tortuous and troubled, for men, ever prone, it seems, to impose their arbitrary will one upon another, have been slow to realize, on the one hand, the social necessity and value of liberty, and, on the other, its source and nature. So essential is liberty in the life of an enlightened society that it ought not to be taken away "even from the most debased wretch in the land"[12] unless for invasion of the liberty of another.[1] Nor is it to be regarded as a creation or gift of government, but as a natural and divine right[2] of everyone within his appropriate sphere, whatever be his color, creed or race, and whether he be rich or poor—a right which a righteous government will admit and which, except for most cogent reasons, none may lawfully abridge or deny. And while liberty implies the absence of arbitrary restraint,[3] it

5 As to religious liberty, see infra §§108-108e

6 Spencer, Justice, §27

7 Internoscia's Internat. L. (1910) xxvii

8 As to the Christian "Law of Liberty," see supra §21

9 Ps. 119:45

10 Matt. 20:15 Heath v Wilson (1903) 139 Cal. 362, 366, 73 P 182; Ferguson v Larson (1934) 139 Cal.App. 133, 33 P 2d 1061

11 See Matt. 20:13 ("Friend, I do thee no wrong"); and see 1 Root's (Conn.) Rep. (1789-1793) pp x, xi

12 In re Lockett 1919) 179 Cal. 581, 583, 178 P 134 (Melvin,J)

But in former times "bond-service" and "slavery" were not considered as being unlawful. See infra §233. A man could "sell" himself, and become a bond-servant. See Isa. 52:3 ("ye have sold yourselves for naught . . .")

1 For it must not be supposed that the liberty of one is more sacred than that of another. If this were true, the liberty of a meek and acquiescent majority would vanish before that of an aggressive and disputatious minority.

2 It is often but inaccurately said that these rights are "granted by the Constitution." Many less fundamental rights, no doubt, can be and are created by law, but these inherent rights are not considered as being dependent upon human law, which can do no more than to admit or recognize them.

3 But not immunity from reasonable regulations. Chicago, B. & Q. R. Co. v McGuire (1911) 219 US 549§ 565, 55 L ed 328, 338 (Hughes,J)

does not consist merely in freedom from physical servitude or imprisonment:[4] it extends to freedoms of the mental and spiritual realms—"where decrees of mundane courts are ineffective to direct the course of men."[5] Thus the broad concept of liberty includes a large and growing category of freedoms, exercisable without permission[6] or purchase:[7] freedom of speech, of the press, and of religion;[8] freedom to live and work as one wills,[9] to use his faculties in all lawful ways and to pursue any lawful calling, occupation or trade;[10] and freedom from unwarranted attack upon, or interference with, one's life, liberty, reputation, and property.[11]

Modern English and American laws have recognized the liberty and rights of the individual more fully, perhaps, than the law of any other age or country. Generally speaking, freedom of action is allowed and every opinion is tolerated, unless the rights of others are interfered with.[12] Nor is any official authorized to prescribe what shall be orthodox in politics, nationalism, religion, or other matters of opinion.[13]

[§26] —— It follows that no greater burden of law should be laid upon the people than is necessary for the general welfare.[14]

"It is not within the competency of government to invade the privacy of a citizen's life and to regulate his conduct in matters in which he alone is concerned, or to prohibit him any liberty the exercise of which will not directly injure society."[15]

But there is no absolute freedom to do as one wills.[15a] The liberty that is sanctioned in the Scriptures is not a lib-

4 Allgeyer v Louisiana (1896) 165 US 578, 41 L ed 832 (Peckham,J); In re Aubrey (1904) 36 Wash. 308, 78 P 900, 104 ASR 952, 1 Ann. Cas. 927

5 Jones v Opelika (1942) 316 US 584, 86 L ed 1691 (Reed,J)

6 Murdock v Pennsylvania (1943) 319 US 105, 87 L ed adv opns 827, 836 (Reed,J, dissenting)

7 One may not be compelled to purchase, through a license fee or tax, or otherwise, a privilege freely conceded by the Constitution. Blue Island v Kozul (1942) 379 Ill. 511, 519, 41 NE 2d 515 (Murphy,CJ)

8 And these freedoms "are available to all, not merely to those who can pay their own way." Murdock v Pennsylvania (1943) 319 US 105, 87 L ed adv opns 827, 831 (Douglas,J)

9 State v Amana Society (1906) 132 Iowa 304, 8 LRANS 909, 916, 109 NW 894, 11 Ann.Cas. 231 (Ladd,J)

10 Allgeyer v Louisiana (1896) 165 US 578, 41 L ed 832 (Peckham,J); In re Aubrey (1904) 36 Wash. 308, 78 P 900, 104 ASR 952, 1 Ann.Cas. 927

11 See Melvin v Reid (1931) 112 Cal. App. 285, 291, 297 P 31 (Marks,J)
One should be "permitted to keep his own . . . and not (be) compelled to do anything contrary to principles of right." 27 Harv. LR (1914) 613, quoting Melanchthon's definition.

12 Ruse v Williams (1913) 14 Ariz 445, 130 P 887, 45 LRANS 927 (Franklin,J)

13 Board of Education (W.Va.) v Barnette (1943) 319 US 624, 87 L ed adv opns 1171, 1180 (Jackson,J)

14 See Acts 15:28

15 Commonwealth v Campbell (1909) 133 Ky. 50, 117 SW 383, 19 AnnCas 159, 24 LRANS 172

15a Chicago, B. & Q. R. Co. v McGuire (1911) 219 US 548, 565, 55 L ed 328, 338 (Hughes,J) erty to "walk every one after the imagination of his evil heart,"[16] nor a liberty to be used "for a cloak of maliciousness."[17] And one may properly be deprived of his liberty as punishment for an offense against the law,[18] or he may lose it by being captured in warfare.[19]

[§27] King David seemingly looked upon the law—Mosaic law—as a supreme good. His views are expressed in numerous passages.[20] And Solomon, who is said to have been wiser than all men[21]—though there were some things past his comprehension[22]—spoke of the law as a "light,"[23] and again as a "fountain of life."[24] Finally St. Paul observed that "the law is holy, and the commandments holy, and just and good,"[25] and that he delighted "in the law of God after the inward man."[26] But he also saw that the law, however good of itself, might be misused, remarking that "the law is good, if a man use it lawfully."[27] And while the meaning of the word "use" is not altogether clear,[28] it is plain that the law should never be permitted to become an instrument of tyranny[28a] or "a weapon of offense by law-breakers."[29]

[§28] The immediate object of laws is to govern human actions,[30] though they are sometimes made for the purpose of controlling or molding men's minds,"[31] It has been said also that "the law was our schoolmaster,"[32] signifying that it is a function of the law to teach proper conduct—to smooth and

16 Jer. 16:12; and see Baruch 1:22

17 1 Pet. 2:16

18 See infra §§419,420

19 See infra §122

20 Ps. 19:7, 19:8, 119:72, 119:77,174, 119:163

21 1 Kings 4:31

22 Ex parte Harkins (1912) 7 Okla. Crim. Rep. 464, 124 P 131, 940 (Furman, J) citing Proverbs 30:18,19

23 Prov. 6:23

24 Prov. 13:14

25 Rom. 7:12

26 Rom. 7:22

27 1 Tim. 1:18

"A human law is good or bad as it agrees or does not agree with the law of God as indicated by the principle of utility." 1 Austin, Lectures on Jurisprudence (1875) 86

28 1 Stephen, English Utilitarians (1900) 271

28a Barnette v Board of Education (1942) 47 F Supp (W.Va.) 251, 253 (Parker, Cir J)

29 Burgess v State (1931) 161 Md 162, 155 A 153, 75 ALR 1471, 1475; People v Kilpatrick (1926) 79 Colo. 303, 245 P 719, 720

Nor should it be so used as to "penalize the diligent and place a premium on laziness." McCarthy v Palmer (1939) 29 F. Supp. 585,586 (Moscowitz, DJ)

"A democratic society . . . naturally guards against the misuse of the law enforcement process." McNabb v United States (1942) 318 US 332, 87 L ed 819 (Frankfurter, J)

30 Reynolds v United States (1879) 98 US 145, 166, 25 L ed 244, 250, (Waite, CJ); Nicholls v Lynn (1937) 297 Mass. 65, 7 NE2d 577, 110 ALR 377, 382

31 See supra §§1, 18, 19

32 Gal. 3:24

perfect civilization.[33] But to what ends are men governed and for what purposes are they taught? As to these things, views have differed through the ages.

[§29] —— According to St. Paul, "all Scripture"—which necessarily includes the law—"is given . . . that the man of God may be perfect, thoroughly furnished unto all good works."[34] Therefore, it has been said of Christian law that it was "intended to secure perfection," whereas Mosaic law was "intended for the government of an imperfect, self-willed, ignorant, stubborn, and hard-hearted people, and for the suppression of vice, injustice, and wrong among them."[35] St. Paul stated further that the law "was not made for a righteous man,"[36] inasmuch as "the desire of the righteous is only good,"[37] and no law is needed to keep him from doing evil.[38] On the contrary the law was made—

> "for the lawless and disobedient, for the ungodly and for sinners, for unholy and profane, for murderers of fathers and murderers of mothers, for manslayers.
>
> "For whoremongers, for them that defile themselves with mankind, for menstealers, for liars, for perjured persons, and if there be any other thing that is contrary to sound doctrine."[39]

So it is evident that law may properly be considered as a means—and law is only a means, not an end[40]—by which the wicked shall be "bridled and restrained from outrageous behavior, and from doing of injuries, whether by fraud or by violence,"[41] so that "there shall no evil happen to the just,"[42] and "the rod of the wicked shall not rest upon the lot of the righteous."[43]

33 9 Am.L.Sch.Rev. (1942) 1297 (Posey)

34 2 Tim. 3:16,17

35 Moore v Strickling (1899) 46 W.Va. 515, 33 SE 274, 50 LRA 279, 282 (Dent.P)

36 1 Tim. 1:9
"For were the impulses of conscience clear, uniform and irresistibly obeyed, man would need no other law-giver." Th. Paine, Common Sense (1776)

37 Prov. 11:23

38 "If all people were truly moral, human laws and government would be unnecessary; for the laws of nature written in their hearts, and perfectly understood by them, would be a sufficient guidance in their dealings with each other. Where no wrongs are committed there exists no necessity for punishment, compensation, or restitution, and human enactments in relation thereto become obsolete. No man need say to his neighbor, 'Know the law;' for all would know it, from the least unto the greatest. But where society is constituted on such an immoral basis as to continually increase the wants and arouse the selfish propensities of mankind, and yet render them proportionally harder of attainment and satisfaction, human law becomes of increasing necessity, to suppress and control these wants and propensities for the common good, otherwise a state of immoral anarchy would be the result, deserving the just condemnation, once requiring his extinction, that 'the imaginations of a man's heart are evil continually from his youth up.'" Moore v Strickling (1899) 46 W.Va. 515, 33 SE 274, 50 LRA 279, 282 (Dent.P)

39 1 Tim. 1:9,10
The law is made to protect the public. Aronberg v Federal Trade Com. (1942) 132 F 2d 165, 167 (Lindley, DJ)

40 9 Am.L.Sch.Rev. (1942) 1297 (Posey)

41 Preface to King James' Version, 1611

42 Prov. 12:21

43 Ps. 125:3

[§30] —— In its broadest sense, as including rules of conduct and also the agencies by which they are made and enforced, law is designed to enable men to live together in peace.[44] Primitive law was essentially a device to keep the peace, giving to those who were injured or wronged a substitute for revenge, thus serving to avert private vengeance and to prevent feuds.[45] Mosaic law was also given, no doubt, that the people might "dwell in a peaceable habitation, and in sure dwellings, and in quiet resting places."[46] Similarly, the Christian teachings are called a "gospel of peace,"[47] and St. Paul observed that it is "good and acceptable in the sight of God" that all men "lead a quiet and peaceable life."[48]

[§31] —— In the modern view, the aims of law are justice, liberty and peace, and the happiness and welfare of the people.[49] Primarily it is the purpose of law, as always, to maintain peace and order,[50] or, as it has been said, "to insure domestic tranquility."[51] Justice and law, as words, have no necessary connection, nor is the law necessarily an instrument by which justice is attained.[52] Yet even under Mosaic law, justice was an ideal, as is seen by the statement of Absalom:

> "Oh that I were made judge in the land, that every man which hath any suit or cause might come unto me, and I would do him justice."[1]

It is also regarded as an ideal, if not the ultimate object, of modern law.[2] "For what is law," it has been said, "but the enforcement of justice amongst men?"[3] Justice has been defined as "the constant, perpetual disposition to render to every

44 See 13 Fla.LJ (1939) 120
"Peace means quiet of mind, and there cannot be quiet of mind where one has not practical certainty, that is high probability, of security as to life, liberty, property, etc." 30 Geo.LJ (1942) 527, n 70

45 27 Harv.LR (1914) 199 (Pound), observing further that "Where modern law seeks a rational mode of trial that will bring forth the exact truth, archaic law sought an acceptable mechanical mode of trial, which would yield a certain, unambiguous result, without opportunity for controversy and consequent disturbance of the peace."

46 Isa. 32:18

47 Rom. 10:15; Eph. 6:15

48 1 Tim. 2:2,3

49 See Preambles to U.S. and Texas constitutions; also 1 Root's (Conn.) Reports (1789-1793) xvi

50 See 14 Or.LR (1934-35) 455
"The triumph of the law is not in always ending conflicts rightly, but in ending them peaceably. And we may be certain that we do less injustice by the worst processes of the law than would be done by the best use of violence." Robt. H. Jackson, Associate Justice US Supreme Court, address before Amer. Bar Assn., Indianapolis, Oct. 2, 1941

51 See note 49, supra
"The law is, after all simply a method of social control." 9 Am.L.Sch.Rev. (1942) 1284 (Shepherd)

52 28 Yale LJ (1918-19) 842, 843

1 2 Sam. 15:4

2 Shaw, CJ, Mass., (1781-1861) eulogizing his predecessor, Parker, CJ

3 McAllister v Marshall (1814) 6 Binney (Pa.) 338, 6 AD 458, 464 (Brackenridge,J)

man his due."[4] But man's conception of justice—of what is one's legal due—in particular circumstances and in the various human relations, differs from age to age.[5] It is coming to mean, not only justice as between the parties to a dispute, but also political, social and economic justice, especially "a more equitable distribution of goods among all the families of the world."[5a]

CHAPTER 5

APPLICATION AND BINDINGNESS OF THE LAW

[§32] Generally the law applies to, or operates upon, all persons and things that are subject to the authority of the law-giver.[6] But it is not always easy to determine who or what is subject to such authority. This may depend upon the character of the law as being, on the one hand a law of the blood—designed for the government of the people of a particular family or tribe wherever they may be—or, on the other hand, a law of the land—for the government of the people in a particular locality or territory whatever their tribe or race.

[§33] —— Primitive law was a law of the family or tribe, and was considered as binding the individual members by reason of an actual or supposed blood relationship. When a tribe moved from place to place, they took with them, not only their cattle and their goods, as did Jacob when he went down into Egypt,[7] but also their law. Similarly when members of a tribe departed, like Abram and Lot, from their own country and from their kindred and went to another land,[8]

4 Justinian, Institutes, I, i

"Justice is the dictate of right, according to the common consent of mankind generally, or of that portion of mankind who may be associated in one government, or who may be governed by the same principles and morals." Duncan v Magette (1860) 25 Tex. 245 (Roberts,J)

5 See 13 Fla.LJ (1939) 120

5a Bishop de Andrea: see Pathfinder (1942) No. 2542, p 9

6 See 25 RCL 778 et seq. Union Pac. R.Co v Anderson (1941) 120 P2d (Ore.) 578 (Lusk,J)

7 Gen. 46:6

8 Gen. 12:1 et seq.

they continued—in theory, at least—to be bound by the tribal laws, though they might of necessity be subject also to the law of the people among whom they sojourned. Mosaic law became a kind of tribal law that was doubtless more or less observed as custom and also for the sake of religion among captive Israelites and Jews after the fall of the kingdoms of Israel about 721 B.C.[9] and Judah about 588 B.C.[10] It has also been observed among the dispersed Jews in various parts of the world since the destruction of Jerusalem by Titus in A.D. 70. This is the kind of law, supported by the bond of blood or religion, of which it may properly be said that "it hath dominion over a man as long as he liveth."[11]

[§34] —— On the other hand, it has come to be generally accepted that the authority of a state or nation, which occupies a definite place upon the earth, is coextensive with the land or territory so occupied. Its law is obligatory upon all persons and things within its borders, and with respect to persons it is binding upon them whether they are citizens or aliens, or whether they are permanent or temporary residents or mere travellers.[11a] This law is thus the law of the land,[12] of which it may be said that "it hath dominion over a man" not "as long as he liveth" but "as long as he dwelleth or sojourneth in the domain." Mosaic law was at one time a law of this character; it was declared as a national law for the Israelites when they had conquered and taken possession of Canaan;[13] and was to be observed by "men, and women, and children, and thy stranger that is within thy gates."[14] Like the laws of most of the modern nations, Mosaic law was a law of the land, binding within but not beyond its borders or "gates."

9 2 Kings 17:6

10 2 Kings 24:14; 2 Chron. 36:20
The Israelites or Jews were sometimes allowed a measure of self-government according to Mosaic law. See 1 Mac. 6:58-60 (covenant of Eupator with the Jews, "that they shall live after their laws, as they did before"); 2 Mac. 11:31 (command of Antiochus that "the Jews shall use their own kind of meats and laws, as before"). But see Mac. 1:42 (where Antiochus commanded that the Israelites give up their law), and 2 Mac. 6:1 (where "the king sent an old man of Athens to compel the Jews to depart from the laws of their fathers")

11 Rom. 7:1

11a The law of the land is "binding on every citizen and every court and enforceable wherever jurisdiction is adequate for the purpose." Miles v Illinois Central R. Co. (1942) 315 US 698, 86 L ed 1129 (Reed,J)

12 Gen. 47:26 ("and Joseph made it a law over the land of Egypt . . .")
The Constitution of the United States (1787) is declared to be the "supreme Law of the Land." Art. VI, ¶2
The notion that English statutes bind British subjects everywhere has found expression in modern times. American Banana Co. v United Fruit Co. (1908) 213 US 347, 53 L ed 826, 832 (Holmes,J)

13 See Deut. 12:1, "These are the statutes and judgments, which ye shall observe to do in the land, which the Lord God of thy fathers giveth thee to possess it, all the days that ye live upon the earth."

14 Deut. 31:12

[§35] But Biblical law as a whole—including the Primitive law as found in Genesis, the Mosaic law contained in Exodus and the ensuing books of the Old Testament, and the Christian law of the New Testament—may be considered neither as a law of the blood nor as a law of the land among Christian nations or peoples, except as its provisions have been adopted or recognized by human or secular law-makers.[14a] Yet the law of the Bible, other than that pertaining to ceremonies and observances, may properly be deemed a law of the faith, binding for the sake of religion upon adherents of Christianity even as the commandments of the Old Testament are still regarded by orthodox Jews as binding upon themselves. Moreover, many of the rules of Biblical law are rules of universal jurisprudence which are essential to the existence of any organized society and which, had they not come down to us in the Scriptures or in some other ancient writing, we would have been obliged to formulate or invent for ourselves. "They are," it has been said, "part of an ancient common law, older than that of England."[15]

[§36] —— So, though the law of Moses was proclaimed to a particular people,[16] much of it has become a universal law to mankind, not of its own force but because—

(1) Christ came not "to destroy . . . but to fulfill" the law,[17] "and by precept and example to illustrate and make plain its true meaning and force according to the divine will;"[18]

(2) The law was not made "void" but was rather established "through faith;"[19]

(3) The early Christians adopted the sacred books of the Jews as their Old Testament; and

(4) With the rise and spread of Christianity, the Scriptures were carried to all parts of the earth and thus became the most influential law book of all times, having profound effect upon the customs and institutions of many peoples.

[§37] —— —— The question as to whether or not converts from among the "Gentiles" must "be circumcised after the manner of Moses"[20] and otherwise "keep the law of Moses" arose among the early Christians, and being the cause of "no small dissention and disputation,"[21]—being in fact the first great Christian controversy—it was considered by the

14a And except, of course, among descendants of ancient Israel, who are entitled to consider Biblical law as being a law of the blood.

15 See 38 Case & Comment (1932) No. 2, p 24

16 Anderson v Winston (1736) Jefferson's (Va.) Reports, 24

17 Matt. 5:17

18 Moore v Strickling (1899) 46 W.Va. 515, 33 SE 274, 50 LRA 279, 282 (Dent,P)

19 Rom. 3:31, "Do we then make void the law through faith? God forbid: yea, we establish the law."

20 Acts 15:1

21 Acts 15:2

apostles and elders at Jerusalem in a council held in A.D. 46 and described in the Fifteenth Chapter of The Acts of the Apostles. The decision or "sentence" of the council, pronounced by James,[22] was embodied in letters reading thus:

"The apostles and elders and brethren send greeting unto the brethren which are of the Gentiles in Antioch and Syria and Cilicia:

"Forasmuch as we have heard, that certain which went out from us have troubled you with words, subverting your souls, saying, Ye must be circumcised, and keep the law; to whom we gave no such commandment:

"It seemed good unto us, being assembled with one accord, to send chosen men unto you with our beloved Barnabas and Paul,

"Men that have hazarded their lives for the name of our Lord Jesus Christ.

"We have sent therefore Judas and Silas, who shall also tell you the same things by mouth.

"For it seemed good to the Holy Ghost, and to us, to lay upon you no greater burden than these necessary things;

"That ye abstain from meats offered to idols, and from blood, and from things strangled, and from fornication: from which if ye keep yourselves, ye shall do well. Fare ye well."[23]

[§38] —— —— Many of the early Christian communities existing not only in Asia Minor but also in Cyprus and in Rome down to the fourth Christian century, did not literally accept the decision of the council of Jerusalem. These Christians, who came to be called Ebionites, held that converts were subject to Mosaic law, that Christianity fulfilled but did not abrogate the law, and that Jesus supplemented the law by his own commandments.

Moreover it appears from a letter of Pliny the Younger to the Emperor Trajan, written near the beginning of the second Christian century, that the Christians of Bithynia observed some, even if not all, of the provisions of Mosaic law. For Pliny quotes an apostate's description of a Christian assembly in that province as follows:

"They met on a certain stated day, before it was light, and addressed themselves in a form of prayer to Christ, as to some god, binding themselves, by a solemn oath, not for the purpose of any wicked design, but never to commit fraud, robbery or adultery, nor to break faith, nor to deny the existence of a deposit when called upon to deliver it up; after which it was their custom to separate and then re-assemble to eat in common a harmless meal."[24]

[§39] —— —— A proper interpretation of the judgment of the council of Jerusalem requires the consideration not only

22 Acts 15:19,20

23 Acts 15:23-29

24 Plinius ad Trajanum, Lib.X, Epistle XCVII (Donaldson's trans., Edinburgh, 1762, 11:251)
See, also, infra §317, n 12b

of the question presented to the council and its decision thereon, but also the circumstances of the controversy so far as they can be perceived.[25] It is evident that the dissension arose between two groups of Jewish Christians, one of which regarded Christianity as a new faith in which there should be "no difference between the Jew and the Greek"[26] or Gentile, while the other viewed it as a new Jewish sect into which Gentiles might be admitted by becoming adopted Jews, that is, by being circumcised and by keeping Mosiac law.[26a] The council chose the former position, relieving the Christians from the necessity of circumcision and the observance of the rules of Mosiac law pertaining to religion, except as to "meats offered to idols, . . . blood, and . . . things strangled," but requiring them to "abstain from fornication,"[27]—a requirement not of Mosaic law but one which seems to have been made necessary by a weakness for that offense among Christians.[28]

[§40] —— —— It will hardly be urged that the council intended that Christians might freely commit the various offenses denounced in Mosaic law—as that, while they must abstain from fornication, they might, with impunity, commit adultery—or that they might disregard the many civil rules embodied in Mosaic law. Had they so intended, their decision would properly have been regarded as "void," for they would thereby have "destroyed" the law in so far as Christians were concerned, in violation of the pronouncement of Jesus that he did not come for that purpose. It must always be considered that Jesus is the highest authority as to Christian law,[29] and that His plain teaching is not to be contradicted and cannot be overcome by any other doctrine.

But even if Christians were not obliged in conscience to observe the non-ceremonial laws of Moses as such, they can scarcely ignore those "things . . . written for our admonition"[30] in the Old Testament, since that part of the Scripture is so intimately connected with the New Testament that both are considered as one work.

25 "The language of a court must always be read in view of the facts before it." Sharon v Sharon (1888) 75 Cal. 1, 16 P. 345, 356 (McKinstry,J)

26 Rom. 10:12
"The general language of decided cases is to be read in the light of what was actually before the courts." Douglas v City of Jeannette (1942) 130 F 2d 652, 661 (Jones, Cir J, dissenting)

26a St. Paul, the Apostle to the gentiles, took pains to show that Christianity was not Judaism continued and reformed, but a New Testament between God and His people.

27 See §37 supra

28 See 1 Cor. 5:1; Eph. 5:3

29 Matt. 28:18, "And Jesus came and spake unto them (the eleven disciples) saying: All power is given unto me in heaven and in earth."

30 1 Cor. 10:11

CHAPTER 6

INTERPRETATION AND OPERATION OF LAWS

[§41] "Like all other ancient writings the Scriptures present many difficulties."[31] Sometimes the meaning of a law is obscure, as though seen "through a glass darkly."[32] More often, questions arise as to whether or how it should be applied. In these circumstances the law must doubtless be interpreted or construed, as the intent of the law-maker and the conditions of life compel.[33] To interpret a law, like any other thing expressed in words, is to discover and declare its true meaning.[33a] To construe a law, on the other hand, is to apply it to a particular situation or state of facts.[34] If the language is so plain that "a wayfaring man, yea any who can read, need not err therein,"[35] there is no room for interpretation outside the words themselves.[36] When the wording is clear and admits but one meaning, it should be given that meaning and none other.[37]

31 "Some of these (difficulties) are not easy of solution, while others may be satisfactorily explained. The existence of difficulties in such a book was to be expected, and therefore cannot be wondered at. It is a matter of astonishment, indeed, that there are not more found in it. This must be evident to any one on reflecting that 'the books of Scripture were written by different persons, in almost every variety of circumstance; that they refer to people whose customs and habits were totally dissimilar to our own; that they narrate histories of which we possess no other authentic document which might reflect light on some obscurity of expression or vagueness of description; that they were written in other languages than those in which we now possess them; and that, in addition to the mutability of language, there are the difficulties of translation out of one tongue into another.'" Holman's Bible, 1881

32 1 Cor. 13:12

33 12 Gr.B (1900) 7
But bearing in mind that the law does not contemplate or require impossibilities. Magnolia Petroleum Co. v Still (1942) 163 SW2d (Tex.Civ.App.) 268, 270 (Johnson,CJ)
Nor vain things. State v Wallace (1942) 131 P2d (Or.) 222, 253 (Kelly,CJ, dissenting)

33a Interpretation originally meant "translation." Ancient rules or statutes were often expressed in a language different from that in common use by the people. It was necessary to make them intelligible by interpretation. See 56 Harv.LR (1942) 397 (Radin)

34 1 Davids NY Law of Wills (1923) 733: "The ascertainment of . . . intention . . . is defined as 'interpretation,' whereas the legal effect of the instrument is described as 'construction.' The court first must interpret the writing, and thereafter may proceed to construe it."

35 Isa. 35:8

36 State v District School Board of Edgerton (1890) 76 Wis. 177, 44 NW 967, 20 ASR 41, 49 (Lyon,J)

37 Deno v Standard Furniture Co. (1937) 190 Wash. 1, 66 P2d 1158, 1162 (Willard,J dissenting)

[§42] —— But when interpretation is needed a law should be interpreted "in newness of spirit, and not in the oldness of the letter,"[38] for "the letter killeth, but the spirit giveth life."[39] The basic rule of interpretation and construction is to find the intent of the law-maker in the whole law, considered in the light of the circumstances under which it was made and the purpose it was intended to serve, and to give proper effect to that intent, though this may result in a departure from the literal meaning of the words used.[40] Yet it is not often permissible when interpreting a law either to add to or take away from the words thereof.[41]

[§43] —— It is to be taken for granted that a law was made for a wholesome purpose, and ordinarily that it was designed to suppress some prevalent wickedness or wrongdoing.[42] If its wording admits of different interpretations, and its purpose is evident or can be seen by those who will "inquire wisely,"[43] it should be so interpreted as to cure the evil toward which it was directed, even though this involves some departure from its literal meaning.[44] On the other hand, it should not be interpreted in such manner as to create other evils. Paraphrasing certain Scriptural passages,[45] where a law "would seek to cast out one evil spirit" it should not be given an interpretation or construction that "would take into the political house thus swept and garnished . . . other more dangerous spirits," thus making "the last condition . . . worse than the first,"[46]

[§43a] ——. Again, it is an old rule, resting on a foundation of solid reason,[46-1] that the contemporaneous exposition of a law—the interpretation or construction given it by those who

38 Rom. 7:6

39 2 Cor. 3:6; Wortham v Walker (1939) 133 Tex. 255, 128 SW 2d 1138, 1150 (Samuel,Spec.CJ); 42 Wash. LR (1914) 773

40 See 25 RCL 961 et seq.; 23 Cal. Jur. 719; 39 Tex.Jur. 155

"Courts are not limited to the lifeless words of a statute but may with propriety recur to the history of the times when it was passed." Great Northern Ry Co. v United States (1941) 315 US 262, 86 L ed 836 (Murphy,J)

41 See Deut. 4:2; Rev. 22:18,19; also Two Ways, 4:13, "Thou shalt . . . keep what thou did receive, neither adding thereto nor taking aught away." And see supra §6

42 So the fact that a nation has many laws signifies that its people are lawless. Law is not made when the people are righteous, but when they are lawless and disobedient. See §29 supra.

43 Ecclesiastes 7:10

44 See §42 supra

45 Matt. 12:43-45: Luke 11:24-26

46 See Stackpole v Hallahan (1895) 16 Mont. 40, 40 P 80, 28 LRA 502, 510

A useful and legitimate statute should not be so construed "as to make of it an instrument of positive fraud and oppression." Keller v Downey (1942) 161 SW2d (Tex.Civ.App.) 803,811 (Combs, J, dissenting)

46-1 Knowles v Yates (1866) 31 Cal. 82 (Currey,CJ)

were living at the time it was made—is in general the best.[46-2] It is entitled to great respect because contemporaries are presumed to have been best acquainted with the language and the circumstances in which the law was made, and to have had opportunities, if need be, of informing themselves of the true intent and purpose of the law-maker,[46-3] whereas those of a later generation, when manners and ideas have changed, may be led to impute their own sentiments to the language of the earlier time or to mistake the intent with which it was used.[46-4] So, the writings of Disciples and Apostles, and known practices of the primitive Christian church as well, seem to be more persuasive in respect of legal teachings of Jesus than later writings or practices. And while new situations arise in human affairs, to which old doctrines are properly applied, it is hardly to be supposed that new meanings, unknown to contemporaries, can be discovered.[46-5]

[§44] —— Much of the law of the Bible is written in broad and general language, and it may therefore be considered as of universal application.[47] The duty to observe this law, like "the obligation to do no hurtful thing toward our fellow man," is one which "rests upon all alike."[48]

"In commandments, such as 'Thou shalt not kill' and 'Thou shalt not steal,' the 'thou,' whatever it may have meant originally, undoubtedly now refers to every human being. Every single person is addressed and . . . is commanded to refrain from these acts. It could not be clearer or more peremptory."[49]

But many provisions of Biblical law concern or are directed to particular persons or classes of persons, such as the king, husbands and wives, parents and children, and masters and servants, and such rules are applicable only to those persons or classes.

[§45] —— When a secular law is to be interpreted, the court may consider the character of the people, as well as the

46-2 Cal.Civ.Code (1872) §3535
"Contemporaneous exposition has ever been esteemed by jurists and statesmen as strong evidence in support of an interpretation or construction of a statute . . . in consonance with such exposition." 5 Cal.Jur. 603.

46-3 Ogden v Saunders (1827) 12 Wheat. (US) 213, 6 L ed 606 (Johnson,J)

46-4 See infra §211, n 37

46-5 See infra §§296, 317, as showing application of the ancient rules against idolatry to the modern flag-salute.

47 See §32 supra

48 Loyd v Pierce (1935) 89 SW2d (Tex. Civ.App.) 1035, 1039 (Martin,J)

49 14 Or.LR (1934) 91, 92 (Radin)

circumstances existing when the law was made. It has been declared that—

"A literal interpretation of a statute which denies to it the historical circumstances under which it was drawn is to make mummery of its provisions."[50]

So in a proper case a court will consider the fact that Americans are a religious or Christian people. For this reason, "no purpose of action against religion can be imputed to any legislation."[51]

"The court starts with the historical fact in view that this nation (the United States) is a religious nation, a Christian people; and therefore accepts, as a conclusive presumption that Congress, or the State legislature, had the same historical fact in view when it passed the act which is to be construed, and that it did not intend to do anything contrary to that accepted condition."[52]

Moreover, a law is to be applied with due regard to the external circumstances in which men live and move and have their being.[53]

[§46] Having seen that law generally operates either upon all persons of the blood or upon all within the domain of the law-maker,[1] it is appropriate here to inquire as to exemptions and certain other matters relating to the operation of laws. Under the Mosaic law, no one was exempt from obedience. Inasmuch as the law was God's, though given by Moses, the priesthood and even the king were bound to obey it.[2] But it does not follow that a rule must be applied in every situation.[3] On the contrary, it is an axiom that "circumstances alter cases,"[4] and it is plain that there are situations in which the

50 Wortham v Walker (1939) 133 Tex. 255, 128 SW2d 1138, 1150 (Samuels, Spec. CJ)
"The notion that because the words of a statute are plain, its meaning is also plain, is merely pernicious over-simplification. It is a wooden English doctrine . . . to which lip service has on occasion been given here, but which since the days of Marshall this Court has rejected, especially in practice. A statute, like other living organisms, derives significance and sustenance from its environment, from which it cannot be severed without being mutilated." United States v Monia (1943) 317 US 424, 87 L ed 376 (Frankfurter,J, dissenting)

51 Holy Trinity Church v United States (1892) 143 US 457, 36 L ed 226 (Brewer, J)

52 42 Wash.LR (1914) 772 (Barnard)

53 Martin v Struthers (1943) 319 US 141, 87 L ed adv opns 861, 867 (Frankfurter,J, concurring)

1 See § 34 et seq., supra

2 See §49 infra

3 "It is impossible to lay down a rule which will govern in every case." Heatherly v Hill (1874) 67 Tenn. 170, 171 (Nicholson,CJ)

4 Payn, Market Overt (1895) xxxix
The law or its application "varies with circumstances." Christie v Callahan (1941) 124 F2d 825, 827 (Rutledge,J)
"The character of every act depends upon the circumstances in which it is done." Kersten v Young (1942) 52 Cal. App.2d 1, 125 P2d 501 (White,J); United States v Pelley (1942) 132 F2d 170, 179 (Evans,Cir.J)
And each particular case must rest (or stand or turn) upon its own facts. Murphy v. St.Claire Brewing Co. (1940) 41 Cal.App.2d 535, 107 P2d 273, 276 (Peters, PJ); Gates v Bisso Ferry Co. (1937) 172 So. (La.App.) 829, 835 (McCaleb,J); Heron v Ramsey (1941) 45 NM 491, 117 P2d 247 (Zinn,J)
It must be decided "with due regard for what went before and no less regard for what may come after." Board of Education (W.Va.) v Barnette (1943) 319 US 624, 87 L ed adv opns 1171, 1190 (Frankfurter,J, dissenting)

application of a given rule, however wholesome it may ordinarily be, would defeat the very purpose of the law-maker.[5] So while no rule is of more general force than the commandment that "Thou shalt not kill," yet there are circumstances in which this fundamental rule does not apply, as where killing is a social or political necessity.[5a]

[§47] —— The priesthood and also the kings and princes of Israel, after the kingdom had been established, were obligated to keep the law of Moses,[6] though no physical means or procedure existed by which they might be compelled to do so. Similarly in the Roman Empire, priests were amenable to the law of the state as well as the canons of the church,[7] and the emperor was supposedly answerable to the civil and criminal laws.[8] Concerning the bindingness of the law upon the sovereign, it was reasoned that—

> "It is just that the prince should obey his own laws. For the authority of his voice is just, only if he is not permitted to do what he has forbidden to the people."[9]

But under the common law it is considered that a rule does not apply to the English king nor to an American government or state, without express words to that effect.[10] It has been said that "there can be no legal right as against the authority that makes the law on which the right depends,"[11] but the better view seems to be merely that the common law, unlike the civil law of Rome, provides no remedy against the king or the government.[12]

[§48] —— In deciding whether one is properly amenable to a rule of Biblical law for a thing that he has done or left undone, it is admissible to consider his knowledge both of law and fact. For in this law it appears that a man is responsible according to that which he knew or should have known.[12a] Gen-

5 "An impeccably 'right' legal rule applied to the 'wrong' facts yields a decision which is as faulty as one which results from the application of the 'wrong' legal rule to the 'right' facts." United States v Forness (1942) 125 F2d 928, 942, 943 (Frank,Cir.J)

5a See infra §367

6 See Neh. 9:34 ("neither have our kings, our princes, our priests, nor our fathers, kept thy law"); Wisdom of Solomon, 6:4 (condemning rulers because they had not "judged aright nor kept the law")

7 See 7 Cal.LR (1918) 101 (Sherman)

8 See 13 Ill.LR (1918-1919) 443 (Zane)

9 St.Isadore of Seville, Sententiae, III: 51

10 See 25 RCL 783 et seq.
But a religious sect is not "above the law," though entitled freely to exercise its religion. Murdock v Pennsylvania (1943) 319 US 105, 87 L ed adv opns 827, 833 (Douglas,J), and see infra §108

11 Kawananokoa v Polybank (1907) 205 US 349, 51 L ed 834 (Holmes,J)

12 30 Harv.LR (1917) 21 (Maguire)

12a See infra §344

erally one is not to be held accountable or molested for a thing "ignorantly done,"[13] whether his ignorance pertained to the law itself or to the nature and consequences of the thing done.[14] Thus it is seen that Ezra was commanded merely to judge "all those that know the law,"[15] and that Jesus prayed in behalf of those who crucified him, saying "Father forgive them; for they know not what they do."[16] But one who is "willingly ignorant,"[17]—who has "rejected knowledge"[18] and scorned the law—may not be held guiltless.

[§49] —— —— The reason for the Biblical doctrine of non-responsibility for things done in ignorance doubtless was that in former times the whole of the law could be read and explained to the people in seven days, so that with proper observance of the directions concerning the reading and teaching of the law to the people they might actually have known and understood the rules by which they were governed. But this reason does not obtain in modern legal systems, and no distinction is recognized, therefore, between those who know the law and those who do not. On the contrary, it is now held that every man must know and conform to the laws of his country.[19] As a practical expedient, "every man is presumed to know the law,"[20] and a violator is not permitted to assert his lack of knowledge.[21]

[§50] —— It is a principle of antiquity that the law should be equal[22] and impartial,[23] and that all should be treated equally[24] "without prefering one before another"

13 2 Mac. 11:31, command of King Antiochus
Ignorance is not "a legal crime." Smith,CJ dissenting in Johnson v State (1942) 204 Ark. 476, 163 SW2d 153, 158
But if one, through ignorance violates any commandment "concerning things which ought not to be done" he is guilty "when he knoweth of it," within the laws relating to sin offerings. Lev. 4:2, 5:3

14 See Gen. 9:21. It is said that by the judgment of the fathers Noah was not guilty of "sin" in being overcome by wine, because he knew not the strength of it.

15 Ezra 7:25; 1 Esd. 8:23

16 Luke 23:34

17 2 Pet. 3:5

18 Hosea 4:6

19 Bixler v Baker (1811) 4 Binney (Pa.) 213, 221 (Yeates,J)

20 Harris v Clap (1805) 1 Mass. 308, 2 AD 27, 32 (Strong,J)

21 10 RCL 873
But a "guilty mind" or "guilty intent" is ordinarily regarded as essential to a crime, though it may be presumed from the circumstances. See 14 Am Jur 782

22 Cicero, Topica, 23, "Justice requires that in equal cases there should be an equal law."

23 See Mal. 2:9, "I . . . have made you contemptible . . . according as ye . . . have been partial in the law."

24 People v Coleman (1942) 53 Cal.App. 2d 18,34, 127 P2d 309 (Ward,J)
"True, the deceased was a Chinaman, a foreigner and a heathen . . . but still he was a human being, and in the estimation of the law his life was as precious, and as much entitled to protection, as that of the most exalted and best beloved citizen of our own State." Duran v State (1883) 14 Tex.Crim.Rep. 195, 199 (Willson,J)

either "in words or in deeds."[25] As bearing upon this doctrine, it has been said:

"If the fortunes of all cannot be equal, if the mental capacities of all cannot be the same, at least the legal rights of all those who are citizens of the same state ought to be equal."[26]

The principle first appears in Exodus, in reference to discrimination against aliens or "strangers," that—

"One law shall be to him that is homeborn, and unto the stranger that sojourneth among you."[27]

It is also embodied in various statements concerning "respect of persons,"[28] as that "Thou shalt not respect persons"[29] and that "It is not good to have respect of persons in judgment."[30] Whether one be poor and friendless or rich and mighty, he is entitled to the same consideration and protection before the law. So, in administering the law, it is improper to show partiality to the rich[31] or to "turn aside the poor in the gate from their right."[32] On the other hand it is also unlawful to "respect the person of the poor."[33]

[§51] ——— ——— But even the doctrine of equality is not applicable in every situation. So, though the general rule declared that the homeborn (native) and the stranger (foreigner) should be governed by "one law," yet it was expressly provided that a stranger should not "eat of the passover"[34] or "enter into the congregation."[35] Moreover, the requirement of impartiality does not mean that the righteous and the unrighteous are to receive equal treatment at the hands of the law. On the contrary, a man is to be judged according to his works[36] and recompensed "according to the cleanness of his hands."[37] The law approves of those who "work righteous-

25 1 Tim. 521 "I charge the . . . observe these things without preferring one before another, doing nothing by partiality."

26 Cicero, De Leg., 2:32,12

27 Ex. 12:49. See also Lev. 24:22; Num. 9:14, 15:15,16

28 "God is no respecter of persons." Acts 10:34. See also Ecclesiasticus 35:12; Rom. 2:11; Eph 6:9; Col. 3:25; 1 Pet. 1:17
"For he which is Lord over all shall fear no man's person, neither shall he stand in awe of any man's greatness: for he hath made the small and great, and careth for all alike." Wisdom of Solomon 6:7

29 Deut. 16:19

30 Prov. 24:23; 3 Ky.St.BJ, No.4, p 22

31 James 2:1-7

32 Amos 5:12
That it may not be truthfully said: "Our laws are like cobwebs, in which the small flies are caught, and the great ones break through." (Rabelais; Defoe)

33 Lev. 19:15

34 Ex. 12:43

35 Deut. 23:3, "An Ammonite or Moabite shall not enter into the congregation." And see Neh. 13:1

36 Prov. 24:12; Ecclesiasticus 16:12; 1 Pet. 1:17
"By their fruits ye shall know them." Matt. 7:16, 20. In re Kirk (1925) 130 Atl. (N.J.) 569, 570 (Minturn,J)
"Even a child is known by his doings." Prov. 20:11

37 2 Sam. 22:21

ness"[38] and condemns those who "work wickedness."[39] It will not "accept the person of the wicked, to overthrow the righteous in judgment."[40]

CHAPTER 7

CONFLICTS AND CHANGES IN THE LAW

[§52] There will occasionally be found two rules, in the same body or system of law, that conflict or seem to conflict, one with the other. In such a case, the rules should, if possible, be interpreted so that they will harmonize and so that proper effect may be given to both, as near as may be.[41] But conflicting rules cannot always be reconciled by sound reasoning, and this will more often be true of rules made at different times or by different authorities. Accordingly the difficulty can usually be solved by giving effect to the more recent rule or to the rule pronounced by the higher authority, if it is apparent that one is superior to the other.

[§53] —— "The latest pronouncement of the law-maker is the law."[42] According to this axiom where two laws have been made by the same authority, or by different authorities of the same dignity, the one last made will prevail over the earlier one in so far as the two conflict. Applying this principle to Biblical law, when a rule of the Old Testament disagrees with one of the New, the older rule must be considered as "abrogated" or "repealed" and the newer rule as being the effective and existing law. So even if a commandment of Jesus were regarded as of the same authority as one given by Moses, the new commandment nevertheless is of greater force and supersedes the old by virtue of its being the latest expression of the law-maker.[43]

38 Ps. 146:8; Acts 10:35

39 Tobit 4:17; Ecclesiasticus 12:6

40 Prov. 18:5

41 A "repeal by implication" is never favored or presumed (25 RCL 918). The intent to repeal must clearly appear (25 RCL 917), and if, by any reasonable construction an early rule and a later one can be reconciled and so construed that both may stand, this must be done (39 Tex Jur 141, 142)

42 25 RCL 914

43 It follows, for example, that Christians are bound to observe the teachings of Jesus concerning divorce, rather than the earlier rule of Moses on that subject. See infra §204

[§54] —— But the doctrine of the supremacy of the most recent law is controlled by one even more fundamental, that an inferior may not be permitted to prevail as against his superior,[44] and consequently that a command of supreme authority is not displaced by that of a subordinate. For example, it is not to be considered that a rule announced by Moses is abrogated or limited by any subsequent pronouncement of a lesser authority. Nor may any notion based upon the saying of an apostle be regarded as valid if it is seen to conflict with a plain doctrine of Jesus.[45]

[§55] —— "No human laws," said Blackstone, "should be suffered to contradict" the law of revelation.[46] In the first American colonial grant in 1584 authority was conferred to enact statutes for the government of the proposed colony provided that "they be not against the true Christian faith."[47] And it may be argued that no law-making body has ever been invested with power to enact statutes in violation of Biblical law. At all events it has been recognized that "there are . . . fundamental principles of morality and justice which no legislature is at liberty to disregard."[48] But this does not mean that an individual may properly set at naught a secular law of the land in which he lives because he considers that it conflicts with the law of the Bible.[48a] For one may have a right to practice his religion and at the same time owe a duty of formal obedience to laws that run counter to his beliefs.[48b]

[§56] Since time immemorial some have desired permanency and stability in human affairs, while others have sought

44 22 Geo.LJ (1934) 426

45 See §40 supra

46 1 Bl.Com. 42

47 See Holy Trinity Church v United States (1892) 143 US 457, 36 L ed 226, 230 (grant by Queen Elizabeth to Sir Walter Raleigh)

48 License Tax Cases (1867) 5 Wall. (US) 462, 18 L ed 497, 500, (Chase,CJ); Appeal of Allyn (1909) 81 Conn. 534, 71 A 794, 23 LRANS 630, 632

"What is morally wrong cannot be made legally right." Lincoln

48a Board of Education (W.Va.) v Barnette (1943) 319 US 624, 87 L ed adv opns 1171, 1181 (Black and Douglass, JJ, concurring) saying that "No well ordered society can leave to the individuals an absolute right to make final decisions . . . as to everything they will or will not do. . . . Religious faiths, honestly held, do not free individuals from responsibility to conduct themselves obediently to laws which are either imperatively necessary to protect society as a whole from grave and pressingly imminent dangers or which, without any general prohibition, merely regulate time, place or manner of religious activity." And see infra §105 et seq.

48b Board of Education (W.Va.) v Barnette (1943) 319 US 624, 87 L ed adv opns 1171, 1187 (Frankfurter,J, dissenting)

change and progress.[48c] This struggle has centered about the law, for law can be an instrument either of stability or progress. Doubtless "it is of great consequence that the law should be settled,"[49] and it has been asserted:

"We must not by any whimsical conceits, supposed to be adapted to the altering fashions of the times, overturn the established law . . . It descended to us as a sacred charge, and it is our duty to preserve it."[50]

On the other hand, the law—as Jesus said of the sabbath[51] —was made for man, and not man for the law,[52] and it has been declared that—

"As the usages of society alter, the law must adapt itself to the various situations of mankind."[53]

[§57] —— Ancient law-makers assumed to speak for all time, and the law was regarded as eternal and unchangeable. Thus it appears in the Scriptures that at the time of Darius, about 537 B.C., "according to the law of the Medes and Persians, which altereth not,"[1]—"no decree nor statute which the king establisheth may be changed."[2] Also it seems that Jesus conceded the everlastingness of Mosaic law in his saying that, "till heaven and earth pass, one jot or one tittle shall in no wise pass from the law, till all be fulfilled."[3] Similarly it was prophesied of the Roman Jus Gentium, that it should not be "one law for Rome, another law for Athens, one law today,

48c Changes ordinarily result from the efforts of the younger generation, which is more sensitive to social injustices and has courage to attempt their rectification. The older generation may also recognize the need for change, but many, being content with their own lot in life, seek to postpone it as long as they live. Others "though they find no content in that which they have, yet they cannot abide to hear of altering." (The Translators to The Reader (1611) When law thus becomes the guardian of stability, bent on maintenance of the status quo, changes required by changing social factors are relegated to the realm of violence.

49 Coggs v Bernard (1703) Lord Raym. 909, 917, 918, 920, 5 English Ruling Cases 247, 260, Smith's Leading Cases, 8th ed., 199 (Holt,CJ) saying, "I have said thus much in this case, because it is of great consequence that the law should be settled in this point, but I don't know whether I may have settled it, or may not rather have unsettled it. But however that happen, I have stirred these points, which wiser heads in time may settle."

"It is not of so much importance what the rule is, as that it be settled." Adams v Delaware Ins. Co. (1811) 3 Binney (Pa.) 287, 294 (Brackenridge,J) See also Clayton v Clayton (1811) 3 Binney (Pa.) 476, 491 (Yeates,J)

50 Clayton v Adams (1796) 6 Durnford & East's Reports 604 (Lord Kenyon)

"Stability . . . and permanency in the laws, are positive blessings. Any change, unless absolutely required by the exigencies of the particular case, is in itself an evil." 18 Mass.LQ (1933) No. 4, p 163 (Inaugural address of Governor Clifford, 1853)

51 Mark 2:27

52 12 Gr.B (1900)

53 Barwell v Brooks (1784) 3 Douglas's Reports 371 (Lord Mansfield)

"Law . . . must adjust itself to the changing needs of . . . life." 27 ABA Journal (1941) No. 2, p 78

"New times demand new measures . . . The old advances and in time outgrows the laws that in our forefathers' day were best." (Lowell) 20 Tex. LR (1942) No. 7, p 62

1 Dan. 6:8,12; see also Est. 1:19

2 Dan. 6:15

3 Matt. 5:18; 42 Wash.LR (1914) 773

another law tomorrow, but one eternal and immutable law for all nations and for all ages."[4] And in some nations "it was made a capital crime, once to motion the making of a new law for the abrogating of an old, though the same were most pernicious."[5]

[§58] —— From the old idea of the immutability of law, it is a far cry to the modern notion of law as something to vary with the fashions of the hour and the shifting currents of politics.[6] The truth, no doubt, is to be found somewhere between these extremes, for parts of the law repose upon fundamental facts of human nature, while other parts are less securely grounded or were designed to meet transitory conditions. Fundamentals—"the weightier matters of the law"[7]—"admit of no substantial change, save in finding the best form of expression."[7a] The basic rules of Biblical law, as finally established in the New Testament, may properly be considered as fundamental and therefore unalterable.

[§59] —— But not all rules, even of Biblical law, are of that character. Many provisions—the greater portion, indeed, of secular law—are merely supplemental to the more fundamental principles, and were intended to apply those principles in certain particulars to the conditions of the time. Such rules will not necessarily fit all people at all times, nor satisfy their sense of justice in all circumstances.[8] On the contrary, they must change from time to time to meet the changing conditions of life—though not so rapidly as to endanger peace and security. This is the law that is meant when it is said "the law must progress,"[9] and that it must adapt

4 Cicero, De Republica

5 Preface to King James' Version, 1611

6 4 J. Marshall LQ (1939) 576
Or "the shifting winds of doctrine." See Board of Education (W.Va.) v Barnette (1943) 319 US 624, 87 L ed adv opns 1171, 1192 (Frankfurter,J, dissenting)

7 Matt. 23:23; Robinson v State (1870) 33 Tex. 342 (Walker,J)

7a 30 Harv. LR (1917) 796, 797

8 13 Fla.LJ (1939) 121
"Rules governing the conduct of persons in their dealings with each other accommodate themselves to the standard of the times." Norvell-Wilder Hardware Co. v McCamey (1926) 290 SW (Tex.Civ.App.) 772 (Pannill,CJ)
"Since experience is of all teachers the most dependable, and since experience also is a continuous process, it follows that a rule . . . at one time thought necessary . . . should yield to the experience of a succeeding generation whenever that experience has clearly demonstrated the fallacy or unwisdom of the old rule." Funk v United States (1933) 290 US 371, 78 L ed 369 (Sutherland,J)

9 38 Case & Comment (1932) No. 1, p 9, per Wm. M. McKinney, saying, "But the law must progress; new legislation is needed to meet changed conditions; fresh interpretations must come from the courts; early precedents must now and then be overruled or given applications to modern circumstances; and lawyers will ever seek and rely upon the latest pronouncements and the newest discussions."

itself "to the new relations and interests which are constantly springing up in the progress of society."[10]

CHAPTER 8

THE WRITING, READING AND TEACHING OF THE LAW

[§60] "The law is in the heart of a righteous man."[11] It is said to be written in the hearts of those who "do by nature the things contained in the law,"[12]—"written not with ink, but with the Spirit of the living God; not in tables of stone, but in fleshly tables of the heart."[13] But the words of the law have also been engraved in stone, lettered in manuscripts, and printed in books, that it might more readily be handed down to posterity and disseminated throughout the earth.

[§61] —— According to the Scriptural record, Primitive law was traditional, which is to say that it was not in writing but was carried in memory and handed down by word of mouth until the time of Moses, to whom we may attribute the recording of such fragments or portions as are now found in the book of Genesis. Mosaic law, on the other hand, "God spake" unto Moses,[14] "and Moses wrote all the words of the Lord,"[15] in the books of Exodus, Leviticus, Numbers and Deuteronomy. The teachings of Jesus, like the primitive commandments and judgments, were given orally and after many years were partially reduced to writing, in the "Four Gospels" of Matthew, Mark, Luke and John.[15a]

10 Hodges v New England Screw Co. (1850) 1 R.I. 312, 356 (Green,CJ)
History shows that it has been in time of war and crisis that the great forward steps in law and government have been made. 20 Tex.LR (1942) No. 7, p 7, quoting Judge John J. Parker.

11 Ps. 37: 31

12 Rom. 2:14,15

13 2 Cor. 3:3

14 Ex. 24:4

15 Ex. 20:1 et seq.

15a Obviously the Bible does not contain all of the law that existed during the Biblical period. Though the statement of Mosaic law seems to be fairly complete, little is known as to the law prevailing before the time of Moses, other than that shown in the Code of Hammurabi. Nor does the New Testament contain all of the teachings of Jesus and the Disciples and Apostles. It does not purport to do so. See John, 21:25 ("And there are also many other things which Jesus did, the which, if they should be written every one, I suppose that even the world itself could not contain the books that should be written."
In subsequent chapters it will be seen that the law pertaining to some subjects is fragmentary, and that it is often necessary to "read between the lines" for matters which are taken for granted.

[§62] —— In Exodus it appears that the Lord "gave unto Moses, when he had made an end of communing with him upon Mount Sinai, two tables of testimony, tables of stone, written with the finger of God."[16] But when "Moses turned, and went down from the mount," seeing the molten calf which the people had made, his "anger waxed hot, and he cast the tables out of his hands, and brake them beneath the mount."[17] Thereafter, at the command of the Lord, Moses hewed two other "tables of stone like unto the first," and again "went up unto Mount Sinai," where he re-wrote "upon the tables the words of the covenant, the ten commandments."[18] A similar account is contained in Deuteronomy,[19] where it is said, however, that the Lord "wrote on the tables, according to the first writing, the ten commandments,"[20] and that Moses, upon coming down from the mount, "put the tables in the ark" which he had made, "and there they be, as the Lord commanded me."[21]

[§63] —— Mosaic law directed that when the people of Israel passed over the river Jordan they should set up "great stones and plaister them with plaister," and that they should write thereon "all the words of this law very plainly."[22] This commandment was performed by Joshua, who set up stones in mount Ebal, and wrote "there upon the stones a copy of the law of Moses . . . in the presence of the children of Israel."[23]

[§64] —— The Bible from the press of Johann Gutenberg in 1454 was the first book to be printed from movable type. Since that time it has been "published according to the language of every people,"[24]—it has been reproduced more frequently and distributed more universally than any other book.[25]

16 Ex. 31:18

17 Ex. 32:15,19

18 Ex. 34:1,4,28

19 Deut. 5:22, 9:15-17

20 Deut. 10:4

21 Deut. 10:5

22 Deut. 27:2-4.8
The code of Hammurabi was inscribed on a monument—a block of black diorite—nearly 8 feet high, which was discovered in Babylonia in 1902. Hughes v Medical Examiners (1926) 162 Ga. 246, 134 SE 42, 49 (Hill,J)

23 Josh. 8:30-32
The "stone Ezal" is mentioned in 1 Sam. 20:19

24 See Est. 1:22, stating that Ahasuerus, king of the Medes and Persians, commanded that the law that a man should bear rule in his own house be published according to the language of every people.

25 In 121 years (1816-1936) the American Bible Society distributed 276,371,654 volumes of Scriptures, and it is said that "The total number of languages in which the Bible or some part of it has been published has now reached the notable figure of 991; the complete Bible in 176 languages; the New Testament in an additional 214; portions consisting of at least one complete book in 520 more; and selections of Scripture, less than a complete book, in still 81 more languages." Report of Board of Managers (1936) p 32
"Unquestionably, among civilized peoples, the Bible is read by and owned by more people than any other book." Stern v State (1943) 171 SW2d (Tex. Cr.App.) 351 (Graves,J)

"There is . . . no book that is so widely used and so highly respected as the Bible; no other that has been translated into as many tongues; no other that has had such marked influence upon the habits and life of the world . . . Many translations of it, and of parts of it, have been made from time to time, since two or three centuries before the beginning of the Christian era. And since the discovery of the art of printing and the manufacture of paper in the sixteenth century, a great many editions of it have been printed."[26]

[§65] The law must be made known to the people in order that they may support it and that ignorance of its requirements may be inexcusable.[27] This is recognized in the Scriptures, which teach that the law should be publicly read and expounded from time to time. Mosaic law commands:

"At the end of every seven years, in the solemnity of the year of release, thou shalt read this law before all Israel in their hearing. Gather the people together, men and women, and children, and thy stranger that is within thy gates, that they may hear and that they may learn . . . and observe to do all the words of this law."[28]

We are not enlightened as to the observance of this provision, but the public reading of the law upon several occasions is mentioned. Thus, it is said that Joshua—

"read all the words of the law . . . before all the congregation of Israel, with the women, and the little ones, and the strangers that were conversant among them."[29]

Shaphan the scribe read unto king Josiah the book of the law found in the house of the Lord,[30] and the king read or caused it to be read to "all the men of Judah and all the inhabitants of Jerusalem . . . and the priests, and the prophets, and all the people, both small and great."[31]

Similarly, during the reign of Artaxerxes of Persia, Ezra the chief priest and reader brought the law before the people upon the first day of the seventh month and read "from morning unto midday"[32] for seven days, "before the men and the

26 Hackett v Brooksville School District (1905) 120 Ky. 608, 87 SW 792, 117 ASR 599, 9 AnnCas 36, 37, 69 LRA 592.

27 22 Geo.LJ (1934) 417; 4 Jn. Marshall LQ (1939) 482

28 Deut. 31:10-12

The Lord "established a testimony . . . and appointed a law . . . which he commanded our fathers, that they should make them known to their children, that the generation to come might know them, even the children which should be born, who should arise and declare them unto their children." Ps. 78:5,6

29 Josh. 8:34,35

30 2 Kings 22:10

In the reign of Josiah, Kilkiah the priest "found the book of the law in the house of the Lord," which he delivered to Shaphan the scribe, who carried it to the king and read it before the king. 2 Chron. 34:14-18

31 2 Kings 23:2

32 1 Esd. 9:41; and see Neh. 9:3, stating that on the twenty and fourth day of this month they "read in the book of the law . . . one fourth part of the day."

women, and those that could understand."[33] And the priests and Levites "caused the people to understand the law: . . . they read . . . distinctly, and gave the sense, and caused them to understand the reading."[34]

[§66] As to the teaching of the law, the Mosiac provision is that—

"Thou shalt teach them (the commandments) diligently unto thy children, and shalt talk of them when thou sittest in thine house, and when thou walkest by the way, and when thou liest down, and when thou risest up. . . . And thou shalt write them upon the posts of thy house, and on thy gates."[35]

The foregoing provision imposes a duty upon parents to instruct their children in the law; other provisions speak of teaching the law to the people, meaning no doubt the public reading and expounding of the law (see §65). Thus it appears that Jehosaphat sent his princes, and with them Levites and priests, and they taught the law throughout all the cities of Judah;[36] also that Artaxerxes, king of Persia, commanded Ezra that "all those that know . . . (the law) thou shalt teach."[37]

CHAPTER 9

LAW OBSERVANCE

[§67] It is not enough that the people "with their lips do honour"[38] the law, "for not the hearers . . . but the doers of the law shall be justified."[39] And surely it is no excuse for disobedience of the law to say that men have never obeyed it as they should or that the law cannot be endured because it is too severe[39a] or because it is directed against common appetites[39b] or popular practices[39c] or that men are no longer subject

33 Neh. 8:1-18; 1 Esd. 9:38-41
Ezra was looked upon as a second Moses. For many centuries the impulse given by him continued to sway the course of Jewish thought.

34 Neh. 8:7,8

35 Deut. 6:7-9

36 2 Chron. 17:7-9

37 1 Esd. 8:23; Ezra 7:25

38 Isa. 29:13; Matt. 15:8

39 Rom. 2:13
"Who is the upright man? He who keeps the decrees of the fathers, the legislation, and the customs." Horace, Epistles, I, 16, 40

39a Heb. 12:20 ("For they could not endure that which was commanded")

39b As was said of the American prohibition law.

39c Such as the charging of interest. See infra §264

to Divine law because they are living in an "age of grace."[39d] Many passages throughout the Scriptures show a deep and constant apprehension—which history shows to have been warranted—that the law would not be properly observed: that pretexts would be seized upon to justify men in defying, evading or ignoring it.[40] In varying phraseology the commandment is reiterated to "do,"[41] "fulfill,"[42] "keep,"[43] "observe,"[44] "remember," [45] and "forget not" the law,[46] the "commandments,"[47] the "ordinances"[48] or "statutes,"[49] and the "judgments."[50] In ancient times obedience to law was encouraged by blessings and enforced by curses.[1] And, as we shall presently see, rewards are promised to those who keep Biblical law and punishments are threatened to those who violate it.

[§68] To them that keep the law, the Scriptures promise the blessings of fruitfulness,[2] happiness,[3] health,[4] longevity,[5] peace,[6] prosperity,[7] and safety.[8] Thus in Leviticus it is declared:

"If ye walk in my statutes, and keep my commandments, and do them:

39d See supra §40

40 See Deut., chaps. 11, 28; Lev., chap. 26; Jer., chap. 7; Ezek., chap. 18; and other citations in notes to this section

41 Lev. 19:37, 20:8,22, 25:18; Deut. 27:10, 30:8; Josh. 23:6 ("do all that is written in the book of the law of Moses")

42 1 Chron. 22:13

43 Lev. 18:30, 19:19, 20:8,22, 25:18; Deut. 5:17, 7:11, 11:1; Josh. 23:6; 1 Chron. 28:8; Prov. 3:1; Ps. 119:4; Tobit 14:9; Ecclesiasticus 28:6 ("abide in the commandments")
"Give me understanding and I shall keep thy law; yea, I shall observe it with my whole heart." Ps. 119:34

44 Lev. 19:37; Deut. 8:1
"Ye shall observe to do therefore as the Lord your God hath commanded you: ye shall not turn aside to the right hand or to the left." Deut. 5:32

45 Mal. 4:4 ("Remember ye the law"); Ecclesiasticus, 28:7 ("Remember the commandments")

46 Prov. 3:1 ("My son, forget not the law"); 2 Mac. 2:1-3 (. . . Jeremy the prophet . . . charged them not to forget the commandments . . . and with other such speeches he exhorted them, that the law should not depart from their hearts")

47 Deut. 5:17, 7:11, 8:1, 11:1; 27:10, 30:8; 1 Chron. 28:8; Prov. 3:1; Tobit 14:19; Ecclesiasticus 28:6,7; 2 Mac. 2:1-3; Matt. 19:17; John 14:21-24

48 Lev. 18:30

49 Lev. 18:26, 19:19,37, 20:8,22, 25:18; Deut. 5:17, 7:11, 11:1, 27:10; Mal. 4:4

50 Lev. 18:26, 19:37, 20:22, 25:18; Deut. 7:11; 11:1; Mal. 4:4

1 See 14 Harv.LR (1901) 509

2 Deut. 7:14 ("Thou shalt be blessed above all people: there shall not be male or female barren among you, or among your cattle"); Deut. 30:9 ("And the Lord thy God will make thee plenteous in every work of thine hand, and in the fruit of thy body, and in the fruit of thy cattle, and in the fruit of thy land, for good")

3 Prov. 29:8 ("he that keepeth the law, happy is he")

4 Deut. 7:15 ("the Lord will take away from thee all sickness")

5 Prov. 3:1,2 ("My son . . . keep my commandments, for length of days, and long life . . . shall they add to thee")

6 Prov. 5:2; Isa. 32:17 ("the work of righteousness shall be peace; and the effect of righteousness quietness and assurance for ever")
"Great peace have they which love thy law." Ps. 119:165

7 Lev. 25:19 ("the land shall yield her fruit, and ye shall eat your fill"); Deut. 30:9; 1 Chron. 22:13 ("Then shalt thou prosper, if thou takest heed to fulfill the statutes and judgments which the Lord charged Moses concerning Israel")

8 Lev. 25:19 ("ye shall . . . dwell . . . in safety"); Tobit 12:7 ("Do that which is good, and no evil shall touch you")
"Blessed" are they "who walk in the law of the Lord." Ps. 119:1

"Then I will give you rain in due season, and the land shall yield her increase, and the trees of the field shall yield their fruit.

"And your threshing shall reach unto the vintage, and the vintage shall reach unto the sowing time: and ye shall eat your bread to the full, and dwell in your land safely.

"And I will give peace in the land, and ye shall lie down, and none shall make you afraid: and I will rid evil beasts out of the land, neither shall the sword go through your land.

"And ye shall chase your enemies, and they shall fall before you by the sword.

"And five of you shall chase a hundred, and a hundred of you shall put ten thousand to flight: and your enemies shall fall before you by the sword.

"For I will have respect unto you, and make you fruitful, and multiply you, and establish my covenant with you.

"And ye shall eat old store, and bring forth the old because of the new.

"And I will set my tabernacle among you: And my soul shall not abhor you.

"And I will walk among you, and will be your God, and ye shall be my people."[9]

Similar expressions may be found in the book of Deuteronomy.[10] And in the New Testament, Jesus declares:

". . . whosoever heareth these sayings of mine, and doeth them, I will liken him unto a wise man, which built his house upon a rock:

"And the rain descended, and the floods came, and the winds blew, and beat upon that house: and it fell not: for it was founded upon a rock."[11]

Nevertheless, the standards of the law are external, [11a] and in a spiritual sense, one is "not justified by the works of the law," that is, Mosaic law, "but by the faith of Jesus Christ."[12]

[§69] On the other hand, a "curse"is pronounced against those "that confirm not all the words of this law to do them,"[13] and the consequences of disregard and disobedience of the law are set forth at length. For example, it is said:

". . . if ye will not hearken unto me, and will not do all these commandments;

"And if ye shall despise my statutes, or if your soul abhor my judgments, so that ye will not do all my commandments, but that ye break my covenant:

"I also will do this unto you; I will even appoint over you terror, consumption, and the burning ague, that shall consume the eyes, and cause sorrow of heart: and ye shall sow your seed in vain, for your enemies shall eat it.

"And I will set my face against you, and ye shall be slain before your

9 Lev. 26:3-12
"He that keepeth the law bringeth offerings enough." Ecclesiasticus 35:1

10 Deut. 5:33, 7:12,13, 11:1-32, 28:1-13; 14 Harv.LR (1901) 510, quoting Deut. 7:12,13, 11:22 et seq.; and see Isa. 33:15, 16; Ezek. 18:5-9

11 Matt. 7:24

11a See supra §1, n 6b

12 Gal. 2:16

13 Deut. 11:28, 27:26; Gal. 3:10

enemies: they that hate you shall reign over you; and ye shall flee when none pursueth you.

"And if ye will not yet for all this hearken unto me, then I will punish you seven times more for your sins.

"And I will break the pride of your power; and I will make your heaven as iron, and your earth as brass:

"And your strength shall be spent in vain: for your land shall not yield her increase, neither shall the trees of the land yield their fruits.

"And if ye walk contrary unto me, and will not hearken unto me; I will bring seven times more plagues upon you according to your sins.

"I will also send wild beasts among you, which shall rob you of your children, and destroy your cattle, and make you few in number: and your high ways shall be desolate.

"And if ye will not be reformed by me by these things, but will walk contrary unto me;

"Then will I also walk contrary unto you, and will punish you yet seven times for your sins.

"And I will bring a sword upon you, that shall avenge the quarrel of my covenant: and when ye are gathered together within your cities, I will send the pestilence among you; and ye shall be delivered into the hand of the enemy.

"And when I have broken the staff of your bread, ten women shall bake your bread in one oven, and they shall deliver you your bread again by weight: and ye shall eat, and not be satisfied.

"And if ye will not for all this hearken unto me, but walk contrary unto me;

"Then I will walk contrary unto you also in fury; and I, even I, will chastise you seven times for your sins.

"And ye shall eat the flesh of your sons, and the flesh of your daughters shall ye eat.

"And I will destroy your high places, and cut down your images, and cast your carcasses upon the carcasses of your idols, and my soul shall abhor you.

"And I will make your cities waste, and bring your sanctuaries unto desolation, and I will not smell the savour of your sweet odours.

"And I will bring the land into desolation: and your enemies which dwell therein shall be astonished at it.

"And I will scatter you among the heathen, and will draw out a sword after you; and your land shall be desolate, and your cities waste."[14]

Moreover it is stated in the New Testament that "Whosoever transgresseth (revolteth), and abideth (continueth) not in the doctrine of Christ, hath not God."[15]

14 Lev. 26:14-33; and see Deut. 28:15-68; Isa. 24:5,6; Jer. 35:17; 14 Harv.LR (1901) 510, quoting from Deut. chaps. 27 and 28

15 2 John, v 9, quoted in Ruse v Williams (1913) 14 Ariz. 445, 130 P 887, 45 LRA NS 923, 928 (Franklin,J)

"Whosoever therefore shall break one of these least commandments, and shall teach men so, he shall be called the least in the kingdom of heaven: but whosoever shall do and teach them, the same shall be called great in the kingdom of heaven." Matt. 5:19

CHAPTER 10

RELATION OF BIBLICAL LAW TO MODERN LAWS

[§70] "Israel's law is the connecting link between the earliest and the latest legal systems and has proved itself one of the most influential forces in the evolution of the world's law."[16] The Scriptures embody fundamental principles that have attained legal effectiveness among nearly all peoples and in remote parts of the earth—principles without which human societies can scarcely continue to exist[17]—and it is not unreasonable to suppose that in many instances these principles were borrowed from the Scriptures or were obtained through contact with those who observed Biblical law.[18] At all events, much of the common law of England was founded upon Mosaic law.[19] The primitive Saxon Codes re-enacted certain precepts taken from the Holy Scriptures,[20] and King Alfred in his Doom Book adopted the Ten Commandments and other selections from the Pentateuch, together with the Golden Rule in the negative form, as the foundation of the early laws of England."[21]

16 4 China LR (1931) 362 (Lobingier)

17 See 42 Wash.LR (1914) 773 (Barnard) saying that "Without the knowledge of right and wrong that is taught by the Lord in the New Testament, in the Sermon on the Mount, and His other sayings and parables, and by His life, men would not know today what laws ought to be established."

18 But see 28 Yale LJ (1919) 782 (Keller) stating that "Human societies are nearly enough alike to be obliged, as a condition of self-preservation, to taboo practices that might be termed anti-social. Such taboos might be thought to be the result of acculturation (contagion, borrowing) if any possible agency of communication could be discovered or even imagined between remote parts of the earth in primitive ages. The better explanation of concurrences is that they are parallelisms—taboos that have sprung up under similar conditions as the only adequate response to them."

19 42 Wash.LR (1914) 770 (Barnard) ". . . our English law never appeared in its strength until after the reformation; until it had come in contact with a free Bible; until it had been softened, subdued and leavened by Bible teaching and Bible precepts, and, by these unmanacled from many of its glaring absurdities and heathenisms and unjust distinctions and inhuman punishments. It was not until then that civil liberty was reinstated after the downfall of the Jewish theocracy." 10 West. Jur. (1876) 92 (Bowman)

20 1 Pomeroy's Eq.Jur. (1881) 5th ed. (1941) §10

21 Moore v Strickling (1899) 46 W.Va. 515, 33 SE 274, 50 LRA 279, 282 (Dent, P); 4 China LR (1931) 359 (Lobingier)

[§71] The Scriptures doubtless have been a potent influence upon American law. In the early colonial period, the Bible seems to have been commonly regarded among the people as law. Several of the colonies formally adopted provisions of Mosaic law.[22] For example, Plymouth Colony in 1636 adopted a "small body of Lawes" largely based upon the laws of Israel.[23] And New Haven Colony in 1639 resolved that "the word of God shall be the only rule to be attended to in ordering the affairs of government in this plantation,"[24] and in 1655 adopted a code in which 47 out of 79 topical statutes were based on the Bible."[25]

Many provisions of Biblical law are still to be seen in American statutes and court decisions.[26] Allusions to the Bible are contained in the reported cases.[27] It has been characterized as "a very ancient authority not inappropriate."[28] "At one time . . . no book was oftener quoted in argument before a jury," but "it is seldom referred to now."[29]

[§72] There is difference of opinion as to whether America is now a Christian land.[30] But it doubtless was so in former times, when the people were predominately Christian

22 See Data of Jurisprudence, Miller, p 416

23 4 China LR (1931) 360

"Historians have emphasized the Biblical element in the founding of Massachusetts. It was to be a Bible commonwealth, a theocracy, the Genevan experiment writ large. Without question the law and theory of the ancient Hebraic order were large factors in shaping and guiding the public polity of the Bay Colony. The influence of the scriptural element is clearly evident in the book of laws (of 1648)." 15 Iowa LR (1930) 181 (Root)

24 10 Encyc. Amer., New Haven Colony (Osborn)

25 Jewish influence on Christian Reform Movements, Newman, p 642

In the early history of Connecticut, the Bible was a rule of political government "in the case of the defect of the law in any particular case." Appeal of Allyn (1909) 81 Conn. 534, 71 A 794, 23 LRANS 630, citing Col. Rec. of Conn., 1, 509

26 42 Wash.LR (1914) 771 (Bernard) also saying that "lawyers and judges frequently refer to and quote from the Bible in the trial of cases."

"The laws" of the Christian system, as embraced in the Bible, "must be respected as of high authority in all our courts. And it cannot be thought improper for the officers of such (our) government to acknowledge their obligation to be governed by its rules." Judge Nathaniel Freeman's Charge to the Grand Jury at the Court of General Sessions of the Peace, holden at Barnstable, Mass. March Term, 1802

27 29 Case & Comment (1923) No. 1, p 3 (Brown) stating that "allusions to the Bible are perhaps more frequent than to any book other than professional law treatises and previous decisions."

"It has been recognized in the courts that generally we acknowledge with reverence the duty of obedience to the will of God." United States v Macintosh (1931) 283 US 605, 75 L ed 1302; Harfst v Hoegen (1942) 349 Mo. 808, 163 SW2d 609, 612 (Douglas,J)

28 Moore v Indian Spring Channel Gold Mining Co. (1918) 37 Cal.App. 370, 381, 174 P 378 (Chipman,PJ)

29 7 Va.L.Reg.(N.S.) (1922) 777

For a case containing many references to and citations of the Bible, see Hampton v North Carolina Pulp Co. (1943) 49 F Supp 625 (Meekins,DJ)

30 See Harold v Parish School Directors (1915) 136 La. 1034, 68 So. 116, LRANS1915D 941, 945

and Protestant.[31] As in Rome after 379 A.D.,[32] Christianity was the established and legally recognized faith among the colonies and also, at first, among the states.[33] Many colonial documents, the Declaration of Independence,[34] the Articles of Confederation,[35] state constitutions,[36] and even the Federal constitution,[37] attest to the religious character of early America.[38] It has been declared:

> "There is a universal language pervading them all, having one meaning; they affirm and reaffirm that this is a religious nation. These are not individual sayings, declarations of private persons; they are organic utterances; they speak the voice of the entire people."[39]

31 Ex parte Newman (1858) 9 Cal. 502, 523 (Field,J) dissenting, saying that "Christianity is the prevailing faith of our people; it is the basis of our civilization; and that its spirit should infuse itself into and humanize our laws, is as natural as that the national sentiment of liberty should find expression in the legislation of the country."

32 7 Cal.LR (1918) 100, 101 (Sherman) observing that "By decree of Constantine the Great in 313 A.D., Christianity was made a lawful Roman religion. In the time of Theodosius the Great, about 379, the pagan religion was completely prescribed and Christianity became the only lawful Roman religion."

33 Runkel v Winemiller (1799) 4 Harris & McHenry (Md.) 429, 1 AD 411, 417 (Chase,J) saying that "By our form of government, the Christian religion is the established religion."

34 In the Declaration of Independence, God is acknowledged as over all and the giver of all good gifts. Herold v Parish School Directors (1915) 136 La. 1034, 68 So. 116, LRA1915D 941, 945

35 God was recognized in the Articles of Confederation (Art.No.13)

36 Holy Trinity Church v United States (1892) 143 US 457, 36 L ed 226 (Brewer,J)

In many states, the constitutions assume Christianity to be the religion of the state and that equality of religions refers to equality among Christian sects. 11 Cal.LR (1923) 186

The Delaware Constitution of 1776 (art.22), prescribed the following formal oath: "I, A.B., do profess faith in God the Father, and in Jesus Christ, His only Son, and in the Holy Ghost, one God, blessed forevermore; and I do acknowledge the Holy Scriptures in the Old and New Testament to be given by divine inspiration."

Preamble to the Constitution of Georgia: "We, the people of Georgia, relying upon the protection . . . of Almighty God, do ordain and establish this constitution." Wilkerson v Rome (1922) 152 Ga. 762, 110 SE 895, 20 ALR 1334, 1343

The Massachusetts Constitution, "in language strong and energetic" established "the religion of Protestant Christians." Avery v People of Tryingham (1807) 3 Mass. 160, 3 AD 105 (Sedgwick,J)

In the preamble to the Constitution of Missouri (1875) the people acknowledge their "profound reverence for the Supreme Ruler of the Universe" and their gratitude for His goodness. Harfst v Hoegen (1942) 349 Mo. 808, 163 SW2d 609, 612 (Douglas,J)

37 God is referred to in the date of the Constitution of the United States.

"In our original Federal Constitution no mention was made of the Bible, or of religion; but religious freedom was what inspired our colonial ancestors to come to this new country, and to declare their independence; and the First Amendment to the Constitution provided that 'Congress shall make no law respecting an establishment of religion, or prohibiting the free exercise thereof'." 42 Wash.LR (1914) 772, 773 (Barnard)

38 42 Wash.LR (1914) 772 (Barnard)

Our government "originating in the voluntary compact of a people, who in that very instrument profess the Christian religion, it may be considered, not as republican Rome was, a Pagan, but a Christian republic." Judge Nathaniel Freeman's Charge to the Grand Jury, 1802

39 Holy Trinity Church v United States (1892) 143 US 457, 36 L ed 226, 231 (Brewer,J)

"Our laws and our institutions must necessarily be based upon and embody the teachings of the Redeemer of mankind. It is impossible that it should be otherwise; and in this sense and to this extent our civilization and our institutions are emphatically Christian." Richmond v Moore (1883) 107 Ill. 429, 435, 47 AR 445 (Walker,J)

As to the original constitutions of the various states, it has been said:

"The constitution of South Carolina adopted in 1778 declared that the 'Christian Protestant religion' was the 'established religion' of that state; but that was modified in 1790, so as to secure freedom and prevent discrimination or preference in worship or religion. The constitution of North Carolina of 1776 excluded from office all non-believers in the Protestant religion or the divine authority of the Old or New Testament; while the constitution of Delaware of the same year made every official subscribe to a confession of faith; but that was abrogated sixteen years afterwards, and equal protection was extended to all sects. So the first constitutions of Maryland, Massachusetts, and New Hampshire, and later, of Connecticut, provided for the support, by taxation or otherwise of the Christian or Protestant Christian religion, with more or less toleration guaranteed to other sets. Such direct sanction and toleration seems to have been inspired by a lingering attachment for, or a sympathy with, the European theory of union between church and state. But the several states of New Jersey, New York, Pennsylvania, Vermont, and Virginia, from the first, and later, Maine and Rhode Island, of the New England States, and every, or nearly every, state admitted into the Union after the organization of the federal government, expressly secured, in effect, in their respective state constitutions, the equal freedom of every religious sect, organization, and society, with a guaranty against preference or discrimination."[40]

[§73] Similarly there is a conflict of authority as to whether Christianity is a part of the common law. Many of the early cases hold that it is.[41] In an early Pennsylvania decision it is said:

"The declaration that Christianity is part of the law of the land is a summary description of an existing and very obvious condition of our institutions. We are a Christian people, in so far as we have entered into the spirit of Christian institutions, and become imbued with the sentiments and principles of Christianity; and we cannot be imbued with them, and yet prevent them from entering into and influencing, more or less, all our social institutions, customs, and relations, as well as all our individual modes of thinking and acting. It is involved in our social nature, that even those among us who reject Christianity cannot possibly get clear of its influence, or reject those sentiments, customs, and principles which it has spread among the people, so that, like the air we breathe, they have become the common stock of the whole country, and essential elements of its life."[42]

40 State v District School Board of Edgerton (1890) 76 Wis. 117, 44 NW 967, 20 ASR 41, 57 (Cassoday,J)

The Constitution of Louisiana, "in the preamble, places God before the state, in the following language: 'We, the people of the state of Louisiana, grateful to Almighty God for the civil, political and religious liberties we enjoy and desiring to secure the continuance of these blessings, do ordain and establish this Constitution.'" Herold v Parish School Directors (1915) 136 La. 1034, 68 So. 116, LRA1915D 941, 946

41 See 49 AD 608, AnnCas1913E 1227

42 Mohney v Cook (1855) 26 Pa.St. 342, 67 AD 419

"It is also said, and truly, that the Christian religion is a part of the common law of Pennsylvania. But this proposition is to be received with its appropriate qualifications, and in connection with the bill of rights of that State, as found in its constitution of government." Vidal v Girard's Executors (1844) 2 Howard (US) 127, 198, 11 L ed 205, 234 (Story,J)

Also, in a Wisconsin case, the court conceded an argument of counsel that—

"the Christian religion is part of the common law of England; that the same was brought to this country by the colonists, and by virtue of the various colonial charters was embodied in the fundamental laws of the colonies; that this religious element or principle was incorporated in the various state constitutions, and in the ordinance of 1787 for the government of the Northwest Territory, by virtue of which ordinance it became the fundamental law of the territory of Wisconsin."[43]

However, the ecclesiastical law was not adopted in America,[44] and some authorities even deny that Christianity is a part of the common law in England and America. Thus, in Thomas Jefferson's Reports it is argued that the common law began with the settlement of the Saxons in England about the middle of the fifth century, and that Christianity was not introduced in England till the seventh century, and was never adopted into the common law by legislative authority.[45] The doctrine that Christianity is part of the common law was rejected in Ohio,[46] and it has been only partially accepted in other states.

Whichever view is taken, it is certain that many of the principles and usages, constantly acknowledged and enforced in courts of justice rest upon the Christian religion.[47]

[§74] Plainness and simplicity are qualities greatly to be desired in law, which ought to be so plain that "he may run that readeth it"[48] and so simple that "wayfaring men, though fools, shall not err therein."[49] Biblical law answers these requirements, for it is a law of fundamentals. Other legal systems, beginning with fundamentals, have developed a maze of

43 State v District School Board of Edgerton (1890) 76 Wis. 117, 20 ASR 41, 46 (Lyon,J), saying further: "Numerous quotations are given by him (counsel) from the above documents, from the utterances of Congress and legislatures, and from the writings of our early statesmen, to prove these propositions. . . . More than that, counsel have proved that many, probably most, of those charters, and some of the state constitutions, not only ordained and enforced some of the principles of the Christian religion, but sectarian doctrines as well."

44 Burtis v Burtis (1825) 1 Hopk. (N Y) 557, 564; Hodges v Hodges (1916) 22 NM 192, 159 P 1007; and see 17 Am Jur p 149, §6

But it does not follow that none of the principles of the ecclesiastical law of divorce are to be applied by an American divorce court. See 30 Harv. LR (1917) 283, 284

Adoption of ecclesiastical law, see 139 ALR 1301

45 Reports of General Court of Virginia, 1730-1740, 1768-1822, published at Charlottesville in 1829; and see 12 Gr.B. (1900) 441

46 Bloom v Richards (1853) 2 Ohio St. 387

47 City Council v Benjamin (1846) 2 Strobhart (SC) 508, 49 AD 608, 609, (O'Neall,J); and see Dunn v Jones (1926) 192 NC 251, 134 SE 487 (1928) 195 NC 354, 142 SE 320

48 Hab. 2:2

"It is most desirable . . . that the law should not be cloudy and confused." Tiller v Atlantic Coast Line (1943) 318 US 54, 87 L ed 610, 143 ALR 967 (Frankfurter,J)

49 Isa. 35:8

rules and forms in which the fundamentals have been buried and lost sight of.[49a] Modern laws, like those of the Romans, have grown "contradictory, some obsolete, some unpractical, some obscure, and the whole bulk of them too voluminous."[50] As Bentham[1] asserted:

"That which we have need of (need we say it?) is a body of law, from the respective parts of which we may each of us, by reading them or hearing them read, learn, and on each occasion know, what are his rights, and what his duties."[2]

And it has been said that—

". . . all the massive bulk of our English and American law may be reduced to a very few grand principles underlying the whole and which were enunciated by Moses, and which Bracton, Blackstone, Kent and the host of our English and American commentators have found a common labor in explaining. And the all but fabulous heaps of our statutes, reports and digests, are but amplifications and applications of these great principles to the various conditions of society."[3]

[§75] The antediluvians are supposed to have had seven great laws, one positive—to do justice, and six negative—not to blaspheme, nor to commit idolatry, murder, incest or robbery, nor to eat the flesh of living animals.[4] The prophet Micah reduced Biblical law to three rules, saying—

". . . what doth the Lord require of thee, but to do justly, and to love mercy, and to walk humbly with thy God?"[5]

And according to the Institutes of Justinian:

"The precepts of right and law are three: to live honorably, not to injure another, and to give to every one his own."[6]

49a The law has become "'encrusted with a mass of barnacles.' From a simple set of rules of conduct it has been gradually transformed into a highly technical system composed of tens of thousands of provisions and pronouncements 'meticulously dealing with minutiae." See 2 FRD (1942) 495 (Holtzoff) speaking of the NY Code of Civ. Proc.

50 Rolle's Abridgement (1668) Preface

1 Jeremy Bentham (1748-1832) English philosopher and jurist

2 18 Harv.LR (1905) 276 (Beale)

3 10 West. Jur. (1876) 91 (Bowman)
But see 28 Cal.LR (1940) 578, (Holdsworth) saying that "the complexity of life, and therefore of the rules of law needed to regulate it, must increase with the complexity of civilization, so that . . (the) ideal of a code of substantive and adjective law, so simple that it could be understood by all" is illusory.

4 13 Gr.B. (1901) 202

5 Micah. 6:8
"If a man be just, and do that which is lawful and right . . . he shall surely live." Ezek. 18:5,9

6 Institutes, I, i, §3
The following sections, based upon maxims of Biblical law, are offered as a substitute for present-day laws:
Section 1. Everyone within the jurisdiction shall, at all times and in all circumstances, do justly and speak the truth.
Sec. 2. Whoever shall violate this law, by doing wrong or speaking falsely to another, shall be liable to the person injured thereby in double the amount of damages actually sustained; and in case of a malicious or wilful violation he shall be subject also to a fine, imprisonment or other punishment, in such amount, for such time, and in such manner, as the judge in his discretion, and in the same proceeding, shall decree.

But secular law-makers have not ordinarily required that one should do good, or even refrain from doing wrong except in specific instances. So it has been said that "Human laws, as a general rule, do not attempt to enforce the positive moral obligation that we should do good, but they do undertake to restrain us from doing harm,"[7] in (it should be added) "certain respects."

7 Furst-Edwards & Co. v St.Louis Southwestern Ry. Co. (1912) 146 SW (Tex.Civ.App) 1024, 1028, error refused (Jenkins,J) observing further that "Our duty in specific instances is written in our statute books, but before human statutes were written, before the law was given at Sinai, the law of God had written upon the hearts of all men the injunction not to harm his fellow man."

D. Law and Gospel

'. Pieper [Concordia Seminary, St. Louis], *Christian Dogmatics* (4 vols.; St. Louis, Mo.: Concordia, 1950-1957), III, 220-47.

LAW AND GOSPEL

(DE DISCRIMINE LEGIS ET EVANGELII)

Because Scripture divides doctrinally into Law and Gospel, one cannot but treat constantly of Law and Gospel and their mutual relation in presenting the Christian doctrine on the basis of Scripture. Already in the very Prolegomena, in distinguishing the Christian religion from pagan religions, we had to demonstrate that the Christian religion is a religion of the Gospel, while all non-Christian religions bear the stamp of the religion of the Law. In describing theology as fitness for the office of public teaching in the Church (ἡ ἱκανότης ἡ ἐκ τοῦ θεοῦ, *facultas docendi*), we had to include in our definition of the theological aptitude also the ability to discern and teach both in what sense Law and Gospel are one and in what sense they are opposites. In the doctrine of God (*De Deo*) we distinguished between the natural concept and the Christian concept of God and pointed out that the Triune God revealed in the Scriptures is the God gracious to sinners, or the God of the Gospel, while the natural concept of God never rises above the Law, and for this reason may indeed produce an evil, but never a good conscience. Because sin is discord with, or departure from, the divine Law (ἀνομία), we had to set forth under the doctrine of sin (*De peccato*) that the divine Law always and everywhere obligates all men. In the doctrine of grace (*De gratia Dei salvifica*) we had to make clear that saving grace is the *favor Dei propter Christum,* is proclaimed in the Gospel, and is the direct opposite of the *iustitia inhaerens vel vitae,* which the Law demands. The doctrine of the procurement of grace by Christ (*De opere Christi*) adds up to this, that in the stead of men Christ took upon Himself both the obligation and the punishment of the Law which God had given to men. In soteriology (*De gratia Spiritus Sancti applicatrice*) the Law was excluded from the means of grace, and the Gospel shown to be the only means of grace because it alone bestows the remission of sins earned by Christ and through such bestowal works and strengthens faith. Conversion of man to God (*conversio*) consists in man's turning from the Law, from his innate *opinio legis,* to the Gospel. The Christian doctrine of the justification of man before God (*De hominis iustificatione coram Deo*) is taught correctly only when the *particulae exclusivae* are meticulously observed, that is, when everything that is Law and work of the Law is carefully weeded out. In the doctrine of sanctification and good works (*De sanctificatione et bonis operibus*) it was necessary to emphasize that not the Law, but only the Gospel produces sanctification and good works.

In proceeding now with a fuller discussion of "Law and Gospel," we can therefore only assemble materials already familiar. Such a compilation, however, is highly necessary and profitable in our day. Though the older Lutheran theologians dealt extensively with *De lege et evangelio* or *De discrimine legis et evangelii,* in newer dogmatic works this topic is either entirely missing, or hardly more than casually mentioned. Among recent theologians also Frank has called attention to this defect. He says: "In our Evangelical Church hardly any other doctrine has been more constantly maintained and elaborated as to both subject matter and practice than the doctrine of Law and Gospel. It was connected so intimately with the way God led Luther, with the cardinal doctrine of the Evangelical Church, justification by grace through faith, with the shaping of the Confessions, with the formulation, in Article V of the Formula of Concord, of the result of the controversy with Agricola and of later related controversies, that one can hardly imagine a continuity of the *publica doctrina* without this doctrine. The relation between the First and the Second Chief Part of the Catechism ever anew leads one to dwell on the difference and the connection between Law and Gospel. Indicative of present-day trends is the fact that also this piece of our evangelical heritage (*paradosis*) is deemed unsuited and declared to conflict with true evangelical knowledge. . . . Many deny that man's original relationship to God is a legal one, with the requirement: 'This do, and thou shalt live,' but that God has now appointed grace and the Gospel to save the transgressors of this Law. . . . Attention may therefore well be called to this point, in which the practical theologian is deeply interested for the spiritual guidance of every evangelical Christian." (*Dogm. Studien,* 1892, p. 104 ff.) Modern theologians have no use for the article "Law and Gospel," more particularly, Law and Gospel look alike to them, because they renounce *satisfactio vicaria* and thus inevitably discard the Gospel, however much they use the term "Gospel" and hold that they have a deeper understanding of the Gospel than former ages.

What we wish to add regarding Law and Gospel and their mutual relation, we shall assemble under the following heads: 1. The Terms Law and Gospel. 2. What Law and Gospel Have in Common. 3. Law and Gospel as Opposites. 4. Their Mutual Relation and Joint Use in Practice. 5. The Difficulty of Properly Distinguishing Between Law and Gospel. 6. The Importance of This Distinction. 7. The Confounders of Law and Gospel.

1

The Terms Law and Gospel

We differentiate between Law and Gospel when both terms are used in their proper sense. The Law in the proper sense (*lex proprie accepta*) is the Word of God in which God demands of men that in their nature and in their thoughts, words, and acts they conform to the standard of His commandments and pronounces the curse on those who fail to comply.[1] The Gospel in the proper sense (*evangelium proprie acceptum*) is the Word of God in which God makes no moral demands whatever on men, hence reproves no transgressions, but, on the contrary, promises His grace for the sake of Christ's vicarious satisfaction to such as have not kept the divine Law.[2]

The term "Law" is used in its proper, i. e., primary, sense in Scripture when it refers to what does not bear on faith, but demands perfect observance on the part of man (Gal. 3:12), pronounces the curse on all transgressors (Gal. 3:10), stops the mouth of all the world (Rom. 3:19), and therefore transmits the knowledge of sin (Rom. 3:20). The term "Gospel" is used in its proper sense in Holy Writ when it refers to what does not call for works, but for faith (Rom. 1:16-17), hence does not condemn sinners, but assures them of grace (Acts 20:24), peace (Rom. 10:15; Eph. 6:15), and salvation (Eph. 1:13).

The term "Law" is used in Holy Writ also in a wider, or general, sense to designate all the divine revelation and, moreover, the divine

---

1 Formula of Concord: "The Law is properly a divine doctrine in which the righteous, immutable will of God is revealed, what is to be the quality of man in his nature, thoughts, words, and works, in order that he may be pleasing and acceptable to God; and it threatens its transgressors with God's wrath and temporal and eternal punishments" (*Trigl.* 957, Sol. Decl., V, 17). Shorter in the Epitome: "We believe, teach, and confess that the Law is properly a divine doctrine which teaches what is right and pleasing to God and reproves everything that is sin and contrary to God's will" (*Trigl.* 801, V, 2).

2 Formula of Concord: "The Gospel is properly such a doctrine as teaches what man, who has not observed the Law and therefore is condemned by it, is to believe, namely, that Christ has expiated and made satisfaction for all sins, and has obtained and acquired for him, without any merit of his, forgiveness of sins, righteousness that avails before God, and eternal life" (*Trigl.* 801, Epit., V, 4). Luther: "The Gospel is such a doctrine or Word of God as does not demand our works nor enjoin us to do something, but bids us simply to receive the offered grace of the remission of sins and eternal salvation and accept it as a present" (St. L. IX:803).

revelation κατ' ἐξοχήν, the Gospel, as in Is. 2:3: "For out of Zion shall go forth the Law (תּוֹרָה)."[3] The term "Gospel," too, is used in Holy Writ to designate the whole body of Christian doctrine. In this case it is a synecdoche, denominating by its principal part all that is to be taught in and by the Church. *Denominatio fit a parte potiori. Ex parte digniori et potiori totum intelligitur.* Thus Mark 1:1 says of the whole Gospel according to St. Mark, in which also the preaching of repentance by John the Baptist is recorded (v. 4 ff.): "The beginning of the Gospel of Jesus Christ." But the term "Gospel" is never used to designate the Law in the proper sense.[4]

This use of the term "Gospel" in the wider and in the proper, or narrower, sense is noted in the Formula of Concord too. A controversy had arisen as to the question whether the Gospel also may be called a preaching of repentance and judgment, more particularly, whether it is correct to say that the Gospel reproves the sin of unbelief. The Formula of Concord answers yes if the term "Gospel" is used in the wider sense (*late*), and no if the term is used in the proper sense (*proprie*). The Formula says: "Now, when we consider this dissent [whether the Gospel should be called a preaching of repentance] aright, it has been caused chiefly by this, that the term "Gospel" is not always employed and understood in one and the same sense, but in two ways, in the Holy Scriptures, as also by ancient and modern church teachers. For sometimes it is employed so that there is understood by it the entire doctrine of Christ, our Lord, which He proclaimed in His ministry upon earth, and commanded to be proclaimed in the New Testament, and hence comprised in it the explanation of the Law and the proclamation of the favor and grace of God, His heavenly Father, as it is written, Mark 1:1: 'The beginning of the Gospel of Jesus Christ, the Son of God.' And shortly afterwards the chief heads are stated: 'Repentance and

---

[3] There can be no doubt that תּוֹרָה here signifies the Gospel, for it is the designation of that Word of God by which the Gentiles are gathered into the Christian Church. Luther: That the Law goes forth out of Zion "is the cause of the increase of the Church and of the expansion of the kingdom of Christ, namely, the preaching of the Gospel. For He here promises a new Word . . . since He adds, 'out of Zion,' as though He would say: Previously I have given the Law on Mount Sinai; now I will give another Word on Mount Zion, which is not to be a doctrine of works, but of faith, not of laws, but of grace, not an accusing Word, but one conferring remission of sins." (St. L. VI:35; *Opp. exeg.* XXII, 42 *sq.*)

[4] Quenstedt (II, 1027) remarks: "In Scripture the designation 'Law' is, indeed, given a number of times to the Gospel, but the appellation 'Gospel' is never given to the Law."

forgiveness of sins.'" (*Trigl.* 953, Sol. Decl., V, 3 f.) This is "the description of the word 'Gospel' when employed in a wide sense and without the proper distinction between the Law and the Gospel." In this "wide sense" the Gospel may be called a preaching of repentance. "Furthermore the term 'Gospel' is employed in another, namely, in its proper sense, by which it comprises not the preaching of repentance, but only the preaching of the grace of God, as follows directly afterwards, Mark 1:15, where Christ says: 'Repent, and believe the Gospel.'" (*Trigl.* 953, *ibid.*, 6.)[5]

2

What Law and Gospel Have in Common

First, both Law and Gospel are the Word of God. "Thou shalt love the Lord, thy God, with all thy heart," and, "Thou shalt love thy neighbor as thyself," including the curse, "Cursed is everyone that continueth not in all things which are written in the Book of the Law to do them" – these words of the Law are as much God's Word and will as the word of the Gospel with which Paul and Silas saved the jailer at Philippi from despair: "Believe on the Lord Jesus Christ, and thou shalt be saved and thy house."

Furthermore, both Law and Gospel apply to all men. As the Word of the Law, "Ye shall be holy, for I am holy," imposes a duty on the king and the beggar, the cultured man and the barbarian, so, too, there is not a man in all the world for whom the Word of the Gospel, releasing all men from guilt and damnation, is not intended.

Finally, both Law and Gospel are to be taught side by side in the Church and by the Church up to the Last Day.[6] The necessity

---

[5] Baier says of the difference in the use of the terms Law and Gospel: "At times the terms are understood in a wider sense, so that Law in this meaning includes the Gospel, and the latter in a measure the former, for example, when the Law is used for the entire Scriptures, Ps. 1:2, or more especially for the Scriptures of the Old Testament, John 15:25; 1 Cor. 14:21, and lastly in particular for the Mosaic Scriptures, Luke 24:44. Gospel is also at times understood in a wider sense for the entire doctrine of the New Testament, delivered by Christ and the Apostles, Mark 1:14; 16:15; Luke 9:6. Here, however, the terms Law and Gospel are understood in so far as they stand in full contradistinction to each other." (Baier-Walther, III, 342.)

[6] Thus Paul in his Epistle to the Romans thoroughly teaches both side by side, first the Law (ch. 1:18—3:20), and then the Gospel (ch. 3:21—5:21 ff.). The Formula of Concord comments: "From the beginning of the world these

of preaching particularly also the Law must be maintained against Antinomianism, which at the time of the Reformation sought to invade the Lutheran Church through Agricola and his followers.[7] Antinomianism is basically the theory that the knowledge of sin must be taught not from the Law, but from the Gospel, and that accordingly the Law does not belong in the Church, but "in the courthouse," in the sphere of the State.[8] The Lutheran Church disowned this error in all its forms in Art. V and VI of the Formula of Concord. See *Trigl.*, Hist. Introd., pp. 161–172.

Nothing can be said, either from a theological angle or from the viewpoint of natural reason, in favor of the position of Agricola and

---

two proclamations [kinds of doctrine] have been ever and ever inculcated alongside of each other in the Church of God, with a proper distinction" (*Trigl.* 959, Sol. Decl., V, 23).

[7] John Agricola, b. 1492 at Eisleben, 1525 pastor of Nicolai-Church at Eisleben, 1536 in Wittenberg, 1540 court preacher in Berlin, d. 1566. — In the Majoristic controversy (see p. 20ff.) regarding the necessity of good works for salvation the pastors Andrew Poach of Erfurt and Anton Otto of Nordhausen defended antinomistic principles.

[8] Agricola and his followers declared: "Repentance is to be taught not from the Decalog or from any Law of Moses, but by means of the Gospel from the wounding of the Son of God." "Christ says in John that not the Law, but the Spirit reproves sin." "Any matter by which the Holy Ghost is not given or men justified need not be taught, neither at the beginning, nor middle, nor end of justification." "Those who teach that first the Law and then the Gospel must be preached pervert the words of Christ." "The Gospel teaches the wrath of God from heaven and at the same time the righteousness of God, Rom. 1." "The Law does not deserve to be called God's Word." "The Decalog belongs in the courthouse, not in the pulpit." — Agricola first (1527) attacked Melanchthon's *Articles of Visitation,* then, ten years later (1537), also Luther. He says against Melanchthon: "In the Saxon *Visitation* [this is impure]: Because Christ commands to preach repentance and remission of sins, the Decalog must be preached." Agricola even names Luther in his attacks: "In his commentary on the Epistle to the Galatians, Luther says that it is the proper office of the Law to plague and terrify the conscience, in order that it might the easier recognize Christ. There are many such passages in this commentary, which we reject as erroneous in order to preserve purity of doctrine." — Agricola's *Positiones inter fratres sparsae* ("Theses Circulated Among Brethren") and other antinomistic propositions advanced by him or his adherents are found in St. L. XX:1624 ff. Luther's six disputations against the Antinomians are also offered (*ibid.*, 1628 ff.). For the Latin see *Opp. v. a.* IV, 424 ff. In addition, Luther's essay *"Wider die Antinomer"* (1539) and *"Luthers Bericht von M. Joh. Eislebens falscher Lehre und schaendlicher Tat"* (1540) pertain to this matter (St. L. XX:1610 ff., 1649 ff.). Also Luther's sermon on the Fifth Sunday after Trinity in his *Gospel Postil* (see *Trigl.* 955, Sol. Decl., V, 12) offers a clear analysis of Agricola's Antinomianism (St. L. XI:1328 ff.). In Schluesselburg's *Catalogus,* Volume IV pertains to this matter. Sufficient material properly to judge the controversy is to be found in Gieseler, III, 2, 137 ff.; Schmid-Hauck, *Dogmengesch.*, 4th ed., p. 360 ff.

his adherents. They did not want the Law taught in the Christian Church. But what they sought to get rid of, they retained under another name. They injected the Law into the Gospel. They made God's wrath an appendix of the Gospel. Luther exactly describes the logical and theological folly of the Antinomians when he says: "They want to abolish the Law and nevertheless teach the wrath, which is exclusively the office of the Law. Therefore all they do is, they throw these letters '*L-a-w*' away, confirm, however, the wrath of God, which is indicated and understood by these letters, not to mention that they attempt to wring the neck of St. Paul and to make the head the tail." "They have invented a new way of putting it, that one is first to preach grace, then the revelation of wrath, in order that one might not be obliged to hear or utter the word 'Law.' That is a handy footstool which pleases them highly, and they hope to draw all of Scripture in and out of it and thus to become *lux mundi*. They make St. Paul teach this in Romans 1. But they do not see that Paul uses exactly the opposite manner of presenting it. He begins with and shows first the wrath of God from heaven and proves all men sinners and guilty before God; then, after they have become sinners, he teaches them how to obtain grace and become righteous. This the first three chapters mightily and clearly show. Moreover this, too, is an exceptional blindness and folly, that they think the revelation of wrath is something else than the Law, which is impossible; for the Law is revelation of wrath wherever it is understood and felt, as St. Paul says: *Lex iram operatur*. Now, didn't they do a perfect job by banning the Law and then reinstating it by teaching the revelation of wrath? Only they wear the heel in front and teach us the Law after the Gospel and wrath after grace!" (St. L. XX:1618 f.)

Just as foolish is the argument of Agricola that the Law is not to be taught because it does not justify.[9] Inverted, the argument makes sense: Because the Law does not justify, but condemns, it must be preached before the Gospel in order that the damnation pronounced by the Law may be canceled by the Gospel. Justification presupposes condemnation by the Law. Luther therefore asked Agricola to consider: "Is not this blindness without measure that he does not want to preach the Law without or before the Gospel? Why, that is an impossible thing. How is it possible to preach of forgiveness of sins if one has not first established the sins? How can one proclaim

---

[9] *Positiones inter fratres sparsae* 6—9; St. L. XX:1625.

life without death being there?" "For grace must war and win in us against the Law and sin that we may be kept from despair." (St. L. XX:1659, 1656.) Luther is therefore not stretching the truth when he claims that Agricola's objection to the preaching of the Law must as a natural result do away with the Gospel, with Christ and His active obedience to the Law, and thus with the whole Christian faith.

Furthermore, Agricola wants contrition or repentance taught from the Gospel and not from the Law, because a contrition or repentance from love of God can come only from the Gospel. The last part of this sentence is true, of course. But when he then says of the contrition which flows from love of God: This is "the first rung of the new birth, the real blowing and breathing upon by the Holy Spirit; after that the heart gains the sincere confidence in God that He will overlook its foolishness,"[10] he is actually making trust in God, or faith in the remission of sins, follow on the contrition which proceeds from love of God, hence dependent on renewal and sanctification. With his new "*methodus*" he is not saving the doctrine of justification, but has turned his steps toward Rome.

Taking into account the further fact that Agricola, in spite of his logical and theological fogginess, presented himself as the savior of the purity of the Christian doctrine[11] and rejected as false the teaching of the Wittenberg faculty, and particularly of Luther, one easily understands why Luther at times employed strong language against Agricola and listed his advent with the "tempests" by which the devil was forever trying to extinguish the restored light of the Gospel. Other details of Antinomianism will be found in the next chapters.[12]

---

[10] *Kurze Summarien,* p. 304; in Schmid-Hauck, p. 361; The "*Kurze Summarien*" of Agricola appeared 1537, but were suppressed because they had been published without being censored; G. Plitt, R. E., 2d ed., I, 452.

[11] *Positiones,* etc., 13: "In order to keep the Christian doctrine pure those must be opposed who teach that the Gospel should be preached only to those whose hearts have previously been terrified and crushed by the Law."

[12] *Wider die Antinomer* (St. L. XX:1619—1623). — A short biography and a striking description of his character by Gustave Plitt is to be found in R. E., 2d ed., I, 214. There, too, the true motive of his attack on Melanchthon is noted. Agricola "was a gifted and not unintelligent man. . . . But all his good sides were nullified by his boundless vanity. Luther, who knew his character well, wrote Dec. 6, 1540: 'If you want to know what vanity itself looks like, you can learn to know it by no better image than that of Agricola.' This character trait made him unfit for service in the Church. Agricola belongs to those assistants of the Reformers who have done more harm than good." The letter mentioned by Plitt is addressed to Jacob Stratner, court preacher in Berlin, and can be found in De Wette, V, 319 f.; St. L. XXIb:2535 ff.

3

Law and Gospel as Opposites

There is no need to apologize for Luther, much less to admit that Luther used language liable to be misunderstood,[13] when he described Law and Gospel as perfect opposites. Indeed, Luther's language in this matter is unequivocal. He says of Law and Gospel that they "differ most widely from each other and are separated farther than opposites" (*inter se longissime distincta et plus quam contradictoria separata sunt, ad Gal.*, St. L. IX:447). And he is entirely right. In content Law and Gospel are actually, like yes and no, perfect opposites. While the Law demands that man perfectly comply with its precepts in his nature and his conduct and proclaims God's wrath to all delinquents, the Gospel makes no moral demands whatever on man and therefore reproves no transgressions – not even the sin of unbelief[14] – but rather, without regard to any good quality or works on their part, promises God's grace for Christ's sake to all transgressors condemned by the Law. We must by all means maintain what a synergistic theology has lost sight of, namely, that the very persons whom the Law pronounces guilty and sentences to death the Gospel acquits of guilt and frees from condemnation. In its promise of grace the Gospel knows of no difference between great and little sinners, between such as conducted themselves properly and such as did not conduct themselves properly, between the more guilty and the less guilty. Rather, there being "no difference, for all have sinned and come short of the glory of God," the Gospel justifies all "freely, by His grace, through the redemption that is in Christ Jesus" (Rom. 3:22 ff.). Men falsify the Gospel through an admixture of Law as soon as they say that the grace promised by the Gospel pertains to other and different, relatively better or less guilty persons than those to whom the Law's verdict of condemnation applies.

The Gospel indeed demands faith. This is the Bible's way of speaking (1 John 3:23) and therefore not to be criticized. But the faith demanded by the Gospel in no wise is a good quality in man or a human accomplishment (*Leistung*), but the very opposite of any accomplishment of man, since "by faith" (διὰ τῆς πίστεως) is tanta-

---

[13] Against Thomasius, *Das Bekenntnis d. ev.-luth. K. in d. Konsequenz seines Prinzips*, p. 47 f.; also *Dogmengesch.*, 2d ed., II, 425.

[14] The Gospel indeed demands faith, but does not reprimand unbelief. More on this at the end of this chapter.

mount to "*not* of works" (οὐκ ἐξ ἔργων), Eph. 2:8-9. God's demand, or command, that the sinner believe proves how earnestly God's Gospel offer of grace is meant. Cf. Vol. II, 441. Moreover, the Gospel itself, without the assistance of man, kindles the faith it demands. This faith is, as Luther says, no "work enjoined" in the Law, such as love, obedience, etc., but a product of the promise (*opus promissionis*). The Gospel imperative: "Believe on the Lord Jesus Christ," breathes faith into the heart, as, for instance, it made a believer of the jailer at Philippi. (Erl. 58, 353 f.)

To show and maintain the complete dissimilarity of Law and Gospel in content, our old theologians have also pointed out the essential difference between the promises of the Law and the promises of the Gospel, calling the former conditional (*promissiones conditionales*) and the latter pure promises of grace (*promissiones gratuitae*). Some Antinomians denied that any promises were added to the Law.[15] But with Scripture we must maintain that the Law promises life to those who keep it. Gal. 3:12: "The man that doeth them [the things written in the Law] shall live in them." Hence the promises of the Law and those of the Gospel in their nature are opposites. Scripture, as we have seen, makes it very clear that the Law promises life only to those who have actually and in all respects kept the Law. Note the character of the promises of the Law by observing how emphatically Christ pointed those who aimed to inherit eternal life by way of the Law to the need of really keeping the Law. "This do," He said (Luke 10:28), "and thou shalt live." On the other hand, if we scrutinize what Scripture has to say of the promises of the Gospel, we note how persistently Scripture stresses the truth that the Gospel promises righteousness and life to those who have not kept the Law. Scripture multiplies the *particulae exclusivae:* "without the Law," "without the deeds of the Law," "not of works," "not by the works of the Law" (Rom. 3:21, 28; Eph. 2:9; Gal. 2:16). In other words, if we compare the promises of the Law with the promises of the Gospel, we find: The Law pronounces the righteous man righteous; the Gospel, however, pronounces the unrighteous man righteous. Faith in the Gospel is faith in the God "that justifieth the ungodly [τὸν ἀσεβῆ]" (Rom. 4:5).

Finally, we must here again keep in mind the fact that the term

---

15 Andrew Poach of Erfurt and Anton Otto of Nordhausen contended that the Law contained no promise of salvation at all. Schluesselburg, *Catalogus*, IV, 276; Schmid-Hauck, p. 363; *Trigl.*, Hist. Introd., p. 170.

"condition" is susceptible of different interpretations. We may not forbid anyone to designate the promises of the Gospel "conditional promises," because the evangelical promises, too, frequently have the grammatical form of conditional statements. Rom. 10:9: "If thou . . . shalt believe in thine heart . . . thou shalt be saved." But the teachers who understand and maintain the difference between Law and Gospel point out that in legal conditional clauses the term "condition" actually denotes a human accomplishment, e. g.: "If you keep the Law, you will obtain life"; but in evangelical conditional clauses, e. g.: "If you believe, you will be saved," "believing" does not denote a product or work of man, but merely the mode and manner of appropriation (*modus applicationis*). The sense of the sentence: "If you believe, you will be saved," is not: "If you furnish the faith, you will be saved," but rather: by way of faith, without any goodness or accomplishment of your own, you will be saved.[16] Quenstedt devotes a special section to the discussion of the question: *An promissiones evangelicae sint conditionales* (*Syst.* II, 1018 ff.).

If, however, we must maintain with Luther that Law and Gospel are *contradictoria* in content, then an insurmountable difficulty seems to arise. When God in the Law sentences sinners to death for their sins, and in the Gospel absolves and awards life to the same sinners – for there is no difference among them – it would seem to follow that neither do the hearers of the Word of God know whether the Word of death or the Word of life applies to them, nor does the minister know whether in applying the Word to individual persons he should say to the individual, "Thou shalt surely die" (2 Sam. 12:5), or, "The Lord also hath put away thy sin; thou shalt not die" (2 Sam. 12:13). To solve this puzzle men have at times resorted to the expedient of announcing the consolation of the Gospel only to those who had apparently mended their ways. We learned above that this is not the solution. To become clear in this matter, we must let Scripture instruct us with regard to a further distinction between Law and Gospel, namely, that each has its separate, sharply defined sphere within which it functions in the order of salvation (οἰκονομία).

The Law is certainly to be preached without diminution (Matt. 5:17-18; Gal. 3:10; Rom. 1:18; 3:9-19), but solely for the purpose of bringing man to a realization of his sinfulness and deserved condemnation. As soon as this purpose is attained, as soon as man asks

---

[16] See the quotations from Heerbrand, Seb. Schmid, and Gerhard in Vol. II, 35, footnote 71.

in contrition, "What must I do to be saved?" the preaching of the Law should cease. It is a divine requirement, and not merely a church regulation, that terrified hearts should hear not the Law, but only the Gospel, which for Christ's sake assures them just as they are ("Just as I Am") of remission of sins and salvation, without the Law and the works of the Law. The Catechism sums up the matter in this fashion: "The Law is to be preached to secure, the Gospel to terrified sinners." In the words of Scripture (Rom. 10:4): "Christ is the end of the Law for righteousness to everyone that believeth," the boundary between Law and Gospel is sharply defined, and Christ asserts the sole authority of the Gospel in the area of broken and humbled hearts when He declares the purpose of His mission to be "to preach the Gospel to the poor, to heal the brokenhearted," (Is. 61:1; Luke 4:18). This line of demarcation between Law and Gospel is clearly fixed in the Scriptures of both the Old and the New Testament, particularly by the practice of Christ and the Apostles.[17] Luther: "The Law has its end, how far it is to go and what it is to achieve, namely, 'unto Christ,' to terrify the impenitent with God's wrath and disfavor. Likewise the Gospel has its peculiar office and function, namely, to preach remission of sins to the troubled consciences. . . . Now, when the conscience is truly smitten, so that it duly feels its sin, experiences the terrors of death, is weighted down with war, pestilence, poverty, shame, and similar misfortune, and the Law then says: You are a dead man and doomed because you have not complied, nor been able to comply, with anything of all that I demanded of you – when the Law, I say, thus crashes down on man and terrifies him with the anguish of death and hell and with despair, it is then high time to know how to separate Law and Gospel from each other and to confine each to its place. Here let him separate who knows how to separate; for here there is occasion and need of separation. To this matter St. Paul's words pertain: 'But before faith came, we were kept under the Law, shut up unto the faith' (Gal. 3:23). . . . Therefore, when the Law accuses me of not having done this or that, of being unrighteous and listed in God's record of debtors, I must confess, it all is true. But the deduction: Therefore you are lost, I must not concede, but in strong faith struggle against it and say: According to the Law, which imputes my guilt unto me, I am

---

[17] Nathan and David (2 Sam. 12:13); Christ and the harlot (Luke 7:47); Peter on Pentecost (Acts 2:37-39); Paul and Silas and the jailer at Philippi (Acts 16:27-31); the congregation at Corinth and the man living in incest (1 Cor. 5:1-5 and 2 Cor. 2:6-8).

indeed a poor, lost sinner, but I appeal from the Law to the Gospel; for God has given another Word over and above the Law, called the Gospel, which makes a gift to us of His grace, remission of sins, eternal righteousness and life, also acquits and delivers me from all your terrors and condemnation and hands me the consolation that all my debt is paid by the Son of God, Jesus Christ Himself. Therefore it is most necessary to know well how to direct and handle both these Words and constantly to take heed that one does not mix them up." (St. L. IX:798 ff.)

It is therefore a part of the proper distinction between Law and Gospel that the Gospel be recognized as the "higher Word," which is to be God's final Word for the terrified sinner. Luther adds: "Now, when both Law and Gospel meet, and the Law declares me a sinner, accuses and condemns me, the Gospel, however, says (Matt. 9:2): 'Be of good cheer; thy sins be forgiven thee,' 'thou shalt be saved,' and both are God's Word, which am I, then, to follow? St. Paul tells you. 'But after faith is come,' he says, 'we are no longer under a schoolmaster,' the Law has come to an end. For as the lesser Word it should and must give way and place to the Gospel. Both are God's Word, the Law and the Gospel, but the two are not equal. One is lower, the other higher; one is weaker, the other stronger; one is lesser, the other greater. When now they wrestle with each other, I follow the Gospel and say, Good-by, Law!" [18]

Law and Gospel differ also as to the sources from which they are known. While natural man still knows the Law, no thought of the Gospel has ever come of itself to even the wisest and civilly most righteous among men. Solely through God's revelation of it in the Word has the Gospel become known among men. Scripture takes great pains to call attention also to this difference between Law and Gospel. Rom. 2:14-15 says of the Law that the Gentiles, who have not the written Law, are a law unto themselves because the work of the Law, that is, the things demanded by the Law, is written in their hearts. But of the Gospel 1 Cor. 2:6 ff. states: "Not the wisdom of this world, nor of the princes of this world, that come to nought but we speak the wisdom of God in a mystery, even the hidden wisdom which God ordained before the world unto our glory, which none of the princes of this world knew; for had they known it, they would

[18] Luther's manner of speaking of a "lesser" and a "higher" Word in reference to the sphere of authority of Law and Gospel within the divine order of salvation is Scriptural, as can be seen from passages such as Rom. 10:4; 5:20-21; 2 Cor. 3:7 ff.; Deut. 18:15 ff.; Jer. 31:31 ff.; Heb. 8:6-13.

not have crucified the Lord of Glory. But as it is written: Eye hath not seen, nor ear heard, neither have entered into the heart of man, the things which God hath prepared for them that love Him. But God hath revealed them unto us by His Spirit." [19]

For this reason all pagan religions, being religions of the Law, have no resemblance whatever to the Christian religion. As a rule, modern studies of comparative religion assert a similarity between, or even a basic identity of, the pagan religions and the Christian religion.[20] They arrive at this conclusion by eliminating the Gospel of Christ Crucified from the Christian religion as unessential, as is done, for example, by Pfleiderer [21] and Frank B. Jevons.[22] Actually, however, the difference between Law and Gospel, in respect to the sources from which they are known, becomes antipodal because natural man insists on opposing the Gospel with his innate religion of the Law. The Gospel of the grace of God in Christ is to him an offense and foolishness (1 Cor. 1:23; 2:14), until the rule of the *opinio legis* in his heart is overcome by the Gospel (*Trigl.* 197, Apol., III, 144).

In considering in what respects Law and Gospel are opposites, theologians have studied the special question whether the Gospel or the Law reproves the sin of unbelief. The Formula of Concord teaches, as stated above (p. 223), that reproof of unbelief is to be regarded as Law and not Gospel if the term "Gospel" is taken in its proper sense. Against this finding it has been and is argued that it is inconceivable that the Law can reprove unbelief, since it knows nothing of faith. Accordingly, the reproof of unbelief necessarily had to belong to the Gospel. This was, as Gerhard remarks upon occasion, the chief argument (*palmarium argumentum*) also of the later Philippists, or crypto-Calvinists.[23] Frank, too, inclines to this view.[24]

---

19 We have repeatedly pointed out that according to the context these words speak not of heaven, but of the Gospel.

20 Max Mueller of Oxford takes a wholly different position. See Vol. I, 15 f.

21 *Religion und Religionen*, 1906, p. 215 ff.

22 *An Introd. to the Study of Compar. Rel.*, 1908, p. 69.

23 Gerhard, *Loci*, "*De ev.*," § 105, points to the fact that Agricola's theses regarding the Gospel as a preaching of repentance were zealously defended by the crypto-Calvinists, "as is apparent from the catecheses and theses published in the year 1570 and 1571 at the same place" (Wittenberg). Cp. Muenscher, *Dogmengesch.* (Neudecker), III, 576.

24 *Dogm. Studien*, p. 114: "The difficulty is that the censuring and reproving function of the Law is nothing more than the reverse side of its demanding and commanding function; in the nature of the case the former cannot extend farther than the latter."

To answer the question, we need but heed two things: 1. According to all that Scripture tells us of the Gospel in its proper sense, one cannot by the remotest chance come to the conclusion that the Gospel reproves the sin of unbelief. 2. According to all that we know of the Law from Scripture, the Law, reproving, as it does, all other sins, surely cannot fail to reprove the sin of unbelief.

Concerning the first point, we recall the exceedingly close relation of the Gospel to the merit of Christ. The Gospel distributes what Christ has merited. But Christ has purchased the remission of all sins for all men, accordingly remission of the sin of unbelief too. The Gospel therefore distributes with the forgiveness of all sins also forgiveness of the sin of unbelief. How, then, could the Gospel, which remits the sin of unbelief, come to reprove it? We should have to disavow Christ's merit and the very essence of the Gospel if we insisted on making reproof of unbelief a part of the Gospel in its proper sense. Moreover, if the Gospel reproved unbelief, it would continually be condemning also the believers, because believers, too, always harbor considerable unbelief along with their faith – a fact that certainly troubles their conscience much. Hence where could we flee with our guilt of unbelief, which we must daily confess? where find consolation if the Gospel reproved the sin of unbelief, instead of forgiving it? Furthermore, if the Gospel reproved the sin of unbelief, no man could ever come to faith in the Gospel, that is, become a Christian, since every man is an unbeliever before he comes to faith. Therefore we shall have to concur in this judgment of the Formula of Concord: "Accordingly we reject and regard as incorrect and injurious the dogma that the Gospel is properly a preaching of repentance or reproof, and not alone a preaching of grace; for thereby the Gospel is again converted into a doctrine of the Law, the merit of Christ and Holy Scripture are obscured, Christians robbed of true consolation, and the door is opened again to [the errors and superstitions of] the Papacy" (*Trigl.* 805, Epit., V, 11. See also 961, Sol. Decl., V, 27).

And now the other point – how the Law comes to reprove unbelief toward the Gospel, whereas the Law by itself knows nothing of Gospel and faith. Here we must recall that Law and Gospel are not abstract concepts suspended in space, but both are God's Word addressed to men. The Law is *Deus propter peccata damnans*, and the Gospel is *Deus propter Christum absolvens sive iustificans.* Now, what should prevent God from extending His punitive activity as

Deus propter peccata damnans also over the sin of despising His grace, that is, over unbelief? The Formula of Concord states the case in this way: "Thus the Law reproves unbelief, [namely,] when men do not believe the Word of God. Now, since the Gospel, which alone properly teaches and commands to believe in Christ, is God's Word, the Holy Ghost, through the office of the Law, also reproves unbelief, that men do not believe in Christ, although it is properly the Gospel alone which teaches concerning saving faith in Christ." (*Trigl.* 957, Sol. Decl., V, 19.) We fully realize that this does not explain how there can be both Law and Gospel simultaneously in God. But our limitation is due to the fact that our mundane knowledge of God bears the stamp: "Now I know in part" (1 Cor. 13:12).

Men have thought to prove that the Gospel is a preaching of repentance and reproof also by pointing to the suffering and death of Christ. The argument took about this form: Christ's suffering and death certainly belongs to the Gospel. But sin is reproved by Christ's suffering because only from His suffering do we learn fully how great God's wrath and man's guilt are. Therefore the Gospel must be a preaching of repentance and reproof. In answer we say: Of course the wrath of God over the sin of men can and should be taught also from the suffering and death of Christ. Christ Himself makes this use of His suffering and death.[25] But in so far as it is thus used, not Gospel, but Law is being preached, both terms taken in their proper sense. This fact, too, the Formula of Concord clearly sets forth in Luther's words: "Anything that preaches concerning our sins and God's wrath, let it be done how or when it will, that is all a preaching of the Law. . . . Yea, what more forcible, more terrible declaration and preaching of God's wrath against sin is there than just the suffering and death of Christ, His Son? But as long as all this preaches God's wrath and terrifies men, it is not yet the preaching of the Gospel nor Christ's own preaching, but that of Moses and the Law against the impenitent. For the Gospel and Christ were never ordained and given for the purpose of terrifying and condemning, but of comforting and cheering those who are terrified and timid." (*Trigl.* 955f., Sol. Decl., V, 12.) In the Epitome terrifying with Christ's suffering and death is called "a foreign work [*alienum opus*] of Christ, by which He arrives at His proper office [*proprium suum officium*], that is, to preach grace" (*Trigl.* 803 V, 10).

---

[25] Luke 23:27 ff. V. 31: "For if they do these things in a green tree, what shall be done in the dry?"

4

How Law and Gospel Are to Be Joined in Practice

While the theologian must differentiate sharply between Law and Gospel, yet he must in practice join them most intimately. This necessity Luther expresses in these words: "Though these two in content [*re ipsa*] are very far apart [*remotissima*], they are at the same time most intimately joined in one and the same heart. Nothing is linked more closely than fear and confidence, Law and Gospel, sin and grace. For they are so bound together, that the one is swallowed by the other (*absorbeatur*). Therefore there can be no mathematical combination that equals this." (St. L. IX:454.)

This intimate connection sets in at conversion, which takes place in the moment when the first ray of faith in the Gospel lights up the heart (Acts 11:21; Col. 2:12; etc.). But only that sinner whom the Law has brought to a knowledge of his deserved condemnation will in faith accept the remission of sins offered in the Gospel. Whoever therefore refuses to preach the Law prevents the Gospel, or Christ in His redemption, from taking effect. This is the theme which Luther developed and thoroughly presented from many angles in his offensive against Antinomianism.

But also objectively, or in regard to content, there is a connection between Law and Gospel inasmuch as the Gospel furnishes and presents man with the very fulfillment which the Law demands. The Gospel of course tells of the redemptive work of Christ, who in the stead of men by His perfect obedience kept the Law given to men (Gal. 4:4-5; Matt. 5:17) and bore the punishment for man's transgression of the Law (Gal. 3:13; Is. 53:4-6). Luther therefore rightly asserts that by their demand that the preaching of the Law be banished from the Church the Antinomians are doing all they can to rob the Church also of the Gospel and Christ. Luther writes: "If the Law is removed, no one knows what Christ is, or what He did when He fulfilled the Law for us." Again: "What will you retain of Christ when the Law, which He fulfilled, has been removed, and you do not know what He has fulfilled?" Again: "Whence shall we learn what Christ is, what He has done for us, if we are not to know what that Law is which He has fulfilled for us, or what sin is, for which He has atoned?" [26]

---

[26] *Fifth Disputation,* Theses 61, 67 (St. L. XX:1646). — *Wider die Antinomer* (*ibid.,* 1616); *Second Disputation Against the Antinomians,* Theses 25—26 (*ibid.,* 1634).

And turning to the mutual relation of the effects of the Law and of the Gospel in the heart of man, we note that the Gospel with its verdict of justification must supersede or "devour" the Law with its verdict of condemnation. "For grace [pledged to us in the Gospel] must war and win in us against the Law and sin, that we may be kept from despair" (St. L. XX:1656). For this reason it is a factual verdict on Antinomianism "that by this 'spiritism' ['*Geisterei*'] the devil does not mean to take away the Law, but Christ, who fulfilled the Law."[27]

But also after a man has become a Christian, Law and Gospel are still joined for him; more exactly, there is still a use of the Law for him, for he cannot do without the preaching of the Law. To be sure, as far as he is a Christian or new man, he no longer needs the Law. This is the clear teaching of Scripture. 1 Tim. 1:9: "The Law is not made for a righteous man, but for the lawless and disobedient, for the ungodly and for sinners." For the Christian according to his new man the Law is superfluous not merely in part, but in its every use. Without the recorded Law, the new man in him knows both what is sinful and what is good; and since the Christian is entirely godly according to the new man, he does not need the Law to keep him in check outwardly by its threats and scourges. According to the new man, the Law is written in the heart of the Christian (Jer. 31:33), even as the first men before the Fall were created with God's Law in their hearts. (*Trigl.* 963, F. C., Sol. Decl., VI, 5.) The Formula of Concord states this truth repeatedly and lucidly. It says: If the Christians had only their new man, "they would do of themselves, and altogether voluntarily, without any instruction, admonition, urging or driving of the Law, what they are in duty bound to do according to God's will; just as the sun, the moon, and all the constellations of

---

[27] *Wider die Antinomer* (*ibid.*, 1614). Chemnitz (*Loci, "De iustif.,"* II, 228) says of the natural connection between Law and Gospel in spite of their divergence: "Two things are to be considered: that there is a difference between Law and Gospel and that Law and Gospel are so joined that there can be no mathematical conjunction like it, as Luther says in his commentary on the third chapter of Galatians. Law and Gospel come together above all in this, that the benefits of Christ of which the Gospel preaches are nothing less than satisfaction for the guilt and punishment which we incurred by transgressing the Law and for the most perfect righteousness of the Law by obedience, and that these two things which the Law requires and vehemently demands are given the believers and imputed unto righteousness. Nor can the magnitude of the benefits of Christ be understood unless one is strictly held in this manner to the rigor and severity of the Law."

heaven have their regular course of themselves, unobstructed, without admonition, urging, driving, force, or compulsion, according to the order of God which God once appointed for them." [28]

But the Christian, considered *in concreto,* as he exists in this world, is not yet entirely a new man; he still has the old man dwelling in him. And in this respect, according to his old man, the Christian still needs the Law in all its uses, no matter how these uses are divided or designated.[29] It is no contradiction, therefore, when Paul, on the one hand, says that "the Law is not made for a righteous man" (1 Tim. 1:9), and, on the other hand, as pointed out by Luther (St. L. IX:880 f.), in that very chapter (v. 18) begins to give commandments, saying: "This charge I commit unto thee, son Timothy." This is no contradiction, because in the one case the Christian comes into consideration according to his new man; in the other case, according to the old man still dwelling in him. Luther asks: "Are, then, Paul and Timothy or the Christians not pious? Or how can Paul say, 'The Law is not made for a righteous man' and then proceed to give Timothy a law?" Luther answers: "According to the spirit the believer is righteous, without any sin, has need of no law whatever; according to his flesh he still has sin. . . . There all manner of filth still clings to him, and evil concupiscence, worry about his daily bread, fear of death, avarice, anger, hatred; the filth always remains beside his faith, for him to contend with it and sweep it out. Now, because this is still in us, Scripture in this respect rates us as of a kind with the unrighteous and sinners, so that according to our flesh we need the Law as much as do they." (St. L. IX:881.) Luther gives it this turn too: "A Christian is in two realms at once. So far as he is flesh,

---

[28] *Trigl.* 965, Sol. Decl., VI, 6; 967, *ibid.,* 17. St. L. IX:879.

[29] Nitzsch-Stephan, *Dogmatik,* p. 509: "In agreement with the doctrine of the Formula of Concord the elder dogmaticians, too, assert some a threefold, some a fourfold *usus* of the Law: (1) an *usus politicus seu civilis,* (2) an *usus elenchticus,* (3) an *usus paedagogicus,* (4) an *usus didacticus seu normaticus.* At times numbers two and three are combined. Where they are distinguished, the distinguishing mark of the *usus elenchticus* is *"peccati manifestatio et redargutio"* (the revealing and refuting of sin); the mark of the *usus paedagogicus* is the *compulsus indirectus ad Christum,* according to Gal. 3:23 f." One need not feel alarmed either at the threefold nor at the fourfold division, so long as the thoughts brought out correspond to Scripture, as in fact they do. When the *usus paedagogicus* is further distinguished from the *usus elenchticus,* this distinction is acceptable because the Law by itself does not lead to Christ, but does so only when Christ takes it in hand. By itself the Law leads only to despair. The Holy Ghost must establish the right, divinely intended connection of Law and Gospel in the heart of man.

he is under the Law; so far as he is spirit, he is under grace." (St. L. IX:452.) But, of course, in such a manner that in the struggle of the two with each other the reign of grace or of the Gospel remains victorious: "When the Law has terrified you, say: Madam Law, you are not alone; and so you are not everything, but besides you there is something still greater and better, namely, grace and faith." But the victorious reign of the Gospel always presupposes the succumbing reign of the Law. Luther: "Therefore the teaching of the Law is necessary in the Church and by all means to be retained, since without it Christ cannot be retained." [30]

And this is what the Formula of Concord confesses on the basis of Scripture over against the current error and doubt: "We believe, teach, and confess that the preaching of the Law is to be urged with diligence, not only upon the unbelieving and impenitent, but also upon true believers, who are truly converted, regenerate, and justified by faith," and it gives this reason: "For although they are regenerate and renewed in the spirit of their mind, yet in the present life this regeneration and renewal is not complete, but only begun." (*Trigl.* 805, Epit., VI, 3–4.)

In addition, the Formula of Concord shows in detail how Law and Gospel are joined in the case of a Christian. First, since the Christian, according to his flesh, still sins daily, but at the same time, according to the same flesh, is inclined not to see the gravity of his sin, rather to imagine "that his work and life are entirely pure and perfect" (*Trigl.* 969, Sol. Decl., VI, 21); and since, as a result, the Christian is in constant danger of falling from faith, the Law must continually reveal and reprove the sin in him, while he, on the other hand, must daily appropriate from the Gospel the consolation that for Christ's sake his sins are remitted unto him. The Formula refers to this process in these words: "Therefore, as often as believers stumble, they are reproved by the Holy Spirit from the Law, and by the same Spirit are raised up and comforted again with the preaching of the Gospel" (*Trigl.* 967, *ibid.*, 14).

Secondly, since the Christian because of his flesh is inclined to err in regard to the good works desired of him by God, he must daily learn from the Law, as the unchanging norm of a God-pleasing life, what God would have him do. "So, too, this doctrine of the Law is

[30] Luther, *Fifth Disputation*, Thesis 66 (St. L. XX:1646). See in the same disputation Theses 40—45.

needful for believers, in order that they may not hit upon a holiness and devotion of their own, and under the pretext of the Spirit of God set up a self-chosen worship, without God's Word and command, as it is written Deut. 12:8, 28, 32: 'Ye shall not do . . . every man whatsoever is right in his own eyes,' etc., but 'observe and hear all these words which I command thee. Thou shalt not add thereto, nor diminish therefrom.'" (*Trigl.* 969, *ibid.*, 20.) The Gospel, however, must continually be employed in this matter of good works in order to work the will and the strength to comply with the divine will which is known from the Law. This fact, too, is sedulously stressed by the Formula: "But we must also explain distinctively what the Gospel does, produces, and works towards the new obedience of believers, and what is the office of the Law in this matter, as regards the good works of believers. For the Law says indeed that it is God's will and command that we should walk in a new life, but it does not give the power and ability to begin and do it; but the Holy Ghost, who is given and received, not through the Law, but through the preaching of the Gospel, Gal. 3:14, renews the heart." (*Trigl.* 965, *ibid.*, 10–11.)

Finally, an application of the Law to the Christian according to his flesh is necessary to keep his flesh outwardly in check. It is no rhetorical overstatement when Luther and the Formula of Concord (*Trigl.* 969, *ibid.*, 19) say that the flesh of the Christians never becomes pious in this life, but retains throughout its characteristic of "enmity against God" (Rom. 8:7). Negatively the Scriptures say of the flesh of the Christian that in it dwells no good thing (Rom. 7:18); and positively, that it wars against the new man (Rom. 7:23). This being the nature of the flesh also of Christians, no more can be achieved than to force the flesh externally to obey the will of God. And this coercion is applied to it both by the threatening of the Law (Mark 9:43 ff.) and by the infliction of punishments (*praedicatio verbalis et realis;* 2 Cor. 12:7 ff.; 1 Cor. 9:27). Formula of Concord: "For the old Adam, as an intractable, refractory ass, is still a part of them, which must be coerced to the obedience of Christ, not only by the teaching, admonition, force, and threatening of the Law, but also oftentimes by the club of punishments and troubles, until the body of sin is entirely put off, and man is perfectly renewed in the resurrection, when he will need neither the preaching of the Law nor its threatenings and punishments, as also the Gospel any longer; for these belong to this [mortal and] imperfect life" (*Trigl.* 969, *ibid.*, 24).

5

The Difficulty of Properly Distinguishing Between Law and Gospel

Properly to distinguish between Law and Gospel is a difficult art. Of course, not in theory, for it is easy to say what is Law and what is Gospel; but in practice the difficulty is present, particularly in one's own heart and conscience. Luther wisely reminds us again and again that the proper differentiation between Law and Gospel exceeds the powers of natural man and is achieved only through the action of the Holy Ghost. The reason lies in man's natural condition. Natural man seeks grace and salvation through the Law, that is, he strives to secure through the Law what can be obtained only through the Gospel. This *opinio legis* is an obsession with him, and continues to be an obsession, until God's grace and power turns his heart from the Law to the Gospel. (*Trigl.* 197, Apol., III, 144 f.)

Also from this standpoint – the discriminating use of Law and Gospel – it again becomes evident that man's conversion, or coming to faith, is solely a work of divine grace and omnipotence, without any assistance on the part of man. In the psychology of conversion the divine verdict of condemnation, spoken by the Law, is replaced by the divine verdict of justification, pronounced by the Gospel. But the conscience-stricken sinner can believe the Gospel verdict only by God's gracious and mighty operation. Therefore Christ says (John 6:44): "No man can come to Me except the Father which hath sent Me draw him," and St. Paul reminds the Christians that their faith in Christ is a gift of grace (Phil. 1:29: "For unto you it is given to believe on Him") and an effect of the same divine power that raised Christ from the dead (Eph. 1:19-20; Col. 2:12). To come to Christ, or to believe in Christ, is in fact nothing else than properly to distinguish between Law and Gospel in one's heart, to believe the verdict of the Gospel over against the contrary verdict of the Law. Men have deemed it incongruous that Christ describes the entrance into the Kingdom of God, which always takes place solely by faith, with the words: "And from the days of John the Baptist until now the kingdom of heaven suffereth violence, and the violent take it by force" (Matt. 11:12). They consider it inappropriate to think of faith, which does not lie in the power of man and is no coercion either, as a "heaven-storming" act of violence. But such people forget that "believing" means, in the face of the condemnatory verdict of the Law, to seize and claim the amnesty proclaimed in the Gospel. Since this is a feat exceeding human powers and always a work of the creative power of God, faith is described as a βιαστής, a man of violence. For this reason Luther, Chemnitz, and other old theologians of ours regard it as self-evident that the words "The kingdom of heaven is gotten by force" refer to faith. Cf. Vol. II, 435, footnote 66. To them this interpretation is obvious because they correctly hold that the faith which makes man a member of the Church is not a dormant quality in the heart (*otiosa qualitas*), but *fides actualis*, the divinely wrought act of distinguishing between Law and Gospel, that is, claiming as one's own the justifying verdict of the Gospel in the face of the condemning verdict of the Law.

And as the first separation of Law and Gospel, making man a Christian, is so difficult that it can be brought about only by divine operation, so, too, the continued lifelong separation, by which man remains a Christian, lies entirely beyond the reach of human ability. Therefore Scripture says of the Christians that they are kept by the power of God through faith unto salvation (1 Pet. 1:5). For thus to be kept is in fact nothing else than, by the power of God, perpetually to distinguish between Law and Gospel, to oppose the condemnatory sentence of the Law, assailing us because of present and past sins, with the acquitting sentence of the Gospel. Luther says: "It is not in the power of man to shake off this frightful terror caused by the Law or any other sorrow of the heart" (St. L. IX:446). Therefore he regards it wise for a Christian not to be alone, but to seek the companionship of a Christian brother, so that, when the reign of the Law and the reign of the Gospel begin to struggle in his heart, the Christian brother is at hand with a word of Gospel to set in motion the divine power of the Gospel against the condemnation of the Law. (*Ibid.*, 421.)

To the difficulty experienced by the pastor in properly differentiating between Law and Gospel Luther's well-known word pertains: "Now, him who is adept at this art of properly dividing Law and Gospel set at the head of the table and declare him a Doctor of the Holy Scriptures" (*ibid.*, 802). The task is so to teach what Law and Gospel have in common, in what they are opposites, and how they are to be joined in use that secure sinners become frightened and the terrified take comfort. To this end the preacher dare not deduct aught from either the Law or the Gospel, dare not rob the Law of its severity by an admixture of Gospel nor the Gospel of its consolation by an admixture of Law. He must know how to keep both within the sphere in which they are to apply according to God's will and order, as we have shown above. Facing this duty, the pastor will despair of his own wisdom and ability [31] and will agree with Luther, who says: "Without the Holy Spirit it is impossible rightly to divide Law and Gospel. I experience it in my own case, also daily observe it in others, how difficult it is to separate the doctrine of the Law from that of the Gospel. The Holy Ghost must here be pedagog and teacher, or no man on earth will ever have the knack of it or be able to teach it. . . . The theory is easy; quickly we can explain how the Law is another Word and doctrine than the Gospel; but to divide them *practice* and to apply the art to life, that is trouble and toil. St. Jerome, too, has written much about it, but like a blind man about colors." [32]

6

The Importance of Proper Discrimination

The importance of properly discriminating between Law and Gospel appears, as we have seen, from the fact that through such discrimination man becomes a Christian and remains a Christian. In other words, without a discriminative use of Law and Gospel there can be no personal or subjective Christianity. Luther places

---

[31] The context indicates that the words in 2 Cor. 3:5 pertain specifically to the proper discernment and application of Law and Gospel. A truly Christian sermon, which properly divides and properly joins Law and Gospel, is in every case a gift from above and must be obtained by prayer. It is very advisable that a pastor subject his carefully prepared sermon to a final review to see whether it applies Law and Gospel correctly, namely, in such a manner that the secure are terrified and those that labor and are heavy laden are consoled.

[32] St. L. IX:802, 806 ff. In this connection a question is occasionally raised about the pastoral activity and success of a man who himself is unbelieving. A preacher who has no personal faith, who in his own heart does not distinguish between Law and Gospel, may nevertheless through his ministry convert other people, that is, teach them to divide Law and Gospel in their heart. This is due to the fact that the efficacy of the Word of God does not depend on the personal state of faith of the preacher. Of course, a preacher who has not learned to divide Law and Gospel in his own heart will in his public preaching, and still more in caring for the individual soul, encounter great difficulty in properly preaching Law and Gospel. Yet such instances are conceivable and *do occur* in which an unbelieving pastor so presents Law and Gospel according to Scripture, from correct theological instruction received and from sound postils, that his hearers come both to know their sin and to believe in the Gospel.

this fact at the head of his sermon of 1532 on "The Difference Between Law and Gospel" (*ibid.*, 798 ff.): "This distinction . . . is the highest art in Christendom, which each and all who pride themselves on or appropriate the name 'Christian' should know and be able to practice. For where there is a lack of this art, one cannot tell a Christian from a heathen or Jew; so absolutely everything depends on this discrimination."

Furthermore, the objective teaching of a theologian is Christian only in so far as the distinction between Law and Gospel is observed in it. See the full discussion of this truth in the chapter "The Doctrine of Justification and the Separation of Law and Gospel," Vol. II, 545 ff. The Christian doctrine of justification is virtually identical with the discrimination between Law and Gospel. Moreover, the elimination of the Law from the article of justification must be absolute. Justification, as Luther reminds us, may not be made to hinge on even one devout Lord's Prayer (Luther is cited in Vol. II, 546, footnote 84) if our teaching is to retain its Christian and consoling character. See Walther's exposition of the thesis "Purity of doctrine also includes that the Word of truth be 'rightly divided,' which means, that Law and Gospel be properly distinguished." (2 Tim. 2:15.) For our warning Walther proceeds to enumerate the most common ways of mixing Law and Gospel. He writes: "Whoever uses the Gospel to deprive the Law of its severity, or the Law to deprive the Gospel of its sweetness; whoever so teaches that secure sinners are comforted and terrified sinners are still more frightened; whoever fails to direct those who have been terrified by the Law to the means of grace and instead directs them simply to pray for grace; whoever explains the demands and threats of the Law to mean that if a Christian do as much as he can, God will be satisfied and overlook the sins of weakness, and so preaches the Gospel as to make it seem to give comfort only to such as already in their life show a change of heart; whoever tries by the demands, threats, and promises of the Law to persuade the unregenerate to do good works, and demands that those who are no Christians (still being without faith) shall desist from sin and love God and their neighbor; whoever demands a certain degree of contrition and comforts only such as have already undergone a change for the better; whoever confounds not being able to believe with not being permitted to believe; and the like: such a one does not rightly divide the Word of Truth, but presents the Law and the Gospel in a tangled and mixed form; even though he otherwise preach the Law and the Gospel and even define it correctly, yet he is guilty of preaching false doctrine." (*Pastorale,* p. 79 f. [Fritz, *Pastoral Theology,* p. 69].)

Furthermore, as mentioned above, it must be stressed particularly that only a precise distinction between Law and Gospel preserves the consoling character of the Christian religion. As an admixture of Law to the Gospel involves a denial of Christ's substitutional fulfillment of the Law and therefore of Christ's merit (Gal. 4:4-5; 2:21), so the same confused and Antichristian procedure also abolishes the certainty of God's grace for men (Gal. 3:10). Thus Christians are robbed of the comfort they sorely need in life and death. There can be no thought of the *certitudo gratiae et salutis,* which Christians should have (Rom. 4:16), till man in his conscience before God is completely free from the Law, that is, by the Holy Spirit's working in the Gospel believes that God does not demand of him even a single work to secure grace and salvation, but for Christ's sake receives him as he is, without regard to what he did or omitted to do. Of this necessary expulsion of the Law from the conscience in the matter of grace and salvation Luther says: "It is impossible that Christ and the Law should dwell together in one heart; either the Law or Christ must give place. But if thou thinkest that Christ and the Law can dwell together, then be thou sure that Christ dwelleth not in thy heart; but the devil, in the likeness of Christ, accusing and terrifying thee, and straitly exacting of thee the Law and the works thereof; for the true Christ (as I have said before) neither calleth thee to a reckoning for thy sins, nor biddeth thee to trust in thine own good works. And the true knowledge of Christ, or faith, disputeth not whether thou hast done good works to righteousness, or evil works to condemnation; but simply concludeth after this sort: If thou hast done good works, thou art not therefore justified; or if thou hast done evil works, thou art not therefore condemned." (St. L. IX:619; *Middleton Transl.,* p. 430.)

Finally it must be pointed out that the differentiation between Law and Gospel is necessary in order to correctly *understand the Scriptures.* The Formula of Concord calls on us to "guard with especial care" this distinction between the Law and the Gospel because it "is a special brilliant light, which serves to the end that God's Word may be rightly divided, and the Scriptures of the holy prophets and apostles may be properly explained and understood" (*Trigl.* 951, Sol. Decl., V, 1). This statement of the Confession is no overstatement. Scripture on the one hand says: "This do, and thou shalt live"; on the other hand: "He that believeth on the Son hath everlasting life."

How can we arrive at a harmonization of these words of Scripture, whose relation is as yes and no? It may not be achieved in the manner of the Antinomians, who relegate the Law to the courthouse. Christ forbids that course when He says: "Whosoever therefore shall break one of these least commandments, and shall teach men so, he shall be called the least in the kingdom of heaven" (Matt. 5:19). Nor may we say, like the Unitarians and modern theologians, that the Gospel, which tells us of Christ's *satisfactio vicaria* and of justification by faith without the deeds of the Law, originated in the Middle Ages or a period of imperfect development of Christian doctrine. Christ's Apostle forbids that, too, when he says: "But though we, or an angel from heaven, preach any other Gospel unto you than that which we have preached unto you, let him be accursed" (Gal. 1:8-9), for the Gospel Paul preached was the Gospel of Christ's substitutional satisfaction and of justification by faith without the deeds of the Law (Rom. 3:23-24, 28). Likewise, we may not harmonize the words of the Law and the words of the Gospel by agreeing on a compromise between them and declaring: "Man is justified and saved in part by grace for Christ's sake, in part by his own works." Scripture rejects this compromise when it says: "And if by grace, then is it no more of works; otherwise grace is no more grace" (Rom. 11:6). There remains but one way of understanding Scripture: We must let both the words of the Law and the words of the Gospel remain in full force, but distinguish between Law and Gospel in this manner, that we confine each to the realm assigned to it by God. The Law is given to reveal sin, not to forgive sin. For the latter purpose the Gospel is given. When therefore the Law has revealed sin, it is to be muzzled, and only the Gospel is to have and hold the floor, as we have shown at length above. Thus, and thus only, will Scripture be understood.

A few details in closing. From Scripture passages such as 1 Cor. 10:12: "Let him that thinketh he standeth take heed lest he fall," and Rom. 8:38 f.: "I am persuaded that neither death nor life . . . shall be able to separate us from the love of God," both Romanists and Protestant synergists of all shades compound a *tertium* and then teach in all seriousness that a Christian may not be certain of his salvation, but must waver between fear and hope. He who knows how to divide Law and Gospel lets both classes of Scripture passages stand in their full import. But he applies the Scripture passages which warn of backsliding to the Christian according to his carnally secure old man, who is to be reproved with the Law. And the Scripture passages asserting the certainty of salvation he applies to the Christian according to the new man, inasmuch as the Christian as a poor sinner should believe and actually believes the Gospel. Cf. Vol. II, 547 f.; Vol. III, p. 96, footnote 14. — Also the text (Heb. 12:14): "Without holiness no man shall see the Lord," has been given most surprising and impossible interpretations to make it harmonize with those Scripture passages that guarantee salvation to faith without the deeds of the Law. The correct exposition (p. 26f.) recognizes these words as Law, as a warning against carnal security, which must be spoken to Christians in so far as they are in danger of succumbing to carnal security. In so far, however, as Christians are of a terrified, humbled spirit and believe the Gospel of salvation for Christ's sake, those threatening and reprimanding words do not at all concern them.

PART TWO

THE STYLE OF LEGAL REASONING

A. Scientific Method and Theological Method

W. Montgomery, "The Theologian's Craft: A Discussion of Theory Formation and Theory Testing": from the author's *The Suicide of Christian Theology* (Minneapolis: Bethany, 1971), pp. 267-313.

The Theologian's Craft: A Discussion of Theory Formation and Theory Testing in Theology*

What is it to "do theology?" Numerous conflicting and inadequate answers (e.g., Bultmannian existentialism, the post-Bultmannian "New Hermaneutic") hold the field today; these have in common a basic misunderstanding as to the relation of theological theorizing to theory construction in other fields of knowledge, and a fundamental misconception in regard to the proper way of confirming or disconfirming theological judgments. In this essay, a detailed comparison between scientific and theological methodologies is set forth, and the artistic and sacred dimensions of theological theorizing are explicated by way of an original structural model suggested by Wittgensteinian philosophical and linguistic analysis.

Scientists are generally at a loss to know precisely what theologians *do.* Mailmen deliver letters; bartenders serve numerous varieties of firewater; otorhinolaryngologists concern themselves with ears, noses, and throats: but what exactly do theologians endeavor to accomplish? The aura of mystery surrounding theological activity troubles not merely the scientist, who generally has a clear-eyed view of his own professional function, but also the so-called "average man," who, though his awareness of his own role in life may be exceedingly vague, is even more troubled by the peculiarities of "religious" vocations. The wry comment of the parishioner, "We take care of pastor in this life and he takes care of us in the next," well illustrates the gulf that, in general, seems to separate theological activity from the meaningful work of the world.

* An invitational paper presented August 24, 1965, at the 20th Annual Convention of the American Scientific Affiliation, convened at The King's College, Briarcliff Manor, New York.

Notes for this section, pages 300-313.

A theologian of course theologizes, i.e., he does theology. But the tautological character of this statement requires us to press on: What is it to "do theology"? Etymologically, as everyone knows, "theology" involves a "speaking-of-God," and this expression should be regarded very carefully, for its double meaning suggests the source of difficulty in understanding the theologian's craft: theology speaks *about* God (the objective genitive of the grammarians), but only because of "God's speaking" to man (the subjective genitive); it is the active presence of the Numinous in the work of theology that renders its task so strange to those who look upon it from the outside. But leaving aside (for the moment only!) the active numinosity in theological endeavor, and concentrating on the object of theological research, we can say very simply that the theologian[1] is one who engages in forming and testing theories concerning the Divine.

Our task in this paper is thus the clarification of what it properly means to form and to test theological theories; and it is hoped that the result will aid both the non-theologian (particularly the scientist) to understand and to appreciate better the nature of theological endeavor, and the theologian himself to keep his methodological sights correctly focused. The center of attention will be neither the historical circumstances attending theological theorizing[2] nor the psychological factors relating to theological discovery[3]—interesting as these subjects are. We shall hold ourselves quite closely to the fundamental realm of theological prolegomena, and seek to discover the nature of the operations that make theology theology. As the reader enters the rarified air of this domain, he is warned to prepare himself for innovation and ground-breaking; it is the writer's conviction that precisely here lie the basic sources of error in much contemporary theological thinking, as well as the relatively untapped resources for theological recovery in our time.

Through a Welter of Confusion

Any attempt to get at the nature of theological theorizing runs the immediate danger of being bogged down in a morass of conflicting interpretations of theological activity. On the one hand, the student of the subject is faced with dogmatically simplistic and pejorative definitions, such as that of Princeton philosopher Walter Kaufmann:

> First, theology is of necessity denominational. Second, theology is essentially a defensive maneuver. Third, it is almost always time-bound and dated quickly.
>
> Theology is the systematic attempt to pour the newest wine into the old skins of a denomination.[4]

To which it may be replied: First, even if all theologians were members of denominations (which is not the case), this would not make theology "denominational"—any more than the (fallacious) assumption that all physicians are members of state medical societies would make medicine political. Secondly, the defense of the faith (technically: apologetics) is but one of the tasks of systematic theology, not the whole or even the center of it. Thirdly, one needs a firm criterion of obsolescence in order to assert that theology is "time-bound"—but the secularist is, *ex hypothesi,* in the worst possible position to establish such a criterion. Finally: to define theological theorizing à la Kaufmann one must gratuitously assume that its content (wine) is forever new and changing, that its interpretative categories (skins) are old and denominational, and that the theorizing process (the pouring) requires no special examination. None of these assumptions, however, is credible enough to warrant pursuing.

Alongside of simplistically objective definitions of theological activity, one encounters existentially subjective descriptions of the theologian's work. In his Cambridge University Stanton Lectures on "Theological Explanation," G. F. Woods asserts, in partial dependence on Tillich:

> The first sense of theological explanation is the ultimate personal being which is the real ground of the world. The second sense is the act of seeking an explanation of what is ultimate, both through our own efforts to make it plain and through its own endeavours to make itself plain to us. The third sense is the act of using ultimate personal being as an explanation of the world in which we live. These manifold acts of explanation take place on particular occasions and are markedly influenced by the circumstances of the day, particularly by the methods of explanation which happen to be dominant at the time. But, throughout the confused series of particular acts of expla-

nation, there is the perpetual trend towards the use of explanatory terms derived from our own being. What we are is the source of all our methods of seeking to explain the actual world.[5]

Here one must unkindly lay stress on the author's phrase "the confused series of particular acts of explanation," for confusion does indeed reign in any theological enterprise where "our own (existential-ontological) being," constitutes the center of the stage. As Carnap showed the analytical nonsensicality of Heidegger's "non-being," so A. C. Garnett has pointed up the unverifiable nonsense involved in "being"-assertions as theological starting-points.[6]

A third major variety of metatheological explanation is illustrated in William Hordern's book, *Speaking of God,* which endeavors to create a bridge between current "ordinary-language philosophy" and theology. Here Hordern, by an exceedingly unfortunate substitution of the later Wittgenstein for the earlier Wittgenstein, leaves the fundamental problem of theological verification aside and attempts to describe theology as a unique, *sui generis* "language game":

> Instead of thinking of theology as the queen of the sciences, can we think of it as the Olympic Games? . . . The Olympic Committee does not legislate the rules of ice hockey, and much less does it train a hockey player how to play hockey. But ice hockey takes its place within the total pattern of the Olympics, and its players must meet the Olympic standard. . . .
>
> By analogy, natural science and other language games are separate and independent, with their own questions, rules, methods of verification, and ways of giving answers. . . . [The] Christian faith cannot answer scientific questions any more than the Olympic Committee can tell a hockey player how to shoot the puck. . . .
>
> Theology, as the Olympics of life. . . . does not pretend to be a superscientific system with answers to all questions left unanswered by science. It is concerned with another kind of question than is science. It does not offer a systematic explanation of the universe; it is a means whereby man is enabled to live his life with a sense of purpose, direction, and integrity.[7]

Such an approach places theology in a mystical cloud of unknowing, and lifts the Mt. Olympus of theology off of the earth entirely.[8] Since theology, in Hordern's view, "cannot answer scientific questions," its axiological ship passes in the night the cognitive vessel of the scientific disciplines, and neither can communicate with the other. Moreover, and most important, the theological "language game" is without external verification, so its theories do not have to be accepted as "Olympic rules" by anyone who is not theologically inclined. It is too bad that Hordern did not see the point behind Wittgenstein's concern that his *Tractatus Logico-Philosophicus* be published along with his *Philosophical Investigations:* the latter, without the former, provides no answer whatever to the fundamental question: how do you know if a "language game" (e.g., theological theorizing) represents reality at all?[9]

In light of fallaciously objectivistic, existentially subjectivistic, and etherially olympian descriptions of theological activity, is it any wonder that tongue-in-cheek humor not infrequently captures the special-pleading character of contemporary theological theorizing? The January 15, 1965, issue of *Christianity Today* carries Lawing's cartoon of Moses' return from Mt. Sinai with the Commandments; a sly Israelite meets him with the suggestion, "Aaron said perhaps you'd let us condense them to 'act responsibly in love.' " Here Bishop Robinson's theological theory as to the "real" meaning of the Commandments is lampooned: the sick humor lies in the fact that the Israelite (probably) and Robinson (certainly) lack awareness of the degree to which cultural conformity and personal preference dictate the content of their theological constructions.

How can we gain clarity in this vital area? Let us, for the moment, step outside of the theological realm and examine the essential nature of theories by way of the discipline in which they have been most thoroughly discussed: the field of science. Here we can gain our bearings and find an immediate and meaningful entrée to the larger question of theological theory formation and testing.

Theory Construction in Science

Though there have been many theories as to the exact nature of scientific theories, a general convergence and agreement among them is not hard to find. Popper uses

Wittgenstein's analogy of the Net: "Theories are nets cast to catch what we call 'the world': to rationalize, to explain, and to master it. We endeavor to make the mesh ever finer and finer."[10] Comments Leonard Nash of Harvard: "He who realizes the existence of such a conceptual fabric, and is capable of lifting it, carries with it all its cords, all the colligative relations it accommodates."[11] The use of an image (the net) to illustrate the nature of scientific theory construction points to an especially vital element in such theories: the employment of "models"—representations that carry "epistemological vividness."[12] So, in speaking of the discovery that "light travels in straight lines," Stephen Toulmin notes that "a vital part of the discovery is the very possibility of drawing 'pictures' of the optical state-of-affairs to be expected in given circumstances—or rather, the possibility of drawing them in a way that *fits the facts.*"[13]

To concretize these abstract remarks on scientific theorizing, let us consider a dramatic and very recent case of successful theory-building: the 1962 Nobel Prize discovery, by James Watson and Francis Crick, of the molecular structure of DNA (the nucleic acid bearing the blueprint of heredity).

> Watson was convinced by reasons based upon genetics that [the] structure could only be built around two spirals arranged "in a certain way." The answer lay in this "certain way."
>
> The only way of representing the three-dimensional structure of an invisible molecule is to replace atoms or groups of atoms by spheres and then build a model of the molecule.
>
> This is exactly what Crick and Watson did, tirelessly attempting to arrange the two spirals. To quote the expression used by one of them, all of their models were "frightful," and quite inadequate to cope with DNA's known qualities ("You couldn't hang anything on these spirals"). . . .
>
> Then came the famous "spiral night." Crick was working late in a laboratory upstairs. On the ground floor, Watson also was going over a list of possible solutions. That night Crick had a revelation, a solution whispered to him by his intuition: there were only two spirals, they were symmetrical, and they coiled in opposite directions, one from "top to bottom" and the other from "bot-

> tom to top" (this hypothesis also reflected certain laws of crystallography).
>
> Crick raced downstairs—it was a spiral staircase—and enthusiastically explained his theory to Watson. Watson received it calmly: it sounded simple to him, much too simple. Then, mentally, he built a spiral form based on this idea, and all the various chemical, biological and physical requirements he put forward were met by it. Now he too was excited; he paced up and down the laboratory, repeating: "It must be true, it must be true." [14]

This lively description of the key point[15] in the discovery of DNA's molecular structure drives home several basic truths about scientific theorizing—truths expressed formally in the definitions previously cited. First, theories do not create facts; rather, they attempt to relate existent facts properly. The DNA molecular model is a "net" thrown to catch the "world" of "chemical, biological and physical requirements" demanded by empirical facticity. The theory maker must never suppose that he is building reality; his task is the fascinating but more humble one of shaping a "conceptual fabric" that, with "epistemological vividness," will correctly mirror the world of substantive reality.[16]

The DNA discovery illustrates, moreover, that theories in science are not formed "either by deductive argument from the experimental data alone, or by the type of logic-book 'induction' on which philosophers have so often concentrated, or indeed by any method for which formal rules could be given." [17] Writers such as Braithwaite have effectively argued the case for the indispensable role of deductive reasoning in scientific explanation; but Braithwaite's concluding paragraphs stress the inductivist side of the coin: "Man proposes a system of hypotheses: Nature disposes of its truth or falsity. Man invents a scientific system, and then discovers whether or not it accords with observed fact." [18] G. H. von Wright has logically demonstrated that "if we wish to call reasoned policies *better* than not-reasoned ones, it follows . . . that induction is of necessity the *best* way"; [19] yet the appealing ghost of Francis Bacon's pure inductivism in science has been laid by such philosophers of science as Joseph Agassi,[20] and as the history of scientific discovery shows beyond question, the great advances in theory have not arisen through static, formalistic induction.[21] Rather than making invidious comparisons between deduction and induction in scientific theory formation, we should see these operations as complementary.[22] Instead of seeking monolithic explanation of scientific method, let us, with Max Black, "think of science as a concrescence, a growing together of variable, interacting, mutually reinforcing factors contributing to a development organic in character." [23] Nash provides the following helpful diagram, illustrating how scientific knowledge is generated by endless cyclical renewal;[24]

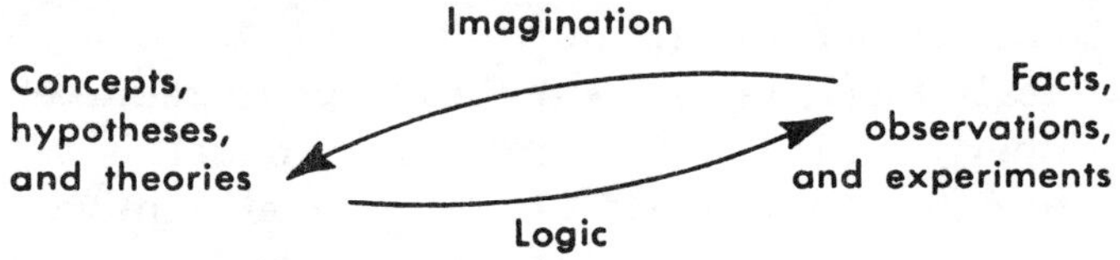

The essential place of "imagination" in scientific theorizing has been greatly stressed by Einstein; and its role can perhaps best be seen by introducing, alongside induction and deduction—as, in fact, the connecting link between them—Peirce's concept of "retroduction" or "abduction," based upon Aristotle's ἀπαγωγή type inference.[25] "Abduction," writes Peirce, "consists in studying facts and devising a theory to explain them. . . . Deduction proves that something *must* be; Induction shows that something *actually is* operative; Abduction merely suggests that something *may be*." [26] N. R. Hanson has well illustrated the centrality of such "retroductive" reasoning to scientific theorizing; consider Hanson's ambiguous "bird-antelope":

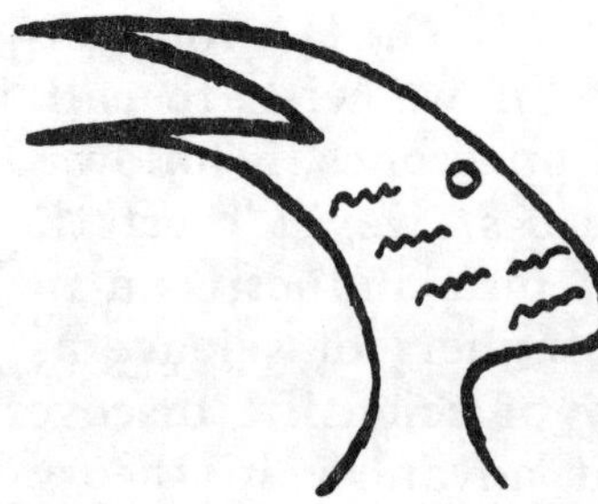

Were this flashed on to a screen I might say "It has four feathers." I may be wrong: that number of wiggly lines on the figure is other than four is a conceptual possibility. "It has four feathers" is thus falsifiable, empirical. It is an observation statement. To determine its truth we need only put the figure on the screen again and count the lines.

The statement that the figure is of a bird, however, is not falsifiable in the same sense. Its negation does not represent the same conceptual possibility, for it concerns not an observational detail but the very pattern which makes those details intelligible. One could not even say "It has four feathers" and be wrong about it, if it was not a feathered object. I can show you your error if you say "four feathers." But I cannot thus disclose your "error" in saying of the bird-antelope that it is a bird (instead of an antelope).

Pattern statements are different from detail statements. They are not inductive summaries of detail statements. Still the statement, "It's a bird" is truly empirical. Had birds been different, or had the bird-antelope been drawn differently, "It's a bird" might not have been true. In some sense it is true. If the detail statements are empirical, the pattern statements which give them sense are also empirical—though not in the same way. To deny a detail statement is to do something within the pattern. To deny a pattern statement is to attack the conceptual framework itself, and this denial cannot function in the same way. . . .

Physical theories provide patterns within which data appear intelligible. They constitute a "conceptual Gestalt." A theory is not pieced together from observed phenomena; it is rather what makes it possible to observe phenomena as being of a certain sort, and as related to other phenomena. Theories put phenomena into systems. They are built up in "reverse"—retroductively. A theory is a cluster of conclusions in search of a premise. From the observed properties of phenomena the physicist reasons his way towards a keystone idea from which the properties are explicable as a matter of course.[27]

Watson and Crick's discovery of the molecular structure of DNA clearly displays the centrality of retroductive inference in scientific theory formation: they sought a "conceptual Gestalt" which would render intelligible the genetic and crystallographic data; and their resultant theory of two symmetrical spirals was successful precisely because it constituted a "keystone idea" from which the various physical, chemical, and biological characteristics of the molecule were "explicable as a matter of course."

It is particularly important to note that the validity of a scientific theory depends squarely upon its applicability as a "conceptual Gestalt"; experimental confirmation through predictive success is of secondary importance and is often, of necessity, dispensed with entirely. In paleobiology, for example, experimental prediction is ruled out by the very nature of the subject matter; and in astrophysics and cosmological theory predictive experiments are seldom able to be formulated. Watson could say of the DNA spiral theory. "It must be true," though several years would elapse before X-ray diffraction patterns of the molecule would become available, for his theory provided a full-scale ordering of the relevant data.

> Galileo knew he had succeeded when the constant acceleration hypothesis patterned the diverse phenomena he had encountered for thirty years. His reasoned advance from insight to insight culminated in an ultimate physical *explicans*. Further deductions were merely confirmatory; he could have left them to any of his students—Viviani or Toricelli. Even had verification of these further predictions eluded seventeenth-century science, this would not have prevented Galileo from embracing the constant acceleration hypothesis, any more than Copernicus and Kepler were prevented from embracing heliocentrism by the lack of a telescope with which to observe Venus' phases. Kepler needed no new observations to realize that the ellipse covered all observed positions. Newton required no predictions from his gravitation hypothesis to be confident that this really did explain Kepler's three laws and a variety of other given data.[28]

The Scientific Level in Theological Theorizing

We have found that scientific theories are conceptual Gestalts, built up retroductively through imaginative attempts to render phenomena intelligible. What relevance does this have for understanding the theologian's labors? Can any application be made to the field of theology? Is not theology a unique realm of the "spirit," unscientific by its very nature? To bring Tertullian's famous question up to date: "What has the Institute of Advanced Study to do with Jerusalem, the Laboratory with the Church?"

The answer to this last question is not "Nothing," but "Everything." Though theology is evidently something *more* than science (precisely what the "more" consists of, we shall see later), it is certainly not anything *less*. I say this, let it be noted, not simply in reference to the fact that any theology can be an object of descriptive, scientific study by specialists in the history, philosophy, or psychology of religion.[29] This is of course true in the case of all the world religions; but Christianity is unique in claiming intrinsic, not merely extrinsic, connection with the empirical reality which is the subject of scientific investigation. Christianity is a *historical* religion—historical in the very special sense that its entire revelational content is wedded to historical manifestations of Divine power. The pivot of Christian theology is the biblical affirmation that **ὁ Λόγος σάρξ ἐγένετο** (John 1:14): God Himself came to earth—entered man's empirical sphere—in Jesus Christ, and the revelation of God in the history of Israel served as a pointer to Messiah's coming, and His revelation in the Apostolic community displayed the power of Christ's Spirit.[30] From the first verse of the Bible to the last God's *contact* with man's world is affirmed. And throughout Scripture human testimony to objective, empirical encounter with God is presented in the strongest terms.[31] Christian theology thus has no fear of scientific, empirical investigation;[32] quite the contrary, the historical nature of the Christian faith—as distinguished from the subjective, existential character of the other world religions[33]—demands objective, scientific theologizing.

Hence we should expect, Barth notwithstanding,[34] that theological theories whatever suprascientific characteristics they may have, will most definitely display the full range of properties of scientific theories. The theological theorist, like his scientific counterpart, will endeavor to formulate conceptual Gestalts—"networks" of ideas capable of rendering his data intelligible. He will employ "models" to achieve epistemological vividness. He will utilize all three types of inference (inductive, deductive, retroductive) in his theory making, but, again like the scientist, he will find himself most usually dependent upon the imaginative operation of retroduction.

Little more than superficial naiveté lies at the basis of the popular opinion that science and theology are in methodological conflict because the former "employs inductive reasoning" while the latter "operates deductively!" In point of fact, both generally proceed retroductively, and neither is less concerned than the other about the concrete verification of its inferences.

And how does verification take place? In science we have seen that the success of a theory depends upon its ability, as Toulmin says, to "fit the facts." The same is true in theology. Ian Ramsey—though he does not see that theology exactly parallels science here—introduces a valuable analogy when he writes that "the theological model works . . . like the fitting of a boot or a shoe."

> In other words, we have a particular doctrine which, like a preferred and selected shoe, starts by appearing to meet our empirical needs. But on closer fitting to the phenomena the shoe may pinch. When tested against future slush and rain it may be proven to be not altogether watertight or it may be comfortable—yet it must not be too comfortable. In this way, the test of a shoe is measured by its ability to match a wide range of phenomena, by its overall success in meeting a variety of needs. Here is what I might call the method of empirical fit which is displayed by theological theorizing.[35]

This is precisely the verifying test that we have encountered in our discussion of scientific theories; the Watson-Crick spiral theory was just such a "shoe" whose adequacy depended squarely upon its ability to "fit" the relevant physical, chemical, and biological characteristics of the DNA molecule. Neither Watson and Crick, nor the great scientific theorists of past ages (we have already referred to Galileo, Copernicus, Kepler, and Newton) achieved their primary success in theory construction through the predictive character of their formulations: both in science and in theology, it is "fit," not "future," that lies at the heart of successful theorizing.[36]

But clearly scientific and theological theories are not identical! Where do the differences lie? One important difference (we leave others until later) is pointed up by Ramsey's "shoe" analogy. This analogy immediately raises two basic questions about theorizing: first and most obvious, How do you make the shoe (the theory or model)? but second, and even more fundamental, What foot (data) do you try to fit? In science, the "foot"—the irreducible stuff which theorizing attempts to grasp in its net—is the natural world, and this includes every phenomenal manifestation in the universe. Science knows no investigative boundaries; its limits are imposed not by the stuff with which it is permitted to deal, but by the manner in which it can treat its data. *Ex hypothesi,* science is methodologically capable of studying the world in an *objective* manner only: it can examine anything that touches human experience, but it can never, qua science, "get inside" its subject matter; it always stands outside and describes. This is, of course, both the glory and the pathos of science: it can analyze everything, but it is prevented from experiencing the heart of anything.

On the objective, scientific level, however, theology has no greater advantage; it likewise stands outside its data and analyzes. But what precisely does it analyze? What are the *Gegenstände* of theological theorizing—the "simples" that the theologian attempts to render intelligible through his conceptual Gestalts? In general, for Christian theology, the "foot to be shod" is revelational experience. Theological theories endeavor to "fit the facts" of such experience; theology on this level is thus one segment of scientific activity as a whole—that segment concerned with revelational, as opposed to non-revelational, phenomena. Jean Racette, in dependence upon the great contemporary Jesuit philosopher-theologian Bernard Lonergan, puts it succinctly and well:

> La théologie n'est pas une science ou une sagesse quelconque. Elle est la science du sacré et du révélé. Elle est une démarche de l'intelligence éclairée par la foi. Elle est une reflexion systématique sur un donné reconnu et accepté comme révélé, et donc comme vrai.[37]

However, the expression "revelational experience" is manifestly ambiguous. What does it signify? This question, without a doubt, is of paramount importance for the entire theological task, since a false step here will tragically weaken the entire process of theological theorizing—either by emasculation (if one excludes from purview genuine revelational data), or by adulteration (if one mixes non-revelational considerations with the truly revelational subject matter). And, ironically, it is exactly at this point that Christian theology has all too often trumpeted forth an uncertain sound—or, worse, a positive discord! To change the metaphor, the theologian has not infrequently played the role of a blind cobbler, trying to make shoes without knowing what kind of foot he is shoeing; at other times, he appears as a bungling apprentice, busily preparing what should be dainty slippers for Queen Revelation when in fact he is putting together clod-hoppers to fit Lumberjack U. (for Unregenerate) Religiosity!

Through Christian history, the "revelational experience" which yields the proper data for theological theorizing has been understood as having either a *single* source or *multiple* sources. Traditional multiple source positions include Roman Catholicism, Greek Orthodoxy, and Anglo-Catholicism (all holding that the Bible and church tradition constitute valid revelational sources), and various sects having sacred books which they use alongside of the Bible as sources of data for theologizing (e.g., Mormonism, with its *Book of Mormon;* Christian Science, with Mrs. Eddy's *Science and Health*). Multiple source approaches also constitute the epistemological core of most avant-garde mainline Protestant theological positions today: a combination of biblical insight, church teaching, and personal religious experience is supposed to provide the fund from which systematic theology should draw its data for doctrinal theorizing. For Paul Tillich, the "survey of the sources of systematic theology has shown their almost unlimited richness: Bible, church history, history of religion and culture." [38] For advocates of the post-Bultmannian "New Hermeneutic" (such as Ernst Fuchs and Gerhard Ebeling), systematic theology has as its subject matter "the word event itself, in which the reality of man comes true," and by "word event" is meant "the event of interpretation";[39] thus theology has its source in a polar dialectic of biblical text and situational interpretation. Heinrich Ott, for all his differences with Fuchs, expresses essentially the same dual-source, dialectic approach when he finds the subject matter of theology in "the Christ event, the reality of revelation and of believing" [40] and proposes that "dogmatics is simply to unfold thoughtfully without presupposing any philosophical schema the meaning-content experienced in believing from within the experience itself";[41] systematic theology thus serves as a "hermeneutical arch that reaches from the text to the contemporary sermon." [42]

All multiple-source views of the subject matter of theology are, however, unstable. They tend to give preference to one source rather than to another, or to seek some single, more fundamental source lying behind the multiple sources already accepted. Among the sects, the Bible has been virtually swallowed up by whatever special "sacred book" has been put alongside of it;[43] tradition has been more determinative than biblical teaching in the theological development of Greek Orthodoxy and Roman Catholicism; and the "New Hermeneutic" seems incapable of withstanding the old Bultmannian gravitational pull away from the biblical text toward the other dialectic pole of contemporary existential interpretation. In the "New Shape" Roman Catholicism of Karl Rahner, Küng, *et al.*, a conscious attempt is being made to get behind the dualism of scripture and tradition through affirming a unity of "Holy Writ *and* Holy Church";[44] yet such a dialectic, like that of the Protestant "New Hermeneutic," does not escape the charge of question-begging. This is the essential, insurmountable difficulty in all multiple-source approaches to theological theorizing. They leave unanswered the question of *final* authority. What do we do as Roman Catholics when Holy Writ and Holy Church *disagree*? What do we do as Tillichians when church history, the Bible and the history of culture are not in accord? Obviously, one must either frankly admit that one source is final, or establish a criterion of judgment over all previously accepted sources—which criterion becomes, *ex hypothesi*, the final source! Multiple source approaches to the subject matter of theology thus logically—whether one likes it or not—reduce to single source interpretations.[45]

If theology must ultimately admit that there is but a single "foot" which its doctrinal theories are to fit, the question becomes one of identifying that foot. The numerous identifications through Christian history contract upon examination, to four: Reason, the Church, Christian Experience, and Scriptural Revelation. During the eighteenth-century "Enlightenment" it was contended that the "natural light of Reason," not any alleged sacred writing or "special revelation," constitutes the final source of valid theological data.[46] Unhappily, however, pure reason (i.e., formal logic) is tautologous and cannot impart any factual data about existent things, whether theological or otherwise;[47] and "reason" understood as "nature" can yield atheistic ideologies almost as easily as deistic theologies.[48] In Romanism, the Church becomes the court of last resort for determining what are or what are not genuine data for theologizing. But the argument that this is necessary because even an infallible Bible requires an infallible interpreter suffers from the fallacy of infinite regress; one can always ask, Then how can the Church itself function without a higher-level interpreter? Moreover, no Divine mandate can be produced to justify the authority of the Church as interpreter of Scripture.[49]

Christian Experience is the most widely accepted Protestant answer to the question of the source of data for theological theorizing. For the unreconstructed Modernism of the Schleiermacher-Ritschl-Fosdick era, "constructive (i.e., subjective) religious empiricism" was expected to yield doctrinal reconstructions in accord with the needs of contemporary man. As a matter of fact, however, such a methodology yielded only the results permitted by the experiential a prioris of the particular theological investigator.[50] Bultmannian existentialism and the post-Bultmannian theologies stemming from his paramount concern with "existential self-understanding"[51] are actually "experience" theologies also: for them the current situation of the theologian, not an objectively unchanging biblical message, is the determinative factor in theological activity. In the same general class fall many of the recent attempts to interrelate theology and "ordinary language philosophy": Ramsey's concern with theological theories in relation to "our empirical needs";[52] Hick's interpretation of theological dogmas as "the basic convictions which directly transcribe Christian experience";[53] etc.

The absolutizing of religious experience commits the "naturalistic fallacy" (sometimes unkindly called the "sociologist's fallacy"): it assumes that the "isness" of the believer's "existential encounter" constitutes an "oughtness." No answer whatever is given to the vital question: How is one to know that the divine and not the demonic is operating in the given experience? Paul Tillich argues with irrefutable cogency that "insight into the human situation destroys every theology which makes experience an independent source instead of a dependent medium of systematic theology."[54] Surely the psychoanalytic discoveries of the twentieth century should give us pause before we commit ourselves to the transparent purity of man's existential life!

> The analogy from human "encounters" suggests that at least some of the experiences which are held to be "encounter with God" really are subjectively produced; can the mere claim that the experiences are "self-verifying" rule out the uncomfortable suspicion that, when dissociated from any empirical personality, they all may be only illusion?[55]

What is clearly needed is an objective check on existential experience — in other words, a source of theological data outside of it, by which to judge it.[56]

Thus we arrive at the Bible[57]—the source by which Reason, Church, and Religious Experience can and must be evaluated theologically. We reach this point not simply by process of elimination, but more especially because only Scripture can be validated as a genuine source of theological truth.[58] It is the biblical message alone that provides the irreducible *Gegenstände* for theological theorizing—the "foot" which all theological theories must "fit." In the words of the Reformation axiom, "Quod non est biblicum, non est theologicum." The Christian theologian, like the scientist, faces a "given": he endeavors, not to create his data, but to provide conceptual Gestalts for rendering them intelligible and interrelating them properly. What Nature is to the scientific theorizer, the Bible is to the theologian. Franz Pieper astutely argued this parallel as follows:

> If we would escape the deceptions which are involved in the attempts to construct a human system of theology,

> we must ever bear in mind that in theology we deal with given and unalterable facts, which human reasoning and the alleged needs of the "system" cannot change in the least. There is, as has been pointed out, an analogy here between natural history and theology. Natural history studies the observable data in the realm of nature; its business is to observe the facts. All human knowledge of natural phenomena extends only so far as man's observation and experience of the given facts extends. The true scientist does not determine the nature and characteristics of plants and animals according to a preconceived and hypothetical system. . . .
>
> This matter has been aptly illustrated by contrasting railroad systems and mountain systems. A railroad system is conceived in the mind of the builders before it exists; its construction follows the blueprint drawn up by the engineers. The mountain system, on the other hand, does not follow our blueprints. We can only report our findings regarding its characteristics, the relation of the different mountain ranges to each other, etc., as we find them. The theologian is dealing with a fixed and unchangeable fact, the Word of God which Christ gave His Church through His Apostles and Prophets.[59]

To be sure, the affirmation that Holy Scripture is the sole source of data for theological theorizing poses questions requiring serious attention. Specifically: (1) Is the Bible an inerrantly reliable source of revelational data? (2) Is the Bible self-interpreting? (3) Does the Bible provide the norms as well as the subject matter for theological theory construction? We cannot hope to discuss any one of these questions fully here, but we can indicate the central considerations which demand affirmative answers in each case.

Elsewhere[60] I have attempted to show that any view of biblical inspiration that rejects the inerrancy of Scripture is not merely incorrect, but in fact *meaningless* from the standpoint both of philosophical and of theological analysis. Anti-inerrancy inspiration positions are based upon dualistic and existentialistic presuppositions that are incapable of being confirmed or disconfirmed (thus their analytically meaningless character), and they fly directly in the face of the scriptural epistemology itself, which firmly joins "spiritual" truth to historical, empirical facticity and regards *all* words spoken by inspiration of God as carrying their Author's guarantee of veracity. Moreover, if in some sense Scripture were not unqualifiedly a reliable source of theological truth, what criteria could possibly distinguish the wheat from the chaff? Not the Scripture itself (by definition), and not anything outside of it (for the "outside" factors would then become revelation, and we have already seen that extra-biblical revelation-claims are incapable of validation)!

This latter point also applies to the question of the self-interpreting nature of the Bible: Were the Scripture not self-interpreting, then a "higher" revelation would be needed to provide interpretative canons for it; but such a Bible-to-the-second-power cannot be shown to exist. And, indeed, there is no reason to feel that one should exist. If God inspired the Scripture, then its self-interpreting perspicuity is established. The Reformers soundly argued that "the clarity of Scripture is demanded by its inspiration. God is able to speak clearly, for He is the master of language and words."[61] True, "there are many impenetrable mysteries in Scripture which are unclear in that they cannot be grasped by human intellect, but these mysteries have been recorded in Scripture in obscure or ambiguous language."[62] Present-day specialists in biblical hermeneutics who have been trained in general literary interpretation make every effort to impress upon their students and readers that the Bible must be approached objectively and allowed to interpret itself. Thus Robert Traina writes in the Introduction to his superlative manual, *Methodical Bible Study: A New Approach to Hermeneutics:*

> Now the Scriptures are distinct from the interpreter and are not an integral part of him. If the truths of the Bible already resided in man, there would be no need for the Bible and this manual would be superfluous. But the fact is that *the Bible is an objective body of literature* which exists because man needs to know certain truths which he himself cannot know and which must come to him from without. Consequently, if he is to discover the truths which reside in this objective body of literature, he must utilize an approach which corresponds in nature with it, that is, an *objective* approach.[63]

Such an hermeneutic approach has been explicitly adopted by the great systematic theologians, past [64] and present,[65] and *must* be presupposed in theological theorizing if one is to avoid exegeting and systematizing one's own subjective opinions and desires instead of God's Word. The "circularity principle" of Bultmann and his former disciples[66] gives carte blanche to this latter error and invariably destroys the possibility of sound theological theorizing; as I have written elsewhere:

> When Bultmann argues that not only historical method but also existential "life-relation" must be presupposed in exegesis, he blurs the aim of objectivity which is essential to all proper literary and historical study. Following Dilthey as well as the general stream of philosophical existentialism, Bultmann attempts to "cut under the subject-object distinction"; he claims that "for historical understanding, the schema of subject and object has validity for natural science is invalid." But in fact the subject-object distinction is of crucial importance in history as well as in natural science, and only by aiming to discover the objective concern of the text (rather than blending it with the subjective concern of the exegete) can successful exegesis take place.[67]

But does the Bible *per se* yield the norms, or only the subject matter, for theological theorizing? Not only from existentially orientated Bultmannians and post-Bultmannian advocates of the "New Hermeneutic," but also from Paul Tillich, who has valiantly endeavored to stiffen theological existentialism by means of ontology, we receive the negative reply that Scripture cannot in itself supply absolute norms for theological construction. After noting the variety of norms employed through church history for imparting significance levels to biblical data, Tillich asserts: "The Bible as such has never been the norm of systematic theology. The norm has been a principle derived from the Bible in an encounter between Bible and church."[68] Now we readily grant that church history presents a number of different normative approaches to Holy Writ: the early Greek church's stress on the Logos as the light shining in the darkness of man's mortality,[69] the sacramental Christology of the Western church in the Middle Ages, the Reformation emphasis on God's gracious forgiveness of sin, Protestant Modernism's concern with social amelioration, Tillich's own concentration on Christ as the New Being, etc. But are we, à la Tillich, to commit the naturalistic fallacy and assume that because varied judgments on the norm of biblical theology *have* existed, they *should* have existed? or that the various historical judgments on the norm have been equally valid, simply because they have met the needs of the time? or that Scripture does not in fact provide its own absolute norms for unifying its content? Tillich's dialectic "encounter between Bible and church" as the source of norms inevitably degenerates to historical relativism, leaving his own norm without justification along with the others.

In point of fact, one can readily detect unsound theological norms (e.g., Modernism's "social gospel") by virtue of their inability to give biblical force to central scriptural teachings, and by their unwarranted elevation of secondary (or even unbiblical) emphases to primary position. In other words, Scripture *does* very definitely supply "weighting factors" for its own teachings. Moreover, the majority of norms displayed in the history of orthodox theology have not really been as divergent as Tillich's discussion implies: most often they have displayed complementary facets of the overarching biblical message that "God was in Christ, reconciling the world unto Himself." Scripture itself makes this Christocentric teaching primary and ranges its other teachings in objective relation to it; and a sinful church learns the fact not through its historical "encounters" (which are always tainted), but from the perspicuous text of Holy Writ. Only Scripture is capable of truly interpreting Scripture; and only Scripture is able to provide the norm-structure for its interpretation and for the construction of theological doctrine based upon its inerrantly inspired content.

Terminating, then, our discussion of the scientific level of theological theorizing, we must reaffirm the fundamental thesis for which proof has been marshalled *in extenso:* science and theology form and test their respective theories in the same way; the scientific theorizer attempts objectively to formulate conceptual Gestalts (hypotheses, theories, laws) capable of rendering Nature intelligible, and the theologian endeavors to provide conceptual Gestalts (doctrines, dogmas)[70] which will "fit the facts" and properly reflect the norms of Holy Scripture. A tabular summary will perhaps offer the best conclusion to the rather involved discussion preceding it, as well as the best background for what is to follow.

	SCIENCE	THEOLOGY
THE DATA (Epistemological certainty presupposed)	Nature	The Bible
CONCEPTUAL GESTALTS	Laws	Ecumenical Creeds (e.g., the Apostles' Creed) and historic Confessions (e.g., the Augsburg Confession)
(In order of decreasing certainty)[71]	Theories	Theological systems (e.g., Calvin's *Institutes*)
	Hypotheses	Theological proposals (e.g., Gustaf Aulen's *Christus Victor*)[72]

The Artistic and Sacral Levels in Theological Theorizing

A recent article describing the sorry Spiritualist phase at the end of Sir Arthur Conan Doyle's distinguished career concludes with this thought-provoking evaluation:

> He was ill suited by personal temperament and life experience to become a religious philosopher. His natural sympathies were located in the outer rather than the inner life of man, as seen in his power to describe actions in his literature and his failure to portray character. Thus he was continually drawn towards the appearance of an event, its overt significance, but denied the ability to perceive its inner meaning.[73]

Leaving aside the disputable point (to which no addict of Sherlock Holmes could possibly agree!) that Doyle was a poor delineator of character, one finds here an exceedingly important reminder that the theological realm requires something more of investigators than scientific objectivity alone: it demands "the ability to perceive inner meaning." What is involved in this "inner meaning," and what connection does it have with theological theorizing?

A powerful hint toward an answer is provided in Luther's description of his theological method, which he characteristically drew from Scripture itself:

> Let me show you a right method for studying theology, the one that I have used. If you adopt it, you will become so learned that if it were necessary, you yourself would be qualified to produce books just as good as those of the Fathers and the church councils. Even as I dare to be so bold in God as to pride myself, without arrogance or lying, as not being greatly behind some of the Fathers in the matter of making books; as to my life, I am far from being their equal. This method is the one which the pious king David teaches in the 119th Psalm and which, no doubt, was practiced by all the Patriarchs and Prophets. In the 119th Psalm you will find three rules which are abundantly expounded throughout the entire Psalm. They are called: *Oratio, Meditatio, Tentatio.*[74]

By *Meditatio,* Luther meant the reading, study, and contemplation of the Bible (i.e., very much what we have spoken of in our foregoing discussion of the objective aspect of theological methodology); by *Tentatio,* he meant internal and external temptation—what we today would doubtless call subjective, experiential involvement; and by *Oratio* ("prayer"), the vertical contact with the Holy One, without which all theologizing is ultimately futile. Much the same threefold approach to theology is suggested by the treatment of the concept of faith in classical Protestant orthodoxy: faith involves *Notitia* ("knowledge"—the objective, scientific element), *Assensus* ("assent"—the subjective element), and *Fiducia* ("trust/confidence"—the vertical, regenerating relation with the Living God).[75] Quenstedt grounds this analysis of faith in John 14:10-12. He notes that "heretics can have the first, the second the orthodox alone, the third the regenerate; and therefore the latter always includes the former, but this order cannot be reversed."[76] Theology, like the faith to which it gives systematic expression, has objective, subjective, and divine levels, no one of which can be disregarded. Having discussed the scientific base in theological theorizing, let us now focus attention on the second, or artistic, level of theological activity.

The Theologian As Artist. John Ciardi, in his excellent introduction to literary criticism, *How Does a Poem Mean?,* quotes the following passage from Dickens' *Hard Times:*

> "Bitzer," said Thomas Gradgrind, "your definition of a horse."

> "Quadruped. Gramnivorous. Forty teeth, namely twenty-four grinders, four eye-teeth, and twelve incisive. Sheds coat in the spring; in marshy countries sheds hoofs too. Hoofs hard, but requiring to be shod with iron. Age known by marks in mouth." Thus (and much more) Bitzer.
> "Now girl number twenty," said Mr. Gradgrind, "you know what a horse is."

Ciardi quite rightly points out that, after having heard this learned description, "girl number twenty" knew "what a horse is" only in a very special and limited way: she knew horses in a formal, objective, scientific manner, but not at all in a personal, experiential way—not in the way in which a poet or an artist endeavors to convey knowledge. In the same vein, Peter Winch argues for the legitimate, and indeed necessary, inclusion of subjective involvement in the work of the social scientist; over against psychological behaviorism he asks the rhetorical question: "Would it be intelligent to try to explain how Romeo's love for Juliet enters into his behaviour in the same terms as we might want to apply to the rat whose sexual excitement makes him run across an electrically charged grid to reach his mate?" [77] Theorizing in the humanities or social sciences requires more than scientific objectivity; it also demands "the language of experience" [78]—"grasping the *point* or *meaning* of what is being done or said." [79]

Is this also true of theology? We have justified the scientific character of theological theorizing by pointing to the empirical, objective nature of God's historical revelation in Holy Scripture; now we must make the equally important point that, by virtue of its historical character, the biblical revelation lies also in the realm of the social sciences and humanities. Because God revealed Himself in history, and the Bible—the source of all true theological Gestalts—is a historical document, theological theories must partake of the dual science-art character of historical methodology. The historian cannot stop with an external, objective examination of facts and records; as Benedetto Croce and R. G. Collingwood have so well shown, he must relive the past in imagination—re-enact it by entering into its very heart.[80] As Jakob Burckhardt's *Civilization of the Renaissance in Italy* and Johan

Huizinga's *Waning of the Middle Ages* magnificently delineate their respective historical epochs by cutting to the essence of them, so theological constructions must meet Ernst Cassirer's standard for every "science of culture": they must teach us "to interpret symbols in order to decipher their latent meaning, to make visible again the life from which they originally came into being." [81]

We cannot enter here into the problem of the logical status of subjective artistic assertions;[82] suffice it to say, as has been effectively shown by Ian Ramsey and others, that such judgments follow from the independent, irreducible nature of the "I," which is in fact presupposed in all statements about the world—including scientific statements.[83] What we do wish to emphasize is the necessity of incorporating the artistic element into all theological theories, in order to avoid a depersonalization of theology and the concomitant freezing of biblical doctrine. Concretely, all valid theological theories must be set within the "invisible quotation marks" of belief,[84] must represent the personal, inner involvement of the theologian with Holy Scripture, and must convey a genuine reliving and re-enactment of historical revelation.

The presence or absence of such artistic criteria as these is to be determined not by formulae, but by individual sensitivity on the part of theologian and Christian believer. Yet the artistic factor is no less real because of that. Just as sensitive social scientist can recognize the greatness of William James' *Varieties of Religious Experience* as compared with pedestrian monographs on the same subject, and the sensitive literary critic has no doubt as to Milton's stature among epic poets, so the Christian who is in tune with Scripture can readily distinguish between theological theorizing that cuts to the heart of biblical revelation and theological theories that (scientifically correct as they may be) operate on a superficial level. Luther's insistence in presenting the doctrine of the Fall of man that "you should read the story of the Fall as if it happened yesterday, and to you" has this requisite inner quality,[85] as does such a creedal statement as the following, extracted from Johann Valentin Andreae's *Christianopolis* of 1619:

Credimus toto corde in Iesum Christum,[86] Dei & Mariae filium, coaequalem patrri, consimilem nobis, Redemptorem, duabus naturis personaliter unitum & utrisque communicatem, Prophetam, Regem, & Sacerdotem nostrum, cujus lex gratia, cujus sceptrum pacis, cujus crucis est sacr(i)ficium.	We believe with our whole heart in Jesus Christ, the Son of God and Mary, coequal with the Father yet like us, our Redeemer, united as to personality in two natures and communicating in both, our Prophet, King, and Priest, whose law is grace, whose scepter is that of peace, whose sacrifice, that of the cross.[87]

The Theologian and the Holy. In common with science, theology formulates its theories with a view to the objective fitting of facts (in this case, the facts of Scripture); in common with the arts, theology seeks by its theoretical formulations to enter personally into the heart of reality (God's revelation in the Bible). But theology is more than science or art, for it possesses a dimension unique to itself: the realm of the Holy. By this expression we do not refer merely to the "Numinous" quality of religion as analyzed by Rudolf Otto in his epochal work, *The Idea of the Holy;* we refer specifically to the unfathomable nature of the God of Scripture, whose ways are not our ways and whose thoughts are not our thoughts (Isa. 55:8), and who demands of the theologian as of Moses, "Draw not nigh hither: put off thy shoes from off thy feet, for the place whereon thou standest is holy ground" (Ex. 3:5; cf. Acts 7:33). Lack of recognition of the distance between sinful man and sinless God or blindness to the absolute necessity of relying upon His Holy Spirit in theologizing will vitiate efforts in this realm, even though the scientific and artist requirements are fully met. Without *Fiducia, Notitia* and *Assensus* are like sounding brass and tinkling cymbal. O. K. Bouwsma makes this point well in his unpublished allegory, "Adventure in Verification," where his hero encounters difficulties in determining how Zeus makes Olympus quake:

> At a meeting of the P.L.B., the Pan-Hellenic Learning Bust, an annual affair at which the feasters eat each other's work, he confided to fellow-ravishers that at the time he was considering his confrontation with the Makers of Fact or the News, on Mt. Olympus, the difficulty that bothered him most was not the matter of protocol but that

> of language. It wasn't that, as he anticipated, they, the interviewed divinities, would not understand him—they are adept in understanding four-hundred and twenty-six languages—but that he would not understand them. . . .
>
> He went down the mountain disappointed. . . . When he got home he wrote an account of his adventure, in order that the future of verification might not lose the benefit of his effort. His own adventure he described as one of weak verification due to sand, quicksand, too quick for the hour-glass. It never occurred to him that, not quick sand, but vanity was the condition which led to his having his eyes fixed on his own good name in the bark of the tree when they should have been fixed on Zeus who made Great Olympus shake, not by waving his ambrosial locks, nor by stamping his foot, nor by a crow-bar, nor by a cough but in his own sweet way.[88]

How many theological theorizers have failed in their herculean labors as a result of vanity—as a result of fixing their eyes on themselves "when they should have been fixed on Zeus who made Great Olympus shake"!

In what way is the dimension of the "Sacred" conveyed in theological theory construction? Essentially, by the admission that (in Bouwsma's phrase) we do not fully understand Zeus' language. That is to say, the theological theorist must always indicate in the statement of his doctrines the limited character of them—the fact that ultimately God works "in his own sweet way" (in the double sense of the phrase!). Michael Foster, by his stress on the irreducible mystery in all sound theological judgments,[89] and Willem Zuurdeeg, with his emphasis on the "convictional" nature of theological assertions,[90] endeavor (albeit by overemphasizing a good thing) to drive this point home. The best analysis of the problem, however, comes from Ian Ramsey, who observes the linguistically "odd" character of genuine theological affirmations. These consist of models taken from experience, so qualified to indicate their sacral (logically "odd") character. Such "qualified models" can be found throughout the range of Christian doctrine, e.g., in the phrases "first cause," "infinite wisdom," "eternal purpose" (where the qualifiying adjective in each case points the empirically grounded noun in the direction of the sacral, so as to reduce anthropomorphism and increase awareness of God's "otherness"). Another example is "creation *ex nihilo*" where "*ex nihilo*" is the sacral qualifier:

> In all the "creation" stories we have told, there has always been *something* from which the "creation" was effected; there have always been causal predecessors. So that "creation" *ex nihilo* is on the face of it a scandal: and the point of the scandal is to insist that when the phrase has been given its appropriate empirical anchorage, any label, suited to that situation, must have a logical behaviour which, from the standpoint of down-to-earth "creation" language, is odd. When creation *ex nihilo* as a qualified model evokes a characteristically religious situation—a sense of creaturely dependence—it further claims for the word "God," which is then posited in relation to such a situation, that it caps all causal stories and presides over and "completes" all the language of all created things. It places "God" as a "key" word for the universe of "creatures." [91]

Ramsey's assertion here that the "odd" qualifier, conveying the sacral dimension, can be "any label, suited to that situation," reminds us again of the single source for all sound theological theorizing: Holy Scripture. Only the Bible can serve as an adequate guide for determining what sacral qualifiers are "suitable" to given doctrinal formulations.[92] On this note the present section of the essay can properly be concluded: Sacred Scripture offers the sole criterion for testing the scientific, the artistic, and the sacral health of theological theories. Does a given theory represent objective truth? Does it incorporate the proper kind of subjective involvement? Does it adequately preserve the sacred dimension? To all three of these questions *sola Scriptura* holds the answers.

The Structure of Theological Theories

Theory formation and testing in theology have now been analyzed from the points-of-view of science, art, and the holy. One final question remains—and it is, if possible, the most consequential of all: How do the three methodological aspects of theology relate to each other? Analysis has now been completed; what about synthesis? So important is the synthetic problem that to neglect it or to embrace a false solution to it is to insure failure in theological theorizing, no matter how honorable one's motives and impeccable one's procedures in other respects.

Let us clear the air by making explicit a fundamental

principle to which we have already arrived by implication. We have seen, from clear scriptural evidence, that each of the three methodological aspects of theology is absolutely essential. Neither the scientific, nor the artistic, nor the sacral element can be removed from theological theorizing without destroying the possibility of results in harmony with God's Word. Thus we can legitimately expect to find deleterious theological climates wherever, in church history or in the present, reductionism is permitted with reference to one or more of the three methodological elements. The following table will indicate the unfortunate end products of the six possible methodological reductionisms:

REDUCTION OF	INTO	PRODUCES
1. Artistic & Sacral	Scientific	Dead Orthodoxy
2. Scientific & Sacral	Artistic	Pietism
3. Scientific & Artistic	Sacral	Mysticism
4. Sacral	Scientific & Artistic	Anthropocentrism
5. Artistic	Scientific & Sacral	"Theology of Glory" [93]
6. Scientific	Artistic & Sacral	Existentialism

In terms of this scheme, many of the unfortunate examples of contemporary theological theorizing already referred to in this paper (G. F. Woods' subjectivism, Hordern's Olympic Game thinking, Bultmannian and "post-Bultmannian" obliteration of the subject-object distinction, etc.) become more understandable: our age is particularly prone to reductionism; (6), which eliminates the scientific element from theology, and produces wooly-minded, unverifiable existentialisms that readily pass into the realm of analytic meaninglessness. But let us not lose perspective; this methodological sin, heinous as it is, is only one of several committed through Christian history, and we must link together the scientific, the artistic, and the sacral elements in theology so that *none* of the six methodological blunders will be permitted.

How shall the elements be related? Certainly not in dialectical fashion,[94] for (as we pointed out earlier) a polar dialectic is an open invitation to reductionism, since, as pressure is brought to bear on theology from the sinful cultural situation, the theologian can readily and almost imperceptibly slide from one pole to another, avoiding the serious demands of each. (It is this dialectic approach, so hospitable to Neo-Orthodox and existentialist viewpoints, that has permitted contemporary theology, under pressure from "scientific" critics of the Bible, to avoid the basic issue of the historical and scientific authority of Holy Writ.) And not by an attempt to find a pivot in man's faculties (e.g., Lonergan's striking "insight" motif[95]) by which the several methodological levels can be tied together, for such a pivot will inevitably shift the focus of theology from the God of Scripture to sinful man. Rather, we must structure the scientific, the artistic, and the sacral factors in theology so that they have a theocentric, Cross-centered focus, and so that the objective provides an epistemological check on the artistic, and the artistic serves as an entrée to the sacral. Consider, then, this structural model of theological explanation:

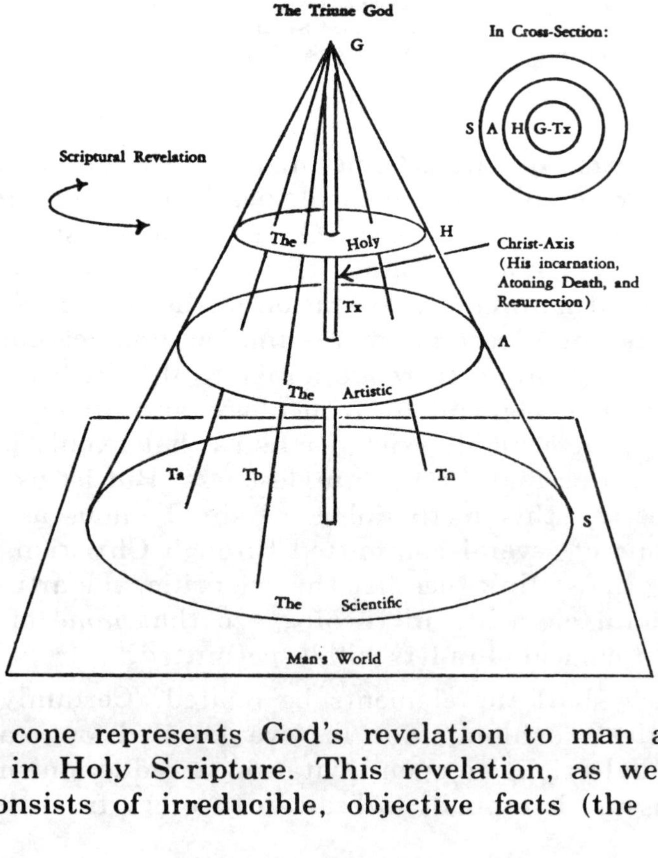

The cone represents God's revelation to man as expressed in Holy Scripture. This revelation, as we have seen, consists of irreducible, objective facts (the scientific level), to which subjective commitment must be made (the artistic level), and over which the divine majesty hovers in grace and judgment (the sacral level). The truths of which God's revelation is composed are legion (T_a, T_b, . . . T_n), but they all center upon the great truth which serves as the axis and focal point of the revelation as a whole: the Word become flesh, who died for the sins of the world and rose again for its justification T_x). The task of systematic theology is to take the truths of revelation as discovered by the exegete, work out their proper relation to the focal center and to each other (in the model, these relations are represented by the distances between T_a, T_b, and T_x), and construct doctrinal formulations that "fit" the revelational truths in their mutual relations. In terms of the model, theological theories can be conceived of as cellophane tubes constructed to fit with maximum transparency the truths of revelation; the theologian will endeavor continually to "tighten" them so that they will most accurately capture the essence of biblical truth.

The theological theorist builds his cellophane tubes from bottom to top: he starts in the realm of objective facticity, employing the full range of scientific skill to set forth revelational truth; and he makes every effort not to vitiate his results by reading his own subjective interests into them.[96]

But as he climbs, he inevitably (because of the personal center of biblical truth) reaches a point where he must involve himself subjectively in his material in order to get at the heart of it; here he passes into what we have called the artistic level, where the semi-transcendent, subjective "I" cannot be ignored. Still he climbs, and eventually—if he is a theologian worthy of the name—he finds that his theory construction has brought him into the realm of the Sacred, where both the impersonal "it" of science and the subjective "I" of the humanities stand on holy ground, in the presence of the living God.

A concrete illustration may be of value here. The doctrine of the Trinity is a theological theory, since the term is not given as a revelational fact. In formulating this theory, the theologian commences by objectively analyzing the biblical data concerning the relations among God the Father, Jesus Christ, and the Holy Spirit—but especially in reference to the character of Jesus Christ, the focal center of theology.[97] He finds that Jesus fully identifies Himself with the Father through His words (e.g., forgiving sin), acts (e.g., miracles), and specific claims ("I and the Father are one"; "he who has seen Me has seen the Father"; etc.), and that He attests His claim to Deity through His resurrection.[98] The theologian discovers, moreover, that this same Jesus asserts that the Holy Spirit is "another of the same kind" (ἄλλον παράκλητον) as Himself,[99] and that in His final charge to His disciples He places Father, Son, and Holy Spirit on precisely the same level.[100] At the same time, the personal identies of Father, Son and Holy Spirit are manifestly evident in Holy Writ, though God is "One" to all the biblical writers. Conclusion: the God of the Bible is (in the words of the Athanasian Creed) "one God in Trinity and Trinity in Unity." The paradoxical character of this theological theory should not disturb us, for it is a conceptual Gestalt demanded by the data; the more "rational" (better: rationalistic) theories of unitarianism and modalism pervert the biblical facts in the interests of a superimposed logical consistency. The orthodox theologian properly and humbly subordinates his theory to the data, as the physical scientist does in formulating the paradoxical "wave-particle" theory to account for the ostensibly contradictory properties of subatomic phenomena:

> Quantum physicists agree that subatomic entities are a mixture of wave properties (W), particle properties (P), and quantum properties (h). High-speed electrons, when shot through a nickel crystal or a metallic film (as fast cathode-rays or even B-rays), diffract like X-rays. In principle, the B-ray is just like the sunlight used in a double-slit or bi-prism experiment. Diffraction is a criterion of wave-like behaviour in substances; all classical wave theory rests on this. Besides this behaviour, however, electrons have long been thought of as electrically charged particles. A transverse magnetic field will deflect an electron beam and its diffraction pattern. Only particles behave in this manner; all classical electromagnetic theory depends upon this. To explain all the evidence electrons must be both particulate and undulatory. An electron is a PWh.[101]

To be sure, the conception of the Trinity in Scripture

is not fully or even principally comprehended by an abstract formula. Though on the scientific level "Trinity" is methodologically analogous to "PWh," the comparison ceases when we rise higher. "PWh" is impersonal, but the Trinity is intensely personal and touches the life of the theologian at its very center. Thus in explaining the Trinitarian articles of the Apostles' Creed, Luther reiterates the subjective, "for me" character of the doctrine: "I believe that God has made me .... I believe that Jesus Christ, true God, begotten of the Father from eternity, and also true man, born of the Virgin Mary, is my Lord .... I believe that ... the Holy Ghost has called me by the Gospel, enlightened me with His gifts, sanctified and kept me in the true faith." [102] Moreover, as the theologian contemplates the Trinitarian character of Holy Scripture, he is caught up in wonder and amazement, finding himself transported to the very gates of glory; with the Athanasian Creed, therefore, he must express by sacral qualifiers the "otherness" of superlative truth: "The Father uncreate, the Son uncreate: and the Holy Ghost uncreate. The Father incomprehensible, the Son incomprehensible: and the Holy Ghost incomprehensible. The Father eternal, the Son eternal: and the Holy Ghost eternal." [103]

Lost in wonder, then, does theological theorizing find its fulfilment. Commencing in the hard-headed realm of science, moving upward into the dynamic sphere of artistic involvement, it issues forth into a land where words can do little more than guard the burning bush from profanation. Here one can perhaps glimpse theology as its Divine Subject sees it: not as man's feeble attempts to grasp eternal verities, but as a cone of illumination coming down from the Father of lights (Jas. 1:17)—a cone whose sacral level brightens the artistic, and the artistic, the scientific level below it. The truly great theologian, like Aquinas, will conclude his labors with the cry: "I can do no more; such things have been revealed to me that everything I have written seems to me rubbish." [104] In the final analysis, the theologian must say of his theologizing what the great Wittgenstein said of his philosophizing:

> My propositions serve as elucidations in the following

way: anyone who understands me eventually recognizes them as senseless, when he has used them—as steps—to climb up beyond them. (He must, so to speak, throw away the ladder after he has climbed up it.)

He must transcend these propositions, and then he will see the world aright.[105]

Notes

[1] It will be observed that in this essay the term "theologian" is being used in the strict sense of "systematic theologian" or "dogmatician," not in the more general and perfectly legitimate sense of "professor on the theological faculty" (a category including exegetes ["biblical theologians"], church historians, homileticians, etc., etc.).

[2] Fascinating studies of this nature are suggested by Etienne Gilson's *History of Christian Philosophy in the Middle Ages* (New York: Random House, 1955). Much needs to be done in the historical study of classical Protestant theological methodologies—e.g., the "analytic" and "synthetic" methods employed by dogmaticians of the 16th and 17th centuries.

[3] A work along the lines of Rosamond E. M. Harding's *An Anatomy of Inspiration and an Essay on the Creative Mood* (3d ed.; Cambridge, England: W. Heffer, 1948) would be an exceedingly valuable addition to the literature of theology.

[4] Walter Kaufmann, *Critique of Religion and Philosophy* (Garden City, New York: Doubleday Anchor Books, 1961), p. 221 (para. 57).

[5] G. F. Woods, *Theological Explanation: A Study of the Meaning and Means of Explaining in Science, History, and Theology, Based upon the Stanton Lectures Delivered in the University of Cambridge, 1953-1956* (Digswell Place, Welwyn: James Nisbet, 1958), p. 151.

[6] Cf. John Macquarrie, *Twentieth-Century Religious Thought: the Frontiers of Philosophy and Theology, 1900-1960* (London: SCM Press, 1963), pp. 274-75. Unhappily, Macquarrie does not personally take Garnett's critique to heart—or he would modify his own existentially-orientated theology!

[7] William Hordern, *Speaking of God: the Nature and Purpose of Theological Language* (New York: Macmillan, 1964), pp. 86-89.

[8] The Christian "Mt. Olympus," as Wittgenstein's student O. K. Bouwsma has well shown in his unpublished essay, "Adventure in Verification," is firmly embedded in the earth, and is indeed subjected to verifiability tests.

[9] Cf. C. B. Daly, "New Light on Wittgenstein," *Philosophical Studies* [St. Patrick's College, Maynooth, Ireland], X (1960), 46-49.

[10] Karl R. Popper, *The Logic of Scientific Discovery* (2d ed.; London: Hutchinson, 1959), p. 59. For Wittgenstein's presentation of the "net" analogy, see his *Tractatus Logico-Philosophicus*, 6.341-6.35. My former professor Max Black, in his exceedingly valuable work, *A Companion to Wittgenstein's 'Tractatus'* (Ithaca, New York: Cornell University Press, 1964), pp. 347-61, finds difficulties in the network analogy, but concludes: "According to the view I have been presenting the principles of mechanics are neither empirical generalizations, nor *a priori* truths. Taken together, they constitute an abstract scheme of explanation, within whose framework specific laws of *predetermined* form can be formulated and tested. If I am correct, Wittgenstein's central idea in his discussion of the philosophy of science has thus been vindicated." On Popper's approach to scientific theorizing, see Thomas H. Leith's unpublished Boston University Ph.D. dissertation, "Popper's Views of Theory Formation Compared with the Development of Post-Relativistic Cosmological Models," and Leith's article, "Some Presuppositions in the Philosophy of Science," *Journal of the American Scientific Affiliation*, XVII (March, 1965), 8-15.

[11] Leonard K. Nash, *The Nature of the Natural Sciences* (Boston: Little, Brown, 1963), p. 61. Cf. Commissioner Tarquin's philosophy of scientific crime detection: "The trick is to surround it [the total crime situation] and then pull it all together" (Sebastien Japrisot, *Compartiment Tueurs* [Paris: Editions Denoël, 1962], chap. 1).

[12] The expression is Frederick Ferré's; see his article, "Mapping the Logic of Models in Science and Theology," *The Christian Scholar*, XLVI (Spring, 1963), 12-15. I am not happy with certain interpretations in this article (e.g., the author's distinction between theories and models; his belief that scientific theories, unlike theological theories, can exist without models), but in general the article deserves the highest commendation for its incisive wrestling with an exceedingly important methodological issue.

[13] Stephen Toulmin, *The Philosophy of Science* (London: Hutchinson University Library, 1953), p. 28 (Toulmin's italics). Cf. also Toulmin's more recent work, *Foresight and Understanding: An Enquiry into the Aims of Science* (Bloomington: Indiana University Press, 1961), *passim;* and Max Black's *Models and Metaphors: Studies in Language and Philosophy* (Ithaca, New York: Cornell University Press, 1962), *passim.*

[14] Roger Louis, "A Team of Experimenters: The Men Who Discovered DNA," *Réalités*, No. 154 (September, 1963), 45-46.

[15] The process of discovery in the case of DNA can be traced back directly to Max Perutz's labors as early as 1936, and the Watson-Crick theory took several years to be collaterally confirmed by Maurice Wilkins, Perutz, and John Kendrew. All five were joint recipients of Nobel prizes (chemistry and medicine) in 1962. For a recent technical overview of the state of research in the DNA area, see Duane T. Gish, "DNA, RNA and Protein Biosynthesis and Implications for Evolutionary Theory," *Journal of the American Scientific Affiliation*, XVII (March, 1965), 2-7.

[16] Cf. the basic distinction made by Wittgenstein between "objects"

or "things" ("Der Gegenstand ist einfach"—*Tractatus Logico-Philosophicus,* 2.02) and "facts" ("Was der Fall ist, die Tatsache, ist das Bestehen von Sachverhalten. Der Sachverhalt ist eine Verbindung von Gegenständen [Sachen, Dingen]" — 2.0, 2.01). Of course, theories can themselves become the substantive grist for the mill of higher level theory, but this in no way lessens the need to distinguish sharply between that which is to be explained (*explicandum*) and that which does the explaining (*explicans*).

[17] Toulmin, *The Philosophy of Science,* p. 43.

[18] R. B. Braithwaite, *Scientific Explanation: A Study of the Function of Theory, Probability and Law in Science* (Cambridge: Cambridge University Press, 1955), p. 368. Braithwaite, it should be noted, is a much more helpful guide in the realm of scientific explanation than he is in the field of theological analysis; in his book, *An Empiricist View of the Nature of Religious Belief* (Cambridge: Cambridge University Press, 1955), he argues the position, grossly inapplicable to the Christian faith, that religious affirmations are meaningful only ethically, not cognitively.

[19] Georg Henrik Von Wright, *The Logical Problem of Induction* (2d ed.; Oxford: Blackwell, 1957), p. 174.

[20] Joseph Agassi, *Towards an Historiography of Science* ("History and Theory Beihefte," 2; The Hague: Mouton, 1963).

[21] Kepler's discovery of Mars' orbit is a particularly good illustration. On the influence of Kepler's Reformation theology upon his scientific labors, see my essay, "Cross, Constellation, and Crucible: Lutheran Astrology and Alchemy in the Age of the Reformation," *Transactions of the Royal Society of Canada,* 4th ser., I (1963), 251-70 (also published in the British periodical *Ambix, the Journal of the Society for the Study of Alchemy and Early Chemistry,* XI [June, 1963]; 65-86; in French in *Revue d'Histoire et de Philosophie Religieuses,* No. 4 [1966] 323-45; and in my *In Defense of Martin Luther* [Milwaukee: Northwestern, 1970]. Cf. W. Pauli, "The Influence of Archetypal Ideas on the Scientific Theories of Kepler," in C. G. Jung and W. Pauli's *The Interpretation of Nature and the Psyche,* trans. Hull and Silz ("Bollingen Series," 51; New York: Pantheon Books, 1955), pp. 147 ff.

[22] See Arthur Pap's chapter on "Deductive & Inductive Inference" in his posthumously published work, *An Introduction to the Philosophy of Science,* with an Epilogue by Brand Blanshard (Glencoe, Ill.: Free Press, 1962), pp. 139-50.

[23] Max Black, "The Definition of Scientific Method," in his *Problems of Analysis: Philosophical Essays* (London: Routledge & Kegan Paul, 1954,) p. 23.

[24] Nash, *op. cit.,* p. 324.

[25] Aristotle, *Prior Analytics,* ii. 25; cf. *Posterior Analytics,* ii. 19.

[26] C. S. Peirce, *Collected Papers,* Harvard ed., V, para. 146, 171. It should go without saying that acceptance of the Peirce-Aristotle retroduction concept in no way commits one to Peirce's pragmatic philosophy; I myself have argued strongly against pragmatic epistemologies in my book, *The Shape of the Past: An Introduction to Philosophical Historiography* ("History in Christian Perspective," I; Ann Arbor, Michigan: Edwards Brothers, 1963), pp. 320-29.

[27] N. R. Hanson, *Patterns of Discovery: An Inquiry into the Conceptual Foundations of Science* (Cambridge: Cambridge University Press, 1958), pp. 87-90; Hanson, following Peirce, illustrates reproductive inference by the classic case of Kepler's theorizing to an elliptical orbit for Mars. With the "bird-antelope," cf. Wittgenstein's detailed philosophical analysis of the psychologist Jastrow's ambiguous "duck-rabbit" (*Philosophical Investigations*, ed. Anscombe and Rhees [New York: Macmillan, 1953], II. xi. 194 ff).

[28] Hanson, *op. cit.*, pp. 89-90. Readers of the present essay who wish to delve further into the nature of scientific theorizing are encouraged to consult J. O. Wisdom's bibliographical article, "The Methodology of Natural Science: Publications in English," *La Philosophie au milieu du vingtième siècle*, ed. Raymond Klibansky (4 vols.; 2d ed.; Firenze: La Nuova Italia Editrice, 1961-1962), I, 164-83.

[29] It is John A. Hutchison's great mistake that he stops here in analyzing the scientific aspect of Christian theology, thereby leaving his reader with the impression that the Christian religion is no more capable of objective validation than are any of the other competing world faiths (*Language and Faith; Studies in Sign Symbol, and Meaning* [Philadelphia: Westminster Press, 1963], especially pp. 244-47, 293).

[30] I made this point *in extenso* in the apologetic lectures I delivered at the University of British Columbia on January 29 and 30, 1963; these have been published in a slightly abridged version as a series of four articles under the general title "History and Christianity," in *His*, December, 1964—March, 1965; the lectures are now available in original form in my *Where Is History Going?* (Grand Rapids, Michigan: Zondervan, 1969), chaps. ii-iii.

[31] See, for example, the accounts of Gideon and the fleece (Judges 6), Elijah on Mount Carmel (I Kings 18), and the primary-source testimonies to empirical contact with the risen Christ (Lk. 24:36-43; Jn. 20:25-28; cf. I Jn. 1:1-4).

[32] To King Agrippa Paul thus defended the empirical facticity of Christ's fulfilment of prophecy and resurrection: "I am speaking the sober truth. For the king knows about these things, and to him I speak freely; for I am persuaded that none of these things has escaped his notice, for this was not done in a corner" (Acts 26:25-26). Peter's Pentecost sermon contains the significant lines: "Men of Israel, hear these words: Jesus of Nazareth, a man attested to you by God with mighty works and wonders and signs which God did through him in your midst, as you yourselves know . . ." (Acts 2:22; cf. F. F. Bruce, *The New Testament Documents: Are They Reliable?* [5th ed.; London: Inter-Varsity Fellowship, 1960], pp. 45-46.

[33] It might seem that such a general statement would not apply to Islam; however, see my article, "The Apologetic Approach of Muhammed Ali and Its Implications for Christian Apologetics," *Muslim World*, LI (April, 1961), 111-22 (see author's "Corrigendum" in the July, 1961 *Muslim World*). No world religion other than Christianity stakes its life on the objective historical facticity of its claims; only the Christian faith dares to make such an assertion as Paul's: "If Christ has not been raised, then our preaching is in vain and your faith is in vain" (I Cor. 15:14).

[34] At the outset of his *Kirchliche Dogmatik,* Barth argues: "If theology allows itself to be called or calls itself a science, it cannot at the same time take over the obligation to submit to measurement by the canons valid for other sciences" (I/1, chap. i. sec. 1). This unwarranted opposition between theology and science directly relates to Barth's scripturally illegitimate distinction between "salvation history" *(Heilsgeschichte)* and ordinary history *(Historie),* to his unqualified rejection of natural revelation, and to the church-directed, anti-apologetic thrust of his entire theology. I have maintained elsewhere that Barth's fundamental difficulties here stem from his over-reaction to Protestant modernism and to his fear of subjecting the Christian faith to the secular examination for which John 1:14 constitutes a specific mandate ("Karl Barth and Contemporary Theology of History," *Evangelical Theological Society Bulletin,* VI [May, 1963], 39-49-; reprinted in *Where Is History Going?* [*op. cit.* in n. 30], chap. v). Gordon H. Clark, in his excellent work, *Karl Barth's Theological Method* (Philadelphia: Presbyterian and Reformed Publishing Co., 1963), chap. iii, points up Barth's irrationalistic tendencies, and correctly notes that in citing and arguing against Heinrich Scholz's six scientific norms (*K.D., loc. cit.*), Barth is in actuality opposing the straw man of nineteenth-century Scientism (Scientific Positivism), not genuine scientific method. Unfortunately, Barth has never cared for science (Henri Bouillard, in his *Genèse et Evolution,* reports that even as a boy Barth disliked physics and mathematics); and his *Church Dogmatics* suffers for it on almost every page.

[35] Ian T. Ramsey, *Models and Mystery* (London: Oxford University Press 1964), p. 17

[36] Ramsey *(ibid.)* perpetuates a common fallacy when he asserts that theological models differ from scientific models in that the letter must generate experimentally verifiable deductions.

[37] Jean Racette, "La Méthode en théologie: Le cours du P. Lonergan au 'Theology Institute' de Toronto" (*Sciences Ecclésiastiques,* XV (Mai-Septembre 1963), 293.

[38] Paul Tillich, *Systematic Theology,* I (Chicago: University of Chicago Press, 1951), 40.

[39] Gerhard Ebeling, *Theologie and Verkündigung; Ein Gespräch mit Rudolf Bultmann* ("Hermeneutische Untersuchungen zur Theologie," 1; Tübingen: J. C. B. Mohr, 1962), pp. 14-15. Cf. James M. Robinson and John B. Cobb, Jr. (eds), *The New Hermeneutic* ("New Frontiers in Theology," 2; New York: Harper, 1964), *passim.*

[40] Heinrich Ott, "Was ist systematische Theologie?," *Zeitschrift für Theologie und Kirche,* Beiheft 2 (1961), pp. 19-46, sec. iii. Ott simultaneously regards "the gospel of Christ" as the subject matter of theology, and here also the dialectic operates: "The Christ event encounters us through the gospel of Christ, but the gospel is encountered through the Gospels and witnesses that are not yet and never will be the gospel itself. What is actually spoken is only the gospel *according to* . . . ., the gospel according to Matthew, according to Mark, according to Luke, according to John, but also according to Paul, and why not also, dependent on those and secondarily, the gospel according to Martin Luther, Calvin, Rudolf Bultmann, or Karl Barth?"

[41] *Ibid.*, sec. v.

[42] *Ibid.*, sec. iii. Cf. James M. Robinson and John B. Cobb, Jr. (eds.), *The Later Heidegger and Theology* ("New Frontiers in Theology," 1; New York: Harper, 1963), *passim.*

[43] A point brought out with particular force in J. K. Van Baalen's fine work, *The Chaos of the Cults* (Grand Rapids, Mich.: Eerdmans, 1955), which has gone through a number of editions.

[44] On this trend, see especially George H. Tavard, who argues that "the authority of the Church's tradition and that of Scripture are not two, but one" (*Holy Writ or Holy Church* [New York: Harper, 1959], p. 244).

[45] Cf. W. N. Clarke's critique of philosopher Paul Weiss' *Modes of Being,* which conceives the universe as having four ultimate dimensions of being: the Weissian system "leaves untouched the . . . fundamental and, for a metaphysician, unavoidable problem of the ultimate origin or source of existence and the ultimate principle of unity of this whole with its four irreducible modes" (*Yale Review,* September, 1958). Cf. my review of Weiss' *History: Written and Lived* in *Christianity Today,* VII (July 19, 1963), 43-44; reprinted in *Where Is History Going?* [*op. cit.* in n. 30], appendix E.

[46] See, for the most influential American example of this approach, Thomas Paine's *Age of Reason,* especially Pt. 2.

[47] Whitehead and Russell, in their great *Principia Mathematica,* showed that this is the case both for formal logic and for mathematics—and that the latter is a special case of the former.

[48] Joseph Lewis' *The Tyranny of God* (New York: The Freethought Press Association, 1921) is a popular example of an atheism built on the natural evils in the world; here the "Nature" which pointed Paine unmistakably (he thought) to a beneficent Creator points Lewis to a universe having no God at all.

[49] See my essay, "The Petrine Theory Evaluated by Philology and Logic," in my *Shape of the Past* (*op. cit.* in n. 26), pp. 351-57.

[50] I have demonstrated this in detail in my essay, "Constructive Religious Empiricism: An Analysis and Criticism," *ibid.*, pp. 257-311.

[51] See especially Bultmann's essay, "The Task and the History of New Testament Theology," included as an Epilogue to his *Theology of the New Testament,* trans. Kendrick Grobel, II (London: SCM Press, 1955), 241.

[52] See above, the quotation corresponding to n. 35. I suspect that Ramsey's overstress on religious experience, combined with relatively little emphasis on biblical authority, is an underlying factor in his defense of F. D. Maurice's uncertainty about the doctrine of eternal punishment (see Ramsey's *On Being Sure in Religion* [London: University of London-Athlone Press, 1963], especially chap. i).

[53] John Hick, *Faith and Knowledge* (Ithaca, New York: Cornell University Press, 1957), p. 198. For Hick, the "catalyst of faith"—the means of theological structuring the "apperceiving mass" of experience—is "the person of Jesus Christ" (p. 196). But this Christ is not seen in the context of a fully reliable biblical revelation. Thus, in his article "Theology and Verification," Hick can make the amazing statement:

"I will only express my personal opinion that the logic of the New Testament as a whole, though admittedly not always its explicit content, leads to a belief in ultimate universal salvation" (*Theology Today*, XVII [April, 1960]. 31). In regard to the existence of God, Hick holds the experiential view that "the important question is not whether the existence of God can be demonstrated but whether . . . faith-awareness of God is a mode of cognition which can properly be trusted and in terms of which it is rational to live" (*The Existence of God*, ed. John Hick [New York: Macmillan, 1964], p. 19).

54 See his full-scale treatment of this issue, *op cit.*, pp. 40-46).

55 Frederick Ferré, *Language, Logic and God* (New York: Harper, 1961), p. 104; Ferré's entire chapter on "The Logic of Encounter" (pp. 94-104) is a masterly critique of much of the wooly "I-Thou," existential-encounter theology popular today.

56 The foregoing criticisms, it is well to point out, also apply to those theologies which attempt to make a "living Christ" (as distinct from the Christ of Scripture) the source of theological theorizing. Such a "living Christ," if He is not known through Scripture, is necessarily known through extra-biblical experience. But, in the latter case, how can one be sure that his "Christ of experience" is the *real* Christ and not a projection of personal or corporate religious needs and desires? The dangers of idolatry here are overwhelming.

57 Limitations of space prevent us from dealing with the question of extra-biblical scriptures which claim to provide the ultimate interpretation of the Bible or revelational data superior to it (e.g., the *Book of Mormon*). Interested readers are referred to Van Baalen (*op. cit.* in n. 43), where the unverifiable nature of these claims is made patent, and where specific refutation of many of them is given.

58 In my *Shape of the Past* (*op. cit.* in n. 26, pp. 138-39), I have summarized what I believe to be the crux validation: "1. On the basis of accepted principles of textual and historical analysis, the Gospel records are found to be trustworthy historical documents—primary source evidence for the life of Christ. 2. In these records, Jesus exercises divine prerogatives and claims to be God in human flesh; and He rests His claims on His forthcoming resurrection. 3. In all four Gospels, Christ's bodily resurrection is described in minute detail; Christ's resurrection evidences His deity. 4. The fact of the resurrection cannot be discounted on *a priori*, philosophical grounds; miracles are impossible only if one so defines them—but such definition rules out proper historical investigation. 5. If Christ is God, then He speaks the truth concerning the absolute divine authority of the Old Testament and of the soon-to-be-written New Testament."

59 Franz Pieper, *Christian Dogmatics*, trans, and edd. T. Engelder, J. T. Mueller, and W. W. F. Albrecht (4 vols.; St. Louis, Mo.: Concordia, 1950-1957), I, 142-43.

60 John Warwick Montgomery, "Inspiration and Inerrancy: A New Departure," *Evangelical Theological Society Bulletin*, VIII, No. 2 (Spring, 1965); reprinted in my *Crisis in Lutheran Theology* (2 vols.; Grand Rapids, Mich.: Baker, 1967), I, chap. i and in the present volume in III. 3.

[61] Robert Preus, *The Inspiration of Scripture: A Study of the Theology of the Seventeenth Century Lutheran Dogmaticians* (Edinburgh: Oliver and Boyd, 1957), p. 159.

[62] *Ibid.*, p. 157.

[63] Introduction, sec. C. 2. a. (p. 7); Traina's italics. This book was first published in 1952 and is available from the Biblical Seminary in New York. Serious application of its principles offers perhaps the best counteractive to such absurdly superficial judgments as Kaufmann's remark on "the overt ambiguity of the Scriptures" (*op. cit.* in n. 5, p. 227): "In no case can a theology really do justice to the Scriptures because it refuses to take into account their heterogeneity and their deep differences."

[64] E.g., the classical Lutheran dogmatician Johann Gerhard (1582-1637), in his *Loci Theologici*, Preuss-Frank ed., I, 237-40.

[65] E.g., my esteemed colleague, J. Oliver Buswell, Jr., in his epochal work, *A Systematic Theology of the Christian Religion* (2 vols.; Grand Rapids, Mich.: Zondervan, 1962-1963), I, 24-25. Edward John Carnell has rightly praised Buswell for his "repeated insistence that a univocal meaning unites the mind of God with the mind of a Christian. The defense of univocal meaning implies a forthright rejection of all species of theology, ancient or modern, that either openly assert or tacitly consent to the hypothesis that truth signifies one thing for God (because he is almighty) and another for a Christian (because he is merely human)" (*Christianity Today*, IX, [February 26, 1965], 40).

[66] Heinrich Ott defends the "hermeneutical circle" as strongly as does Bultmann; see Ott's "Was ist systematische Theologie?" (*op. cit.*), sec. ii. The "hermeneutical circle" approach is, of course, an outgrowth and corollary of Heideggerian existentialism.

[67] John Warwick Montgomery, "The Fourth Gospel Yesterday and Today," *Concordia Theological Monthly*, XXXIV [April, 1963], 204; reprinted in the present volume in III. 5.

[68] Tillich, *op. cit.*, pp. 50-51.

[69] Cf. Jaroslav Pelikan's *The Light of the World: A Basic Image in Early Christian Thought* (New York: Harper, 1962), and *The Shape of Death: Life, Death, and Immortality in the Early Fathers* (New York: Abingdon, 1961).

[70] Hick (*Faith and Knowledge*, pp. 198 ff.) distinguishes between "dogmas" and "doctrines": the former "define the religion in question by pointing to the area of primary religious experiences from which it has arisen" (example: The Apostles' Creed), while the latter are "the propositions officially accepted as interpreting [the religion's] dogmas and as relating them together in a coherent system of thought." This is a useful distinction in practice, but Hick errs at several points in developing it; (1) Not "religious experiences" but the Holy Scriptures are the proper source of data from which Christian dogmas are developed (see above, our text at n. 53). (2) Doctrinal systems are not to be built upon "dogmatic foundations"; doctrines, no less than dogmas, are Gestalts that conceptualize *biblical* data. (3) The difference between dogmas and doctrines does not lie in the "fixed and unchangeable" character of the former as contrasted with the variable nature of the latter

(*both* are theoretically alterable for only scripture is inerrant), nor in the fact that dogmas are formulated by "a descriptive and empirical process" while the construction of doctrines is "speculative in method," involving "philosophical thinking" (*both* are Wittgensteinian "nets" to catch Scripture—not descriptive assertions *or* philosophical speculations). In actuality, the distinction between dogmas and doctrines is *quantitative*: the former are more stable because they are based on a greater wealth of biblical evidence, whereas the latter express theological convictions for which less scriptural support can be adduced. It follows that no strict or absolute line can be drawn between dogmas and doctrines, or between heresy (the rejection of orthodox dogma) and heterodoxy (the rejection of orthodox doctrine). Christian churches, in formulating tests of fellowship, should proceed with great care so as to avoid twin errors of laxity (stemming from an insufficiently defined or enforced dogmatic-doctrinal position) and bigotry (the bruising of consciences through required subscription to biblically doubtful doctrines). Thomas Campbell's rule remains the best guide: "Where the Scriptures speak, we speak; where the Scriptures are silent, we are silent."

[71] *Absolute* certainty, both in science and in theology, rests only with the data (for the former, natural phenomena; for the latter, scriptural affirmations). All conceptualizations on the basis of these data lack ultimate certainty (in science the Einsteinian revolution helped to make this clear), but some formulations are so well attested by the data that they acquire a practically (though not a theoretically) "certain" status; in science we call such Gestalts "laws," in theology, "creeds" and "confessions." Just as a denial of scientific laws removes one from the scientific community (cf. modern alchemists such as Tiffereau and Jollivet-Castelot), so denial of creeds and confessions results in one's separation from ecclesiastical circles. Scientific hypotheses and theological proposals, however, are never proper tests of "fellowship," for they lie, by definition, in the realm of open questions—which, hopefully, more investigation will either raise to a higher status or cause to be discarded. Scientific "theories" (in the narrow sense) and theological systems occupy an intermediate of Immanuel Velikovsky's catastrophism).

It is, of course, possible to develop a more extensive classification of conceptual Gestalts in Science and theology (since only *quantitative* differences exist among the respective levels), but the above scheme appears to be the most generally useful; in Roman Catholic dogmatics, at least ten "theological grades of certainty" are distinguished, from "immediately revealed truths" to "tolerated opinion" (see Ludwig Ott, *Fundamentals of Catholic Dogma,* trans. Patrick Lynch and ed. James Bastible; [2d ed.; St. Louis, Mo.: Herder, 1958], pp. 9-10 para. 8).

[72] On the "Christus Victor" atonement motif, set forth in historical context in Aulén's book of that title (English translation by A. G. Hebert published by Macmillan of New York in 1956), see the Appendix to my *Chytraeus on Sacrifice: A Reformation Treatise in Biblical Theology* (St. Louis, Mo.: Concordia, 1962), pp. 139-46, where I compare the Aulén

approach with Anselm's "Latin doctrine" of the atonement and with Abelard's "subjective view."

[73] Sherman Yellen, "Sir Arthur Conan Doyle: Sherlock Holmes in Spiritland," *International Journal of Parapsychology*, VII (Winter, 1965), 54.

[74] This passage appears in the Preface to the German section of the first edition of Luther's collected writings (Wittenberg, 1539). For an excellent discussion of it, see Pieper, *op. cit.*, I, 186-90.

[75] A particularly attractive presentation of this threefold conception of faith is given by Johann Gerhard (*op. cit.* in n. 64), III, 354 ff. A similar treatment can be found in Martin Chemnitz's *Loci Theologici*, II, 270.

[76] Johann Andreas Quenstedt (1617-1688), *Theologia didactico-polemica*, IV, 282. For Quenstedt, as for many of the other classical Protestant dogmaticians, both *Notitia* and *Assensus* pertain to the intellect, and *Fiducia* to the will; however, *assensus* is better regarded as bridging the gap between intellect and will, for, as Chemnitz correctly asserts, it involves "not merely a general assent, but that by which each one determines with firm persuasion, which Paul calls assurance (πληροφορία, Heb. 10:22), that the universal promise belongs privately, individually, and specifically to him, and that he also is included in the general promise" (*loc. cit.*).

[77] Peter Winch, *The Idea of a Social Science and Its Relation to Philosophy* (London: Routledge & Kegan Paul, 1958), p. 77.

[78] John Ciardi, "How Does a Poem Mean?", in *An Introduction to Literature*, ed. Gordon N. Ray (Boston: Houghton Mifflin, 1959), p. 666.

[79] Winch, *op. cit.*, p. 115. Winch illustrates with Wittgenstein's hypothetical society where the people sold their wood by piling the timber "in heaps of arbitrary, varying height and then sold it at a price proportionate to the area covered by the piles. And what if they even justified this with the words: 'Of course, if you buy more timber, you must pay more'?" (*Remarks on the Foundations of Mathematics* [Oxford: Blackwell, 1956], pp. 142 ff.). To *understand* such behavior, notes Winch, requires much more than the formulation of statistical laws concerning it. ("Understanding" is here used, let it be noted, not in an abstract, purely cerebral way, but in Max Weber's sense of *Verstehen*—"empathic comprehension"; see Talcott Parsons, "Unity and Diversity in the Modern Intellectual Disciplines: The Role of the Social Sciences," *Daedalus: Journal of the American Academy of Arts and Sciences*, XCIV [Winter, 1965], 59 ff.)

[80] On the historical philosophies of Croce and Collingwood, see my *Shape of the Past* (*op. cit.* in n. 26), pp. 90 ff. Crime detection, like history, is both a science and an art; thus Commissioner Tarquin (see above n. 11) also recommends in the investigation of a woman's murder: "Put yourself inside this woman's skin, get to know her better than she knew herself, become her twin. Get to understand her from the inside out, if you see what I mean" (Japrisot, *op. cit.*, chap. iii).

[81] Ernst Cassirer, *The Logic of the Humanities*, trans. C. S. Howe

(New Haven, Conn.: Yale University Press, 1961), p. 158.

[82] A good beginning can be made with Virgil C. Aldrich's *Philosophy of Art* (Engelwood Cliffs, N.J.: Prentice-Hall, 1963).

[83] "In every situation, when 'I' and 'me' have been distinguished. 'I' cannot be given an exhaustive 'objective' analysis without denying ourselves in fact, or without supposing that the subject-object relation in the construction of language is merely subject-predicate, which seems a quite unnecessary, indeed a quite disastrous, assumption. It is what Whitehead calls 'extreme objectivism' which even objectifies the subject" (Ian T. Ramsey, *Miracles; an Exercise in Logical Mapwork. An Inaugural Lecture delivered before the University of Oxford on 7 December 1951* [Oxford: Clarendon Press, 1952], p. 15). Cf. Karl Heim, *Christian Faith and Natural Science,* trans N. Horton Smith (New York: Harper Torchbooks, 1957), *passim*.

[84] Ramsey, *Models and Mystery,* p. 27: "There can—and it is a logical 'can'—be no objects without a subject which cannot itself be reducible to objects. The ideal of logical completion is never a third-person assertion; it is first-person assertion. *He does X* necessarily carries with it a pair of invisible quotation marks, so that it is to be set in some such frame as 'I am saying . . .', and without this wider frame the third-person assertion is logically incomplete."

[85] Cf. my article, "The Cause and Cure of Sin," *Resource,* III (February, 1962), 2-4.

[86] "Credimus in" followed by the accusative is the Latin equivalent of Greek **πιστεύομεν εἰς** . . . , signifying the highest level of faith (*Fiducia,* confidence). Andreae's Creed thus reaches beyond assent to trust, as must all genuine Christian doctrinal affirmations.

[87] For the full text of this Creed, with accompanying English translation and detailed analysis, see my dissertation for the degree of Docteur de l 'Université, mention Théologie Protestante: "Cross and Crucible: Johann Valentin Andreae's *Chymical Wedding*" (3 vols.; University of Strasbourg, France, 1964), I, 272 ff. As a contemporary example of a theological system manifesting biblically sound artistic-subjective quality throughout, I particularly recommend the late Erlangen professor Werner Elert's *An Outline of Christian Doctrine,* trans. C. M. Jacobs (Philadelphia: United Lutheran Publication House, 1927).

[88] Bouwsma, (*op. cit.* in n. 8), pp. 8, 10.

[89] Michael B. Foster, *Mystery and Philosophy* (London: SCM Press, 1957).

[90] Willem F. Zuurdeeg, *An Analytical Philosophy of Religion* (New York: Abingdon, 1958).

[91] Ian T. Ramsey, *Religious Language: An Empirical Placing of Theological Phrases* (London: SCM Press. 1957), p. 73.

[92] Unhappily, as we have seen (the text at nn. 35 and 52), Ramsey makes "religious experience" rather than Holy Writ his touchstone for confirming or disconfirming theological models and their qualifiers.

[93] Luther used the expression *Theologia gloriae* to characterize the presumptive, god-like attempts of late medieval scholastic theologians to embrace all reality in their systems; his own approach he designated

simply as a *Theologia crucis* ("Theology of the Cross"); see Philip S. Watson, *Let God Be God! An Interpretation of the Theology of Martin Luther* (London: Epworth Press, 1947), p. 78. The scholastics erred through neglecting the *Tentatio* element requisite to the theologian's activity; their impossible endeavor to theologize from as it were, the perspective of God's throne would not have come about if they had retained awareness of their own subjective involvement in the theological task.

94 E.g., "in the tension between analysis and existentialism" (Walter Kaufmann's philosophical maxim, characteristically endorsed by Willem F. Zuurdeeg in his article, "The Implications of Analytical Philosophy for Theology," *Journal of Bible and Religion*, XXIX[July, 1961], 210). In point of fact, only a solid analytical *base* can keep existential affirmations from dribbling off into unverifiable nonsensicality; thus not a "tension" but a *structure* is required for the proper relating of objective analysis and subjective-sacral existentialism. No better illustration of this exists than Wittgenstein's arrival at "das Mystische" at the end of his *Tractatus Logico-Philosophicus*, and the manner in which this work of logical analysis prepared the ground for his later *Philosophical Investigations*.

95 Bernard J. F. Lonergan, S. J., *Insight: A Study of Human Understanding* (London: Longmans, 1958), *passim*. The Autumn, 1964, number of the Saint Xavier College quarterly *Continuum* is a Festschrift entirely devoted to the exceedingly important work of this Wittgenstein-like professor at Rome's Gregorian University. In matters of theological methodology, Lonergan is far more worth reading than most contemporary Protestant writers on the subject, since he is well aware of the debilitating effect of current existentialism on theological method, and is thoroughly versed in post-Einsteinian scientific theory. Cf. Lonergan's review of Johannes Beumers *Theologie als Glaubensverständnis*, in *Gregorianum*, XXXV [1954], 630-48; and see also the accounts of Lonergan's institute on theological methodology held in July, 1962, at Regis College, Toronto (*Sciences Ecclésiastiques*, XV, 291-93 [*op. cit.* in n. 37], and F. E. Crowe, "On the Method of Theology," *Theological Studies*, XXIII [1962], 637-42).

96 The mingling of the subjective with the objective is deadly to any scientific theorizing. Theologians who would disregard this fact in their eagerness to existentialize Christian theology might ponder the following quotation from Rupert T. Gould's *Enigmas* (New Hyde Park, N.Y.: University Books, 1965), p. 321: "A novel and interesting theory respecting the origin—wholly, or in part—of Schiaparelli's (Martian) 'canals' was communicated to me in November, 1944, by Dr. G. S. Brock, F.R.S.E. He draws attention to the possibility that some or all of the appearances which the Italian astronomer believed that he had discovered on the Martian disc were actually situated *in the lens of his own eye*, and were symptomatic of incipient cataract.

"It is undoubtedly true that in certain conditions of lighting an image of the lens of the eye (together with any defects which this may have) can be projected on to the object which its owner is observing. Dr. Brock informs me that this fact was first announced by an Austrian scientist c.1842, but was afterwards lost sight of in consequence of Helmholtz' invention of the ophthalmoscope some ten years later. He considers it quite possible that some, at least, of Schiaparelli's 'canals' were caused by light from Mars, reflected from his retina, causing defects in the lens of his eye to be apparently projected on to the planet's disc—and, not improbably, blended with markings actually existing there" (italics Gould's). Whether or not this explanation of the famed "canals" of Mars is sound, it should give pause to contemporary theologians; for not a few of the theological theories of our day reflect the inner life of their proponents far more than the objective revealed truth of Holy Writ.

[97] Historically, as is well known, the Church arrived at its Trinitarian doctrine primarily through just such reflection on the christological problem of Jesus' relation to the Father.

[98] See Jn. 2:18-22, and cf. my *Shape of the Past* (*op. cit.* in n. 26), pp. 138-45. What in our structural model we have called the "Christ-axis" thus becomes the epistemological support for the entire theological endeavor.

[99] Jn. 14:16; ἄλλος is sharply distinguished in the Greek from ἕτερος ("another of a different kind")—cf. Gal. 1:6.

[100] Mt. 28:19

[101] Hanson (*op. cit.* in n. 27), p. 144. Cf. Jean E. Charon, *La Connaissance de l 'Univers* (Paris: Editions du Seuil, 1963), *passim.* Lutheran theology has always cautioned against violating revelational paradox, while Roman Catholic and Calvinist theologies have emphasized the need of achieving maximum rational consistency in doctrinal construction; the above parallel between the Trinity and PWh illustrates the complementary truth in the two views: the theologian must always strive for rationality in his theorizing, but he must sacrifice this ideal to the accurate "fitting of the facts" when the latter do not perit logically consistent formulation. Reason properly has a ministerial, not a magisterial role in theology.

[102] Luther, *The Small Catechism,* Arts. 1, 2, and 3 of the Creed.

[103] Cf. Ramsey, *Religious Language,* pp. 174-79.

[104] Cf. Jacques Maritain, *St. Thomas Aquinas* (London: Sheed, 1931), pp. 44-46, 51. The eminent Jesuit philosopher Frederick Copleston writes: "The Christian recognizes in the human nature of Christ the perfect expression in human terms of the incomprehensible Godhead, and he learns from Christ how to think about God. But at the same time it is certainly no part of the Christian religion to say that God in Himself can be adequately comprehended by the human mind. And that He cannot be so comprehended seems to me to be at once a truth vital to religion, in the sense that it prevents us from degrading the idea of God and turning Him into an idol, and a truth which follows necessarily from the fact that our natural knowledge begins with sense-experience. For my own part, I find the thought that the reality, the 'objective meaning,' far exceeds in richness the reach of our analogical concepts the very reverse of depressing. St. Paul tells us that we see through a glass darkly, and the effect of a little linguistic analysis is to illuminate the truth of this statement" (*Contemporary Philosophy: Studies of Logical*

Positivism and Existentialism [London: Burns & Oates, 1956], pp. 101-102).

[105] *Tractatus Logico-Philosophicus,* 6.54. On the famous concluding assertion (7.0) that immediately follows, Foster (*op. cit.* in n. 89, p. 28), perceptively comments: "When Zechariah says 'Be silent all flesh before the Lord,' this is not wholly different from Wittgenstein's 'Whereof one cannot speak, thereof one must be silent'."

B. How Lawyers Think

. Abrahams [Barrister-at-Law], "Argument by Layman and Lawyer": from his *The Legal Mind* (London: H. F. L., 1954), pp. 15-30.

aaw, C. J., in *Commonwealth v. Webster* (from John Romain Rood [Prof. of Law, Michigan], *Criminal Law: 3 American Law and Procedure* 115 (Chicago: LaSalle Extension University, 1954).

ARGUMENT BY LAYMAN AND LAWYER

If a layman, that is to say a person who is not a lawyer, were asked what an advocate is, he would probably reply that an advocate is somebody who pleads or argues; and he will have in mind either a person who, with histrionic gesture, persuades by the power of his personality; or else a person who obstinately contradicts and disputes in the way that ordinary people do when they are said to argue, only more cunningly. But these ideas are misleading. When a lawyer argues he is presenting a case in a legal setting. When he pleads (in one sense of that term) he is presenting arguments pertinent to the defence of persons accused of crime. Even more misleading is the common idea that, in some way, emotion and argument are blended in advocacy. The resultant picture of a lawyer who, with passionate declamation, makes bad argument good —' a robustious periwig-pated fellow ' who can ' tear a passion to tatters '— is as unjust to the lawyer as that which presents him as a cold blooded wrangler, thriving on ' the law's delays,' with no sentiment to spare for human wrongs and sufferings.

To anyone who contemplates, or who is embarking upon, a career in the law, it is important to understand that a lawyer is someone expert in legal principle and procedure. In so far as the lawyer is an advocate, he argues and he pleads in a way that can only be appreciated in the light of an understanding of legal principle and procedure. His arguments and his pleas (the word is here used in a non-technical sense) would often be difficult to appreciate for the ordinary debater, or disputant, or haggler. They would not be completely un-understandable, because the law is closely related to common sense. But there is sufficient difference between the principles of law (or, for that matter, the principles of any science) and the rough rules of common

All footnotes to this chapter will be found on pages 29-30

sense, for an argument acceptable to a layman not to be acceptable to a lawyer, and for an argument appreciated by a lawyer not to be appreciated by a layman.

Some examples may serve to make this clear.

A pedestrian is crossing the road and is knocked down by a motor car. This is the type of occurrence that is apt to bring about a request for legal advice. Indeed, in recent years, the injuries of pedestrians have provided the life blood of the legal profession. The layman is apt to think that the pedestrian's right to recover damages arises automatically and is correspondingly easy to establish. Says the layman: 'It was the driver's fault, he had no right to knock an innocent man down. If he hadn't been driving his car, this poor man would not have been injured. He ought to compensate him. Besides, he was probably insured.' Now, this is very elementary, and very bad, argument; and general intelligence and general knowledge may be sufficient to enable anybody to counter it. But the fallacies are instructive enough to merit the dwelling on them. First, the fact that the motorist is insured (even granting that he is so insured as to be covered in respect of that particular accident in those particular circumstances, including the terms of his policy, the identity of the driver, the purpose of the journey, etc.) is completely irrelevant.[1]

By 'irrelevant,' a lawyer means not only that it is beside the point (it may be that as well), but that it would not even be listened to in a court of law. The important word 'relevance' is a relatively simple one; but it is of crucial importance. Irrelevant means 'not to be considered.' It is irrelevant to consider the accidental fact that a man was insured, when the question at issue is whether or not his conduct has involved him in a legal liability. This is unsentimental, and the kind of fact that makes some people say that the law is heartless. Be that as it may. But woe betide any advocate who opened his case to a jury, as one old, but inexperienced, advocate is reported to have done, by suggesting that his impoverished client had been injured by a defendant who was in a position to pay. What the Judge would say to such an advocate would be worth hearing intrinsically, but, substantially, would only amount to the fact that what had been opened was irrelevant.

Then we are back to the question whether or not the driver is liable; and it is not inaccurate in any degree to say that that means whether or not it was the driver's fault. But a lawyer would point out that the argument presented by a layman is, on this issue, quite inadequate. To say that the pedestrian had a right to be on the road, and nobody had a right to knock him down, takes us nowhere, because the motorist has a right to be on the road as well; and the motorist's duty is so to drive that he does not knock the pedestrian down in ordinary circumstances; *i.e.* not to drive so as to make his conduct wrongful. The wrongfulness is what requires to be proved. And to say that he had no right to knock the pedestrian down, though it sounds true enough, is in this case circular argument — *i.e.* assuming what is required to be proved; namely, that he has done something wrong.

When a law book says that a motor vehicle is not an intrinsically dangerous thing[2] or that a motor accident is an occurrence that ' does not speak for itself,' it is saying something that sounds very trite, as many very important statements in lawbooks appear; but it is the epitome of legal arguments, and judicial decisions, which resulted in important contributions to the law of procedure and evidence that requires to be followed in this particular action of negligence.

To revert to the layman's argument, it is also unhelpful to say that if the motorist had not been there the accident would not have happened. When a lawyer says that somebody's conduct ' caused ' something else he does not mean that had X not done anything at all the next event could not have happened. He means that there is a much more direct relationship between the two events than that one is a sine qua non of the other. Without going into the difficulties of logic and law involved in this (and there are many), it can usefully be said that causation is understood in the law usually to mean fairly isolable, recognisable, conduct followed by an effect, as a fall follows a blow.[3]

Further, when it is said that the motorist's conduct caused the accident, then, assuming that it is proved that the conduct of the pedestrian did not help in the causation, did not contribute to the causation, or did not make it an inevitable accident from the Defendant's point of view, it still does not follow that the motorist is liable, because it still remains to be established that the latter bore an element of fault; that he did something that he should not have done, or that he omitted to do something that he should have done. The test here is whether he behaved in the circumstances as a reasonable man would have behaved in the circumstances.[4] And those words ' in the circumstances ' are important because they bring in the standpoint of the motorist as such. What would the reasonable motorist have done?

In the result we see that the question whether that pedestrian is entitled to damages reduces itself to a quite detailed analysis of the happening, in the light of reasonably detailed knowledge of the ordinary methods of driving motor cars.[5]

In the consideration of what has happened, very little will be taken for granted that is not deposed to by witnesses who saw things, or proved by inference from the facts so presented. When a lawyer speaks of ' proving ' a case, he means having facts sworn to on oath and having inferences or inductions drawn from those facts. In this process many things are excluded that a layman would think relevant. What the injured man said in hospital before he died is not evidence that can be used by his dependants as showing the cause of the accident. What he said immediately after the impact may, on the other hand, be evidence. What the driver of the alleged offending vehicle admitted may not be admissible in an action against the owner of the vehicle, because the driver may not be an agent authorized to make admissions.[6] Further, the previous history of pedestrian and driver can only become relevant in certain circumstances, *e.g.* in cross-examination. And, generally, many things that have an appearance of pertaining to the issue are rigorously excluded.

In fine, the investigation of liability seems to take a pedantic form. The type of argument that arises is reasonably clear, but differs from laymen's argument by reason of the frame of legal relationships in which it is confined, and by reason of the rigorous exclusion of what lawyers consider inessential. The total effect is an apparently arid technicality, the compensation for which, and the justification for which, consists partly in the element of certainty that a strict procedure gives to any science in which it is important to anticipate results.

From the foregoing example, two important truths of legal

procedure can be induced. (1) that argument in law is useful so far as it helps to bring a set of facts within some legal category. These legal categories are similar to the categories of common sense; but they are sufficiently distinctive to make reliance on common sense unwise, and common sense conclusions misleading. (2) that argument in law centres round, and is controlled and limited by, evidence. In the absence of sufficient evidence, all the sympathies in the world are of no avail. Evidence has its strict meaning in law; and the rules of evidence (which again are misleadingly near to rules of common-sense) require considerable elucidation before they can be effectively used and applied by a newcomer to the law.

These consideration are even more strikingly realised in the Criminal Court than in the Civil Court. Suppose the driver of the motor car, in the case already mentioned, happens to have killed his pedestrian, and finds himself charged with Manslaughter. The advocate defending him is likely to be engaged, paradoxically, in at least as severe and unemotional a work of analysis as his colleague defending the Civil claim. Before occasion arises for any emotional appeal to the jury to safeguard the freedom of the road, and the importance of transport in the evolution of society, there takes place a rigorous examination of events that have happened in a narrow context of time and place. Witnesses are called to give an account of the speed of the vehicle, the manner in which it appeared to be driven, the boldness or hesitancy of the pedestrian, the state of the road, the state of the brakes, the sobriety or otherwise of the driver at the time; also the prevailing light, and any manifestation of heat. It is important to prosecuting Counsel to present evidence which can be valued by a jury as amounting to evidence of recklessness, which is integral to the conduct that is is Manslaughter. It is important for the advocate for the defence to work out, and elicit by cross-examination, if it is safe and necessary to try to do so, what the witnesses do not say. His concern is to know and meet the case against him, and no other. He must see to it that irrelevancies are excluded. Other behaviour of his client must not be referred to in the case against him. Equally, he must be careful about making reference to his client's good driving record; and should not make this reference unless he is sure that the prosecution cannot take advantage of the opportunities which, under the appropriate Statute, this policy makes available to them.[7]

It is only when a case has been made by the prosecution and an answer to it is in the course of being made by the Defence — usually by evidence denying or explaining away the Prosecutor's evidence — that the advocate finds scope for the kind of plea that the layman understands by 'pleading,' or for the disputation that the layman understands by 'argument.' The address to the jury will be considered in a later chapter. Suffice it to say here that the psychological considerations, the emotional considerations, while they serve to enrich legal oratory, are only available to the advocate against a background of fact, and as considerations that arise in the detailed analysis of the evidence that is before the jury. Compendiously, the only claim that can be made on the jury's sympathy is, not that they shall find facts as the advocate wishes because of their sentiments, but that, putting themselves into the position of the accused, sympathetically (in the sense of constructively, uncynically), they shall understand his case and appreciate the possibility that his story is credible, however improbable. And always what matters is whether a series of facts alleged are proved, and the inferences or inductions from them warranted.

The technical characteristics of the criminal law would be even more strikingly illustrated, if your client were charged, not with driving the motor car dangerously, or killing people with it, but with receiving it knowing it to have been stolen. There you are not primarily concerned with general questions as to the social desirability of informal trading. Those considerations only enter indirectly. What is important here is for you to be sure that the prosecution has proved that the motor car was stolen, and that very shortly afterwards it was found in your client's possession in circumstances that were not to be expected from his ordinary way of life or trading. And the prosecution must satisfy the Court that your client actually had possession of it, and was not merely driving it for somebody else, or selling it to somebody else's order. You may have read in a law-book that an agent's possession is sufficient to enable him to accuse one who takes it from him of theft. Do not be alarmed by this. The law, you have learned, is empirical. A rule in the law of Bailment does not apply to the law of Receiving. The logic of law is not only not common sense. It is not always what is normally understood by logic.[8] Certainly the logic of particular cases can be difficult to grasp. Assume, then, that the possession is proved. Then, when the prosecution has set out all its facts, if you can show that your client can give, and has given at an early opportunity, an explanation of his possession of the car which is not impossible of belief, and which is not demonstrated by the prosecution's evidence to be untrue (if the prosecution is believed), you find that you do not have to urge the moral merits of your client. Perhaps to your surprise, you have answered the charge by exposing to the Court considerations which leave the prosecution in the position of not having established its case beyond reasonable doubt. There was a case to answer, but the burden of evidence was not on you, and has not been discharged by the prosecution.[9]

Incidentally, it is worth remarking that the common use of that phrase 'beyond reasonable doubt' is another instance of the lay misunderstanding of professional practice. It must be understood that evidence is never required to prove guilt with mathematical certainty; only with such a high degree of probability that to refuse to accept the probabilities would be violently contrary to the dictates of common-sense and common prudence. And, a further point, the considerations to be borne in mind are always in the context of the evidence. The jury must not speculate on possibilities not directly suggested by evidence for or against the accused. It has been repeatedly said that a jury is panelled to determine not whether a man is guilty, but whether he is guilty according to the evidence. Thus they may have learned by accident that the man has a bad character; they may have heard him accused in an unsworn statement by a fellow-prisoner, which they believe; but if they are told by the Judge to disregard these things they must do so, even if that consideration would be sufficient to satisfy reasonable men that the probability of the accused person's guilt was sufficiently high to justify a conviction.[10]

Always, both in the Criminal Court and in the Civil Court, the advocate's emphasis is on evidence. This is easy enough to say; but it requires concentration and experience to enable a man to isolate and confine his attention to evidence; and to evidence relevant to some legal relationship. Suppose your client is a motor salesman working on commission. He has been getting 10% on sales of cars varying between £100 and £500 in price. One day, however, he sells a car at £2,000. His dealer is reluctant to give him as large a sum as £200 and offers him £75, pointing out that this incident is quite exceptional. The salesman comes to you full of indignation and very conscious of the profit that the dealer has made. The dealer may have pointed out to him that the sale of that £2,000 car was not an unmixed advantage. You, however, are not concerned with this. Laymen find it surprisingly difficult to approach such a case from the right end, and to ask themselves, in these circumstances, what was the agreement pursuant to which the agent looks to the dealer for commission? Was it in writing? Was it ambiguous? If the writing is clearly and unambiguously in favour of the agent, was it ever varied? And you have to consider the purely legal point as to whether a variation of this agreement could be effected by conduct, or whether it would require further writing. It may transpire that the agreement takes the form of a letter asking the agent to see what he can do with a group of cars of low price; and that subsequently the agent has sold other cars than those mentioned in that letter, and received a similar commission. Then it becomes not at all easy to determine the exact nature of an agreement constituted part in writing and part by conduct; and considerations relating to the unscrupulousness of motor dealers only become relevant to, as it were, the atmosphere, when you are satisfied that you have an arguable contention that the agreement provides for the commission your client claims, and that your opponent's client is now retreating from his word.[11]

The law of Evidence is full of rules and principles that break the continuity between the claim of common sense and the claim in law.

You, a layman, are negotiating with a dealer for the purchase and sale of a secondhand car. The letters that pass between you consist of offers and counter-offers, none of which is completely acceptable to the recipient. Eventually you resort to the telephone. Over the telephone the dealer agrees with you that he will supply the car for £100 to be paid on delivery; and will, in addition, guarantee its performance for one year. You thereupon refuse somebody else's offer of an equally acceptable car, you write to the dealer confirming your bargain, and await delivery of your purchase. Eventually, the dealer forgets or neglects to reply to your letter; and, just before the date of delivery gets a better offer from somebody else, to whom he sells; and never delivers to you. You are forced to go into the open-market and spend more than £100 to get what you want. From a layman's point of view it would appear that you have a good case. The dealer made you a promise, and he has not kept it; and you have been put to expense on that account. Therefore, you think, you have suffered a loss, and should be able to get damages. Some might even suggest that you could claim delivery of the car, and get it from the man who has purported to buy it. And if the dealer protested that he had put nothing in writing, you would reply that that was his negligence, or wickedness, and that you yourself had put it into writing; and you have plenty of letters from the dealer before these events which show his intention to sell.

To cut a long story short, the layman here is doomed to disappointment. Not only has the claimant got no action for delivery of the car, and no action against the buyer (because the property had not passed to the Plaintiff, and the buyer had no agreement with him); but he has not even got an action for Damages against the dealer; because by reason of Section 4 of the Sale of Goods Act, no action can be brought on this alleged agreement in the absence of a document signed by the party to be charged — *i.e.* the person to be sued, in this case the dealer. This illustrates, forcibly, the fact that legal claims are grounded, as explained above, in evidence. In every case the lawyer requires to consider what is likely to be proved in evidence before he considers the claim properly so-called. Or rather, he sees a claim in a mass of potential evidence as an artist sees a figure in marble, or as a doctor diagnoses a disease in a certain minimum of symptoms. In this case, owing to a clear rule, there is demonstrably no evidence of an agreement.

It remains to be added, that had you been concerned, not

with something priced £100, but with an article costing less than £10, or with services up to any amount, you could recover damages if all the evidence you had was your own sworn testimony that a promise was made. Thus if you had ordered the dealer to reconstruct a car for you, it may be that you would recover Damages without documentary evidence. He undertook to do work, and has failed to do so.[12]

Another situation is that you may have said to the dealer, in writing, 'Put that car aside for me. I'll bring the money next week.' You may have received an acknowledgement of your instruction. Here you may not recover. The Court may hold that you asked for an option, and were granted it, but that you gave no consideration for the option: consequently it is not binding.[13] Incidentally, given a situation in which Documents are not necessary, the layman still finds himself unable to appreciate a feature of the law. He says: 'It's only my word against his.' He does not realise that, in law, the sworn evidence of one witness, if believed by the Court, can ground a successful claim if no rule of evidence exists to the contrary. Moreover, such an action can succeed even if the sworn evidence is contradicted on oath; because the Judge can believe one and disbelieve the other. 'My word against his' can be valid; equally it can fail. The result will not be, as in haggling, a compromise.

Another illustration from ordinary life may prove helpful in order to show the way in which the legal categories of liability differ from those that present themselves to commonsense. Your charwoman is cleaning the bathroom of your house, and falls through the floor, which has collapsed for reasons that you did not know about, but which a careful examination would have revealed. She will probably recover damages. Now, suppose that the person who falls through is not your servant, but a guest, whom you have invited to visit you. A layman might be inclined to argue in the following way. If a servant, who gets paid for working on your floors, can recover, surely a guest whom you invited, and is not paid to take this kind of risk, should recover. Unfortunately for the guest, this, like many another plausible argument, is not valid in English law. By a paradoxical use of language, the charwoman is called an 'Invitee'[14]; the guest, who was invited, is not an Invitee, but a bare Licensee. The duty to the charwoman was to make the premises reasonably safe for her. The duty to the guest was only to warn of hidden dangers the existence of which you knew.

But, if it happens that you are not the owner of the house, and the defect in the floor is such that it was not reasonable for you to know about it, and, by your lease, the landlord is bound to repair the house, and it was reasonable for the landlord to know the defects because he had had the floors inspected recently, the charwoman cannot recover. She cannot recover from you, because you are not in breach of duty. And she cannot recover from the landlord; because she was not an Invitee of the Landlord's. Nor had she any contractual relationship with him. Not even a member of your family could recover against the landlord in these circumstances.[15] The moral of this story is that the categories of law, while sensible and rational enough, are not self-evident to that form of apprehension which is called commonsense.

On the other hand, what is remarkable is the number of occasions on which the law operates exactly along lines of commonsense.

The law is not fixed and settled. It is always for the Court to find in a particular case what the duty of a given person was in given circumstances. In the course of searching his bosom[16] for the principle to guide him, the common law Judge is incidentally searching a repository of commonsense. His finding of what a commercial man would do in the course of a certain transaction is quite likely to be that which appeals to commonsense. He will depart from commonsense at certain points. He will not, for example, attach quite the same importance as a layman would to a failure to reply to a letter. In particular cases he will attach more importance, or less. On the other hand, he will put a commonsense construction on whatever commercial letter was written; and he will adopt criteria which are the criteria of the man in the street in deciding whether the contract has been performed or not performed, or whether certain conduct can be said to be careless; on whether in certain circumstances something should have been known.

In contrast, advocacy differs from ordinary argument, and common law differs from commonsense, not only because the principles of the former are more specialised, but because there is a good deal of law which is detailed enough to require knowing; and for this detailed knowledge commonsense is no substitute. Particular branches of the criminal law and the civil law require learning; and above all other things, the law of evidence; because whatever category of law the claim or charge you are considering falls into, and whatever the special rules that apply to it, it must be considered always as the possible subject matter of a case in court. In court the rules that matter above all others, and are of most general application, are the laws of evidence.

The rules of evidence are empirical and numerous. Without detailed investigation of them, suffice it here to say that a conception of evidence, and the knowledge of some rules of evidence, is a *sine qua non* of the acquisition of a technique of advocacy. We have seen above at least one illustration of this, *viz.* that the lawyer who has a conception of evidence sees his case analytically, and in stages, in a way that the layman does not. The lawyer, like the layman, must see things as a whole, but he must also see them articulated into detailed allegation and detailed defence, both set in a frame of legal concepts.

A further consequence of the conception of evidence is also very important. The need for proof of facts brings it about that the law is never quite analogous to debating.

Your opponent expects a high degree of care from your client: and seems to be satisfied with much less on the part of his own. That is a debating point, but it does not assist the Court very much, when the questions at issue are, what was the duty? and was the duty discharged? Debating points matter less in Court than they do in Parliament, where it is *vieux jeu* to present the Prime Minister with quotations from his speeches when in Opposition.

Your case and your opponent's case stand on the proof of them. The lines of proof are usually at an early stage made clear. In this connection the theory of pleading (*i.e.* the drawing of documents setting out claims, and, particularly for our purpose, civil defences) can be very misleading to the beginner in advocacy. You plead, very often, along the lines of what Maitland has called the ' broken pitcher ' argument. I don't admit you had a pitcher. I don't admit that it has been broken. I don't admit that you have suffered any loss by its being broken. I don't admit that I broke it; and if I broke it, it was not my fault, etc. But when the case finally takes shape in Court, you will find that you are tied to only one of these lines of defence, or at the most, to two. Those are the lines that you will have indicated in your cross-examination.[17]

Noting, *en passant*, that the law does not allow you to spring surprises, but makes you expose your defence, playing as it were with the cards on the table (which again is something that laymen do not regard as reasonable) you will find that your arguments are tied very closely to your proven facts. You cannot debate against your opponent in the following way; he is in a dilemma; if he had his lights on he dazzled me; if he didn't have his lights on he was not in a position to see me. You will find that the Court is saying to you: 'Mr Smith, or Mr Jones, are you saying that the lights were on, or are you saying that the lights were off?' And your answer has to be: 'My evidence is that I and my witnesses saw lights,' or did not see lights, as the case may be. But you cannot have it both ways. And further you will find that a number of tempting logical arguments are useless to you. It has been held, for example, that the court will attach little importance to the 'dilemma' as such. If you say: either he saw me and should have stopped, or he did not see me and was driving beyond the limits of his vision, the court will reverse your dilemma for you, and ignore it. In general, the court, in considering a dynamic situation, will not allow the over-simplification which a formal logical argument is apt to introduce.

In conclusion, the reader may be now be saying: 'Well, the law is evidently a mere presentation of facts with an invitation to believe or disbelieve. Where, then, does advocacy come in?' First let it be said that in framing this question the questioner has already emancipated himself from a degree of error. He has realised that the music-hall conception of the lawyer as a type of dishonest tinkerer with facts is even inaccurate as caricature. If dishonesty is the telling of lies then no man is more honest than the lawyer; for the simple reason that it is never in his province to make statements of fact on his own responsibility.

The lawyer never states in Court his own belief, or even opinion; always it is his submission, or his suggestion, based on the evidence. If ever his statement is categorical, it is subject to the unstated but understood hypothesis that the Court is accepting evidence before it. That evidence is the evidence of witnesses, of whom the lawyer is never one.[18]

What then is the task? Quite simply the ordering and interpretation of facts and contention in support of that order and interpretation. With facts, the advocate does everything except swear to them.

Even within the limits set by the conception of evidence there is plenty of scope. Facts are inveterately ambiguous. The fact that the driver did not see the pedestrian is at once an explanation of the collision in terms of accident rather than recklessness, and also a suggestion that he was not keeping a proper look-out.

The same facts which prove that your opponent is a rascal prove that your client should have had no dealings with him. The situation in which it may be suggested that it was reasonable to make a reply, is also a situation in which it is arguable that a certain type of man would not make a reply, etc. Further, facts are interpretable by way of valuation. Do they add up to carelessness, or do they not? Or do the proved facts support a certain inference? And facts and inferences from them are always subject to the argument that is entailed in fitting them into a legal frame of liability, criminal or civil. You will find that in the law there is plenty of scope for argument. What you need to learn is how your ability in argument must be controlled by the rules of law, the rules of procedure, and the conception of evidence, *i.e.* the realisation of the importance of facts. These rules, it cannot be too often emphasized, cannot be properly visualised, if your merely learn them from books. The student must acquire imaginative understanding of them. That understanding will bring with it an understanding of the principles of advocacy, of which the practicality is not easy to appreciate at the outset, but which, being mastered, become part of a forensic technique that can never be lost.

* * *

[1] Gower v. Hales, [1928] 1 K.B. 191. Since Motor Insurance against Third Party Risks became compulsory (Road Traffic Act, 1930) it is arguable that where a Defendant is not so insured the Court should be informed of the situation. It may be mentioned that twenty years ago the Irish Free State made itself, in effect, the insurer of the public against the consequences of road accidents. In some Continental Courts awards of Damages are inflicted and exacted as if they were fines.

[2] Wing *v.* L.G.O.C., [1909] 2 K.B. 652. For the meaning of *Res Ipsa Loquitur* see Byrne *v.* Boadle [1863], 2 H. & C. 722.

[3] The Author has contended that this conception of Causation is better than that of the logicians (*see* Philosophy: 1946: The Verb to Cause). It should be added that in one branch of the law (Workmen's Compensation) Causation seems to be less strictly treated. The law there is (roughly) that, given an accident of which the work is a *sine qua non*, the Applicant is compensated. The accident must be one 'arising out of and in the course of the employment '— a looser expression than ' caused by the work. For a recent discussion of Causation, see Stapley *v.* Gypsum Mines Ltd. (*Times*, 25th June, 1953) in which a fellow workman's omission was held (by a majority of the law lords) to be a cause, not a *sine qua non*, of the accident.

[4] Blyth *v.* Birmingham Waterworks Co. [1856], 11 Ex. When it is said that the criterion of negligence is ' objective ' not ' subjective,' mental factors (knowledge etc.) are not excluded: but the test of a motorist's judgment is 'public' not 'private.' Great allowance cannot be made for idiosyncrasies, ignorance and stupidity.

[5] A good deal of case law has developed round the defence of Contributory Negligence. This is not a question of duty, but of causation. Did the Plaintiff do something voluntary or unnecessary which enables it to be said that the Defendant did not cause the accident at all? Or did the Plaintiff contribute to the causation of the accident by his carelessness? There are many cases on ' agony of the moment ' ' last opportunity,' etc., but the House of Lords has said that one cannot evade the simple question, ' Who caused the accident?' By modern statute, a Plaintiff who is found to have contributed to the accident can receive a part of the Damages that he would have been awarded had he not so contributed.

[6] Cf. G.W.R. Co. *v.* Willis [1865], 34 L.J.C.P. 195. Not high 'authority.'

[7] See Chap. XII.

[8] A neat example of this truth is the situation in the Divorce Court, where the Court can hold it proved that A committed adultery with B, but not that B committed adultery with A. The reason is that what is evidence against A may not be admissible against B. Apparently against common sense, but not against the logic of evidence is that a man can be sent to prison for Attempted Murder of his wife; but, later, when a charge of Cruelty is brought, the facts must be proved again. The conviction is *RES INTER ALIOS ACTA*.

[9] R *v.* Schama, [1915] C.A.R. 45.

[10] If a jury hears (or sees in the Press) something that it should not be told, the Court can and will dismiss the jury and order a recommencement of the trial with a new jury. On one accasion, when, after three days of Trial, a prisoner complained that he had heard a juror say ' He's guilty,' the Judge dismissed the jury and recommenced the Trial. When Counsel for the Prosecution challenged the truth of the prisoner's complaint, Lawrence, J. as he then was (later to be on the Bench at Nuremberg) pointed out that, even if it were proved untrue, the jury would be affected by it (R. *v.* Morton and James, 1934, unreported, a very striking example of the English conception of justice as a result to be obtained through the severe application of strict rules).

[11] In the realms of contract, even good lawyers find scope for error. Thus in Whall *v.* Bulman (1953, 2 All Eng. R. 306) premises had been let for use as ' office accommodation only.' In an Action for possession, based on the Defendant's user of the premises as a dwelling-house, both Parties, and the County Court Judge, overlooked the fact that the agreement contained no clause providing for a forfeiture in the event of the premises being used otherwise than as agreed.

C

[12] The Painter of a Picture is selling work, not goods (Robinson *v.* Craves, [1935 1 K.B. 574), but Tailors and Furriers, making clothes 'to measure,' have been held to be selling goods for the purpose of the Act (*see* Marcel Ltd. *v.* Tapper, (1953 1 All Eng. R. 15) and Lee *v.* Griffin [1861], 1 B & S. 272).

[13] A comparable surprise is experienced, by the layman dealing with agreements, when he discovers that a 'contractor's' figures are not binding. They were an 'estimate,' not a promise.

[14] Some Judges would set the standard for the protection of servants on an even higher level.

[15] Cavalier *v.* Pope, [1906] A.C. 428.

[16] The old formula under which Judges maintained that they were not making law, but finding it — a theory no longer maintained. See: *The Changing Law* by Sir Alfred Denning (Stevens, 1953).

[17] The two most frequent pleas are: 1. Traverse — *i.e.*, Denial (of which 'Don't admit' is a variation). 2. Confession and Avoidance, *e.g.*, if the agreement was made as alleged the Plaintiff broke alternatively determined the said agreement.

Confession and Avoidance can be modified by inserting the words 'which is not admitted' after the protasis.

The Draftsman pleads in the light of a 'differential diagnosis' of the future total effect of the evidence. It may emerge that there was no agreement: it may emerge that there was an agreement but that it was broken by the Plaintiff.

But some allegations of fact rapidly become proved or disproved by evidence, *e.g.*, that a document was signed, etc. So that, in practice, the advocate, quite early in the Court stages of a case, finds himself with rather less latitude than the pleadings might suggest. Also certain conclusions may become evident early. Thus it may soon become clear in an 'Invitee' case that the defect 'should have been known' to the Defendant. Then the main struggle may take place round the issue whether the danger was clear to the Plaintiff or not.

Complex cases can be quite protean. In the Workington Harbour Case, [1936] 1 All. E.R., after fifteen years of 'progress,' the matter came to the House of Lords, where a completely new construction was put upon the contract. The result was a new start which after another twelve years proved to be abortive.

But generally, it is safe to be guided by a dictum of that celebrated advocate Hastings that most cases turn upon one point.

[18] 'A Counsel's position is one of the utmost difficulty. He is not to speak of that which he knows. He is not called upon to consider whether the facts with which he is dealing are true or false. What he has to do is to argue as best he can, without degrading himself, in order to maintain the proposition which will carry with it either the protection or the remedy which he desires for his client. If amidst the difficulties of his position, he were called upon during the heat of his argument to consider whether what he says is true or false, whether what he says is relevant or irrelevant, he would have his mind so embarrassed that he could not do the duty which he is called upon to perform' (Brett, M. R., in Munster *v.* Lamb [1883], 11 Q.B.D. at pp. 603 *et seq.*). The reference to relevance must be taken carefully. The context is a barrister's possible liability for Defamation. Also this must be read in the light of the truth that as a citizen a barrister dare not connive at Perjury.

§ 105. The evidence and proof in homicide cases. In order to convict there must be proof that someone is dead, —that death was criminally induced, and that the accused is the guilty party. The burden is on the prosecution to establish these facts and all of them to a moral certainty,

(8) State v. Hardie, 47 Iowa 647.

or, as it is commonly expressed, beyond a reasonable doubt. This proof may be by the direct testimony of persons who saw the acts, or by indirect and circumstantial evidence, or partly by one and partly by the other. It is believed that the law of this subject can be best explained by giving an extended quotation from the instructions to the jury in the celebrated trial of Dr. Webster of Harvard, for the murder of Dr. Parkman (9) who was seen going towards Dr. Webster's laboratory in the medical college about 1:45 p. m., Nov. 23, 1849, and was never seen afterwards. Diligent search was made in and about Boston and vicinity, but he could not be found. Five witnesses testified on the trial to have seen him after this time, but they were not well acquainted with him, and had no occasion at the time to take special notice. Suspicion being cast on Dr. Webster, his laboratory was searched. In the furnace were found bones like those of Dr. Parkman, which could not have been part of a body dissected at the college, for they had not been chemically treated. It was shown that Dr. Webster was indebted to Dr. Parkman, had promised to meet and pay him at the college at that time, then had no means to pay, and the note was afterwards found in his possession.

§ 106. **Same (continued).** The following instruction was given to the jury by Chief Justice Shaw of the supreme court, after consultation with all the other judges: "The rule, as deduced from the authorities, is that the implication of malice arises in every case of intentional homicide; and, the fact of killing being first proved, all

(9) Commonwealth v. Webster, 5 Cushing 295.

the circumstances of accident, necessity, or infirmity, are to be satisfactorily established by the party charged, unless they arise out of the evidence produced against him to prove the homicide, and the circumstances attending it. If there are, in fact, circumstances of justification, excuse, or palliation, such proof will naturally indicate them. But where the fact of killing is proved by satisfactory evidence, and there are no circumstances disclosed, tending to show justification or excuse, there is nothing to rebut the natural presumption of malice. This rule is founded on the plain and obvious principle, that a person must be presumed to intend to do that which he voluntarily and wilfully does in fact do, and that he must intend all the natural, probable, and usual consequences of his own acts. Therefore, when one person assails another violently with a dangerous weapon, likely to kill and which does in fact destroy the life of the party assailed, the natural presumption is, that he intended death or other great bodily harm; and, as there can be no presumption of any proper motive or legal excuse for such a cruel act, the consequence follows, that, in the absence of all proof to the contrary, there is nothing to rebut the presumption of malice. * * * The prisoner at the bar is charged with the wilful murder of Dr. George Parkman. This charge divides itself into two principal questions, to be resolved by the proof: first, whether the party alleged to have been murdered came to his death by an act of violence inflicted by any person; and if so, secondly, whether the act was committed by the accused. Under the first head we are to inquire and ascertain, whether the party alleged to have been slain is actually dead; and, if so, whether the evidence is such as to exclude, beyond reasonable doubt, the supposition that such death was occasioned by accident or suicide, and to show that it must have been the result of an act of violence. When the dead body of a person is found, whose life seems to have been destroyed by violence, three questions naturally arise. Did he destroy his own life? Was his death caused by accident? Or was it caused by violence inflicted on him by others? In most instances, there are facts and circumstances surrounding the case, which, taken in connection with the age, character, and relations of the deceased, will put this beyond doubt.

"This case is to be proved, if proved at all, by circumstantial evidence; because it is not suggested that any direct evidence can be given, or that any witness can be called to give direct testimony, upon the main fact of killing. It becomes important, therefore, to state what circumstantial evidence is; to point out the distinction between that and positive or direct evidence; and to give some idea of the mode in which a judicial investigation is to be pursued by the aid of circumstantial evidence.

"The distinction, then, between direct and circumstantial evidence, is this. Direct or positive evidence is when a witness can be called to testify to the precise fact which is the subject of the issue on trial; that is, in a case of homicide, that the party accused did cause the death of the deceased. Whatever may be the kind or force of the evidence, this is the fact to be proved. But suppose no person was present on the occasion of the death, and of course that no one can be called to testify to it; is it wholly unsusceptible of legal proof? Experience has shown that circumstantial evidence may be offered in such a case; that is, that a body of facts may be proved of so conclusive a character, as to warrant a firm belief of the fact, quite as strong and certain as that on which discreet men are accustomed to act, in relation to their most important concerns. It would be injurious to the best interests of society, if such proof could not avail in judicial proceedings. If it was necessary always to have positive evidence, how many criminal acts committed in the community, destructive of its peace and subversive of its order and security, would go wholly undetected and unpunished?

"The necessity, therefore, of resorting to circumstantial evidence, if it is a safe and reliable proceeding, is obvious and absolute. Crimes are secret. Most men, conscious of criminal purposes, and about the execution of criminal acts, seek the security of secrecy and darkness. It is therefore necessary to use all other modes of evidence besides that of direct testimony, provided such proofs may be relied on as leading to safe and satisfactory conclusions; and, thanks to a beneficent providence, the laws of nature and the relations of things to each other are so linked and combined together, that a medium of proof is often thereby furnished, leading to inferences and conclusions as strong as those arising from direct testimony.

" 'Perhaps strong circumstantial evidence, in cases of crimes like this, committed for the most part in secret, is the most satisfactory of any from whence to draw the conclusion of guilt; for men may be seduced to perjury by many base motives, to which the secret nature of the offence may sometimes afford a temptation; but it can scarcely happen that many circumstances, especially if they be such over which the accuser could have no control, forming together the links of a transaction, should all unfortunately concur to fix the presumption of guilt on an individual, and yet such a conclusion be erroneous' (10). Each of these modes of proof has its advantages and disadvantages; it is not easy to compare their relative value. The advantage of positive evidence is, that it is the direct testimony of a witness to the fact to be proved, who, if he speaks the truth, saw it done, and the only question is, whether he is entitled to belief. The disadvantage is, that the witness may be false and corrupt, and that the case may not afford the means of detecting his falsehood.

"But, in a case of circumstantial evidence where no witness can testify directly to the fact to be proved, it is arrived at by a series of other facts, which by experience have been found so associated with the fact in question, that in the relation of cause and effect, they lead to a satisfactory and certain conclusion; as when footprints are discovered after a recent snow, it is certain that some animated being has passed over the snow since it fell; and, from the form and number of footprints, it can be determined with equal certainty, whether they are those of a man, a bird, or a quadruped. Circumstantial evidence,

(10) East's Pleas of the Crown. c 5. § 11.

therefore, is founded on experience and observed facts and coincidences, establishing a connection between the known and proved facts and the fact sought to be proved. The advantages are, that, as the evidence commonly comes from several witnesses and different sources, a chain of circumstances is less likely to be falsely prepared and arranged, and falsehood and perjury are more likely to be detected and fail of their purpose. The disadvantages are, that a jury has not only to weigh the evidence of facts, but to draw just conclusions from them; in doing which, they may be led by prejudice or partiality, or by want of due deliberation and sobriety of judgment, to make hasty and false deductions; a source of error not existing in the consideration of positive evidence.

"From this view, it is manifest, that great care and caution ought to be used in drawing inferences from proved facts. It must be a fair and natural, and not a forced or artificial conclusion; as when a house is found to have been plundered, and there are indications of force and violence upon the windows and shutters, the inference is that the house was broken open, and that the persons who broke open the house plundered the property. It has sometimes been enacted by positive law, that certain facts proved shall be held to be evidence of another fact; as where it is provided by statute, that if the mother of a bastard child gives no notice of its expected birth and is delivered in secret, and afterwards is found with the child dead, it shall be presumed that it was born alive and that she killed it. This is a forced and not a natural presumption, prescribed by positive law, and not conformable to the rule of the common law. The common law appeals to the plain dictates of common experience and sound judgment; and the inference to be drawn from the facts must be a reasonable and natural one, and, to a moral certainty, a certain one. It is not sufficient that it is probable only; it must be reasonably and morally certain.

§ 107. **Same (continued).** "The next consideration is, that each fact which is necessary to the conclusion must be distinctly and independently proved by competent evidence. I say, every fact necessary to the conclusion; because it may and often does happen, that, in making out a case on circumstantial evidence, many facts are given in evidence, not because they are necessary to the conclusion sought to be proved, but to show that they are consistent with it and not repugnant, and go to rebut any contrary presumption. As in the present case, it was testified by a witness, that, the day before the alleged homicide, he saw Dr. Parkman riding through Cambridge and inquiring for Dr. Webster's house; this evidence had a slight tendency to show that he was then urgently pressing his claim; but not being necessary to the establishment of the main fact, if the witness was mistaken in the time or in the fact itself, such failure of proof would not prevent the inference from other facts, if of themselves sufficient to warrant it. The failure of such proof does not destroy the chain of evidence; it only fails to give it that particular corroboration, which the fact if proved, might afford.

"So to take another instance arising out of the evidence

in the present case. The fact of the identity of the body of the deceased with that of the dead body, parts of which were found at the medical college, is a material fact, necessary to be established by the proof. Some evidence has been offered, tending to show, that the shape, size, height, and other particulars respecting the body, parts of which were found and put together, would correspond with those of the deceased. But inasmuch as these particulars would also correspond with those of many other persons in the community, the proof would be equivocal and fail in the character of conclusiveness upon the point of identity. But other evidence was then offered, respecting certain teeth found in the furnace, designed to show that they were the identical teeth prepared and fitted for Dr. Parkman. Now, if this latter fact is satisfactorily proved, and if it is further proved to a reasonable certainty, that the limbs found in the vault and the burnt remains found in the furnace were parts of one and the same dead body, this would be a coincidence of a conclusive nature to prove the point sought to be established; namely, the fact of identity. Why, then, it may be asked, is the evidence of height, shape, and figure of the remains found, given at all? The answer is, because it is proof of a fact not repugnant to that of identity, but consistent with it, and may tend to rebut any presumption that the remains were those of any other person; and therefore, to some extent, aid the proof of identification. The conclusion must rest upon a basis of facts proved, and must be the fair and reasonable conclusion from all such facts taken together.

"The relations and coincidences of facts with each other from which reasonable inferences may be drawn, are some of a physical or mechanical, and others of a moral nature. Of the former, some are so decisive as to leave no doubt; as where human footprints are found on the snow (to use an illustration already adduced), the conclusion is certain, that a person has passed there; because we know, by experience, that that is the mode in which such footprints are made. A man is found dead, with a dagger-wound in his breast; this being the fact proved, the conclusion is, that his death was caused by that wound, because we know that it is an adequate cause of death, and no other cause is apparent.

"We may also take an instance or two from actual trials. A recent case occurred in this court, where one was indicted for murder by stabbing the deceased in the heart, with a dirk-knife. There was evidence tending to show that the prisoner had possession of such a knife on the day of the homicide. On the next morning, the handle of a knife, with a small portion of the blade remaining, was found in an open cellar, near the spot. Afterwards, upon a post mortem examination of the deceased the blade of a knife was found broken in his heart, causing a wound in its nature mortal. Some of the witnesses testified to the identity of the handle, as that of the knife previously in the possession of the accused. No one, probably, could testify to the identity of the blade. The question, therefore, still remained, whether that blade belonged to that handle. Now, when these pieces came to be placed together the toothed edges of the fracture so exactly fitted each other, that no person could doubt that they had belonged together; because, from the known qualities of steel, two knives could not have been broken in such a manner as to produce edges that would so precisely match.

"So, an instance is mentioned of a trial before Lord Eldon, when a common-law judge, where the charge was of murder with a pistol. There was much evidence tend ing to show that the accused was near the place at the time, and raising strong suspicions that he was the person who fired the pistol; but it fell short of being conclusive,—of fastening the charge upon the accused. The surgeon had stated in his testimony, that the pistol must have been fired near the body, because the body was blackened, and the wad found in the wound. It was asked, by the judge, if he had preserved that wad; he said he had, but had not examined it. On being requested to do so, he unrolled it carefully, and on an examination it was found to consist of paper, constituting part of a printed ballad; and the corresponding part of the same ballad,—as shown by the texture of the paper and the purport and form of stanza of the two portions,—was found in the pocket of the accused. This tended to identify the defendant as the person who loaded and fired the pistol.

"These are cases where the conclusion is drawn from known relations and coincidences of a physical character. But there are those of a moral nature, from which conclusions may as legitimately be drawn. The ordinary feelings, passions, and propensities under which parties act, are facts known by observation and experience; and they are so uniform in their operation, that a conclusion may be safely drawn, that if a person acts in a particular manner he does so under the influence of a particular motive. Indeed, this is the only mode in which a large class of crimes can be proved. I mean crimes, which consist not merely in an act done, but in the motive and intent with which they are done. But this intent is a secret of the heart, which can only be directly known to the searcher of all hearts; and if the accused makes no declaration on the subject, and chooses to keep his own secret, which he is likely to do if his purposes are criminal, such criminal intent may be inferred, and often is safely inferred, from his conduct and external acts.

"A few other general remarks occur to me upon this subject, which I will submit to your consideration. Where, for instance, probable proof is brought of a state of facts tending to criminate the accused, the absence of evidence tending to a contrary conclusion is to be considered,—though not alone entitled to much weight; because the burden of proof lies on the accuser to make out the whole case by substantive evidence. But when pretty stringent proof of circumstances is produced, tending to support the charge, and it is apparent that the accused is so situated that he could offer evidence of all the facts and circumstances as they existed, and show, if such was the truth, that the suspicious circumstances can be accounted for consistently with his innocence, and he fails to offer such proof, the natural conclusion is, that the proof, if produced, instead of rebutting, would tend to sustain the charge. But this is to be cautiously applied, and only in cases where it is manifest that proofs are in the power of the accused, not accessible to the prosecution.

"To the same head may be referred all attempts on the part of the accused to suppress evidence, to suggest false and deceptive explanations, and to cast suspicion, without just cause, on other persons: all or any of which tend somewhat to prove consciousness of guilt, and, when proved, to exert an influence against the accused. But this consideration is not to be pressed too urgently; because an innocent man, when placed by circumstances in a condition of suspicion and danger, may resort to deception in the hope of avoiding the force of such proofs.

§ 108. **Same (continued).** "Another rule is, that the circumstances taken together should be of a conclusive nature and tendency, leading on the whole to a satisfactory conclusion, and producing in effect a reasonable and moral certainty, that the accused, and no one else, committed the offense charged. It is not sufficient that they create a probability, though a strong one; and if, therefore, assuming all the facts to be true which the evidence tends to establish, they may yet be accounted for upon any hypothesis which does not include the guilt of the accused, the proof fails. It is essential, therefore, that the circumstances taken as a whole, and giving them their reasonable and just weight, and no more, should to a moral certainty exclude every other hypothesis. The evidence must establish the corpus delicti, as it is termed, or the offense committed as charged; and, in case of homicide, must not only prove a death by violence, but must, to a reasonable extent, exclude the hypothesis of suicide, and a death by the act of any other person. This is to be proved beyond reasonable doubt.

"Then, what is reasonable doubt? It is a term often used, probably pretty well understood, but not easily defined. It is not mere possible doubt; because every thing relating to human affairs, and depending on moral evidence, is open to some possible or imaginary doubt. It is that state of the case, which, after the entire comparison and consideration of all the evidence, leaves the minds of jurors in that condition that they cannot say they feel an abiding conviction, to a moral certainty, of the truth of the charge. The burden of proof is upon the prosecutor. All the presumptions of law independent of evidence are in favor of innocence; and every person is presumed to be innocent until he is proved guilty. If upon such proof there is reasonable doubt remaining, the accused is entitled to the benefit of it by an acquittal. For it is not sufficient to establish a probability, though a strong one arising from the doctrine of chances, that the fact charged is more likely to be true than the contrary; but the evidence must establish the truth of the fact to a reasonable and moral certainty; a certainty that convinces and directs the understanding, and satisfies the reason and judgment, of those who are bound to act conscientiously upon it. This we take to be proof beyond reasonable doubt; because if the law, which mostly depends upon considerations of a moral nature, should go further than this, and require absolute certainty, it would exclude circumstantial evidence altogether."

Defendant was found guilty, sentenced to death, and hanged. While in prison after the trial he confessed to the killing of Parkman.

C. Legal Reasoning as Model for Philosophical Reasoning

ephen Toulmin [Prof. of Philosophy, Leeds],
The Uses of Argument (Cambridge, Eng.: Cambridge University Press, 1958), pp. 1-10.

THE USES OF ARGUMENT

BY

STEPHEN EDELSTON TOULMIN

Professor of Philosophy
University of Leeds

CAMBRIDGE
AT THE UNIVERSITY PRESS
1958

INTRODUCTION

Πρῶτον εἰπεῖν περὶ τί καὶ τίνος ἐστὶν ἡ σκέψις, ὅτι περὶ ἀπόδειξιν καὶ ἐπιστήμης ἀποδεικτικῆς.

ARISTOTLE, *Prior Analytics*, 24a10

THE PURPOSE of these studies is to raise problems, not to solve them; to draw attention to a field of inquiry, rather than to survey it fully; and to provoke discussion rather than to serve as a systematic treatise. They are in three senses 'essays', being at the same time experimental incursions into the field with which they deal; assays or examinations of specimen concepts drawn rather arbitrarily from a larger class; and finally *ballons d'essai*, trial balloons designed to draw the fire of others. This being so, they may seem a little inconsequent. Some of the themes discussed will recur, certain central distinctions will be insisted on throughout, and for literary reasons I have avoided too many expressions of hesitancy and uncertainty, but nothing in what follows pretends to be final, and I shall have fulfilled my purpose if my results are found suggestive. If they are also found provoking, so much the better; in that case there is some hope that, out of the ensuing clash of opinions, the proper solutions of the problems here raised will become apparent.

What is the nature of these problems? In a sense they are *logical* problems. Yet it would perhaps be misleading to say that they were problems *in* logic, for the whole tradition of the subject would lead a reader to expect much that he will not find in these pages. Perhaps they had better be described as problems *about* logic; they are problems which arise with special force not within the science of logic, but only when one withdraws oneself for a moment from the technical refinements of the subject, and inquires what bearing the science and its discoveries have on anything outside itself—how they apply in practice, and what connections they have with the canons and methods we use when, in everyday life, we actually assess the soundness, strength and conclusiveness of arguments.

Must there be any such connections? Certainly the man-in-the-street (or the man-out-of-the-study) expects the conclusions of logicians to have some application to his practice; and the first words of the first systematic treatise on the subject seem to justify his

1 TUA

expectation. 'As a start', says Aristotle, 'we must say what this inquiry is about and to what subject it belongs; namely, that it is concerned with *apodeixis* [i.e. the way in which conclusions are to be established] and belongs to the science (*episteme*) of their establishment.' By the twentieth century A.D. it may have become possible to question the connection, and some would perhaps want to say that 'logical demonstration' was one thing, and the establishment of conclusions in the normal run of life something different. But when Aristotle uttered the words I have quoted, their attitude was not yet possible. For him, questions about 'apodeixis' just were questions about the proving, making good or justification—in an everyday sense—of claims and conclusions of a kind that anyone might have occasion to make; and even today, if we stand back for once from the engrossing problems of technical logic, it may still be important to raise general, philosophical questions about the practical assessment of arguments. This is the class of questions with which the present essays are concerned; and it may be surprising to find how little progress has been made in our understanding of the answers in all the centuries since the birth, with Aristotle, of the science of logic.

Yet surely, one may ask, these problems are just the problems with which logic ought to be concerned? Are these not the central issues from which the logician starts, and to which he ought continually to be returning? About the duties of logicians, what they *ought* to do or to have been doing, I have neither the wish nor the right to speak. In fact, as we shall discover, the science of logic has throughout its history tended to develop in a direction leading it away from these issues, away from practical questions about the manner in which we have occasion to handle and criticise arguments in different fields, and towards a condition of complete autonomy, in which logic becomes a theoretical study on its own, as free from all immediate practical concerns as is some branch of pure mathematics; and even though at all stages in its history there have been people who were prepared to raise again questions about the application of logic, some of the questions vital for an understanding of this application have scarcely been raised.

If things have worked out this way, I shall argue, this has been at least partly because of an ambition implicit in Aristotle's opening words: namely, that logic should become a formal science—an *episteme*. The propriety of this ambition Aristotle's successors have rarely questioned, but we can afford to do so here; how far logic *can* hope to be a formal science, and yet retain the possibility of being applied in the critical assessment of actual arguments, will be a central question for us. In this introduction I want to remark only on two effects which this programme for logic has had; first, of distracting attention from the problem of logic's application; secondly, of substituting for the questions to which that problem would give rise an alternative set of questions, which are probably insoluble, and which have certainly proved inconclusive.

How has this come about? If we take it for granted that logic can hope to be a science, then the only question left for us to settle is, what sort of science it can hope to be. About this we find at all times a variety of opinions. There are those writers for whom the implicit model seems to be psychology: logic is concerned with the laws of thought—not perhaps with straightforward generalisations about the ways in which people are as a matter of fact found to think, since these are very varied and not all of them are entitled equally to the logician's attention and respect. But just as, for the purpose of some of his inquiries, a physiologist is entitled to put on one side abnormal, deviant bodily processes of an exceptional character, and to label them as 'pathological', so (it may be suggested) the logician is concerned with the study of proper, rational, normal thinking processes, with the working of the intellect in health, as it were, rather than disease, and is accordingly entitled to set aside as irrelevant any aberrant, pathological arguments.

For others, logic is a development of sociology rather than psychology: it is not the phenomena of the individual human mind with which the logician is concerned, but rather the habits and practices developed in the course of social evolution and passed on by parents and teachers from one generation to another. Dewey, for instance, in his book *Logic: the Theory of Enquiry*, explains the character of our logical principles in the following manner:

> Any habit is a way or manner of action, not a particular act or deed. When it is formulated it becomes, as far as it is accepted, a rule, or more generally, a principle or 'law' of action. It can hardly be denied that there are habits of inference and that they may be formulated as rules or principles.

Habits of inference, in other words, begin by being merely customary, but in due course become mandatory or obligatory. Once more the distinction between pathological and normal habits and practices may need to be invoked. It is conceivable that unsound methods of argument could retain their hold in a society, and be passed on down the generations, just as much as a constitutional bodily deficiency or a defect in individual psychology; so it may be suggested in this case also that the logician is justified in being selective in his studies. He is not simply a sociologist of thought; he is rather a student of *proper* inferring-habits and of *rational* canons of inference.

The need to qualify each of these theories by adding words like 'proper' or 'rational' has led some philosophers to adopt a rather different view. Perhaps, they suggest, the aim of the logician should be to formulate not generalisations about thinkers thinking, but rather maxims reminding thinkers how they should think. Logic, they argue, is like medicine—not a science alone, but in addition an art. Its business is not to discover laws of thought, in any scientific sense of the term 'law', but rather laws or rules of argument, in the sense of tips for those who wish to argue soundly: it is the *art de penser*, the *ars conjectandi*, not the *science de la pensée* or *scientia conjectionis*. From this point of view the implicit model for logic becomes not an explanatory science but a technology, and a text-book of logic becomes as it were a craft manual. 'If you want to be rational, here are the recipes to follow.'

At this stage many have rebelled. 'If we regard logic as being concerned with the nature of thinking, this is where we end up—either by making the laws of logic into something psychological and subjective, or by debasing them into rules of thumb. Rather than accept either of these conclusions, we had better be prepared to abandon the initial assumption.' Logic, they insist, is a science, and an objective science at that. Its laws are neither tips nor tentative generalisations but established truths, and its subject matter is not 'thinking' but something else. The proper ambition for logic becomes in their eyes the understanding of a special class of objects called 'logical relations', and its business is to formulate the system of truths governing relations of this kind. References to 'thinking' must be sternly put on one side as leading only to sophistry and illusion: the implicit model for logic is now to be neither an explanatory science nor a technology, but rather pure mathematics. This view has been both the explicit doctrine of philosophers such as Carnap and the practice of many contemporary symbolic logicians, and it leads naturally enough to a conception of the nature, scope and method of logic quite different from those implied by the other views.

The dispute between these theories has many features of a classic philosophical dispute, and all the resultant interminability. For each of the theories has clear attractions, and equally undeniable defects. In the first place, there is the initial presumption, acknowledged by Aristotle, that logic is somehow concerned with the ways in which men think, argue and infer. Yet to turn logic into a branch of psychology, even into the psychopathology of cognition, certainly makes it too subjective and ties it too closely to questions about people's actual *habits* of inference. (There is, after all, no reason why mental words should figure at all prominently in books on logic, and one can discuss arguments and inferences in terms of propositions asserted and facts adduced in their support, without having to refer in any way to the particular men doing the asserting and adducing.) In the second place, the sociological approach has its merits: the logic of such a science as physics, for instance, can hardly be discussed without paying some attention to the structure of the arguments employed by current practitioners of the science, i.e. physicists' customary argument-forms, and this gives some plausibility to Dewey's remarks about the way in which customary inferences can become mandatory. Yet again, it cannot be custom alone which gives validity and authority to a form of argument, or the logician would have to wait upon the results of the anthropologist's researches.

The counter-view of logic as a technology, and its principles as the rules of a craft, has its own attractions. The methods of computation we learn at school serve us well as inferring-devices, and calculations can certainly be subjected to logical study and criticism. Again, if one is asked why it is that the principles of logic apply to reality, it is a help to be reminded that 'it is not so much the world which is logical or illogical as *men*. Conformity to logic is a merit in argumentative performances and performers, not a sign of any radical docility in the things argued about, so the question why logic applies to the world does not, as such, arise.' Yet the idea that inferring is a kind of performance to be executed in accordance with rules, and that the principles of logic play the part of these rules, leads in turn to its own paradoxes. Often enough we draw our conclusions in an instant, without any of the intermediate stages essential to a rule-governed performance—no taking of the plunge, no keeping of the rules in mind or scrupulous following of them, no triumphant reaching of the end of the road or completion of the inferring performance. Inferring, in a phrase, does not always involve calculating, and the canons of sound argument can be applied alike whether we have reached our conclusions by way of a computation or by a simple leap. For logic is concerned not with the *manner* of our inferring, or with questions of *technique*: its primary business is a retrospective, justificatory one—with the arguments we can put forward afterwards to make good our claim that the conclusions arrived at are acceptable, because justifiable, conclusions.

This is where the mathematical logician comes on the scene. For, he can claim, an argument is made up of propositions, and the logician's objects of study are the formal relations between propositions; to ask whether an argument is valid is to ask whether it is of the right form, and the study of form is best undertaken in a self-consciously mathematical manner; so we must sweep away all references to thinking and rationality and the rest, and bring on the true objects of logical study, the formal relations between different sorts of propositions....But this is where we came in, and the ensuing paradox is already in sight. We can hardly sweep away *all* references to thinking without logic losing its original practical application: if this is the price of making logic mathematical, we shall be forced to pose the Kantian-sounding problem, 'Is mathematical logic at all *possible*?'

The question, 'What sort of a science is logic?', leads us into an impasse: we cannot, accordingly, afford to get too involved with it at the very outset of our inquiries, but must put it on one side to be reconsidered later. For our purposes, fortunately, we can justifiably do so. This question is one about logical *theory*, whereas the starting-point of our studies will be logical *practice*. So let us begin by attempting to characterise the chief concepts we employ in logical practice: when this is done, the time may have come to return and ask what a 'theoretical' logic might be—what sort of a theory men might build up which could have the kind of application required.

A further precaution will be necessary. In tackling our main problems about the assessment of arguments, it will be worth while clearing our minds of ideas derived from existing logical theory, and seeing by direct inspection what are the categories in terms of which we actually express our assessments, and what precisely they mean to us. This is the reason why, in the earlier of these studies at any rate, I shall deliberately avoid terms like 'logic', 'logical', 'logically necessary', 'deductive' and 'demonstrative'. All such terms carry over from logical theory a load of associations which could prejudice one main aim of our inquiry: to see how—if at all—the formal analysis of theoretical logic ties up with the business of rational criticism. For suppose there did prove to have been a systematic divergence between the fundamental notions of logical theory and the categories operative in our practical assessment of arguments; we might then have reason to regret having committed ourselves by the use of theory-loaded terms, and find ourselves led into paradoxes which we could otherwise have avoided.

One last preliminary: to break the power of old models and analogies, we can provide ourselves with a new one. Logic is concerned with the soundness of the claims we make—with the solidity of the grounds we produce to support them, the firmness of the backing we provide for them—or, to change the metaphor, with the sort of *case* we present in defence of our claims. The legal analogy implied in this last way of putting the point can for once be a real help. So let us forget about psychology, sociology, technology and mathematics, ignore the echoes of structural engineering and *collage* in the words 'grounds' and 'backing', and take as our model the discipline of jurisprudence. Logic (we may say) is generalised jurisprudence. Arguments can be compared with law-suits, and the claims we make and argue for in extra-legal contexts with claims made in the courts, while the cases we present in making good each kind of claim can be compared with each other. A main task of jurisprudence is to characterise the essentials of the legal process: the procedures by which claims-at-law are put forward, disputed and determined, and the categories in terms of which this is done. Our own inquiry is a parallel one: we shall aim, in a similar way, to characterise what may be called 'the rational process', the procedures and categories by using which claims-in-general can be argued for and settled.

Indeed, one may ask, is this really an analogy at all? When we have seen how far the parallels between the two studies can be pressed, we may feel that the term 'analogy' is too weak, and the term 'metaphor' positively misleading: even, that law-suits are just a special kind of rational dispute, for which the procedures and rules of argument have hardened into institutions. Certainly it is no surprise to find a professor of jurisprudence taking up, as problems in his own subject, questions familiar to us from treatises on logic—questions, for instance, about causation—and for Aristotle, as an Athenian, the gap between arguments in the courts and arguments in the Lyceum or Agora would have seemed even slighter than it does for us.

There is one special virtue in the parallel between logic and jurisprudence: it helps to keep in the centre of the picture the *critical* function of the reason. The rules of logic may not be tips or generalisations: they none the less apply to men and their arguments—not in the way that laws of psychology or maxims of method apply, but rather as *standards of achievement* which a man, in arguing, can come up to or fall short of, and by which his arguments can be judged. A sound argument, a well-grounded or firmly-backed claim, is one which will stand up to criticism, one for which a case can be presented coming up to the standard required if it is to deserve a favourable verdict. How many legal terms find a natural extension here! One may even be tempted to say that our extra-legal claims have to be justified, not before Her Majesty's Judges, but before the Court of Reason.

In the studies which follow, then, the nature of the rational process will be discussed with the 'jurisprudential analogy' in mind: our subject will be the *prudentia*, not simply of *jus*, but more generally of *ratio*. The first two essays are in part preparatory to the third, for it is in Essay III that the crucial results of the inquiry are expounded. In Essay I the chief topic is the variety of the claims and arguments we have occasion to put forward, and the question is discussed, in what ways the formalities and structure of argument change and do not change, as we move from one sort of claim to another or between arguments in different 'fields': the main innovation here is a distinction between the 'force' of terms of logical assessment and the 'grounds' or 'criteria' for their use, a distinction which is taken up again later. Essay II is a study of the notion of probability, which serves here as a pilot investigation, introducing us to a number of ideas and distinctions which can throw a more general light on the categories of rational assessment.

In Essay III we reach the central question, how we are to set out and analyse arguments in order that our assessments shall be logically *candid*—in order, that is, to make clear the functions of the different propositions invoked in the course of an argument and the relevance of the different sorts of criticism which can be directed against it. The form of analysis arrived at is decidedly more complex than that which logicians have customarily employed, and forces on us a number of distinctions for which the normal analysis leaves no room; too many different things (I shall suggest) have been run together in the past under the name of 'major premisses', and a single division of arguments into 'deductive' and 'inductive' has been relied on to mark at least four different distinctions. When these various distinctions are separated out, it begins to look as though formal logic has indeed lost touch with its application, and as if a systematic divergence has in fact grown up between the categories of logical practice and the analyses given of them in logicians' text-books and treatises.

The philosophical origins of this divergence and its implications for logic and epistemology are the subjects of the two final essays. In Essay IV the origins of the divergence are traced back to the Aristotelian ideal of logic as a formal science comparable to geometry: in the field of jurisprudence, the suggestion that we should aim to produce theories having the formal structure of mathematics has never become popular, and it turns out here that there are objections also to the idea of casting the whole of logical theory into mathematical form. Essay V traces some of the wider consequences of the deviation between the categories of working logic and the analysis of them given by philosophers and, in particular, its effect on the theory of knowledge. There, as in logic, pride of place has been given to arguments backed by entailments: wherever claims to knowledge have been seen to be based on evidence not entailing analytically the correctness of the claim, a 'logical gulf' has been felt to exist which the philosopher must find some way either of bridging or of conjuring away, and as a result a whole array of epistemological problems has grown up around scientific, ethical, aesthetic and theological claims alike. Once, however, we recognise the sources of the deviation between working logic and logical theory, it becomes questionable whether these problems should have been raised in the first place. We are tempted to see deficiencies in these claims only because we compare them with a philosopher's ideal which is in the nature of the cases unrealisable. The proper task of epistemology would be not to overcome these imagined deficiencies, but to discover what actual merits the arguments of scientists, moralists, art critics or theologians can realistically hope to achieve.

The existence of this 'double standard', this divergence between the philosopher's question about the world and the ordinary man's, is of course a commonplace: no one has expressed it better than David Hume, who recognised both habits of mind in one and the same person—namely, himself. Usually, the divergence has been treated as a matter for pride, or at any rate tolerance; as a mark (at best) of superior penetration and profundity in the thought of philosophers, or (at worst) as the result of a pardonable psychological quirk. It seems almost mean of one to suggest that it may be, in fact, a consequence of nothing more than a straightforward fallacy—of a failure to draw in one's logical theorising all the distinctions which the demands of logical practice require.

The studies which follow are, as I have said, only essays. If our analysis of arguments is to be really effective and true-to-life it will need, very likely, to make use of notions and distinctions that are not even hinted at here. But of one thing I am confident: that by treating logic as generalised jurisprudence and testing our ideas against our actual practice of argument-assessment, rather than against a philosopher's ideal, we shall eventually build up a picture very different from the traditional one. The most I can hope for is that some of the pieces whose shape I have here outlined will keep a place in the finished mosaic.

PART THREE

THE JUSTIFICATION OF LAW

A. Natural Law

Blackstone, Burke, Kent: selections from John C. H. Wu [Prof. of Law, Seton Hall; Member, Permanent Court of Arbitration, The Hague], *Cases and Materials on Jurisprudence* (St. Paul, Minn.: West, 1958), pp. 188-93.

C. S. Lewis [Prof. of Mediaeval and Renaissance English Literature, Cambridge] on the Tao: from his *The Abolition of Man* (New York: Macmillan, 1947), pp. 51-61.

A. P. d'Entrèves [D. Phil., Prof. of Political Theory, Turin], "The Ideal Law": from his *Natural Law: An Introduction to Legal Philosophy* (rev. ed.; London: Hutchinson University Library, 1970), pp. 93-107.

BLACKSTONE, in Commentaries, Introd. Sec. 2, pp. 39–43:—Man, considered as a creature, must necessarily be subject to the laws of his Creator, for he is entirely a dependent being. * * * And consequently, as man depends absolutely upon his Maker for every thing, it is necessary that he should, in all points, conform to his Maker's will.

This will of his Maker is called the law of nature. For as God, when he created matter, and endued it with a

[2] Justinian, Institutes, I. 2. 1. "Natural law is what nature has taught all animals, * * * such as the union of male and female and the education of children."—Ed.

principle of mobility, established certain rules for the perpetual direction of that motion, so, when he created man, and endued him with free-will to conduct himself in all parts of life, he laid down certain immutable laws of human nature, whereby that free-will is in some degree regulated and restrained, and gave him also the faculty of reason to discover the purport of those laws. * * *

This law of nature, being coeval with mankind, and dictated by God himself, is of course superior in obligation to any other. It is binding over all the globe in all countries, and at all times: no human laws are of any validity, if contrary to this; and such of them as are valid derive all their force and all their authority, mediately or immediately, from this original.

* * *

Upon these two foundations, the law of nature and the law of revelation, depend all human laws; that is to say, no human laws should be suffered to contradict these. There are, it is true, a great number of indifferent points in which both the divine law and the natural leave a man at his own liberty, but which are found necessary, for the benefit of society, to be restrained within certain limits. And herein it is that human laws have their greatest force and efficacy; for, with regard to such points as are not indifferent, human laws are only declaratory of, and act in subordination to, the former. To instance in the case of murder: this is expressly forbidden by the divine, and demonstrably by the natural law; and, from these prohibitions, arises the true unlawfulness of this crime. Those human laws that annex a punishment to it do not at all increase its moral guilt, or superadd any fresh obligation, in foro conscientiae, to abstain from its perpetration. Nay, if any human law should allow or enjoin us to commit it, we are bound to transgress that human law, or else we must offend both the natural and the divine. But, with regard to matters that are in themselves indifferent, and are not commanded or forbidden by those superior laws,—such, for instance, as exporting of wool into foreign countries,—here the inferior legislature has scope and opportunity to interpose, and to make that action unlawful which before was not so.

Peter J. Stanlis on Edmund Burke:[1] —Burke's most extended and eloquent attack on Hastings' claim of arbitrary power, made on February 16, 1788, derives wholly from his ardent faith in the Natural Law as an emanation of God's justice:

> Will you ever hear the rights of mankind made subservient to the practice of government? It will be your lordships' duty and joy, it will be your pride and triumph, to teach men, that they are to conform their practice to their principles, and not to derive their principles from the wicked, corrupt, and abominable practices of any man whatever. Where is the man that ever before dared to mention the practice of all the villains, of all the notorious depredators, as his justification? To gather up, and put it all into one code, and call it the duty of a British governor? . . . "He had arbitrary power!" My lords, the East India Company have not arbitrary power to give him. The king has no

1 Reprinted by permission of University of Detroit Law Journal from Peter J. Stanlis, "Edmund Burke and the Natural Law," 33 U of Detroit L.J. 150, at pp. 178–181. Notes renumbered.

arbitrary power to give. Neither your lordships, nor the Commons, nor the whole legislature, have arbitrary power to give. Arbitrary power is a thing which no man can give. My lords, no man can govern himself by his own will; much less can he be governed by the will of others. We are all born —high as well as low—governors as well as governed—in subjection to one great, immutable, pre-existing law, a law prior to all our devices and all our conspiracies, paramount to our feelings, by which we are connected in the eternal frame of the universe, and out of which we cannot stir. This great law does not arise from our combinations and compacts; on the contrary, it gives to them all the sanction they can have. Every good and perfect gift is of God: all power is of God; and He who has given the power, and from whom alone it originates, will never suffer it to be corrupted. Therefore . . . if this great gift of government be the greatest and best that was ever given by God to mankind, will he suffer it to be the plaything of man, who would place his own feeble and ridiculous will on the throne of divine justice? It is not to be overturned by conquest; for by conquest, which is the more immediate designation of the hand of God, the conqueror succeeds to that alone which belonged to the sovereign before him. He cannot have absolute power by succession; he cannot have it by compact; for the people cannot covenant themselves out of their duty to their rights.[2]

To Burke, the norms of law and claims to arbitrary power are eternally at war. As Burke maintained that since the introduction of the Roman law into Britain, "the law of nature and nations (always a part of the law of England) came to be cultivated," Hastings' theory of sovereignty based upon arbitrary will contradicted the ethical norms of both the common law and Natural Law.

Hastings' claim that arbitrary power was normal in Asia implied there was no universal law of just conduct on essential principles, as taught by the Natural Law. Burke's rejection of this claim reaffirmed the Natural Law:

> This gentleman has formed a geographical morality, by which the duties of men in public and private stations are not to be governed by their relation to the great Governor of the universe, and by their relation to one another, but by climates. After you have crossed the equinoxial line, all the virtues die. . . . Against this geographical morality I do protest, and declare therefore, that Mr. Hastings shall not screen himself under it, because . . . the laws of morality are the same everywhere; and actions that are stamped with the character of peculation, extortion, oppression and barbarity in England, are so in Asia, and the world over.[3]

WIGHTMAN v. WIGHTMAN

Chancery Court of New York, 1820.
4 Johnson Chancery 343.

THE CHANCELLOR [KENT]. The fact of insanity of the plaintiff, at the time of the marriage, as charged in the bill, and the fact that the parties have never since lived together, or in any manner cohabited with each other, are proved to my satisfaction. It follows, as a necessary consequence, from these facts, that

[2] Speeches, IV, pp. 357–368.

[3] Ibid. IV, p. 354.

the marriage was null and void, from the beginning, by reason of the want of capacity in the plaintiff to contract, and has never since obtained any validity, because the plaintiff has never, since the return of her lucid interval, ratified or consummated it.

It is too plain a proposition to be questioned, that idiots and lunatics are incapable of entering into the matrimonial contract. In Morrison's case, before the Delegates, (cited in 1 Bl.Com. 439, and 1 Collinson on Lunacy, 554.) it was held, that the marriage of a lunatic, not being in a lucid interval, was absolutely void. I cite this case, not so much for the rule which it declares, as to show, that though such marriages be, *ipso facto,* void, yet that it is proper that there should be a judicial decision to that effect, by some Court of competent jurisdiction; and that, in England, the *Spiritual* Court is the appropriate tribunal. * * *

The fitness and propriety of a judicial decision, pronouncing the nullity of such a marriage, is very apparent, and is equally conducive to good order and decorum, and to the peace and conscience of the party. The only question, then, is, to what Court does the jurisdiction of such a case belong? There must be a tribunal existing with us competent to investigate such a charge, and to afford the requisite relief; and the power, I apprehend, must reside in this Court, which has not only an exclusive jurisdiction over cases of lunacy, but over matrimonial causes. The Chancery powers, in cases of lunacy, have never been applied to this case, because, there existed in England, another and peculiar jurisdiction for the case; but as such a jurisdiction does not exist here, the case seems to belong, incidently to the more general jurisdiction of this Court over those subjects. * * *

For the more full examination of this very interesting point of jurisdiction, let us suppose the abominable case of a marriage between parent and child, or other persons in the lineal or ascending and descending line, is there no Court that can listen to the voice of nature and reason, and sustain a suit *instituted purposely* to declare such a marriage void? If a man marry his mother, or his sister, they are husband and wife, say the old cases, until a divorce, and the marriage be judicially dissolved. [Citations.] Are the principles of natural law, and of christian duty, to be left unheeded and inoperative, because we have no Ecclesiastical Courts recognised by law, as specially charged with the cognisance of such matters? * * * I apprehend, then, that the power is necessarily cast upon this Court, which has, by statute, the sole jurisdiction over the marriage contract in certain specified cases. The Legislature has, in that respect, pointed to this Court as the proper organ of such a jurisdiction.

We are placed in a singular situation, in this state, and, probably, one unexampled in the christian world, since we have no statute regulating marriage, or prescribing the solemnities of it, or defining the forbidden degrees. It remains to be settled, not only where the jurisdiction, in some of these cases, resides, but what are the sound and binding principles of common law, under which that jurisdiction is to be exercised.

It was said by Vaughan, Ch. J., in Harrison v. Buswell, (Vaug. 206. 2 Vent. 9. S.C.) in delivering the opinion, which he declared to be given upon consultation with all the judges of England, that by the ancient common law, some marriages were within forbidden degrees, and unlawful, and that the cognisance of such questions belonged to the Spiritual Courts.

But he observed, that if it were not for the statutes of Hen. VIII., (and which we have not re-enacted,) it would be difficult to prove, that they were civilly bound by the Levitical degrees, in respect to the lawfulness of marriage connections, unless the prohibition was, also, clearly dictated by the natural law. He held, that marriages, in the ascending and descending line, as between parents and children, were monstrous connections, and repugnant to the law of nature, and that, so far, the Levitical was a moral, as contradistinguished from a positive, prohibition to the Jews, and binding upon all mankind.

Divorces ***a vinculo,*** says Lord Coke, (1 Inst. 235. a.) are *causa metus, causa impotentiæ, causa affinitatis, causa consanguinitatis,* & c. & c. * * * The principles of canonical jurisprudence, and the rules of the common law, are the same, in respect to some of those strong instances which I have mentioned, and there must be a tribunal to apply them. If it were otherwise, there would be a most deplorable and distressing imperfection in the administration of justice.

Besides the case of lunacy, now before me, I have, hypothetically, mentioned the case of a marriage between persons in the direct lineal line of consanguinity, as clearly unlawful by the law of the land, independent of any church canon, or of any statute prohibition. That such a marriage is criminal and void by the Law of Nature, is a point universally conceded. And, by the Law of Nature, I understand those fit and just rules of conduct which the Creator has prescribed to Man, as a dependent and social being; and which are to be ascertained from the deductions of right reason, though they may be more precisely known, and more explicitly declared by Divine Revelation. There is one other case, in which the marriage would be equally void, *causa consanguinitatis,* and that is the case of brother and sister; and, since it naturally arises, in the consideration of this subject, I will venture to add a few incidental observations. I am aware, that when we leave the lineal line, and come to the relation by blood or affinity in the collateral line, it is not so easy to ascertain the exact point at which the Natural Law has ceased to discountenance the union. Though there may be some difference in the theories of different writers on the Law of Nature, in regard to this subject, yet the general current of authority, and the practice of civilized nations, and certainly, of the whole christian world, have condemned the connection in the second case which has been supposed, as grossly indecent, immoral, and incestuous, and inimical to the purity and happiness of families, and as forbidden by the Law of Nature. (Grotius de Jure, & c. lib. 2. c. 5. s. 13. Puffend. de Jure Gent. lib. 6. c. 1. s. 34. Id. de off. Hom. lib. 2. c. 2. s. 8. Heinec. Op. tom. 8. pars 2. p. 203. Taylor's Elem.Civ.Law, 326. Montesq.Esq. des Loix, liv. 26. c. 14. Payley's [Paley] Moral Philosophy, b. 3. part 3. c. 5.) We, accordingly, find, such connections expressly prohibited in different Codes. (Dig. lib. 23. tit. 2. 18. lib. 23. tit. 2. l. 14. s. 2. lib. 45. tit. 1. l. 35. s. 1. Just.Inst. lib. 1. tit. 10. De Nuptiis. Vinnius, h. t. Heinecc. ubi supra. Code Civile de France, n. 161, 162, 163, 164. Inst. of Menu, by Sir William Jones, c. 3. s. 5. Staunton's Ta-Tsing-Leu-Lee, s. 107, 108. Sale's Koran, c. 4. Marsden's Sumatra, p. 194. 221.) And whatever may have been the practice of some ancient nations, originating, as Montesquieu observes, in the madness of superstition, the objection to such marriages, is undoubtedly, founded in reason and nature. It grows out of the institution of families, and the rights and duties, habits, and affections, flowing from that relation, and which may justly be considered as part of the Law of our Nature, as *rational* and *social* beings. Marriages among such near relations, would not only lead to domestic licentiousness, but by blending in one object, duties and feelings incompatible with each other, would perplex and confound the duties, habits, and affections proceeding from the family state, impair the perception and corrupt the purity of moral taste, and do violence to the moral sentiments of mankind. Indeed, we might infer the sense of mankind, and the dictates of reason and nature, from the language of horror and detestation in which such incestuous connexions have been reprobated and condemned in all ages. (Plato de Leg. lib. 8. Cic.Orat. pro Mil. 27. Hermion, in Eurip.Androm. v. 175. Byblis.Ovid.Met. lib. 9. Tacit.Ann. lib. 12. c. 4. Vell.Paterc. Hist. lib. 2. ch. 45. Corn.Nep.Excel. Imp.Prefat.) The general usage of mankind is sufficient to settle the question, if it were possible to have any doubt on the subject; and it must have proceeded from some strong uniform and natural principle. Prohibitions of the Natural Law are of absolute, uniform, and universal obligation. They become rules of the Common Law, which is founded in the common reason and acknowledged duty of mankind, sanctioned by immemorial usage, and, as such, are clearly binding. To this extent, then, I apprehend it to be within the power and within the duty of this Court, to enforce the prohibition. Such marriages should be declared void, as *contra bonos mores*. But as to the other collateral degrees, beyond brother and sister, I should incline to the intimation of the judges in Harrison v. Buswell, already cited, that as we have no statute on the subject, and no train of common law decisions independent of any statute authority, the Levitical degrees are not binding, as a rule of municipal obedience. Marriages out of the lineal line, and in the collateral line, beyond the degree of brothers and sisters, could not well be declared void, as against the first principles of society. The laws or usages of all the nations to whom I have referred, do, indeed, extend the prohibition to remoter degrees, but this is stepping out of the family circle; and I cannot put the prohibition on any other ground than positive institution. There is a great diversity of usage on this subject. *Neque teneo, neque dicta refello.* The limitation must be left, until the legislature thinks proper to make some provision in the case, to the injunctions of religion, and to the control of manners and opinion.

I have been led further than I, at first, intended, by these remarks, which have been made merely by way of argument, and in illustration of the question touching the power and duty of the Court to declare void the marriage of the lunatic in the case before me. I trust I have shown that there must exist such a power for this and other cases; and I, also, trust that this Court will never be under the painful necessity of making a more solemn and direct application of the doctrine.

I shall, accordingly, declare the marriage null and void, and that the parties are free from the obligations of marriage with each other.

Decree accordingly.

ILLUSTRATIONS OF THE *TAO*

THE following illustrations of the Natural Law are collected from such sources as come readily to the hand of one who is not a professional historian. The list makes no pretence of completeness. It will be noticed that writers such as Locke and Hooker, who wrote within the Christian tradition, are quoted side by side with the New Testament. This would, of course, be absurd if I were trying to collect independent testimonies to the *Tao*. But (1) I am not trying to *prove* its validity by the argument from common consent. Its validity cannot be deduced. For those who do not perceive its rationality, even universal consent could not prove it. (2) The idea of collecting *independent* testimonies presupposes that 'civilizations' have arisen in the world independently of one another; or even that humanity has had several independent emergences on this planet. The biology and anthropology involved in such an assumption are extremely doubtful. It is by no means certain that there has ever (in the sense required) been more than one civilization in all history. It is at least arguable that every civilization we find has been derived from another civilization and, in the last resort, from a single centre—'carried' like an infectious disease or like the Apostolical succession.

I. THE LAW OF GENERAL BENEFICENCE

(*a*) *Negative*

'I have not slain men.' (Ancient Egyptian. From the Confession of the Righteous Soul, 'Book of the Dead.' v. *Encyclopedia of Religion and Ethics* [=*ERE*], vol. v, p. 478.)

'Do not murder.' (Ancient Jewish. Exodus xx. 13.)

'Terrify not men or God will terrify thee.' (Ancient Egyptian. Precepts of Ptahhetep. H. R. Hall, *Ancient History of Near East*, p. 133 n.)

'In Nástrond (= Hell) I saw . . . murderers.' (Old Norse. *Volospá* 38, 39.)

'I have not brought misery upon my fellows. I have not made the beginning of every day laborious in the sight of him who worked for me.' (Ancient Egyptian. Confession of Righteous Soul. *ERE* v. 478.)

'I have not been grasping.' (Ancient Egyptian. Ibid.)

'Who meditates oppression, his dwelling is overturned.' (Babylonian. *Hymn to Samaš*. *ERE* v. 445.)

'He who is cruel and calumnious has the character of a cat.' (Hindu. Laws of Manu. Janet, *Histoire de la Science Politique*, vol. i, p. 6.)

'Slander not.' (Babylonian. *Hymn to Sama*. *ERE* v. 445.)

'Thou shalt not bear false witness against thy neighbour.' (Ancient Jewish. Exodus xx. 16.)

'Utter not a word by which anyone could be wounded.' (Hindu. Janet, p. 7.)

'Has he . . . driven an honest man from his family? broken up a well cemented clan?' (Babylonian. List of Sins from incantation tablets. *ERE* v. 446.)

'I have not caused hunger. I have not caused weeping.' (Ancient Egyptian. *ERE* v. 478.)

'Never do to others what you would not like them to do to you.' (Ancient Chinese. *Analects of Confucius*, trans. A. Waley, xv. 23; cf. xii. 2.)

'Thou shalt not hate thy brother in thy heart.' (Ancient Jewish. Leviticus xix. 17.)

'He whose heart is in the smallest degree set upon goodness will dislike no one.' (Ancient Chinese. *Analects*, iv. 4.)

(*b*) *Positive*

'Nature urges that a man should wish human society to exist and should wish to enter it.' (Roman. Cicero, *De Officiis*, I. iv.)

'By the fundamental Law of Nature Man [is] to be preserved as much as possible.' (Locke, *Treatises of Civil Govt.* ii. 3.)

'When the people have multiplied, what next should be done for them? The Master said, Enrich them. Jan Ch'iu said, When one has enriched them, what next should be done for them? The Master said, Instruct them.' (Ancient Chinese. *Analects*, xiii. 9.)

'Speak kindness . . . show good will.' (Babylonian. *Hymn to Samaš. ERE* v. 445.)

'Men were brought into existence for the sake of men that they might do one another good.' (Roman. Cicero, *De Off.* I. vii.)

'Man is man's delight.' (Old Norse. *Hávamál* 47.)

'He who is asked for alms should always give.' (Hindu. Janet, i. 7.)

'What good man regards any misfortune as no concern of his?' (Roman. Juvenal xv. 140.)

'I am a man: nothing human is alien to me.' (Roman. Terence, *Heaut. Tim.*)

'Love thy neighbour as thyself.' (Ancient Jewish. Leviticus xix. 18.)

'Love the stranger as thyself.' (Ancient Jewish. Ibid. 33, 34.)

'Do to men what you wish men to do to you.' (Christian. Matt. vii. 12.)

II. The Law of Special Beneficence

'It is upon the trunk that a gentleman works. When that is firmly set up, the Way grows. And surely proper behaviour to parents and elder brothers is the trunk of goodness.' (Ancient Chinese. *Analects*, i. 2.)

'Brothers shall fight and be each others' bane.' (Old Norse. Account of the Evil Age before the World's end, *Volospá* 45.)

'Has he insulted his elder sister?' (Babylonian. List of Sins. *ERE* v. 446.)

'You will see them take care of their kindred [and] the children of their friends . . . never reproaching them in the least.' (Redskin. Le Jeune, quoted *ERE* v. 437.)

'Love thy wife studiously. Gladden her heart all thy life long.' (Ancient Egyptian. *ERE* v. 481.)

'Nothing can ever change the claims of kinship for a right thinking man.' (Anglo-Saxon. *Beowulf*, 2600.)

'Did not Socrates love his own children, though he did so as a free man and as one not forgetting that the gods have the first claim on our friendship?' (Greek. Epictetus, iii. 24.)

'Natural affection is a thing right and according to Nature.' (Greek. Ibid. I. xi.)

'I ought not to be unfeeling like a statue but should fulfil both my natural and artificial relations, as a worshipper, a son, a brother, a father, and a citizen.' (Greek, Ibid. III. ii.)

'This first I rede thee: be blameless to thy kindred. Take no vengeance even though they do thee wrong.' (Old Norse. *Sigrdrifumál*, 22.)

'Is it only the sons of Atreus who love their wives? For every good man, who is right-minded, loves and cherishes his own.' (Greek. Homer, *Iliad*, ix. 340.)

'The union and fellowship of men will be best preserved if each receives from us the more kindness in proportion as he is more closely connected with us.' (Roman. Cicero, *De Off.* I. xvi.)

'Part of us is claimed by our country, part by our parents, part by our friends.' (Roman. Ibid. I. vii.)

'If a ruler . . . compassed the salvation of the whole state, surely you would call him Good? The Master said, It would no longer be a matter of "Good." He would without doubt be a Divine Sage.' (Ancient Chinese. *Analects*, vi. 28.)

'Has it escaped you that, in the eyes of gods and good men, your native land deserves from you more honour, worship, and reverence than your mother and father and all your ancestors? That you should give a softer answer to its anger than to a father's anger? That if you cannot persuade it to alter its mind you must obey it in all quietness, whether it binds you or beats you or sends you to a war where you may get wounds or death?' (Greek. Plato, *Crito*, 51 A, B.)

'If any provide not for his own, and specially for those of his own house, he hath denied the faith.' (Christian. I Tim. v. 8.)

'Put them in mind to obey magistrates.' . . . 'I exhort that prayers be made for kings and all that are in authority.' (Christian. Tit. iii. 1 and I Tim. ii. 1, 2.)

III. Duties to Parents, Elders, Ancestors

'Your father is an image of the Lord of Creation, your mother an image of the Earth. For him who fails to honour them, every work of piety is in vain. This is the first duty.' (Hindu. Janet, i. 9.)

'Has he despised Father and Mother?' (Babylonian. List of Sins. *ERE* v. 446.)

'I was a staff by my Father's side. . . . I went in and out at his command.' (Ancient Egyptian. Confession of the Righteous Soul. *ERE* v. 481.)

'Honour thy Father and thy Mother.' (Ancient Jewish. Exodus xx. 12.)

'To care for parents.' (Greek. List of duties in Epictetus, III. vii.)

'Children, old men, the poor, and the sick, should be considered as the lords of the atmosphere.' (Hindu. Janet, i. 8.)

'Rise up before the hoary head and honour the old man.' (Ancient Jewish. Lev. xix. 32.)

'I tended the old man, I gave him my staff.' (Ancient Egyptian. *ERE* v. 481.)

'You will see them take care . . . of old men.' (Redskin. Le Jeune, quoted *ERE* v. 437.)

'I have not taken away the oblations of the blessed dead.' (Ancient Egyptian. Confession of the Righteous Soul. *ERE* v. 478.)

'When proper respect towards the dead is shown at the end and continued after they are far away, the moral force (*tê*) of a people has reached its highest point.' (Ancient Chinese. *Analects*, i. 9.)

IV. Duties to Children and Posterity

'Children, the old, the poor, etc. should be considered as lords of the atmosphere.' (Hindu. Janet, i. 8.)

'To marry and to beget children.' (Greek. List of duties. Epictetus, III. vii.)

'Can you conceive an Epicurean commonwealth? . . . What will happen? Whence is the population to be kept up? Who will educate them? Who will be Director of Adolescents? Who will be Director of Physical Training? What will be taught?' (Greek. Ibid.)

'Nature produces a special love of offspring' and 'To live according to Nature is the supreme good.' (Roman. Cicero, *De Off*. I. iv, and *De Legibus*, I. xxi.)

'The second of these achievements is no less glorious than the first; for while the first did good on one occasion, the second will continue to benefit the state forever.' (Roman. Cicero, *De Off*. I. xxii.)

'Great reverence is owed to a child.' (Roman. Juvenal, xiv. 47.)

'The Master said, Respect the young.' (Ancient Chinese. *Analects*, ix. 22.)

'The killing of the women and more especially of the young boys and girls who are to go to make up the future strength of the people, is the saddest part . . . and we feel it very sorely.' (Redskin. Account of the Battle of Wounded Knee. *ERE* v. 432.)

V. The Law of Justice

(*a*) *Sexual Justice*

'Has he approached his neighbour's wife?' (Babylonian. List of Sins. *ERE* v. 446.)

'Thou shalt not commit adultery.' (Ancient Jewish. Exodus xx. 14.)

'I saw in Nástrond (= Hell) . . . beguilers of others' wives.' (Old Norse. *Volospá* 38, 39.)

(b). Honesty

'Has he drawn false boundaries?' (Babylonian. List of Sins. *ERE* v. 446.)

'To wrong, to rob, to cause to be robbed.' (Babylonian. Ibid.)

'I have not stolen.' (Ancient Egyptian. Confession of Righteous Soul. *ERE* v. 478.)

'Thou shalt not steal.' (Ancient Jewish. Exodus xx. 15.)

'Choose loss rather than shameful gains.' (Greek. Chilon Fr. 10. Diels.)

'Justice is the settled and permanent intention of rendering to each man his rights.' (Roman. Justinian, *Institutions*, I. i.)

'If the native made a "find" of any kind (e.g. a honey tree) and marked it, it was thereafter safe for him, as far as his own tribesmen were concerned, no matter how long he left it.' (Australian Aborigines. *ERE* v. 441.)

'The first point of justice is that none should do any mischief to another unless he has first been attacked by the other's wrongdoing. The second is that a man should treat common property as common property, and private property as his own. There is no such thing as private property by nature, but things have become private either through prior occupation (as when men of old came into empty territory) or by conquest, or law, or agreement, or stipulation, or casting lots.' (Roman. Cicero, *De Off.* I. vii.)

(c) Justice in Court, &c.

'Whoso takes no bribe . . . well pleasing is this to Samaš.' (Babylonian. *ERE* v. 445.)

'I have not traduced the slave to him who is set over him.' (Ancient Egyptian. Confession of Righteous Soul. *ERE* v. 478.)

'Thou shalt not bear false witness against thy neighbour.' (Ancient Jewish. Exodus xx. 16.)

'Regard him whom thou knowest like him whom thou knowest not.' (Ancient Egyptian. *ERE* v. 482.)

'Do no unrighteousness in judgement. You must not consider the fact that one party is poor nor the fact that the other is a great man.' (Ancient Jewish. Leviticus xix. 15.)

VI. The Law of Good Faith and Veracity

'A sacrifice is obliterated by a lie and the merit of alms by an act of fraud.' (Hindu. Janet, i. 6.)

'Whose mouth, full of lying, avails not before thee: thou burnest their utterance.' (Babylonian. Hymn to Samaš. *ERE* v. 445.)

'With his mouth was he full of *Yea*, in his heart full of *Nay?*' (Babylonian. *ERE* v. 446.)

'I have not spoken falsehood.' (Ancient Egyptian. Confession of Righteous Soul. *ERE* v. 478.)

'I sought no trickery, nor swore false oaths.' (Anglo-Saxon. *Beowulf*, 2738.)

'The Master said, Be of unwavering good faith.' (Ancient Chinese. *Analects*, viii. 13.)

'In Nástrond (= Hell) I saw the perjurers.' (Old Norse. *Volospá* 39.)

'Hateful to me as are the gates of Hades is that man who says one thing, and hides another in his heart.' (Greek. Homer. *Iliad*, ix. 312.)

'The foundation of justice is good faith.' (Roman. Cicero, *De Off*. I. vii.)

'[The gentleman] must learn to be faithful to his superiors and to keep promises.' (Ancient Chinese. *Analects*, I. 8.)

'Anything is better than treachery.' (Old Norse. *Hávamál* 124.)

VII. The Law of Mercy

'The poor and the sick should be regarded as lords of the atmosphere.' (Hindu. Janet, i. 8.)

'Whoso makes intercession for the weak, well pleasing is this to Samaš' (Babylonian. *ERE* v. 445.)

'Has he failed to set a prisoner free?' (Babylonian. List of Sins. *ERE* v. 446.)

'I have given bread to the hungry, water to the thirsty, clothes to the naked, a ferry boat to the boatless.' (Ancient Egyptian. *ERE* v. 478.)

'One should never strike a woman; not even with a flower.' (Hindu. Janet, i. 8.)

'There, Thor, you got disgrace, when you beat women.' (Old Norse. *Hárbarthsljóth* 38.)

'In the Dalebura tribe a woman, a cripple from birth, was carried about by the tribes-people in turn until her death at the age of sixty-six.' . . . 'They never desert the sick.' (Australian Aborigines. *ERE* v. 443.)

'You will see them take care of . . . widows, orphans, and old men, never reproaching them.' (Redskin. *ERE* v. 439.)

'Nature confesses that she has given to the human race the tenderest hearts, by giving us the power to weep. This is the best part of us.' (Roman. Juvenal, xv. 131.)

'They said that he had been the mildest and gentlest of the kings of the world.' (Anglo-Saxon. Praise of the hero in *Beowulf*, 3180.)

'When thou cuttest down thine harvest . . . and hast forgot a sheaf . . . thou shalt not go again to fetch it: it shall be for the stranger, for the fatherless, and for the widow.' (Ancient Jewish. Deut. xxiv. 19.)

VIII. The Law of Magnanimity

A.

'There are two kinds of injustice: the first is found in those who do an injury, the second in those who fail to protect another from injury when they can.' (Roman. Cicero, *De Off.* I. vii.)

'Men always knew that when force and injury was offered they might be defenders of themselves; they knew that howsoever men may seek their own commodity, yet if this were done with injury unto others it was not to be suffered, but by all men and by all good means to be withstood.' (English. Hooker, *Laws of Eccl. Polity*, I. ix. 4.)

'To take no notice of a violent attack is to strengthen the heart of the enemy. Vigour is valiant, but cowardice is vile.' (Ancient

Egyptian. The Pharaoh Senusert III. cit. H. R. Hall, *Ancient History of the Near East*, p. 161.)

'They came to the fields of joy, the fresh turf of the Fortunate Woods and the dwellings of the Blessed . . . here was the company of those who had suffered wounds fighting for their fatherland.' (Roman. Virgil, *Aen.* vi. 638–9, 660.)

'Courage has got to be harder, heart the stouter, spirit the sterner, as our strength weakens. Here lies our lord, cut to pieces, our best man in the dust. If anyone thinks of leaving this battle, he can howl forever.' (Anglo-Saxon. *Maldon*, 312.)

'Praise and imitate that man to whom, while life is pleasing, death is not grievous.' (Stoic. Seneca, *Ep.* liv.)

'The Master said, Love learning and if attacked be ready to die for the Good Way.' (Ancient Chinese. *Analects*, viii. 13.)

B.

'Death is to be chosen before slavery and base deeds.' (Roman. Cicero, *De Off.* I. xxiii.)

'Death is better for every man than life with shame.' (Anglo-Saxon. *Beowulf*, 2890.)

'Nature and Reason command that nothing uncomely, nothing effeminate, nothing lascivious be done or thought.' (Roman. Cicero, *De Off.* I. iv.)

'We must not listen to those who advise us "being men to think human thoughts, and being mortal to think mortal thoughts," but must put on immortality as much as is possible and strain every nerve to live according to that best part of us, which, being small in bulk, yet much more in its power and honour surpasses all else.' (Ancient Greek. Aristotle, *Eth. Nic.* 1177 B.)

'The soul then ought to conduct the body, and the spirit of our minds the soul. This is therefore the first Law, whereby the highest power of the mind requireth obedience at the hands of all the rest.' (Hooker, op. cit. I. viii. 6.)

'Let him not desire to die, let him not desire to live, let him wait for his time . . . let him patiently bear hard words, entirely abstaining from bodily pleasures.' (Ancient Indian. Laws of Manu. *ERE* ii. 98.)

'He who is unmoved, who has restrained his senses . . . is said to be devoted. As a flame in a windless place that flickers not, so is the devoted.' (Ancient Indian. *Bhagavad gita. ERE* ii. 90.)

C.

'Is not the love of Wisdom a practice of death?' (Ancient Greek. Plato, *Phaedo*, 81 A.)

'I know that I hung on the gallows for nine nights, wounded with the spear as a sacrifice to Odin, myself offered to Myself.' (Old Norse. *Hávamál*, l. 10 in *Corpus Poeticum Boreale;* stanza 139 in Hildebrand's *Lieder der Älteren Edda.* 1922.)

'Verily, verily I say to you unless a grain of wheat falls into the earth and dies, it remains alone, but if it dies it bears much fruit. He who loves his life loses it.' (Christian. John xii. 24, 25.)

NATURAL LAW

AN INTRODUCTION TO LEGAL PHILOSOPHY

A. P. d'Entrèves
MA, D.PHIL
Professor of Political Theory in the University of Turin
and formerly Serena Professor of Italian Studies
in the University of Oxford

HUTCHINSON UNIVERSITY LIBRARY
LONDON

THE IDEAL LAW

It has been the purpose of this enquiry to show that the theory of natural law provided answers to many problems which still face the modern legal philosopher. No assessment of that theory would, however, be complete without taking into account what may well be said to constitute its most constant feature all through the ages: the assertion of the possibility of testing the validity of all laws by referring them to an ultimate measure, to an ideal law which can be known and appraised with an even greater measure of certainty than all existing legislation. Natural law is the outcome of man's quest for an absolute standard of justice. It is based upon a particular conception of the relationship between the ideal and the real. It is a dualist theory which presupposes a rift, though not necessarily a contrast, between what is and what ought to be.

This must not be taken to mean that the doctrine of natural law is at heart a revolutionary doctrine. Nothing indeed would be more remote from the truth. If natural law played a revolutionary part at certain epochs of Western history, it is equally true that, during most of its age-long development, the doctrine was limited to a mildly progressive, and at times to a frankly conservative function. The recognition of the existence of an ideal law did not necessarily imply that positive law should be overruled by it in cases of conflict. Natural law could serve as well to support revolutionary claims as to justify an existing legal order. It could even lead to the glorification of a particular system of law, as when Roman law, after its reception on the Continent as the 'common' law of Europe, came to be considered as the *ratio scripta*, or as when Sir Edward Coke described the English Common law as 'nothing else but reason'.[1] Justice Holmes humorously described this particular outcome of natural law by remarking:

> It is not enough for the knight of romance that you agree that his lady is a very nice girl—if you do not admit that she is the best that God ever made or will make, you must fight. There is in all men a demand for the speculative, so much so that the poor devil who has no other way of reaching it obtains it by getting drunk. It seems to me that this demand is at the bottom of the philosopher's effort to prove that truth is absolute and of the jurist's search for criteria of universal validity which he collects under the head of natural law.
>
> (Holmes,'Natural Law' in *Harvard Law Review*, 1918)

This is not a very charitable judgment: but there is no doubt that natural law was the *belle dame sans merci* who inspired the crusading spirit of old-time jurisprudence. That spirit has gone. It has given way to a realistic approach which is in keeping with an age of prosaic undertakings. The study of the ideal law is no longer conceived as being of any relevance to the lawyer. 'The juridical science of the nineteenth and twentieth century expressly declares itself incapable of drawing the problem of justice into the scope of its enquiries' (Kelsen). It actually prides itself on being able to master and to construct into a system any given legal material without resorting to the delusion of natural law. The abandonment of natural law marks the rise of modern jurisprudence. This is the fundamental fact which we must keep in mind in order to understand, if only from a negative angle, what natural law ultimately stood for. It may well be that after we have examined the achievements and limitations of modern jurisprudence, the case for natural law may once again be assessed in a positive manner.

The rise of modern jurisprudence is marked by the abandonment of natural law and by a new or 'positive' approach to legal experience. But the notion of natural law as the embodiment of justice and as the ultimate ground of the validity of all laws had been criticised long before the advent of positive jurisprudence. Nor can the new approach be described as the outcome of any particular doctrinal standpoint. The word 'positivism', if one cares to use it in this connection, can indicate only an attitude rather than a definite philosophical creed. Indeed, the oldest argument

[1] *The Institutes of the Laws of England*, pt. I (1628).

against natural justice is the sceptical argument. It goes back to the very beginnings of speculative thought. It has a long history which stretches down from the Sophists to the present day. I need only refer the reader, for a classical treatment of the subject, to Hume's *Treatise of Human Nature*, book II, part ii, or to the section in Cicero's *Republic* (III, vi–xx), where Carneades' argument is set forth with sufficient vigour and clearness to remind us how little there is that can be called entirely new in legal and political philosophy.

Modern or positive jurisprudence is not necessarily based upon scepticism, nor does it imply a denial that the problem of justice exists. Modern jurists may be willing to leave the discussion of the ultimate reason why law should be regarded as binding to the legal philosopher, without taking a definite stand about the existence of natural law. Nor do they accept as a matter of course the 'monist' view of the coincidence of the ideal and the real which, as we have seen in a preceding chapter, consecrated the law of the State as the embodiment of moral values. All they do is to put the problem of the ideal or natural law, as it were, within brackets. However influenced they may have been or still are by one or other philosophical current, their implicit or explicit philosophy is not the determining factor. They are indeed anxious to convince us that theirs is not a philosophical, but a 'scientific' concern.

This, I understand, is apparent among English jurists. To the foreign observer English jurisprudence—with some notable exceptions—may still seem to have a flavour of utilitarianism as a distinctive national characteristic. And indeed, if we think of Austin, we may well believe that the cradle of modern English jurisprudence was utilitarian philosophy. But Austin himself, if I am not mistaken, was careful not to tie his notion of jurisprudence to any particular philosophical assumption. He actually avoided any final pronouncement on the possibility of evaluating legal experience from a standpoint other than that of the 'analytical' jurist. Of general jurisprudence he wrote:

> It is concerned directly with principles and distinctions which are common to various systems of particular or positive law; and which each of these various systems inevitably involves, let it be worthy of praise or blame, or let it accord or not with an assumed measure or test.
> (Austin, *Lectures*, Campbell's ed., I, 33)

He seems clearly to admit that 'the goodness or badness of

laws' might be tried 'by the test of utility (or by any of the various tests which divide the opinions of mankind)'. He contented himself with declaring that with this kind of undertaking general jurisprudence 'has no immediate concern'. The problem of the ideal law is neither denied nor declared insoluble. It is simply put within brackets as irrelevant to the task of the jurist.

Very similar remarks can be made about Continental jurisprudence. This was, as is well known, the outcome of the 'Historical school', and it is significant that the standard-bearer of that school—F. C. von Savigny (1779–1861)—was also the founder, or at any rate the most authoritative exponent, of the systematic treatment of law which still obtains general recognition and application in the law-schools of the Continent. Now the Historical school—the programme of which was laid down in Savigny's famous book, published in 1814, *Of the Vocation of Our Age for Legislation and Jurisprudence*—meant, if not a new philosophical theory of law, at least the expression in the field of law of a great philosophical revolution. It was an aspect as well as a result of the great tide of Romanticism which, foreshadowed in the eighteenth century, swept Europe as a counterblow to the French revolution.

As its name clearly indicates, the Historical school was essentially a vindication of growth and development against the abstract rationalism which had become the distinguishing mark of natural law theory in its last stage of development. It stressed that the origin and the explanation of legal phenomena must not be sought in the individual, but in collective life; that law is the product of the particular genius of each nation (*Volksgeist*); that legal experience should not be arrested and as it were crystallised in statutes and codes, but allowed to grow and bear fruit in its full vigour and vitality.

How then can it be explained that the untiring advocate of the historical study of law should also have been the exponent of a systematic treatment which seems to be mainly inspired by the rationalist quest for order, coherence and unity? Savigny's *System of Present-day Roman Law* (1840–49) brought to perfection a method which had long been applied, in Germany and elsewhere, in the study of the common (Roman) law of Continental Europe. It added little or nothing to the pattern that the great *Pandektisten* had elaborated, which had come to be considered as the necessary introductory or 'general' part (*Allgemeiner Teil*) of jurisprudence. Under that heading the notions of law, objective and subjective right, juridical relationship, personality, facts, things and so forth, had been abstractly assessed and defined. These notions have remained down to the present day the elements of legal study and training on the Continent.

Now it might well be questioned whether the acceptance by Savigny of any of these abstract categories was not in contradiction to the notion of law which he championed. These categories were derived from the essentially individualistic conception of law which had inspired the Continental law-schools for centuries. Surely they needed recasting if they were to be fitted to a new conception of law as the expression of the organic life of society. It must also be remembered that the final outcome of the Historical school, as Sir Ernest Barker has pointed out,[1] was a vindication of 'national' law (in the particular case of Germany, of German law) as against Roman law, the impact of which was bound to be more and more resented as alien. The 'Germanist' doctrine of group-personality, the 'organic theory of the State', the struggle against individualism in the field of public and even of private law, all trace their beginnings to the Historical school.

But the point which must here receive our attention is the paradox of the parallel birth of the historical interpretation of law and of modern, positive jurisprudence. The Historical school had begun by stressing the growth and development of law, it ended by fostering its scientific study. It had begun with an apology for history. It ended with an apology for jurisprudence. The paradox is worth considering more closely, for it is one of the crucial episodes in the rise of modern juristic thought, and it throws light upon its fundamental nature.

The explanation of the riddle can be found only in the correct interpretation of Savigny's intentions, as well as of the real aims and purposes of the historical doctrine. Already in the *Vocation* Savigny had pointed out that the life of law is, as it were, twofold. Law has a 'political' life inasmuch as it expresses the realities of a given social structure. But law has also a 'technical' life, which begins the very moment it undergoes its 'scientific' elaboration at the hands of the jurist.[2] Law is no doubt the product of the *Volkgeist* and the outcome of history. But it can be assessed and appraised only through the labours of the professional lawyer.

The complete change of front from the old natural law approach

[1] Introduction to Gierke, *Natural Law and the Theory of Society*, pp. liv–lv.
[2] F. C. von Savigny, *Of the Vocation of Our Age for Legislation and Jurisprudence*, trans. Hayward, 1831, pp. 22–29, 62.

G

is here apparent. The rationalist school had led to an exaltation of the law-giver as the agent for the realisation of justice. The Historical school led to an exaltation of the jurist as the interpreter of historical growth and development. But this does not mean that the followers of the Historical school intended to substitute historical growth and development for the notion of absolute justice. Its greatest representatives, such as Savigny, Puchta and Stahl, remained unshaken in their Christian belief in an order of justice based upon the existence of a transcendent God. They must not be mistaken for Hegelians. Theirs was at bottom a 'dualist' theory: they never accepted the fundamental assumption of Hegel's legal philosophy, that the ideal finds its revelation in history. The cult of history they had in common with all the Romantics. But historicism was a method to them, rather than a philosophy. They, too, were putting the ideal law within brackets. Jurisprudence was called in to fill the vacuum.

It filled it so well and so thoroughly that, for a time, the old quest for the ideal law seemed to have been written off from the tasks of the jurist and the lawyer. The achievement of nineteenth century jurisprudence is a great and positive one. The age of science produced a science of law worthy of its ambitions. Anyone who is acquainted with the immense amount of ingenuity which generation after generation of jurists spent in constructing the majestic edifice of modern jurisprudence, cannot easily believe that such labours could have been in vain.

To bring order, coherence and unity into the system of law, to provide the law-giver with a clear map of his province, the lawyer and the judge with a body of concepts which should enable them to perform their duties with the greatest amount of precision and ease: this was, for nearly a century, the distinguishing mark of legal theory on the Continent. And it is indeed on the Continent rather than in English-speaking countries that Austin's programme of a 'general jurisprudence' has been carried out to the full. 'As principles abstracted from positive systems are the subject of general jurisprudence, so is the exposition of such principles its exclusive or appropriate object.' German *Rechtwissenschaft*, with its relentless pursuit of an ever-increasing degree of systematic perfection and of formal abstraction, can and must be taken as the best illustration of the fate of legal theory after the spell of natural law had been broken.

This is not the place to discuss the character and value of legal science, or, if we may indeed identify the two terms, of modern jurisprudence: its claim, that is, to possess the character of a science, as well as the possibility of its universal application. These are not two different problems, but one: for indeed, if we admit the claim of jurisprudence to be 'the formal science of positive law'—as Holland defined it—I can see no reason why we should not admit that jurisprudence may be 'particular' or 'general' according to the greater or lesser degree of induction and generalisation which has been performed in the collection and elaboration of legal material. If jurisprudence is an empirical science, then clearly it is so from beginning to end, nor is there any substantial change, either in its methods or in its results, whether it restricts itself to the *Dogmatik* or scientific elaboration of a particular legal order, or whether it progresses to a 'general theory of law' (*Allgemeine Rechtslehre*) which 'takes up . . . several systems of law and seeks for legal institutions which have appeared in history on more than one occasion' (Stammler).

What I am concerned with here is a different question. It is the claim of modern jurisprudence to have entirely eliminated the problems which had for centuries been considered and discussed under the heading of the natural or ideal law, the claim to self-sufficiency, if I may so call it, of modern jurisprudence, viz., to provide the student of the law with the sufficient and necessary criteria for the understanding and interpretation of legal phenomena. In order to assess to what extent that claim is justified we must now examine the answer which modern jurisprudence has given to the problem of the validity of the laws which are the object of its study.

The existence of that problem was certainly never denied by the 'positive' jurist. On the contrary, it is because it purported to restrict itself only to the study of laws 'actually valid' that modern jurisprudence was led to lay all the emphasis on the adjective 'positive'. That term can have a meaning only as a term of contrast. 'There is no law but positive law', wrote Stahl;[1] natural law precepts 'possess neither the requisite definiteness nor the binding force of law'. But Bergbohm, the 'diligent tracker of natural law', was perfectly right to point out that, from the point of view of legal positivism, the very use of the adjective 'positive' with regard to law is nothing but a pleonasm.[2]

The real question was to determine which laws are sufficiently 'definite', or 'binding', or 'positive' to deserve the name of laws.

[1] F. J. Stahl, quot. by H. Rommen, *The Natural Law*, p. 117.
[2] K. Bergbohm, *Jurisprudenz und Rechtsphilosophie*, I, 1892, p. 49, 51 ff.

It is on this point that the difficulties began, and that the peculiarities of legal empiricism soon became apparent. It gradually dawned upon lawyers and jurists that the validity or 'positiveness' of law cannot consist, or at least cannot consist solely, in the mere fact of its enforcement. The use of force, or the possibility of its use, is only the outward or material aspect of positive law. From a strictly juridical or 'formal' point of view the validity of a particular law cannot depend upon its varying degree of effectiveness. It consists in the fact that that particular law belongs to a system which is singled out and recognised as the only positive and valid system.

That this system, to nineteenth-century jurists, was the system or legal order of the State, has only a relative importance. The formal or logical side of their argument is the side which calls for attention. To say that the positiveness of law derives from its belonging to a positive system is in fact only a different way of saying that the recognition of its validity as a law depends on the possibility of referring it back, directly or indirectly, to a common source from which all legal precepts ultimately proceed. This is what the jurists, borrowing an old term with which we are already acquainted, indicated under the name of sovereignty. Sovereignty became the sacred dogma of positive jurisprudence, because it was the condition of the positiveness of law. Sovereignty may be, and indeed is, a fact. But from the juridical angle it was also, and essentially, a formal criterion: the criterion which made it possible to recognise a rule or a body of rules as part of a positive order, and therefore to pronounce on their validity as laws.

Thus the restriction of all law to positive law and the quest for a systematic construction of the legal order went hand in hand. They are indeed the two fundamental aspects of modern jurisprudence. Its tendency to become more and more 'formal' was only a consequence of its purpose to be a 'positive' science, that is, to steer clear of any criterion of validity of law—such as natural law—extraneous to the system.

We have of late grown accustomed to consider this 'formal' character of jurisprudence as self-evident. I have no doubt that we are greatly indebted to the 'pure theory of law', developed by Kelsen and his school, for a sounder appreciation of the logical issues of the juristic method. But the process which led modern jurisprudence to an increasing degree of abstraction had long been at work. It is interesting to look back upon it and to see how the concepts which had at first provided the basis of positive jurisprudence were gradually transformed, as it were by an internal logic. The process is curiously reminiscent of the old discussions about the essence of law which have been examined in a preceding chapter.

Positive jurisprudence had started from the identification of law and command. It ended with the elimination of will from the field of law altogether. This is apparent not only in the sphere of 'public law', in the untiring efforts of 'classical' German jurisprudence (Jellinek, Laband, etc.) to construe the State as a *Rechtsstaat*. It is equally apparent in the sphere of 'private law', as anyone can easily gather who is acquainted with the great debate on the *Willenstheorie* which divided nineteenth-century jurists.

The tendency was to eliminate any intrinsic, original power of the will, whether of the State or of the individual. To admit such a power, it was argued, is nothing but a natural law proposition: for where can will derive its juridical value from except from law itself? Surely, if we admit, as Savigny admitted, a 'natural capacity' of the human person to set in motion legal consequences; or if we ascribe, as Windscheid ascribed, a 'creative force' to the individual will in laying down legal precepts, we deprive State sovereignty of its essential function as the ultimate source of all rules which have positive validity.

In turn, even sovereignty is a misnomer. It seems to indicate that the will of a man or of a body of men is endowed with some original legal value—a natural law proposition! From a purely juridical, that is, from a strictly 'formal' and 'positive' standpoint, it is clear that the will of this or that man or body of men is creative of law only because there is a superior law (the law of the constitution) which attributes to that will a juridical relevance.

The tendency among up-to-date writers is in fact to substitute some other expression for the word 'sovereignty', wherever it would have been used in the past. Thus we hear it now said that the legal order can be conceived only as 'complete' and 'exclusive'. Exclusive, because the recognition of a particular legal order as positive implies that the rules which compose it are, for the jurist, the only valid ones: all other rules are not properly laws but mere facts.[1] Complete, because the admission that there may be 'gaps' in the law is nothing but a delusion, which springs from the belief that there may be situations or facts 'intrinsically' juridical—a residue of natural law thinking. From a really 'positive' standpoint,

[1] This principle has been applied with remarkable success in the theory of Conflict of Laws, or Private International Law, as it is called on the Continent.

unless these situations or facts are given relevance by a law, they are, as far as the legal order is concerned, simply non-existent.

We seem to be forced to the conclusion that command is not the essential attribute of law. The function of law is to qualify, to provide, as it were, a term of reference for certain situations and facts by ascribing a particular meaning to them, or inserting them in a relation of condition and sequence. The widespread adoption of the word 'norm' in modern juristic terminology is, from this point of view, particularly significant. For that word does, it is true, involve the notion of an 'ought', but also and primarily that of a standard or model or pattern; and the 'injunctive' character is at any rate in no way essential to an 'ought' proposition. Thus, modern legal thought has been led to emphasise more and more the logical character of law, and to conceive of juridical categories as mere symbols or names for indicating the relevance of certain situations and facts from a given 'normative' angle. The parallel between law and language is ready to hand, as well as the comparison of jurisprudence and grammar.[1]

This description of the characteristics of modern legal thought may sound strange to English ears. The tendencies which I have described may perhaps be suspected as fundamentally alien. Jurisprudence on this side of the Channel has preserved a solid core of commonsense which has guarded it from the perils of over-abstraction. It may also be doubted whether all the conclusions of Continental juristic thinking are applicable to a type of legal experience such as that of the Common law, entirely different from the tradition of Roman law on the Continent.[2]

There is, however, one point which of late has attracted attention in England also. I would like to refer to it as one of the best illustrations of the final outcome of present-day legal theory, as well as one of the most carefully thought-out attempts to provide an answer to the problem of the validity of law which, as I have pointed out, was from the outset one of the inspiring motifs of positive jurisprudence. It is the notion of the 'basic norm', which Kelsen and his followers have stressed as the necessary presupposition for a systematic construction of the legal order. The notion is well known, and readily understood in the light of what has already been said about the logical issues of the juristic method.

[1] See below, pp. 114.
[2] For the 'typically English approach' to the problems of legal theory I need only refer the reader to Professor Goodhart's stimulating lecture, *English Contributions to the Philosophy of Law*, New York, 1949.

The 'basic norm' is, according to Kelsen, the condition of completeness and self-sufficiency in a given legal order—in other words, of its 'positiveness'. 'The basic norm of a legal order is the postulated ultimate rule according to which the norms of this order are established and annulled, receive and lose their validity.' 'The quest for the reason of validity of a norm is not—like the quest for the cause of an effect—a *regressus ad infinitum*; it is terminated by a highest norm which is the last ground of validity within the normative system.' In other words, the basic norm is the necessary hypothesis on which the jurist sets to work: his first and primary task is indeed that of discovering the common ground of validity in each and every norm or group of norms which constitute the system.

This, Kelsen maintains, is possible for any given legal material: for the determination of the basic norm 'implies no categorical statement as to the value of the method of law-making or of the person functioning as the positive legal authority; this value is a hypothetical assumption'. Thus the basic norm of national law in the modern sovereign State is that the commands of the sovereign (a man or a body of men) are to be obeyed; the basic norm of the international legal order is that *pacta sunt servanda*, and so forth. Each and every order will appear as a hierarchical system, every part of which derives from the basic norm its ultimate ground of validity.

I can see no serious objection to Kelsen's theory of the 'basic norm' as the condition of correct legal thinking. On the contrary, I think that the theory throws considerable light upon the real nature of jurisprudence. In grounding his whole construction upon a hypothetical premise, the jurist may well claim that he is doing nothing but what is done in all other empirical sciences. But what should always be borne in mind is that scientific constructions are based upon 'working' hypotheses. The fundamental task is therefore for the scientist to choose his hypothesis correctly. The moment it ceases to work, the question of rejecting it arises, and of superseding it with another and better one.

I find it difficult to see how the jurist who accepts the postulates of the 'pure theory of law' for what they are worth—as an admirable system of formal logic applied to the law[1]—can avoid asking himself some similar question. The basic norm of a national system of law—that the commands of the sovereign are to be obeyed—can have a meaning for the jurist (who will then be able to declare that the system is a positive system) only inasmuch as

[1] H. J. Laski, *Grammar of Politics*, 4th ed., p. vi.

the commands of the sovereign are in fact obeyed. Similarly, the basic norm of international law, *pacta sunt servanda*, can provide the foundation of the international order only inasmuch as there is such an order in which *pacta sunt servata*: which is, I suppose, what international lawyers, from Grotius onwards, have, correctly or incorrectly, assumed.

In other words there is, and must be, a point at which the basic norm—the hypothesis—is converted into a fact—a thesis—unless its validity be derived from some other or further hypothesis, from a norm which will no longer be positive but can only be a proposition of 'natural law', a pronouncement on justice.

Thus, in its latest and most up-to-date developments, modern jurisprudence has really done nothing more than shift to a higher plane the old problem which used to be discussed under the heading of the ideal or natural law. The following quotation from Kelsen seems to me particularly significant:

> That a norm of the kind just mentioned is the basic norm of the national legal order does not imply that it is impossible to go beyond that norm. Certainly one may ask why one has to respect the first constitution as a binding norm. The answer might be that the fathers of the first constitution were empowered by God. The characteristic of so-called legal positivism is, however, that it dispenses with any such religious justification of the legal order. The basic norm is only the necessary presupposition of any positivistic interpretation of legal material. (Kelsen, *General Theory of Law and State*, p. 116)

How this passage reveals the Achilles' heel of modern legal positivism! For the recognition that the ultimate test of the validity of law lies *beyond* law itself is nothing but a natural law proposition. In peaceful days, when the actual observance of law (be it of the commands of the State or of treaties solemnly entered upon) was unchallenged, 'positivism' could find in 'facts' its ground and perhaps its justification. But the moment 'facts' are called into question, the moment a 'choice' must be made between two or more possible alternatives,[1] I can see no reason why the old argument of natural law, which purported to value the facts and to direct the choice, should not be reconsidered.

[1] Kelsen gives an example of such an alternative in the case of the relationship between national and international law. The choice between the two hypotheses of the 'primacy' of the one or the other he declares to be merely a matter of 'political ideology'.

The typically German dilemma of either blind force or blind faith with which Kelsen leaves us stranded can never be entirely satisfactory. Positivism may indeed dispense with the quest for the ultimate foundation of the legal order. But this makes it entirely powerless when a vital issue is involved, such as the defence or the destruction of that order. It is tragically significant that the country where formal jurisprudence was developed to its utmost perfection was also the country where legality offered least resistance to the challenge of new and disruptive forces. Events seem to have brought us back once again to long-forgotten responsibilities.

I would like to conclude this long argument with the mention of some recent examples of the inadequacy of legal positivism to solve the problem of the ultimate validity of law. Examples of this kind are, in our troubled days, only too frequent. I remember a time, not very remote, when there was in my country not one but four different legal orders, all of which could have claimed some degrees of 'positiveness'. I prefer to use a simpler example which was given by Professor Goodhart in an interesting article.[1]

A statute is promulgated during the war by the Netherlands Government in London, purporting to bind Dutch subjects in Holland. Professor Goodhart asks 'is this law?'—by which he means, I presume, 'is it positive law?', law the validity of which can be ascertained by the criteria of positive jurisprudence. Now, as Professor Goodhart points out, the statute was certainly a law from the point of view of the Netherlands Government, who regarded themselves as having the right to issue it, independently of the fact whether it could ever be made efficacious. Yet, on the other hand, the German authorities would never have regarded it as a law, not even if every citizen in Holland had obeyed it. From the standpoint of a third party, such as the British courts, the question might have been dubious. 'The real difficult question arises, however, when we consider the position of the inhabitant of Holland.'

Professor Goodhart suggests that, at the end of the war, the Netherlands courts would have considered his particular views as immaterial. They would have confined themselves to assessing the actual observance or violation of the statute. And, indeed, so they should according to 'positive' jurisprudence. But, as Professor Goodhart frankly admits, 'this does not mean that the view of the

[1] 'An Apology for Jurisprudence', in *Interpretations of Modern Legal Philosophies*, 1947.

individual is unimportant. On the contrary, a large part of political history has been concerned with disputes between individuals and governments regarding the authority of the latter to declare law.'

I submit that what Professor Goodhart seems to consider a political issue is what our benighted ancestors would have called a clear issue of natural law. I submit that this issue can be solved only on the traditional lines of calling the validity of positive law into question, and that it is impossible for the individual to do so unless he decides on the justice of the law which he is asked to obey. But I further submit that it is possible to find in quite recent developments of legal theory and practice a clear indication of a return to the obsolete notions which positivism had criticised and declared to be unacceptable.

That the whole question of the trial of war criminals at the end of the war would raise a 'natural law' issue was an authoritative opinion which events have fully confirmed.[1] No doubt the provisions for the Nürnberg Tribunal were based, or purported to be based, on existing or 'positive' international law. Apart from the preliminary and controversial question of individual responsibility under international law, the violation of international treaties, of the laws and customs of war, and above all of Article I of the Preamble to the Fourth Hague Convention of 1907 (the 'Martens clause' which formally included the 'laws of humanity' and the 'dictates of the public conscience' within the boundaries of international law) certainly provided a 'positive' basis for the prosecution.

But I strongly suspect that the boundaries of legal positivism were overstepped, and had to be overstepped, the moment it was stated that the trials were a 'question of justice'. The principle *nullum crimen sine poena*, on which the sentences were grounded, was a flat contradiction of one of the most generally accepted principles of positive jurisprudence, the principle *nulla poena sine lege*. Whether or not the assertion of that principle constitutes a dangerous precedent is not for me to judge. All I suggest is that the words used by the Court ('So far from it being unjust to punish him, it would be unjust if his wrong were allowed to go unpunished')[2] are clearly reminiscent of old natural law argumentations. The rejection of the defence of superior orders makes that

[1] Lord Wright, 'Natural Law and International Law' in *Interpretations of Modern Legal Philosophies*, 1947; 'War Crimes under International Law' in *Law Quarterly Review*, 1946.

[2] *The Times*, October 1946.

reminiscence even more poignant: for it is nothing less than the old doctrine that the validity of laws does not depend on their 'positiveness', and that it is the duty of the individual to pass judgment on laws before he obeys them.

Thus, after a century of effort to eliminate the dualism between what is and what ought to be from the field of legal and political experience, natural law seems to have taken its revenge upon the very champions of the pernicious doctrine that there is no law but positive law, or that might equals right, since for all practical purposes the two propositions are perfectly equivalent.

R. POUND, *Outline of Lectures on Jurisprudence*, 5th ed., 1943 (a complete bibliographical guide).

SIR P. VINOGRADOFF, *Common-sense in Law*, 10th imp., 1933.

C. K. ALLEN, 'Jurisprudence—What and Why?' in *Legal Duties*, 1931.

Modern Theories of Law, Ed. by J. JENNINGS, 1933.

J. W. JONES, *Historical Introduction to the Theory of Law*, 1940.

W. FRIEDMANN, *Legal Theory*, 1944.

W. W. BUCKLAND, *Some Reflections on Jurisprudence*, 1945.

G. W. PATON, *A Text-Book of Jurisprudence*, 1946.

J. STONE, *The Province and Function of Law*, 1946.

H. KELSEN, *General Theory of Law and State*, 1946, with an Appendix on *Natural Law Doctrine and Legal Positivism.*

Interpretations of Modern Legal Philosophies, Essays in honour of Roscoe Pound, 1947.

A useful selection from authors can be found in J. HALL's *Readings in Jurisprudence.*

For the interpretation of Savigny, which is outlined in this chapter, I wish to acknowledge my indebtedness to an excellent Italian book by G. SOLARI, *Storicismo e diritto privato*, 1940.

For a further analysis of 'formal' jurisprudence and for a survey of the immense literature on the subject, I must refer to my book, *Il Negozio Giuridico*, 1934.

Mention should be made here of the remarkable efforts made by French jurisprudence to disentangle itself from the impact of positivism. Under the influence especially of Gény (*Science et technique en droit privé positif*, 1914–1924), a renaissance of natural law thinking has taken place among French legal writers which could well be the object of a separate study.

B. Revealed Law

Hugo Grotius [author of *De jure belli et pacis;* "father of international law"] on Jesus Christ: from his *The Truth of the Christian Religion,* ed. Le Clerc, trans. John Clarke (new ed.; London, 1825), pp. 79-88.

Sir Matthew Hale [author of *The History of the Pleas of the Crown;* Lord Chief Justice in the reign of Charles II], *A Letter of Advice to his Grand-Children* (2d ed.; London, 1823), pp. 44-48.

Thomas Sherlock [Bishop of London], *The Tryal of the Witnesses of the Resurrection of Jesus* (London, 1729).

Thomas Erskine [advocate; defended Hadfield in the classic trial for attempted regicide in 1800], *Remarks on the Internal Evidence for the Truth of Revealed Religion* (7th ed.; Edinburgh, 1823), pp. 192-99.

I. H. Linton [member of the D. C. Bar and the Bar of the U. S. Supreme Court], *A Lawyer Examines the Bible* (Boston: W. A. Wilde, 1943), pp. 13-44, 220-23.

J. W. Montgomery, "Is Man His Own God?": from his *Christianity for the Tough Minded* (Minneapolis: Bethany, 1973), pp. 21-34.

________________, "The Relevance of Scripture in Today's Philosophical Climate": from *The Bible - The Living Word of Revelation,* ed. Merrill C. Tenney (Grand Rapids, Mich.: Zondervan, 1968), pp. 201-218, 227-28.

________________, "The Quest for Absolutes": based on the author's *Shape of the Past* (Ann Arbor, Mich.: Edwards Brothers, 1963) and here published for the first time in book form.

________________, "The Divine Imperative": from his *Shape of the Past,* pp. 358-74.

THE TRUTH

OF THE

CHRISTIAN RELIGION.

IN SIX BOOKS.

BY HUGO GROTIUS.

CORRECTED, AND ILLUSTRATED WITH NOTES,
BY MR. LE CLERC.

TO WHICH ARE ADDED,
TWO BOOKS BY THE SAID MR. LE CLERC.

BOOK I.
Concerning the choice of our opinion amongst the different Sects of Christians.

BOOK II.
Against Indifference in the choice of our Religion.

TRANSLATED BY JOHN CLARKE, D.D.
DEAN OF SARUM.

A New Edition.

LONDON:
PRINTED FOR WILLIAM BAYNES & SON
Paternoster Row;
AND H. S. BAYNES, EDINBURGH.
1825.

THE TRUTH

OF THE

CHRISTIAN RELIGION.

BOOK II.

SECT. I. That the Christian religion is true.

THE design, then, of this second book (after having put up our petitions to Christ the King of heaven, that he would afford us such assistances of his holy Spirit, as may render us sufficient for so great a business) is not to treat particularly of all the opinions in Christianity, but only to shew that the Christian religion itself is most true and certain; which we attempt thus:—

SECT. II. The proof that there was such a person as Jesus.

THAT Jesus of Nazareth formerly lived in Judæa, in the reign of Tiberius the Roman emperor, is constantly acknowledged, not only by Christians dispersed all over the world, but also by all the Jews which now are, or have ever wrote since that time: the same is also testified by heathens, that is, such as did not write either of the Jewish or of the Christian religion, Suetonius,*

* In his Claudius, chap. 25. where *Chresto* is put for *Christo*, because that name was more known to the Greeks and Latins.

Tacitus,* Pliny the younger,† and many after these.

That he died an ignominious death.

THAT the same Jesus was crucified by Pontius Pilate, the president of Judæa, is acknowledged by all the same

* Book xv. where he is speaking of the punishment of the Christians. "The author of that name was Christ, who, in the reign of Tiberius, suffered punishment under his procurator Pontius Pilate." Where the great crimes, and hatred to human-kind, they are charged with, is nothing else but their contempt of false gods; which same reason Tacitus had to curse the Jews; and Pliny the elder, when he calls the Jews "a people remarkable for contempt of the gods." That is, very many of the Romans were come to this, that their consciences were not affected by that part of their theology which was civil, (which Seneca commends), but they feigned it in their outward actions, and kept it as a command of the law; looking upon worship as a thing of custom, more than in reality. See the opinion of Varro and Seneca about this matter, which is the same with that of Tacitus, in Augustine, book v. chap. 33. and book vi. chap. 10. of his city of God. In the mean time, it is worth observing, that Jesus, who was punished by Pontius Pilate, was acknowledged by many at Rome, in Nero's time, to be the Christ. Compare that of Justin in his second Apologetic concerning this history; where he addresses himself to the emperors and Roman senate, who might know those things from the Acts.

† The epistle is obvious to every one, viz. book x. chap. 97. which Tertullian mentions in his Apologetic, and Eusebius in his Chronicon; where we find, that the Christians were used to say a hymn to Christ as God, and to bind themselves not to perform any wicked thing, but to forbear committing theft, robbery, or adultery; to be true to their word, and strictly perform their trust. Pliny blames their stubbornness and inflexible obstinacy in this one thing; that they would not invoke the gods, nor do homage with frankincense and wine before the shrines of deities, nor curse Christ; nor could they be compelled to do it by any torments whatsoever. The epistle in answer to that of Trajan says, that he openly declares himself to be no Christian who supplicates the Roman gods. Origen, in his fourth book against Celsus, tells us, there was a certain history of Jesus extant in Numenius the Pythagorean.

Christians, notwithstanding it might seem dishonourable to them who worship such a Lord. It is also acknowledged by the Jews,* though they are not ignorant how much they lie under the displeasure of the Christians, under whose government they every where live, upon this account, because their ancestors were the cause of Pilate's doing it. Likewise, the heathen writers we mentioned have recorded the same to posterity; and, a long time after, the acts of Pilate were extant, to which the Christians sometimes appealed.† Neither did Julian, or other opposers of Christianity, ever call it in question. So that no history can be imagined more certain than this; which is confirmed by the testimonies, I don't say, of so many men, but of so many people, which differed from each other. Notwithstanding which, we find him worshipped as Lord throughout the most distant countries of the world.‡

SECT. III. *And yet, after his death, was worshipped by wise men.*

And that not only in our age, or those immediately foregoing, but also even in the first, the age next to that in which it was done, in the reign of the emperor Nero; at which time the fore-mentioned Tacitus and others attest, that very many were punished because they professed the worship of Christ.

SECT. IV. *The cause of which could be no other but those miracles which were done by him.*

And there were always very many amongst the worshippers of Christ who were men of good judgment, and of no small learning; such as (not to mention Jews) Sergius the presi-

* Who call him תלוי, that is, *hanged*. Benjaminis Tudelensis, in his Itinerary, acknowledges that Jesus was slain at Jerusalem.

† See Epiphanius in his Tessarescædecatitæ.——(It were better to have omitted this argument, because some imprudent Christians might appeal to some spurious acts; for it does not appear there were any genuine ones. *Le Clerc.*)

‡ Chrysostom handles this matter at large, upon 2 Cor. v. 7.

dent of Cyprus,* Dionysius the Areopagite,† Polycarp,‡ Justin,|| Irenæus,§ Athenagoras,¶ Origen,** Tertullian,†† Clemens Alexandrinus, and others: ‡‡ who being such men, why they should themselves be worshippers of a man that was put to an ignominious death, especially when almost all of them were brought up in other religions, and there was neither honour nor profit to be had by the Christian religion; why, I say, they should do thus, there can be no reason given but this one; that upon a diligent inquiry, such as becomes prudent men to make, in a matter of the highest concern to them, they found, that the report which was spread abroad, concerning the miracles that were done by him, was true, and founded upon sufficient testimony; such as healing sore diseases, and those of a long continuance, only by a word, and this publicly; restoring sight to him that was born blind; increasing bread for the feeding of many thousands, who were all witnesses of it; restoring the dead to life again, and many other such like.

SECT. V. Which miracles cannot be ascribed to any natural or diabolical power, but must be from God.

WHICH report had so certain and undoubted a foundation, that neither Celsus,|||| nor Julian,§§ when they wrote

* Acts xiii. 12.

† Acts xvii. 34.

‡ Who suffered martyrdom in Asia, in the clxviiith year of Christ, according to Eusebius.

|| Who published writings in defence of the Christians in the cxliid year of Christ. See the same Eusebius.

§ He flourished at Lyons, in the clxxxiiid year of Christ.

¶ This man was an Athenian. He flourished about the clxxxth year of Christ, as appears from the inscription of his book.

** He flourished about the ccxxxth year of Christ.

†† Who was famous in the ccviiith year of Christ.

‡‡ About the same time. See Eusebius.

|||| Whose words, in book ii. of Origen, are, "You think he is the Son of God, because he healed the lame and the blind."

§§ Nay, he plainly confesses the thing, when he says, in the words recited by Cyril, book vi. "Unless any one will reckon amongst the most difficult things, healing the lame and the blind, and casting out devils in Bethsaida and Bethany."

against the Christians, dared to deny that some miracles were done by Christ; the Hebrews also confess it openly in the books of the Talmud.* That they were not performed by any natural power, sufficiently appears from hence, that they are called wonders or miracles; nor can it ever be that grievous distempers should be healed immediately, only by a word speaking, or a touch, by the power of nature. If those works could have been accounted for by any natural efficacy, it would have been said so at first, by those who either professed themselves enemies of Christ when he was upon earth, or of his gospel. By the like argument, we gather, that they were not juggling tricks, because very many of the works were done openly, in the sight of all the people;† and amongst whom were many learned men, who bore no good-will to Christ, who observed all his works. To which we may add, that the like works were often repeated, and the effects were not of a short continuance, but lasting. All which, rightly considered, as it ought to be, it will plainly follow, according to the Jews' own confession, that these works were done by some power more than human, that is, by some good or bad spirit; that these works were not the effects of any bad spirit, is from hence evident, that this doctrine of Christ, for the proof of which these works were performed, was opposite to those evil spirits: for it forbids the worship of evil spirits; it draws men off from all immorality, in which such spirits delight. It appears also, from the things themselves, that wherever this doctrine has been received, the worship of demons and magical arts have ceased;‡ and the one God has been worshipped, with an abhorrence of demons; whose strength and power, Porphyry acknowledges, were broken upon the coming of Christ.|| And it is not at all credible,

* In the title Aboda Zara.

† Acts xxvi. 26. Luke xii.

‡ The books about which were burnt by the advice of the disciples of Christ, Acts xix. 19.

|| The place is in Eusebius's Prep. book v. chap. 1. "After Christ was worshipped, nobody experienced any public benefit from the gods."

that any evil spirits should be so imprudent, as to do those things, and that very often, from which no honour or advantage could arise to them, but, on the contrary, great loss and disgrace. Neither is it any way consistent with the goodness or wisdom of God, that he should be thought to suffer men, who were free from all wicked designs, and who feared him, to be deceived by the cunning of devils; and such were the first disciples of Christ, as is manifest from their unblameable life, and their suffering very many calamities for conscience-sake. If any one should say, that these works were done by good beings, who yet are inferior to God; this is to confess, that they were well-pleasing to God, and redounded to his honour; because good beings do nothing but what is acceptable to God, and for his glory. Not to mention that some of the works of Christ were such as seem to declare God himself to be the author of them, such as the raising more than one of those that were dead to life. Moreover, God neither does nor suffers miracles to be done without a reason; for it does not become a wise lawgiver to depart from his laws without a reason, and that a weighty one. Now, no other reason can be given why these things were done, but that which is alleged by Christ, viz. to give credit to his doctrine;* nor could they who beheld them conceive any other reason in their minds: amongst whom, since there were many of a pious disposition, as was said before, it would be profane to think God should do them, to impose upon such. And this was the sole reason why many of the Jews, who lived near the time of Jesus, who yet could not be brought to depart from any thing of the law given by Moses,† (such as

* We may add, that the event itself, in that so great a part of mankind embraced the Christian religion, shews that it was a thing so worthy of God, as for him to confirm it with miracles at the beginning. If he did so many for the sake of one nation, and that no very great one, I mean the Jewish; how much more agreeable to his goodness was it to bestow this heavenly light to so great a part of mankind, who lay in the thickest darkness! *Le Clerc.*

† See Acts xv. Rom. xiv. Jerom in the Eusebian Chronicon, for the year of Christ cxxv. after he had named fifteen Christian

they who were called Nazarenes and Ebionites), nevertheless owned Jesus to be a teacher sent from heaven.

SECT. VI. *The resurrection of Christ proved from credible testimony.*

CHRIST'S coming to life again in a wonderful manner, after his crucifixion, death, and burial, affords us no less strong an argument for those miracles that were done by him. For the Christians of all times and places assert this not only for a truth, but as the principal foundation of their faith: which could not be, unless they, who first taught the Christian faith, had fully persuaded their hearers that the thing did come to pass. Now, they could not fully persuade men of any judgment of this, unless they affirmed themselves to be eye-witnesess of it; for, without such an affirmation, no man in his senses would have believed them, especially at that time, when such a belief was attended with so many evils and dangers. That this was affirmed by them with great constancy, their own books, and the books of others,* tell us; nay, it appears from those books, that they appealed to five hundred witnesses, who saw Jesus after he was risen from the dead.† Now, it is not usual for those that speak untruths to appeal to so many witnesses.

bishops of Jerusalem, adds, "These were all bishops of the circumcision, who governed till the destruction of Jerusalem under the emperor Adrian." Severus Sulpitius, concerning the Christians of those times and places, says, "They believed Christ to be God, whilst they observed also the law; and the church had a priest out of those of the circumcision." See Epiphanius, where he treats of the Nazarenes and Ebionites. Nazarenes was a name not for any particular part, but all the Christians in Palestine were so called, because their master was a Nazarene.

* Even of Celsus, who wrote against the Christians. See Origen, book ii.

† Paul, 1 Cor. xv. 6. He says, some of them were dead at that time, but their children and freinds were alive, who might be hearkened to, and testify what they had heard. But the greater part of them were alive when Paul wrote this. This appearance was in a mountain in Galilee.

H

Nor is it possible so many men should agree to bear a false testimony. And if there had been no other witnesses but those twelve known first propagators of the Christian doctrine, it had been sufficient. Nobody has any ill design for nothing. They could not hope for any honour, from saying what was not true, because all the honours were in the power of the heathens and Jews, by whom they were reproached and contemptuously treated: nor for riches, because, on the contrary, this profession was often attended with the loss of their goods, if they had any; and if it had been otherwise, yet the gospel could not have been taught by them, but with the neglect of their temporal goods. Nor could any other advantages of this life provoke them to speak a falsity, when the very preaching of the gospel exposed them to hardship, to hunger and thirst, to stripes and imprisonment. Fame, amongst themselves only, was not so great, that for the sake thereof, men of upright intentions, whose lives and tenets were free from pride and ambition, should undergo so many evils. Nor had they any ground to hope that their opinion, which was so repugnant to nature, (which is wholly bent upon its own advantages), and to the authority which every where governed, could make so great a progress, but from a divine promise. Further, they could not promise to themselves that this fame, whatever it was, would be lasting; because (God on purpose concealing his intention in this matter from them) they expected that the end of the whole world was just at hand, as is plain from their own writings, and those of the Christians that came after them.* It remains, therefore, that they must be said to have uttered a falsity, for the sake of defending their religion; which, if we consider the thing aright, can never be said of them; for either they believed from their heart that their religion was true, or they did not believe it. If they had not believed it to have been the best, they would never have chosen it from all

* See 1 Thess. iv. 15, 16. 1 Cor. xv. 52. Tertullian, of having but one wife: "Now the time is very short." Jerom to Gerontias: "What is that to us, upon whom the ends of the world are come?"

other religions, which were more safe and honourable. Nay, though they believed it to be true, they would not have made profession of it, unless they had believed such a profession necessary; especially when they could easily foresee, and they quickly learnt by experience, that such a profession would be attended with the death of a vast number; and they would have been guilty of the highest wickedness, to have given such occasion, without a just reason. If they believed their religion to be true, nay, that it was the best, and ought to be professed by all means, and this after the death of their Master; it was impossible this should be, if their Master's promise concerning his resurrection had failed them; for this had been sufficient to any man, in his senses, to have overthrown that belief which he had before entertained.* Again, all religion, but particularly the Christian religion, forbids lying and false witness, especially in divine matters:† they could not therefore be moved to tell a lie out of love to religion, especially such a religion. To all which may be added, that they were men who led such a life as was not blamed even by their adversaries;‡ and who had no objection made against them, but only their simplicity, the nature of which is the most distant that can be from forging a lie. And there was none of them who did not undergo even the most grievous things for their profession of the resurrection of Jesus. Many of them endured the most exquisite death for this testimony. Now, suppose it possible, that any man in his wits could undergo such things for an opinion he had entertained in his mind; yet for a falsity, and which is known to be a falsity, that not only one man, but very many, should be willing to endure such hardships, is a thing plainly incredible. And that they were not mad,

* Chrysostom handles this argument at large, upon 1 Cor. i. towards this end.

† Matt. xii. 36. John viii. 44, 45. Eph. iv. 25. Rom. ix. 1. 2 Cor. vii. 14. xi. 31. Gal. i. 20. Col. iii. 9. 1 Tim. i. 10. and ii. 7. Jam. iii. 14. Matt. xxii. 16. Mark xii. 14. Luke xx. 21. John xiv. 16. Eph. v. 9. and elsewhere.

‡ Even Celsus. See Origen, book i.

H 2

both their lives and their writings sufficiently testify. What has been said of these first, the same may also be said of Paul, who openly declared that he saw Christ reigning in heaven,* and he did not want the learning of the Jews, but had great prospect of honour, if he had trod in the paths of his fathers.† But, on the contrary, he thought it his duty, for this profession, to expose himself to the hatred of his relations; and to undertake difficult, dangerous, and troublesome, voyages all over the world, and at last to suffer an ignominious death.

A

LETTER OF ADVICE

TO HIS

GRAND-CHILDREN,

MATTHEW, GABRIEL, ANNE, MARY, AND FRANCES HALE.

BY SIR MATTHEW HALE,

LORD CHIEF JUSTICE IN THE REIGN OF CHARLES II.

THE SECOND EDITION.

PRINTED FROM AN ORIGINAL MANUSCRIPT, AND COLLATED WITH THE COPY IN THE BRITISH MUSEUM.

"Believe it, children, if I could leave you the wealth of both the Indies, possessions as ample as principalities, great and honourable titles; yet all these are not to be valued in comparison with the good advice I shall herein give you."—P. 7.

LONDON:

PRINTED FOR TAYLOR AND HESSEY,

93, FLEET STREET;

AND 13, WATERLOO PLACE, PALL MALL.

1823.

H.R. Cook. sculp.

Sir Matthew Hale,

Lord Chief Justice of the Kings Bench.

Published Jan. 18.. by Taylor & Hessey 93 Fleet Street

CHAPTER VI.

CONCERNING RELIGION AS IT IS REVEALED IN THE WRITTEN WORD OF GOD OF THE OLD AND NEW TESTAMENT, AND ESPECIALLY CHRISTIAN RELIGION.

ALTHOUGH Religion, as it is before described, or Natural Religion, is in truth the foundation and groundwork of all true religion, yet the Almighty, in love to mankind, hath made a more full and clear discovery of himself and his will, and the manner of his worship, and of the means to attain everlasting happiness, and his purpose concerning the children of men, in his written word, contained in the Old and New Testaments.

In the Old Testament he hath given us the true relation of the world, and of mankind, and the doctrinal and historical discoveries of his providence and government of all things in the world, and the instances of his foresight and knowledge of all events, in the prophecies and writings of his prophets; but especially he hath set forth his power, wisdom, nature, essence, and attributes, and likewise his will and laws which he requires men to observe, contained in that abridgment or sum of moral duties contained in the ten commandments, and those additional precepts and directions of piety and moral duties contained in the writings of that sacred volume. But in the New Testament he hath yet given us a clearer manifestation of his council, will, and purposes, touching the children of men: namely—

That he sent his Son into the world, to take upon him human nature, and to become man for our sakes; and in that nature to acquaint us more perfectly what the future state of mankind after death should be, namely, the state of rewards and punishments; and to acquaint us what we are to believe, and to do, and to avoid, in order to obtain everlasting happiness and glory; and to give us all the assurance possible for the truth of that message, by his holy life, by his miracles, by his death, resurrection, and ascension into heaven; and to become our Sacrifice, our Intercessor, at the right hand of God. And this divine doctrine and instruction he also illustrated and confirmed, by sending abroad his disciples and apostles to preach and teach, which accordingly they did. The most necessary part of Christian doctrine and history, was by the divine providence committed to writing, by the four evangelists and apostles in their epistles.

By the advantage, therefore, of the doctrine and history of Christ and his apostles, true religion is more clearly and fully revealed and discovered, in all things necessary to be believed, in order to the obtaining of everlasting happiness. And among other great advantages given to men by the Christian religion, these that follow are of great moment and remark.

1. That the souls of men have most certainly a being and continuance, notwithstanding the death of their bodies.

2. That there shall be a time, when the souls shall be united to the bodies again, which is called the Resurrection.

3. That there shall certainly be a state of reward to the good and righteous, of everlasting happiness and glory; and to the wicked and disobedient, of everlasting shame and misery.

4. That in the gospel there is a clear discovery of the will of God, which he would have all mankind to obey; the tenor of all those excellent precepts of piety towards God and righteousness towards men, sobriety towards ourselves, repentance for sins committed, and faith in God and his Son Jesus Christ.

5. That the Son of God, becoming man, offered himself as a sacrifice for the satisfaction of the sin of the world, and for the reconciling God to man, and bringing man to God.

6. That he is ascended, and abides in the glorious heavens, as a Mediator and Intercessor of the children of men with the glorious God, presenting their supplications to him, and applying his merits to them.

7. That all those that obey the will of God revealed in this gospel, shall, through the efficacy of the sacrifice of Christ, infallibly attain everlasting happiness; and for the farther strengthening of our faith, and for a perpetual seal of the truth of the evangelical promises, and of our profession of Christian faith, and obedience to the precepts of Christ contained therein, he did institute the two Sacraments of baptism and the Lord's supper.

In short, the Christian religion contains, 1. The things to be believed; the sum and abstract whereof is contained in the creed, commonly called the Apostles' Creed.

2. The things to be done; the sum whereof is contained in the ten commandments, and the commentaries and expositions thereof, given by Christ and his apostles — together with those

additional duties contained in the gospel, the principal whereof are faith in Christ, repentance towards God, and love and charity towards men.

3. The things to be prayed for and desired of God; the sum whereof is contained in the Lord's prayer.

This is the Christian religion. * * *

THE

TRYAL

OF THE

WITNESSES

OF THE

Resurrection of *Jesus*.

by Dr. Sherlock Bp. of Bangor

LONDON:

Printed for J. ROBERTS, near the *Oxford-Arms* in *Warwick-Lane*. MDCCXXIX.

THE

TRYAL

OF THE

Witneſſes of the Reſurrection of JESUS.

WE were, not long ſince, ſome Gentlemen of the Inns of Court, together, each to other ſo well known, that no Man's Preſence was a Confinement to any other from ſpeaking his Mind on any Subject that happened to ariſe in Converſation. The Meeting was without Deſign, and the Diſcourſe, as in like Caſes, various. Among other Things we fell upon the Subject of *Woolſton*'s Tryal and Conviction, which had happened ſome few Days before: That led to a Debate how the Law ſtands in ſuch Caſes, what Puniſhment it inflicts; and, in general, whether the Law ought at all to interpoſe in Controverſies of this kind. We were not agreed in theſe Points. One, who maintained the favourable ſide to *Woolſton*, diſcovered a great Liking and Approbation of his Diſcourſes againſt the Miracles of

Chriſt, and ſeemed to think his Arguments unanſwerable. To which another reply'd, I wonder that one of your Abilities, and bred to the Profeſſion of the Law, which teaches us to conſider the Nature of Evidence, and its proper Weight, can be of that Opinion; I am ſure you wou'd be unwilling to determine a Property of Five Shillings upon ſuch Evidence, as you now think material enough to overthrow the Miracles of Chriſt.

It may eaſily be imagined that this opened a Door to much Diſpute, and determined the Converſation for the Remainder of the Evening to this Subject. The Diſpute ran thro' almoſt all the Particulars mentioned in *Woolſton*'s Pieces; but the Thread of it was broken by ſeveral Digreſſions, and the Purſuit of Things which were brought accidently into the Diſcourſe. At length one of the Company ſaid, pleaſantly, Gentlemen, you don't argue like Lawyers; if I were Judge in this Cauſe, I wou'd hold you better to the Point. The Company took the Hint, and cry'd they ſhou'd be glad to have the Cauſe re-heard, and him to be the Judge. The Gentlemen who had engaged with Mettle and Spirit in a Diſpute which aroſe accidentally, ſeem'd very unwilling to be drawn into a formal Controverſy; and eſpecially the Gentleman who argued againſt *Woolſton*, thought the Matter grew too ſerious for him, and excuſed himſelf from undertaking a Controverſy in Religion, of all others the moſt momentous: But he was told, that the Argument ſhould be confined merely to the Nature of the Evidence, and that might be conſidered without entring into any ſuch Controverſy

as

as he wou'd avoid; and to bring the Matter within Bounds, and under one View, the Evidence of Chriſt's Reſurrection, and the Exceptions taken to it, ſhou'd be the only Subject of the Conference. With much Perſuaſion he ſuffered himſelf to be perſuaded, and promiſed to give the Company, and their new-made Judge, a Meeting that Day fortnight. The Judge and the reſt of the Company were for bringing on the Cauſe a Week ſooner; but the Council for *Woolſton* took the Matter up, and ſaid, Conſider, Sir, the Gentleman is not to argue out of *Littleton*, *Plowden*, or *Cook*, Authors to him well known; but he muſt have his Authorities from *Matthew*, *Mark*, *Luke*, and *John*; and a Fortnight is time little enough of all conſcience to gain a Familiarity with a new Acquaintance; and, turning to the Gentleman, he ſaid, I'll call upon you before the Fortnight is out, to ſee how reverend an Appearance you make behind *Hammond* on the New Teſtament, a Concordance on one hand, and a Folio Bible with References on the other. You ſhall be welcome, Sir, reply'd the Gentleman, and perhaps you may find ſome Company more to your own Taſte; he is but a poor Council who ſtudies one ſide of the Queſtion only, and therefore I will have your Friend *Woolſton*, *T—l*, and *C—s*, to entertain you when you do me the Favour of the Viſit. Upon this we parted in good Humour, and all pleaſed with the Appointment made, except the two Gentlemen who were to provide the Entertainment.

The

The SECOND DAY.

THE Company met at the Time appointed: But it happened in this, as in like Cases it often does, that some Friends to some of the Company, who were not of the Party the first Day, had got Notice of the Meeting; and the Gentlemen who were to debate the Question, found they had a more numerous Audience than they expected or desired. He especially who was to maintain the Evidence of the Resurrection, began to excuse the Necessity he was under of disappointing their Expectation, alledging that he was not prepared; and he had persisted in excusing himself, but that the Strangers, who perceived what the Case was, offered to withdraw, which the Gentleman wou'd by no means consent to: They insisting to go, he said, he would much rather submit himself to their Candor, unprepared as he was, than be guilty of so much Rudeness, as to force them to leave the Company. Upon which one of the Company, smiling, said, It happens luckily that our Number is increased; when we were last together, we appointed a Judge, but we quite forgot a Jury, and now, I think, we are good Men and true, sufficient to make one. This Thought was pursued in several Allusions to legal Proceedings, which created some Mirth, and had this good Effect, that it dispersed the solemn Air which the mutual Compliments upon the Difficulty before-mentioned had introduced, and restored the Ease and Good-Humour natural to the Conversation of Gentlemen.

2 The

The Judge perceiving the Difpofition of the Company, thought it a proper Time to begin, and called out, Gentlemen of the Jury take your Places; and immediately feated himfelf at the upper End of the Table: The Company fat round him, and the Judge called upon the Council for *Woolfton* to begin.

Mr. A. *Council for* Woolfton, addreffing himfelf to the Judge, faid,

May it pleafe your Lordfhip; I conceive the Gentleman on the other fide ought to begin, and lay his Evidence, which he intends to maintain, before the Court; till that is done, it is to no purpofe for me to object. I may perhaps object to fomething which he will not admit to be any part of his Evidence, and therefore, I apprehend, the Evidence ought in the firft Place to be diftinctly ftated.

Judge. Mr. *B.* What fay you to that?

Mr. B. *Council on the other Side:*

My Lord, If the Evidence I am to maintain, were to fupport any new Claim, if I were to gain any thing which I am not already poffeffed of, the Gentleman wou'd be in the right; but the Evidence is old, and is Matter of Record, and I have been long in poffeffion of all that I claim under it. If the Gentleman has any thing to fay to difpoffefs me, let him produce it, otherwife I have no reafon to bring my own Title into queftion. And this I take to be the known Method of Proceeding in fuch Cafes; no Man is obliged to produce his Title to his Poffeffion; it is fufficient if he maintains it when it is called in queftion.

Mr. *A.*

Mr. *A*. Surely, my Lord, the Gentleman mistakes the Caſe; I can never admit myſelf to be out of Poſſeſſion of my Underſtanding and Reaſon; and ſince he wou'd put me out of this Poſſeſſion, and compel me to admit Things incredible, in vertue of the Evidence he maintains, he ought to ſet forth his Claim, or leave the World to be directed by common Senſe.

Judge. Sir, you ſay right; upon Suppoſition that the Truth of the Chriſtian Religion were the Point in Judgment. In that Caſe it would be neceſſary to produce the Evidence for the Chriſtian Religion; but the Matter now before the Court is, Whether the Objections produced by Mr. *Woolſton*, are of weight to overthrow the Evidence of Chriſt's Reſurrection. You ſee then the Evidence of the Reſurrection is ſuppoſed to be what it is on both Sides, and the Thing immediately in Judgment, is the Value of the Objections, and therefore they muſt be ſet forth. The Court will be bound to take notice of the Evidence, which is admitted as a Fact on both Parts. Go on Mr. *A*.

Mr. *A*. My Lord, I ſubmit to the Direction of the Court. I cannot but obſerve that the Gentleman on the other ſide, unwilling as he ſeems to be to ſtate his Evidence, did not forget to lay in his Claim to Preſcription, which is, perhaps, in Truth, tho' he has too much Skill to own it, the very Strength of his Cauſe. I do allow that the Gentleman maintains nothing but what his Father and Grandfather, and his Anceſtors, beyond time of Man's Memory, maintain'd before him: I allow too, that Preſcription in many Caſes makes a good Title;

Title; but it muſt always be with this Condition, that the thing is capable of being preſcribed for: And I inſiſt, that Preſcription cannot run againſt Reaſon and Common Senſe. Cuſtoms may be pleaded by Preſcription; but if upon ſhewing the Cuſtom, any thing unreaſonable appears in it, the Preſcription fails; for length of Time works nothing towards the eſtabliſhing any thing that cou'd never have a Legal Commencement. And if this Objection will overthrow all Preſcriptions for Cuſtoms; the Miſchief of which extends perhaps to one poor Village only, and affects them in no greater a Concern, than their Right of Common upon a ragged Mountain; ſhall it not much more prevail when the Intereſt of Mankind is concern'd, and on no leſs a Point than his Happineſs in this Life, and in all his Hopes for Futurity? Beſides, if Preſcription muſt be allowed in this Caſe, how will you deal with it in others? What will you ſay to the Ancient *Perſians*, and their Fire-Altars? Nay, what to the *Turks*, who have been long enough in Poſſeſſion of their Faith to plead ——

Mr. *B*. I beg Pardon for interrupting the Gentleman. But it is to ſave him Trouble. He is going into his favourite Common-Place, and has brought us from *Perſia* to *Turkey* already; and if he goes on, I know we muſt follow him round the Globe. To ſave us from this long Journey, I'll wave all Advantage from the Antiquity of the Reſurrection, and the general Reception the Belief of it has found in the World; and am content to conſider it as a Fact which happen'd but laſt

Year, and was never heard of either by the Gentleman's Grandfather, or by mine.

Mr. A. I ſhould not have taken quite ſo long a Journey as the Gentleman imagines, nor, indeed, need any Man go far from home to find Inſtances to the Purpoſe I was upon. But ſince this Advantage is quitted, I am as willing to ſpare my Pains, as the Gentleman is deſirous that I ſhould. And yet I ſuſpect ſome Art even in this Conceſſion, fair and candid as it ſeems to be. For I am perſuaded that one Reaſon, perhaps the main Reaſon, why Men believe this Hiſtory of Jeſus, is, that they cannot conceive that any one ſhould attempt, much leſs ſucceed in ſuch an Attempt as this, upon the Foundation of meer human Cunning and Policy; and 'tis worth the while to go round the Globe, as the Gentleman expreſs'd himſelf, to ſee various Inſtances of the like Kind, in order to remove this Prejudice. But I ſtand corrected, and will go directly to the Point now in Judgment.

Mr. *B.* My Lord, The Gentleman in Juſtification of his firſt Argument, has entred upon another of a very different Kind. I think he is ſenſible of it, and ſeeming to yield up one of his popular Topicks, is indeed, artfully getting rid of another; which has made a very good Figure in many late Writings, but will not bear in any Place, where he who maintains it may be asked Queſtions. The mere Antiquity of the Reſurrection I gave up; for if the Evidence was not good at firſt, it can't be good now. The Gentleman is willing, he ſays, to ſpare us his Hiſtory of Antient Errors, and intimates, that upon this account he paſſes

over

over many Inftances of Fraud, that were like in Circumftances to the Cafe before us. By no means, my Lord, let them be paffed over. I wou'd not have the main Strength of his Caufe betrayed in Complaifance to me. Nothing can be more material, than to fhew a Fraud of this Kind that prevailed univerfally in the World. Chrift Jefus declared himfelf a Prophet, and put the Proof of his Miffion on this; that he fhou'd dye openly and publickly, and rife again the third Day. This furely was the hardeft Plot in the World to be managed: And if there be one Inftance of this Kind, or in any degree like it, by all means let it be produced.

Mr. *A.* My Lord, There has hardly been an Inftance of a falfe Religion in the World, but it has alfo afforded a like Inftance to this before us. Have they not all pretended to Infpiration? Upon what Foot did *Pythagoras*, *Numa*, and others fet up? did they not all converfe with the Gods, and pretend to deliver Oracles.

Mr. *B.* This only fhews that Revelation is by the common Confent of Mankind, the very beft Foundation of Religion, and therefore every Impoftor pretends to it? But is a Man's hiding himfelf in a Cave for fome Years, and then coming out into the World, to be compared to a Man's dying and rifing to Life again? So far from it, that you and I and every Man may do the one, but no Man can do the other.

Mr. *A.* Sir, I fuppofe it will be allowed to be as great thing to go to Heaven and converfe with Angels, and with God, and to come down to the

B 2 Earth

Earth again, as it is to dye and riſe again. Now this very thing *Mahomet* pretended to do, and all his Diſciples believe it. Can you deny this Fact?

Mr. *B.* Deny it, Sir? No. But tell us who went with *Mahomet?* who were his Witneſſes? I expect before we have done, to hear of the Guards ſet over the Sepulchre of Chriſt, and the Seal of the Stone: What Guard watched *Mahomet* in his going or returning? What Seals and Credentials had he? He himſelf pretends to none. His Followers pretend to nothing but his own Word. We are now to conſider the Evidence of Chriſt's Reſurrection, and you think to parallel it by producing a Caſe, for which no one ever pretended there was any Evidence. You have *Mahomet*'s Word; and no Man ever told a Lye, but you had *his* Word for the Truth of what he ſaid; and therefore you need not go round the Globe to find ſuch Inſtances as theſe. But this Story, 'tis ſaid, has gained great Credit, and is receiv'd by many Nations: Very well: And how was it receiv'd? Was not every Man converted to this Faith with the Sword at his Throat? In our Caſe, every Witneſs to the Reſurrection, and every Believer of it was hourly expoſed to Death: In the other Caſe, whoever refuſed to believe, died, or what was as bad, lived a wretched conquered Slave: And will you pretend theſe Caſes to be alike? One Caſe indeed there was within our own Memory, which in ſome Circumſtances came near to the Caſe now before us. The *French* Prophets put the Credit of their Miſſion upon the Reſurrection of Dr. *Emmes*, and gave publick Notice of it. If the Gentleman pleaſes to to make uſe of this Inſtance, it is at his Service.

Mr. *A.* The Inſtance of Dr. *Emmes* is ſo far to the Purpoſe, that it ſhews to what Lengths Enthuſiaſm will carry Men. And why might not the ſame thing happen at *Jeruſalem*, which happen'd but a few Years ago in our own Country? *Matthew*, and *John*, and the reſt of them, manag'd that Affair with more Dexterity than the *French* Prophets; ſo that the Reſurrection of Jeſus gained Credit in the World, and the *French* Prophets ſunk under their ridiculous Pretenſions. That's all the Difference.

Mr. *B.* Is it ſo? And a very wide Difference, I promiſe you. In one Caſe, every thing happen'd that was proper to convince the World of the Truth of the Reſurrection; in the other, the Event manifeſted the Cheat: and upon the View of theſe Circumſtances, you think it ſufficient to ſay, with great Coolneſs, That's all the Difference. Why, what Difference do you expect between Truth and Falſhood? What Diſtinction——

Judge. Gentlemen, you forget that you are in a Court, and are falling into Dialogue. Courts don't allow of Chit-chat. Look ye, the Evidence of the Reſurrection of Jeſus is before the Court, recorded by *Matthew*, *Mark*, and others. You muſt take it as it is; you can neither make it better nor worſe. Theſe Witneſſes are accuſed of giving falſe Evidence. Come to the Point; and let us hear what you have to offer, to prove the Accuſation.

Mr. *B.*

Mr. *B.* Is it your Meaning, Sir, that the Objections should be stated and argued all together, and that the Answer should be to the whole at once? Or would you have the Objections argued singly, and answered separately by themselves.

Judge. I think this Court may dispense with the strict Forms of legal Proceedings, and therefore I leave this to the Choice of the Jury.

After the Jury had consulted together, the Foreman rose up.

The Foreman of the Jury. We desire to hear the Objections argued and answered separately. We shall be better able to form a Judgment by hearing the Answer, whilst the Objection is fresh in our Minds.

Judge. Gentlemen, You hear the Opinion of the Jury. Go on.

Mr. *A.* I am now to disclose to you a Scene, of all others the most surprizing. * "The Resurrection has been long talked of, and to the Amazement of every one who can think freely, has been believed thro' all Ages of the Church". This general and constant Belief creates in most Minds a Presumption that it was founded on good Evidence. In other Cases the Evidence supports the Credit of the History; but here the Evidence itself is presum'd only upon the Credit which the Story has gain'd. † I wish the Books dispersed

* *Sixth Discourse*, p. 17.

† Ibid. *p.* 4.

against

againſt Jeſus by the ancient *Jews* had not been loſt; for they would have given us a clear Inſight into this Contrivance. But 'tis happy for us, that the very Account given by the pretended Witneſſes of this Fact is ſufficient to deſtroy the Credit of it.

The Reſurrection was not a thing contrived for its own Sake. No! It was undertaken to ſupport great Views, and for the Sake of great Conſequences that were to attend it. It will be neceſſary therefore to lay before you theſe Views, that you may the better judge of this Part of the Contrivance, when you have the whole Scene before you.

The *Jews* were a weak ſuperſtitious People, and, as is common among ſuch People, gave great Credit to ſome traditionary Prophecies about their own Country. They had beſides, ſome old Books among 'em, which they eſteemed to be Writings of certain Prophets, who had formerly lived among them, and whoſe Memory they had in great Veneration. From ſuch old Books and Traditions they formed many extravagant Expectations; and among the reſt one was, That ſome time or other a great victorious Prince ſhould ariſe among them, and ſubdue all their Enemies, and make 'em Lords of the World. * In *Auguſtus*'s Time they were in a low State, reduced under the *Roman* Yoke; and as they never wanted a Deliverer more, ſo the Eagerneſs of this Hope, as it happens to weak Minds, turned into a firm Expectation that he would ſoon come. This proved a Temptation to ſome bold,

* See *Scheme of Literal Prophecy*, p. 26.

and

and to ſome cunning Men, to perſonate the Prince ſo much expected; and † "nothing is more natu- "ral and common to promote Rebellions, than to "ground them on new Prophecies, or new Inter- "pretations of old ones: Prophecies being ſuited "to the vulgar Superſtition, and operating with "the Force of Religion". Accordingly many ſuch Impoſtors roſe, pretending to be the victori- ous Prince expected; and they and the People who followed them periſhed in the Folly of their At- tempt.

But Jeſus, knowing that Victories and Triumphs are not Things to be counterfeited; that the Peo- ple were not to be delivered from the *Roman* Yoke by Sleight of Hand; and having no Hope of being able to cope with the Emperor of *Rome* in good earneſt, took another and more ſucceſsful Method to carry on his Deſign. He took upon him to be the Prince foretold in the ancient Prophets; but then he inſiſted that the true Senſe of the Prophe- cies had been miſtaken; that they related not to the Kingdoms of this World, but to the King- dom of Heaven; that the Meſſias was not to be a conquering Prince, but a ſuffering one; that he was not to come with Horſes of War, and Cha- riots of War, but was to be meek and lowly, and riding on an Aſs. By this means he got the com- mon and neceſſary Foundation for a new Revela- tion, which is to be built and founded on a prece- dent Revelation *

† *Scheme of Literal Prophecy*, p. 27.
* See *Diſcourſe of the Grounds*, &c. Ch. iv.

To

To carry on this Deſign, he made choice of Twelve Men of no Fortunes or Education, and of ſuch Underſtandings as gave no Jealouſy that they would diſcover the Plot. And what is moſt wonderful, and ſhews their Ability; whilſt the Maſter was preaching the Kingdom of Heaven, theſe poor Men, not weaned from the Prejudices of their Country, expected every Day that he would declare himſelf a King, and were quarrelling who ſhould be his firſt Miniſter. This Expectation had a good Effect on the Service, for it kept them conſtant to their Maſter.

I muſt obſerve farther, that the *Jews* were under ſtrange Apprehenſions of ſupernatural Powers; and as their own Religion was founded on the Belief of certain Miracles, ſaid to be wrought by their Lawgiver *Moſes*; ſo were they ever running after Wonders and Miracles, and ready to take up with any Stories of this Kind. Now as ſomething extraordinary was neceſſary to ſupport the Pretenſions of Jeſus, he dextrouſly laid hold on this Weakneſs of the People; and ſet up to be a Wonder-Worker. His Diſciples were well qualified to receive this Impreſſion; they ſaw, or thought they ſaw, many ſtrange things, and were able to ſpread the Fame and Report of them abroad.

This Conduct had the deſired Succeſs. The whole Country was alarmed, and full of the News of a great Prophet's being come among them. They were too full of their own Imagination, to attend to the Notion of a Kingdom of Heaven: Here was one Mighty in Deed and in Word; and they concluded, he was the very Prince their Nation expected. Accordingly they once attempted to ſet him up for a King; and at another time attended him in Triumph to *Jeruſalem.* This natural Conſequence opens the natural Deſign of the Attempt. If things had gone on ſucceſsfully to the End, 'tis probable the Kingdom of Heaven would have been changed into a Kingdom of this World. The Deſign indeed failed, by the Impatience and Over-haſtineſs of the Multitude, which alarmed not only the Chief of the *Jews*, but the *Roman* Governor alſo.

The Caſe being come to this Point, and Jeſus ſeeing that he could not eſcape being put to Death; he declared, that the ancient Prophets had foretold that the Meſſias ſhould dye upon a Croſs, and that he ſhould riſe again on the third Day. Here was the Foundation laid for the continuing this Plot; which otherwiſe had died with its Author. This was his Legacy to his Followers; which having been well managed by them and their Succeſſors, has at laſt produced a Kingdom indeed; a Kingdom of Prieſts, who have governed the World for many Ages, and have been ſtrong enough to ſet Kings and Emperors at Defiance. But ſo it happens, the ancient Prophets appealed to are ſtill extant; and there being no ſuch Prophecies of the Death and Reſurrection of the Meſſias, they are a ſtanding Evidence againſt this Story. As he expected, ſo it happen'd, that he died on a Croſs. And the proſecuting of this Contrivance was left to the Management of his Diſciples and Followers. Their Part is next to be conſider'd——

Mr. *B.*

Mr. *B.* My Lord, Since it is your Opinion that the Objections should be consider'd singly, and the Gentleman has carry'd his Scheme down to the Death of Christ, I think he is come to a proper Rest; and that it is agreeable to your Intention, that I should be admitted to answer.

Judge. You say right, Sir. Let us hear what you answer to this Charge.

Mr. *B.* My Lord, I was unwilling to disturb the Gentleman by breaking in upon his Scheme; otherwise I should have reminded him, that this Court sits to examine Evidence, and not to be entertained with fine Imaginations. You have had a Scheme laid before you, but not one bit of Evidence to support any Part of it; no, not so much as a Pretence to any Evidence. The Gentleman, I remember, was very sorry that the old Books of the *Jews* were lost, which wou'd, as he supposes, have set forth all this Matter; and I agree with him, that he has much Reason to be sorry, considering his great Scarcity of Proof. And since I have mention'd this, that I may not be to return to it again, I would ask the Gentleman now, How he knows there ever were such Books? And since if ever there were any, they are lost, How he knows what they contained? I doubt I shall have frequent Occasion to ask such Questions. It wou'd indeed be a sufficient Answer to the whole, to repeat the several Suppositions that have been made, and to call for the Evidence upon which they stand. This wou'd plainly discover every Part of the Story to be mere Fiction. But since the Gentleman seems to have endeavour'd to bring under one View, the many Insinuations which have of late been spread abroad by different Hands, and to work the whole into a consistent Scheme; I will, if your Patience shall permit, examine this Plot, and see to whom the Honour of the Contrivance belongs.

The Gentleman begins with expressing his "Amazement, that the Resurrection has been believed in all Ages of the Church". If you ask him, Why? he must answer, Because the Account of it is a Forgery: For 'tis no Amazement to him surely, that a true Account should be generally well received. So that this Remark proceeds indeed from Confidence rather than Amazement; and comes only to this, that he is sure there was no Resurrection: And I am sure this is no Evidence that there was none. Whether he is mistaken in his Confidence, or I in mine, the Court must judge.

The Gentleman's Observation, That the general Belief of the Resurrection creates a Presumption that it stands upon good Evidence, and therefore People look no farther, but follow their Fathers, as their Fathers did their Grandfathers before them, is in great measure true; but it is a Truth nothing to his Purpose. He allows that the Resurrection has been believed in all Ages of the Church; that is, from the very Time of the Resurrection: What then prevailed with those who first receiv'd it? They certainly did not follow the Example of their Fathers. Here then is the Point, How did this Fact gain Credit in the World at first? Credit it has gained, without

2 doubt.

doubt. If the Multitude at preſent go into this Belief thro' Prejudice, Example, and for Company ſake, they do in this Caſe no more, nor otherwiſe, than they do in all Caſes. And it cannot be denied, but that Truth may be receiv'd thro' Prejudice (as it is call'd) *i. e.* without examining the Proof or Merits of the Cauſe, as well as Falſhood. What general Truth is there, the Merits of which all the World, or the hundredth Part, has examin'd? It is ſmartly ſaid ſomewhere, *That the Prieſt only continues what the Nurſe began:* But the Life of the Remark conſiſts in the Quaintneſs of the Antitheſis between the *Nurſe* and the *Prieſt*; and owes its Support much more to Sound than to Senſe. For is it poſſible that Children ſhou'd not hear ſomething of the common and popular Opinions of their Country, whether thoſe Opinions be true or falſe? Do they not learn the common Maxims of Reaſon this way? Perhaps every Man firſt learnt from his Nurſe, that two and two makes four; and whenever ſhe divides an Apple among her Children, ſhe inſtils into them this Prejudice, That the Whole is equal to its Parts, and all the Parts equal to the Whole; and yet Sir *Iſaac Newton* (ſhame on him) what Work has he made, what a Building has he erected upon the Foundation of this Nurſery-Learning? As to Religion, there never was a Religion, there never will be one, whether true or falſe, publickly owned in any Country, but Children have heard, and ever will hear, more or leſs of it from thoſe who are placed about them. And if this is, and ever muſt be the Caſe, whether the Religion be true or falſe; 'tis

'tis highly abſurd to lay ſtreſs on this Obſervation, when the Queſtion is about the Truth of any Religion; for the Obſervation is indifferent to both ſides of the Queſtion.

We are now, I think, got thro' the Common-place Learning, which muſt for ever, it ſeems, attend upon Queſtions of this Nature; and are coming to the very Merits of the Cauſe.

And here, the Gentleman on the other ſide thought proper to begin with an Account of the People of the *Jews*: The People, in whoſe Country the Fact is laid, and who were originally, and in ſome reſpects principally concerned in its Conſequences.

They were, he ſays, a weak ſuperſtitious People, and lived under the Influence of certain pretended Prophecies and Predictions; that upon this Ground they had, ſome time before the Appearance of Chriſt Jeſus, conceived great Expectations of the coming of a victorious Prince, who ſhou'd deliver them from the *Roman* Yoke, and make them all Kings and Princes. He goes on then to obſerve, how liable the People were, in this ſtate of things, to be impoſed on, and led into Rebellion, by any one who was bold enough to take upon him to perſonate the Prince expected. He obſerves further, that in Fact many ſuch Impoſtors did ariſe, and deceived Multitudes to their Ruin and Deſtruction.

I have laid theſe things together, becauſe I do not intend to diſpute theſe Matters with the Gentleman. Whether the *Jews* were a weak and ſuperſtitious People, and influenc'd by falſe Prophecies, or whether they had true Prophecies among

among them, is not material to the present Question. It is enough for the Gentleman's Argument, if I allow the Fact to be as he has stated it; that they did expect a victorious Prince, that they were upon this Account exposed to be practised on by Pretenders; and in Fact were often so deluded.

This Foundation being laid, it was natural to expect, and I believe your Lordship, and every one present did expect, that the Gentleman wou'd go on to shew, that Jesus laid hold of this Opportunity, struck in with the Opinion of the People, and profess'd himself to be the Prince who was to work their Deliverance. But so far, it seems, is this from being the Case, that the Charge upon Jesus is, that he took the contrary Part, and set up in Opposition to all the popular Notions and Prejudices of his Country: That he interpreted the Prophecies to another Sense and Meaning than his Countrymen did; and by his Expositions took away all Hopes of their ever seeing the victorious Deliverer so much wanted and expected.

I know not how to bring the Gentleman's Premises and his Conclusion to any Agreement; they seem to be at a great variance at present. If it be the likeliest Method for an Impostor to succeed, to build on the popular Opinions, Prejudices and Prophecies of the People; then surely an Impostor cannot possibly take a worse Method than to set up in Opposition to all the Prejudices and Prophecies of the Country. Where was the Art and Cunning then of taking this Method? Cou'd any thing be expected from it, but Hatred, Contempt, and

and Persecution? And did Christ in Fact meet with any other Treatment from the *Jews*? And yet when he found, as the Gentleman allows he did, that he must perish in this Attempt, did he change his Note? Did he come about, and drop any Intimations agreeable to the Notions of the People? It is not pretended. This, which in any other Case, which ever happened, wou'd be taken to be a plain Mark of great Honesty, or great Stupidity, or of both, is in the present Case, Art, Policy, and Contrivance.

But it seems, Jesus dared not set up to be the victorious Prince expected, for Victories are not to be counterfeited. I hope it was no Crime in him that he did not assume this false Character, and try to abuse the Credulity of the People: If he had done so, it certainly wou'd have been a Crime; and therefore in this Point at least he is innocent. I do not suppose, the Gentleman imagines that the *Jews* were well founded in their Expectation of a Temporal Prince; and therefore when Christ opposed this Conceit at the manifest hazard of his Life; as he certainly had Truth on his side, so the Presumption is, that it was for the sake of Truth that he exposed himself.

No; he wanted, we are told, the *Common* and *Necessary* Foundation for a new Revelation, the Authority of an old one, to build on. Very well; I will not enquire how common or how necessary this Foundation is to a new Revelation; for be that Case as it will, it is evident that in the Method Christ took, he had not, nor cou'd have the supposed Advantage of such Foundation. For why is this Foun-

Foundation neceſſary? A Friend of the Gentleman's ſhall tell you. " Becauſe * it muſt be difficult, if not impoſſible, to introduce among Men " (who in all civilized Countries are bred up in " the Belief of ſome revealed Religion) a revealed " Religion wholly new, or ſuch as has no Reference to a preceding one; for that wou'd be to " combat all Men on too many Reſpects, and not " to proceed on a ſufficient Number of Principles " neceſſary to be aſſented to by thoſe, on whom the " firſt Impreſſions of a new Religion are propoſed " to be made." You ſee now the Reaſon of the Neceſſity of this Foundation; it is that the new Teacher may have the Advantage of old popular Opinions, and fix himſelf upon the Prejudices of the People. Had Chriſt any ſuch Advantages, or did he ſeek any ſuch? The People expected a victorious Prince; he told them they were miſtaken: They held as ſacred the Traditions of the Elders; he told them thoſe Traditions made the Law of God of none Effect: They valued themſelves for being the peculiar People of God; he told them, that People from all Quarters of the World ſhou'd be the People of God, and ſit down with *Abraham*, *Iſaac*, and *Jacob*, in the Kingdom: They thought God cou'd be worſhipped only at *Jeruſalem*; he told them God might and ſhou'd be worſhipped every where: They were ſuperſtitious in the Obſervance of the Sabbath; he, according to their Reckoning, broke it frequently: In a word, their Waſhings of Hands and Pots, their ſuperſti-

* *Diſcourſe of the Grounds*, p. 24.

tious Diſtinctions of Meats, their Prayers in publick, their Villanies in ſecret, were all reproved, expoſed, and condemned by him; and the Cry ran ſtrongly againſt him, that he came to deſtroy the Law and the Prophets. And now, Sir, what Advantage had Chriſt of your common and neceſſary Foundation? What *ſufficient Number of Principles*, owned by the People, did he build on? If he adhered to the old Revelation in the true Senſe, or (which is ſufficient to the preſent Argument) in a Senſe not received by the People, it was, in truth, the greateſt Difficulty he had to ſtruggle with. And therefore what cou'd tempt him, but purely a Regard to Truth, to take upon himſelf ſo many Difficulties which might have been avoided, cou'd he have been but ſilent as to the old Revelation, and left the People to their Imaginations?

To carry on this Plot, we are told, that the next Thing which Jeſus did, was to make Choice of proper Perſons to be his Diſciples. The Gentleman has given us their Character; but, as I ſuppoſe, he has more Employment for them before he has done, I deſire to defer the Conſideration of their Abilities and Conduct, till I hear what Work he has for them to do. I wou'd only obſerve, that thus far this Plot differs from all that ever I heard of. Impoſtors generally take Advantage of the Prejudices of the People; generally too they make choice of cunning dextrous Fellows to manage under them: But in this Caſe, Jeſus oppoſed all the Notions of the People, and made choice of Simpletons, it ſeems, to conduct his Contrivances.

But

But what Design, what real End was carrying on all this while? Why, the Gentleman tells us, that the very thing disclaimed, the temporal Kingdom, was the real thing aimed at under this Disguise. He told the People there was no Foundation to expect a temporal Deliverer, warned them against all who shou'd set up those Pretensions: He declared there was no Ground from the ancient Prophecies, to expect such a Prince; and yet by these very Means he was working his way to an Opportunity of declaring himself to be the very Prince the People wanted. We are still upon the marvellous; every Step opens new Wonders. I blame not the Gentleman; for what but this can be imagined, to give any Account of these Measures imputed to Christ? Be this never so unlikely, yet this is the only thing that can be said. Had Christ been charged with Enthusiasm, it wou'd not have been necessary to assign a Reason for his Conduct: Madness is unaccountable: *Ratione modoque tractari non vult.* But when Design, Cunning, and Fraud, are made the Charge, and carry'd to such an Height, as to suppose him to be a Party to the Contrivance of a sham Resurrection for himself; it is necessary to say, to what End this Cunning tended. It was, we are told, to a Kingdom; and indeed the Temptation was little enough, considering that the chief Conductor of the Plot was to be crucify'd for his Pains. But were the Means made use of, at all probable to attain the End? Yes, says the Gentleman, that can't be disputed; for they had really this Effect. The People wou'd have made him King. Very well;

D 2 Why

Why was he not King then? Why, it happened unluckily that he wou'd not accept the Offer, but withdrew himſelf from the Multitude, and lay concealed till they were diſperſed. It will be ſaid, perhaps, that Jeſus was a better Judge of Affairs than the People, and ſaw that it was not yet time to accept the Offer. Be it ſo: Let us ſee then what follows.

The Government was alarmed, and Jeſus was looked on as a Perſon dangerous to the State; and he had Diſcernment enough to ſee, that his Death was determined and inevitable. What does he do then? Why, to make the beſt of a bad Caſe, and to ſave the Benefit of his Undertaking to thoſe who were to ſucceed him, he pretends to propheſy of his Death, which he knew cou'd not be avoided: And further, that he ſhould riſe again the Third Day.—Men do not uſe to play Tricks *in articulo mortis*; but this Plot had nothing common, nothing in the ordinary way. But what if it ſhould appear, that after the foretelling of his Death, (thro' Deſpair of his Fortunes, 'tis ſaid) he had it in his Power to ſet up for King once more, and once more refuſed the Opportunity? Men in Deſpair lay hold on the leaſt Help, and never refuſe the greateſt. Now the Caſe was really ſo; after he had foretold his Crucifixion, he came to *Jeruſalem* in the triumphant manner the Gentleman mentioned: The People ſtrew'd his Way with Boughs and Flowers, and were all at his Devotion; the *Jewiſh* Governors lay ſtill for fear of the People. Why was not this Opportunity laid hold on to ſeize the Kingdom, or at leaſt to ſecure himſelf from

from the ignominious Death he expected? For whose Sake was he contented to die? For whose Sake did he contrive this Plot of his Resurrection? Wife and Children he had none; his nearest Relations gave little Credit to him; his Disciples were not fit even to be trusted with the Secret, nor capable to manage any Advantage that cou'd arise from it. However, the Gentleman tells us, a Kingdom has arisen out of this Plot, a Kingdom of Priests. But when did it arise? Some hundred Years after the Death of Christ, in Opposition to his Will, and almost to the Subversion of his Religion. And yet, we are told, this Kingdom was the thing he had in view. I am apt to think the Gentleman is persuaded, that the Dominion he complains of is contrary to the Spirit of the Gospel; I am sure some of his Friends have taken great Pains to prove it so. How then can it be charged as the Intention of the Gospel to introduce it? Whatever the Case was, it cannot surely be suspected, that Christ died to make Popes and Cardinals. The Alterations which have happened in the Doctrines and Practices of Churches, since the Christian Religion was settled by those who had an authentick Commission to settle it, are quite out of the Question, when the Enquiry is about the Truth of the Christian Religion. Christ and his Apostles did not vouch for the Truth of all that shou'd be taught in the Church in future Times. Nay, they foretold and forewarned the World against such corrupt Teachers. 'Tis therefore absurd to challenge the Religion of Christ, because of the Corruptions which have spread among

mong Chriſtians. The Goſpel has no more Concern with them, and ought no more to be charged with them, than with the Doctrines of the *Alcoran*.

There is but one Obſervation more, I think, which the Gentleman made under this Head. Jeſus, he ſays, referred to the Authority of Ancient Prophecies to prove that the Meſſias was to die and riſe again: The ancient Books referr'd to are extant, and no ſuch Prophecies, he ſays, are to be found. Now whether the Gentleman can find theſe Prophecies, or no, is not material to the preſent Queſtion. It is allowed, that Chriſt foretold his own Death and Reſurrection; if the Reſurrection was managed by Fraud, Chriſt was certainly in the Fraud himſelf, by foretelling the Fraud that was to happen: Diſprove therefore the Reſurrection, and we ſhall have no further Occaſion for Prophecy. On the other ſide; by foretelling the Reſurrection, he certainly put the Proof of his Miſſion on the Truth of the Event. Whether it be the Character of the Meſſias, in the ancient Prophets or no, that he ſhould die and riſe again; without doubt Jeſus is not the Meſſias, if he did not riſe again. For by his own Prophecy he made it part of the Character of the Meſſias. If the Event juſtified the Prediction, it is ſuch an Evidence as no Man of Senſe and Reaſon can reject. One would naturally think, that the foretelling his Reſurrection, and giving ſuch publick Notice to expect it, that his keeneſt Enemies were fully apprized of it, carried with it the greateſt Mark of ſincere dealing. It ſtands thus far

far clear of the Sufpicion of Fraud; and had it proceeded from *Enthufiafm*, and an heated Imagination, the dead Body at leaft would have refted in the Grave, and without further Evidence have confuted fuch Pretenfions. And fince the dead Body was not only carried openly to the Grave, but there watched and guarded, and yet could never afterwards be found, never heard of more, as a dead Body; there muft of neceffity have been either a real Miracle, or a great Fraud in this Cafe. *Enthufiafm* dies with the Man, and has no Operation on his dead Body. There is therefore here no Medium; you muft either admit the Miracle, or prove the Fraud.

Judge. Mr. *A*. You are at Liberty either to reply to what has been faid under this Head, or to go on with your Caufe.

Mr. *A*. My Lord, The Obfervations I laid before you, were but introductory to the main Evidences on which the Merits of the Caufe muft reft. The Gentleman concluded, that here muft be a real Miracle, or a great Fraud; a Fraud, he means, to which Jefus in his Life-time was a Party. There is, he fays no Medium: I beg his Pardon: Why might it not be an *Enthufiafm* in the Mafter which occafioned the Prediction, and Fraud in the Servants who put it in Execution?

Mr. *B*. My Lord, This is new Matter, and not a Reply: The Gentleman opened this Tranfaction as a Fraud from one end to the other. Now he fuppofes Chrift to have been an honeft, poor *Enthufiaft*, and the Difciples only to be Cheats.

Judge.

Judge. Sir, If you go to new Matter, the Council on the other ſide muſt be admitted to anſwer.

Mr. *A*. My Lord, I have no ſuch Intention. I was obſerving, that the Account I gave of Jeſus was only to introduce the Evidence that is to be laid before the Court. It cannot be expected that I ſhould know all the ſecret Deſigns of this Contrivance; eſpecially conſidering that we have but ſhort Accounts of this Affair, and thoſe too conveyed to us thro' Hands of Friends and Parties to the Plot. In ſuch a Caſe, it is enough if we can imagine what the Views probably were. And in ſuch Caſe too, it muſt be very eaſy for a Gentleman of Parts to raiſe contrary Imaginations, and to argue plauſibly from them. But the Gentleman has rightly obſerved, that if the Reſurrection be a Fraud, there is an End of all Pretenſions, good or bad, that were to be ſupported by it. Therefore I ſhall go on to prove this Fraud, which is one main Part of the Cauſe now to be determined.

I beg Leave to remind you, that Jeſus, in his Life-time, foretold his Death, and that he ſhould riſe again the third Day. The firſt Part of his Prediction was accompliſhed; he died upon the Croſs, and was buried. I will not trouble you with the Particulars of his Crucifixion, Death, and Burial. 'Tis a well known Story.

Mr. *B*. My Lord, I deſire to know whether the Gentleman charges any Fraud upon this Part of the Hiſtory; perhaps he may be of Opinion by and by, that there was a Sleight of Hand in the

the Crucifixion, and that Christ only counterfeited Death.

Mr *A.* No, no; have no such Fears: he was not crucify'd by his Disciples, but by the *Romans* and the *Jews*; and they were in very good earnest. I will prove beyond Contradiction, that the dead Body was fairly laid in the Tomb, and the Tomb sealed up; and it will be well for you, if you can get it as fairly out again.

Judge. Go on with your Evidence.

Mr. *A.* My Lord, The Crucifixion being over, the dead Body was conveyed to a Sepulchre; and, in the general Opinion, there seem'd to be an End of the whole Design. But the Governors of the *Jews*, watchful for the Safety of the People, called to mind, that Jesus in his Life-time had said, that he wou'd rise again on the third Day. It may at first sight seem strange, that they shou'd give any Attention to such a Prophecy; a Prophecy big with Confidence and Presumption, and which, to the common Sense of Mankind, carried its Confutation along with it. And " there's no other " Nation in the World, which would not have " slighted such a vain Prognostication of a known " Impostor". But they had Warning to be watchful. It was not long before that the People " had like to have been fatally deluded, and im- " posed on by him, in the pretended Resuscitati- " on of *Lazarus*". They had fully discover'd the Cheat in the Case of *Lazarus*, and had narrowly escaped the dangerous Consequences of it. And tho' Jesus was dead, yet he had many Disciples and Followers alive, who were ready enough to com-

E bine

bine in any Fraud to verify the Prediction of their Master. Shou'd they succeed, the Rulers foresaw the Consequences in this Case wou'd be more fatal, than those which before they had narrowly escaped. Upon this Account they addressed themselves to the *Roman* Governor; told him how the Case was; and desired that he wou'd grant them a Guard to watch the Sepulchre; that the Service would not be long, for the Prediction limited the Resurrection to the third Day; and when that was over, the Soldiers might be released from the Duty. *Pilate* granted the Request; and a Guard was set to watch the Sepulchre.

This was not at all. The chief Priests took another Method to prevent all Frauds, and it was the best that could possibly be taken; which was to seal up the Door of the Sepulchre. To understand to what Purpose this Caution was used, you need only consider what is intended by sealing up Doors and Boxes, or Writings. Is it not for the Satisfaction of all Parties concerned, that they may be sure things are in the State they left them, when they come and find their Seals not injured? This was the Method used by *Nebuchadnezzar*, when *Daniel* was cast into the Lions Den; he sealed the Door of the Den. And for what Purpose? Was it not to satisfy himself and his Court, that no Art had been used to preserve *Daniel?* And when he came and saw *Daniel* safe, and his own Seal untouch'd, he was satisfy'd. And indeed if we consider the thing rightly, a Seal thus used imports a Covenant: If you deliver Writings to a Person sealed, and he accepts them so, your Delivery and his

his Acceptance, implies a Covenant between you, that the Writings ſhall be deliver'd, and the Seal whole. And ſhou'd the Seal be broken, it wou'd be a manifeſt Fraud and Breach of Truſt. Nay, ſo ſtrongly is this Covenant implied, that there needs no ſpecial Agreement in the Caſe. 'Tis a Compact which Men are put under by the Law of Nations, and the common Conſent of Mankind. When you ſend a Letter ſealed to the Poſt-houſe, you have not indeed a ſpecial Agreement with all Perſons thro' whoſe Hands it paſſes, that it ſhall not be opened by any Hand, but his only to whom it is directed: Yet Men know themſelves to be under this Reſtraint, and that it is unlawful and diſhonourable to tranſgreſs it.

Since then the Sepulchre was ſealed; ſince the Seal imported a Covenant, conſider who were the Parties to this Covenant. They cou'd be no other than the chief Prieſts on one Side, the Apoſtles on the other. To prove this, no ſpecial Agreement need be ſhewn. On one ſide, there was a Concern to ſee the Prediction fulfilled; on the other, to prevent Fraud in fulfilling it. The Sum of their Agreement was naturally this: That the Seals ſhou'd be opened at the time appointed for the Reſurrection, that all Parties might ſee and be ſatiſfied, whether the dead Body was come to Life, or no.

What now wou'd any reaſonable Man expect from theſe Circumſtances? Don't you expect to hear that the chief Prieſts and the Apoſtles met at the time appointed, opened the Seals, and that the matter in diſpute was ſettled beyond all Con-

E 2 troverſy

troverſy one way or other? But ſee how it happen'd. The Seals were broken, the Body ſtolen away in the Night by the Diſciples; none of the chief Prieſts preſent, or ſummon'd to ſee the Seals open'd. The Guards, when examin'd, were forc'd to confeſs the Truth, tho' joined with an Acknowledgment of their Guilt, which made them liable to be puniſh'd by *Pilate*; they confeſſed that they were aſleep, and in the mean time that the Body was ſtolen away by the Diſciples.

This Evidence of the *Roman* Soldiers, and the far ſtronger Evidence ariſing from the clandeſtine Manner of breaking up the Seals, are ſufficient Proofs of Fraud.

But there is another Circumſtance in the Caſe of equal Weight. Tho' the Seals did not prevent the Cheat entirely, yet they effectually falſified the Prediction. According to the Prediction, Jeſus was to riſe on the third Day, or after the third Day. At this Time the chief Prieſts intended to be preſent, and probably wou'd have been attended by a great Multitude. This made it impoſſible to play any Tricks at that time, and therefore the Apoſtles were forced to haſten the Plot; and accordingly the Reſurrection happened a Day before its time. For the Body was buried on the *Friday*, and was gone early in the Morning on *Sunday*.

Theſe are plain Facts; Facts drawn from the Accounts given us by thoſe who are Friends to the Belief of the Reſurrection. The Gentleman won't call theſe Imaginations, or complain that I have given him Schemes inſtead of Evidence.

Mr. *B.*

Mr. *B*. My Lord, I am now to consider that Part of the Argument upon which the Gentleman lays the greatest Stress. He has given us his Evidence; mere Evidence, he says, unmixed and clear of all Schemes and Imaginations. In one thing indeed he has been as good as his word; he has proved beyond Contradiction, that Christ died, and was laid in the Sepulchre; for without doubt when the *Jews* sealed the Stone, they took care to see that the Body was there; otherwise their Precaution was useless. He has proved too, that the Prediction of Christ concerning his own Resurrection, was a thing publickly known in all *Jerusalem*; for he owns that this gave Occasion for all the Care that was taken to prevent Fraud. If this open Prediction implies a fraudulent Design, the Evidence is strong with the Gentleman; but if it shall appear to be, what it really was, the greatest Mark that cou'd be given of Sincerity and plain Dealing in the whole Affair, the Evidence will be still as strong, but the Weight of it will fall on the wrong side for the Gentleman's Purpose.

In the next place, the Gentleman seems to be at a great Loss to account for the Credit which the chief Priests gave to the Prediction of the Resurrection, by the Care they took to prevent it. He thinks the Thing in itself was too extravagant and absurd to deserve any Regard; and that no one wou'd have regarded such a Prediction in any other Time or Place. I agree with the Gentleman entirely: But then I demand of him a Reason why the chief Priests were under any Concern about this Prediction: Was it because they had plainly discovered

vered him to be a Cheat and an Impoſtor? 'Tis impoſſible. This Reaſon wou'd have convinced them of the Folly and Preſumption of the Prediction. It muſt therefore neceſſarily be, that they had diſcovered ſomething in the Life and Actions of Chriſt, which raiſed this Jealouſy, and made them liſten to a Prophecy in his Caſe, which in any other Caſe they wou'd have deſpiſed. And what could this be but the ſecret Conviction they were under, by his many Miracles, of his extraordinary Powers? This Care therefore of the chief Prieſts over his dead, helpleſs Body, is a laſting Teſtimony of the mighty Works which Jeſus did in his Life-time. For had the *Jews* been perſuaded that he performed no Wonders in his Life, I think they wou'd not have been afraid of ſeeing any done by him after his Death.

But the Gentleman is of another mind. He ſays they had diſcovered a plain Cheat in the Caſe of *Lazarus*, whom Chriſt had pretended to raiſe from the Dead; and therefore they took all this Care to guard againſt a like Cheat.

I begin now to want Evidence; I am forbid to call this Imagination; what elſe to call it, I know not. There is not the leaſt Intimation given from Hiſtory, that there was any Cheat in the Caſe of *Lazarus*, or that any one ſuſpected a Cheat. *Lazarus* lived in the Country after he was raiſed from the Dead; and tho' his Life was ſecretly and baſely ſought after, yet no body had the Courage to call him to a Tryal for his part of the Cheat. It may be ſaid, perhaps the Rulers were terrify'd. Very well: But they were not terrify'd when they had

had Chriſt in their Poſſeſſion, when they brought him to a Tryal; why did they not then object this Cheat to Chriſt? It wou'd have been much to their Purpoſe. Inſtead of that, they accuſe him of a Deſign to pull down their Temple, to deſtroy their Law, and of Blaſphemy; but not one word of any Fraud in the Caſe of *Lazarus*, or any other Caſe.

But not to enter into the Merits of this Cauſe, which has in it too many Circumſtances for your preſent Conſideration; let us take the Caſe to be as the Gentleman ſtates it, That the Cheat, in the Caſe of *Lazarus*, was detected. What Conſequence is to be expected? In all other Caſes, Impoſtors, once diſcovered, grow odious and contemptible, and quite incapable of doing further Miſchief: So little are they regarded, that even when they tell the Truth they are neglected. Was it ſo in this Caſe? No, ſays the Gentleman, the *Jews* were the more careful that Chriſt ſhou'd not cheat them in his own Reſurrection. Surely this is a moſt ſingular Caſe: When the People thought him a Prophet, the chief Prieſts ſought to kill him, and thought his Death wou'd put an End to his Pretenſions: When they and the People had diſcovered him to be a Cheat, then they thought him not ſafe, even when he was dead, but were afraid he ſhou'd prove a true Prophet, and, according to his own Prediction, riſe again. A needleſs, a prepoſterous Fear!

In the next place, the Gentleman tells us how proper the Care was that the chief Prieſts took. I agree perfectly with him. Human Policy cou'd not

invent

invent a more proper Method to guard againſt and prevent all Fraud. They delivered the Sepulchre, with the dead Body in it, to a Company of *Roman* Soldiers, who had Orders from their Officer to watch the Sepulchre. Their Care went further ſtill, they ſealed the Door of the Sepulchre.

Upon this Occaſion, the Gentleman has explained the uſe of Seals when applied to ſuch Purpoſes. They imply, he ſays, a Covenant that the Things ſealed up ſhall remain in the Condition they are, till the Parties to the ſealing are agreed to open them. I ſee no Reaſon to enter into the Learning about Seals: Let it be as the Gentleman has opened it. What then?

Why then, it ſeems, the Apoſtles and chief Prieſts were in a Covenant that there ſhould be no Reſurrection, at leaſt no opening of the Door, till they met together at an appointed Time to view and unſeal the Door.

Your Lordſhip and the Court will now conſider the Probability of this Suppoſition. When Chriſt was ſeized and carried to his Tryal, his Diſciples fled, and hid themſelves for fear of the *Jews*, out of a juſt Apprehenſion that they ſhou'd, if apprehended, be ſacrificed with their Maſter. *Peter* indeed followed him, but his Courage ſoon failed, and 'tis well known in what manner he denied him. After the Death of Chriſt, his Diſciples were ſo far from being ready to engage for his Reſurrection, or to enter into Terms and Agreements for the Manner in which it ſhould be done, that they themſelves did not believe it ever wou'd be. They gave over all Hopes and Thoughts of it; and

2

and far from entring into Engagements with the Chief Priests, their whole Concern was to keep themselves concealed from them. This is a well known Case, and I will not trouble you with particular Authorities to prove this Truth. Can any Man now in his right Senses, think that the Disciples, under these Circumstances, entred into this Covenant with the *Jews?* I believe the Gentleman don't think it, and for that Reason says, that Seals so used import a Covenant without a special Agreement. Be it so; and it must then be allowed, that the Apostles were no more concerned in these Seals, than every other Man in the Country, and no more answerable for them; for the Covenant reached to every body as well as to them, since they were under no special Contract.

But I beg Pardon for spending your time unnecessarily; when the simple plain Account of this Matter, will best answer all these Jealousies and Suspicions. The *Jews*, 'tis plain, were exceedingly sollicitous about this Event. For this Reason they obtain'd a Guard from *Pilate*; and when they had, they were still suspicious lest their Guards should deceive them, and enter into Combination against them. To secure this Point, they sealed the Door, and required of the Guards to deliver up the Sepulchre to them sealed as it was. This is the natural and true Account of the Matter. Do but consider it in a parallel Case; suppose a Prince should set a Guard at the Door of his Treasury; and the Officer who placed the Guard should seal the Door, and say to the Soldiers, you shall be answerable for the Seal if I find it broken:

F Wou'd

Wou'd not all the World underſtand the Seal to be fixed to guard againſt the Soldiers, who might, tho' employed to keep off others, be ready enough to pilfer themſelves? This is in all ſuch Caſes but a neceſſary Care; you may place Guards, and when you do, all is in their Power; *Et quis cuſtodes cuſtodiat ipſos?*

But it ſeems, that notwithſtanding all this Care, the Seals were broken, and the Body gone: If you complain of this, Sir, demand Satisfaction of your Guards, they only are reſponſible for it. The Diſciples had no more to do in it, than you or I.

The Guards, the Gentleman ſays, have confeſſed the Truth, and owned that they were aſleep, and that the Diſciples in the mean Time ſtole away the Body. I wiſh the Guards were in Court, I wou'd ask them, how they came to be ſo punctual in relating what happen'd when they were aſleep; what induced them to believe that the Body was ſtolen at all; what, that it was ſtolen by the Diſciples; ſince by their own Confeſſion they were aſleep, and ſaw nothing, ſaw nobody. But ſince they are not to be had, I wou'd deſire to ask the Gentleman the ſame Queſtions; and whether he has any Authorities in Point, to ſhew that ever any Man was admitted as an Evidence in any Court to prove a Fact which happen'd when he was aſleep. I ſee the Gentleman is uneaſy; I'll preſs the Matter no further.

As this Story has no Evidence to ſupport it, ſo neither has it any Probability. The Gentleman has given you the Character of the Diſciples, that they were weak ignorant Men, full of the popu-

lar

lar Prejudices, and Superſtitions of their Country; which ſtuck cloſe to them, notwithſtanding their long acquaintance with their Maſter. The Apoſtles are not much wronged in this Account. And is it likely that ſuch Men ſhou'd engage in ſo deſperate a Deſign as to ſteal away the Body, in Oppoſition to the combined Power of the *Jews* and *Romans?* What cou'd tempt them to it? What good cou'd the dead Body do them? or if it cou'd have done them any, what Hope had they to ſucceed in their Attempt? A dead Body is not to be removed by ſleight of Hand; it requires many Hands to move it. Beſides, the great Stone at the Mouth of the Sepulchre was to be removed; which could not be done ſilently, or by Men walking on tiptoes to prevent diſcovery; ſo that if the Guards had really been aſleep, yet there was no Encouragement to go on this Enterprize: for it is hardly poſſible to ſuppoſe, but that rolling away the Stone, moving the Body, the Hurry and Confuſion in carrying it off, muſt awaken them.

But ſuppoſing the thing practicable, yet the Attempt was ſuch as the Diſciples conſiſtently with their own Notions cou'd not undertake. The Gentleman ſays, they continued all their Maſter's Life-time to expect to ſee him a temporal Prince; and a Friend of the Gentleman's * has obſerved, what is equally true, that they had the ſame Expectation after his Death. Conſider now their Caſe. Their Maſter was Dead; and they are to contrive to ſteal away his Body.

* *Grounds, pag.* 33.

For what? Did they expect to make a King of the dead Body, if they cou'd get it into their Power? Or did they think, if they had it, they cou'd raiſe it to Life again? If they truſted ſo far to their Maſter's Prediction, as to expect his Reſurrection, (which I think is evident they did not) cou'd they yet think the Reſurrection depended on their having the dead Body? It is in all Views abſurd. But the Gentleman ſuppoſes, that they meant to carry on the Deſign for themſelves in their Maſter's Name, if they cou'd but have perſuaded the People to believe him riſen from the Dead. But he does not conſider, that by this Suppoſition he ſtrips the Diſciples of every part of their Character at once, and preſents to us a new Set of Men in every reſpect different from the former. The former Diſciples were plain weak Men; but theſe are bold, hardy, cunning, and contriving. The former were full of the Superſtition of their Country, and expected a Prince from the Authority of their Prophets; but theſe are Deſpiſers of the Prophets, and of the Notions of their Countrymen, and are deſigning to turn theſe Fables to their own Advantage: For it cannot be ſuppoſed that they believed the Prophets, and at the ſame time thought to accompliſh, or defeat them, by ſo manifeſt a Cheat, to which they themſelves, at leaſt, were conſcious.

But let us take leave of theſe Suppoſitions, and ſee how the true Evidence in this Caſe ſtands. Guards were placed, and they did their Duty. But what are Guards and Centinels againſt the Power of God! An Angel of the Lord opened the Sepulchre,

pulchre, the Guards ſaw him, and became like dead Men. This Account they gave to the chief Prieſts; who ſtill perſiſting in their Obſtinacy, bribed the Guards to tell the contradictory Story, of their being aſleep, and the Body ſtolen.

I cannot but obſerve to your Lordſhip, that all theſe Circumſtances, ſo much queſtioned and ſuſpected, were neceſſary Circumſtances, ſuppoſing the Reſurrection to be true. The Seal was broken, the Body came out of the Sepulchre, the Guards were placed in vain to prevent it. Be it ſo: I deſire to know whether the Gentleman thinks that the Seal put God under Covenant; or cou'd preſcribe to him a Method of performing this great Work? Or whether he thinks the Guards were placed to maintain the Seal, in Oppoſition to the Power of God? If he will maintain neither of theſe Points, then the opening the Seals, notwithſtanding the Guard ſet upon them, will be an Evidence, not of the Fraud, but of the Power of the Reſurrection; and the Guards will have nothing to anſwer for, but only this, that they were not ſtronger than God. The Seal was a proper Check upon the Guards; the *Jews* had no other Meaning in it; they cou'd not be ſo ſtupid, as to imagine that they cou'd by this Contrivance diſappoint the Deſigns of Providence. And it is ſurprizing to hear theſe Circumſtances made uſe of to prove the Reſurrection to be a Fraud, which yet cou'd not but happen, ſuppoſing the Reſurrection to be true.

But there is another Circumſtance ſtill, which the Gentleman reckons very material, and upon which, I find, great Streſs is laid. The Reſur-

2 rection

rection happened, we are told, a Day sooner than the Prediction imported. The Reason assigned for it is, that the Execution of the Plot at the Time appointed, was rendred impracticable, because the Chief Priests, and probably great Numbers of the People, were prepared to visit the Sepulchre at that Time; and therefore the Disciples were under a Necessity of hastening their Plot.

This Observation is entirely inconsistent with the Supposition upon which the Reasoning stands. The Gentleman has all along supposed the Resurrection to have been managed by Fraud, and not by Violence; and indeed Violence, if there had been an Opportunity of using it, wou'd have been insignificant. Beating the Guards, and removing the dead Body by Force, wou'd have destroyed all Pretences to a Resurrection. Now surely the Guards, supposing them not to be enow in Number to withstand all Violence, were at least sufficient to prevent, or to discover Fraud. What Occasion then to hasten the Plot for fear of Numbers meeting at the Tomb, since there were Numbers always present sufficient to discover any Fraud; the only Method that cou'd be used in the Case?

Suppose then that we cou'd not give a satisfactory Account of the way of reckoning the Time from the Crucifixion to the Resurrection; yet this we can say, That the Resurrection happened during the Time that the Guards had the Sepulchre in keeping; and 'tis impossible to imagine what Opportunity this cou'd give to Fraud. Had the Time been delayed, the Guards removed, and then a Resurrection pretended, it might with some colour

lour of Reaſon have been ſaid, Why did he not come within his Time? Why did he chuſe to come after his Time, when all Witneſſes, who had patiently expected the appointed Hour, were withdrawn? But now what is to be objected? You think he came too ſoon. But were not your Guards at the Door when he came? Did they not ſee what happened? And what other Satisfaction cou'd you have had, ſuppoſing he had come a Day later?

By ſaying of this, I do not mean to decline the Gentleman's Objection, which is founded upon a Miſtake of a way of ſpeaking, common to the *Jews* and other People; who, when they name any Number of Days and Years, include the firſt and the laſt of the Days or Years to make up the Sum. Chriſt, alluding to his own Reſurrection, ſays, *In three Days I will raiſe it up.* The Angels report his Prediction thus, *The Son of Man ſhall be crucify'd, and the third Day riſe again.* Elſewhere it is ſaid, *after three Days*; and again, that he was to be in the Bowels of the Earth *three Days and three Nights.* Theſe Expreſſions are equivalent to each other, for we always reckon the Night into the Day, when we reckon by ſo many Days. If you agree to do a thing ten Days hence, you ſtipulate for Forbearance for the Nights as well as Days; and therefore in Reckoning, two Days, and two Days and two Nights, are the ſame thing. That the Expreſſion, *after three Days*, means incluſive Days, is proved by *Grotius* on *Matt.* xxvii. 63. and by others. The Prediction therefore was, that he wou'd wou'd riſe on the third Day. Now, he was crucify'd on *Friday*, and buried; he lay in the Grave all *Saturday*, and roſe early on *Sunday* Morning. But the Gentleman thinks he ought not to have riſen till *Monday*. Pray try what the Uſe of common Language requires to be underſtood in a like Caſe. Suppoſe you were told, that your Friend ſickned on *Friday*, was let blood on *Saturday*, and the third Day he died; what Day wou'd you think he died on? If you have any Doubt about it, put the Queſtion to the firſt plain Man you meet, and he will reſolve it. The *Jews* cou'd have no Doubt in this Caſe; for ſo they practiſed in one of the higheſt Points of their Law. Every Male Child was to be circumciſed on the eighth Day. How did they reckon the Days? Why, the Day of the Birth was one, and the Day of the Circumciſion another; and tho' a Child was born towards the very End of the firſt Day, he was capable of Circumciſion on any time of the eighth Day. And therefore it is not new nor ſtrange, that the third Day, in our Caſe, ſhou'd be reckoned into the Number, tho' Chriſt roſe at the very beginning of it. It is more ſtrange to reckon whole Years in this manner; and yet this is the conſtant Method obſerved in *Ptolemy*'s Canon, the moſt valuable Piece of ancient Chronology, next to the Bible, now extant. If a King lived over the firſt Day of a Year, and died the Week after, that whole Year is reckoned to his Reign.

I have now gone through the ſeveral Objections upon this Head; what Credit they may gain in this Age, I know not; but 'tis plain they had no Credit

Credit when they were firſt ſpread abroad; nay 'tis evident that the very Perſons who ſet abroad this Story of the Body being ſtolen, did not believe it themſelves. And not to inſiſt here upon the plain Fact, which was, that the Guards were hir'd to tell this Lye by the chief Prieſts, it will appear from the After-Conduct of the chief Prieſts themſelves, that they were conſcious that the Story was falſe. Not long after the Reſurrection of Chriſt, the Diſciples having received new Power from above, appeared publickly in *Jeruſalem*, and in the very Temple, and teſtified the Reſurrection of Chriſt, even before thoſe who had murdered him. What now do the chief Prieſts do? They ſeize upon the Apoſtles, they threaten them, they beat them, they ſcourge them, and all to ſtop their Mouths, inſiſting that they ſhould ſay no more of the Matter. But why did they not, when they had the Diſciples in their Power, charge them directly with their notorious Cheat in ſtealing the Body, and expoſe them to the People as Impoſtors? This had been much more to their Purpoſe, than all their Menaces and ill Uſage, and would more effectually have undeceived the People. But of this not one Word is ſaid. They try to murder them, enter into Combinations to aſſaſſinate them, prevail with *Herod* to put one of them to Death; but not ſo much as a Charge againſt them of any Fraud in the Reſurrection. Their Orator *Tertullus*, who could not have miſſed ſo fine a Topick of Declamation, had there been but a Suſpicion to ſupport it, is quite ſilent on this Head, and is content to flouriſh on the Common-Place of Sedition and Heresy, profaning the Temple, and the like; very Trifles to his Cause, in comparison to the other Accusation, had there been any Ground to make use of it. And yet as it happens, we are sure the very Question of the Resurrection came under Debate; for *Festus* tells King *Agrippa*, that the *Jews* had certain Questions against *Paul*, *of one Jesus, which was dead, whom Paul affirmed to be alive*. After this, *Agrippa* hears *Paul* himself; and had he suspected, much less had he been convinced that there was a Cheat in the Resurrection, he would hardly have said to *Paul* at the End of the Conference, *Almost thou persuadest me to be a Christian*.

But let us see what the *Council* and *Senate* of the Children of *Israel* thought of this Matter, in the most solemn and serious Deliberation they ever had about it. * Not long after the Resurrection, the Apostles were taken; the High Priest thought the Matter of that Weight, that he summoned the Council and Senate of the Children of *Israel*. The Apostles are brought before them, and make their Defence. Part of their Defence, is in these Words; *The God of our Fathers raised up Jesus, whom ye slew, and hanged on a Tree*. The Defence was indeed a heavy Charge upon the Senate, and in the Warmth of their Anger, their first Resolution was to slay them all. But *Gamaliel*, one of the Council, stood up, and told them, that the Matter deserved more Consideration. He recounted to them the History of se-

* Acts v.

veral

veral Impoſtors who had periſhed, and concluded with reſpect to the Caſe of the Apoſtles then before them; *If this Work be of Men, it will come to nought; But if it be of God, ye cannot overthrow it, leſt haply ye be found to fight againſt God.* The Council agreed to this Advice, and after ſome ill Treatment, the Apoſtles were diſcharged. I ask now, and let any Man of common Senſe anſwer; Could *Gamaliel* poſſibly have given this Advice, and ſuppoſed that the Hand of God might be with the Apoſtles, if he had known that there was a Cheat diſcovered in the Reſurrection of Jeſus? Could the whole Senate have followed this Advice, had they believed the Diſcovery of the Cheat? Was there not among them one Man wiſe enough to ſay, How can you ſuppoſe God to have any thing to do in this Affair, when the Reſurrection of Jeſus, upon which all depends, was a notorious Cheat, and manifeſtly proved to be ſo? I ſhould but leſſen the Weight of this Authority by ſaying more; and therefore I will reſt here, and give way to the Gentleman to go on with his Accuſation.

Mr. *A.* My Lord, before I proceed any further, I beg leave to ſay a few Words in Reply to what the Gentleman has offered on this Head.

The Gentleman thinks that the Detection in the Caſe of *Lazarus* ought to have made the *Jews* quite unconcerned in the Caſe of *Jeſus*, and ſecure as to the Event of his own Reſurrection. He ſays very true, ſuppoſing their Care had been for themſelves: But Governors have another Care upon their hands, the Care of their People; and 'tis not enough for them to guard againſt being im-

G 2 poſed

posed on themselves, they must be watchful to guard the Multitude against Frauds and Deceits. The chief Priests were satisfied indeed of the Fraud in the Case of *Lazarus*, yet they saw the People deceived by it; and for this Reason, and not for their own Satisfaction, they used the Caution in the Case of the Resurrection of Jesus, which I before laid before you. In so doing, they are well justified; and the Inconsistency charged on the other side, between their Opinion of Jesus, and their Fear of being imposed on by his pretended Resurrection, is fully answered.

The next Observation relates to the Seal of the Sepulchre. The Gentleman thinks the Seal was used as a Check upon the *Roman* Soldiers. But what Reason had the *Jews* to suspect them? They were not Disciples of Jesus; they were Servants of the *Roman* Governor, and employed in the Service of the *Jews*: And I leave it to the Court to judge, whether the *Jews* set the Seal to guard against their Friends, or their Enemies. But if the Seals were really used against the Guards, then the breaking of the Seals is a Proof that the Guards were corrupted: And if so, 'tis easy to conceive how the Body was removed.

As to the Disciples, the Gentleman observes, that the Part allotted them in the Management of the Resurrection supposes an unaccountable Change in their Character. It will not be long before the Gentleman will have Occasion for as great a Change in their Character; for these weak Men you will find soon employed in converting the World, and sent to appear before Kings and Princes in the Name

Name of their Maſter; ſoon you will ſee them grow wiſe and powerful and every way qualified for their extenſive and important Buſineſs. The only difference between me and the Gentleman on the other ſide will be found to be this, that I date this Change a little earlier then he does. A ſmall matter ſurely, to determine the Right of this Controverſy.

The laſt Obſervation relates to King *Agrippa*'s Complaiſance to *Paul*, and *Gamaliel*'s Advice. I cannot anſwer for *Agrippa*'s Meaning, but certainly he meant but little; and if this matter is to be tryed by his Opinion, we know that he never did turn Chriſtian. As for *Gamaliel*, 'tis probable that he ſaw great numbers of the People engaged zealouſly in favour of the Apoſtles, and might think it prudent to paſs the Matter over in ſilence, and not to come to extremities. This is a common Caſe in all Governments; the Multitude and their Leaders often eſcape Puniſhment, not becauſe they do not deſerve it, but becauſe it is not in ſome Circumſtances, prudent to exact it.

I paſs over theſe things lightly, becauſe the next Article contains the great, to us indeed, who live at this diſtance, the only great Queſtion; for whatever Reaſon the *Jews* had to believe the Reſurrection, it is nothing to us, unleſs the Story has been conveyed to us upon ſuch Evidence as is ſufficient to ſupport the weight laid on it.

My Lord, we are now to enter upon the laſt and main Article of this Caſe; the Nature of the Evidence upon which the Credit of the Reſurrection ſtands. Before I enquire into the Qualifications of the particular Witneſſes whoſe Words

we

we are desired to take in this Case; I wou'd ask, why this Evidence, which manifestly relates to the most essential Point of Christianity, was not put beyond all exception? Many of the Miracles of Christ are said to be done in the Streets, nay even the Temple, under the Observation of all the World; but the like is not so much as pretended as to this; nay, we have it upon the Confession of *Peter*, the Ringleader of the Apostles, that Christ appeared * *Not to all the People, but unto witnesses chosen before of God.* Why picking and culling of Witnesses in this Case more than in any other? Does it not import some Suspicion, raise some Jealousy that this Case wou'd not bear the publick Light?

I wou'd ask more particularly, Why did not Jesus after his Resurrection appear openly to the chief Priests and Rulers of the *Jews?* Since his Commission related to them in an especial manner, why were not his Credentials laid before them? The Resurrection is acknowledged to be the chief Proof of his Mission, why then was it concealed from those who were more than all others concerned in the Event of his Mission? Suppose an Ambassador from some foreign Prince, shou'd come into *England*, make his publick Entry thro' the City, pay and receive Visits, and at last refuse to shew any Letters of Credence, or to wait on the King, what wou'd you think of him? Whatever you wou'd think in that Case, you must think in this, for there is no Difference between them.

But we must take the Evidence as it is; it was thought proper in this Case, to have select chosen Witnesses;

* Acts x. 41.

Witnesses; and we must now consider who they were, and what reason we have to take their Word.

The first Witness was an Angel, or Angels: They appeared like Men to some Women who went early to the Sepulchre. If they appeared like Men, upon what ground are we to take them for Angels? The Women saw Men, and therefore they can witness only to the seeing of Men: But I suppose it is the Womens Judgment, and not their Evidence that we are to follow in this Case. Here then we have a Story of one Apparition to support the Credit of another Apparition; and the first Apparition hath not so much as the Evidence of the Women to support it, but is grounded on their Superstition, Ignorance, and Fear. Every Country can afford an hundred Instances of this Kind; and there is this common to them all, that as Learning and Common Sense prevail in any Country, they die away and are no more heard of.

The next Witnesses are the Women themselves: The wisest Men can hardly guard themselves against the fears of Superstition; poor silly Women therefore in this Case must needs be unexceptionable Witnesses; and fit to be admitted into the number of the chosen Witnesses to attest this Fact. One part of the Account given of them is very rational, that they were surprized and frightned beyond Measure; and I leave it to your Lordship and the Court to judge, how well qualified they were to give a just Relation of what passed.

After

After this, Jeſus appears to two of his Diſciples as they were upon a Journey; he joins them, and introduces a Diſcourſe about himſelf; and ſpent much time, till it began to grow dark, in expounding the Prophecies relating to the Death and Reſurrection of the Meſſias. All this while the Diſciples knew him not. But then going into an Houſe to lodge together, at Supper he broke Bread, and gave it to them; immediately they knew him, immediately he vaniſh'd. Here then are two Witneſſes more: But what will you call them? Eye-Witneſſes? Why their Eyes were open, and they had their Senſes, when he reaſoned with them and they knew him not. So far therefore they are Witneſſes that it was not he. Tell us therefore upon what Account you reject the Evidence of their Senſe, before the breaking of the Bread, and inſiſt on it afterwards? And why did Jeſus vaniſh as ſoon as known; which has more of the Air of an Apparition, than of the Appearence of a real Man reſtored to Life?

Cleopas, who was one of theſe two Diſciples, finds out the Apoſtles, to make the Report of what had paſſed to them. No ſooner was the Story told, but Jeſus appears among them. They were all frighten'd and confounded, and thought they ſaw a Spectre. He rebukes them for Infidelity, and their Slowneſs in believing the Prophecies of his Reſurrection; and tho' he refuſed before to let the Women touch him, (a Circumſtance which I ought not to have omitted); yet now he invites the Apoſtles to handle him, to examine his Hands and Feet, and ſearch the Wounds of the Croſs.

But

But what Body was it they examin'd? The ſame that came in when the Doors were ſhut; the ſame that vaniſh'd from the two Diſciples; the ſame that the Women might not touch: In a word, a Body quite different from an human Body, which we know cannot paſs thro' Walls, or appear or diſappear at pleaſure. What then cou'd their Hands or Eyes inform them of in this Caſe? Beſides; is it credible that God ſhou'd raiſe a Body imperfectly, with the very Wounds in it of which it died? Or if the Wounds were ſuch as deſtroy'd the Body before, how cou'd a natural Body ſubſiſt with them afterwards?

There are more Appearences of Jeſus recorded, but ſo much of the ſame kind, ſo liable to the ſame Difficulties and Objections, that I will not trouble your Lordſhip and the Court with a diſtinct Enumeration of them. If the Gentleman on the other ſide finds any Advantage in any of them more than in theſe mention'd, I ſhall have an Opportunity to conſider them in my Reply.

It may ſeem ſurprizing to you perhaps, that a Matter of this Moment was truſted upon ſuch Evidence as this: But it will be ſtill more ſurprizing to conſider, that the ſeveral Nations who receiv'd the Goſpel, and ſubmitted to the Faith of this Article, had not even this Evidence: For what People or Nation had the Evidence of the Angels, the Women, or even of all the Apoſtles? So far from it, that every Country had its ſingle Apoſtle, and receiv'd the Faith upon the Credit of his ſingle Evidence. We have follow'd our Anceſtors without Enquiry; and if you examine the thing to the

H bottom,

bottom, our Belief was originally built upon the Word of one Man.

I ſhall trouble you, Sir, but with one Obſervation more, which is this: That altho' in common Life we act in a thouſand Inſtances upon the Faith and Credit of human Teſtimony; yet the Reaſon for ſo doing is not the ſame in the Caſe before us. In common Affairs, where nothing is aſſerted but what is probable, and poſſible, and according to the uſual Courſe of Nature, a reaſonable Degree of Evidence ought to determine every Man. For the very Probability, or Poſſibility of the thing, is a Support to the Evidence; and in ſuch Caſes we have no Doubt but a Man's Senſes qualify him to be a Witneſs. But when the thing teſtified is contrary to the Order of Nature, and, at firſt ſight at leaſt, impoſſible, what Evidence can be ſufficient to overturn the conſtant Evidence of Nature, which ſhe gives us in the uniform and regular Method of her Operations? If a Man tells me he has been in *France*, I ought to give a Reaſon for not believing him; but if he tells me he comes from the Grave, what Reaſon can he give why I ſhou'd believe him? In the Caſe before us, ſince the Body raiſed from the Grave differed from common natural Bodies, as we have before ſeen; how can I be aſſured that the Apoſtles Senſes qualified them to judge at all of this Body, whether it was the ſame, or not the ſame which was buried? They handled the Body, which yet cou'd paſs through Doors and Walls; they ſaw it, and ſometimes knew it, at other times knew it not. In a word, it ſeems to be a Caſe exempt from human Evidence.

2 Men

Men have limited Senſes, and a limited Reaſon; when they act within their Limits, we may give Credit to them; but when they talk of things removed beyond the Reach of their Senſes and Reaſon, we muſt quit our own, if we believe theirs.

Mr. *B.* My Lord, In anſwering the Objections under this Head, I ſhall find myſelf obliged to change the Order in which the Gentleman thought proper to place them. He began with complaining, that Chriſt did not appear publickly to the *Jews* after his Reſurrection, and eſpecially to the chief Prieſts and Rulers; and ſeem'd to argue, as if ſuch Evidence wou'd have put the Matter in queſtion out of all doubt; but he concluded with an Obſervation, to prove that no Evidence in this Caſe can be ſufficient; that a Reſurrection is a thing in Nature impoſſible, at leaſt impoſſible to be proved to the Satisfaction of a rational Enquirer. If this be the Caſe, why does he require more Evidence, ſince none can be ſufficient? Or to what Purpoſe is it to vindicate the particular Evidence of the Reſurrection of Chriſt, ſo long as this general Prejudice, that a Reſurrection is incapable of being proved, remains unremoved? I am under a Neceſſity therefore to conſider this Obſervation in the firſt place, that it may not lie as a dead Weight upon all I have to offer in Support of the Evidence of Chriſt's Reſurrection.

The Gentleman allows it to be reaſonable in many Caſes to act upon the Teſtimony and Credit of others; but he thinks this ſhould be confined to ſuch Caſes, where the Thing teſtified is *probable*, *poſſible*, and *according to the uſual Courſe of Nature.*

The Gentleman does not, I ſuppoſe, pretend to know the Extent of all natural Poſſibilities, much leſs will he ſuppoſe them to be generally known; and therefore his Meaning muſt be, that the Teſtimony of Witneſſes is to be receiv'd only in Caſes which appear to us to be poſſible. In any other Senſe we can have no Diſpute; for mere Impoſſibilities which can never exiſt, can never be proved. Taking the Obſervation therefore in this Senſe, the Propoſition is this: That the Teſtimony of others ought not to be admitted, but in ſuch Matters as appear probable, or at leaſt poſſible to our Conceptions. For Inſtance: A Man who lives in a warm Climate, and never ſaw Ice, ought upon no Evidence to believe that Rivers freeze and grow hard in cold Countries; for this is improbable, contrary to the uſual Courſe of Nature; and impoſſible according to his Notion of Things. And yet we all know that this is a plain manifeſt Caſe, diſcernible by the Senſes of Men, of which therefore they are qualified to be good Witneſſes. An hundred ſuch Inſtances might be named, but 'tis needleſs; for ſurely nothing is more apparently abſurd, than to make one Man's Ability in diſcerning, and his Veracity in reporting plain Facts, depend upon the Skill or Ignorance of the Hearer. And what has the Gentleman ſaid, upon this Occaſion, againſt the Reſurrection, more than any Man, who never ſaw Ice, might ſay againſt an hundred honeſt Witneſſes, who aſſert that Water turns to Ice in cold Climates?

'Tis very true, that Men do not ſo eaſily believe upon Teſtimony of others, things which to them

them ſeem improbable or impoſſible; but the Reaſon is not, becauſe the Thing itſelf admits no Evidence, but becauſe the Hearer's preconceived Opinion outweighs the Credit of the Reporter, and makes his Veracity to be called in queſtion. For Inſtance: 'Tis natural for a Stone to roll down Hill, 'tis unnatural for it to roll up Hill: but a Stone moving up Hill is as much the Object of Senſe, as a Stone moving down Hill; and all Men in their Senſes are as capable of ſeeing and judging, and reporting the Fact in one Caſe, as in the other. Shou'd a Man then tell you, that he ſaw a Stone go up Hill of its own accord, you might queſtion his Veracity, but you cou'd not ſay the thing admitted no Evidence, becauſe it was contrary to the Law and uſual Courſe of Nature: For the Law of Nature formed to yourſelf from your own Experience and Reaſoning, is quite independent of the Matter of Fact which the Man teſtifies; and whenever you ſee Facts yourſelf, which contradict your Notions of the Law of Nature, you admit the Facts, becauſe you believe yourſelf: when you do not admit like Facts upon the Evidence of others, it is becauſe you do not believe them; and not becauſe the Facts in their own Nature exclude all Evidence.

Suppoſe a Man ſhou'd tell you, that he was come from the Dead: You wou'd be apt to ſuſpect his Evidence. But what wou'd you ſuſpect? That he was not alive, when you heard him, ſaw him, felt him, and converſed with him? You cou'd not ſuſpect this, without giving up all your Senſes, and acting in this Caſe as you act in no other. Here then

then you wou'd queſtion, whether the Man had ever been dead. But wou'd you ſay, that it is incapable of being made plain by human Teſtimony, that this or that Man died a Year ago? It can't be ſaid. Evidence in this Caſe is admitted in all Courts perpetually.

Conſider it the other way. Suppoſe you ſaw a Man publickly executed, his Body afterwards wounded by the Executioner, and carry'd and laid in the Grave; that after this you ſhou'd be told, that the Man was come to Life again: What wou'd you ſuſpect in this Caſe? Not that the Man had never been dead; for that you ſaw your ſelf: But you wou'd ſuſpect whether he was now alive. But wou'd you ſay, this Caſe excluded all human Teſtimony; and that Men cou'd not poſſibly diſcern, whether one with whom they convers'd familiarly, was alive or no? Upon what Ground cou'd you ſay this? A Man riſing from the Grave is an Object of Senſe, and can give the ſame Evidence of his being alive, as any other Man in the World can give. So that a Reſurrection conſider'd only as a Fact to be proved by Evidence, is a plain Caſe; it requires no greater Ability in the Witneſſes, than that they be able to diſtinguiſh between a Man dead, and a Man alive: A Point, in which I believe every Man living thinks himſelf a Judge.

I do allow that this Caſe, and others of like nature, require more Evidence to give them Credit than ordinary Caſes do. You may therefore require more Evidence in theſe, than in other Caſes; but it is abſurd to ſay, that ſuch Caſes admit no

Evi-

Evidence,' when the Things in queſtion are manifeſtly Objects of Senſe.

I allow further, that the Gentleman has rightly ſtated the Difficulty upon the Foot of common Prejudice; and that it ariſes from hence, that ſuch Caſes appear to be contrary to the Courſe of Nature. But I deſire him to conſider what this Courſe of Nature is. Every Man, from the loweſt Countryman to the higheſt Philoſopher, frames to himſelf from his Experience and Obſervation a Notion of a Courſe of Nature; and is ready to ſay of every thing reported to him that contradicts his Experience, that it is contrary to Nature. But will the Gentleman ſay that every thing is impoſſible, or even improbable, that contradicts the Notion which Men frame to themſelves of the Courſe of Nature? I think he will not ſay it. And if he will, he muſt ſay that Water can never freeze, for it is abſolutely inconſiſtent with the Notion which Men have of the Courſe of Nature, who live in the warm Climates. And hence it appears, that when Men talk of the Courſe of Nature, they really talk of their own Prejudices and Imaginations, and that Senſe and Reaſon are not ſo much concerned in the Caſe as the Gentleman imagines. For I ask, Is it from the Evidence of Senſe, or the Evidence of Reaſon, that People in warm Climates think it contrary to Nature, that Water ſhould grow ſolid and become Ice? As for Senſe, they ſee indeed that Water with them is always Liquid, but none of their Senſes tell them that it can never grow Solid; as for Reaſon it can never ſo inform them, for right Reaſon can never contradict

contradict the Truth of things. Our Senſes then inform us rightly what the uſual Courſe of Things is; but when we conclude that things cannot be otherwiſe, we outrun the Information of our Senſes, and the Concluſion ſtands upon Prejudice, and not upon Reaſon. And yet ſuch Concluſions form what is generally called the Courſe of Nature. And when Men upon proper Evidence and Informations admit things contrary to this preſuppoſed Courſe of Nature, they do not, as the Gentleman expreſſes it, *quit their own Senſe and Reaſon*, but, in truth, they quit their own Miſtakes and Prejudices.

In the Caſe before us; the Caſe of the Reſurrection, the great Difficulty ariſes from the like Prejudice: We all know by Experience that all Men die, and riſe no more. Therefore we conclude, that for a dead Man to riſe to Life again, is contrary to the Courſe of Nature: and certainly it is contrary to the uniform and ſettled Courſe of Things. But if we argue from hence, that it is contrary and repugnant to the real Laws of Nature, and abſolutely impoſſible on that Account, we argue without any Foundation to ſupport us either from our Senſes or our Reaſon. We cannot learn from our Eyes, or Feeling, or any other Senſe, that it is impoſſible for a dead Body to live again: If we learn it at all, it muſt be from our Reaſon; and yet what one Maxim of Reaſon is contradicted by the Suppoſition of a Reſurrection? For my own part, when I conſider how I live; that all the Animal Motions neceſſary to my Life are independent of my Will; that my Heart beats without

without my Consent, and without my Direction; that Digestion and Nutrition are performed by Methods to which I am not conscious; that my Blood moves in a perpetual round; which is contrary to all known Laws of Motion; I cannot but think that the Preservation of my Life, in every Moment of it, is as great an Act of Power, as is necessary to raise a dead Man to Life. And whoever so far reflects upon his own Being, as to acknowledge that he owes it to a superior Power, must needs think that the same Power which gave Life to senseless Matter at first, and set all the Springs and Movements a going at the beginning, can restore Life to a dead Body. For surely it is not a greater thing to give Life to a Body once dead, than to a Body that never was alive.

In the next Place must be considered the Difficulties which the Gentleman has laid before you, with regard to the Nature of Christ's Body after the Resurrection. He has produced some Passages which, he thinks, imply, that the Body was not a real natural Body, but a mere Phantom, or Apparition; and thence concludes, that there being no real Object of Sense, there can be no Evidence in the Case.

Presumptions are of no Weight against positive Evidence; and every Account of the Resurrection assures us, that the Body of Christ was seen, felt, and handled by many Persons; who were called upon by Christ so to do, that they might be assured that he had Flesh and Bones, and was not a mere Spectre, as they, in their first Surprize, imagined him to be. 'Tis impossible that they, who give this Account, ſhou'd mean by any thing they report, to imply that he had no real Body. 'Tis certain then, that when the Gentleman makes uſe of what they ſay to this purpoſe, he uſes their Sayings contrary to their Meaning. For 'tis not pretended that they ſay, that Chriſt had not a real human Body after the Reſurrection; nor is it pretended they had any ſuch Thought, except only upon the firſt Surprize of ſeeing him, and before they had examined him with their Eyes and Hands. But ſomething they have ſaid, which, the Gentleman, according to his Notions of Philoſophy, thinks, implies that the Body was not real. To clear this Point therefore, I muſt lay before you the Paſſages referred to, and conſider how juſtly the Gentleman reaſons from them.

The firſt Paſſage relates to *Mary Magdalen*, who, the firſt time ſhe ſaw Chriſt, was going to embrace his Feet, as the Cuſtom of the Country was: Chriſt ſays to her *, *Touch me not, for I am not yet aſcended to my Father; but go to my Brethren, and tell them*, &c. Hence the Gentleman concludes, that Chriſt's Body was not ſuch an one as wou'd bear the Touch. But how does he infer this? Is it from theſe Words, *Touch me not?* It cannot be: For Thouſands ſay it every Day, without giving the leaſt Suſpicion that their Bodies are not capable of being touched. The Concluſion then muſt be built on thoſe other Words, *For I am not yet aſcended to my Father.* But what have theſe Words to do with the Reality of his Body? It might be real or not real, for any thing that is here ſaid. There is a Difficulty in theſe Words, and it may be

* John xx. 17.

be hard to give the true Senſe of them; but there is no Difficulty in ſeeing that they have no relation to the Nature of Chriſt's Body; for of his Body nothing is ſaid. The natural Senſe of the Place, as I collect by comparing this Paſſage with *Matt.* xxviii. 9. is this: *Mary Magdalen*, upon ſeeing Jeſus, fell at his Feet, and laid hold of them, and held them as if ſhe meant never to let them go: Chriſt ſaid to her, "Touch me not, or hang not "about me now, you will have other Opportuni-"ties of ſeeing me, for I go not yet to my Father; "loſe no time then, but go quickly with my Meſ-"ſage to my Brethren." I am not concerned to ſupport this particular Interpretation of the Paſſage; it is ſufficient to my Purpoſe, to ſhew that the Words cannot poſſibly relate to the Nature of Chriſt's Body one way or other.

The next Paſſage relates to Chriſt's joining two of his Diſciples upon the Road, and converſing with them without being known by them: It grew dark, they preſſed him to ſtay with them that Night; he went in with them, broke Bread, and bleſſed it, and gave it them, and then they knew him; and immediately he diſappeared.

The Circumſtance of diſappearing, ſhall be conſidered under the next Head, with other Objections of the like kind: At preſent I ſhall only examine the other Parts of this Story, and enquire whether they afford any Ground to conclude that the Body of Chriſt was not a real one. Had this Piece of Hiſtory been related of any other Perſon, I think no ſuch Suſpicion cou'd have ariſen: For what is there unnatural or uncommon in this Ac-

I 2 count?

count? Two Men meet an Acquaintance whom they thought dead; they converſe with him for ſome time without ſuſpecting who he was; the very Perſuaſion they were under that he was dead, contributed greatly to their not knowing him; beſides, he appeared in an Habit and Form different from what he uſed when he convers'd with them; appeared to them on a Journey, and walked with them ſide by ſide; in which Situation no one of the Company has a full View of another. Afterwards, when they were at Supper together, and Lights brought in, they plainly diſcerned who he was. Upon this Occaſion, the Gentleman asks what ſort of Witneſſes theſe are; Eye-Witneſſes? No; before Supper they were Eye-Witneſſes, ſays the Gentleman, that the Perſon whom they ſaw was not Chriſt: And then he demands a Reaſon for our rejecting the Evidence of their Senſe, when they did not know Chriſt, and inſiſting on it when they did.

It is no uncommon thing for Men to catch themſelves and others by ſuch notable acute Queſtions, and to be led by the Sprightlineſs of their Imagination out of the Road of Truth and common Senſe. I beg leave to tell the Gentleman a ſhort Story, and then to ask him his own Queſtion. A certain Gentleman who had been ſome Years abroad, hapned in his Return to *England* through *Paris* to meet his own Siſter there. She not expecting to ſee him there, nor he to ſee her, they converſed together with other Company, at a publick Houſe, for great part of a Day, without knowing each other. At laſt the Lady began to ſhew great

great Signs of Disorder; her Colour came and went, and the Eyes of the Company were drawn towards her; and then she cryed out, Oh my Brother! and was hardly held from fainting. Suppose now this Lady were to depose upon Oath in a Court of Justice, that she saw her Brother at *Paris*; I would ask the Gentleman, Whether he would object to the Evidence, and say that she was as good an Eye-witness that her Brother was not there, as that he was; and demand of the Court, why they rejected the Evidence of her Senses when she did not know her Brother, and were ready to believe it when she did? When the Question is answered in this Case, I desire only to have the Benefit of it in the Case now before you. But if you shall be of Opinion that there was some extraordinary Power used on this Occasion, and incline to think that the Expression, (their Eyes were holden) imports as much; then the Case will fall under the next Article. In which

We are to consider Christ's vanishing out of Sight; his coming in and going out when the Doors were shut; and such like Passages; which, as they fall under one Consideration, so I shall speak to them together.

But 'tis necessary first to see what the Apostles affirm distinctly in their Accounts of these Facts; for I think more has been said for them, than ever they said, or intended to say for themselves. In one Place* it is said, *he vanished out of their sight.* Which Translation is corrected in the Margin of

* Matth. xxviii. 31

our

our Bibles thus, *he ceased to be seen of them.* And the Original † imports no more.

It is said in another Place, that the Disciples being together, *and the doors shut*, Jesus came and stood in the midst of them. How he came is not said: Much less is it said that he came through the Door, or the Key-hole; and for any thing that is said to the contrary, he might come in at the Door, tho' the Disciples saw not the Door open, nor him, till he was in the midst of them. But the Gentleman thinks these Passages prove that the Disciples saw no real Body, but an Apparition. I am afraid that the Gentleman after all his Contempt of Apparitions, and the Superstition on which they are founded, is fallen into the Snare himself, and is arguing upon no better Principles than the common Notions which the Vulgar have of Apparations. Why else does he imagine these Passages to be inconsistent with the Reality of Christ's Body? Is there no way for a real Body to disappear? Try the Experiment now; do but put out the Candles, we shall all disappear: If a Man falls asleep in the Day-time, all things disappear to him; his Senses are all lock'd up; and yet all things about him continue to be real, and his Senses continue perfect. As shutting out all Rays of Light would make all things disappear; so intercepting the Rays of Light from any particular Body would make that disappear. Perhaps something like this was the Case; or perhaps something else, of which we know nothing. But be the

† ἄφαντος ἐγένετο.

Case

Case what it will, the Gentleman's Conclusion is founded on no Principle of true Philosophy: For it does not follow that a Body is not real, because I lose sight of it suddenly. I shall be told perhaps, that this way of accounting for the Passages, is as wonderful, and as much out of the common Course of Things as the other. Perhaps it is so; and what then? Surely the Gentleman does not expect, that in order to prove the Reality of the greatest Miracle that ever was, I should shew that there was nothing miraculous in it, but that every thing happen'd according to the ordinary Course of things? My only Concern is to shew, that these Passages do not infer that the Body of Christ after the Resurrection was no real Body. I wonder the Gentleman did not carry his Argument a little further, and prove that Christ, before his Death, had no real Body; for we read, that when the Multitude would have thrown him down a Precipice, he went through the midst of them unseen. Now nothing happen'd after his Resurrection more unaccountable than this that happen'd before it; and if the Argument be good at all, it will be good to prove that there never was such a Man as Jesus in the World. Perhaps the Gentleman may think this a little too much to prove; and if he does, I hope he will quit the Argument in one Case, as well as in the other; for Difference there is none.

Hitherto we have been called upon to prove the Reality of Christ's Body, and that it was the same after the Resurrection that it was before; but the next Objection complains, that the Body was too much

much the ſame with that which was buried; for the Gentleman thinks that it had the ſame mortal Wounds open and uncured, of which it died. His Obſervation is grounded upon the Words which Chriſt uſes to *Thomas*, * *Reach hither thy finger, and behold my hands, and reach hither thy hand, and thruſt it into my ſide.* Is it here affirmed that *Thomas* did actually put his hands into his Side, or ſo much as ſee his Wounds freſh and bleeding? Nothing like it. But 'tis ſuppoſed from the Words of Chriſt; for if he had no Wounds, he would not have invited *Thomas* to probe them. Now the Meaning of Chriſt will beſt appear by an Account of the Occaſion he had to uſe this Speech. He had appeared to his Diſciples, in the Abſence of *Thomas*, and ſhewn them his Hands and Feet, which ſtill had the Marks of his Crucifixion: The Diſciples report this to *Thomas*: He thought the Thing impoſſible, and expreſſed his Unbelief, as Men are apt to do when they are poſitive, in a very extravagant manner: You talk, ſays he, of the Prints of the Nails in his Hands and Feet; for my part, I'll never believe this thing, *except I ſhall ſee in his Hands the Print of the Nails, and put my Finger into the Print of the Nails, and thruſt my Hand into his Side.* Now in the firſt place, here is nothing ſaid of open Wounds; *Thomas* talks only of putting his Finger into the Print, that is, the Scar of the Nails, and of thruſting his Hand into his Side. And in common Speech, to thruſt an Hand into any one's Side,

* John xx. 27.

does

does not ſignify to thruſt it through the Side into the Bowels. Upon this Interpretation of the Words, which is a plain and natural one, the Gentleman's Objection is quite gone. But ſuppoſe *Thomas* to mean what the Gentleman means; in that Caſe the Words of Chriſt are manifeſtly a ſevere Reproach to him for his Infidelity: Here, ſays Chriſt, are my Hands and my Side; take the Satisfaction you require; thruſt your Fingers into my Hands, your Hand into my Side; repeating to him his own Words, and calling him to his own Conditions; which, to a Man beginning to ſee his Extravagance, is of all Rebukes the ſevereſt. Such Forms of Speech are uſed on many Occaſions, and are never underſtood to import that the thing propoſed is proper, or always practicable. When the *Grecian* Women reproached their Sons with Cowardice, and called to them as they were flying from the Enemy, to come and hide themſelves once more, like Children as they were, in their Mothers Wombs; he would have been ridiculous who had asked the Queſtion, Whether the Women really thought that they cou'd take their Sons into their Wombs again?

I have now gone through the Objections which were neceſſarily to be removed before I could ſtate the Evidence in this Caſe. I am ſenſible I have taken up too much of your Time; but I have this to ſay in my Excuſe; That Objections built on popular Notions and Prejudices, are eaſily conveyed to the Mind in few Words; and ſo conveyed, make ſtrong Impreſſions: But whoever anſwers the Objections, muſt encounter all

K the

the Notions to which they are allied, and to which they owe their Strength; and 'tis well if with many Words he can find Admittance.

I come now to consider the Evidence on which our Belief of the Resurrection stands. And here I am stopped again. A general Exception is taken to the Evidence, that it is imperfect, unfair; and a Question is asked, Why did not Christ appear publickly to all the People, especially to the Magistrates? Why were some Witnesses culled and chosen out, and others excluded?

It may be sufficient perhaps to say, that where there are Witnesses enow, no Judge, no Jury complains for want of more; and therefore, if the Witnesses we have are sufficient, 'tis no Objection that we have not others, and more. If three credible Men attest a Will, which are as many as the Law requires, would any Body ask, Why all the Town were not called to set their Hands? But why were these Witnesses culled and chosen out? Why? For this Reason, that they might be good ones. Does not every wise Man chuse proper Witnesses to his Deed and to his Will? And does not a good Choice of Witnesses give Strength to every Deed? How comes it to pass then, that the very thing which shuts out all Suspicion in other Cases, should in this Case only, be of all others, the most suspicious thing it self?

What reason there is to make any Complaints on the behalf of the *Jews*, may be judged, in part, from what has already appeared. Christ suffered openly in their sight; and they were so well

well apprized of his Prediction, that he ſhould riſe again, that they ſet a Guard on his Sepulchre; and from their Guards they learnt the Truth. Every Soldier was to them a Witneſs of the Reſurrection of their own chuſing. After this, they had not one Apoſtle, (which the Gentleman obſerves was the Caſe of other People) but all the Apoſtles, and many other Witneſſes with them, and in their Power. The Apoſtles teſtified the Reſurrection to them; not only to the People, but to the Elders of *Iſrael* aſſembled in Senate: To ſupport their Evidence, they were enabled to work, and did work Miracles openly in the Name of Chriſt. Theſe People therefore have the leaſt Reaſon to complain; and had of all others the fulleſt Evidence; and in ſome reſpects ſuch as none but themſelves cou'd have, for they only were Keepers of the Sepulchre. I believe, if the Gentleman was to chuſe an Evidence to his own Satiſfaction in a like Caſe, he wou'd deſire no more than to keep the Sepulchre, with a ſufficient number of Guards.

But the Argument goes further. It is ſaid that Jeſus was ſent with a ſpecial Commiſſion to the *Jews*, that he was their Meſſias; and as his Reſurrection was his main Credential, he ought to have appeared publickly to the Rulers of the *Jews* after his Reſurrection: that in doing otherwiſe, he acted like an Ambaſſador pretending Authority from his Prince, but refuſing to ſhew his Letters of Credence.

I was afraid, when I ſuffered myſelf to be drawn into this Argument, that I ſhou'd be led into Matters fitter to be decided by Men of another Profeſſion, than by Lawyers. But ſince there is no Help now, I will lay before you what appears to me to be the natural and plain Account of this Matter; leaving it to others, who are better qualified, to give a fuller Anſwer to the Objection.

It appears to me, by the Accounts we have of Jeſus, that he had two diſtinct Offices: One, as the Meſſias particularly promiſed to the *Jews*; another, as he was to be the great High Prieſt of the World. With reſpect to the firſt Office, he is called * *the Apoſtle* of the *Hebrews*; the † *Miniſter of the Circumciſion*; and ſays himſelf, || *I am not ſent, but unto the loſt ſheep of the houſe of Iſrael.* Accordingly when he ſent out his Apoſtles in his Life-time to preach, he expreſsly forbids them to go to the *Gentiles* or *Samaritans*; but go, ‡ ſays he, *to the loſt ſheep of the houſe of Iſrael.* Chriſt continued in the Diſcharge of this Office during the Time of his natural Life, till he was finally rejected by the *Jews*. And it is obſervable, that the laſt time he ſpoke to the People, according to St. *Matthew*'s Account, he ſolemnly took leave of them, and cloſed his Commiſſion. He had been long among them publiſhing glad Tidings; but when all his Preaching, all his Miracles, had proved to be in vain, the laſt thing he did was to denounce the Woes they had brought on themſelves. The 23[d] Chapter of St. *Matthew* recites theſe Woes; and at the End of them Chriſt takes this paſſionate Leave of *Jeruſalem*: " O *Jeruſalem, Je-*

* Heb. iii. 1.

† Rom. xv. 8.

|| Matth. xv. 24.

‡ Matth. x. 5, 6.

" *ruſalem,*

" *rusalem*, thou that killest the Prophets, and stonest them which are sent unto thee; how often wou'd I have gathered thy Children together, even as a Hen gathereth her Chickens under her Wings, and ye would not! Behold, your House is left unto you desolate. For I say unto you, Ye shall not see me henceforth, till ye shall say, Blessed is he that cometh in the Name of the Lord". 'Tis remarkable, that this Passage, as recorded by St. *Matthew*, and St. *Luke* twice over, is determin'd, by the Circumstances, to refer to the near Approach of his own Death, and the extreme Hatred of the *Jews* to him: And therefore those Words, *Ye shall not see me henceforth*, are to be dated from the Time of his Death, and manifestly point out the End of his particular Mission to them. From the making this Declaration, as it stands in St. *Matthew*, his Discourses are to his Disciples; and they chiefly relate to the miserable and wretched Condition of the *Jews*, which was now decreed, and soon to be accomplish'd. Let me now ask, Whether, in this state of things, any farther Credentials of Christ's Commission to the *Jews* cou'd be demanded or expected? He was rejected, his Commission was determin'd, and with it the Fate of the Nation was determin'd also: What Use then of more Credentials? As to appearing to them after his Resurrection, he cou'd not do it consistently with his own Prediction; *Ye shall see me no more, till ye shall say, Blessed is he that cometh in the name of the Lord.* The *Jews* were not in this Disposition after the Resurrection, nor are they in it yet.

The

The Resurrection was the Foundation of Christ's new Commission, which extended to all the World. Then it was he declared, that *all Power was given unto him in heaven and in earth.* Then he gave a new Commission to his Disciples, not restrained to the House of *Israel*, but to go and *teach all Nations.* This Prerogative the *Jews* had under this Commission, that the Gospel was every-where first offered to them; but in no other Terms than it was offered to the rest of the World. Since then this Commission, of which the Resurrection was the Foundation, extended to all the World alike; What Ground is there to demand special and particular Evidence to the *Jews?* The Emperor and the Senate of *Rome* were a much more considerable Part of the World, than the chief Priests and the Synagogue; Why does not the Gentleman object then, that Christ did not shew himself to *Tiberius* and his Senate? And since all Men have an equal Right in this Case, Why may not the same Demand be made for every Country; nay, for every Age? And then the Gentleman may bring the Question nearer home; and ask, Why Christ did not appear in *England* in King *George*'s Reign? There is, to my Apprehension, nothing more unreasonable, than to neglect and despise plain and sufficient Evidence before us, and to sit down to imagine what Kind of Evidence wou'd have pleased us; and then to make the Want of such Evidence an Objection to the Truth; which yet, if well consider'd, wou'd be found to be well establish'd.

The

The Obſervation I have made upon the Reſurrection of Chriſt, naturally leads to another; which will help to account for the Nature of the Evidence we have in this great Point. As the Reſurrection was the opening a new Commiſſion, in which all the World had an Intereſt; ſo the Concern naturally was, to have a proper Evidence to eſtabliſh this Truth, and which ſhou'd be of equal Weight to all. This did not depend upon the Satisfaction given to private Perſons, whether they were Magiſtrates or not Magiſtrates; but upon the Conviction of thoſe, whoſe Office it was to be, to bear Teſtimony to this Truth in the World. In this Senſe the Apoſtles were choſen to be Witneſſes of the Reſurrection, becauſe they were choſen to bear Teſtimony to it in the World; and not becauſe they only were admitted to ſee Chriſt after his Reſurrection: For the Fact is otherwiſe. The Goſpel indeed, concerned to ſhew the Evidence on which the Faith of the World was to reſt, is very particular in ſetting forth the ocular Demonſtration which the Apoſtles had of the Reſurrection; and mentions others, who ſaw Chriſt after his Reſurrection, only accidentally, and as the Thread of the Hiſtory led to it. But yet 'tis certain, there were many others, who had this Satisfaction, as well as the Apoſtles. St. *Luke* tells us, that when Chriſt appeared to the eleven Apoſtles, there were others with them *; who they were, or how many they were, he ſays not. But it appears in the *Acts*, when an Apoſtle was to be choſen in the room of *Judas*; and the chief Qualification requi-

* Luke xxiv. 33.

2 red

red was, that he ſhou'd be one capable of being a Witneſs of the Reſurrection; that there were preſent an hundred and twenty ſo qualified *. And St. *Paul* ſays, that Chriſt after his Riſing was ſeen by 500 at once, many of whom were living when he appealed to their Evidence. So that the Gentleman is miſtaken, when he imagines that a few only were choſen to ſee Chriſt after he came from the Grave. The Truth of the Caſe is, that out of thoſe who ſaw him, ſome were choſen to bear Teſtimony to the World, and for that Reaſon had the fulleſt Demonſtration of the Truth, that they might be the better able to give Satisfaction to others. And what was there in this Conduct to complain of? What to raiſe any Jealouſy or Suſpicion?

As to the Witneſſes themſelves; the firſt the Gentleman takes notice of, are the Angels and the Women. The Mention of Angels led naturally to Apparitions; and the Women were called poor ſilly Women; and there is an End of their Evidence. But to ſpeak ſeriouſly: Will the Gentleman pretend to prove, that there are no intelligent Beings between God and Man; or that they are not Miniſters of God; or that they were improperly employed in this great and wonderful Work, the Reſurrection of Chriſt? Till ſome of theſe Points are diſproved, we may be at reſt; for the Angels were Miniſters, and not Witneſſes of the Reſurrection. And it is not upon the Credit of the poor ſilly Women that we believe Angels were

* Acts i. *Compare Verſes* 15, 21, 22 *together*.

con-

concerned, but upon the Report of thoſe who wrote the Goſpels, who deliver it as a Truth known to themſelves, and not merely as a Report taken from the Women.

But for the Women, what ſhall I ſay? Silly as they were, I hope at leaſt they had Eyes and Ears, and cou'd tell what they heard and ſaw. In this Caſe they tell no more; they report that the Body was not in the Sepulchre; but ſo far from reporting the Reſurrection, that they did not believe it, and were very anxious to find to what Place the Body was removed. Further, they were not employed. For, I think, the Gentleman in another Part obſerves rightly, that they were not ſent to bear Teſtimony to any People. But ſuppoſe them to be Witneſſes; ſuppoſe them to be improper ones; yet the Evidence of the Men ſurely is not the worſe, becauſe ſome Women happened to ſee the ſame thing which they ſaw. And if Men only muſt be admitted, of them we have enow to eſtabliſh this Truth.

I will not ſpend your Time in enumerating theſe Witneſſes, or in ſetting forth the Demonſtration they had of the Truth which they report. Theſe Things are well known. If you queſtion their Sincerity, they lived miſerably, and died miſerably, for the ſake of this Truth. And what greater Evidence of Sincerity can Man give or require? And what is ſtill more, they were not deceived in their Expectation by being ill treated; for he who employed them, told them before-hand, that the World would hate them, and treat them with Contempt and Cruelty.

L But

But leaving these weighty and well-known Circumstances to your own Reflexion, I beg leave to lay before you another Evidence, paſſed over in Silence by the Gentleman on the other Side. He took notice that a Reſurrection was ſo extraordinary a Thing, that no human Evidence cou'd ſupport it. I am not ſure that he is not in the right. If twenty Men were to come into *England* with ſuch a Report from a diſtant Country, perhaps they might not find twenty more here to believe their Story. And I rather think the Gentleman may be in the right, becauſe in the preſent Caſe I ſee clearly, that the Credit of the Reſurrection of Chriſt was not truſted to mere human Evidence. To what Evidence it was truſted, we find by his own Declaration: *The Spirit of Truth which proceedeth from the Father, he ſhall teſtify of me*; and *ye alſo* (ſpeaking to his Apoſtles) *ſhall bear witneſs, becauſe ye have been with me from the beginning* *. And therefore tho' the Apoſtles had convers'd with him forty Days after his Reſurrection, and had received his Commiſſion to go teach all Nations, yet he expreſly forbids them entring upon the Work, till they ſhou'd receive Powers from Above †. And St. *Peter* explains the Evidence of the Reſurrection in this manner: *We* (the Apoſtles) *are his Witneſſes of theſe Things, and ſo is alſo the Holy Ghoſt, whom God hath given to them who obey him* ‖.

Now, What were the Powers received by the Apoſtles? Were they not the Powers of Wiſdom

* John xv. 26, 27. † Acts i. 14. ‖ Acts v. 32.

and

and Courage, by which they were enabled to appear before Rulers and Princes in the Name of Chriſt; the Power of Miracles, even of raiſing the Dead to Life, by which they convinc'd the World, that God was with them in what they ſaid and did? With reſpect to this Evidence, St. *John* ſays, *If we receive the Witneſs of Men, the Witneſs of God is greater**. Add to this, that the Apoſtles had a Power to communicate theſe Gifts to Believers. Can you wonder that Men believed the Reality of thoſe Powers of which they were Partakers, and became conſcious to themſelves? With reſpect to theſe communicated Powers, I ſuppoſe St. *John* ſpeaks, when he ſays, *He that believeth on the Son of God, hath the Witneſs in himſelf* †. Appealing not to an inward Teſtimony of the Spirit, in the Senſe of ſome modern Enthuſiaſts, but to the Powers of the Spirit, which Believers received, and which were ſeen in the Effects that followed.

It was objected, that the Apoſtles ſeparated themſelves to the Work of the Miniſtry, and one went into one Country, another to another; and conſequently, that the Belief of the Reſurrection was originally receiv'd every where upon the Teſtimony of one Witneſs. I will not examine this Fact: Suppoſe it to be ſo. But did this one Witneſs go alone, when he was attended with the Powers of Heaven? Was not every blind Man reſtored to Sight, and every lame Man to his Feet, a new Witneſs to the Truth reported by the firſt? Beſides, when the People of different Countries

* 1 John v. 9. † Ibid. *ver.* 10.

L 2 came

came to compare Notes, and found that they had all received the ſame Account of Chriſt, and of his Doctrine; then ſurely the Evidence of theſe diſtant Witneſſes thus united, became ſtronger than if they had told their Story together: For twelve Men ſeparately examined, form a much ſtronger Proof for the Truth of any Fact, than twelve Men agreeing together in one Story.

If the ſame Thing were to happen in our own Time; If one or two were to come into *England*, and report that a Man was raiſed from the Dead; and in conſequence of it, teach nothing but that we ought to love God and our Neighbours: If to confirm their Report, they ſhou'd, before our Eyes, cure the Blind, the Deaf, the Lame, and even raiſe the Dead to Life; if endow'd with all theſe Powers, they ſhould live in Poverty and Diſtreſs, and patiently ſubmit to all that Scorn, Contempt, and Malice cou'd contrive to diſtreſs them; and at laſt ſacrifice even their Lives in Juſtification of the Truth of their Report: If upon Enquiry we ſhou'd find, that all the Countries in *Europe* had received the ſame Account, ſupported by the ſame miraculous Powers, atteſted in like manner by the Sufferings, and confirmed by the Blood of the Witneſſes: I wou'd fain know what any reaſonable Man wou'd do in this Caſe? Wou'd he deſpiſe ſuch Evidence? I think he wou'd not; and whoever thinks otherwiſe, muſt ſay, That a Reſurrection, tho' in its own Nature poſſible, is yet ſuch a Thing, in which we ought not to believe either God or Man.

Judge. Have you done, Sir?

Mr. *B.*

Mr. *B*. Yes, My Lord.

Judge. Go on Mr. *A*. if you have any Thing to ſay in Reply.

Mr. *A*. My Lord, I ſhall trouble you with very little. The Objections and Anſwers under this Head, I ſhall leave to the Judgment of the Court; and beg leave only to make an Obſervation or two upon the laſt Part of the Gentleman's Argument.

And firſt, with reſpect to the Sufferings of the Apoſtles and Diſciples of Jeſus; and the Argument drawn from thence for the Truth of their Doctrines and Aſſertions; I beg leave to obſerve to you, That there is not a falſe Religion or Pretence in the World, but can produce the ſame Authority, and ſhew many Inſtances of Men, who have ſuffered even to Death for the Truth of their ſeveral Profeſſions. If we conſult only modern Story, we ſhall find Papiſts ſuffering for Popery, Proteſtants for their Religion; and among Proteſtants, every Sect has had its Martyrs; Puritans, Quakers, Fifth-Monarchy Men. In *Henry* VIIIth's Time, *England* ſaw both Popiſh and Proteſtant Martyrs; in Queen *Mary*'s Reign the Rage fell upon Proteſtants; in Queen *Elizabeth*'s, Papiſts and Puritans were called ſometimes, tho' rarely, to this Tryal. In later Times, ſometimes Churchmen, ſometimes Diſſenters, were perſecuted. What muſt we ſay then? All theſe Sufferers had not Truth with them; and yet, if there be any Weight in this Argument from Suffering, they have all a Right to plead it.

But I may be told, perhaps, that Men by their Sufferings, tho' they do not prove their Doctrines to be true, yet prove at leaſt their own Sincerity: As

As if it were a thing impossible for Men to dissemble at the Point of Death! Alas! How many Instances are there of Men's denying Facts plainly proved, asserting Facts plainly disproved, even with the Rope about their Necks? Must all such pass for innocent Sufferers, sincere Men? If not, it must be allowed, that a Man's Word at the Point of Death is not always to be relied on.

Another Observation I wou'd make, is with respect to the Evidence of the Spirit, on which so much Stress is laid. It has been hitherto insisted on, that the Resurrection was a Matter of Fact, and such a Fact, as was capable and proper to be supported by the Evidence of Sense. How comes it about, that this Evidence, this which is the proper Evidence, is given up as insufficient, and a new improper Evidence introduced? Is it not surprizing, that one great Miracle shou'd want an hundred more to prove it? Every Miracle is itself an Appeal to Sense, and therefore admits no Evidence but that of Sense. And there is no Connection between a Miracle done this Year and last Year. It does not follow therefore, because *Peter* cured a lame Man (allowing the Fact) that therefore Christ rose from the Dead.

But allowing the Gentleman all he demands, what is it to us? They who had the Witness within them, did perhaps very well to consult him, and to take his Word; but how am I, or others, who have not this Witness in us, the better for it? If the first Ages of the Church saw all the Wonders related by the Gentleman, and believed, it shews at least, in his Opinion, that this strong Evidence

dence was neceſſary to create the Belief he requires; why then does he require this Belief of us, who have not this ſtrong Evidence?

Judge. Very well. Gentlemen of the Jury, you have heard the Proofs and Arguments on both Sides, and it is now your Part to give a Verdict.

Here the Gentlemen whiſpered together, and the Foreman ſtood up.

Foreman. My Lord, The Cauſe has been long, and conſiſts of ſeveral Articles, therefore the Jury hope you will give them your Directions.

Judge. No, no; you are very able to judge without my Help.

Mr. *A.* My Lord, Pray conſider, you appointed this Meeting, and choſe your Office. Mr. *B.* and I have gone through our Parts, and have ſome Right to inſiſt on your doing your Part.

Mr. *B.* I muſt join, Sir, in that Requeſt.

Judge. I have often heard, that all Honour has a Burden attending it; But I did not ſuſpect it in this Office, which I conferred upon myſelf. But ſince it muſt be ſo, I will recollect, and lay before you, as well as I can, the Subſtance of the Debate.

Gentlemen of the Jury; The Queſtion before you, is, Whether the Witneſſes of the Reſurrection of Chriſt are guilty of giving falſe Evidence, or no.

Two ſorts of Objections, or Accuſations are brought againſt them. One charges Fraud and

Deceit

Deceit on the Tranſaction itſelf; the other charges the Evidence as forged, and inſufficient to ſupport the Credit of ſo extraordinary an Event.

There are alſo three Periods of Time to be conſidered.

The firſt takes in the Miniſtry of Chriſt, and ends at his Death. During this Period the Fraud is ſuppoſed to be contrived.

The ſecond reaches from his Death to his Reſurrection. During this Period the Fraud is ſuppoſed to be executed.

The third begins from the Reſurrection, and takes in the whole Miniſtry of the Apoſtles. And here the Evidence they gave the World for this Fact is the main Conſideration.

As to the firſt Period of Time, and the Fraud charged upon Jeſus, I muſt obſerve to you, that this Charge had no Evidence to ſupport it; all the Facts reported of Jeſus ſtand in full Contradiction to it. To ſuppoſe, as the Council did, that this Fraud might poſſibly appear, if we had any *Jewiſh* Books written at the Time, is not to bring Proof, but to wiſh for Proof; for as it was rightly obſerved on the other ſide, how does Mr. *A.* know there were any ſuch Books? And ſince they are loſt, how does he know what was in them? Were ſuch Books extant, they might probaly prove beyond Diſpute the Facts recorded in the Goſpels.

You were told that the *Jews* were a very ſuperſtitious People, much addicted to Prophecy, and particularly that they had a ſtrong Expectation about the Time that Chriſt appeared, to have a victorious Prince riſe among them. This is laid

as

as the Ground of Suspicion; and in fact, many Impostors you are told, set up upon these Notions of the People; and thence it is inferred that Christ built his Scheme upon the Strength of these popular Prejudices. But when this Fact came to be examined on the other Side, it appeared that Christ was so far from falling in with these Notions, and abusing the Credulity of the People, that it was his main Point to correct these Prejudices, to oppose these Superstitions; and by these very Means, he fell into Disgrace with his Countrymen, and suffered as one, who in their Opinion, destroyed the Law and the Prophets. With respect to temporal Power, so far was he from aiming at it, that he refused it when offered: So far from giving any Hopes of it to his Disciples, that he invited Men upon quite different Terms; *To take up the Cross, and follow him.* And it is observable, that after he had foretold his Death and Resurrection, he continued to admonish his Disciples of the Evils they were to suffer; to tell them that the World would hate them, and abuse them; which surely to common Sense has no Appearence that he was then contriving a Cheat, or encouraging his Disciples to execute it.

But as ill supported as this Charge is, there was no avoiding it; it was Necessity, and not Choice, which drove the Gentleman to it: For since Christ had foretold his Resurrection, if the whole was a Cheat, he certainly was conscious to it, and consequently the Plot was laid in his own Time. And yet the supposing Christ conscious to such a Fraud in these Circumstances, is contrary to all Probabi-

M lity.

lity. Is is very improbable, that He, or any Man, ſhould without any Temptation, contrive a Cheat to take place after his Death. And if this could be ſuppoſed, 'tis highly improbable that he ſhould give publick Notice of it, and thereby put all Men on their guard; eſpecialy conſidering there were only a few Women, and twelve Men of low Fortunes, and mean Education, to conduct the Plot; and the whole Power of the *Jews* and *Romans* to oppoſe it.

Mr. *A.* ſeemed ſenſible of theſe Difficulties, and therefore would have varied the Charge, and have made Chriſt an Enthuſiaſt, and his Diſciples only Cheats. This was not properly moved, and therefore not debated; for which Reaſon I ſhall paſs it over with this ſhort Obſervation; that Enthuſiaſm is as contrary to the whole Character and Conduct of Chriſt as even Fraud is. Beſides, this Imagination, if allowed, goes only to Chriſt's own part; and leaves the Charge of Fraud, in its full extent, upon the Management from the time of his Death, and therefore is of no uſe, unleſs the Fraud afterwards be apparent. For if there really was a Reſurrection, it will ſufficiently anſwer the Charge of Enthuſiaſm.

I paſs on then to the ſecond Period, to conſider what happen'd between the Death and Reſurrection of Chriſt. And here it is agreed that Chriſt died, and was buried. So far then there was no Fraud.

For the better underſtanding the Charge here, we muſt recollect a material Circumſtance reported by one of the Evangeliſts; which is this:

2 After

After Chriſt was buried, the chief Prieſts and *Phariſees* came to *Pilate* the *Roman* Governor, and informed him that this Deceiver, (meaning Jeſus) had in his Life-time foretold, that he would riſe again after three Days; that they ſuſpected his Diſciples would ſteal away the Body, and pretend a Reſurrection; and then the *laſt Error would be worſe than the firſt.* They therefore deſire a Guard to watch the Sepulchre, to prevent all Fraud. They had one granted; accordingly they placed a Watch on the Sepulchre, and ſealed up the Stone at the Mouth of it.

What the Event of this Caſe was, the ſame Writer tells us. The Guards ſaw the Stone removed by Angels, and for Fear they became as dead Men: When they came to the City, they reported to the chief Prieſts what had happen'd: A Council is called, and a Reſolution taken to bribe the Soldiers to ſay, that the Body was ſtolen while they were aſleep; and the Council undertook to excuſe the Soldiers to *Pilate*, for their Negligence in falling aſleep when they were on Duty.

Thus the Fact ſtands in the original Record. Now the Council for *Woolſton* maintains, that the Story reported by the Soldiers, after they had been bribed by the chief Prieſts, contains the true Account of this pretended Reſurrection.

The Gentleman was ſenſible of a Difficulty in his way, to account for the Credit which the *Jews* gave to the Prediction of Chriſt; for if, as he pretends, they knew him to be an Impoſtor,

M 2

poſtor, what Reaſon had they to take any Notice of his Prediction? And therefore, that very Caution in this Caſe betrayed their Concern, and ſhewed that they were not ſatisfied that his Pretenſions were groundleſs. To obviate this, he ſays, that they had diſcovered before, one great Cheat in the Caſe of *Lazarus*, and therefore were ſuſpicious of another in this Caſe. He was anſwered, That the Diſcovery of a Cheat in the Caſe before mentioned, ought rather to have ſet them at eaſe, and made them quite ſecure as to the Event of the Prediction. In Reply he ſays, that the chief Prieſts, however ſatisfied of the Cheat themſelves, had found that it prevailed among the People; and to ſecure the People from being farther impoſed on, they uſed the Caution they did.

This is the Subſtance of the Argument on both Sides.

I muſt obſerve to you, that this Reaſoning from the Caſe of *Lazarus* has no Foundation in Hiſtory; there is no Pretence for ſaying, that the *Jews* in this whole Affair had any particular Regard to the raiſing of *Lazarus*: And if they had any ſuch juſt Suſpicion, why was it not mention'd at the Trial of Chriſt? There was an Opportunity of opening the whole Fraud, and undeceiving the People. The *Jews* had a plain Law for puniſhing a falſe Prophet; and what cou'd be a ſtronger Conviction, than ſuch a Cheat made manifeſt? Why then was this Advantage loſt?

The Gentleman builds this Obſervation on theſe Words, *So the laſt Error ſhall be worſe than the firſt.* But

But is there here any thing ſaid about *Lazarus?* No; the Words are a proverbial Form of Speech, and probably were uſed without relation to any particular Caſe. But if a particular Meaning muſt be aſſigned, it is more probable, that the Words being uſed to *Pilate*, contained a Reaſon applicable to him. Now *Pilate* had been drawn in to conſent to the Crucifixion, for fear the *Jews* ſhou'd ſet up Jeſus to be their King in Oppoſition to *Cæſar*; therefore ſay the chief Prieſts to him, If once the People believe him to be riſen from the dead, the laſt Error will be worſe than the firſt; *i.e.* they will be more inclined and encourag'd to rebel againſt the *Romans* than ever. This is a natural Senſe of the Words, as they are uſed to move the *Roman* Governor to allow them a Guard. Whether *Lazarus* were dead or alive; whether Chriſt came to deſtroy the Law and the Prophets, or to eſtabliſh or confirm them, was of little moment to *Pilate*. It is plain, he was touched by none of theſe Conſiderations; and refus'd to be concern'd in the Affair of Chriſt, till he was alarm'd with the Suggeſtions of Danger to the *Roman* State. This was the *firſt* Fear that moved him; muſt not therefore the *ſecond* now ſuggeſted to him be of the ſame Kind?

The next Circumſtance to be conſider'd, is that of the Seal upon the Stone of the Sepulchre. The Council for *Woolſton* ſuppoſes an Agreement between the *Jews* and Diſciples about ſetting this Seal. But for this Agreement there is no Evidence; nay, to ſuppoſe it, contradicts the whole Series of the Hiſtory, as the Gentleman on the other

other Side obſerv'd. I will not enter into the Particulars of this Debate; for it is needleſs. The plain natural Account given of this Matter, ſhuts out all other Suppoſitions. Mr. *B*. obſerv'd to you, that the *Jews* having a Guard, ſet the Seal to prevent any Combination among the Guards to deceive them: which ſeems a plain and ſatisfactory Account. The Council for *W*. replies, Let the Uſe of the Seals be what they will, it is plain they were broken; and if they were uſed as a Check upon the *Roman* Soldiers, then probably they conſented to the Fraud; and then 'tis eaſily underſtood how the Body was removed.

I muſt obſerve to you here, that this Suſpicion agrees neither with the Account given by the Evangeliſt, nor with the Story ſet about by the *Jews*; ſo that it is utterly unſupported by any Evidence.

Nor has it any Probability in it. For what cou'd move *Pilate*, and the *Roman* Soldiers, to propagate ſuch a Cheat? He had crucify'd Chriſt for no other Reaſon, but for fear the People ſhou'd revolt from the *Romans*; perhaps too he conſented to place a Guard upon the Sepulchre, to put an end to the People's Hope in Jeſus; and is it likely at laſt that he was conſenting to a Cheat, to make the People believe him riſen from the dead? The thing, of all others, which he was oblig'd, as his Apprehenſions were, to prevent.

The next Circumſtance inſiſted on as a Proof of the Fraud, is, that Jeſus roſe before the Time he had appointed. Mr. *A*. ſuppoſes that the Diſciples haſten'd the Plot, for fear of falling in with Multi-

Multitudes, who waited only for the appointed Time to be at the Sepulchre, and to ſee with their own Eyes. He was anſwer'd, that the Diſciples were not, cou'd not be concern'd, or be preſent at moving the Body; that they were diſpers'd, and lay conceal'd for fear of the *Jews*: that haſtning the Plot was of no Uſe, for the Reſurrection happen'd whilſt the Guards were at the Sepulchre; who were probably enow to prevent Violence; certainly enow to diſcover it, if any were uſed.

This Difficulty then reſts merely upon the reckoning of the Time. Chriſt died on *Friday*, roſe early on *Sunday*. The Queſtion is, Whether this was riſing the third Day according to the Prediction? I will refer the Authorities made uſe of in this Caſe to your Memory, and add only one Obſervation, to ſhew that it was indeed the third Day according as the People of the Country reckon'd. When Chriſt talked with the two Diſciples who knew him not, they gave him an Account of his own Crucifixion, and their Diſappointment; and tell him, *To day is the third Day ſince theſe things were done* *. Now this Converſation was on the very Day of the Reſurrection. And the Diſciples thought of nothing leſs than anſwering an Objection againſt the Reſurrection, which as yet they did not believe. They recount only a Matter of Fact, and reckon the Time according to the Uſage of their Country, and call the Day of the Reſurrection *the third Day* from the Crucifixion; which is a plain Evidence, in what manner the *Jews* reckon'd in this and like Caſes.

* Luke xxiv. 21.

As

As the Objections in this Caſe are founded upon the Story reported by the *Jews*, and the *Roman* Soldiers; Mr. *B*. in his Anſwer, endeavour'd to ſhew from ſome hiſtorical Paſſages, that the *Jews* themſelves did not believe the Story.

His firſt Argument was, That the *Jews* never queſtion'd the Diſciples for this Cheat, and the Share they had in it, when they had them in their Power. And yet who ſees not that it was very much to their Purpoſe ſo to do? To this there is no Reply.

The ſecond Argument was from the Treatment St. *Paul* had from King *Agrippa*, and his ſaying to St. *Paul*, *Almoſt thou perſuadeſt me to be a Chriſtian*. A Speech, which he reckons cou'd not be made by a Prince, to one concern'd in carrying on a known Cheat. To this the Gentleman replies, That *Agrippa* never did become a Chriſtian, and that no great Streſs is to be laid upon his Complaiſance to his Priſoner. But allowing that there was ſomething of Humanity and Civility in the Expreſſion, yet ſuch Civility could hardly be paid to a known Impoſtor. There is a Propriety even in Civility; a Prince may be civil to a Rebel, but he will hardly compliment him for his Loyalty; he may be civil to a poor Sectary, but if he knows him to be a Cheat, he will ſcarcely compliment him with Hopes that he will be of his Party.

The third Argument was from the Advice given by *Gamaliel* to the Council of the *Jews*, to let the Apoſtles alone, *for fear they themſelves ſhould be found to fight againſt God*: A Suppoſition which the Gentleman thinks

thinks absolutely inconsistent with his or the Council's being persuaded, that the Apostles were guilty of any Fraud in managing the Resurrection of Christ.

The Gentleman replies, That *Gamaliel's* Advice respected only the Numbers of People deceived, and was a Declaration of his Opinion, that it was not prudent to come to Extremities till the People were in a better Temper. This deserves Consideration.

First, I observe, that *Gamaliel's* Words are express, *lest ye be found to fight against God*, which Reason respects God, and not the People. And the Supposition is, that the *Hand of God* might possibly be in this Work: A Saying which cou'd not have come from him, or have been received by the Council, if they had believed the Resurrection to have been a Cheat.

Secondly, It is remarkable, that the Miracles wrought by the Apostles after the Death of Christ, those especially which occasioned the calling this Council, had a much greater Effect upon the *Jews*, than even the Miracles of Christ himself. They held out against all the Wonders of Christ, and were perpetually plotting his Death, not doubting but that wou'd put an End to their Trouble: But when after his Death, they saw the same Powers continue with the Apostles, they saw no End of the Affair, but began to think in earnest there might be more in it than they were willing to believe. And upon the Report made to them of the Apostles Works, they make serious Reflexion, *and doubted whereunto this wou'd grow*. And tho' in their Anger and Vexation of Heart they thought

N of

of desperate Remedies, and were for killing the Apostles also, yet they hearkened willingly to *Gamaliel's* Advice, which at another Time might have been dangerous to the Adviser. So that it appears from the History, that the whole Council had the same Doubt that *Gamaliel* had, that possibly the Hand of God might be in this Thing. And cou'd the *Jews*, if they had manifestly discovered the Cheat of the Resurrection a little time before, have entertained such a Suspicion?

The last Period commences at the Resurrection, and takes in the Evidence upon which the Credit of this Fact stands.

The Council for *Woolston*, among other Difficulties, started one, which, if well-grounded, excludes all Evidence out of this Case. The Resurrection being a Thing out of the Course of Nature, he thinks the Testimony of Nature, held forth to us in her constant Method of working, a stronger Evidence against the Possibility of a Resurrection, than any human Evidence can be for the Reality of one.

In answer to this, it is said, on the other Side,

First, That a Resurrection is a Thing to be judged of by Men's Senses; and this cannot be doubted. We all know when a Man is dead; and shou'd he come to Life again, we might judge whether he was alive or no, by the very same Means by which we judge those about us to be living Men.

Secondly, That the Notion of a Resurrection contradicts no one Principle of right Reason, interferes with no Law of Nature. And that whoever admits

mits that God gave Man Life at firſt, cannot poſſibly doubt of his Power to reſtore it when loſt.

Thirdly, That appealing to the ſettled Courſe of Nature, is referring the Matter in diſpute, not to Rules or Maxims of Reaſon and true Philoſophy, but to the Prejudices and Miſtakes of Men; which are various and infinite, and differ ſometimes according to the Climate Men live in; becauſe Men form a Notion of Nature from what they ſee; and therefore in cold Countries all Men judge it to be according to the Courſe of Nature for Water to freeze, in warm Countries they judge it to be unnatural. Conſequently, that it is not enough to prove any Thing to be contrary to the Laws of Nature, to ſay that it is uſually, or conſtantly, to our Obſervation, otherwiſe. And therefore, tho' Men in the ordinary Courſe die, and do not riſe again, (which is certainly a Prejudice againſt the Belief of a Reſurrection) yet is it not an Argument againſt the Poſſibility of a Reſurrection.

Another Objection was againſt the Reality of the Body of Chriſt after it came from the Grave. Theſe Objections are founded upon ſuch Paſſages as report his appearing or diſappearing to the Eyes of his Diſciples at pleaſure; his coming in among them when the Doors were ſhut; his forbidding ſome to touch him, his inviting others to do it; his having the very Wounds whereof he died, freſh and open in his Body, and the like. Hence the Council concluded that it was no real Body, which was ſometimes viſible, ſometimes inviſible; ſome-

N 2 times

times capable of being touched, ſometimes incapable.

On the other Side, it was anſwered, That many of theſe Objections are founded on a miſtaken Senſe of the Paſſages referred to; particularly of the Paſſage in which Chriſt is thought to forbid *Mary Magdalen* to touch him; of another, in which he calls to *Thomas* to examine his Wounds; and probably of a third, relating to Chriſt's Converſation with his Diſciples on the Road, without being known by them.

As to other Paſſages, which relate his appearing and diſappearing, and coming in when the Doors were ſhut, it is ſaid, that no Concluſion can be drawn from them againſt the Reality of Chriſt's Body: That theſe Things might happen many Ways, and yet the Body be real; which is the only Point to which the preſent Objection extends: That there might be in this, and probably was, ſomething miraculous; but nothing more wonderful than what happened on another Occaſion in his Life-time; where the Gentleman who makes the Objection, allows him to have had a real Body.

I mention theſe Things but briefly, juſt to bring the Courſe of the Argument to your Remembrance.

The next Objection is taken from hence, That Chriſt did not appear publickly to the People, and particularly to the Chief Prieſts and Rulers of the *Jews*. It is ſaid, that his Commiſſion related to them in an eſpecial manner; and that it appears ſtrange, that the main Proof of his Miſſion, the

I Reſur-

Reſurrection, ſhou'd not be laid before them; but that Witneſſes ſhou'd be picked and culled to ſee this mighty Wonder. This is the Force of the Objection.

To which it is anſwer'd, *Firſt*, That the particular Commiſſion to the *Jews* expired at the Death of Chriſt, and therefore the *Jews* had, on this Account, no Claim for any particular Evidence. And it is inſiſted, that Chriſt, before his Death, declared the *Jews* ſhou'd not ſee him, till they were better diſpoſed to receive him.

Secondly, That as the whole World had a Concern in the Reſurrection of Chriſt, it was neceſſary to prepare a proper Evidence for the whole World; which was not to be done by any particular Satiſfaction given to the People of the *Jews*, or their Rulers.

Thirdly, That as to the choſen Witneſſes, it is a Miſtake to think that they were choſen as the only Perſons to ſee Chriſt after the Reſurrection; and that in truth many others did ſee him; but that the Witneſſes were choſen as proper Perſons to bear Teſtimony to all People; an Office to which many others who did ſee Chriſt, were not particularly commiſſioned. That making Choice of proper and credible Witneſſes, was ſo far from being a Ground of juſt Suſpicion, that it is in all Caſes the moſt proper way to exclude Suſpicion.

The next Objection is pointed againſt the Evidence of the Angels, and the Women. It is ſaid, that Hiſtory reports that the Women ſaw young Men at the Sepulchre; that they were advanced into Angels merely thro' the Fear and Superſtition of of the Women: That at the beſt, this is but a Story of an Apparition; a Thing in Times of Ignorance much talked of, but in the Days of Knowledge never heard of.

In anſwer to this, it is ſaid, That the Angels are not properly reckoned among the Witneſſes of the Reſurrection; they were not in the Number of the choſen Witneſſes, or ſent to bear Teſtimony in the World: That they were indeed Miniſters of God appointed to attend the Reſurrection: That God has ſuch Miniſters, cannot be reaſonably doubted; nor can it be objected that they were improperly employed, or below their Dignity, in attending on the Reſurrection of Chriſt: That we believe them to be Angels, not on the Report of the Women, but upon the Credit of the Evangeliſt who affirms it. That what is ſaid of Apparitions on this Occaſion, may paſs for Wit and Ridicule, but yields no Reaſon or Argument.

The Objection to the Women was, I think, only that they were Women; which was ſtrengthned by calling them ſilly Women.

It was anſwered, that Women have Eyes and Ears as well as Men, and can tell what they ſee and hear. And it happened in this Caſe, that the Women were ſo far from being credulous, that they believed not the Angels, and hardly believed their own Report. However, that the Women are none of the choſen Witneſſes; and if they were, the Evidence of the Men cannot be ſet aſide, becauſe Women ſaw what they ſaw.

This is the Subſtance of the Objections and Anſwers.

The

The Council for the Apostles insisted further; That they gave the greatest Assurance to the World, that possibly cou'd be given, of their sincere Dealing, by suffering all Kinds of Hardship, and at last Death itself, in Confirmation of the Truth of their Evidence.

The Council for *Woolston*, in Reply to this, told you, That all Religions, whether true or false, have had their Martyrs; that no Opinion, however absurd, can be named, but some have been content to die for it; and then concluded, that Suffering is no Evidence of the Truth of the Opinions for which Men suffer.

To clear this Matter to you, I must observe how this Case stands. You have heard often, in the Course of this Argument, that the Apostles were Witnesses chosen to bear Testimony to the Resurrection; and, for that Reason, had the fullest Evidence themselves of the Truth of it; not merely by seeing Christ once or twice after his Death, but by frequent Conversations with him for forty Days together, before his Ascension. That this was their proper Business, appears plainly from History, where we find, that to ordain an Apostle, was the same thing as *ordaining* one *to be a Witness of the Resurrection* *. If you look further to the preaching of the Apostles, you will find this was the great Article insisted on †. And St. *Paul* knew the Weight of this Article, and the Necessity of teaching it, when he said, *If Christ be*

* Acts i. 22.

† Acts ii. 2, 22, *&c.* iii. 15. iv. 10. v. 30.

not

not risen, our Faith is vain. You see then, that the thing which the Apostles testified, and the thing for which they suffered, was the Truth of the Resurrection; which is a mere Matter of Fact.

Consider now how the Objection stands. The Council for *Woolston* tells you, that 'tis common for Men to die for false Opinions; and he tells you nothing but the Truth. But even in those Cases their suffering is an Evidence of their Sincerity; and it wou'd be very hard to charge Men who die for the Doctrine they profess, with Insincerity in the Profession. Mistaken they may be; but every mistaken Man is not a Cheat. Now if you will allow the Suffering of the Apostles to prove their Sincerity, which you cannot well disallow; and consider that they died for the Truth of a Matter of Fact which they had seen themselves, you will perceive how strong the Evidence is in this Case. In Doctrines and Matters of Opinion, Men mistake perpetually; and it is no Reason for me to take up with another Man's Opinion, because I am persuaded he is sincere in it. But when a Man reports to me an uncommon Fact, yet such an one, as in its own Nature is a plain Object of Sense; if I believe him not, it is not because I suspect his Eyes, or his Sense of Feeling, but merely because I suspect his Sincerity. For if I was to see the same thing myself, I should believe myself; and therefore my Suspicion does not arise from the Inability of human Senses to judge in the Case, but from a Doubt of the Sincerity of the Reporter. In such Cases therefore there wants nothing to be proved,

proved, but only the Sincerity of the Reporter: and ſince voluntary Suffering for the Truth, is at leaſt a Proof of Sincerity; the Sufferings of the Apoſtles for the Truth of the Reſurrection, is a full and unexceptionable Proof.

The Council for *Woolſton* was ſenſible of this Difference, and therefore he added, that there are many Inſtances of Mens ſuffering and dying in an obſtinate Denial of the Truth of Facts plainly proved. This Obſervation is alſo true. I remember a Story of a Man who endured with great Conſtancy all the Tortures of the Rack, denying the Fact with which he was charged. When he was asked afterwards, how he could hold out againſt all the Tortures? He anſwered, I had painted a Gallows upon the Toe of my Shoe, and when the Rack ſtretched me, I looked on the Gallows, and bore the Pain, to ſave my Life. This Man denied a plain Fact, under great Torture, but you ſee a Reaſon for it. In other Caſes, when Criminals perſiſt in denying their Crimes, they often do it; and there is Reaſon to ſuſpect they do it always, in Hopes of a Pardon or Reprieve. But what are theſe Inſtances to the preſent purpoſe? All theſe Men ſuffer againſt their Will, and for their Crimes; and their Obſtinacy is built on the Hope of eſcaping, by moving the Compaſſion of the Government. Can the Gentleman give any Inſtances of Perſons who died willingly in Atteſtation of a falſe Fact? We have had in *England* ſome weak enough to die for the Pope's Supremacy; but do you think

O a Man

a Man could be found to die in Proof of the Pope's being actually on the Throne of *England*.

Now the Apostles died in asserting the Truth of Christ's Resurrection. It was always in their Power to quit their Evidence, and save their Lives. Even their bitterest Enemies, the *Jews*, required no more of them than to be silent.* Others have denied Facts, or asserted Facts, in hopes of saving their Lives, when they were under Sentence of Death: But these Men attested a Fact at the expence of their Lives, which they might have saved by denying the Truth. So that between Criminals dying and denying plain Facts, and the Apostles dying for their Testimony, there is this material Difference: Criminals deny the Truth in hopes of saving their Lives; the Apostles willingly parted with their Lives, rather than deny the Truth.

We are come now to the last, and indeed the most weighty Consideration.

The Council for the Apostles having in the Course of the Argument allowed, that more Evidence is required to support the Credit of the Resurrection, it being a very extraordinary Event, than is necessary in common Cases; in the latter Part of his Defence sets forth the extraordinary Evidence upon which this Fact stands. This is the Evidence of the Spirit; the Spirit of Wisdom and Power, which was given to the Apostles, to enable them to confirm their Testimony by Signs and Wonders, and mighty Works. This Part of

* Acts iv. 17. v. 28.

the

the Argument was well urged by the Gentleman, and I need not repeat all he ſaid.

The Council for *Woolſton* in his Reply, made two Objections to this Evidence.

The firſt was this; That the Reſurrection having all along been pleaded to be a Matter of Fact, and an Object of Senſe; to recur to Miracles for the Proof of it, is to take it out of its proper Evidence, the Evidence of Senſe; and to reſt it upon a Proof which cannot be applied to it; for ſeeing one Miracle, he ſays, is no Evidence that another Miracle was wrought before it; as healing a ſick Man, is no Evidence that a dead Man was raiſed to Life.

To clear this Difficulty, you muſt conſider by what Train of Reaſoning Miracles come to be Proofs in any Caſe. A Miracle of itſelf proves nothing, unleſs this only, that there is a Cauſe equal to the producing the Effect we ſee. Suppoſe you ſhou'd ſee a Man raiſe one from the dead, and he ſhou'd go away and ſay nothing to you, you wou'd not find that any Fact, or any Propoſition, was prov'd or diſprov'd by this Miracle. But ſhou'd he declare to you, in the Name of him, by whoſe Power the Miracle was wrought, that Image-Worſhip was unlawful, you wou'd then be poſſeſs'd of a Proof againſt Image-Worſhip. But how? Not becauſe the Miracle proves any thing, as to the Point itſelf; but becauſe the Man's Declaration is authorized by him who wrought the Miracle in Confirmation of his Doctrine. And therefore Miracles are directly a Proof of the

Authority of Perſons, and not of the Truth of Things.

To apply this to the preſent Caſe: If the Apoſtles had wrought Miracles, and ſaid nothing of the Reſurrection, the Miracles wou'd have proved nothing about the Reſurrection, one way or other. But when as Eye-witneſſes they atteſted the Truth of the Reſurrection, and wrought Miracles to confirm their Authority; the Miracles did not directly prove the Reſurrection; but they confirmed and eſtabliſh'd beyond all Suſpicion the proper Evidence, the Evidence of Eye-witneſſes. So that here is no Change of the Evidence from proper to improper; the Fact ſtill reſts upon the Evidence of Senſe, confirmed and ſtrengthen'd by the Authority of the Spirit. If a Witneſs calls in his Neighbours to atteſt his Veracity; they prove nothing as to the Fact in queſtion, but only confirm the Evidence of the Witneſs. The Caſe here is the ſame; tho' between the Authorities brought in Confirmation of the Evidence, there is no Compariſon.

The ſecond Objection was, That this Evidence, however good it may be in its kind, is yet nothing to us. It was well, the Gentleman ſays, for thoſe who had it; but what is that to us, who have it not?

To adjuſt this Difficulty, I muſt obſerve to you, that the Evidence, now under Conſideration, was not a private Evidence of the Spirit, or any inward Light, like to that which the Quakers in our Time pretend to; but an Evidence appearing in the manifeſt and viſible Works of the Spirit: And this

this Evidence was capable of being tranſmitted, and actually has been tranſmitted to us upon unqueſtionable Authority: And to allow the Evidence to have been good in the firſt Ages, and not in this, ſeems to me to be a Contradiction to the Rules of Reaſoning. For if we ſee enough to judge that the firſt Ages had Reaſon to believe, we muſt needs ſee at the ſame time, that it is reaſonable for us alſo to believe. As the preſent Queſtion only relates to the Nature of the Evidence, it was not neceſſary to produce from Hiſtory the Inſtances to ſhew in how plentiful a manner this Evidence was granted to the Church. Whoever wants this Satisfaction, may eaſily have it.

Gentlemen of the Jury, I have laid before you the Subſtance of what has been ſaid on both Sides. You are now to conſider of it, and to give your Verdict.

The Jury conſulted together, and the Foreman roſe up.

Foreman. My Lord, We are ready to give our Verdict.

Judge. Are you all agreed?

Jury. Yes.

Judge. Who ſhall ſpeak for you?

Jury. Our Foreman.

Judge. What ſay you? Are the Apoſtles guilty of giving falſe Evidence in the Caſe of the Reſurrection of Jeſus, or not guilty?

Foreman. Not guilty.

Judge,

Judge. Very well; and now Gentlemen I resign my Commission, and am your humble Servant.

The Company rose up, and were beginning to pay their Compliments to the Judge and the Council; but were interrupted by a Gentleman, who went up to the Judge, and offer'd him a Fee. What's this? says the Judge. A Fee, Sir, said the Gentleman. A Fee to a Judge is a Bribe, said the Judge. True, Sir, said the Gentleman; but you have resign'd your Commission, and will not be the first Judge who has come from the Bench to the Bar without any Diminution of Honour. Now *Lazarus*'s Case is to come on next, and this Fee is to retain you on his Side. There follow'd a confus'd Noise of all speaking together, to persuade the Judge to take the Fee: But as the Trial had lasted longer than I expected, and I had lapsed the time of an Appointment for Business, I was forc'd to slip away; and whether the Judge was prevailed on to undertake the Cause of *Lazarus*, or no, I cannot say.

FINIS.

ERRATA.

Page 5. *line* 13. *for* Cook, *read* Coke.
Page 9. *line* 16. *for* on, *read* in.
Page 28. *line* 18. *for* articula, *read* articulo.
Page 34. *In a Paſſage taken from Mr.* Woolſton, Nubuchadnezzar *is put inſtead of* Darius.
Page 61. *line* 8. *for* o, *read* of.

N. B. *Not only Mr.* Woolſton's *Objections in his* Sixth Diſcourſe, *but thoſe alſo which he and others have publiſhed in other Books, are here conſidered.*

E R R A T A

[illegible]

[illegible]

REMARKS

ON THE

INTERNAL EVIDENCE

FOR THE TRUTH OF

Revealed Religion.

By THOMAS ERSKINE, Esq.

ADVOCATE.

SEVENTH EDITION.

EDINBURGH:

PRINTED FOR WAUGH AND INNES:

AND OGLE, DUNCAN AND CO. LONDON.

M.DCCC.XXIII.

If the gospel really was a communication from heaven, it was to be expected that it would be ushered into the world by a miraculous attestation. It might have been considered as giving a faithful delineation of the Divine character, although it had not been so attested; but it could never have impressed so deep a conviction, nor have drawn such reverence from the minds of men, had it not been sanctioned by credentials which could come from none other than the King of kings. As this conviction and this reverence were necessary to the accomplishment of its moral object, the miracles which produced them were also necessary. Under the name of miraculous attestations, I mean merely those miracles which were extrinsic to the gospel, and did not form an essential part of it; for the greatest miracles of all—namely, the conception, resurrection, and ascension of our Lord—constitute the very substance of the Divine communication, and are essential to the development of that Divine character which gives to the gospel its whole importance.

The belief of the miraculous attestation of the gospel, then, is just so far useful as it excites our reverence for, and fixes our attention on the truth contained in the gospel. All the promises of the gospel are to faith in the gospel, and to those moral qualities which faith produces; and we cannot believe that which we do not understand. We may believe that there is more in a thing than we can understand; or we may believe a fact, the causes or modes of which we do not understand; but our ac-

K

tual belief is necessarily limited by our actual understanding. Thus, we understand what we say when we profess our belief that God became man, although we do not understand *how*. This *how*, therefore, is not the subject of belief; because it is not the subject of understanding. We however understand *why*,—namely, that sinners might be saved, and the Divine character made level to our capacities; and therefore this is a subject of belief. In fact, we can as easily remember a thing which we never knew, as believe a thing that we do not understand. In order, then, to believe the gospel, we must understand it; and in order to understand it, we must give it our serious consideration. An admission of the truth of its miraculous attestation, unaccompanied with a knowledge of its principles, serves no other purpose than to give a most mournful example of the extreme levity of the human mind. It is an acknowledgment that the Almighty took such a fatherly interest in the affairs of men, that he made a direct manifestation of himself in this world, for their instruction; and yet they feel no concern upon the subject of this instruction. Nevertheless, they say, and perhaps think, that they believe the gospel. One of the miraculous appearances connected with our Saviour's ministry places this matter in a very clear light. When on the mount of transfiguration, he for a short time anticipated the celestial glory in the presence of three of his disciples, a voice came from Heaven saying, "This is my beloved Son; *hear ye him.*" He was sent to tell men something which they did not know. Those, therefore, who believed the reality of this miraculous appearance, and yet did not listen to what he taught, rejected him on the very ground on which it was of prime importance that they should receive him.

The regeneration of the character is the grand object; and this can only be effected by the pressure of the truth upon the mind. Our knowledge of this truth must be accurate, in order that the image impressed upon the heart may be correct; but we must also know it in all the awfulness of its authority, in order that the impression may be deep and lasting. Its motives must be ever operating on us,—its representations ever recurring to us—its hopes ever animating us. This will not relax, but rather increase our diligence in the business of life. When we are engaged in the service of a friend, do we find that the thought of that friend and of his kindness retards our exertions?—No. And when we consider all the business of life as work appointed to us by our Father, we shall be diligent in it for his sake. In fact, however clearly we may be able to state the subject, and however strenuous we may be in all the orthodoxy of its defence, there must be some flaw in our view of it, if it remains only a casual or an uninfluential visitor of our hearts. Its interests are continually pressing: eternity is every moment coming nearer; and our characters are hourly assuming a form more decidedly connected with the extreme of happiness or misery. In such circumstances, trifling is madness. The professed infidel is a reasonable man in comparison with him who admits the Divine inspiration of the gospel, and yet makes it a secondary object of his solicitude.

The Monarch of the Universe has proclaimed a general amnesty of rebellion, whether we give or withhold our belief or our attention; and if an amnesty were all that we needed, our belief or our attention would probably never have been required. Our notions of pardon and punishment are taken from our experience of human laws. We are in the habit of considering punishment and transgression as two distinct and separate things, which have been joined together by authority, and pardon as nothing more than the dissolution of this arbitrary connexion. And so it is amongst men; but so it is not in the world of spirits. Sin and punishment there are one thing. Sin is a disease of the mind which necessarily occasions misery; and therefore the pardon of sin, unless it be accompanied with some remedy for this disease, cannot relieve from misery.

This remedy, as I have endeavoured to explain, consists in the attractive and sanctifying influence of the Divine character manifested in Jesus Christ. Pardon is preached through him, and those who really believe are healed; for this belief implants in the heart the love of God and the love of man, which is only another name for spiritual health. Carelessness, then, comes to the same thing as a decided infidelity. It matters little in what particular way, or on what particular grounds we put the gospel from us. If we do put it from us either by inattention or rejection, we lose all the benefits which it is fitted to bestow; whilst, on the other hand, he who does receive it, receives along with it all those benefits, whether his belief has originated from the external evidence, or simply from the conviction of guilt and the desire of pardon, and the discovery that the gospel meets his necessities as a weak and sinful creature,—just as a voyager gains all the advantage of the information contained in his chart, whatever the evidence may have been, on which he at first received it.

This last illustration may explain to us why God should have declared *faith* to be the channel of all his mercies to his intelligent creatures. The chart is useless to the voyager, unless he believes that it is really a description of the ocean which he has to pass, with all its boundaries and rocks and shoals and currents; and the gospel is useless to man, unless he believes it to be a description of the character and will of that Great Being on whom his eternal interests depend. Besides, the nature of the gospel required such a reception in another point of view: It was necessary to its very object that its blessings should be distinctly marked out to be of free and unmerited bounty. When we speak of benefits freely bestowed, we say of them, "You may have them by asking for them,"—distinguishing them by this mode of expression as gifts, from those things for which we must give a price. Precisely the same idea is conveyed by the gospel declaration, "Believe and ye shall be saved." When it is asked, How am I to obtain God's mercy? the gospel answers, that "God has already declared himself reconciled through Jesus Christ; so you may have it by believing it." Faith, therefore, according to the gospel scheme, both marks the freeness of God's mercy, and is the channel through which that mercy operates on the character.

A LAWYER EXAMINES THE BIBLE

An Introduction to Christian Evidences

I

ADDRESSED ESPECIALLY TO LAWYERS

"If a close examination of the evidences of Christianity may be expected of one class of men more than another, it would seem incumbent upon us [lawyers] who make the law of evidence one of our peculiar studies. Our profession leads us to explore the mazes of falsehood, to detect its artifices, to pierce its thickest veils, to follow and expose its sophistries, to compare the statements of different witnesses with severity, to discover truth and separate it from error."

THUS wrote Simon Greenleaf, the greatest authority known to England and America on the subject of legal evidence, in dedicating to the members of the bar his great but up to recently almost forgotten work, "The Testimony of the Evangelists." It is because the subject of the Christian Evidences has proven both to me and to scores whom I have interested in it the most interesting, satisfactory, thrilling and informing encountered in a lifetime of study, that I make this appeal to anyone not familiar with it to address himself to it forthwith. I urge upon my fellow lawyers especially that they give themselves at least once before they die the benefit of their own skilled professional services in examining, by every acid test known to the law, the evidence and reasoning in support of the formally recorded opinions of many of the most famous members of our learned and skeptical profession that a thing proved beyond a reasonable doubt is the claim of the Christian religion and the Holy Bible to be in deed and in fact the one religion and book with the inspiration and sanction of Almighty God behind them.

Legal scrutiny is the last thing to which any form of imposture is willing to submit, courts and their officers being especially skilled and daily exercised in its exposure; and yet it is investigation at the hands of men of this profession that Christianity especially courts and from which it uniformly emerges triumphant.

There is deep significance in the fact adverted to both by the evangelist Charles G. Finney, and by David Nelson, the author of the famous old book, "Nelson on the Cause and Cure of Infidelity."

Writes David Nelson, long an infidel doctor, later a Christian minister:

"I do not know why it is so, but it is the result of eighteen years' experience that lawyers, of all those with whom I have examined, exercise the clearest judgment while investigating the evidence of Christianity. I am unable to account for the fact, yet so it is, that the man of law excels. He has when examining the evidence of the Bible's inspiration shown more common sense in weighing proof and appreciating argument, where argument really existed, than any other class of men I have ever observed."

And, confirming this statement of Dr. David Nelson, we find the most famous of all evangelists, Charles G. Finney, writing as follows:

"I have always been particularly interested in the salvation of lawyers, and all men of the legal profession. To that profession I was myself educated. I understood pretty well their habits of reading and thinking, and knew that they were more certainly controlled by argument, by evidence and by logical statements than any other class of men. I have always found, wherever I have labored, that when the Gospel was properly presented, they were the most accessible of men; and I believe it is true that, in proportion to their relative number in any community, more have been converted than of any other class. I have been particularly struck with this, in the manner in which a clear presentation of the Law and the Gospel of God will carry the intelligence of judges, men who are in the habit of sitting and hearing testimony and weighing argument on both sides. I have never, to my recollection, seen a case in which judges were not convinced of the truth of the Gospel, where they have attended meetings, in the revivals which I have witnessed. I have often been very much affected, in conversing with members of the legal profession, by the manner in which they would consent to propositions to which persons of ill disciplined minds would have objected. . . .

". . . Indeed, as a general thing, they take a more intelligent view of the whole plan of salvation than any other class of men to whom I have ever preached or with whom I have ever conversed."

We have before us here a phenomenon for which a " reasonably prudent man " will seek an explanation.

Why should it be that the one class of men whose lives are largely spent in the work of sifting and weighing evidence about disputed matters, trained by their profession " to explore the mazes of falsehood, to detect its artifices, to pierce its thickest veils, to follow and expose its sophistries, to compare the statements of different witnesses with severity, to discover truth and separate it from error," should be the very class of men who, after such dubious scrutiny as it becomes a lawyer's second nature to bestow upon any proposition, are surest to assent to the Bible's claims to divine inspiration and its presentation of Jesus Christ as the very incarnate, crucified, resurrected Son of God? Is not the answer strongly suggested: Because Christianity is true " in manner and form as alleged "?

But is the opinion of a lawyer or the whole profession of the law particularly valuable in regard to matters so abstruse as religion, morals, theology and life in another world? Would not the view of a master of some of the more abstract sciences be more significant: the metaphysician, psychologist, physicist, biologist, physician or the like? Gentlemen of these professions are frequently called upon to take the witness stand as " experts " in court trials, and some of their most famous members will testify to the disintegrating effect of skilled cross-examination at the hands of able lawyers, whose profession leads them to study at one time or another almost all branches of knowledge.

I am not minimizing but rejoicing in the firm faith in Christianity and testimony to it of great scientists of all branches of research, from Newton to Lord Kelvin and our recently deceased famous Christian brother in the Lord Dr. Howard A. Kelly; but it seems to me that most significant is the fact that of all learned callings, it is the followers of that profession which gives the keenest ability to detect imposture and unproven claims, who most promptly, firmly and universally, when they bring to consideration of the matter their training and skill, accept the Bible as truly the inspired word of God and the Christ as the divine Son of God.[1]

The lawyer does indeed deal more with facts than with theology and philosophy, but one of the fundamental and blessed facts about the Christian religion is that it is a (and the only) *fact based religion.* In distinction from all other and false religions and isms of the world, which rest on unverifiable theories, assumptions, postulates and chains of syllogisms, each often using as a major premise a very poorly established conclusion of the previous one, our Christian faith, with its glad assurance of a rapturous resurrection and life after death, rests on definite, historical facts and events—facts and historical events of such nature that if they really took place, the religion is true, and established by so direct, so strong and so great a variety of independent and converging proofs that it has been said again and again by great lawyers that they cannot but be regarded as proved under the strictest rules of evidence used in the highest American and English courts.

We have, then, the well-reasoned opinions of that profession and class of men most skeptical and skilled by training to discern falsehood and imposture that the Christian religion, presenting ponderable, factual proofs, is neither, but is what it purports to be.

True, there have been many lawyers of this and other days infidel or agnostic. But their legal training gives their views no value unless their attention has seriously been given to a consideration of this matter. And it may safely be believed of all infidel lawyers that no one of them has ever made a careful, lawyer-like, two-sided investigation of the claims of the " Bible and its Christ," studying and digesting any of the great " briefs " or works on the " Christian Evidences " which gather together and sum up the proofs in support of the claim of the Lord Jesus Christ to deity and of the Bible to divine inspiration. I have never found one, and I have hunted for twenty-five years.

---

[1] William James once expressed himself: " When you defer to what you suppose a certain authority in scientists as confirming these negations, I am surprised. Of all insufficient authorities as to the total nature of reality, give me the ' scientists ' from Munsterberg up or down. Their interests are most incomplete. Their only authority at large is for method."—" Life and Letters of William James," Vol. II, p. 270.

I have never read of one and I have studied this matter for thirty-five years. And in the last twenty years I have more than once, with no result, challenged large audiences to produce any man, lawyer or layman, who was an unbeliever who had ever read even one of the old classics on the Christian Evidences. I have sometimes followed this inquiry for an instructed unbeliever by the statement that "if you do not believe the Bible, I know what you do believe. You believe in evolution," and then I have asked if there were present a man or woman who believed in this theory who had ever read a single one of the scholarly works against it—still without ever finding one such man or woman.

Surely we have here another phenomenon to be accounted for!

But the general statement that legal training coupled with an investigation of the Bible's proofs practically always results in Christian conviction should be fortified by some examples, and the first I would cite is Sir Matthew Hale, the great Lord Chancellor under Oliver Cromwell. I have a priceless copy of his book "Contemplations Moral and Divine," which was one of the few volumes in the library of George Washington's father. We find inscribed on the fly-leaf of the volume at Mt. Vernon first the name of "Jane, Butler, her book," then this name struck out, apparently by the hand of her successor in Augustine Washington's affections, Mary Ball, the mother of George, who substituted her own name as owner, and probably read this book assiduously to her son, to his great edification. The profound Christian faith and piety of this great English lawyer and his ability to express theological as well as legal matters with force and precision make this old volume, with its f-like ss, worthy of any man's careful study; but the one poem in the book will suffice to make clear the piety of this lawyer whose fame is second to none in the annals of English law:

"CHANGES AND TROUBLES"

Peace wayward Soul! let not those various storms,
Which hourly fill the World with fresh Alarms,
Invade thy Peace; nor discompose that Rest,
Which thou maist keep untoucht within thy Breast,
Amidst those whirlwinds, if thou keep but free
Thy Intercourse betwixt thy God and thee.

The Region lies above these Storms: and know
Thy thoughts are earthly, and they creep too low,
If these can reach this, or access can find,
To bring or raise like Tempests in thy Mind.
But yet in these disorders something lies,
That's worth thy notice, out of which the Wise
May trace, and find that just and Powerful Hand,
That secretly, but surely doth Command
And Manage these distempers with that skill,
That while they seem to cross they Act his Will.
Observe that Silver Thred, that Steers and bends
The worst of all disorders, to such Ends,
That speak his Justice, Goodness, Providence,
Who closely guides it by his Influence.
And though these Storms are loud, yet listen well,
There is another message that they tell:
This World is not thy Country; 'tis thy Way;
Too much contentment would invite thy stay
Too long upon thy journey; make it Strange
Unwelcome News, to think upon a Change:
Whereas this rugged entertainment fends
Thy thoughts before thee to thy journey's end;
Chides thy desires homeward; tells thee plain,
To think of resting here it is but vain;
Makes thee to set an equal estimate,
On this uncertain World, and a just rate
On that to come: It bids thee wait and Stay,
Until thy Master calls, and then with joy
To entertain it. Such a Change as this
Renders thy Loss, thy Gain; improves thy Bliss.

That poem with which Sir Matthew Hale comforted his heart in his days of distress has a message for us in ours!

Somewhat earlier we have John Selden, a Christian equally famous as a lawyer, and a scholar so profound that it is said the learned men who gathered together under the auspices of King James to produce that priceless gift to the English-speaking world, the "King James Version" of the Scriptures, were wont to refer to John Selden for solution many problems of translation confronting them as their work progressed.

In our own day we had Sir Robert Anderson, both a lawyer and the head of "Scotland Yard," knighted by Queen Victoria for his services along lines that called for the utmost skill in "exploring the mazes of falsehood . . . in discovering truth and separating it from error." The meticulous care and acid cross-examination with which he tested the Bible appear on every page of his numerous works, such as "The Coming Prince," "The Silence of God" and others. The reader is referred to Appendix "A" for a sample of his method, and an illustration of the amazing, to-the-day accuracy of Bible prophecy, as this accuracy is demonstrated by this great lawyer-detective, with the aid of the British Astronomer Royal, G. B. Airy.

Lord George Lyttleton, who played an important part in English politics during the reign of George II and was Chancellor of the Exchequer until his lack of aptitude for figures caused him to resign, contended in a work to which Dr. Samuel Johnson declared "infidelity has never been able to fabricate a specious answer" that "the conversion and apostleship of St. Paul alone, duly considered, is of itself sufficient to prove the truth of Christianity," a thesis that the arguments he brings forth make clear.

The scholarly work of Gilbert West, Esq., in showing the real harmony and probative force of the various accounts of the resurrection of Christ is often mentioned in connection with that of Lord Lyttleton, as Lyttleton was much moved to his investigation of the foundations of Christianity by the deep conviction West had formed as the result of his own research. Lyttleton's great work was written at a time when his heart was breaking over the impending death of his wife and, as Cowper exclaims, "How readily does affliction make us Christians"—or at least incline us to that serious consideration of eternal issues which are often neglected in times of health and prosperity.

The death of Abraham Lincoln's little son is said to have been a contributing cause to his investigation of the proofs of Christianity which resulted in his conversion. Up to his fortieth year, though "a great reader of the Bible," he was an agnostic and deist. About that time Dr. James Smith, pastor of the First Presbyterian Church of Springfield, Ill., gave him to read his own work on the Christian Evidences called "The Christian's Defense," with the result that, in the words of Dr. Smith, "at the conclusion of his examination he came forth, his doubts scattered to the winds and his reason convinced by the arguments in support of the inspired and infallible authority of the Old and New Testaments—a believer in God, in His providential government, in His son, the way, the truth and the life." [1] However one's political views may chance to differ from those of Lincoln, all recognize in his inaugural addresses and constant humble expressions of faith in God the reality of his Christian faith and conversion.

Daniel Webster, the force of whose intellect so showed in his face that a sculptor once working on his bust was accosted by a friend with the remark that he observed he was sculpturing the head of Olympian Jove, wrote a confession of his faith from which the following paragraphs are taken:

> " I believe the Scriptures of the Old and New Testaments to be the will and word of God.
>
> " I believe Jesus Christ to be the Son of God. The miracles which he wrought [note that he does not indicate the slightest deficiency in the evidence supporting them] establish in my mind his personal authority and render it proper for me to believe whatever he asserts. I believe, therefore, all his declarations, as well when he declares himself the Son of God as when he declares any other proposition. And I believe there is no other way of salvation than through the merits of his atonement.
>
> " I believe that things past, present, and to come are all equally present in the mind of Deity; that with him there is no succession of time nor of ideas; that, therefore, the relative terms past, present and future, as used among men, cannot with strict propriety be applied to Deity. I believe in the doctrines of foreknowledge and predestination as thus expounded. I do not believe in those doctrines as imposing any fatality or necessity on men's actions or infringement of free agency."

The most famous members of the English and American bars have shared Webster's Christian faith. I have said that I doubted whether a single infidel lawyer had ever read a work on the Christian Evidences and I am almost as confident that very few believing lawyers have failed to follow a law-trained man's inveterate habit of " studying the other side " and obeying the old Latin injunction "*Audi et alterem partem.*" An *ex parte* consideration of any question is unworthy the name, and the fact that so many of the famous Christian lawyers have not only adopted their views as a result of careful study of the arguments for both infidelity and Christianity, but have written

[1] " Abraham Lincoln the Christian," by Wm. J. Johnson, pp. 51–2.

notable books (as in the case of Lyttleton, as well as Greenleaf, Lord Erskine, Sir Robert Anderson and many others) in support of their convictions, lends special value to their conclusions. But Christianity does not at all rely upon authority for its support, and lawyers themselves regard lightly mere *obiter dicta* and unreasoned opinions, valuing and weighing the reasoning behind judicial decisions as the thing of real value in every precedent. Christianity offers and asks the most dubious and careful consideration for every one of the " many infallible proofs " of its truth and reality on the part of every inquirer. St. Paul, himself, urges us to let no man fool us, but " to prove all things, hold fast that which is good." " Search the Scriptures " said our Lord to the Pharisees. " Come now, let us reason together " is the gracious invitation of the " High and Holy One who dwelleth in the high and holy place "; and those who " have laid hold on God's covenant " and taken the trouble to weigh the superabundant proofs God has provided for the assurance of all who will examine the credentials of the Gospel, are almost as grateful for the mental rest which such study produces as for the spiritual peace resulting from assurance of forgiven sins, eternal life, an assured bodily resurrection, reunion with radiant, restored, lost-awhile loved ones and " an inheritance incorruptible and undefiled and that fadeth not away reserved in heaven " for those " who are kept by the power of God, through faith unto salvation."

I have mentioned so far only the research made by lawyers into this most important of all questions confronting a human being; but personal experiences with business acquaintances who were not lawyers further illustrate the overwhelming effect on serious minds of the proofs on which Christian faith rests:

One of Washington's prominent real estate brokers is a schoolmate of mine. We parted when we finished the graded schools, and I did not see him again until I came back from college, my brain tingling with the great discovery that the religion of Christ was not a dubious thing to be regarded as a hopeful possibility, but a great reality which, while calling for the exercise of faith, was willing and eager to have its credentials most meticulously examined before it asked that confidence be reposed in it. In our talk I soon got my chance to find out what his religious convictions were. Said he:

"Irwin, I have looked into all that, and there is nothing in it."

"Charlie, what have you read along this line?"

"Paine's 'Age of Reason,'" he replied, then he paused.

"What else?" I asked. "Go on."

"That's all."

"Haven't you read any on the other side?"

"I don't think there is more than about one side to it," was his answer.

"Will you read even one book on the side of the Bible?" I asked him.

"Certainly," he answered, "if there are any books an intelligent man can find worth reading."

Because it is so readable and, by using the author's experience in dealing with unbelievers so freely with his argument, stirs the interest and emotions more than pure close-knit reasoning, I gave him a copy of an old book I have already mentioned, Nelson's "Cause and Cure of Infidelity"—about which I shall have more to say later.

Several weeks passed. Then he came to my office to return the book, and said: "Irwin, I didn't know such things existed." He said more in explanation and amplification of his astonishment at the proofs that supported the Christian's faith in the Bible and Christ, but these are the only words I remember literally. He had not a word to say in opposition to Dr. Nelson's arguments or in support of his own unbelief.

As I write, it was some fifteen years ago, that Dr. R. C. Grier, then and now president of Erskine (my old "Scotch Covenanter Presbyterian") College in South Carolina, happened to be in my office when the telephone rang. I found I was connected with Baltimore, and at the other end of the line was a gentleman who was one of the officers of the Baltimore Association of Commerce, a highly educated German professional man to whom I had lent my old copy of Paley's "Evidences" about two weeks before. He had come into my office about a business matter, and before he left, rather unexpectedly, I fancy, found himself replying, to some leading questions, that his early faith in Christ and the Bible was so in eclipse that there was hardly a vestige left.

He accepted with a smile my statement that, so far as his brain and intellectual belief were concerned, I would undertake to guarantee that he could not retain his unbelief if he would study the matter a bit, and start in with a book or two I offered then and there to lend him. Paley was handy in my bookcase, and he took it with him, after he had told me that he really had not known there were any noteworthy books in opposition to the agnostic and infidel writers.

Before this point was reached I had said to him:

"Mr. Von B——, for twenty years I have looked for the unbeliever in these things who at the same time was thoroughly familiar with the proofs in support of them. I haven't found him yet. You may be the exception, and if so you will spoil a generalization in which I have often indulged. Have you studied carefully any of the great works on the Christian Evidences?"

"No, I have not," he answered, "though I have read many of the opposite sort."

"That exception is still to find, then," I remarked, as I asked that he would report to me after he had finished Paley.

This long distance telephone call was the report. My friend said: "I certainly thank you for lending me that book. I am ninety-nine and nine-tenths converted, and I have still one chapter to read before I finish." (I have his letter to the same effect.)

This message, coming at the moment when I was telling the president of my old college of my experiences with unbelievers and the really amusing uniformity and completeness with which an agnostic's self-satisfied unbelief collapsed before the assault of almost any one of the old Christian apologists, was a most timely confirmation of my statement, and a most heart-warming encouragement to "carry on" in this line so long as life is in me.

I cannot resist mentioning a third somewhat similar experience when a client, educated in the German universities, spoke with contempt of the claims of Christianity. I defied him to despise them after he had read even one book I might pick out for him. It so happened that it was another copy of the same old Paley. My client came into my office a few days later and said: "That man nearly drove me crazy. I lay awake all last night."

He was a clear thinker and loved to think, and he could not find any flaw or weakness in the argument. He went away, and I have not seen or heard of him for many years. Whether he has been converted I do not know. But I do know that he was a meek and silenced agnostic after he had received the mental broadside of that old "ship of the line" Paley, in defense of the faith once delivered and ever since committed to the saints as a sacred treasure and thrilling issue to maintain against all comers and at all hazards until the Prince come back again.

It takes proof of some cogency to silence an agnostic full of Huxley, and Hume's "Essay on Miracles," and with a superiority complex toward believing men and women. So many questions in life are left in doubt even after they are carefully pondered; but the blessed thing about this, the most important of all questions, is that when you are through, or really when you just make a fair beginning, there is no room for doubt left. The thing is simply demonstrated, that is all. A man who studies and uses the multiplication table knows it is true; and a man who studies and uses the Bible knows it is true. It can be proved theoretically, and it proves itself empirically.

You, my reader, may be the exception I did not find in any of the three men mentioned—but I doubt it. If you have never read Paley, or Alexander, or Mark Hopkins' "Evidences," for example, or if you read them long ago and have forgotten, read them again. If you have never, or for many years have not, read Paley's "Natural Theology," a work whose reasoning is as sound and unanswerable now as it ever was, read it; and if you have been hearing or reading the proponents of evolution, see if his argument from design does not sound like "words of truth and soberness" after the maunderings of a madhouse.

And I make no apology for referring back to these old books, any more than the English professor does for studying Shakespeare and Homer. While there has been a great accumulation of information, the vigor and power of the human mind and its ability to draw sound conclusions have not increased as sin- and disease-stricken generations have interposed one step after another between them and the mighty intellect with which Jehovah endowed his first man, "Adam, which was the son of God." The son who inherits and adds to his father's fortune is not therefore a greater financier than the father who accumulated it; and the present-day scientists and "men of modern mind" who are the "heirs of all the ages" of accumulated knowledge are not necessarily stronger of mind and power to reason than those nearer the source of originally perfect mentality. Surely archeology does much to support the great English preacher who declared "Aristotle but the ruins of an Adam, and Athens but the relic of Eden." Do not let anyone dissuade you from reading Paley by saying his works are out of date. Sound reasoning is never out of date; and there were ample data in Paley's time to support his contention ten times over. There are many fine recent works on the evidences, but often an old book is like an old matured bond, and studying it is a safer investment. But, by all means, let everyone study this subject for himself, and be "ready always to give . . . a reason of the hope" that is in him—not only reasons from his own personal experience and altogether valid for him, but such as can penetrate the armor of any unbeliever. If you already believe, considering the unanswerable reasons for your faith will make it more vivid; if you are not now a believer, you will be before you are through.

II

OPENING THE CASE

Prophecy

But in this day of fast motion and hurried thinking, there is a widespread belief that religion is something which from its nature no one can know enough about to make worth while the effort to arrive at a well-founded conclusion in regard to it; and the President of the American Association for the Advancement of Atheism has put a popular argument against Christianity succinctly when he writes: "There are twenty-seven Bibles in the world; the Christian rejects twenty-six of them. The atheist rejects only one more than the Christian does," the persuasive inference being that since the Christian agrees with the atheist that twenty-six of these Bibles are false, the only reasonable thing to do is to reject the twenty-seventh also. A popular "conclusion of the whole matter" is that "it makes no difference what you believe, just so you are sincere": that a man's sincerity in following whatever faith he is inclined or was born to in the midst of bewildering and equally unverifiable claims of divine origin for rival religious books and leaders is assuredly all that a reasonable God can require.

Every trace of plausibility for this contention evaporates, however, in the burning light of the fact that uncertainty as to which is God's Book and who is God's Son is possible only to one who carelessly neglects to examine (largely as a result of criminal neglect on the part of Christians to advertise) the proofs God's forethought has provided for the conviction of any man who will take half as much care in investigating the religion he lives and dies by as he does the title to a house he plans to purchase and live in. And he who relies on this theory of the all-sufficiency of sincerity has to admit that, if this rule operates in spiritual matters of eternal importance, it certainly does not here and in this life, where it can be tested in advance, and where sincerity in mistaking, for instance, mercuric for mecurous chloride (corrosive sublimate for calomel) has never been known to prevent or mitigate the deadly effects of the error.

The Bible tells us that there is one, and only one way to escape eternal death and secure eternal life: " If thou shalt confess with thy mouth the Lord Jesus, and shalt believe in thine heart that God hath raised him from the dead, thou shalt be saved " (Rom. 10: 9). The way of salvation is many times declared, but always to the same effect. If the Bible is God's inspired, infallible Word, all who trust any other way of escape from God's eternal prison house are doomed. So the most important question in the world for every man of us to settle as quickly as possible is: Is this " twenty-seventh Bible," the " Holy Bible," God's one revelation of Himself and His covenant to men? But since men are confronted, as Mr. Smith tells us, with twenty-seven Bibles all making the same claim, what reason is there to justify a lawyer or any other intelligent man in rejecting utterly twenty-six Bibles and accepting the twenty-seventh? This is a fair question and calls for a satisfactory answer.

And now, first, to " clear the decks " of the twenty-six false Bibles, whose claims to divine inspiration are presented by the infidel as reducing to absurdity a claim for inspiration for any Bible, let us invoke the rule of law and logic that puts the burden of proof upon any plaintiff or proponent of establishing his contention by sufficient evidence; and when we do so, we find at once that not one of the twenty-six alleged Bibles presents even a " scintilla of proof " such as a law-trained man would consider in support of any claim of divine origin.

Has any one of us ever heard of a reason which would convince any rationally skeptical man that the Koran or the Book of Mormon, for instance, or the book written by Mrs. Mary Baker Eddy, are to be regarded as anything more than normal or subnormal productions? Could not everything to be found in any of these books be readily duplicated and bettered? Is there known a single indubitably supernatural thing about them?

Mohammed declared that he was God's inspired prophet in giving the world the Koran. If a man believed him, often with a sword at his throat to convince him, he became a Mohammedan. A shred of proof was never offered. If anyone found himself able to " swallow " the story Joseph Smith told of his finding the golden plates from which he wrote his Bible, he became a Mormon. Smith never proved his assertion. A man or woman who is not firmly " rooted and grounded " in " the faith which was once for all delivered unto the saints " and who has never found the all-sufficient peace and power to meet life's sorrows and vicissitudes inherent in the " apostles' doctrine," in which is every good thing to be found in Christian Science with no admixture of its pagan pantheism, may become, as a matter of pure credulity and bewilderment, a " Christian Scientist."

Not so with the Christian. He is offered " many infallible proofs "—proofs such as would stand in a court of law. And to prove the truth of the gospel facts and the unmistakable supernaturalness of the Bible is the very thing that any Christian instructed in the " Evidences " longs for a chance to do for any unbelieving friend who will attend to this matter. And good it is to reflect that the one religion that has any proofs at all has all conceivable proofs, and that it is the religion which offers and promises the most which is the one and only religion which, while received by faith, is proved by evidence and logic which have led such great lawyers as those mentioned to declare it conclusive.

Everlasting life in an environment beautiful beyond conception, " Joys inexpressible in degree and eternal in duration," to be had as a free gift accompanied by the unswerving and unfathomable love of the eternal Son of God who, disguised as a Man, submitted Himself to the torturous death of a condemned felon to procure this eternal life for us—such is what Christianity offers us.

Supernatural and stupendous events, established by historical evidence which Greenleaf, in common with every other lawyer who has carefully studied the record, declares impregnable, and a standing miracle increasing in marvelousness as we now look upon it—such are samples of the proofs attesting the solid reality of the offer and the accompanying warning of unendurable but eternal woe if it is not availed of in time.

Now to deal first with the latter of the two samples of Christian proofs above mentioned:

Keeping in mind the fact that neither the Koran nor any other false Bible, as far as I know, has ever attempted to foretell the future at all and that even the Pope of Rome, though claiming divine inspiration when speaking on matters of faith and doctrine, has never ventured on such an unmistakable test or proof of supernatural knowledge, when we open the Holy Bible we find on almost every page future events in multiplied and varied detail foretold as if as good as already done. And then when we read history, we find accomplished and being accomplished before our eyes the very things centuries ago foretold.[1] As surely as only God knows in advance what numerous free agents will do in a world where uncontrollable natural forces and unpredictable combinations of events make the happenings of the next moment uncertain, the men who wrote the Old Testament over two thousand years ago (to claim for it only the antiquity of the Septuagint Version which was translated from the Hebrew into the Greek in 285 B. C., by order of Ptolemy Philadelphus) wrote "as they were moved by the Holy Ghost" in foretelling with absolute precision the things which have subsequently come to pass, and many of which are happening before our eyes.

Can any man rationally ignore such a phenomenon as is presented by the correspondence between historical facts and the words of the prophet Ezekiel foretelling that, while Sidon's streets should run with blood (Ezek. 28: 22, 23), though the city should not be ended, Tyre should have the very dust scraped from off her (Ezek. 26: 4, 5)—as Alexander the Great literally did to the city; that she should be merely a top of a bare rock in the midst of the sea, and a place for the spreading of nets and nevermore be rebuilt (Ezek. 26: 14), exactly according to her fate and her present condition as illustrated in a photograph published in a recent number of the *National Geographic Magazine.*

---

[1] See Alexander Keith, "Demonstration of the Truth of the Christian Religion," Harper Bros., 1844, for more detailed consideration.

Can anyone intelligently disregard the words of Daniel—centuries before Christ—that Babylon, Persia, and Greece should be followed by a kingdom as much stronger than the others as iron is than gold, silver, or brass, which should obliterate the lines of previous kingdoms, divide into two parts (in fulfillment, the eastern and western empires of Rome), and finally into ten toes or kingdoms of Europe, whose governments are characterized today as foretold, on the one hand by the incohesiveness of clayey democracies and Communism, and on the other by the iron rule of the Fascism which originated with Mussolini in the capital of the ancient iron Roman Empire. And, to leave out of account all reference to the scores of other millennia-old prophecies giving names, exact dates and places and compound events, can any man read without amazement and awe the newspaper accounts of what is happening to the Jews in Germany, Poland, Roumania, Austria, and practically all over the world at this time and then consider the words of Moses to be found in this at least two-thousand-year-old Book in telling the Jews he was then leading into Palestine what would happen to them as a result of their forsaking the law and worship of their God:

> "The Lord shall bring thee, and thy king which thou shalt set over thee, unto a nation which neither thou nor thy fathers have known; and there shalt thou serve other gods, wood and stone. And thou shalt become an astonishment, a proverb, and a byword, among all nations whither the Lord shall lead thee. . . . And the Lord shall scatter thee among all people, from the one end of the earth even unto the other; and there thou shalt serve other gods, which neither thou nor thy fathers have known, even wood and stone. And among these nations shalt thou find no ease, neither shall the sole of thy foot have rest; but the Lord shall give thee there a trembling heart, and failing of eyes, and sorrow of mind: And thy life shall hang in doubt before thee; and thou shalt fear day and night, and shalt have none assurance of thy life: In the morning thou shalt say, Would God it were even! And at even thou shalt say, Would God it were morning! for the fear of thine heart wherewith thou shalt fear, and for the sight of thine eyes which thou shalt see" (Deut. 28: 36, 37, 64–67).

Other fulfilled and improbable prophecies predicted that while the nations then surrounding the Jews would be completely ended, though subject to no such scattering and banishment of their people as foretold for the Jews, the Jews alone should not be ended and should not lose their racial identity (though it is obvious their persecution has, through the ages, presented every inducement to them to intermarry and escape their troubles by merging with other nationalities) and should, when came the time of the "twilight of the Gentiles," return to their long-deserted and desolate land, as they are doing at the present day.

The fact that the prophecies about the Jews—as about the coming Messiah—should be not only numerous and specific (in contrast with the Delphic and other Pagan oracles who felt and found it necessary to hedge against mistake in making even one single prediction by giving their words a "double aspect" to cover either contingency)—that these Bible prophecies are not only so numerous as to make accidental fulfillment almost infinitely improbable, but were of such nature that the events predicted seemed beforehand mutually destructive and were and are unparalleled in human history, multiplies the marvel of exact fulfillment by an element itself almost infinite in its effect on the miracle.

Should such a striking phenomenon be ignored in our thinking about these matters as is presented by the fact that the Jewish Passover has been celebrated continuously to this very year during these three or four thousand years (although the sacred fires of Persia and those tended by the Vestal Virgins of Rome which were to be kept burning forever have been out for centuries), in the light of the words we find in this same old Book:

> "And this day shall be unto you for a memorial; and ye shall keep it a feast to the Lord throughout your generations: ye shall keep it a feast by an ordinance forever" (Ex. 12: 14).

In this matter of prophecy two facts are self-evident: If the prophecy was not assuredly delivered long before the event, we have nothing to be astonished at; if the events did not and do not fulfill the prophecy, we have a demonstration that it was fraudulent. But here the predictions are found in a Book completed and translated into the world-famous Septuagint Version over two thousand years ago, the events fulfilling them are matters of personal knowledge and newspaper notoriety, and the chance of accidental fulfillment of the prophecies in the Bible which have been actually and exactly done and accomplished has been compared by a great mathematician (Olinthus Gregory) to a fraction whose numerator is a grain of sand and whose denominator is the bulk of the earth many times magnified. Does any lawyer of us know of any other issue or item of human certainty established by such an overwhelming "weight of evidence" as this prophetic fulfillment which proves that the God who alone controls and knows the future put this supernatural thing in the Bible? Will any man deny his own eyesight that it is there? Will he deny his own reason that it is a miracle? And if a miracle, who but God could perform the thing which our very senses attest has been done?

We have an answer, therefore, to the infidel's argument, know that any number of imitations can never disprove the existence of the genuine and have a reason to concentrate our investigation on the claims of the one Book in all the world which presents to us the unmistakable and only possible miraculous feature a book can possess: genuine prophecy.

Before leaving this subject of prophecy, however, which St. Peter declared was so sure a proof of the joyful and supernatural things he declared (and what more joyful thing can be heard and known than that the "supernatural" is real and actual? with its angels, its heaven of beauty and delight, its radiant life beyond the grave, its miraculous answers to prayer?) —brief attention should be paid in passing to the present day widely advertised "prophecies" of Nostradamus, Mother Shipton, Thomas Jefferson, George Washington and so many others that it would seem that predicting future events is within the powers of almost anyone with a high school education.

Now that only the One—if there be such an One—who controls the future can make it certain and thereby know it and make it known would seem to be a truism, not of faith or theology, but of simple arithmetic and common sense. And I, for one, am willing to concede the supernatural in any case where the three elements of real prophecy are united: delivery unquestionably long before the event, exact fulfillment ("divine prophecy admits of no failure or approximate fulfillment") and sufficient details to eliminate the chance of mere coincidence. These criteria are not to be found anywhere but in the Bible, as far as my research goes. If they were I would believe there had been a " leak " in the heavenly counsels or that God had given prophetic knowledge outside of inspiration.

Satan's concern lest the culminating fulfillment of the Bible's prophecies at this time startle mankind into repentance and regard for the Bible is manifestly at the bottom of the widespread advertisements (the last of which I received today) in which at least twenty-two prophets, from Mother Shipton and Nostradamus to Generals Grant and McClellan are presented as revealing the future. The argument for anyone to draw is too obvious to escape notice: If anyone from Mother Shipton and Madam Blavatsky to Joseph Smith and Thomas Jefferson can foretell the future, manifestly St. Peter was foolish in speaking of the " sure word of prophecy " and a Christian is in laying any stress upon it. That which can be done by almost everyone affords no evidence that the hand of the Lord was involved in its doing by anyone.

But it takes no prophetic revelation for a man versed in history to predict, as the men mentioned did, that like causes will in the future produce generally similar effects to those of the past. Anyone whose views of political economy are based on the fundamental principles Adam Smith made clear in his " Wealth of Nations " can easily foretell the ultimate result of the violation of these basic laws in scattering into fragments for consumption (by the nine spenders to one saver of which statistics show mankind consists) of the accumulations of savings in the form of capital which alone make possible the sheltering and tooling needed for the production by the workman of that excess of production over consumption which is the only source of wealth and even of taxes. Such shrewd predictions as Jefferson and Washington made and notably the one by Macaulay as to the final effect of giving equal voice in directing the government to the many who had all to gain and nothing to lose with the few who had a " stake " in the country, something to lose through unwise legislation as well as something to gain by well considered laws, can be presented as matching Bible prophecy only by those " for whom it maketh " in Bacon's phrase " that there be no God" as the source of the Bible's solemn and dread predictions.

As for Mother Shipton, it seems to have been forgotten that her supposed prophecy of 1448 was edited and amended even after its concoction by Charles Hindley in 1862; and the scattering predictions of Nostradamus, as I am only slightly familiar with them, remind me of the time I failed to hit a difficult target with a rifle and brought it down quickly with my shotgun. The utter folly of one of his definite predictions is before us in the failure of the world to end on the first day that Easter came at its latest possible date—which happened in 1886 as well as this year.

A certain famous Latin writer once hazarded the prediction that some day a land would be discovered to the west of the Atlantic Ocean, and this happy guess that there would be a repetition of discoveries often made in the past has been cited by deists as a triumphant match to the prophecies of Scripture. If Seneca had prophesied that a continent greater than Europe would be discovered by a man named Christopher Columbus in the exact year 1492 (more than matched by Isaiah's[1] naming the very Persian king who should restore Jerusalem centuries before his birth, the foretelling of the exact length of the Babylonian captivity, and by Daniel centuries in advance[2] of the exact day when Messiah the Prince should be revealed[3]) every Christian as well as Pagan would have strong reason to believe that we had here an "act of God." But we find nothing even approaching such exacting precision outside the Bible.

The ambiguity of the predictions of the Delphic and other ancient oracles are matters of common knowledge. "Ille die hostem Romanorum periturum esse" (on that day the enemy of Rome will perish) pronounced the Delphic Oracle to Maxentius about to fight Constantine, to his great encouragement until the fact of his own perishing made clear that the oracle had not committed itself after all. "Kroisos Halun diabas, megalan arkan katelusei" (if Croesus cross the Halys he will destroy a mighty empire) declared the same Oracle to Croesus when he

[1] Isaiah 44: 28.
[2] Daniel 9: 25.
[3] Appendix A.

sought to know in advance the result of his contemplated campaign against Persia. But a certain incident connected with this matter as related by Herodotus is worthy of comment,[1] as it illustrates the limitations of the supernormal power this Oracle, (along with many other people to this day) possessed; and that is the power of mental telepathy and of the daemons of Christ's day, the disembodied spirits with which Scripture forbids us to have dealings, and psychical research indicates are a dangerous reality, to make known things done at a distance and not observable by the five senses.

Herodotus tells us that Croesus, with a healthy skepticism about the supernatural powers of the Delphic and other oracles, devised a test which he thought would be conclusive if met. He instructed his servants on the hundredth day after their departure to ask the oracle what he, Croesus, was doing, on which day he cut up and seethed in a brazen pot a sheep and a tortoise. The Pythoness at Delphi responded to his inquiry with the following verse:

> "I count the sands and know the measures of ocean;
> I understand the dumb and hear him that speaketh not.
> On my sense there stole the savor of a strong shelled tortoise
> Boiling in a caldron with the flesh of a lamb.
> Brass is the couch beneath it and brass the robe upon it."

On reading this Croesus "performed an act of adoration." The Oracle had met his test and he gave complete confidence therefore to its prediction which he interpreted to mean that he would destroy Persia—instead, as the event turned out, of Persia destroying his own mighty empire. The unseen beings with whom the Delphic Oracle had contact could tell what was being done at a distance but they could not tell what the future would bring forth, and so had recourse to the usual oracular ambiguity.

We may know assuredly then that real prophecy is an act of God which no man or devil can duplicate and that the one book which has this miraculous thing woven through it like a water mark has no rival.

---

[1] See Pember's "Earth's Earliest Ages," p. 285.

III

THE FACTUAL FOUNDATION

EVEN as the Bible has no rival in being the only book containing supernaturally given and fulfilled prophecy, so the Christian religion is the only religion based upon and inseparably connected with historical facts—facts of such nature that if established, so also is established the religion based upon them.

In dealing with this phase of the proofs of Christianity, no better or greater authority can be called upon than the Simon Greenleaf from whom we have already briefly quoted. Of him the *London Law Journal* wrote in 1874:

"It is no mean honor to America that her schools of jurisprudence have produced two of the first writers and best esteemed legal authorities of this century—the great and good man, Judge Story, and his eminent and worthy associate, Professor Greenleaf. Upon the existing law of evidence (by Greenleaf) more light has shone from the New World than from all the lawyers who adorn the courts of Europe."

And Chief Justice Fuller, of the United States Supreme Court, once asserted of Greenleaf that "he is the highest authority cited in our courts."

In giving his "Testimony of the Evangelists" to the bar, Greenleaf writes:

"To the members of the legal profession:
"Gentlemen:
"The subject of the following work I hope will not be deemed so foreign to our professional pursuits as to render it improper for me to dedicate it, as I now respectfully do, to you.

"If a close examination of the evidence of Christianity may be expected of one class of men more than another, it would seem incumbent upon us who make the law of evidence one of our peculiar studies.

Our profession leads us to explore the mazes of falsehood, to detect its artifices, to pierce its thickest veils, to follow and expose its sophistries, to compare the statements of different witnesses with severity, to discover truth and separate it from error.

"Our fellow men are well aware of this, and probably they act upon this knowledge more generally and with more profound repose than we are in the habit of considering. The influence too of the legal profession upon the community is unquestionably great, conversant as it daily is with all classes and grades of men in their domestic and social relations and in all the affairs of life from the cradle to the grave. This influence we are constantly exerting for good or ill; and hence to refuse to acquaint ourselves with the evidences of the Christian religion, or to act as though, having fully examined, we lightly esteem them is to assume an appalling amount of responsibility.

"The things related by the evangelists are certainly of the most momentous character, affecting the principles of our conduct here and our happiness forever.

"The religion of Jesus Christ aims at nothing less than the utter overthrow of all other systems of religion of the world; denouncing them as inadequate to the wants of man, false in their foundations and dangerous in their tendency. It not only solicits the grave attention of all, to whom its doctrines are presented, but it demands their cordial belief as a matter of vital concernment. These are no ordinary claims; and it seems hardly possible for a rational being to regard them with even a subdued interest; much less to treat them with mere indifference and contempt. If not true, they are little else than the pretensions of a bold imposture which, not satisfied with having already enslaved millions of the human race, seeks to continue its encroachments upon human liberty until all nations shall be subjugated under its iron rule. But if they are well founded and just they can be no less than the high requirements of Heaven, addressed by the voice of God to the reason and understanding of man, concerning things deeply affecting his relations to his sovereign and essential to the formation of his character and of course to his destiny, both for this life and for the life to come. Such was the estimate taken of religion, even the religion of pagan Rome, by one of the greatest lawyers of antiquity, when he argued that it was either nothing at all, or was everything. *Aut undique religionem tolle, aut usquequaque conserva* (Cicero, Phillip. II, par. 43).

"With this view of the importance of the subject, and in the hope that the present work may in some degree aid or at least incite others to a more successful pursuit of this interesting study, it is submitted to your kind regard by

"Your obedient servant,

"SIMON GREENLEAF."

At one place in the great book thus dedicated Greenleaf remarks:

" The essential marks of difference between true narratives of fact and works of fiction are unmistakable,"

and to quote further,

" the attributes of truth are strikingly apparent throughout the Gospel histories, and the absence of all others is equally remarkable."

Here is an illustration of one of these differences which Greenleaf does not even mention.

While romances, legends and false testimony are careful to place the events related in some distant place and some indefinite time, thereby violating the first rules we lawyers learn of good pleading, that " the declaration must give time and place," the Bible narratives give us the date and place of the things related with the utmost precision, as for instance when Luke tells us when Christ's ministry, immediately preceded by John's proclamation, began:

" Now in the fifteenth year of the reign of Tiberius Caesar, Pontius Pilate being governor of Judaea, and Herod being tetrarch of Galilee, and his brother Philip tetrarch of Ituraea and of the region of Trachonotis, and Lysanias the tetrarch of Abilene,

" Annas and Caiaphas being the high priests " (Luke 3: 1–2)

then came the beginning of Christ's ministry and the doing of the " mighty works " which so convinced the apostolic observers and recorders of them of His deity that they devoted the rest of their lives to spreading the news of them and making known to all the men they could reach, Jew and Gentile, that there was pardon for sin and everlasting life to be had by believing and relying upon the atoning death and bodily resurrection of the Jewish Messiah who had turned out to be the light and salvation of the Gentiles also.

How significant of a consciousness of utter truth and certainty this prodigality of detail in lining up seven public officials as holding office contemporaneously in a definite year of Tiberius' reign!

The Apostle John in concluding his testimony or record of the things he said he saw Christ do and heard Him say, explains the purpose of his writing his account:

> " And many other signs truly did Jesus in the presence of his disciples which are not written in this book; but these are written that ye might believe that Jesus is the Christ, the Son of God, and that believing ye might have life through his name" (John 20: 30–31).

But the first step in arriving at certainty that Jesus Christ lived and died and rose from the dead and performed the miracles attributed to Him is to make sure of the authenticity of the records of these things.

This we can do with the utmost certainty by applying fundamental laws of thought to unquestionable facts. A fact known to all who have given any study at all to this subject is that these books were quoted, listed, catalogued, harmonized, cited as authority by different writers, Christian and Pagan, right back to the time of the apostles. Celsus, for instance, a bitter opponent of Christianity who was born only fifty years after the life of St. John, mentioned the four Gospels as being in his day the sacred books of the Christians. The Gospels, then, were written before the time of Celsus and Justin Martyr and Polycarp, the disciple of John, Irenaeus and the others who quoted them, as surely as a book has to be written by someone before it can be quoted by anyone.

On this important but obvious point let Greenleaf speak again:

> " If any ancient document concerning our public rights had been lost, copies which had been as universally received and acted upon as the four gospels have been would have been received in evidence in any of our courts, without the slightest hesitation. The entire text of the Corpus Juris Civilis is received as authority in all the courts of Continental Europe upon much weaker evidence of genuineness."

Unless one, therefore, desires to apply to the Gospels the theory Mark Twain satirized with the remark that Shakespeare's plays were not written by him but by another man of the same name, and to believe that the Gospels were not written by the apostles to whom they have been universally attributed from the earliest times, but by some other remarkable men of the same names, there is no room for question that the records of the words and acts of Jesus of Galilee came from the pens of the men who, with John, wrote what they had "heard" and "seen" and their hands had "handled of the Word of life."

Among the things they reported were Christ's cure of cripples, blind men, lepers (one having "confluent leprosy" as Dr. Luke reports) under conditions of roadside publicity that made imposture and mistake impossible; that He stopped a storm with a word; that three dead people (one in the tomb four days) returned to life at His command and that He, Himself, in exact accordance with His prediction, returned to them from the grave three days after being publicly executed, and that He consorted with them after His resurrection for a period of about a month and ten days. If He truly did these things I believe no man will or could question His divine nature and authority. It remains, therefore, only to ascertain whether the laws of thought and rules of evidence can enable us to know for a certainty that He did do the supernatural things reported in these documents, or Gospels, that were written by some persons at or shortly after the time they were done and, from conclusive internal evidence, by men who were, at least as to three of them, eyewitnesses as they allege. On this point let us hear again from Greenleaf:

"The great truths which the apostles declared were that Christ had risen from the dead, and that only through repentance from sin, and faith in him, could men hope for salvation. This doctrine they asserted with one voice, everywhere, not only under the greatest discouragements, but in the face of the most appalling terrors that can be presented to the mind of man. Their master had recently perished as a malefactor, by the sentence of a public tribunal. His religion sought to overthrow the religions of the whole world. The laws of every country were against the teachings of his disciples. The interests and passions of all the rulers and great men in the world were against them. The fashion of the world was against them. Propagating this new faith, even in the most inoffensive and peaceful manner, they could expect nothing but contempt, opposition, revilings, bitter persecutions, stripes, imprisonments, torments and cruel deaths. Yet this faith they zealously did propagate; and all these miseries they endured undismayed, nay, rejoicing. As one after another was put to a miserable death, the survivors only prosecuted their work with increased vigor and resolution. The annals of military warfare afford scarcely an example of the like heroic constancy, patience and unblenching courage. They had every possible motive to review carefully the grounds of their faith, and the evidences of the great facts and truths which they asserted; and these motives were pressed upon their attention with the most melancholy and terrific frequency. It was therefore impossible that they could have persisted in affirming the truths they have narrated had not Jesus actually risen from the dead, and had they not known this fact as certainly as they knew any other fact. If it were morally possible for them to have been deceived in this matter, every human motive operated to lead them to discover and avow their error. To have persisted in so gross a falsehood, after it was known to them, was not only to encounter, for life, all the evils which man could inflict, from without, but to endure also the pangs of inward and conscious guilt; with no hope of future peace, no testimony of a good conscience, no expectation of honor or esteem among men, no hope of happiness in this life, or in the world to come.

"Such conduct in the apostles would moreover have been utterly irreconcilable with the fact that they possessed the ordinary constitution of our common nature. Yet their lives do show them to have been men like all others of our race; swayed by the same motives, animated by the same hopes, affected by the same joys, subdued by the same sorrows, agitated by the same fears, and subject to the same passions, temptations and infirmities, as ourselves. And their writings show them to have been men of vigorous understandings. If then their testimony was not true, there was no possible motive for this fabrication.

"It would also have been irreconcilable with the fact that they were good men. But it is impossible to read their writings, and not feel that we are conversing with men eminently holy, and of tender consciences, with men acting under an abiding sense of the presence and omniscience of God, and of their accountability to him, living in his fear, and walking in his ways. Now, though, in a single instance, a good man may fall, when under strong temptations, yet he is not found persisting, for years, in deliberate falsehood, asserted with the most solemn appeals to God, without the slightest temptation or motive, and against all the opposing interests which reign in the human breast. If, on the contrary, they are supposed to have been bad men, it is incredible that such men should have chosen this form of imposture; enjoining, as it does, unfeigned repentance, the utter forsaking and abhorrence of all falsehood and of every other sin, the practice of daily self-denial, self-abasement and self-sacrifice, the crucifixion of the flesh with all its earthly appetites and desires, indifference to the honors, and hearty contempt of the vanities of the world; and inculcating perfect purity of heart and life, and intercourse of the soul with heaven. It is incredible that bad men should invent falsehoods to promote the religion of the God of truth. The supposition is suicidal. If they did believe in a future state of retribution, a heaven and a hell hereafter, they took the most certain course, if false witnesses, to secure the latter for their portion. And if, still being bad men, they did not believe in future punishment, how came they to invent falsehoods the direct and certain tendency of which was to destroy all their prospects of worldly honor and happiness, and to insure their misery in this life? From these absurdities there is no escape but in the conviction and admission that they were good men, testifying to that which they had carefully observed and considered and well knew to be true."

And again:

"The attributes of truth are strikingly apparent throughout the Gospel histories and the absence of all others is equally remarkable.

"The writers allude, for example, to the existing manners and customs and to the circumstances of the times and of their country, with the utmost minuteness of reference. And these references are never formally made, nor with preface and explanation, never multiplied and heaped on each other, nor brought together, as though introduced by design; but they are scattered broadcast and singly over every part of the story, and so connect themselves with every incident related, as to render the detection of falsehood inevitable. This minuteness, too, is not peculiar to any one of the historians, but is common to them all. Though they wrote at different periods and without mutual concert, they all alike refer incidentally to the same state of affairs, and to the same contemporary and collateral circumstances. Their testimony, in this view, stands on the same ground with that of four witnesses, separately examined before different commissioners, upon the same interrogatories, and all adverting incidentally to the same circumstances as surrounding and accompanying the principal transaction, to which alone their attention is directed. And it is worthy of observation that these circumstances were at that time of a peculiar character. Hardly a state or kingdom in the world ever experienced so many vicissitudes in its government and political relations as did Judea during the period of the gospel history. It was successively under the government of Herod the Great, of Archelaus, and of a Roman magistrate; it was a kingdom, a tetrarchate, and a province; and its affairs, its laws, and the administration of justice, were all involved in the confusion and uncertainty naturally to be expected from recent conquest. It would be difficult to select any place or period in the history of nations, for the time and scene of a fictitious history or an imposture, which would combine so many difficulties for the fabricator to surmount, so many contemporary writers to confront with him, and so many facilities for the detection of falsehood.[1]

* * * * * * * * *

"There is also a striking naturalness in the characters exhibited in the

[1] See Chalmers' "Evidences," Chapter 3.

sacred historians, rarely if ever found in works of fiction, and probably nowhere else to be collected in a similar manner from fragmentary and incidental allusions and expressions, in the writings of different persons. Take, for example, that of Peter, as it may be gathered from the evangelists, and it will be hardly possible to conceive that four persons, writing at different times, could have concurred in the delineation of such a character, if it were not real; a character too, we must observe, which is nowhere expressly drawn, but is shown only here and there, casually, in the subordinate parts of the main narrative. Thus disclosed, it is that of a confident, sanguine, and zealous man; sudden and impulsive, yet humble and ready to retract; honest and direct in his purposes; ardently loving his master, yet deficient in fortitude and firmness in his cause. When Jesus put any question to the apostles, it was Peter who was foremost to reply; and if they would inquire of Jesus, it was Peter who was readiest to speak. He had the impetuous courage to cut off the ear of the High Priest's servant, who came to arrest his master; and the weakness to dissemble before the Jews, in the matter of eating with Gentile converts. It was he who ran with John to the sepulchre, on the first intelligence of the resurrection of Jesus, and with characteristic zeal rushed in, while John paused without the door. He had the ardor to desire and the faith to attempt to walk on the water, at the command of his Lord; but as soon as he saw the wind boisterous, he was afraid. He was the first to propose the election of another apostle in the place of Judas; and he it was who courageously defended them all, on the day of Pentecost, when the multitude charged them with being filled with new wine. He was forward to acknowledge Jesus to be the Messiah; yet having afterwards endangered his own life by wounding the servant of the High Priest, he suddenly consulted his own safety by denying the same Master, for whom, but a few hours before, he had declared himself ready to die. We may safely affirm that the annals of fiction afford no example of a similar but not uncommon character, thus incidentally delineated.

"There are other internal marks of truth in the narratives of the evangelists, which, however, need here be only alluded to, as they have been treated with great fullness and force by able writers, whose works are familiar to all. Among these may be mentioned the nakedness of the narratives; the absence of all parade by the writers about their own integrity, of all anxiety to be believed, or to impress others with a good opinion of themselves or their cause, of all marks of wonder, or of desire to excite astonishment at the greatness of the events they record, and of all appearance of design to exalt their Master. On the contrary, there is apparently the most perfect indifference on their part, whether they are believed or not; or rather, the evident consciousness that they are recording events well known to all, in their own country and times, and undoubtedly to be believed, like any other matter of public history, by readers in all other countries and ages. It is worthy, too, of especial observation, that though the evangelists record the unparalleled sufferings and cruel death of their beloved Lord, and this, too, by hands and with the consenting voices of those on whom he had conferred the greatest benefits, and their own persecutions and dangers, yet they have bestowed no epithets of harshness or even of just censure on the authors of all this wickedness, but have everywhere left the plain and unincumbered narrative to speak for itself, and the reader to pronounce his own sentence of condemnation; like true witnesses, who have nothing to gain or to lose by the event of the cause, they state the facts, and leave them to their fate. Their simplicity and artlessness, also, should not pass unnoticed, in readily stating even those things most disparaging to themselves. Their want of faith in their master, their dullness of apprehension of his teachings, their strifes for pre-eminence, their inclination to call fire from heaven upon their enemies, their desertion of their Lord in his hour of extreme peril; these and many other incidents tending directly to their own dishonor are nevertheless set down with all the directness and sincerity of truth as by men writing under the deepest sense of responsibility to God. Some of the more prominent instances of this class of proofs will be noticed hereafter, in their proper places, in the narratives themselves.

". . . The narratives of the evangelists are now submitted to the reader's perusal and examination, upon the principles and by the rules already stated. With the relative merits of modern harmonists, and with points of controversy among theologians, the writer has no concert. His business is that of a lawyer, examining the testimony of witnesses by the rules of his profession, in order to ascertain whether, if they had thus testified on oath, in a court of justice, they would be entitled to credit; and whether their narratives, as we now have them, would be received as ancient documents, coming from the proper custody. If so, then it is believed that every honest and impartial man will act consistently with that result by receiving their testimony in all the extent of its import."

And now note what disintegrating violence the rejecter of Christianity must do to his mind and every trusted rule and principle of reasoning to maintain his unbelief. He must either maintain that the signs and earmarks of truth and reality in the testimony of the evangelists which so impressed Greenleaf are not to be found in such testimony at all or are, Greenleaf to the contrary notwithstanding, inconclusive and without significance. That they exist everyone who can verify Greenleaf's references from his own Testament knows; that they are the indicia of historic truth and reality the world's greatest expert, the uniform experience of lawyers for centuries and every man's common sense agree in declaring. Which horn of the dilemma shall he take?

APPENDIX "A"

"THE COMING PRINCE"

By Sir Robert Anderson

The following is from Chapter X of "The Coming Prince," by Sir Robert Anderson, and is quoted for the purpose of illustrating an exactly fulfilled prophecy and the care with which this Christian lawyer examined the Bible.

"'The secret things belong unto the Lord our God; but those things which are revealed belong unto us and to our children' (Deut. 29: 29). And among the 'things which are revealed,' fulfilled prophecy has a foremost place. In presence of the events in which it has been accomplished, its meaning lies upon the surface. . . . The writings of Daniel have been more the object of hostile criticism than any other portion of the Scripture, and the closing verses of the ninth chapter have always been a principal point of attack. And necessarily so, for if that single passage can be proved to be a prophecy it establishes the character of the book as a Divine revelation."

The words of Daniel with which Sir Robert Anderson here deals are the following (Daniel 9):

"Seventy weeks are determined upon thy people and upon thy holy city, to finish the transgression and to make an end of sins and to make reconciliation for iniquity, and to bring in everlasting righteousness, and to seal up the vision and prophecy and anoint the most Holy.

"Know therefore and understand that from the going forth of the commandment to restore and build Jerusalem unto the Messiah the Prince shall be seven weeks and threescore and two weeks: the street shall be built again and the wall even in troublous times.

"And after three score and two weeks shall Messiah be cut off, but not for himself . . ."

Resuming the quotation from "The Coming Prince":

"The sceptre of earthly power which was entrusted to the house of David was transferred to the Gentiles in the person of Nebuchadnezzar, to remain in Gentile hands 'until the times of the Gentiles be fulfilled.'

"The blessings promised to Judah and Jerusalem were postponed till after a period described as 'seventy weeks'; and at the close of the sixty-ninth week of this era the Messiah should be 'cut off.'

"These seventy weeks represent seventy times seven prophetic years of 360 days, to be reckoned from the issuing of the edict for the rebuilding of the city—'the street and rampart' of Jerusalem.

"The edict in question was the decree issued by Artaxerxes Longimanus in the twentieth year of his reign, authorizing Nehemiah to rebuild the fortifications of Jerusalem.

"The date of Artaxerxes' reign can be definitely ascertained—not from elaborate disquisitions by Biblical commentators and prophetic writers, but by the united voice of secular historians and chronologers.

"The statement of St. Luke is explicit and unequivocal, that our Lord's public ministry began in the fifteenth year of Tiberius Caesar. It is equally clear that it began shortly before the Passover. The date of it can thus be fixed as between August A. D. 28 and April A. D. 29. The Passover of the crucifixion therefore was in A. D. 32, when Christ was betrayed on the night of the Paschal Supper, and put to death on the day of the Paschal Feast.

"If then the foregoing conclusions be well founded we should expect to find that the period intervening between the edict of Artaxerxes and the Passion was 483 prophetic years. And accuracy as absolute as the nature of the case permits is no more than men are here entitled to demand. There can be no loose reckoning in a Divine chronology; and if God has deigned to mark on human calendars the fulfillment of His purposes as foretold in prophecy, the strictest scrutiny shall fail to detect miscalculation or mistake.

"The Persian edict which restored the autonomy of Judah was issued in the Jewish month Nisan. It may in fact have been dated the 1st Nisan, but no other date being named, the prophetic period must be reckoned, according to a practice common with the Jews, from the Jewish New Year's Day.[1] The seventy weeks are therefore to be computed from the 1st Nisan B. C. 445.

"Now the great characteristic of the Jewish sacred year has remained unchanged ever since the memorable night when the equinoctial moon beamed down upon the huts of Israel in Egypt, bloodstained by the Paschal sacrifice; and there is neither doubt nor difficulty in fixing within narrow limits the Julian date of the 1st of Nisan in any year whatever. In B. C. 445 the new moon by which the Passover was regulated was on the 13th of March at 7h. 9m. A. M.[2] And accordingly the 1st Nisan may be assigned to the 14th March.

"But the language of prophecy is clear: 'From the going forth of the

---

[1] "On the 1st of Nisan is a new year for the computation of the reign of kings and for festivals."—Misha, treatise "Rosh Hash."

[2] For this calculation I am indebted to the courtesy of the Astronomer Royal, whose reply to my inquiry on the subject is appended:

"Royal Observatory, Greenwich.
June 26th, 1877.

"Sir:—

I have had the moon's place calculated from Largeteau's Tables in Additions to the Connaisance des Tems 1846, by one of my assistants, and have no doubt of its correctness. The place being calculated for 444, March 12d. 20h, French reckoning, or March 12d. 8h. P. M., it appears that the said time was short of New Moon by about 8h. 47m., and therefore the New Moon occurred at 4h. 47m. A. M., March 13th, Paris time.

"I am, etc.,
"(Signed) G. B. AIRY."

"The new moon, therefore, occurred at Jerusalem on the 13th March, B. C. 445 (444 Astronomical) at 7h. 9 m. A. M."

commandment to restore and build Jerusalem unto Messiah the Prince shall be seven weeks and threescore and two weeks.' An era therefore of sixty-nine 'weeks' or 483 prophetic years reckoned from the 14th March B. C. 445 should close with some event to satisfy the words 'unto Messiah the Prince.'

* * * * * * * * *

"No student of the gospel narrative can fail to see that the Lord's last visit to Jerusalem was not only in fact, but in the purpose of it, the crisis of His ministry, the goal toward which it had been directed. After the first tokens had been given that the nation would reject His Messianic claims, He had shunned all public recognition of them. But now the twofold testimony of His words and His works had been fully rendered, and His entry into the Holy City was to proclaim His Messiahship and to receive His doom. Again and again His apostles even had been charged that they should not make Him known. But now He accepted the acclamations of the 'whole multitude of the disciples,' and silenced the remonstrance of the Pharisees with the indignant rebuke, 'I tell you if these should hold their peace the stone would immediately cry out.' . . .

"The time of Jerusalem's visitation had come, and she knew it not. Long ere then the nation had rejected Him, but this was the predestined day when their choice must be irrevocable;—the day so distinctly signalized in Scripture as the fulfillment of Zechariah's prophecy, 'Rejoice greatly, O daughter of Zion! shout, O daughter of Jerusalem! behold thy King cometh unto thee.' Of all the days of the ministry of Christ upon earth, no other will satisfy so well the angel's words 'unto Messiah the Prince.'

"And the date of it can be ascertained. In accordance with the Jewish custom, the Lord went up to Jerusalem on the 8th Nisan, 'six days before the Passover.'[1] But as the 14th, on which the Paschal Supper was eaten, fell that year upon a Thursday, the 8th was the preceding Friday. He must have spent the Sabbath, therefore, at Bethany; and on the evening of the 9th, after the Sabbath had ended, the Supper took place in Martha's house. Upon the following day, the 10th Nisan, He entered Jerusalem as recorded in the Gospels (Lewin, "Fasti Sacri," p. 230).

"The Julian date of that 10th Nisan was Sunday the 6th April, A. D. 32. What then was the length of the period intervening between the issuing of the decree to rebuild Jerusalem and the public advent of 'Messiah the Prince'—between the 14th March, B. C. 445, and the 6th April, A. D. 32?

[1] "When the people were come in great crowds to the feast of unleavened bread on the eighth day of the month Xanthicus," *i. e. Nisan* (Josephus, Wars, vi: 5, 3).

"And the Jews' Passover was nigh at hand, and many went out of the country up to Jerusalem, before the Passover, to purify themselves. . . . Then Jesus, six days before the Passover, came to Bethany" (John 11: 55; 12: 1).

" THE INTERVAL CONTAINED EXACTLY AND TO THE VERY DAY 173,880 DAYS, OR SEVEN TIMES SIXTY-NINE PROPHETIC YEARS OF 360 DAYS, the first sixty-nine weeks of Gabriel's prophecy.[1]

" Much there is in Holy Writ which unbelief may value and revere, while utterly refusing to accept it as Divine; but prophecy admits of no half faith. The prediction of the 'seventy weeks' was either a gross and impious imposture, or else it was in the fullest and strictest sense God-breathed (Τεοπνεοστος, 2 Tim. 3: 16). . . . To believe that the facts and figures here detailed amount to nothing more than happy coincidences involves a greater exercise of faith than that of the Christian who accepts the book of Daniel as divine. There is a point beyond which unbelief is impossible, and the mind in refusing truth must needs take refuge in a misbelief which is sheer credulity."

---

[1] " The 1st Nisan in the twentieth year of Artaxerxes (the edict to rebuild Jerusalem) was 14th March B. C. 445.

" The 10th Nisan in Passion Week (Christ's entry into Jerusalem) was 6th April, A. D. 32.

" The intervening period was 476 years and 24 days (the days being reckoned inclusively, as required by the prophecy, and in accordance with Jewish practice).

" But 476 × 365 =	173,740 days
Add (14th March to 6th April, both inclusive)	24 days
Add for leap years	116 days
	173,880 days

And 69 weeks of prophetic years of 360 days (or 69 × 7 × 360) = 173,880 days.

" It may be well here to offer two explanatory remarks: First: in reckoning years from B. C. to A. D. one year must always be omitted; for it is obvious, ex. gr., that from B. C. 1 to A. D. 1 was not two years, but one year. B. C. 1 ought to be described as B. C. 0, and it is so reckoned by astronomers, who would describe the historical date B. C. 445 as 444 (see note p. 124 ante). And secondly, the Julian year is 11m. 10. 46s., or about the 129th part of a day longer than the mean solar year. The Julian calendar, therefore, contains three leap years too many in four centuries, an error which had amounted to eleven days in A. D. 1752, when our English calendar was corrected by declaring the 3rd September to be the 14th September, and by introducing the Gregorian reform which reckons three secular years out of four as common years: ex. gr., 1700, 1800 and 1900 are common years, and 2000 is a leap year. 'Old Christmas day' is still marked on our calendars, and observed in some localities, on the 6th of January: and to this day the calendar remains uncorrected in Russia."

Is Man His Own God? *

Currently making the rounds on American college campuses is the question, "How are you going to recognize God when you get to heaven?" Answer: "By the big 'G' on his sweatshirt." This litany has more metaphysical profundity than meets the eye, for it reflects the contemporary philosophical dilemma as to the meaningfulness of God-language—a dilemma to which we shall be addressing ourselves shortly. But it is essential to make one basic point at the very outset: in the philosophy of life of every person without exception, someone or something is invested with the sweatshirt lettered "G." There are no atheists; everyone has his god. In the language of Paul Tillich (who was ironically called an atheist by some of his less perceptive critics), all of us have our "ultimate concerns," and the sad thing is that so few of them are truly ultimate or worthy of worship. As one of William James' "twice-born" (having come to Christian belief as an adult), I am especially concerned that idols be properly identified and the true owner of the cosmic sweatshirt wear it. As a modest contribution to that end, we shall first consider how much ultimacy ought to be attributed to three prominent alternatives to biblical theism, and then devote ourselves to the crucial arguments in behalf of the Christian view of God.

The Unreality of Major Non-Theistic Positions

Pantheism à la Spinoza

I recall but one occasion when my old Greek professor

* An invitational presentation at DePaul University, Chicago, February 5, 1969, in debate with humanist Julian J. Steen, dean of the Chicago School for Adults. The debate was sponsored by DePaul's theology department; Professor Robert Campbell, O.P. served as moderator. This same essay was also presented at Harvard University on February 14, 1969, as one of a series of "Christian Contemporary Thought Lectures."

at Cornell was drawn into a religious discussion, and—in a state of obvious discomfort—he defended his unorthodoxy somewhat as follows: "But do not conclude that I am an atheist. Far from it. For me the universe as a whole, with all its mystery, is God, and I reverence it." This viewpoint (which can, of course, be stated in many different ways) has perhaps best been set forth and defended by Spinoza. In Part One of his *Ethics*, the philosopher endeavors to show that the universe is a single, all-embracing unity and that that unity is God. This is proved by the fact that the universe obviously consists of some thing—Spinoza calls it Substance—and this Substance "is in itself and is conceived through itself"; now since God is properly defined as "a being absolutely infinite" and Substance is infinite and unique, it follows that Substance is God.

The fallacy in this piece of geometrically-modeled legerdemain has been well stated by C. E. M. Joad in his *Guide to Philosophy*: "If we assume that Substance in the original definition means simply 'all that there is,' then the initial definition contains within itself the conclusion. Such a conclusion is not worth proving. It is, indeed, merely a tautology—that is to say, an asserting of the same thing in two different ways." Pantheism, in other words (and this applies equally to all forms of it, whether derived from Spinoza or not), is neither true nor false; it is something much worse, viz., entirely trivial. We had little doubt that the universe was here anyway; by giving it a new name ("God") we explain nothing. We actually commit the venerable intellectual sin of Word Magic, wherein the naming of something is supposed to give added power either to the thing named or to the semantic magician himself.

Humanism

If the universe cannot be meaningfully deified, why not man himself? Can we not regard as strictly literal the question posed in the title of this presentation, "Is Man His Own God?" and answer it affirmatively? For the humanist, man is himself the proper "ultimate concern," and human values are the only eternal verities.

But which "human values" do we mean? Anthropologists such as Ruth Benedict have discovered a most bewildering variety of human value systems, styles of life, and ethical norms. And what is worse, these morals and mores are often entirely incompatible. Some peoples reverence their parents and others eat them. Among cannibals it is doubtless both good ethics and good table manners to clean your plate.

How is the humanist going to decide among these competing value systems? He has no absolute vantage point from which to view the ethical battle in the human arena. He is in the arena himself; or, to use beatnik poet Kerouac's expression, he is "on the road"—not in a house by the side of the road where he can watch the world go by and arbitrate it. All value systems that arise from within the human context are necessarily conditioned by it and are therefore relative. Out of flux, nothing but flux. As Wittgenstein correctly observed in the *Tractatus Logico-Philosophicus*: "If there is any value that does have value, it must lie outside the whole sphere of what happens and is the case . . . . Ethics is transcendental."

Yet a transcendental perspective is exactly what the humanist does not have. He is therefore left to *consensus gentium* (majority values), cultural totalitarianism (the values of one's own society) or sheer authoritarianism (*my* values, not yours). But, sad to say, fifty million Frenchmen *can* be wrong; the ethical perspective of an entire society can be cruelly immoral; and the individual who considers himself the true barometer to moral worth may simply be suffering from overactive glands or an advanced stage of messianic complex.

To establish absolute ethical values for human action is both logically and practically impossible apart from transcendence. To move the world Archimedes rightly noted that he would need a fulcrum outside the world. The assassination of biblical revelation in the 18th century left man without a clear conception of or confidence in God, and God's resultant death in the 19th century (in the work of Nietzsche and others) set the stage for the dehumanization of man in the 20th. Nietzsche recognized full well that apart from God only man remains to establish his own value; and the stronger has every right under such conditions to impose his self-centered value system on the weaker—and eliminate him if he does not learn his lessons well. The anti-Semitism of the deists of the 18th century Enlightenment (as definitively researched by Arthur Hertzberg in his 1968 publication, *The French Enlightenment and the Jews),* the Nietzschean transvaluation of values, will-to-power, and antichristic treatment of the weak, and the National Socialist extermination of racial and political minorities demonstrate only too clearly what happens when man becomes the measure of all things. It is curious that humanists presently (and commendably) striving for racial equality in this country do not ask themselves why, in any absolute sense, their goals are more justifiable than the genocide practiced by an equally passionate and idealistic generation of young people in the Germany of the 1930s and 1940s. As for me, I'm for absolute racial justice, and I'm unwilling to see it—or any comparable value—left at the mercy of relativistic humanism. If man is his own god, then religion is *really* in trouble. Personally, I'd be willing to join a Man-is-dead movement!

Agnosticism

High on the popularity poll of non-theistic ultimate concerns today is agnosticism. What is seldom recognized, however, by either its advocates or its opponents, is that the term agnosticism embraces two very different positions. The first might be called "hard-boiled" agnosticism: "I know that I am unable to know that there is a God"; the second, "soft-boiled" agnosticism: "I am not sure whether knowledge of God is possible."

Little time should be spent on hard-boiled agnosticism, since it is tantamount to traditional atheism, and suffers from its basic fallacy: it presumes that one can (apart from any revelation of God, to be sure!) know the universe so well that one can assert the non-existence of God or the non-existence of compelling evidence for his existence. But such comprehensive knowledge of the universe would require either (a) revelation, which is excluded on principle, or (b) divine powers of observation on the part of the atheist or hard-boiled agnostic. In the latter case, atheism and the extreme agnostic position become self-defeating, since the unbeliever perforce creates a god by deifying himself.

As for soft-boiled agnosticism, it is highly commendable *if actually practiced* (which is very seldom). A genuine agnostic of this school will of course bend every effort to see whether in fact evidence does exist in behalf of theistic claims. His view of the universe is open-ended; he is a passionate seeker for truth; and he recognizes that his best energies must be put to this quest, since one's happiness in this world, to say nothing about one's eternal destiny in the next, is directly at stake if God in fact exists and makes demands on his creatures. The true agnostic, then, might be thought of as a person in this room who was not sure whether or not to believe a report that a bomb was planted in the building and would go off in two hours. Because of the cruciality of the *possibility,* he would not sit here in blasé indifference (the usual agnostic posture), but would clear the room and engage in a most diligent search of the premises to determine whether concrete evidence supported the claim or not.

It is now our task to perform a brief, but hopefully constructive, check of the universal premises to see if divine power is there revealed.

The Reality of the Biblical God

Where to look for the footprints of Deity? Virtually anywhere but in the arguments of some modern theologians, clerics, and mystics, of whom it might well be said: "With friends like that God doesn't need any enemies." I refer, for example, to those Anglican canons who parachuted from the top of St. Paul's Cathedral, to "bring the young people back to the church" (eliciting the remark in *Esquire* magazine: "If God isn't dead, maybe he wishes he were"); or the Protestant-Roman Catholic-Jewish death-of-God school; or Aldous Huxley's World Controller, who declared in *Brave New World* that God now "manifests himself as an absence; as though he weren't there at all." Once having stated this small *caveat,* however, not even the sky is the evidential limit. As Jacques Maritain so well expressed it in *Approaches to God:* "There is not just one way to God, as there is to an oasis across the desert or to a new mathematical idea across the breadth of the science of number. For man there are as many ways of approach to God as there are wanderings on the earth or paths to his own heart." We shall consider four such pathways.

God and the World

In his famous 1948 BBC debate with Bertrand Russell, the great historian of philosophy F. C. Copleston succinctly stated the fundamental "argument from contingency" for God's existence:

> First of all, I should say, we know that there are at least some beings in the world which do not contain in themselves the reason for their existence. For example, I depend on my parents, and now on the air, and on food, and so on. Now, secondly, the world is simply the real or imagined totality or aggregate of individual objects, none of which contain in themselves alone the reason for their existence. There isn't any world distinct from the objects which form it, any more than the human race is something apart from the members. Therefore, I should say, since objects or events exist, and since no object of experience contains within itself the reason of its existence, this reason, the totality of objects, must have a reason external to itself. That reason must be an existent being. Well, this being is either itself the reason for its own existence, or it is not. If it is, well and good. If it is not, then we must proceed farther. But if we proceed to infinity in that sense, then there's no explanation of existence at all. So, I should say, in order to explain existence we must come to a being which contains within itself the reason for its existence, that is to say, which cannot not-exist.

This argument is not only regarded by most philosophical advocates of theism as the keystone of the so-called "classic proofs" of God's existence; it is today reinforced by a most impressive battery of evidence from the physical sciences. For example (one may on the point consult the engineering publications of University of Michigan professor Gordon J. Van Wylen), the second law of thermodynamics states that for irreversible processes in any closed system left to itself, the entropy (loss of available heat energy) will increase with time; thus the universe, viewed as such a system, is moving to the condition of maximum entropy (heat death); *but* (and this is the significant aspect of the matter for our purposes) if the irreversible process had begun an infinite time ago—if, in other words, the universe were uncreated and eternal—the earth would *already* have reached maximum entropy; and since this is not the case, we are driven to the conclusion that the universe is indeed contingent and finite, and requires a creative force from the outside to have brought it into existence.

It should be carefully noted that this *a posteriori* argument from contingency is empirically grounded in testable experience; it is neither a disguised form of the highly questionable ontological argument, which asserts *a priori* that God's essence establishes his existence, nor an attempt at allegedly "synthetic *a priori*" reasoning. And unlike the "causal argument," it does not gratuitously presuppose an unalterable cause-and-effect structure in the universe (a very doubtful assumption in light of Einsteinian physics and the Heisenberg uncertainty principle which requires us to give serious consideration to all event-claims, even those "miraculously uncaused").

But what about the standard rebuttal: "You just beg the question; now tell us why God exists"? Though this question evidently started Bertrand Russell on the downhill slide into intellectual anticlericalism at an early age, it is not especially profound. We have just seen some of the evidence for the contingency of the universe we live in; to regard this world as eternal is out of the question. But to regard its creator as likewise contingent ("Who created *him?*") *would* beg the question, for it would force us to pose the very same query again—and again. Only by stopping with a God who is the final answer to the series do we *avoid* begging the question—and only then do we offer any adequate account for the contingent universe with which we began. Moreover, the "why God?" question suffers an acute case both of artificiality and of absurdity, as philosopher Plantinga has shown in his essay on "Necessary Being" (in his *Faith and Philosophy* [1964]):

> We should note that the question "Why does God exist?" never does, in fact, arise. Those who do not believe that God exists will not, of course, ask *why* He exists. But neither do believers ask that question. Outside of theism, so to speak, the question is nonsensical, and in-

side of theism, the question is never asked. . . .

Now it becomes clear that it is absurd to ask why God exists. To ask that question is to presuppose that God does exist; but it is a necessary truth that if He does, He has no cause. And it is also a necessary truth that if He has no cause, then there is no answer to a question asking for His causal conditions. The question "Why does God exist?" is, therefore, an absurdity.

God and Personhood

Robert Benchley tells of the disastrous college biology course in which he spent the term meticulously drawing in his lab manual the image of his own eyelash as it fell across the microscopic field. The catastrophe occurred because he lost track of the necessary distinction between himself as subject (his subjectivity) and the external object to be observed (the objectivity of the outside world). Such results and others no less dire are inevitable when one engages in what Whitehead well termed "extreme objectivism"—an objectivism which even objectifies the subject. A person is an "irreducible I": he can never be fully comprehended as an object. No matter how complete a list you make of your own characteristics—or of the characteristics of that stunning coed you are dating—you and the coed *transcend* the list. Persons are grounded in the clay of the contingent world we discussed above, but at the same time they transcend it; human personhood warrants the designation "semi-transcendent." This semi-transcendent, irreducible character of the human person is the quality that has escaped (and logically must escape) the behaviorist who always treats his subjects as objects; it is to the credit of contemporary psychological (especially psychoanalytic) thought that efforts are now made to get beyond such hyper-objectivism. Indeed, in those cases where human subjectivity and freewill are consistently denied, the deterministic objectivist loses all right to claim volitional action and purpose as an experimenter. His refusal to recognize the "semi-transcendent I" finally results in his own epistemological evaporation.

Now, as philosophical theologians such as Ian Ramsey have shown in considerable detail in recent years, the partial transcendence of the human subject establishes both the possibility of metaphysical assertions and the legitimacy of God-language. We cannot meaningfully talk about the universe around us without presupposing our own subjectivity, and the partial transcendence we possess demands an unqualifiedly transcendent integrating subjectivity to make *it* meaningful. As Ramsey puts it in an essay in his *Prospect for Metaphysics* (1961): "Just as 'I' acts as an integrator word for all kinds of scientific and other descriptive assertions about myself, 'I exist' being a sort of conceptual presupposition for them all, so also may 'God' be regarded as a contextual presupposition for the Universe."

This perspective sheds considerable light on two fundamental problems raised by theistic belief: the existence of evil and the question of meaningful God-talk (the problem of the "sweatshirt," as alluded to at the outset of this presentation). Opponents of theism have perennially argued that the natural and moral evils in the universe make the idea of an omnipotent and perfectly good God irrational. But if subjectivity (and its correlative, freewill) must be presupposed on the level of human action, and if God's character as fully transcendent divine Subject serves to make human volition meaningful, then the existence of freewill in itself provides a legitimate explanation of evil. To create personalities without genuine freewill would not have been to create persons at all; and freewill means the genuine possibility of wrong decision, i.e., the creation of evil by God's creatures (whether wide-ranging natural and moral evil by fallen angels or limited chaos on earth by fallen mankind). As for the argument that a good God should have created only those beings he would foresee as choosing the right—or that he should certainly eliminate the effects of his creatures' evil decisions, the obvious answer is (as Plantinga develops it with great logical rigor in his *God and Other Minds* [1967]) that this would be tantamount to not giving freewill at all. To create only those who "must" (in any sense) choose good is to create automata; and to whisk away evil effects as they are produced is to whisk away evil itself, for an act and its consequences are bound together. C. S. Lewis has noted that God's love enters into this issue as well, since the biblical God created man out of love, and genuine human love is impossible without freewill—without the free possibility of accepting love or rejecting it. Just as a boy who offers himself and his love to a girl must count on the real possibility of rejection, so when God originated a creative work that made genuine love possible, it by definition entailed the concomitant possibility of the evil rejection of his love by his creatures.

By the "sweatshirt" problem we refer to an objection to theism posed by such analytical philosophers as Kai Nielsen and Antony Flew, who claim that God's very uniqueness makes it irrational to say anything about him: since, in the absence of any perfect analogy, he must always be described in negatives, God-talk becomes totally meaningless. The sweatshirt with the big "G," we are told, is necessarily empty. But again note how the understanding of God as transcendent integrating Subject in relation to semi-transcendent human subjects clears the air. Human persons are *likewise* unique—no person is just like another, and the very meaning of "subject" and individual "freewill" entails this irreducible uniqueness. To call God-talk meaningless, then, is at the same time to render man-talk nonsensical! Conversely, if we once accept what is involved in the concept of human subjective existence (and how can we avoid it?) then we simultaneously open the gate to meaningful God-talk. As Ramsey neatly suggests, "We might perhaps then say that we are as certain of God as we are of ourselves."

However, it would be conceding far too much if we were to allow that talk about God involves only negatives—the so-called "death by a thousand qualifications." Here we find ourselves immediately drawn into discussion of

God in Christ

The following parable, formulated by philosophers Flew and Wisdom, is a good statement of the view that God-claims are too vague to be sensible and offer no adequate empirical evidence in their behalf:

> Once a time two explorers came upon a clearing in the jungle. In the clearing were growing many flowers and many weeds. One explorer says, "Some gardener must

> tend this plot." The other disagrees, "There is no gardener." So they pitch their tents and set a watch. No gardener is ever seen. "But perhaps he is an invisible gardener." So they set up a barbed-wire fence. They electrify it. They patrol with bloodhounds. (For they remember how H. G. Wells' *The Invisible Man* could be both smelt and touched though he could not be seen.) But no shrieks ever suggest that some intruder has received a shock. No movements of the wire ever betray an invisible climber. The bloodhounds never give cry. Yet still the Believer is not convinced. "But there is a gardener, invisible, intangible, insensible to electric shocks, a gardener who has no scent and makes no sound, a gardener who comes secretly to look after the garden which he loves." At last the Sceptic despairs, "But what remains of your original assertion? Just how does what you call an invisible, intangible, eternally elusive gardener differ from an imaginary gardener or even from no gardener at all?"

This parable may echo the religious claims of many sincere people, but it has little to do with the Christian affirmation of God. Why? Because central to the Christian position is the historically grounded assertion that *the Gardener entered the garden*: God actually appeared in the empirical world in Jesus Christ and fully manifested his deity through miraculous acts in general and his resurrection from the dead in particular. Christian talk about God therefore becomes in the most rigorous sense affirmative, for when asked to "define God" or "tell us what he looks like," the Christian simply points to Christ. Dr. Jowett was supposed to have been asked by an effusive young lady, "Do tell me—what do you think about God?" and his reply was: "That, my dear young lady, is a very unimportant question; the only thing that signifies is what he thinks about me." The Christian knows what God thinks about him—and the human race; he knows what God's eternal value system is (and how desperately the human race needs that knowledge, as we saw in our discussion of humanism!); and he knows that in spite of man's self-centered trampling of God's values, God's love has reached down to earth. How does he know this? Because God tells him this in Christ.

Now it cannot be stressed too strongly that this claim to divine intervention in history is solidly grounded in historical evidence. The textual case for the New Testament documents which record Christ's divine utterances and acts is so excellent that Sir Fredric G. Kenyon, director and principal librarian of the British Museum, could write in 1940 in *The Bible and Archaeology*: "Both the *authenticity* and the *general integrity* of the books of the New Testament may be regarded as finally established" (Kenyon's italics). The world's foremost living biblical archeologist, W. F. Albright of Johns Hopkins University, has identified the New Testament materials as primary source documents for the life of Jesus, dating all of them (including John's Gospel) "between the forties and the eighties of the first century A.D. (very probably sometime between about 50 and 75 A.D.)" (interview in *Christianity Today,* January 18, 1963). The New Testament writers claim eyewitness contact with the events of Jesus' career, and describe his death and post-resurrection appearances in minute detail. In A.D. 56, for example, Paul wrote (I Cor. 15) that over five hundred people had seen the risen Jesus and that most were still alive. The New Testament writers explicitly affirm that they are presenting historical facts, not religious fables; writes Peter (II Pet. 1:16): "We have not followed cunningly devised myths when we made known to you the power and coming of our Lord Jesus Christ, but were eyewitnesses of his majesty." And if deception and fabrication were here involved, why didn't the numerous religious enemies of the early Christians blast the whole business? F. F. Bruce of the University of Manchester has shrewdly observed in his book, *The New Testament Documents* (5th ed., 1960), that if the early proclaimers of Christ's deity had had any tendency to depart from the facts, the presence of hostile witnesses in the audience would have served as a most powerful corrective.

The central attestation for Jesus' deity is his resurrection, and to deny its facticity isn't easy. To oppose it on historical grounds is so difficult that, if one succeeds, the victory is entirely Pyrrhic: any argument that will impugn the New Testament documents will at the same time remove confidence from virtually all other ancient, and numerous modern, historical sources; the result, then, is a general (and entirely unacceptable) historiographical solipsism. To oppose the resurrection on the ground that miracles do not occur is, as we have noted earlier, both philosophically and scientifically irresponsible: philosophically, because no one below the status of a god could know the universe so well as to eliminate miracles *a priori;* and scientifically, because in the age of Einsteinian physics (so different from the world of Newtonian absolutes in which Hume formulated his classic anti-miraculous argument) the universe has opened up to all possibilities, "any attempt to state a 'universal law of causation' must prove futile" (logician Max Black), and only a careful consideration of the empirical testimony for a miraculous event can determine whether in fact it has or has not occurred.

Success in opposing the evidence for Christ's resurrection is so hard to come by that some objectors to Christian theism (e.g. humanist Corliss Lamont) are reduced to arguing that the event is trivial. "Even if Christ rose from the dead, would that prove his claims? And would it necessarily mean anything for us?" In a recent public discussion following a lecture I delivered at Roosevelt University, I was informed by a philosophy professor that Christ's conquest of death was no more significant qualitatively than a medical victory over pattern baldness. To which I offered the inevitable reply: "A knock comes at the door. It's the faculty secretary with the message that your wife and children have just been killed in a traffic accident. Your comment would of course be: 'Oh well, what's death? Just like pattern baldness'." In point of fact, we all recognize the overarching significance of death, and a very large proportion of our individual and societal energies are expended in trying to postpone it (medicine), indirectly overcome it (familial, vocational, and artistic achievement), ignore it (escapist entertainment), or kid ourselves about it (funeral practices). Whether we look to anthropological evidence, psychoanalytic studies (E. Herzog's *Psyche and Death* [1967]), philosophical treatments (Jacques Choron's *Death and Western Thought* [1963]), or literary expressions of the human dilemma (Camus' *La Peste*), the reality of the problem of death for all mankind is displayed with appalling clarity. If Christ did in fact conquer this most basic of all human enemies and claimed on the basis of it to be God incarnate, able to give eternal life to those who believe in him, it would be sheer madness not to take with full seriousness the biblical affirmation that "God was in Christ, reconciling the world unto himself."

God and Human Experience

Contemplation of the centrality of death and man's quest for immortality vis-à-vis the God question leads us quite naturally to a striking new book which treats the existence of God from the standpoint of man's sociological experience. I refer to *A Rumor of Angels: Modern Society and the Rediscovery of the Supernatural* (1969) by Peter Berger, a professor of sociology at the New School for Social Research. Berger argues that such human experiences as hope in the face of death and the conviction that there must be a retribution transcending inadequate human justice for the commission of monstrous evil in this life are most sensibly explained in terms of God's existence. Other analogous empirical pointers to the existence of the transcendent are man's affirmation of societal ordering (cf. Voegelin's *Order and History*) and unshakeable conviction that such ordering extends to the universe as a whole (cf. the reassurance given by mothers to their frightened children since the world began, "Everything is all right"); man's humor, reflecting his basic awareness that a radical discrepancy exists between life as he lives it (in finitude) and life as it ought to be (in transcendent rightness); and man's play experiences—his brief transmigrations out of time into realms where finitude is momentarily transcended:

> Some little girls are playing hopscotch in the park. They are completely intent on their game, closed to the world outside it, happy in their concentration. Time has stood still for them—or, more accurately, it has been collapsed into the movements of the game. The outside world has, for the duration of the game, ceased to exist. And, by implication (since the little girls may not be very conscious of this), pain and death, which are the law of that world, have also ceased to exist. Even the adult observer of this scene, who is perhaps all too conscious of pain and death, is momentarily drawn into the beatific immunity.
>
> In the playing of adults, at least on certain occasions, the suspension of time and of the "serious" world in which people suffer and die becomes explicit. Just before the

> Soviet troops occupied Vienna in 1945, the Vienna Philharmonic gave one of its scheduled concerts. There was fighting in the immediate proximity of the city, and the concertgoers could hear the rumbling of the guns in the distance. . . . It was . . . an affirmation of the ultimate triumph of all human gestures of creative beauty over the gestures of destruction, and even over the ugliness of war and death. . . .
>
> All men have experienced the deathlessness of childhood and we may assume that, even if only once or twice, all men have experienced transcendent joy in adulthood. Under the aspect of inductive faith, religion is the final vindication of childhood and of joy, and of all gestures that replicate these.

Professor Berger's arguments carry us from the lowlands of sociology to the heights of philosophical ontology for they conjoin with a very important passage in Norman Malcolm's classic essay on Anselm's ontological proof of God's existence (*Philosophical Review*, January, 1960). Asks Malcolm: Why have human beings formed the concept of "a being a greater than which cannot be conceived"? This is his suggested answer, based, as are Berger's arguments, on "an understanding of the phenomena of human life:"

> There is the phenomenon of feeling guilt for something that one has done or thought or felt or for a disposition that one has. One wants to be free of this guilt. But sometimes the guilt is felt to be so great that one is sure that nothing one could do oneself, nor any forgiveness by another human being, would remove it. One feels a guilt that is beyond all measure, a guilt "a greater than which cannot be conceived." Paradoxically, it would seem, one nevertheless has an intense desire to have this incomparable guilt removed. One requires a forgiveness that is beyond all measure, a forgiveness "a greater than which cannot be conceived." Out of such a storm in the soul, I am suggesting, there arises the conception of a forgiving mercy that is limitless, beyond all measure.

The experiences of death, judgment, order, humor, play, and guilt point beyond themselves—as does the very "I" who is conscious of them—and the direction of the signpost is to a Cross where the transcendent God offered "forgiving mercy that is limitless, beyond all measure." In the words of the Apostle (Rom. 4:25), he was "delivered for our offences and was raised again for our justification." Is man his own God? No, for man could never attain such limitless mercy. But God became man to offer that mercy, which no one could buy at any price, as a free gift. The evidence of God's existence and of his gift is more than compelling, but those who insist that they have no need of him or it will always find ways to discount the offer. As Pascal trenchantly observed (*Pensées*, No. 430): "Il y a assez de lumière pour ceux qui ne désirent que de voir, et assez d'obscurité pour ceux qui ont une disposition contraire." This statement is, of course, but a corollary of Jesus' words (Matt. 9:13; 18:3): "I am not come to call the righteous, but sinners to repentance. Except you be converted and become as little children, you shall not enter into the kingdom of heaven."

The Relevance of Scripture in Today's Philosophical Climate

The great Anglican divine E. A. Litton emphasized the unanimity of all branches of the Christian Church in regard to the plenary inspiration of the Bible: "If there ever was a general consent of the Church Catholic on any question, it exists on this. East and West, from the earliest to the latest times, concurred in assigning to Scripture a pre-eminence which consisted in its being—as no other collection of writings is—the Word of God" (*Introduction to Dogmatic Theology*, ed. Philip E. Hughes [1960], p. 19). For classical Protestant theology, the Bible in its entirety is a message introduced by the eternal God into the human situation, and is therefore totally veracious both in its facts (its descriptive content) and in its values (its normative content). Moreover, having God as its Author, Scripture is a clear book whose teachings can be objectively determined through the study and comparison of one portion of the Bible with another. When the objective truths of God's Word—and particularly the factual reality of Christ's death for man's sin and resurrection for his justification—are brought to bear on human life, they have the power to transform existence totally: "If any man be in Christ," declares the Apostle, "he is a new creature: old things are passed away; behold, all things are become new" (II Cor. 5:17).

In a striking number of ways, this high view of biblical authority maintained by orthodox Protestantism can establish ideological links with the latest and most fruitful advances in contemporary philosophical thought. Orthodox Christians of the 19th and early 20th centuries had a hard row to hoe vis-à-vis the ideological climate of their day, for the 19th century was characterized by a philosophical idealism (Hegel and Bradley come immediately to mind) that confidently endeavored to set forth absolute truth apart from revelation, and, when these endeavors hopelessly failed, 20th-century existentialism (Heidegger, Sartre) gave up in principle the search for absolutes and substituted for objective truth and value a subjective relativism in which the individual determines the nature of his world through his own decisions. The 19th century tried to reach God through human reason, and the early 20th century, having failed in constructing this Tower of Babel and finding its language confused, gave up all hope of eternal truth and saw no other recourse than to make a philosophy of life out of the hopelessness of a confused existence. Both idealism and existentialism had been right and wrong simultaneously: idealism was right in believing that man desperately needed an absolute Word, but wrong in thinking that man could attain it by pulling himself to heaven by his own ideological bootstraps; existentialism was right in recognizing man's inability to arrive at absolute truth and value through his philosophical efforts, but wrong in giving up all hope of an eternal Word. The most recent developments in philosophical thinking point the way beyond this impasse and offer powerful testimony to the continuing relevance of the orthodox doctrine of biblical authority.

At the root of the new look in 20th-century philosophy

is Ludwig Wittgenstein (1889-1951), a strange, eccentric, passionate seeker after philosophical integrity who combined mathematical-logical genius with intense mysticism. Says Justus Hartnack—and he does not exaggerate —"Wittgenstein holds the key to modern philosophical activity." In his remarkable *Tractatus Logico-Philosophicus,* Wittgenstein effectively argued that "the sense of the world must lie outside the world" (6.41), that is, man never has sufficient perspective from within the world situation to build an eternal structure of truth and value. Absolute truth and eternal value, if they exist at all, must take their origin from outside the flux of the human situation.

This insight has revolutionized all branches of philosophy and has dealt a virtual deathblow to metaphysical idealism. Consider the realms of philosophy of history and ethics. The grandiose 19th- and early 20th-century attempts (Hegel, Spengler, *et al.)* to construct universally valid interpretations of history apart from revelation are now seen to be impossible in principle; the philosopher simply cannot gain the perspective outside the world needed to explain the human drama (cf. my article, "Where Is History Going?", *Religion in Life,* Spring, 1964; reprinted in my *Where Is History Going?* [Zondervan, 1969]). As Arthur C. Danto has shown, following in Wittgenstein's footsteps, the only "substantive philosophy of history" which is logically possible would be in reality *prophetic:* "It involves speaking in a prophetic vein, i.e. describing the present in the light of things which have not as yet happend ('Unto you a Saviour is born')" (*Analytical Philosophy of History* [Cambridge: Cambridge University Press, 1965], pp. 12-13).

Likewise in the realm of ethics. G. E. Moore, who considered Wittgenstein his best student and, with Bertrand Russell, examined him for his doctorate, labeled as the "naturalistic fallacy" any attempt to define "goodness' absolutely in the human sphere—particularly the attempt to create an absolute value system simply on the basis of what people do (*Principia Ethica,* chap. i). More recently, Kurt Baier, one of the foremost ethical thinkers to benefit from Wittgensteinian insights, has admitted that from within the human situation ethical values can never rise above the societal level: "Outside society, the very distinction between right and wrong vanishes" (*The Moral Point of View* [New York: Random House, 1965], p. 157). Human beings, in other words, are incapable of reaching absolute ethical norms by unaided reason; their ethic will always reflect their stance in society. As Wittgenstein put it in the *Tractatus:* "If there is any value that does have value, it must lie outside the whole sphere of what happens and is the case. . . . Ethics is transcendental" (6.41-6.421).

The plain consequence is that the only possible answer to modern man's quest for the ultimate meaning of history and for an absolute ethical standard would have to lie in a revelation from outside the world. If such a revelation does not exist, man will of logical (not merely practical) necessity remain forever bound to his cultural relativities, forever ignorant of life's meaning. But if such a revelation should exist, it would explode the world —turn it, as men said the early Christians did, upside down (Acts 17:6). Wittgenstein himself understood this very clearly, as one sees from the following passage in the only popular lecture he is known to have composed (the text remained unpublished until its appearance in the January, 1965, *Philosophical Review*):

> And now I must say that if I contemplate what Ethics really would have to be if there were such a science, this result seems to me quite obvious. It seems to me obvious that nothing we could ever think or say should be *the* thing. That we cannot write a scientific book, the subject matter of which could be intrinsically sublime and above all other subject matters. I can only describe my feeling by the metaphor, that, if a man could write a book on Ethics which really was a book on Ethics, this book would, with an explosion, destroy all the other books in the world.

It is the conviction of orthodox Christianity that in Holy Scripture just such a book exists: a Book "intrinsically sublime and above all other subject matters" because its Author is the transcendent Lord God, who is unconditioned by the human predicament that corrupts even our best attempts to find life's meaning, and who alone knows and is Absolute Truth.

But is the Bible the revelation Christians claim it is? Has it the power to explode the world of human speculation? Sad to say, neither Wittgenstein himself nor the analytical philosophy movement that stems from his work has seriously investigated the question (cf. Wittgenstein's *Lectures & Conversations on Aesthetics, Psychology and Religious Belief*, ed. Cyril Barrett [Oxford: Blackwell, 1966], pp. 57-59). In Wittgenstein's personal life, one sees only the profound and pathetic longings of one who recognized man's overwhelming need for a Word from God but did not think any avenue existed for its transmission; as his biographer Malcolm described it: "Often as we walked together he would stop and exclaim 'Oh, my God!', looking at me almost piteously, as if imploring a divine intervention in human events." But the analytical philosophy movement—Wittgenstein's continuing legacy—has provided the tools by which early 20th-century existential skepticism toward objective biblical truth can be effectively countered, and the fact of "divine intervention" through Scripture meaningfully proclaimed.

Characteristic of existential modes of thinking is Wilhelm Dilthey's historical relativism. Dilthey argued that the historian is never able to obtain a genuinely objective view of the past, for his own subjectivity inevitably enters into his investigations of earlier times. This viewpoint has been picked up by theological existentialists such as radical New Testament critic and demythologizer Rudolf Bultmann ("always in your present lies the meaning in history"), by post-Bultmannians such as Heinrich Ott ("the objective mode of knowledge is entirely inappropriate to historical reality because there are no such things as objectively verifiable facts"), and by death-of-God theologians such as Thomas J. J. Altizer (who, on the basis of his belief that objective knowledge of the past is impossible, freely creates a "hidden Christ" in terms of his own present experience).

The insights of Wittgenstein-inspired analytical philosophy have done much to show the fallacy in this kind of approach to historical reality and to the literary products of the past. Summarizing the results, J. W. N. Watkins notes that, over against the Dilthey tradition, analytical work by such philosophers as Ryle "dispels the old presumption . . . that to understand Ghengis Khan the historian must be someone very like Ghengis Khan" (*La Philosophie au milieu du vingtième siècle,* ed. R. Klibansky [2nd ed.; Firenze, 1961-1962], III, 159). One can most definitely arrive at an objective knowledge of a Ghengis Khan—or of a Moses or of Jesus Christ! The most recent and important collection of papers reflecting an analytical approach to historiography is William H. Dray's *Philosophical Analysis and History* (New York: Harper, 1966); the essays by C. G. Hempel and J. A. Passmore are especially devastating to the Dilthey-existential variety of historical skepticism. Hempel's closely reasoned paper on "Explanation in Science and in History" demonstrates "the methodological unity of all empirical science," i.e., the common ground between scientific and historical investigations. Passmore, in his essay on "The Objectivity of History," effectively argues in the same vein that skepticism toward history will necessarily involve one in skepticism both toward science and toward one's present experience, resulting in total solipsism; he concludes: "If we mean by 'science' the attempt to find out what really happens, then history is a science. It demands the same kind of dedication, the same ruthlessness, the same passion for exactness, as physics." Comparable realization in the literary field that objectivity of interpretation is possible can be seen in the work of the "neo-Aristotelians" such as Elder Olson, who shows that existential blendings of literary texts with their interpreters have produced "an endless succession of free improvisations" instead of an objective understanding of the great literary products of the past ("Hamlet and the Hermeneutics of Drama," *Modern Philology,* February, 1964; cf. R. S. Crane, *Critics and Criticism* [Chicago: University of Chicago Press, 1952]). The biblical implications of this recovery of confidence in historical and literary objectivity are no less than revolutionary: now the orthodox Christian claim that Scripture is objectively true historical revelation, capable of yielding a clear message to all who without prejudice study its literary content, must be taken with utmost seriousness.

The analytical philosophy movement has provided still another inestimable boon for evangelicals concerned to maintain the classic view of biblical truth. Analytical philosophers have had much to say about "verifiability" and "meaningfulness"; they stress that truth-claims which are in principle unable to be confirmed or disconfirmed have no meaningful content. Philosopher Paul Edwards makes this point well in his critique of Tillich's theology (*Mind*, April, 1965):

> We normally regard as empty, as devoid of (cognitive) meaning or content a sentence which, while pretending to assert something, is on further examination found to be compatible with any state of affairs. If, for example, I say "Bomba is going to wear a red tie tonight" and if I do not withdraw my statement even if he shows up wearing a brown or a black or a grey tie, and if it further becomes clear that I will not consider my statement refuted even if Bomba wears no tie at all and in fact that I will consider it "true," no matter what happens anywhere, then it would be generally agreed that I have really said nothing at all.

Tillich and other contemporary theologians much influenced by existentialist modes of thought have been particularly prone to make religious statements that, being "compatible with any state of affairs" and totally without the possibility of confirmation or disconfirmation, are really meaningless. The attitudes toward Scripture taken by dialectic theologians such as Barth and by existential theologians such as Bultmann and his disciples precisely fit this category. For example, we are told that the Bible, though an erroneous book, is revelatory because "God encounters us there" (Barth) or because "self-understanding" occurs in contact with it (Bultmann) or because "the text interprets us" (Fuchs, Ebeling; cf. Merrill Abbey's *The Word Interprets Us* [1967]). These subjectivistic approaches to biblical inspiration are now revealed as hopelessly weak; they are in fact technically meaningless, for they are still maintained by the modern theologian regardless of the errors he purports to find in Scripture and regardless of the untestability of subjective experience.

The orthodox Christianity of the Reformers and of the evangelical divines has never fallen into this pit: orthodoxy has consistently affirmed that the dynamic effect of Scripture on man's personal life occurs because

Scripture is in fact objectively true. Personal truth is grounded in objective truth. Historic Christianity has always maintained a meaningful doctrine of inspiration which rests the case for the Bible's subjective validity on its *de facto* objective truthfulness. By a very precise and confirmable argument (the historical reliability of the New Testament documents *qua* documents; the demonstrable Deity of Christ in those records; Christ's stamp of approval on the Old Testament and his promise of identical, Spirit-led remembrance of His Word among the apostles under whose aegis the New Testament would be written), evangelical Christians offer to the world today the only meaningful revelation-claim for the truth of Holy Scripture.

Today, as never before, philosophical thought manifests a passion for objective, empirical truth, and the ordinary-language philosophers (whose work stems from Wittgenstein's *Philosophical Investigations*) are stressing the importance of verbal expression in conveying truth. Idealistic castles-in-air have been deflated and existential wanderings in the labyrinth of subjectivity have been discredited. Evangelicals of the second half of the 20th century have an unparalled opportunity to affirm the philosophical relevance of their high view of Scripture. The "divine intervention" for which Wittgenstein longed can with confidence be offered to modern man in the totally veracious, inscripturated Word of God.

THE QUEST FOR ABSOLUTES: AN HISTORICAL ARGUMENT*

John Warwick Montgomery, Ph.D., D. Théol.

THE STARTING POINT--METHODOLOGY

A. Summary

Where to begin in the quest for absolutes? The usual beginning is made in the realm of philosophy; we see a typical example of this in the recent book by George P. Grant, Philosophy in the Mass Age. In this book Grant argues that an examination of the human situation forces one to place limits on human conduct and activity--and that these limits constitute a "natural law". However, such a procedure will never provide a list of natural laws--or even one natural law--upon which there will be universal agreement. The reason for the failure of this method is that it attempts to reach universal permanent, absolute principles by analyzing the human situation from within. Such an analysis can never provide absolutes, for the human situation is never in itself permanent; rather, it is in constant flux. As a Pre-Socratic philosopher put it, "You can never step into the same river twice". This basic fact applies to the philosopher as much as to any one else (though the philosopher seems seldom to recognize it). No one can "sit in a house by the side of the road and watch the world go by"; everyone is caught up in the flux of human life, and there is no universal, absolute perspective on the universe or man's life. Philosophy has served its purpose when it has shown the logical errors in attempts to reach absolutes by analyzing the human situation; as someone has cleverly said, "Philosophy doesn't know the answers, but it can sure state the problems".

The basic question, then, it that of starting point. Every argument or position begins with presuppositions--but obviously it is desirable to incorporate as little content in one's presuppositions as possible. In other words, one should assume as little as possible, and attempt to discover as much as possible. The best way to do this is to accept presuppositions of method (which will yield truth) rather than presuppositions of substantive content (which aasume a body of truth already). In our modern world we have found that the presuppositions of empirical or scientific method best fulfil this condition. Historical method has the same advantages, the only differe being that "experiments" as such cannot be conducted, for one cannot duplicat the conditions of the past. Let us begin, then, by seeing how much better it is to employ empirical method than to start from other presuppositions.

B. Methods of Acquiring Truth

The chief methods of arriving at truth are four, the first two of which are commonly employed by the layman and the last two of which are the usual

---

*This mimeograph is a summary of material from the author's book, The Shape of the Past.

methods of the educated investigator. These are: common sense, authority, intuition, and empirical or scientific method.[1] Common sense, the most unsophisticated of these methods, is in reality a combination of the other three; it may be defined as the almost unconscious and certainly uncritical activity of acquiring self-evident and commonly held beliefs through experience. The authoritarian method requires that the individual relinquish his independent efforts to determine what is true or false, and transfer this function to another individual, group of individuals, or institution which seems to be in a better position to exercise it. Typical authorities are custom, tradition, revelation, consensus gentium. Intuition presupposes that truth can be known by direct insight or immediate awareness--that there are certain principles which need not be tested for error, because being self-evident, they guarantee their own truth. The intuitive approach is used both by mystics and by rationalist philosophers and theologians, the latter often deducing complex systems from principles which they hold to be intuitively true. Empirical or scientific method is a process which consists of (1) the investigation of the universe by observations, (2) the verification of these observations by others, (3) the drawing of generalizations (hypotheses) from these verified observations (4) the verification of these hypotheses by others, etc., etc.

C. Critique of the Methods of Acquiring Truth

We have just stated and explained the four principle methods of acquiring truth, viz.: common sense, authority, intuition, and empirical or scientif method. Let us now evaluate these methods. Common sense, since it is completely uncritical, must be rejected wherever possible by the educated investigator. The chief fallacy in the authoritarian method lies in the fact that it begs the question: how did the given authority acquire the truth it holds in the first place? Since all human authorities are fallible, the must be screened from without for truth or error. Even in the case of an alleged divine authority, it would be necessary to test by some means or an other whether the authority is truly an infallible one before accepting as true all of its decrees. Thus authority must be rejected as a primary meth of acquiring truth.

The intuitive method, although it has been defended vigorously by many thinl ers, has at least one serious disadvantage: since the only self-evident tru is the tautology (if A then A)--which reveals no factual information whatsoever--and since no philosophies have been deduced from tautologies, all intuitive principles and systems likewise must be screened from without for their truth-value. Of course, a prioris must lie at the basis of every procedure,[2] but because of this disadvantage they should be kept to a minimum, and be as self-evident and beyond dispute as possible.

Empirical or scientific method is the truly valid way of approaching truth because it alone can accomplish to the satisfaction of all what the other methods which we have discussed cannot; not only do its results not need to be tested for error independently, but it is in itself capable of determining what authority to follow and what common sense beliefs and presuppositions to hold.

"The evidence that science accumulates is public. It is open to the scrutiny of all. If a scientific result is to be refuted, it must be refuted by the same kind of evidence. When a biologist experiments in order to test the soundness of a biological theory, his experiments are such as could be performed and observed by all who have the requisite training and competence. If the experimental results are favourable to the theory, everyone must, in spite of extra-scientific considerations, regard the theory as more acceptable than it was previously. It is not because the biologist says so (authority); not because of any ethical or emotional reasons (faith); not because of any feelings of certainty (intuition); it is because the evidence is of the kind that compels assent."[3]

It is true that empirical method, like all other disciplines, has its presuppositions, but these a prioris are few, self-evident, and more generally agreed upon than those of any other system. Dr. Edward J. Carnell states the empirical presuppositions as follows:

"1. Epistemology. If a law is to be meaningful, it must be true. Every successful scientist, then, must assume that knowledge is possible . . .
2. Metaphysics. Science assumes that the universe is regular but how can that hypothesis be made significant without a world-view which allows for regularity? . . .
3. Ethics. All scientists know that a man must be honest before his conclusions can be trusted, but how can the empiricist show, by a laboratory experiment, that honesty is a normative affair? Science can only describe."[4]

It might seem that since empirical method is based on intuitive premises, even empiricism is a variety of rationalism.[5] Strictly speaking this is true, but the distinction between the two methods lies in the fact that whereas rationalists attempt to deduce their world-views from their presupposition(s), empiricists use their presuppositions only to justify investigation of the universe--this investigation providing the data for their world-view.

Because empiricism avoids the disadvantages of the other three methods of approaching truth it should be employed wherever possible. An important ramification of the scientific method should be noted at this point: nothing is certain (other than the presuppositions of empiricism and the data with which the empiricist works, by definition): thus one must make his decisions on probability, for the conclusions of empirical method are always hypothetical (to varying degrees, of course, depending upon the strength of present evidence and the probability of relevant new evidence arising).

D. An Important Warning: Empirical Method is not the "Religion of Science'

The presuppositions of Modern Science as world-view (Dr. Burtt calls it the "Religion of Science") are many more than the presuppositions of empirical or scientific method, given above.

"THE MAJOR DISPUTED ASSUMPTIONS OF THE RELIGION OF SCIENCE

1. Assumptions Concerning Man's Moral Situation
   a. He needs certainty to attain his highest good, whose nature is indicatedby the experience of disappointed attachment.

   b. He can attain the needed certainty through the power of his own reason.

2. Assumption Concerning Metaphysical Knowledge
   a. The ultimate criterion of truth is the clarity of direct apprehension of an object's essence.
      (1) Supplementation of human reason by supernatural revelatio: is therefore superfluous and irrational.

   b. The ultimate structure of the world is mathematical in its determinate order and its unconcern for human welfare.

   c. Good and evil are relative to human desire.

3. Psychological Assumptions
   a. Knowledge of the structure of the world on which we depend produces love of that which is known.

   b. Love of truth and reality is capable of indefinite growth.

   c. Such love can transform desire and emotion into harmony with itself."[6]

As can readily be seen by comparing the a prioris of the Religion of Scienc and those of the scientific method, the former are hospitable to the latter but the converse is not necessarily true.

II. APPLICATION OF EMPIRICAL METHODOLOGY TO THE CENTRAL EVENT OF AN HISTORICAL RELIGION

A. Summary

At the outset we noted that human beings cannot, by the very nature of the case, arrive at absolutes by examining their own relativistic human situation. But suppose--just for the sake of argument--that a "god" (or God?) entered the human situation and stated absolutes. Obviously, if such an entrance could be demonstrated, the quest for absolutes would be fulfilled, for a "god", not being himself involved in the flux of human life, could see the real nature of man and of the universe and provide the permanent principles which men seek. Many religions, it should be noted, talk about "revelations", "divine Truths", etc., but only one religion provides an objective, empirical test for its claims. All the religions of the world except Christianity say, "Try me out and you'll see that I have the truth"; but the rational man cannot engage in such a procedure, for once one becomes emotionally involved in a faith, it becomes less and less possible to examine other faiths with impartiality. But Christianity rests its case on an historical event which, if it indeed happened, attests its claim to know absolutes. This event is the resurrection of Christ from the dead. When the Jewish religious leaders expressed disbelief in his claim to be God-come-to-earth, Jesus said, "Destroy this temple (his body) and in three days I will raise it up" (John 2:18 ff.), and Paul based his entire claim for the truth of Christianity on this same resurrection (I Cor. 15). The obvious question is, of course, does this event hold up under historical investigation? A second question, of almost as great significance, is the troublesome one: Can miracles occur?

B. The Argument in Outline

1. The Gospels are reasonable historical documents--primary source material. All scholars (even non-Christians) admit that Matt., Mark, and Luke were written within 50 years after Christ's death, and John within 65 years of Christ's death. The objector can check this in any encyclopedia.
2. In the Gospels, Christ claims to be God in human flesh. Matthew 11:27; John 12:45; John 10:30; Matthew 16:13-17.
3. In all four Gospels, Christ's bodily Resurrection is described in great detail. Christ's Resurrection proves His claim to Deity.
4. If Christ is God, whatever He says is true.
5. Christ stated that the O.T. was infallible (Matthew 5:17-19) and that the New Testament (written by Apostles or close associates of Apostles) would be infallible (John 14:26-27; John 16:12-15; of Acts 1:21-26).
6. The New Testament and the Old Testament contain religious, philosophical, and ethical absolutes; these thus take on the character of divine or "natural" law, and remain valid even if vast numbers of human beings--or entire societies--are foolish enough to ignore them.

C. The Historical Argument in Detail

The historical consideration which throws the scale of probability far to the side of supernaturalism, is the man Jesus Christ--His claims and the validation which He gave for His claims. First I shall discuss the claims themselves, then the attestation which He provided for them, and lastly their ramification for this discussion.

Jesus of Nazareth--the "humble carpenter"--made the most stupendous claims of any one who has ever lived. He claimed the following things, which if validated, would mean the annihilation of the materialist point of view:

1. That there exists a perfectly just, wise, powerful, holy, and loving personal Being;
2. That He, Jesus Christ, was the human incarnation of this Being[8], come to earth vicariously to save its inhabitants from eternal death,[9] and to reveal God to man.[10];
3. That the universe--including the earth and the human--had been created by God,[11] that God has a continual interest in the most minute things which happen on the earth[12], and that the termination of the present age will be brought about in God's own time and by His command;[13] in short, that the creation is in every sense teleologically and supernaturalistically operated.

These claims of Christ, together with all the data we have concerning Him, are included in four books--the Gospels of Matthew, Mark, Luke and John. These records, which no competent scholar today maintains were written later than 50 years (Synoptics) and 65 years (John) after Christ's death,[14] contain the record of His crucifixion and resurrection from the dead--this latter event being the one upon which He placed the most emphasis while alive, and which He considered to provide the ultimate verification for His claims.[15] We should note carefully that the dates of the Gospels remove any doubt as to their authorship by attesting their claim to have been written by Christ's contemporaries; and furthermore that since they were written while eye-witnesses of the events recorded in them were still alive, their contents could be tested at first hand for truth or error by anyone desiring to do so.

According to the Gospel records, Jesus of Nazareth was put to death by the Roman governor of Palestine during the passover celebration which took place in Jerusalem in 33 A.D. The official charge was treason against Rome (Jesus had claimed to be a King), although the Jewish religious leaders, who gave Jesus over to the Roman governor, had hated Him chiefly because He had in their eyes blasphemed--claimed to be God, and to exercise divine prerogatives.[16] The city of Jerusalem was packed during the passover week, and Jesus' crucifixion was witnessed by many.[17] Upon His death, which was accompanied by an earthquake, darkness over the land, and other phenomena,[18] His body was placed in a tomb belonging to a rich man of the Jews.[19] The huge boulder at the entrance to the tomb[20] was sealed, and a Roman guard was stationed, in response to the pleas of the high-priests and rabbis, who, knowing that Jesus had said that He would rise from the dead after three days to verify His claims, desired to prevent anyone's spiriting away the body and spreading the story that Jesus had risen.[21] On the morning of the third day, however, Jesus did rise, the guard having been rendered completely ineffective through fear.[22] During the forty days following, Jesus appeared in bodily form[23] on at least eight occasions,[24] making His identity a matter of unquestioned authenticity. He charged His followers that since He had attested His claim by conquering death, that they should "go into all the world and preach the gospel to the whole creation. He who believes and is baptized will be saved; but he who does not believe will be condemned."[25] The disciples, who had been fearful and faithless before and during the events of the Passion week now boldly went forth to spread the message of salvation throughout the then-known world.[26]

Out of the first century A.D., when the Resurrection, if untrue, could have been easily disproved by anyone who took the trouble to talk with those who had been present in Jerusalem during the passover week of 33, no contrary historical evidence has come; instead, during that century the number of conversions to Christianity increased by geometric progression, the influence of the Gospel story spreading out of Jerusalem like a gigantic web. If Christ did not rise as He promised, how can we rationally explain this lack of negative evidence and number of conversions? Furthermore, if the body of the crucified Jesus naturally left the tomb, how did He leave? Not by its own accord, for Jesus was unquestionably dead.[27] Not through the efforts of the Jewish religious leaders or the Romans, for they had placed a guard at the tomb for the express purpose of keeping the body there. Not Jesus' followers, for to perform such an act would have been to deny the principles of truth upon which their later lives were predicated, and which they preached until killed for their convictions.[26] If Jesus did not rise from the dead, what happened to His body in the city teeming with the passover crowd, a great number of whom had been members of the mob which required us to admit the truth of the Resurrection; probability, which is the criterion of truth of the historian, must rule over any *a priori* considerations in the making of historical judgments. Can miracles occur? History and not philosophy must answer this question.

D. Can Miracles Such as the Resurrection Occur? Montgomery vs. Hume

The most formidable argument against the miraculous--and that which has generally carried most weight with modernists and humanists--is the argument which Hume stated in his *Enquiry Concerning Human Understanding*.[28] The substance of Hume's argument runs as follows:

"A miracle is a violation of the laws of nature; and as a firm and unalterable experience has established these laws, the proof against a miracle, from the very nature of the fact, is as entire as any argument from experience can possibly be imagined. Why is it more than probable, that all men must die; that lead cannot, of itself, remain suspended in the air; that fire consumes wood, and is extinguished by water, unless it be, that these events are found agreeable to the laws of nature and there is required a violation of these laws, or in other words, a miracle to prevent them? Nothing is esteemed a miracle, if it ever happens in the common course of nature. It is no miracle that a man, seemingly in good health, should die on a sudden; because such a kind of death, though more unusual than any other, has yet been frequently observed to happen. But it is a miracle, that a dead man should come to life; because that has never been observed in any age or country. There must, therefore, be a uniform experience against every miraculous event, otherwise the event would not merit that appellation. And as a uniform experience amounts to a proof, there is here a direct and full proof, from the nature of the fact, against the existence of any miracle; nor can such a proof be destroyed, or the miracle rendered incredible, but by an opposite proof, which is superior.

"The plain consequence is (and it is a general maxim worthy of our attention), 'That no testimony is sufficient to establish a miracle, unless the testimony be of such a kind, that its falsehood would be more miraculous, than the fact, which it endeavours to establish; and even in that case there is a mutual destruction of arguments, and the superior only gives us an assurance suitable to that degree of force, which remains, after deducting the inferior.' When anyone tells me that he saw a dead man restored to life, I immediately consider with myself, whether it be more probable, that this person should either deceive or be deceived, or that the fact, which he relates, should really have happened. I weigh the one miracle against the other; and according to the superiority, which I discover, I pronounce my decision, and always reject the greater miracle. If the falsehood of his testimony would be more miraculous, than the event which he relates; then, and not till then, can he pretend to command by belief or opinion."

* * * * * * *

The invalidity of Hume's argument lies in his definition of the word "miracle"--a definition entirely in accordance with Newtonion physics, but one which in the physics of today (a physics transformed by the concept of Relativity) no longer has meaning. Hume's definition of a miracle is given in the first sentence of the above quoted passage: "a miracle is a violation of the laws of nature". For fear of not making his definition clear, Hume writes in a footnote to this section: "A miracle may be accurately defined, <u>a transgression of a law of nature by a particular volition of the Deity, or by the interposition of some invisible agent</u>". (Italics Hume's). It is evident that were there no rigorous structure of natural law for a miraculous event to violate, it would be impossible <u>a priori</u> to rule out an alleged miracle as Hume has done. Hume says that the ordinary course of events is such powerful evidence against the occurrence of unique events, that the latter can be rejected regardless of the authority or evidence attesting them. Under only one condition would Hume's argument hold, namely, if there were irrefutable evidence for the existence of a rigorous framework of natural law in the universe which would render absurd the idea of its violation.[29] Do we have such evidence? Newton thought so, and so has the traditional Religion of Science.[30] Yet, since Einstein, science has gradually given up this notion. Rather than looking at natural law as <u>a structure which is already present in the universe and which is progressively being discovered</u>, scientists of today see natural law as <u>the human description of what is observed to happen in the universe</u>.

Such a conception of natural law is the only truly empirical one, for it places all events, regardless of their uniqueness, on equal footing -- all are to be tested for error by a study of the empirical evidence for them, not ruled out a priori because they have not happened as many times as other events.

> "Laws of nature are a description of what happens, not a handbook of rules to tell us what cannot happen. In choosing his laws of nature, therefore, the scientist 'should first consult history, and after deciding by historical evidence what has happened, should then choose his laws within the limits of historical actuality. The non-christian thinker, intent on repudiating miracles, proceeds by a reverse method. He chooses his law without regard to historical limits, and then tries to rewrite history to fit his law. But surely this method is not only the reverse of the Christian method, it is clearly the reverse of rational procedure as well.'"[31]

That the conception of natural law of Newton and Hume is indeed the "reverse of rational procedure", may be seen even more clearly by means of an illustration. Gulliver, of Jonathan Swift's Gulliver's Travels, was said to have been shipwrecked on the island of Lilliput--an island inhabited by men six inches high. Before Gulliver's arrival, the Lilliputians had had no contact whatsoever with the rest of the world--no contact whatever with creatures taller than themselves. Suppose the Lilliputians who discovered Gulliver had followed Hume's reasoning: Never before had a man one foot, much less six feet, tall been seen--either by themselves or by anyone within the course of recorded Lilliputian history. Which then, would be more miraculous--that they themselves were deluded, or that Gulliver really existed?

Obviously the former would be the greater miracle, so Gulliver does not exist at all. He may plead with the Lilliputians to evaluate the overwhelming, objective evidence that he does exist--the fact that he takes up space, eats, etc.--but to no avail. No Lilliputians have ever seen a six foot man; therefore Gulliver a priori does not exist.

Such an example illustrates well the fallaciousness of Hume's argument. In order to determine what natural laws are it is necessary for us to evaluate, without a priori, the particular evidence for each alleged event, no matter how unique it is. If the evidence for a singular occurrence is equal to that ordinarily required to verify events, we must accept the unique happening, and consider it when plotting or revising the laws of nature. The significance of a miracle does not lie in the fact that it transgresses some universal framework of natural law (we should remember that if God exists, natural law is nothing more than the expression of His will), but in the fact that it is unique--that its very degree of uniqueness gives strong evidence for the truth of the claim of the one who performed it and/or of the claim of the book in which it is recorded.

We pointed out above the distinction between the presuppositions of the Religion of Science and those of empirical or scientific method. It was noted that whereas the presuppositions of Sciences include those of scientific method, the converse is not true. The more progressive scientists, since Einstein's revolutionary Theory of Relativity, have come to see this distinction, and have gradually abandoned the presuppositions of Science as a Religion, while retaining and re-emphasizing those of empirical method. Our discussion of the miraculous brings this out clearly; specific empirical evidence for an alleged event, not the number of events dissimilar to it which have occurred, is the proper determinant of the validity of the event. The universe, previously closed by Newton, Hume, et al. to the possibility of unique events, now opens to full empirical investigation.

C. S. Lewis vs. Hume*

The ordinary procedure of the modern historian, even if he accepts the possibility of miracle, is to admit no particular instance of it until every possibility of 'natural' explanation has been tried and failed. That is, he will accept the most improbable 'natural' explanations rather than say that a miracle occurred. Collective hallucination, hypnotism of unconsenting spectators, widespread instantaneous conspiracy in lying by persons not otherwise known to be liars and not likely to gain by the lie--all these are known to be very improbable events: so improbable that, except for the special purpose of excluding a miracle, they are never suggested. But they are preferred to the admission of a miracle. Such a procedure is, from the purely historical point of view, sheer midsummer madness unless we start by knowing that any Miracle whatever is more improbable than the most improbable natural event. Do we know this?

We must distinguish the different kinds of improbability. Since miracles are, by definition, rarer than other events, it is obviously improbable beforehand that one will occur at any given place and time. In that sense every miracle is improbable. But that sort of improbability does not make the story that a miracle has happened incredible; for in the same sense all events whatever were once improbable. It is immensely improbable beforehand that a pebble dropped from the stratosphere over London will hit any given spot, or that any one particular person will win a large lottery. But the report that the pebble has landed outside such and such a shop or that Mr. So-and-So has won the lottery is not at all incredible. When you consider the immense number of meetings and fertile unions between ancestors which were necessary in order that you should be born, you perceive that it was once immensely improbable that such a person as you should come to exist; but once you are here, the report of your existence is not in the least incredible. With the probability of this kind--antecedent probability of chances--we are not here concerned. Our business is with historical probability.

*C. S. Lewis, Miracles, Ch. XIII. (Miracles is now available in Fontana paperbacks for only fifty cents; it is highly recommended.)

Ever since Hume's famous Essay it has been believed that historical statements about miracles are the most intrinsically improbable of all historical statements. According to Hume, probability rests on what may be called the majority vote of our past experiences. The more often a thing has been known to happen, the more probable it is that it should happen again and the less often the less probable. Now the regularity of Nature's course, says Hume, is supported by something better than the majority vote of past experiences: it is supported by their unanimous vote, or, as Hume says, by 'firm and unalterable experience'. There is, in fact, 'uniform experience' against Miracle: otherwise, says Hume, it would not be Miracle. A Miracle is therefore the most improbable of all events. It is always more probable that the witnesses were lying or mistaken than that a Miracle occurred.

Now of course we must agree with Hume that if there is absolutely 'uniform experience' against miracles, if in other words they have never happened, why then they never have. Unfortunately, we know the experience against them to be uniform only if we know that all the reports of them are false. And we can know all the reports to be false only if we know already that miracles have never occurred. In fact, we are arguing in a circle.

There is also an objection to Hume which leads us deeper into our problem. The whole idea of Probability (as Hume understands it) depends on the principle of the Uniformity of Nature. Unless Nature always goes on in the same way, the fact that a thing had happened ten million times would not make it a whit more probable that it would happen again. And how do we know the Uniformity of Nature? A moment's thought shows that we do not know it by experience. We observe many regularities in Nature. But of course all the observations that men have made or will make while the race lasts cover only a minute fraction of the events that actually go on. Our observations would therefore be of no use unless we felt sure Nature when we are not watching her behaves in the same way as when we are: in other words, unless we believed in the Uniformity of Nature. Experience therefore cannot prove Uniformity, because Uniformity has to be assumed before experience proves anything. And mere length of experience does not help matters.

It is no good saying, 'Each fresh experience confirms our belief in Uniformity and therefore we reasonably expect that it will always be confirmed'; for that argument works only on the assumption that the future will resemble the past--which is simply the assumption of Uniformity under a new name. Can we say that Uniformity is at any rate very probable? Unfortunately not. We have just seen that all probabilities depend on it. Unless Nature is uniform, nothing is either probable or improbable. And clearly the assumption which you have to make before there is any such thing as probability cannot itself be probable.

The odd thing is that no man knows this better than Hume. His Essay on Miracles is quite inconsistent with the more radical, and honourable, scepticism of his main work.

The question, 'Do miracles occur?' and the question, 'Is the course of Nature absolutely uniform?' are the same question asked in two different ways. Hume, by sleight of hand treats them as two different questions. He first answers, 'Yes', to the question whether Nature is absolutely uniform: and then uses this 'Yes' as a ground for answering 'No' to the question, 'Do miracles occur?'. The single real question which he set out to answer is never discussed at all. He gets the answer to one form of the question by assuming the answer to another form of the same question.

NOTES

1. My list of four methods for acquiring truth has been culled from Randall and Buchler, Philosophy: An Introduction (1947) Chs. V-VII, XI; and Edward John Carnell, An Introduction to Christian Apologetics (1948), Ch. III. In both of these works many more than four methods of arriving at truth are given, but most of these result from a confusion of the problem. "Methods of acquiring truth" and "methods of testing for truth" (e.g., pragmatism, systematic consistency) are intermixed. Randall and Buchler consider even faith as a method of acquiring truth! See also Max Black, Critical Thinking (1947), Ch. XIII; Ambrose and Lazerowitz, Fundamentals of Symbolic Logic, (1950), pp. 16-19.

2. Carnell, op. cit., pp. 91-2: "It may be asked why we make assumptions at all. Why not stay with the facts? The answer to this is very easy indeed! We make assumptions because we must make assumptions to think at all. All knowledge is inferential and all inferences are assumptions. Knowledge is the mind's construction of meaning, and properly construed meaning is truth. It is therefore useless to say, 'Stay with the facts', unless we mean, 'Keep your hypotheses in conformity to facts.' Facts just are. Knowledge is inference drawn from facts. A fact is any unit of being which is capable of bearing meaning, but it is the meaning, not the fact, which is the knowledge."

3. Randall and Buchler, op. cit., p. 58. See the whole of Ch. VI.

4. Carnell, op. cit., p. 94.

5. See Randall and Buchler, op. cit., Ch. VII.

6. Burtt, Types of Religious Philosophy (1939), p. 196.

7. See for example, Matt. 5:44-5,48; 6:7-13; 19:26; 22:29; Luke 6:35-36; 13:23-29; 18:27; John 3:16; 4:10,24; 5:26; 7:18; 14:31; 15:9; 20:17. See especially John 17. N.B. The reader is very strongly encouraged to look up and examine carefully all Bible references cited in this and the following footnotes. The Revised Standard Version of 1946 is recommended and has been used throughout this paper.

8. Matt. 11:27: "All things have been delivered to me by my Father; and no one knows the Son except the Father, and no one knows the Father except the Son and any one to whom the Son chooses to reveal him." John 12:45: "And he who sees me sees him who sent me." John 10:30: "I and the Father are one." Matt. 16:13-17; "Now when Jesus came into the district of Caesarea Philippi, he asked his disciples, 'Who do men say that the Son of man is?' And they said, 'Some say John the Baptist, others say Elijah, and others Jeremiah or one of the prophets.' He said to them, 'But who do you say that I am?' Simon Peter replied, 'You are the Christ, the Son of the living God.' And Jesus answered him, 'Blessed are you, Simon Bar-Jona! For flesh and blood has not revealed this to you, but my Father who is in heaven.'" See also Matt. 12:8, 26:63-5; Mark 2:5-7; Luke 3:21-2; 6:5; 22:66-71; John 3:13-18; 5:23; 8:58; 10:38.

9. Mark 10:45: "For the Son of man also came not to be served but to serve, and to give his life as a ransom for many." Matt. 26:26-8: "Now as they were eating, Jesus took bread and blessed, and broke it, and gave it to the disciples and said 'Take, eat; this is my body.' And he took a cup, and when he had given thanks he gave it to them, saying, 'Drink of it, all of you; for this is my blood of the covenant, which is poured out for many for the forgiveness of sins.'" John 10:11: "I am the good shepherd. The good shepherd lays down his life for the sheep." See also Matt. 18:11; 20:28; Luke 12:50; 19:10; 22:37; John 3:14-17; 10:17-18.

10. John 14:6-11: "Jesus said to him, 'I am the way, and the truth, and the life; no one comes to the Father, but by me. If you had known me, you would have known my Father also; henceforth you know him and have seen him.' Philip said to him, 'Lord, show us the Father, and we shall be satisfied.' Jesus said to him, 'Have I been with you so long, and yet you do not know me, Philip? He who has seen me has seen the Father; how can you say, "Show us the Father"? Do you not believe that I am in the Father and the Father in me? The words that I say to you I do not speak on my own authority; but the Father who dwells in me does his works. Believe me that I am in the Father and the Father in me; or else believe me for the sake of the works themselves'."

11. Jesus claimed in such passages as Matt. 5:17-18 that the Old Testament was the valid revelation of God. (The Law=the first five books of the Old Testament; the "Prophets"=the rest.) In Genesis, Chs. 1 and 2, we find the account of God's creation activity.

12. Luke 12:6-7: "Are not five sparrows sold for two pennies? And not one of them is forgotten before God. Why, even the hairs of your head are all numbered. Fear not; you are of more value than many sparrows." Cf. Matt. 10:29-31.

13. John 5:25-9: "Truly, truly, I say to you, the hour is coming, and now is, when the dead will hear the voice of the Son of God, and those who hear will live. For as the Father has life in himself, so he has granted the Son also to have life in himself, and has

given him authority to execute judgment, because he is the Son of man. Do not marvel at this; for the hour is coming when all who are in the tombs will hear his voice and come forth, those who have done good, to the resurrection of life, and those who have done evil, to the resurrection of judgment." Matt. 13:36-43: "Then he left the crowds and went into the house. and his disciples came to him, saying, 'Explain to us the parable of the weeds of the field.' He answered, 'He who sows the good seed is the Son of man: the field is the world, and the good seed means the sons of the kingdom: the weeds are the sons of the evil one, and the enemy who sowed them is the devil; the harvest is the close of the age, and the reapers are angels. Just as the weeds are gathered and burned with fire, so will it be at the close of the age. The Son of man will send his angels, and they will gather out of his kingdom all causes of sin and all evil-doers and throw them into the furnace of fire; there men will weep and gnash their teeth. Then the righteous will shine like the sun in the kingdom of their Father. He who has ears, let him hear!" See also Matt. 7:21-3; 16:24-7; 25:31-46; 26:64; Mark 8:38; 14:62; Luke 12:35-40; 21; John 14:3.

14. With regard to the dates of the Synoptic Gospels (Matthew, Mark, and Luke), Dr. Wilbur M. Smith, Professor of English Bible at Fuller Theological Seminary, Pasadena, says, after surveying the opinions of scholars who are authorities on this subject: "I think...we would be safe in saying that the general consensus of opinion among the outstanding New Testament scholars of our generation is, that all three of the synoptic gospels were written by 80 A.D. in other words, Matthew, Mark, and Luke...were all written within half a century of our Lord's death" (The Supernaturalness of Christ, p. 39). Dr. Hugo Odeburg, Professor of New Testament Interpretation at the University of Lund, Sweden, says of the Gospel of John: "The oldest fragment of a copy of a New Testament Scripture which has so far been discovered is the fragment of the Gospel of John found in 1935. This fragment was in a group of papyrus which had been classified under the nineties of the first century A.D., and could not be placed later than the very beginning of the second century. But let us remember that this papyrus is only a copy. This proves that the Gospel of John was known and that copies of it had been spread as far as Egypt by about A.D. 100. Clearly then, the original, the Gospel of John itself, must have been in existence before any copies of it could be made. All theories about the Gospel which rest on the assumption that the Gospel originally dates from some decade in the second century, long after the death of the Apostle John, have therefore become entirely unhistorical." ("The Authorship of St. John's Gospel," Concordia Theological Monthly, April, 1951, p. 246.)

15. John 2:18-22: "The Jews then said to him, 'What sign have you to show us for doing this?' Jesus answered them, 'Destroy this temple, and in three days I will raise it up.' The Jews then said, 'It has taken forty-six years to build this temple, and will you raise it up in three days?' But he spoke of the temple of his body. When therefore he was raised from the dead, his disciples remembered that he had said this; and they believed the scripture and the word which Jesus had spoken." Matt. 16:21: "From that time Jesus began to show his

disciples that he must go to Jerusalem and suffer many things from the elders and chief priests and scribes, and be killed, and on the third day be raised." Also see Matt. 20:17-19; 26:31-2; Mark 8:31-32a; 9:9; 14:27-8; Luke 9:22.

Mark 2:5-7: "And when Jesus saw their faith, he said to the paralytic, 'My son, your sins are forgiven.' Now some of the scribes were sitting there, questioning in their hearts, 'Why does this man speak thus? It is blashpemy! Who can forgive sins but God alone,'" Mark 14:55-65; "Now the chief priests and the whole council sought testimony against Jesus, to put him to death; but they found none. For many bore false witness against him, and their witness did not agree. And some stood up and bore false witness against him, saying, 'We heard him say, "I will destroy this temple that is made with hands, and in three days I will build another, not made with hands.'" Yet not even so did their testimony agree. And the high priest stood up in the midst, and asked Jesus, 'Have you no answer to make? What is it that these men testify against you?' But he was silent and made no answer. Again the high pries asked him, 'Are you the Christ, the Son of the Blessed?' and Jesus said, 'I am; and you will see the Son of man sitting at the right hand of Power and coming with the clouds of heaven.' And the high priest tore his mantle, and said, 'Why do we still need witnesses? You have heard his blasphemy. What is your decision?' And they all condemned him as deserving death. And some began to spit on him, and to cover his face, and to strike him, saying to him, 'Prophesy!' And the guards received him with blows." Luke 23:1-5: "Then the whole company of them arose, and brought him before Pilate. And they began to accuse him, saying, "We found this man perverting our nation, and forbidding us to give tribute to Caesar, and saying that he himself is Christ a king! And Pilate asked him, 'Are you the King of the Jews?' And he answered him, 'You have said so.' And Pilate said to the chief priests and the multitudes, 'I find no crime in this man.' But they were urgent, saying, 'He stirs up the people, teaching throughout all Judea, from Galilee even to this place.'" John 19:6-7,12: "Upon this Pilate sought to release him, but the Jews cried out, 'If you release this man, you are not Caesar friend; everyone who makes himself a king sets himself against Caesar." See also Matt. 26:63-5; Luke 22:66-71; John 10:30-33.

Matt. 26:47,55: "While he was still speaking, Judas came, one of the twelve, and with him a great crowd with swords and clubs, from the chief priests and the elders of the people. At that hour Jesus said to the crowds, 'Have you come out as against a robber with swords and clubs to capture me? Day after day I sat in the temple teaching and you did not seize me!" Matt. 27:22-5: "Pilate said to them, 'Then what shall I do with Jesus who is called Christ? They all said, 'Let him be crucified.' And he said, 'Why, what evil has he done?' But they shouted all the more, 'Let him be crucified.' So when Pilate saw that he was gaining nothing, but rather that a riot was beginning, he took water and washed his hands before the crowd, saying, 'I am innocent of this man's blood; see to it yourselves.' And all the people answered, 'His blood be on us and on our children!" See also Matt. 21:8-11; 27:39-43.

18. Matt. 27:45,50-53: "Now from the sixth hour there was darkness over all the land until the ninth hour. And Jesus cried again with a loud voice and yielded up his spirit. And behold, the curtain of the temple was torn in two, from top to bottom; and the earth shook, and the rocks were split; the tombs also were opened, and many bodies of the saints who had fallen asleep were raised, and coming out of the tombs after his resurrection they went into the holy city and appeared to many."

19. Luke 23:50-53: "Now there was a man named Joseph from the Jewish town of Arimathea. He was a member of the council, a good and righteous man, who had not consented to their purpose and deed, and he was looking for the kingdom of God. This man went to Pilate and asked for the body of Jesus. Then he took it down and wrapped it in a linen shroud, and laid him in a rock-hewn tomb, where no one had ever yet been laid."

20. Matt. 27:59-60: "And Joseph took the body, and wrapped it in a clean linen shroud and laid it in his own new tomb, which he had hewn in the rock; and he rolled a great stone to the entrance of the tomb, and departed. Mark 16:1-4: "And when the sabbath was past, Mary Magdalene, and Mary the mother of James, and Salome, brought spices, so that they might go and anoint him. And very early on the first day of the week they went to the tomb when the sun had risen. And they were saying to one another, 'Who will roll away the stone for us from the door of the tomb?' And looking up, they saw that the stone was rolled back; for it was very large."

21. Matt. 27:62-6: "Next day, that is after the day of Preparation, the chief priests and the Pharisees gathered before Pilate and said, 'Sir, we remember how that impostor said, while he was still alive, "After three days I will rise again." Therefore order the tomb to be made secure until the third day, lest his disciples go and steal him away, and tell the people, "He has risen from the dead," and the last fraud will be worse than the first.' Pilate said to them, 'You have a guard of soldiers go, make it as secure as you can.' So they went and made the tomb secure by sealing the stone and setting a guard."

22. Matt. 28:1-10: "Now after the sabbath, toward the dawn of the first day of the week Mary Magdalene and the other Mary went to see the tomb. And behold, there was a great earthquake; for an angel of the Lord descended from heaven and came and rolled back the stone, and set upon it. His appearance was like lightning, and his raiment white as snow. And for fear of him the guards trembled and became like dead men. But the angel said to the women, 'Do not be afraid; for I know that you seek Jesus who was crucified. He is not here; for he is risen, as he said. Come, see the place where he lay. Then go quickly and tell his disciples that he has risen from the dead, and behold, he is going before you to Galilee; there you will see him. Lo, I have told you.' So they departed quickly from the tomb with fear and great joy, and ran to tell his disciples. And behold, Jesus met them and said, 'Hail!' And they came up and took hold of his feet and worshiped him. Then Jesus said to them, 'Do not be afraid; go and tell my brothers to go to Galilee, and there they will see me.'"

23. Luke 24:36-43: "As they were saying this, Jesus himself stood among them. But they were startled and frightened and supposed that they saw a spirit. And he said to them, 'Why are you troubled, and why do questionnings rise in your hearts? See my hands and my feet, that it is I myself; handle me, and see; for a spirit has not flesh and bones as you see that I have. And while they still disbelieved for joy, and wondered, he said to them, 'Have you anything here to eat?' They gave him a piece of broiled fish, and he took it and ate before them." John 20:25-28: "So the other disciples told him, 'We have seen the Lord.' But he said to them, 'Unless I see in his hands the prints of the nails, and place my finger in the mark of the nails, and place my hand in his side, I will not believe.' Eight days later, his disciples were again in the house, and Thomas was with them. The doors were shut, but Jesus came and stood among them, and said, 'Peace be with you.' Then he said to Thomas, 'Put your finger here, and see my hands; and put out your hand, and place it in my side; do not be faithless, but believe-ing.' Thomas answered him, 'My Lord and my God.'

24. See Matt. 28; Luke 24; John 20,21.

25. Mark 16:15-16 (traditional statement of the Great Commission); cf. parallel passage in Matthew.

26. See Luke 22:54-62.

27. John 19:32-35: "So the soldiers came and broke the legs of the first, and of the other who had been crucified with him; but when they came to Jesus and saw that he was already dead, they did not break his legs. But one of the soldiers pierced his side with a spear, and at once there came out blood and water."

28. Sec. X ("Of Miracles"). The Enquiry is contained in Burtt's English Philosophers from Bacon to Mill (1939).

29. See C. S. Lewis, Miracles, esp. Chs. VIII and XIII.

30. Writing as late as 1902, William James says (The Varieties of Religious Experience (Modern Library ed.), pp. 483-4): "The God whom science recognizes must be a God of universal laws exclusively, a God who does wholesale, not a retail business."

31. Carnell, op. cit., p. 258.

* * *

N.B. The best available work on the historicity of the Gospel records is F. F. Bruce, The New Testament Documents: Are They Reliable? This is available in paperback, and well worth purchasing.

A CRITICAL EXAMINATION OF EMIL BRUNNER'S *THE DIVINE IMPERATIVE*, BK. III

The Content of Book III of "The Divine Imperative"

Those who have read one or more of Professor Brunner's publications--whether in the original German or in authorized English translation--need not be told that the author's style is so lucid and his organization of material so well conceived that detailed *précis* of his works have doubtful value. The present examination of *The Divine Imperative*, Book III, does not, therefore, attempt to provide a complete restatement of the contents of the volume; yet, because accurate exposition is the only sound basis for meaningful criticism, a summary of the author's argument and a review of the high points of his presentation will be set forth before proceeding to a critique of the work.

The title of Book III of *The Divine Imperative* indicates the book's subject-matter: "The Orders," i.e., the Divine orders, or orders of Creation (*Schöpfungsordnungen*). For Brunner's definition of the term "orders," one should turn first to Chapter 14 of Book I, where the following explanation is given:[1]

> It is characteristic of our present existence (as an actuality created by God, and yet sinful) that it is embedded in a framework of "orders" of a most varied kind. The individual human being does not enter into the sphere of social and natural relations as a free master of himself but, as a psycho-physical and historical being, he is born into the life which is already present, and--as always--already "ordered," and he grows--at first instinctively, more or less unconsciously, within this "organism" composed of a people and of humanity as a whole, as one of its "members." When conscious self-determination and faith awaken, man has already been moulded both by nature and by history, he has already been absorbed into the intricate web of human life with its manifold claims; duties of all kinds chain him to a certain way of living; he is burdened and tied down by a thousand ties.

According to Brunner, then, an order is first and foremost a necessary configuration of human existence, within which the individual finds himself by the very fact of his humanity. Werner Elert likewise points up this characteristic of the orders when he asserts that they "have validity in individual situations" and that their "existential orderliness always becomes apparent in the fact that they allow no substitution."[2] But something more is involved in the concept of the orders. In the Introduction to Book III, Brunner writes: "We see not merely particular spheres of life within which we are to act, but orders in accordance with which we have to act, because in them, even if only in a fragmentary and indirect way, God's Will meets us. Hence we call them 'Divine orders'" (p. 291). Thus the orders must be viewed not only as structures required by the nature of human life, but also as areas in which God meets man and requires of him responsible existence. Elert has this latter aspect in mind when he states that the "formal criterion" of the orders is "the fact that man can break them and that they are therefore subject to divine legislation."[3]

As background for his discussion of the particular Divine orders, Brunner begins Book III with a general treatment of "The Individual, the Community, and the Orders of Society." Here he points out that the traditional opposition between individualism and corporate life is a false dichotomy which can be solved only in the agape-love of the Christian faith; for "real communio is simply and solely love without conditions, which is only possible in reply to God's way of loving, which is without conditions," and "the individual essence of a human being only prospers where its development is not deliberately sought" (pp. 306, 307). The author deals in a very penetrating manner with the fundamental ethical problem of the relation between God, the neighbor, and the self; he affirms correctly that "there are no duties towards God, in the way in which there are duties towards our neighbour. We do not bring anything to God, we simply receive" (p. 310),[4] and he notes that "the command to love one's neighbour 'as oneself' is not to be understood as an imperative but as an indicative" (p. 316).[5] The fact that "the distinctive mark of the Christian Ethos--not merely of the Middle Ages, with its ascetic errors, but also of Primitive Christianity and of all genuine Christianity--is passive love, self-sacrificing surrender--which, from the psychological point of view is the highest activity" leads one to ask, "What am I to do if these [individual neighbor-] claims conflict with each other ?" (p. 328). The answer to this question necessarily involves the author in the whole problem of the orders--within which responsible human action is to be carried out. The various orders, being the product of Divine creation and yet also suffering from sinful human perversion, are all to be viewed by the Christian with "a watchful, aggressive, determined attitude of hostility to all that is contrary to the will of God within human life; but this critical and reforming temper must always be based upon a grateful acceptance of human life, coupled with a readiness to serve wherever we may be" (p. 338). At this point the author has laid a sufficient foundation for discussing each of the Divine orders individually.

Marriage and family are treated first. Brunner begins by setting forth a methodological principle which will govern his discussion both of this order and of the others to follow:

> Just as it is useless to appeal to tradition on this question, so also it is useless to appeal to isolated passages in the Bible. Devotees of the literalist interpretation of the Bible are particularly prone to this practice, especially on this question, but such procedure reveals a very unevangelical, legalistic idea of the authority of the Bible. . . . We may . . . demand of a theological ethic that it should not make its statements as apodictic doctrines without considering whether they have any relation to human reality or not, but that it should develop its doctrines in view of reality, and that means the reality of the present day. (Pp. 341-42.)

The case for monogamy is built on two arguments, one objective, the other subjective. The former presents what Brunner terms a "trinity of being"--the fact "that every human being is irrevocably the child of one man and one woman, that every father, with this woman, and every mother, with this man, is, irrevocably, the father and the mother of this child" (p. 345). The subjective argument for monogamy is the assertion that "genuine natural love is in its essence monistic" (p. 347). These objective and subjective considerations are bound together in the concept of Divine Creation. "Only where--in the recognition of the order of creation--husband and wife bind themselves together in love and know themselves bound--marriage means 'binding'--has a marriage (on its subjective as well as on its objective side) been 'concluded'" (p. 348). Such marriage serves as "a symbol and a way of approach to true community" (p. 350). Human sin colors the picture, however; one must recognize that marriage is indeed a remedium concupiscentiae, and that monogamy "is the optimum which, as experience has proved, lies between complete asceticism and a form of sex relation which is more accommodating to the sex desire" (p. 352). Moreover, since in thought if not in actual deed "we are all adulterers, the difference between the different orders of the sex relation become relative" (p. 353). This latter conclusion leads logically to such statements as the following: "It is conceivable that a case might arise in which, in order to obey the Divine Command, one might have to act 'against the law.' Such a case, for instance, would occur if the dissolution of a marriage had become a duty" (p. 354). "A marriage without love, and this means also without sex attraction, should never be contracted. . . . For the sake of the love of our neighbour the only moral thing to do is to dissolve a marriage of this kind" (p. 361). "The worth of a law is to be measured not by its 'strictness' in the abstract sense, but by the wisdom with which the legislation is adjusted to reality, in order to attain a maximum of social health and decency. From this point of view it is even possible that the State may have to resolve to renounce the exclusive protection of monogamous marriage, and be compelled to extend it to sex relations which are still further removed from monogamous marriage, since, in any case, the present form of marriage can be easily dissolved" (p. 363). "It must certainly be admitted that the gratifying decline in the number of prostitutes is due in whole or in part to the increase in the practice of free relationships among 'decent people'" (p. 653). Brunner concludes his discussion of the order of marriage and the family with a plea for "responsible motherhood" (in reference to the birth-control issue), for an understanding of the economic difficulties which today confront young people seeking marriage, and for a recognition of the complex role which modern Western civilization has forced upon both the wife and the unmarried woman.[6]

The economic order is next examined. The author begins by stressing the basic principles that God wills that men work; that He also desires that they experience sufficient rest and constructive recreation; and that He regards as demonic any unrestrained attempt to dominate the world or any form of enslavement to the things of this world. "It is essential to the Divine purpose of labour that labour can only make people happy in so far as it fulfils its purpose, that is, in so far as it helps man to be truly man, and serves the purpose of life in community" (p. 393). The economic order--involving the soil, tools, human workers, finished goods, and the consumption of these goods--is both the product of Divine creation ("If any will not work, neither let him eat"--II Thess. 3:10), and an area in which sin has particular power ("On the one hand, it has been spoilt by its false tendency to become an end in itself, and on the other by egoistic exploitation by the individual which always works out both as sin and as a curse"--p. 399). Granting this, however, "the first question the Christian ought to ask in this economic world should not be: 'How can I alter it?' but: 'How can I serve within it?'" (p. 401). Brunner answers this latter question via three principles: (1) "Man is not to engage in economic activity for its own sake, but in order to live, to live in a human way" (p. 402). (2) "The economic system should never be regarded merely as an individual concern, but also as the concern of the community" (p. 404). It follows from this, of course, that private property can per se neither be affirmed nor be denied. (3) "Every person capable of rendering service is under an obligation to render service" (p. 406). As a means of adjusting the "comparative monopolies" which exist in the economic sphere due to differences among individuals and among groups, the capitalistic system is vigorously rejected as the "objectification of the striving for gain" (p. 419 - from Sombart in the Handwörterbuch der Soziologie). Capitalism is "irresponsibility developed into a system" (p. 423); yet a Christian must not shirk his economic responsibility even where this system is present, for "none of us knows whether he will ever know any better order" (p. 424). Communism offers no more desirable economic Weltanschauung, for "it is just as much opposed to the Divine order in creation as its counterpart; it is the same system, with the signs reversed" (p. 427).[7] Certain socialistic approaches (e.g., the English consumers' Co-operative and the Danish agricultural producers' co-operative Movement--see p. 670) offer fruitful suggestions toward a more Christian economic approach; however, we should never allow ourselves to think that any economic program--regardless of its attractiveness--can cancel out the radical selfishness of fallen man. Within whatever economic system the Church finds itself, it is called to preach the Gospel, engage in social service, offer prophetic criticism of existing evils and idols, and present an example of genuine community based on love.

The order of the State now comes under discussion. The author's concern is not with political theory (the Idea of the State--whether Positivistic, Idealistic, or Romantic), but with political reality; and in every actual State three elements exist: community, disciplinary order, and the exercise of power. True community is of course not created by the State, for compulsion, not love, is its principle of action; yet the State, like the family, provides men with a faint approximation of the interdependent life which characterizes God's Kingdom. The nature of the State as the Divine institution of the power of order is evidenced by its numinous authority--expressed in rational legislation and in irrational power. And it is axiomatic that "the greater the power of the State, and the certainty that every one who breaks the law will be dealt with by the law, the less will the power of coercion be felt" (p. 453).[8] However, the State has no right to assume totalitarian control over the other orders.[9] "A too close connection with the State, or even a subordination in principle of these spheres of life to the State, must take away their meaning and destroy their vitality; and--this should be noted as very significant--it must also destroy the force and meaning of the State" (p. 458). Brunner holds that "in itself there is no Christian and non-Christian form of the State" (p. 465); whether one proceeds from the standpoint of the twofold purpose of the State (to achieve both the most competent form of government and the maximum degree of community), or from the fact of sin and evil in the State, one is forced to conclude that "neither complete autocracy nor unqualified government by the people, that is, democracy (which is the ideal of Liberalism), can, as a rule, be the right form of government" (p. 466). The author rejects absolute pacifism as not taking into account the extent of human depravity, but suggests that modern war may have become a greater evil than any alternative to it. With regard to the penal treatment of criminals, Brunner declares that punishments must expiate the wrongs both of society as a whole and of the lawbreakers themselves; he believes that "forcible education" (p. 477) at state expense is the best means of achieving this.

The several cultural orders are next analyzed.[10] Here especially Christian faith must perform its regulative function, for "the symbol of all actual--but not true--creation of culture is the Tower of Babel" (p. 488). The particular danger inherent in science is its "one-sided emphasis on the freedom of man from the world, without any consideration for the fact that man belongs to the world" (p. 492). Art, on the other hand, can easily lend support to mysticism and pantheism; it is often "sought because it does not demand decision, as faith does, but merely the attitude of a spectator, or of one who is swayed hither and thither by the artistic influences around him" (p. 500). To be sure, science and art, like the other orders, are Divine gifts and tasks; Christians are to participate in them with thankfulness to God and in reliance upon His grace. With respect to education, Brunner makes several interesting points:[11] The Idealistic philosophy of education needs to be corrected and supplemented by the Christian stress on integrating the individual into the community and increasing his sense of personal responsibility toward his fellows. Education is primarily the concern of the family--not of the school, or even of the State; indeed, "the State as a legal organization requires centralization, the building up from above, downwards. Culture, which begins, essentially, with the individual, and as a fellowship, needs the intimacy of the small group, requires to be built up from below" (p. 513). The Church, though it should employ sound pedagogical method, is "not an education institution, but it is the community of the redeemed" (p. 511). The "free forms of community" (friendship, custom, public opinion) receive brief treatment. "As friendship is the nearest approach of the natural spiritual element to personal community, so, on the other hand, custom is the impersonal medium between the truly ethical and the natural" (p. 519). Public opinion is "a kind of secular parallel to the 'invisible Church'" (p. 521), and "it is the duty of Christendom to create public opinion, in the sense that through it and in it Christ should exercise His Sovereignty even over those who do not know Him, so far as this is possible" (ibid.).

Lastly, Brunner deals with the Church as a Divine order. He defines the Church by combining the three classic statements of its nature: coetus electorum; communio sanctorum; corpus Christi; and at the same time he makes quite clear that "the Church and perfection are mutually exclusive ideas; the Church is the community of those who are still sinners" (p. 526). This Divine-human institution is characterized primarily by the preaching and believing of the Word (even where only two or three are gathered); but it must also move out into the community of faith with other believers (here the Sacraments and Church order enter the picture) and into a community of love with those who do not believe (here the missionary effort and social service come into play). Brunner distinguishes between the "Church of faith" and the "worshipping community"; the former "makes its influence felt beyond the bounds of the worshipping community in the natural secular relations between human beings, in the natural orders of the family, the economic order, the State and culture" (p. 535). Church discipline is necessary to prevent the Church as worshipping community from becoming absorbed in the world. The significance of the worshipping community lies in the fact that it "is the preferred, distinctive necessary order, which in far greater measure than the other orders, because in more direct and necessary connexion with it, serves the Church of faith" (p. 538). Church union "ought never to be achieved at the expense of the primary element; the primary element is that the local congregation should fulfil its particular calling, as fully as it possibly can, a calling which is unique and wholly peculiar to itself" (p. 540). No denomination or type of Church-State relationship (State Church, National Church, Free Church) can honestly be considered the "true" Church--for sin exists in all. Sin within the churches shows itself especially in legalism--which either "confuses the letter of Scripture with the Word of God" (p. 545) or blurs "the distinction between the human confession of faith (dogma) and the Word of God" (ibid.), or identifies ecclesiastical legislation ("canon law") or church organization with the Word of God. "True ecclesiasticism . . . consists in the fact that the divine and the human are not separated, but also that they are not regarded as identical with one another" (p. 562). "False churchmanship, or clericalism," on the other hand, "does not consist in an excessive concern for the visible Church, but it is churchmanship which lacks any real foundation because it seeks that foundation in itself. . . . The watchword of genuine churchmanship is never 'the Church,' but always and only 'Jesus Christ'" (pp. 565-66).

A Critique of Book III of "The Divine Imperative"

Brunner's analysis of the Divine orders is almost sure to leave the Christian reader with two equally strong, but conflicting, impressions. One of these is that in many respects the author succeeds wonderfully in showing the application of the Christian message to the real world of human experience. When he deals with science and art, Brunner does not attempt to force from the Christian revelation standards of propositional truth or of aesthetic value by which to judge the work of scholars, researchers, and artists.[12] In his presentation of the political and economic orders, he wisely observes the sin rampant in all the various human panaceas and programs, and therefore refuses to justify any existing economic or political system from the standpoint of Christ's Gospel.[13] In all these areas the author employs the Christian message as a regulative principle, thereby pointing up the idolatrous tendencies which inhere in each of them; yet at the same time he stresses the responsibility which believers have to enter these spheres and serve the Creator to the best of their ability in them.

But this positive impression is not the only one which the Christian reader carries away with him after studying The Divine Imperative, Book III. Brunner's discussion of the Church as a Divine order is characterized by an unfortunate vagueness. No denomination, in his opinion, deserves the designation of the "true" Church; with this almost all

Protestant Christians would agree, but since every Christian is duty-bound to align himself with other believers in a worshipping community, some criteria should be presented for choosing among the welter of denominational bodies. Brunner gives no such criteria; his assertion that the sine qua non of the Church is the preaching of the Word offers little help, for he cautions us not to confuse the letter of Scripture, or confessions of faith, with that Word. Similar vagueness is manifested in his attitude toward church union. No principles of union are stated; in fact, as we have seen, the author recommends that such union ought not to be considered as important as the local congregation's fulfilment of its "wholly peculiar" calling. Brunner's discussion of the marital order reveals further difficulties. From the truth that we are all adulterers, if only in thought, the author makes the questionable deductions that divorce is normally justifiable when marriage has occurred "without sex attraction," and that the State would be right in renouncing "the exclusive protection of monogamous marriage" if by doing so greater "social health and decency" would be promoted.

How are we to view such doubtful or inadequate arguments as those just cited? Do we have here merely isolated examples of lapsus theologi? Or is there a more basic explanation for the difficulties in certain areas of Brunner's presentation, as contrasted with a thoroughgoing soundness in other areas? I believe that a fundamental problem lies at the root of Brunner's treatment of the orders--a problem which exists also in more than a few other analyses of the Schöpfungsordnungen.

The problem of which I speak has to do with the relationship between the two defining characteristics of an order which were stated at the outset of this paper. Brunner and Elert (and other theologians who have dealt with the orders) agree that an order is (1) a necessary configuration of human existence, and (2) an area of life in which God encounters man and requires of him responsible existence. Now a basic question (given no precise answer by Brunner) is: How does one determine the proper content of an order--i.e., the content which accords with the Divine Will? Is the proper content of an order already inherent in it as a necessary structure of existence? Or does the "necessity" of the orders refer merely to their form (their proper content being determined only by Special Revelation)? Or does the proper content of an order stem in part from the already-existing order, and in part also from God's revealed Will? If the latter is the correct answer, what is the final arbiter when the actually-existing order and God's Revelation concerning that order are at variance? The importance of this problem becomes evident when one realizes that by assuming no more than a natural content for the political order, Gogarten and other German theologians of the Third Reich concluded that the Nazi régime was consistent with God's Will; and that by assuming a revealed content for the artistic order, Zwingli and others refused to allow music to be employed in Divine services.

The final determinative of the content of an order must be the Divine Revelation--for the orders have been, and continue to be, corrupted by sin. Once this latter fact is admitted, it necessarily follows that the existing content of an order need not be identical with God's Will for that order; and that without some Word from outside the orders themselves, it would forever be impossible to determine their proper content. However, this does not say that God's Revelation has fully or equally outlined the proper content of each order; it simply says that wherever the Revelation does speak with regard to an order, its assertions must be taken as final.

Brunner, however, does not approach the orders with this principle as his guide. His fear of being classed with Biblical literalists and fundamentalists causes him again and again to warn that "the Bible itself is not simply the Word of God" (p. 528),[14] and to base his statements with regard to the proper content of the orders not principally upon Scriptural ground, but primarily upon "the reality of the present day" (p. 342).[15] The result is not particularly serious where Scripture is silent or virtually silent on the content of an order, but it becomes a matter of real concern where Scripture makes detailed apodictic assertions on the Divine Will for an order. And when does Scripture speak on the content of orders? Brunner himself suggests the answer in another connection when he writes: "The further the sphere of science is from the personal sphere the more autonomous does the science become, the more legitimate is its abstract conception of scientific law; the nearer it is to the personal sphere, the more the real human being needs to be known, the more faith gains not merely a regulative but a constitutive significance" (p. 496). A careful study of Scriptural statements bearing directly on the orders will show, I am convinced, that the more personal the order, the more the Christian Revelation has to say about its proper content; and the less personal the order, the less the Bible deals with its content. Brunner's discussion of the orders is, then, understandably strongest where the orders are the most impersonal (science, art, the State, economics)--where, in other words, the content of the orders is not a matter of Revelation, and where faith acts largely as a regulative, not a constitutive, principle. And Brunner's presentation is weakest, as we have seen, in the highly personal orders of the Church and the family, where Scripture has much to say in criticism of the current content of these orders.

More specifically: If the orders are arranged in a continuum from less personal to more personal, it will be seen that the single continuum represents both an increasing amount of Scriptural teaching on the proper content of the orders, and a decreasing strength in Brunner's treatment of these same Divine configurations.

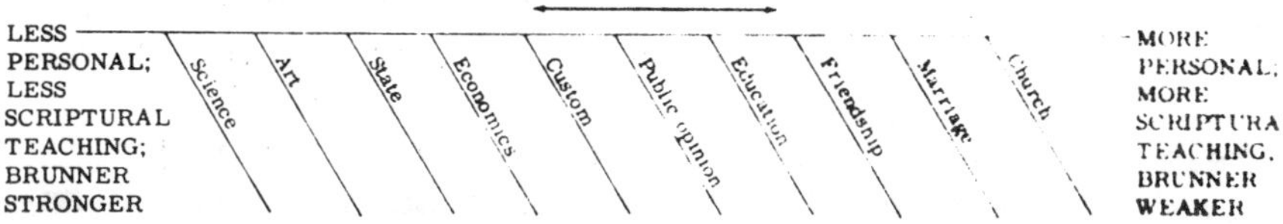

Where science and art are involved, Scripture presents only simple regulative principles, e.g., "Avoid the . . . contradictions of what is falsely called knowledge, for by professing it some have missed the mark as regards the faith" (I Tim. 6:20-21),[16] and "Little children, keep yourselves from idols" (I Jn. 5:21). Such principles as these Brunner has competently developed in The Divine Imperative, Book III. With regard to the slightly less impersonal realms of the State and economics, Scripture is only a bit more full in its assertions (Rom. 13:1-7 and similar passages; Acts 5:29; II Thess. 3:10); these passages, though of vital importance, are still regulative, not constitutive, in character, and Brunner, as we have seen, presents their implications quite effectively. Custom Brunner rightly calls "the impersonal medium between the truly ethical and the natural" (p. 519), and here again Scripture does not attempt to set down absolute rules as to proper or improper customs;[17] the regulative principle is, "Whether you eat or drink, or whatever you do, do all to the glory of God" (I Cor. 10:31). Brunner catches the spirit of this Apostolic approach when he writes, "It should be an urgent concern of the Church that custom should be moulded into shape as a deposit of faith and not of unbelief, of personal responsibility and not of irresponsibility" (p. 519). Unfortunately, however, he does not in this connection work out the full implications of such a passage as Phil. 4:8.

The Christian Revelation is at many points concerned with public opinion--that "secular parallel to the 'invisible Church.'"

Again and again the New Testament exhorts Christians to conduct themselves in the world in such a way that the best possible climate of opinion is created for the furtherance of God's Kingdom; such a verse as Mt. 5:16 is representative: "Let your light so shine before men, that they may see your good works and give glory to your Father who is in heaven" (cf. also Phil. 1:27; II Cor. 6:3-8). Brunner, however, in his brief discussion of public opinion, does not directly present any Biblical teaching on the subject. "Education," the author agrees, in that it "has more to do with the personal centre than any other aspect of cultural life, has a particularly close connexion with faith or with its opposite" (p. 507), but he does not apparently recognize the wealth of Scriptural material on this very personal sphere of life. Brunner stresses as the proper aim of education "integrating the individual into the community and increasing his sense of personal responsibility toward his fellows"--goals which closely parallel those of American progressive educationists. The Biblical Revelation, on the other hand, emphasizes the educational importance of thoroughly comprehending the objective works of God in nature and history (Deut. 6:6-7; Ps. 104; II Tim. 2:15, 3:14-17). Community and responsibility are of course genuine Biblical concerns, but from the standpoint of the "fruits of the Spirit," not as an educational goal. The sphere of friendship thrusts us even more into the personal realm, and by that very fact it places us more definitely within the area of Scriptural teaching. The close connection between philia (love as friendship) and agape is evidenced by Jn. 21:15-17 (Gk. txt.); and the New Testament tells us that our closest associations should be made within the circle of true believers (II Cor. 6:14ff.; II Jn. 10-11), but also that we should seek worldly friends for the sake of spiritual goals (Lk. 16:9). These constitutive principles receive no mention in Brunner's work.

The marital order is more personal in character than any other order except the Church (cf. Eph. 5:23-32), and Scripture makes far more constitutive assertions about it than with regard to the configurations to the left of it in the continuum given above. Monogamy was instituted prior to the Fall; polygamy, concubinage, and easy divorce were permitted under the Old Covenant only due to the hardness of human hearts (Mk. 10:2-12; Mt. 19:3-9), and with the coming of Christ, who fulfilled the Law, the situation is radically and unalterably changed (Mt. 5:27-32). The content of the marital order is clearly defined by Revelation--it is permanent monogamy; and current cultural trends, population statistics, etc. have nothing to do with the issue. The fact that all are adulterers before God because of sins of the heart in no way provides an escape-hatch for church or state policy on the marriage and divorce problem. We must find our solutions within the framework of Scriptural teaching, not by circumventing it. More time spent in evangelism, premarital counselling, sex education, etc., and less on speculations concerning polygamous solutions to a high female birthrate, and the hygenic advantages of pre-marital intimacies among "decent people," will accord better with the total Christian ethos.

The most personal of the Divine orders is the Church, for through it men enter into a living, intimate relationship with the Lord of the universe. The Christian Revelation sets forth the content of this Church in greater detail than it does for any of the other orders. Brunner instinctively recognizes this when he terms this order "the Church," and not simply "Religion." From the purely natural viewpoint, one might well assert that Religion, but not the Christian Church, is a necessary configuration of existence for human beings. Only Revelation tells us that one religion alone--Christianity--is truly worthy of the designation "Divine order" (Jn. 14:6; Acts 4:12)--even as only that same Christian Revelation tells us that one form of marriage alone--monogamy--is Divinely ordered. But our author does not attempt rigorously to examine Scriptural teaching on the Church; instead he concentrates on the Church as one actually finds it in the world, as if its legitimate content can be determined naturally like that of science or the State--as if Scripture sets up only regulative principles to govern the Church's life. Brunner presents the work of the local congregation as of more fundamental significance than the larger perspective of church cooperation and world-wide witness; yet Scripture clearly stresses the latter to a much greater degree than the former (Jn. 17:20-21; Mt. 28:18-20; Acts 1:7-8). Moreover, the New Testament Revelation is in no sense indifferent to the problem of the "true" Church; true doctrine determines the truth of a church body (Acts 2:42; Gal. 1:6-9); and it is safe to say that if Christians were really convinced of this, efforts in the ecumenical direction might not be quite as frustrating as they have been in the past.

In conclusion, then, the central point growing out of this critique may well be reiterated, namely, that it is not legalism, or bibliolatry, or fundamentalism to take the Scriptural Revelation seriously when it speaks--to let "our consciences become captive to the Word of God," both in the written and in the living sense. Thomas Campbell's motto provides an excellent guide for all those who would understand the Divine orders: "Where the Scriptures speak, we speak; where the Scriptures are silent, we are silent."[18]

NOTES

1. Emil Brunner, The Divine Imperative, tr. by Olive Wyon (Philadelphia, Westminster Press, c1947), p. 140. All succeeding page references to The Divine Imperative assume this edition.

2. Werner Elert, The Christian Ethos, tr. by Carl J. Schindler (Philadelphia, Muhlenberg Press, c1957), p. 79. (A 2d and revised edition of this translation has now been published.)

3. Elert, op. cit., p. 78.

4. Cf. Paul Ramsey, Basic Christian Ethics (New York, Scribner, c1950), pp. 116ff. ("Is Love for God Part of the Meaning of Christian Love?").

5. Ramsey emphasizes this also: "Pointing to the existence of self-love is one thing, making it an injunction would be another. The words, 'You shall love your neighbor as yourself,' certainly contain a reference to love for self, yet they by no means include a commandment, 'You shall love yourself'" (op. cit., p. 100).

6. These latter issues are also carefully examined by Harold Haas in his chapter on "Christian Faith and Family Life" in Christian Social Responsibility, Vol. III (Life in Community), ed. by Harold C. Letts (Philadelphia, Muhlenberg Press, c1957), pp. 148ff.

7. The fundamental individualism at the root of Marxist Communism as well as of Western Capitalism is seldom noticed. Karl Löwith (professor of history at Heidelberg) points up this individualism when he writes, "In a perfect communist commonwealth each individual has realized his human essence as a common sociopolitical existence" (Meaning in History [Chicago, University of Chicago Phoenix Books, c1949], p. 50).

8. Cf. the principle stated in Justinian's Institutes: "Melius

est in tempore occurrere, quam post causam vulneratam remedium quaerere" (2 Inst. 299).

9. For thought-provoking literary depictations of such totalitarianisms, see Thomas Hobbes' Leviathan and George Orwell's 1984.

10. A very valuable work on this subject is Emile Cailliet's The Christian Approach to Culture (New York, Abingdon-Cokesbury, c1953).

11. Note in this connection Gordon H. Clark's A Christian Philosophy of Education (Grand Rapids, Eerdmans, 1946).

12. Fundamentalists have been especially prone to judge scientific work by what they believe to be the "truth of revelation"; Calvinists have done the same in the artistic realm.

13. Brunner thus does not fall into the error committed by the many theologians who have identified an economic system (Capitalism, Communism, etc.) or a political system (Nazism, Americanism, etc.) with the Christian faith. C. S. Lewis sums up this failing when he has Screwtape write: "The real trouble about the set your patient is living in is that it is merely Christian. . . . What we want, if men become Christians at all, is to keep them in the state of mind I call 'Christianity And.' You know--Christianity and the Crisis, Christianity and the New Psychology, Christianity and the New Order. . . . Substitute for the faith itself some Fashion with a Christian colouring" (The Screwtape Letters [New York, Macmillan, 1944], p. 126).

14. This distinction, frequently made today (e.g. by Joseph Sittler among Lutherans), between the Scriptures and the living Word of God (Christ) is very misleading and results in more difficulties than it resolves. The only "living Word" any Christian knows is the Word whose characteristics are set forth in the "written Word"; any inner experience of Christ which contradicts the Christ of Revelation is, ipso facto, not the real Christ. Moreover, the Bible does not merely contain the Word of God, it is the Word of God--otherwise, as the Lutheran Confessions have asserted unequivocally (Formula of Concord, para. 1), it could not be the standard by which all other writings and teachings are to be judged, but would itself have to be judged by some

other standard. Professor Lavik correctly notes that the Brunner-Sittler view "assumes as a philosophic and rationalistic principle that the finite is not capable of the infinite (finitum non est capax infiniti)"--a tenet which harks back to Greek philosophical conceptions of the Absolute (John R. Lavik, The Christian Church in a Secularized World [Minneapolis, Augsburg, c1952], p. 73). Brunner recognizes that he deviates from the Reformers on this matter; he writes: "This is the point at which the theology and the Church of the present day must move most definitely away from the view of the Reformers. . . . Calvin . . . and Luther . . . at this point . . . were more closely bound by the ecclesiastical tradition than we have any right to be" (p. 716). Recent Lutheran doctrinal affirmations have fortunately followed the Reformers and not the Neo-Orthodox; the Federation of Evangelical Lutheran Churches in India stated in 1951: "All believers will, as our Lord and His apostles did with regard to the Holy Scriptures of the Old Testament, listen to every word and passage of the biblical text with the reverent faith that is due to the holy Word of God" (Doctrinal Statement Presenting the Confessional Basis of the Federation of Evangelical Lutheran Churches in India [Guntur, India, Lutheran Press, 1951], p. 14).

15. The basic role to be played in theology by "the reality of the present day" is, as Tillich so well points out, not to offer theological solutions in contradistinction to those of Revelation, but to reveal the vital and truly significant questions and problems to which Revelation must supply the answers. See Paul Tillich, Systematic Theology, Vol. I (Chicago, University of Chicago Press, c1951), pp. 3 ff.

16. Scripture does not necessarily present constitutive scientific data in such passages as Gen. 1-2. The Hebrew employed in the Creation account is highly poetic in character, and the clear intention of the writer is theological, not cosmological or scientific.

17. One might at first glance think that the New Testament makes a considerable number of apodictic, constitutive assertions with regard to customs (e.g. the "braided hair" passages--I Tim. 2:9; I Pet. 3:2-3). Here, however, the principle applies in Biblical interpretation which has been universally accepted in Anglo-American common law: "The reasoning, illustrations, or references contained in the

opinion of a court are not authority, not precedent, but only the points in judgment arising in the particular case before the court" (L. & N.R.R. Co. v. County Court of Davidson County, 1 Sneed [Tenn.] 637). The New Testament writers use such matters as braided hair simply as examples to illustrate their point that women "should adorn themselves modestly and sensibly in seemly apparel."

18. Quoted by Kenneth Scott Latourette, A History of Christianity (New York, Harper, c1953), p. 1042.

PART FOUR

POSITIVE LAW AND ETERNAL LAW

A. Case Study: Abortion

AMA Symposium: "When Does Life Begin?", 214 *Journal of the American Medical Association* 1893.

J. W. Montgomery, "The Christian View": from *Birth Control and the Christian*, ed. W. O. Spitzer and C. L. Saylor (Wheaton, Ill.: Tyndale; London: Coverdale, 1969), pp. 67-89.

Questions and Answers

When Does Life Begin?

Q *Much of the debate that has been provoked by the legalization of abortions in a number of states centers about the question: "When does life begin?" Judging from what I have heard and read, objective opinions on this complex question are not readily found. Specifically, would you define life as beginning (1) with the first cell that forms when sperm and egg meet, or (2) when the cell has demonstrated life with the first cell division, or (3) with the first heart beat, or (4) when the first wave activity can be demonstrated on the electroencephalogram, or (5) at the first possible time when life can be sustained outside the uterus or (6) when? Would it be possible for the American Medical Association to help shed some light on one of the most sensitive problems confronting our contemporary society?*

MD, Ohio

THIS QUESTION WAS REFERRED TO SIX CONSULTANTS: A LAWYER; PROTESTANT, CATHOLIC, AND JEWISH THEOLOGIANS; A BEHAVIORAL SCIENTIST; AND AN OBSTETRICIAN-GYNECOLOGIST, WHOSE DISCUSSIONS, RESPECTIVELY, ARE AS FOLLOWS:

A In most legal systems, legal personality begins at live birth.[1 (p579)] However, there are several important exceptions to this general rule, such as the law of property which grants to a fetus yet unborn a conditional legal personality. That is to say, if a fetus is subsequently born alive it may immediately receive a legacy, obtain an injunction, have a guardian, or even be an executor, even though it was, at the critical moment, en ventre sa mère.

Moreover, according to a steadily growing number of recent cases in the area of tort law, a fetus can maintain an action for the death of a parent while it is still in utero. It has also been recently held by several courts that an action can be maintained on behalf of a child who was born deformed because of prenatal injuries negligently inflicted upon it; and, that an action can be maintained against a tort-feasor if the child dies—regardless of whether the death occurred before or after birth. Depending therefore on the particular jurisdiction involved, if the law of torts is concerned, human life may begin as soon as the child is capable of living apart from its mother (viable). Moreover, as of early 1965 eight American courts when dealing with cases in tort law followed a biological approach and now hold that life begins at conception; thereby according legal personality to the zygote.[1 (pp589-590)]

In the area of criminal law there is yet another exception to the general statement that life begins at birth, in that our state laws customarily define homicide as the killing of a fetus after it is viable.

Finally, it should be understood that in addition to the fact that the law first asks for what purpose we wish to know when life begins, our legal system proceeds on an ad hoc basis. Consequently, we cannot positively say that a future ruling will follow an earlier decision.

DOUGLAS STRIPP, Attorney at Law
Kansas City, Mo

1. *The Unborn Plaintiff*. Michigan Law Review, 63, 1965.

A Human life can, of course, be arbitrarily "defined" to begin at any of the points mentioned. The ancient common law emphasis on "quickening" illustrates how arbitrary such definitions often are, and how pragmatic are the considerations giving rise to them (in this case, workable sanctions against socially harmful abortion).

The medical profession and the Christian religion, however, are so fully committed to the irreducible dignity and worth of individual human life that neither can be satisfied with arbitrary or pragmatic definitions capable of investing the nonhuman with humanity or of lowering the genuinely human to subhuman status. Though variations in theological and medical judgment can certainly be observed historically on the question, it is remarkable how closely biblical teaching (Exodus 21:22-25)[1] and scientific evidence today enter into accord on the absolute cruciality of egg-and-sperm union as the point of origin of individual human life as discussed by Dr. Melville Vincent and myself in separate symposium papers for the Christian Medical Society.[1]

The force of such biblical passages as Psalms 51:5 and Luke 1:15,41 is entirely consistent with current biological evidence as summarized, for example, by Jules Carles, director of research at France's National Center for Scientific Research (CNRS):

> This first cell [formed by sperm-and-egg union] is already the embryo of an autonomous living being with individual hereditary patrimony, such that if we knew the nature of the spermatozoid and the chromosomes involved, we could already at that point predict the characteristics of the child, the future color of his hair, and the illnesses to which he would be subject. In his mother's womb, where he will grow, he will not accept everything she brings to him, but only that which is necessary to his existence: thereby he will realize his hereditary patrimony. In that first cell the profound dynamism and the precise direction of life appears. . . . In spite of its fragility and its immense

The answers here published have been prepared by competent authorities. They do not, however, represent the opinions of any medical or other organization unless specifically so stated in the reply. Anonymous communications cannot be answered. Every letter must contain the writer's name and address, but these will be omitted on request. All inquiries receive a direct mail reply.

needs, an autonomous and genuinely living being has come into existence. . . . It is rather surprising to see certain physicians speak here of 'potential life' as if the fertilized egg began its real life when it nests in the uterus. Modern biology does not deny the importance of nidation, but it sees it only as a condition—indispensable, to be sure—for the *development* of the embryo and the *continuation* of a life already in existence (*La Fécondation*, ed 5. Paris, Presses Universitaires de France, 1967, pp 81-82).

John Warwick Montgomery, PhD, DTheol
Trinity Evangelical Divinity School
Deerfield, Ill

1. Christian Medical Society: *Birth Control and the Christian*. Wheaton, Ill, Tyndale House, 1969, pp 86-89.

A Roman Catholic moral teaching has traditionally held that human life begins when God infuses the soul, the distinguishing feature of human existence. Man's life and God-given destiny, then, are necessarily intertwined. From the first moments of his existence he is caught up into an ongoing personal relationship with his Creator, one that reaches fulfillment in final and eternal union.

In the past, various theories have been advanced as to when the soul is infused. Aquinas, working from inadequate biological evidence, posited 40 to 80 days after fertilization. Although we have had no certain knowledge as to the precise moment that ensoulment takes place, theologians have always held that in practice the fetus must be accorded all the rights of the human person from the moment of conception.

In our day, the theologian relies more and more upon the scientist to provide accurate scientific information as the background for ethical reflection. In regard to the question at hand, some scientists would see conception, ie, the beginning of human life, as a process that is only fully completed and verifiable at implantation. Geneticists would argue that at the moment of fertilization the genetic blueprint is set up for each human person, and all that follows is a natural consequence of this determined plan. The ethician has no revealed knowledge of when life begins or when ensoulment takes place, but he can reasonably rely on the scientific evidence. He can conclude that human life is an ongoing process at least from implantation, and most probably from fertilization.

Roman Catholic teaching has always placed a high value on human life, coming as it does from the creative hand of God and the biological potentiality of man and woman. Life then is to be supported and maintained from its first moment of existence, and accepting our human inability to pinpoint precisely the moment of its beginning, the theologian chooses the safest course and assumes that human life is present from the time of fertilization, that is, with the first cell formation when sperm and egg are joined. Ethical questions concerning maternal health care, prenatal care of the fetus, and abortion are all founded on this presupposition.

Rev James T. McHugh
United States Catholic Conference
Washington, DC

A The question, "When does life begin?" as any other problem relating to life, when posed to a Jewish theologian, must be viewed from the vantage point of a tradition. In Judaism, this is Scripture as illumined by rabbinic literature.

The Bible makes reference to the status of a fetus in the following passage from Exodus (21: 22-23):

> If men strive and hurt a woman with child so that her fruit depart from her, and yet no mischief follow, he shall surely be punished according as the woman's husband will lay upon him; and he shall pay as the judge determines. And if any mischief follow, then thou shalt give life for life.

The death of the unborn child is punishable by fine only, because the unborn child is not considered a living person.

The text is further interpreted in the rabbinic literature, where we learn when life begins. We are told that when a woman is having difficulty in giving birth, it is permissible to "cut up the child inside her womb and take it out limb by limb." The commentaries further tell us that "as long as the child did not come out into the world it is not called a living being and it is, therefore, permissible to take its life in order to save the life of its mother."

It is clear from all the authorities in Judaism that the embryo is not considered a living being, and that "once the head has appeared, this being must not be touched, for we may not set aside one human life to save another." The fetus is considered "the loin of its mother," or *pars viscera matrum*.

According to Jewish sources the period to be considered is three months after conception; prior to this period, life has not yet begun.

Rabbi David Graubart, DD, PhD,
The Bet Din
Chicago

A Philosophers and scientists tend to agree that human life, as all life, is continuous, being passed through the germ cells from person to person. When a specific human life begins, however, is a question of ethical belief rather than one of science. The answer to this question depends upon how one defines a human life, and on this we are no closer to agreement than were the Greeks.

The professional definitions employed for the purpose of vital statistics and death registration were developed in cooperation with the World Health Assembly in 1950. Nearly all states now require that stillbirths be registered when the criterion of 20 weeks or more of gestation is satisfied. Most states, in addition, employ the criteria of (1) heart action, (2) breathing, and (3) movement of voluntary muscles. Death registration identifies the stillborn as a human death, and accordingly, requires that disposal of the body be in accord with state regulations as regards human burial or cremation.

Hospital rules and procedures, medical codes, and other regulations concerned with health practice must, at a minimum, employ state definitions regarding the beginning of a human life and require action in conformity to those definitions in professional practice. In some settings, definitions may be employed which define a human life as beginning at an earlier point than that defined by law.

Studies of health professionals reveal wide variations in their personal beliefs. For one group of 350 health professionals, about 50% say a new life is a human life by the end of the first trimester; 30% during the second or third trimester or at birth; and 20% at viable birth or later. These findings have recently been corroborated (AL Knutson, unpublished data). Religion and sex appear to be significant factors related to such beliefs; professional education and experience do not seem to contribute greatly to their formation. Most important, however, are beliefs about the definition of a human life, the acceptance and definition of the concept of a human soul, and the time of the infusion of the soul into the new life. Conflicts are found to exist between personal beliefs and legal and medical codes which require conformity in professional behavior. Such conflicts tend to be the sources of considerable personal difficulty and discomfort in the performance of responsibilities.

Publications which discuss some of the views of other professionals are listed below.[1,2]

ANDIE L. KNUTSON, PhD
University of California
Berkeley

1. Knutson AL: When does a human life begin? Viewpoints of public health professionals. *Amer J Public Health* 57:2163-2177, 1967.

2. Knutson AL: The definition and value of a new human life. *Soc Sci Med* 1:7-29, 1967.

A Concerning when life begins, a particular aggregate of hereditary tendencies (genes and chromosomes) is first assembled at the moment of fertilization when an ovum is invaded by a spermatozoon. This restores the normal number of required chromosomes, 46, for survival, growth, and reproduction of a new composite individual.

By this definition a new composite individual is started at the moment of fertilization. However, to survive, this individual needs a very specialized environment for nine months, then extended care for an indefinite period. But from the moment of fertilization a new hereditary composite is formed which, under appropriate conditions, will grow into a recognizable personality. From the union of the germ cells, there is under normal development a living, definite going concern. To interrupt a pregnancy at any stage is like cutting the link of a chain; the chain is broken no matter where the link is cut. Naturally the earlier a pregnancy is interrupted, the less the physical, objective encounter.

LANDRUM B. SHETTLES, MD
Columbia University
College of Physicians & Surgeons
New York

THE CHRISTIAN VIEW OF THE FETUS

by John Warwick Montgomery

INTRODUCTION

A superficial glance at the subject of this paper may suggest exactly that: superficiality. In the mid-20th century, is it really possible that theologians are still engaged in the kind of scholastic nit-picking that led St. Thomas,[1] following Aristotle,[2] to assert that the male receives his "rational soul" forty days after conception while the female has to wait eighty to ninety days for hers? Does our topic imply a revival of theological interest in intrauterine movement, such as led Samuel Pepys to write in his diary: "Lady Castlemaine quickened at my Lord Gerard's at dinner."?[3]

The relation of "soul" to "fetus" is of crucial importance

[1] *Summa Theologica,* Pt. I, quest. 75, art. i; cf. quest. 76, art. iii ad 3; quest. 118, art. ii ad 2.

[2] *Hist. Anim.,* vii. 3.

[3] Entry for 1 January 1662/3.

for the whole abortion issue. Is abortion morally wrong, and if so, *how* wrong? The answer to this question depends squarely on the nature of the unborn child. Is it in fact a person prior to attaining viability? In theological parlance, does it possess a soul? Is it a being destined for eternal life or merely a physiological growth within the mother (analogous to a tumor) ? On the basis of responses to these questions the Christian will decide whether or not abortion is murder, and whether under any circumstances it can be morally justified.

The complexity, rather than superficiality, of our task comes from the necessity of interrelating at least five disciplines. First we must discuss the nature of the "soul" (theology), then the nature of the "fetus" (medical science). The answers to basic questions in those areas will force us to pose the ontological riddle concerning the nature of "personhood" (philosophy). And, finally, we must face the pressing moral and societal problem as to whether abortion ought to be allowed (ethics and the law).

WHAT IS THE SOUL?

As a descriptive tool Hegel's dialectic is not limited to history and economics. Most fields of endeavor manifest from time to time ideological trends that swing from one extreme (thesis) to another (antithesis). In medicine, for example, preventive tonsillectomy has been vehemently accepted at certain times ("yank 'em") and equally vehemently rejected at others ("forget 'em"). Theology is not immune from such trends, and the issue as to the nature of the soul is a good example demonstrating this.

The traditional, "orthodox" theology of the church, both Roman Catholic and Protestant, has maintained a trichotomistic (body, soul, spirit) or dichotomistic/dualistic (body, soul) view of man. In this conception, which has had definite historical alignments with "faculty psychology," [4] the soul has generally been regarded as the separable and immortal part of man, as contrasted with his mortal body.

Protestant liberalism of the early 20th century, which flowered on the soil of 19th century philosophical idealism, likewise stressed man's "immortal soul" (but for humanistic, rather than for strictly theological, reasons). Thus in the Neo-Orthodox reaction of liberalism (beginning in the 1920's), a powerful reaction to this entire mode of thinking entered the picture. In an effort to oppose the anthropocentrism of the liberals, and influenced by the salutary psychosomatic trend in the science and medicine of the time, Neo-Orthodox theologians and their compatriots in biblical studies (the so-called "biblical theology movement") argued for a totally monistic view of man. Undoubtedly the most influential product of this thinking in German has been the articles dealing with *ψυχή, σῶμα, πνεῦμα, σάρξ, καρδία,* etc. in Kittel's *Theologisches Wörterbuch zum Neuen Testament,* and in English the slim volume, *The Body,* by Bishop John A. T. Robinson (subsequently famous—or infamous—for his *Honest to God*). Here an attempt was made, conjointly with the emphasis in the biblical research of those decades, to distinguish as sharply as possible "Greek thinking" (supposedly foreign to the true biblical message) from genuine "Hebrew thought." One result was the rejection as a Greek import into Christian theology the entire concept of a separable, immortal soul. Thus Robinson categorically regarded the antithesis of body and soul as "foreign to the Hebrew," described the "Greek" dualistic position as the "angel in a slot machine," and asserted: "Man does not

[4] See Gardner Murphy, *Historical Introduction to Modern Psychology* (rev. ed.; New York: Harcourt, Brace, 1949), *passim.* This work is of particular interest because of Murphy's stature in the field of parapsychology (cf. his *Challenge of Psychical Research* [New York: Harper, 1961]).

have a body, he *is* a body. . . . The soul does not survive a man—it simply goes out, draining away with the blood."[5] In this view, the terms "body" and "soul" (as, indeed, such other expressions of biblical anthropology as "flesh," "spirit," "heart," and "will") do not designate separate ontological entities: they rather speak of the same "psycho-physical unity" from different angles. In recent years, this same position has been accepted and promoted by theological existentialists[6] and by a number of "new shape" Roman Catholic biblical scholars.[7]

Much can be said for this "holistic" understanding of man. The textual support for it in Scripture is powerful, and it has received qualified acceptance among conservative theologians.[8] The term "soul" both in the Old Testament (נֶפֶשׁ) and in the New (ψυχή) frequently designates simply an entity that breathes and therefore has life; both men and animals are so described.[9] Occasionally, "soul" is applied in a simple enumeration of persons, obviously without any attempt to delineate a separable aspect of man.[10] The vital biblical theme of the resurrection of the body argues in the strongest terms, over against the σῶμα-σῆμα motif in Eastern thought and Greek mysticism, that man's restoration in Christ must be a total, psychosomatic renewal. Liberalism deserved to be severely criticized for maintaining that man, because of his alleged native virtue, possesses a

---

[5] Robinson, *The Body: A Study in Pauline Theology* ("Studies in Biblical Theology," No. 5; London: SCM Press, 1952), p. 14.

[6] See Rudolf Bultmann, *Theology of the New Testament*, trans. Kendrick Grobel, I (London: SCM Press, 1951), 190–259.

[7] See, for example, Claude Tresmontant, *Essai sur la pensée hébraïque* (Paris: Éditions du Cerf, 1953), pp. 87–143. Tresmontant, significantly, has published an appreciation of the thought of Teilhard de Chardin.

[8] That this is no exaggeration may be seen by comparing the editorial notes at Gen. 1:26 and I Thess. 5:23—and even the index references to them in the editions of 1917 and 1967 (1st edition: "Man, tripartite nature of"; 2d ed.: "Man, nature").

[9] Gen. 2:7, 1:20 ff. (cf. Rom. 13:1 and Rev. 16:3); 9:12 ff.; Ezek. 47:9; Prov. 12:10 (cf. Gen. 44:30).

[10] Acts 2:41; 7:14.

natural immortality; Scripture makes the whole man totally dependent on God not only for his present but also for his future life. And the excuses offered by dualism for depreciating the body (medieval monasticism and clerical celibacy) and avoiding dynamic involvement in the physical secular world (blue-law fundamentalism) warranted the most rigorous theological opposition.

Yet the "monists" must themselves be faulted for extremism. In their eagerness to make a legitimate point, they committed the all-too-common human error of misusing and ignoring evidence on the other side. James Barr, in his epochal and badly needed critique of the methods of the "biblical theology movement," has shown that both the contributors to Kittle's *Wörterbuch* and Robinson's *The Body* sadly misuse philological data in an effort to build a case for the "Hebrew theological mentality." Barr rightly slaps Robinson's attempt to obliterate distinctions between such New Testament terms as σῶμα and σάρξ (so as to achieve more "psycho-physical unity")—and the same judgment could equally apply to σῶμα and ψυχή: "No one supposes that the two words are completely synonymous in Paul." [11] For Barr, Robinson manifests "a total neglect of linguistic semantics." [12] This point is well taken, for though there is much scriptural evidence in behalf of the holistic view, there are, at the same time, not only passages in which a "faculty" approach is taken to man's nature,[13] but—even more important—passages clearly showing that the soul can be separated from the body and that it is capable of existence after the body's dissolution.[14] In Scripture all life (whether here or hereafter) depends squarely on the God

[11] James Barr, *The Semantics of Biblical Language* (London: Oxford University Press, 1961), p. 37.

[12] *Ibid.*, p. 35.

[13] Deut. 4:29; 26:16; I Kings 8:48; II Kings 23:25; Micah 7:1; Mt. 16:26; 22:37 (cf. Deut. 6:5); Acts 4:32; Heb. 4:12.

[14] Mt. 10:28; Rev. 6:9; 20:4.

who creates and redeems it;[15] but an unqualified monism and a denial of life in the intermediate state between physical death and the general resurrection lose biblical warrant. It is highly significant in this connection that the force of total biblical teaching has led the world's foremost specialist on Luther's pneumatology to affirm a "dichotomisch (zweistufig)" theological anthropology.[16] The biblical scholar—or the lay Christian, for that matter—must take into account *all* scripture data in arriving at biblical teaching; as a faithful inductivist, he must not make his theories a procrustean bed into which some data are forced and from which others are selectively excluded.

But how can the "holistic" and the "dualistic" views be reconciled? If man is a body-soul unity, how can he continue to exist after the dissolution of his body? The best answer seems to be that during the intermediate state between death and the general resurrection, some kind of "clothing" is given to the soul, whose "nakedness" is an abnormal condition.[17] This "clothing" or "tabernacle" could

[15] Léon-Dufour makes the vital point, on the basis of James 1:21 and I Pet. 1:8–9, that the "souls under the altar" (Rev. 6:9; 20:4) are there only by "un appel à la résurrection, oeuvre de l'Esprit de vie, non d'une force immanente. Dans l'âme Dieu a déposé une semence d'éternité qui germera en son temps" (Xavier Léon-Dufour [ed.], "Ame," *Vocabulaire de Théologie Biblique* [Paris: Editions du Cerf, 1964], 29). Léon-Dufour, a French Jesuit, is, like Claude Tresmontant (see above, our note 7), a representative of the post-Vatican II "new shape" Roman Catholic theology, with both its positive and its negative characteristics (see my forthcoming book, *Ecumenicity, Evangelicals and Rome* [Grand Rapids, Michigan: Zondervan, 1969]).

[16] Regin Prenter, "Anthropologie. IV. Dogmatisch," *Die Religion in Geschichte und Gegenwart*, I (3. Aufl.; Tübingen, 1957), 420–24. Prenter's work on Luther, *Spiritus Creator*, contains detailed discussions of biblical anthropology.

[17] II Cor. 5:1–10; Rev. 6:9–11. This point has been well developed by Oscar Cullmann in his influential book, *Immortalité de l'âme ou Résurrection des morts?* (Neuchâtel & Paris: Delachaux & Niestlé, 1956; translated in *Immortality and Resurrection*, ed. Krister Stendahl [New York: Macmillan, 1965], pp. 9–53). It is too bad that Cullmann made such an invidious comparison between "immortality" and "resurrection" in his work; much of the criticism his book received has been due to unfortunate semantic overtones for which he was himself unwittingly responsible.

with some legitimacy be called a body (if we mean by "body" no more than a "soul covering"), for the New Testament makes clear that in God's creative activity there are many kinds of bodies, terrestrial and celestial.[18] On the other hand, it is definitely not the physical body of earthly life, since this has decayed; in this sense man's soul is most certainly separable from his body and can function in dualistic isolation from it. Assuredly this is not "normal": it is a temporary state, mitigated by temporary "clothing," and ending at the time of the general resurrection. But it cannot be ignored.

THE FETUS AND PERSONHOOD

Our examination of the biblical concept of the soul brought us to the conclusion that it is intimately, though not absolutely, connected with the life of the physical body. In general we may regard "soul" as a theological term for the "person"—who, though he exists without his earthly body after physical death, is "clothed" temporarily even in that condition. Evidently, then, to conceive of the "person" apart from any and every "body" is not a biblical mode of thought. So considerable is the importance of the earthly body that one thinks naturally of the intermediate "tabernacle" as having a close enough relation with it to maintain continuity of the total person.

The intimate connection of soul and body in scripture establishes a predisposition against the idea of a divine "superadding" of the soul to an already existent body, but such a possibility cannot be excluded *a priori*, since, as we have seen, the soul and the physical body must be considered ontologically distinct. The question of a possible superaddition of the soul to the fetus requires a brief glance at

[18] I Cor. 15:35–44.

the venerable conflict between the *creationists* and the *traducianists*.[19]

"Creationism," or (better) "concreationism," is a theological position held by Pelagius, Peter Lombard, St. Thomas, the Roman Catholic ordinary magisterium (though that Church has never given the position solemn definition), and by most Calvinists. This view affirms that God creates souls *ex nihilo* and supplies them to developing individuals at conception or during the intrauterine period.

Dissent has existed in the creationist camp in regard to the time when God supplies the soul to the developing person: Does this occur at the moment of conception or at a later point? Though St. Thomas, as we have noted, held to the latter viewpoint, the pressure of modern embryological knowledge has pushed creationist theologians more and more to the view that the soul is supplied by God when conception itself occurs. When sperm and ovum unite and the two pronuclei fuse, a process commences, governed by the DNA molecular pattern, that fixes the new individual's characteristics—and this occurs prior to the first division of the zygote. The following argument by the director of research at France's Centre National de Recherche Scientifique is typical of the judgments which have influenced creationists to focus their attention on the moment of conception:

> Cette [première] cullule est déjà le premier embryon d'un vivant autonome avec son patrimoine héréditaire bien à lui, tant et si bien que si l'on connaissait le spermatozoïde qui est venu et les chromosomes qui se sont rencontrés, on pourrait déjà prévoir le tempérament de cet enfant, la couleur future de ses cheveux et les maladies auxquelles il sera sujet. Dans la mère

---

19 On the issue, see especially R. Lacroix, *L'origine de l'âme humaine* (Québec, 1945); R. Boigelot, *L'homme et l'univers* (Bruxelles, 1946); C. Fabro, *L'anima* (Roma, 1955; with valuable bibliography); and P. Overhage & Karl Rahner, *Das Problem der Hominisation* (Freiburg i.Br., 1961).

> où il va croître et grandir, il prendra, non pas tout ce que celle-ci lui apportera, mais ce qui lui sera nécessaire: il réalisera son patrimoine héréditaire. En lui vient d'apparaître le dynamisme profond et l'orientation précise de la vie: un nouvel être est conçu. (. . .) Malgré sa fragilité et ses immenses besoins, un être autonome et bien vivant, dont on peut désormais briser mais non pas modifier le destin biologique, entre dans l'existence. (. . .) Il est assez surprenant de voir certains médecins parler ici de vie potentielle comme si l'ovule fécondé commençait sa vie réelle lorsqu'il s'est fixé sur l'utérus. La biologie moderne ne nie pas l'importance de la nidation, mais elle y voit seulement une condition, évidemment indispensable, pour le développement de l'embryon et la continuation d'une vie qui existe déjà.[20]

But does not the phenomenon of identical twins demand a later point for the introduction of the soul? Identical twins result—just as does the ordinary single individual—from the fertilization of one ovum by one spermatozoid; but splitting brings about *two* developing embryos with identical hereditary patterns.[21] Must not the soul therefore enter the picture at the point when the two individuals become truly distinct? And what can be done with the analogous conundrum posed by Ettinger?

> *Experiment 4*. Applying biochemical or microsurgical techniques to a newly fertilized human ovum, we force it to divide and separate, thereby producing identical twins where the undisturbed cell would have developed as a single individual. (Similar experiments have been performed with animals.)
>
> An ordinary individual should probably be said to originate at the "moment" of conception. At any rate, there does not seem to be any other suitable time—certainly not the time of birth, because a Caesarean operation would have produced a living individual as

---

[20] Jules Carles, *La fécondation* (5. éd.; Paris: Presses Universitaires de France, 1967), pp. 81–82.

[21] *Ibid.*, pp. 86–90. See also *L'hérédité humaine* by Jean Rostand of the Académie Française (7 éd.; Paris: Presses Universitaires de France, 1966), pp. 9–11.

> well; and choice of any other stage of development of the foetus would be quite arbitrary.
>
> Our brief, coarse, physical interference has resulted in two lives, two individuals, where before there was one. In a sense, we have created one life. Or perhaps we have destroyed one life, and created two, since neither individual is quite the same as the original one would have been.[22]

A minority of Roman Catholic theologians—the most persuasive being Hudeczek—have seen such arguments as definitive support for St. Thomas' mediate animation theory. But a close examination of Hudeczek's case reveals that it stands or falls on the scholastic principle that the soul, as a "rational" or "spiritual" entity, must be indivisible (*simplex*).[23] Our study of the biblical data on the soul certainly established no such *a priori* principle, and on what other ground could such a principle be asserted definitively? Perhaps the soul is as divisible as is the fertilized egg! If the resultant identical twins show remarkable affinities in appearance, temperament, habits, etc., and if (as we have seen) scripture sets forth an intimate soul-body relationship, perhaps one can as legitimately speak of "twin souls" as of twin bodies!

But as we have found ourselves imperceptibly moving back toward the motif of psycho-physical unity, we have in fact been approaching the domain of the theological traducianists. "Materialistic" traducianism holds either that parents generate from inanimate matter not only the body but also the soul of the child, or that the soul is actually contained in the sperm and conveyed by organic generation. More attractive by far has been "spiritual" traducianism,

---

22 Robert C. W. Ettinger, *The Prospect of Immortality* (Garden City, New York: Doubleday, 1964), p. 132. I have discussed the central thesis of Ettinger's book in my article, "Cryonics and Orthodoxy," *Christianity Today*, XII (May 10, 1968), 816.

23 M. Hudeczek, "De tempore animationis foetus humani secundum Embryologiam hodiernam," *Angelicum* (Roma), XXIX (1952), 162–81 (especially p. 175).

often called "generationism," which asserts that the soul of the child derives from the souls of the parents. Augustine, in opposing the Pelagians and in his insistence on man's total depravity, held to generationism,[24] as did Luther and most theologians influenced by him. The Roman Church, while not solemnly defining creationism (as we noted), has seen fit through its ordinary magisterium to condemn both forms of traducianism.[25]

The contemporary orthodox Protestant systematician Mueller is quite right to use the traducianist-creationist dispute as an example of an "open question"—a question "on which the Word of God is silent."[26] In a sense it is a pseudo-problem: a special case of the more general question as to whether the appearance of a new human individual is an act of direct or mediate creation by God. But the conflict is very instructive from the point of view of the abortion question, for we see how, whether more obviously as in traducianism or less obviously in creationism, the point of origin of the individual is pushed backwards in time. For the traducianist, it would be absurd to regard the individual as commencing later than conception, for even his soul derives from his parents. For most creationists, the moment of conception is the point when the soul is bestowed. Even those theologians who follow Aquinas in his mediate animation theory now argue from the case of identical twins, analysis of which leads directly to the original fertilized egg as supplying what will become the total and identical hereditary constellation of genes and chromosomes for both individuals. Moreover, the Roman Church has long condemned the viewpoint that if one grants that the soul is

---

[24] Augustine, *Epist.*, 166.8.25–26; 190.4.14–15.

[25] See P. B. T. Bilaniuk, "Creationism," *New Catholic Encyclopedia*, IV (New York, 1967), 428–29; "Traducianism," *ibid.*, XIV, 230.

[26] J. Theodore Mueller, *Christian Dogmatics* (St. Louis, Missouri: Concordia, 1934), p. 58.

supplied subsequent to conception, abortion would not be murder. Pope Innocent XI, in a decree of 2 March 1679, condemned this position;[27] the encyclical *Casti connubii* (1930) reinforced the Church's unqualified opposition to abortion; and very recently (3 October 1964), Paul VI, in reviewing the doctrine for a group from the New England Obstetrical and Gynecological Society,[28] repeated Pius XII's condemnation of abortion (26 November 1951).[29]

But cannot the force of the embryological evidence be reduced simply by recourse to contemporary philosophical attempts at defining "personhood" functionally? Granted that from the moment of conception everything has been supplied to produce an individual; can it really be said to *be* an individual prior to, say, the onset of its brain functions, or its viability, or its manifestation of rational activity—in short, prior to its genuine *functioning* as a human being? Should we not, with Van Peursen, choose as our starting-point "the whole man in his ordinary, day-to-day conduct, attitudes and decisions. These things are not accretions to the human being who exists in himself *qua* substance (body plus soul), but they are the indispensable essence or core of man, without which he would not be man at all"?[30] If this is the case, abortion could hardly be murder, for the fetus lacks this "indispensable essence or core of man." Glanville Williams suggests brain-functioning as the *point de départ:*

---

27 Condemned was the following proposition: "Videtur probabile omnem foetum (quamdiu in utero est) carere anima rationali et tunc primum incipere eamdem habere, cum paritur: ac consequenter dicendum erit, in nullo abortu homicidium committi" (Denzinger, *Enchiridion*, § 1052).

28 *Pope Speaks*, X (1964), 1.

29 *Discorsi e radio messagi di Sua Santità Pio XII*, 13.415. By the papal bull *Apostolicae sedis* (12 October 1869), the canon law penalty of excommunication was levied against those persons responsible for procuring abortions of nonviable fetuses.

30 C. A. Van Peursen, *Body, Soul, Spirit: A Survey of the Body-Mind Problem*, trans. from the Dutch by H. H. Hoskins (London: Oxford University Press, 1966), p. 181 (cf. pp. 188, 193–94).

> The soul, after all, is frequently associated with the mind, and until the brain is formed there can be no mind. By placing electrodes on the maternal abdomen over the foetal head, electric potentials ("brain waves") are discernible in the seventh month, i.e., shortly before the time of viability. If one were to compromise by taking, say, the beginning of the seventh month as the beginning of legal protection for the foetus, it would practically eliminate the present social problem of abortion.[31]

The answer to this is two-fold. First, even from a totally secular viewpoint, the "functionalist" definition of man will not wash. What functions will be regarded as *truly* human —as *sine quibus non* for genuine humanity? Movement? (But what about total paralysis?) Intelligence? (But what degree of it?) Personhood escapes all such definitional attempts, and the reason appears to be that personality is a transcendent affair: the subjective "I" can never be totally objectified without destroying it.[32] If this is true, then one can hardly look for the origin-point of personhood anywhere other than at the moment when all potentialities necessary for its functioning enter the picture: namely, at conception. To argue otherwise is to become caught inextricably in a maze which would deny true humanity to those who, through organic defect, are incapable of carrying out certain rational activities (e.g., some mental cases). The efforts of the Third Reich "eugenically" to eliminate such "non-humans" should give us no little pause here. Can we say that when a human being on the operating table undergoes suspension of activity he ceases to be human? As long as the native potentiality to function as a human being

---

[31] Glanville Williams, *The Sanctity of Life and the Criminal Law* (London: Faber & Faber, 1958), p. 210.

[32] See my treatment of the "irreducible I" in "The Theologian's Craft: A Discussion of Theory Formation and Theory Testing in Theology," *American Scientific Affiliation Journal*, XVIII (September, 1966), 74.

exists, one must be treated as human and must have his human rights protected.[33] Though the new-born child does little at the time to justify its humanity (except to make an immediate pest of itself), its potentiality to exercise a range of human functions later rightly causes the law to regard its wanton destruction as murder in the full sense; and the same may be said by simple extension for the nonviable fetus.

Theologically, the argument is even stronger. Man is not man because of what he does or accomplishes. He is man because God made him. Though the little child engages in only a limited range of human activities, Jesus used him as the model for the Kingdom [34]—evidently because, as one of the "weak things of this world that confound the wise," he illustrates God's grace rather than human works-righteousness. Even the term *βρέφος*, "unborn child, embryo, infant," is employed in one of the parallel passages relating children to God's Kingdom.[35] The same expression appears in the statement that when Mary visited Elizabeth, the unborn John the Baptist "leaped for joy" in Elizabeth's womb and she was filled with the Holy Spirit.[36] Peter parallels the ideal Christian with a *βρέφος*,[37] and Paul takes satisfaction that from Timothy's infancy (*ἀπὸ βρέφους*) he had had contact with God's revelation.[38] Moreover, the Bible regards personal identity as beginning with conception, and one's involvement in the sinful human situation as commencing at that very point: "Behold, I [not "it"] was shapen in iniquity; and in sin did my mother conceive me [not "it"]." [39]

[33] The legal practice of "ascription of rights" well illustrates this point (see especially the writings of H. L. A. Hart): though the fetus cannot defend himself in court (any more than an infant can), society ascribes genuine legal rights to him and seeks to uphold them.

[34] Mt. 19:13–15; Mark 10:13–16.

[35] Luke 18:15.

[36] Luke 1:41, 44.

[37] I Pet. 2:2.

[38] II Tim. 3:15.

[39] Ps. 51:5.

For the biblical writers, personhood in the most genuine sense begins no later than conception; subsequent human acts illustrate this personhood, they do not create it. Man *does* because he *is* (not the reverse) and he *is* because God brought about his psycho-physical existence in the miracle of conception.

ABORTION IN LIGHT OF THE CHRISTIAN ETHIC

We have now reached the point where ethical judgment can be made on the abortion question. Four considerations warrant the strongest possible emphasis.

1. Abortion is in fact homicide, for it terminates a genuine human life. God's revealed moral law in Holy Scripture, with its high view of the sanctity of life, is an absolute, and therefore to cut off human existence is always an evil, regardless of changing circumstances or "situations." [40]

2. Nonetheless, it must be clearly seen that Christians have no business "legislating morality" in such a way that their non-Christian neighbors are forced to adhere to laws which create impossible stresses for them. The divorce laws in some countries and in some states of the United States are of such severity that many non-Christians who never contracted their marriage on a proper foundation are forced to greater sin in attempting to circumvent the legislation against divorce. Abortion problems are often analogous: the individual has put himself or herself in a situation where abortion might conceivably be the lesser of evils. Still an evil, definitely, and the law of the land must unflinchingly say so; but the penalties could well reflect the ambiguity of the sinner's condition. As the law recognizes gradations of homicide, it should look with some under-

---

[40] The most effective presentation of this viewpoint in all its aspects is, in this writer's judgment, *Le respect de la vie* (Paris: Beauchesne, 1963), by the eminent French medical scientist Paul Chauchard. Cf. also Rousas J. Rushdoony, "Abortion," *The Encyclopedia of Christianity*, ed. Edwin H. Palmer, I (Wilmington, Delaware: National Foundation for Christian Education, 1964), 20–23.

standing on abortions where the lesser-of-evils principle unquestionably comes into play. Certainly there is some social difference between an abortion-homicide and the murder of a full member of society, whose life intermeshes with the lives of many others.[41] We are not here advocating legal laxity, but we are underscoring a fact often forgotten by Christians, namely that the purpose of a human court of law is not identical with that of the Great Assize.

3. Christians must not, however, tolerate the fallacious argument that the establishment of legal abortion would *per se* constitute a lesser of evils by allegedly eliminating illegal abortion. A recent and careful study of ten years of legal abortion practice in Sweden reached the conclusion the "the frequency of illegal abortion has if anything increased," [42] and recommended that "a more restrictive attitude should be adopted in the evaluation of the grounds for legal abortion." [43] The causes of legal abortion stem from much deeper considerations than can be touched through legalizing such operations. As a Planned Parenthood Federation conference on the subject recommended, sensing the underlying moral problems involved: "There

---

[41] The following judgment is admittedly overdrawn, but is there not some truth in it? "In comparison with other cases of murder, a minimum of harm is done by it [abortion]. . . . The victim's mind is not sufficiently developed to enable it to suffer from the contemplation of approaching suffering or death. It is incapable of feeling fear or terror. Nor is its consciousness sufficiently developed to enable it to suffer pain in appreciable degree. Its loss leaves no gap in any family circle, deprives no children of their breadwinner or their mother, no human being of a friend, helper or companion. The crime diffuses no sense of insecurity. No one feels a whit less safe because the crime has been committed. It is a racial crime, purely and solely. Its ill effect is not on society as it is, but in striking at the provision of future citizens, to take the place of those who are growing old; and by whose loss in the course of nature, the community must dwindle and die out, unless it is replenished by the birth and upbringing of children" (Charles Mercier, *Crime and Insanity* [London, 1911], pp. 212–13).

[42] Per Arén, *On Legal Abortion in Sweden: Tentative Evaluation of Justification of Frequency during Last Decade* ("Acta Obstetricia et Gynecologica Scandinavica," Vol. XXXVII, Supp. 1; Lund, 1958), p. 62.

[43] *Ibid.*, p. 70.

should be encouragement . . . of higher standards of sexual conduct and of a greater sense of responsibility toward pregnancy." [44]

4. The lesser-of-evils principle referred to above can (and frequently does) apply to Christian ethical decisions in abortion cases. The Christian, no less than the non-Christian, lives in an ambiguous and sinful world, where few decisions can be regarded as unqualifiedly good—untainted by evil consequences. Thus the Christian physician may be called on to sacrifice the fetus for the mother, or the mother for the fetus. Decisions in cases like this will be agonizing, but there is no *a priori* way of knowing what to do: given the particular medical problem, the Christian doctor will endeavor with all his skill to cheat the grim reaper to the maximum and bring the greatest good possible out of the given ambiguity.[45] And the Protestant, unlike his Roman Catholic confrère, will not casuistically endeavor to "justify" himself through his decisions. Though in particular instances the Protestant may well arrive at the very same action as his Catholic counterpart, he will find his decisions —in which lesser evils still remain evils—driving him continually to the Cross for forgiveness.[46] "Abortion" will

---

[44] Mary S. Calderone (ed.), *Abortion in the United States* (New York: Hoeber-Harper, 1958), p. 183.

[45] It is perhaps well to note that even for Protestant Christians (such as this writer) who are members of communions where infant baptism holds a place of great theological importance, the baptism issue does not automatically place the unborn child's welfare above the mother's. No possible interpretation of Scripture can yield the belief that children who die without baptism are ipso facto consigned to hell or to a "limbo" state, and even the most "orthodox" of Lutheran theologians (e.g., Martin Chemnitz) made this perfectly clear; the destiny of such a child, though beyond human ken (as is, note well, the specific destiny of every individual, old or young—Mt. 25:31–46), rests in the hands of the Father of all mercies. As Augustine and Luther rightly maintained: *Contemptus sacramenti damnat, non privatio.* Thus the Christian physician must not decide a question of physical life or death on the basis of the unknown quantity of a given individual's ultimate personal salvation. (Cf. Mueller, *op. cit.* [in note 26 above], pp. 499–500.)

[46] A point well made by George Forell in his writings on the Protestant social and individual ethic.

suggest to him first and foremost the total human drama as well as his own life: an "arrested development" due to neglect of God's creative love—yet wondrously redeemable through the sacrifice of Christ for us all.

ADDENDUM

The reader of the preceding paper will have observed that its author has become convinced of the truly human character of the fetus, and that he has reached this conclusion on the basis both of medical and of theological considerations. The essayist therefore looks with particular severity on the practice of abortion, allowing it only in instances where abortion unquestionably constitutes the lesser of evils. This is in substance the viewpoint held by medical scientists such as Dr. M. O. Vincent (whose papers on the subject appear in the present volume) and theologians such as Helmut Thielecke:

> The fetus has its own autonomous life, which, despite all its reciprocal relationship to the maternal organism, is more than a mere part of this organism and possesses a certain independence. . . . These elementary biological facts should be sufficient to establish its status as a human being. . . . This makes it clear that here it is not a question—as it is in the case of contraception—whether a proffered gift can be responsibly accepted, but rather whether an already bestowed gift can be spurned, whether one dares to brush aside the arm of God after this arm has already been outstretched. Therefore here [in abortion] the order of creation is infringed upon in a way that is completely different from that of the case of contraception. (Thielecke, *The Ethics of Sex*, trans. Doberstein [New York: Harper, 1964], pp. 227–28.)

It would be less than fair to imply, however, that this "strong view" was universally represented by participants at the Symposium on the Control of Human Reproduction. Some medical men (e.g., Drs. R. L. Willows and C. T. Reilly) and theologians (e.g., Drs. Bruce Waltke and Kenneth

Kantzer) have definite reservations as to the genuine humanity of the fetus and as to its possession of a human soul from the moment of conception. I shall not speak further in regard to the medical evidence bearing on this point, for I have already given a summary statement of what would appear to be the definitive considerations bearing on the question: the fact that the DNA molecular pattern, established at conception, is a package containing the entire hereditary makeup of the individual—the sum total of his characteristics as an independent individual (see above, the quotation from Jules Carles, corresponding to note 20). But an additional word is necessary in respect to a theological, or rather exegetical, argument introduced by Professor Waltke which strongly influenced the thinking of a number of Symposium participants (cf. the news report on the Symposium which appeared in *Christianity Today,* September 27, 1968, pp. 33–34).

This argument, contained in Dr. Waltke's paper (Chapter 1), regards Exod. 21:22–25 as definitive biblical proof that "in contrast to the mother, the fetus is not reckoned as a soul [*nephesh*]." But, wholly apart from specific exegetical considerations, one might raise the general hermeneutic question as to whether a statement of penalty in the legislation God gave to ancient Israel ought to establish the context of interpretation for the total biblical attitude to the value of the unborn child (including not only specific and non-phenomenological Old Testament assertions such as Ps. 51:5, but the general New Testament valuation of the βρέφος, as illustrated especially in Luke 1:41, 44). Should a passage such as Exod. 21 properly outweight the analogy of the Incarnation itself, in which God became man at the moment when "conception by the Holy Ghost" occurred—not at a later time as the universally condemned and heretical adoptionists alleged? Do we not have in the very nature of Dr. Waltke's argument a common hermeneutical blunder:

the erroneous perspective that does not properly distinguish Law from Gospel and that tends to view the New Testament in light of the Old, instead of the Old Covenant as comprehensible only in terms of the New?

Moreover, even on strictly exegetical grounds, Exod. 21:22–25 does not say what Dr. Waltke thinks it does. He follows the interpretation of David Mace [47] over against virtually all serious exegetes, classical and modern, in claiming that the passage distinguishes between a pregnant mother (whose life has to be compensated for by another life if killed) and her fetus (unworthy of such compensation). But Keil and Delitzsch,[48] after explaining that the passage demands *exactly* the same penalty for injuring the mother *or* the child ("but if injury occur [to the mother or the child], thou shalt give soul for soul, eye for eye, . . . wound for wound"), comment in a lengthy note as to how the Septuagint translation of the Hebrew text has misled vernacular translators (and a few commentators like the Hellenizing Jew Philo) to adopt the view that

> "the fruit, the premature birth of which was caused by the blow, if not yet developed into a human form, was not to be regarded as in any sense a human being, so that the giver of the blow was only required to pay a pecuniary compensation." [49]
>
> "But," continue Keil and Delitzsch, "the arbitrary character of this explanation is apparent at once; for יֶלֶד only denotes a child, as a fully developed human being, and not the fruit of the womb before it has assumed a human form. . . . The omission of לָהּ, also, apparently renders it impracticable to refer the words to injury done to the woman alone." [50]

The full meaning of the passage is, then: "If men strove

---

[47] David Mace, *Hebrew Marriage*, note 6, p. 11.

[48] C. F. Keil and Franz Delitzsch, *Biblical Commentary on the Old Testament: The Pentateuch*, trans. James Martin, II (small reprint ed; Grand Rapids, Michigan: Eerdmans, [n.d.]), 134–35.

[49] Keil and Delitzsch, *op. cit.*

[50] *Ibid.*

and thrust against a woman with child, who had come near or between them for the purpose of making peace, so that her children come out (come into the world), and no injury was done either to the woman or the child that was born, a pecuniary compensation was to be paid. . . . A fine is imposed, because even if no injury had been done to the woman and the fruit of her womb, such a blow might have endangered life."[51] But where injury occurred either to mother or unborn child (as we have noted), the *lex talionis* applied indiscriminately—to the genuinely human fetus as well as to his genuinely human parent.

This interpretation is presented not only by a classic Old Testament scholar such as the 19th century Protestant Delitzsch, but equally by such contemporary Jewish exegetes as Cassuto, whose *Commentary on the Book of Exodus* is a landmark. Here are the relevant portions of Cassuto's explanatory rendering:

> "When men strive together and they hurt unintentionally a woman with a child, and her children come forth but no mischief happens—that is, the woman and the children do not die—the one who hurt her shall surely be punished by a fine. But if any mischief happen, that is, if the woman dies or the children die, then you shall give life for life."[52]

To interpret the passage in any other way is to strain the text intolerably, and efforts at emendation (such as what S. R. Driver commended as Budde's "clever" suggestions) are neither necessary nor helpful. The original text places a value on fetal life equal to that accorded to adult life, and in doing so perfectly conjoins with the rest of Holy Writ.

---

[51] *Ibid.*

[52] Umberto Cassuto, *Commentary on The Book of Exodus* translated by Abrahams Jerusalem: Magnes Press, The Hebrew University, 1967, p. 275.

B. Summing Up

Sir Alfred Denning [Lord Justice of Her Majesty's Court of Appeal], "The Influence of Religion": from his *The Changing Law* (London: Stevens, 1953), pp. 99-122.

THE
CHANGING LAW

BY

THE RIGHT HONOURABLE

SIR ALFRED DENNING

One of the Lords Justices of Her Majesty's
Court of Appeal in England

LONDON

STEVENS & SONS LIMITED

1953

THE INFLUENCE OF RELIGION

In primitive societies, the influence of religion on law was obvious, but it is not so obvious in modern societies. In primitive communities religion, morals and law were indistinguishably mixed together. In the Ten Commandments, for instance, you find the first Commandment which is *religious*: "God spake these words and said, 'I am the Lord thy God: Thou shalt have none other Gods but me.'" You find the fifth Commandment which is a *moral* precept: "Honour thy father and thy mother: that thy days may be long in the land which the Lord thy God giveth thee." You find the eighth Commandment which is a *legal* duty: "Thou shalt not steal." This intermingling is typical of all early communities. The severance of the three ideas—of law from morality, and of religion from law—belongs very distinctly to the later stages of mental progress.

This severance has gone a great way. Many people now think that religion and law have nothing in common. The law, they say, governs our dealings with our fellows: whereas religion concerns our dealings with God. Likewise they hold that law has nothing to do with morality. It lays down rigid rules which must be obeyed without questioning whether they are right or wrong. Its function is to keep order, not to do justice.

The severance has, I think, gone much too far. Although religion, law and morals can be separated, they are nevertheless still very much dependent on each other. Without religion there can be no morality: and without morality there can be no law. I will try to show you how many of the fundamental principles of our law have been derived from the Christian religion:

and in so doing I will try to indicate how they are challenged by a changing world which knows no religion, or at any rate treats religion as something which is of no moment in practical affairs.

TRUTH

Let me start first with truth. No one here doubts, I hope, that it is his duty to tell the truth. Nevertheless if your actions were governed by expediency alone, without regard to the precepts of law, religion or morals, you would soon find that there is as much to be said for lying as there is for telling the truth. You would discard the old saying that " honesty is the best policy " as a maxim fit for fools but not for clever people like yourself. If it were necessary in order to attain your ends that you should tell a lie, then tell it you would : for the end would justify the means. For instance, if your friend was charged with being drunk in charge of a car, and it would help him for you to say he was sober, then say it you would, although you knew he was drunk.

The reason why that reasoning is not acceptable to most of us is, I believe, because we have been taught the contrary from our mother's knee. The Christian religion has always stressed the importance of truth, absolute truth, in all our dealings. Just as the psalmist commends the man who " speaketh the truth from his heart,"[1] so also St. Paul enjoins the early Christians in these words : " Wherefore putting away lying, speak every man truth with his neighbour : for we are members one of another."[2] If there is one thing that gives rise to more resentment than anything else it is to be deceived—to be told a lie. It is an affront to the whole

[1] Psalm xv, 2.
[2] Ephesians iv, 25.

personality. Just as we do not wish others to deceive us, so we should not deceive them.

"PIOUS FRAUD"

Some theologians have argued that it is permissible to tell a lie for a just cause. The Roman Catholic Church itself did so at one time. For instance they invented legendary incidents relating to the life of Our Lord and the saints, and portrayed them as true. It was done with the best of motives so as to help people to believe, but nevertheless it was a fraud. Hence the phrase "pious fraud" which has become part of our language. A parallel in modern times is when doctors sometimes deceive their patients because they believe it is for their good to do so. I am not sure, however, that it is ever permissible for any man to tell a lie to his neighbour. St. Augustine held that the duty of truth is absolute and he would permit no exceptions to it: and he gave as a sufficient reason that, by lying, eternal life is lost. In modern times Kant and other philosophers take the view that truth is absolute. What then, you may ask, is to be said about stratagems made by our military men for deceiving the enemy? Some of them are downright lies but no one sees any wrong in them. On the contrary it is matter for congratulation when they succeed. The answer for the Christian is, I suggest, that an enemy, who is seeking to destroy you, can hardly be considered your neighbour.

THE TAKING OF AN OATH

Turning now to the law, it has insisted upon the truth being told on all occasions without exception. It is not difficult to see the reason why. Justice cannot be done unless the truth be known. The judges have to rely on the statements of witnesses. If it were permissible for a witness to tell a lie to help his friend, it would be the end of any attempt to do justice. I must remark, however, in parenthesis that this reasoning assumes that the law itself is just, and that the judges decide the cases justly. If the law is harsh and unjust, or is unjustly administered, then witnesses may be tempted to permit themselves a "pious fraud." In the old days when stealing anything worth more than 40 shillings was punishable with death, a jury solemnly found that a £5 bank-note was only worth 39s.: and no one thought it reprehensible. Hence the importance of seeing that the law is not only certain, but also that it is just.

On the assumption that the law is just, the judges insist on absolute truth: and to emphasise its importance, they require the witness to take an oath that he will tell the truth. There is nothing, perhaps, in our legal procedure which so clearly shows the influence of religion as the taking of an oath. Ever since there has been a system of law in this country, it has proceeded on the footing that each man believes in God. And it still proceeds on that footing. When a man goes into the witness box the first thing he has to do is to take the oath. Silence is demanded in court to emphasise the solemnity of what he is about to do. The witness takes the book in his hand and says these words: "I swear by Almighty God that the evidence I shall give shall be the truth, the whole truth, and nothing but the truth." The book that is handed to him, unless he asks for another, is the New Testament. By that oath the witness is not merely making a solemn affirmation to the judge. He is binding himself to God that he will tell the truth: and before God there is no room for half-truths or pious frauds. This is well known to ordinary folk who come to give evidence. Some of the more emphatic sort have been known to protest too much the truth of their answer by adding "May God strike me dead if I have told a lie." It is recorded that on one occasion on the Western Circuit a witness who made such an exclamation, did fall down dead, and a stone is set up to note the fact. Witnesses of other religious faiths take the oath according to the form of their own religion, but it must always be an oath which is binding on their conscience.

NO HALF-TRUTHS

So much for witnesses. But the law does not only insist on people telling the truth on oath. It insists on truth in all affairs of life where one person acts on the word of another. There is nothing upon which the law is more strict. It allows no evasions. Half-truths are condemned as much as real falsehoods. If a statement is literally true but conveys a wrong impression because of what is left unsaid, that is fraud, as the late Lord Kylsant once found out to his cost. He had inserted in a company's prospectus figures for the years which had shown profits but omitted those for the years which had shown losses, and the net result was to make the company's position look much better than it was. He was sent to prison for 12 months.[3] The principle underlying all the rules of law on these subjects, fraud, misrepresentation, estoppel and the like is this: No man shall get a benefit from a lie if the law can prevent him. No excuse or justification is permitted. It is not allowable to tell a lie in order to achieve a just result. A good end does not justify a bad means.[4]

The law therefore is sound enough on this point: but what I would observe is that law is not sufficient by itself.

[3] *R.* v. *Kylsant* [1932] 1 K.B. 442.
[4] *Hobbs* v. *Pinling* [1929] 2 K.B. at p. 53.

If the people have not true religion, then all the ordinances of the law are of little use. May not this be the reason why honesty has declined in recent times? Many people do not seem nowadays to pay much regard to the sanctity of an oath. They say that which they think helps their case, whether it be true or not.

GOOD FAITH

Akin to truth is the requirement of good faith. Just as you must tell the truth, so you must keep your promises. The just man in the Psalms is not only "he that hath used no deceit on his tongue," but also "he that sweareth unto his neighbour and disappointeth him not: though it were to his own hindrance."[5] This precept finds its place in the law also. Our law of contract has passed through many phases. At one time promises were not binding unless they were made in the form of a covenant under seal. Later on they were not binding unless there was consideration for them, that is, something given or done as the price for them. Nowadays nearly all formalities have been eliminated. If a man makes a promise which is intended to be binding and to be acted upon by the party to whom it is addressed, then once he has acted upon it, it is enforceable at law.

STANDARDISED CONTRACTS

So far so good. But the law on this matter has on occasions over-reached itself. The best instance is perhaps the way it has treated standardised contracts. Large concerns, such as hire-purchase companies, insurance companies, and others often issue printed forms containing many conditions of contract. The small individual member of the public has no choice but either to accept them or else go without the benefit of any

[5] Psalm xv, 3, 5.

contract at all. More often than not, he does not read them, and even if he did, he would probably not understand them. Yet he is bound by their conditions as if he had deliberately promised to fulfil them. Again, when it comes to the interpretation of contracts, the law holds the man bound to the letter of his contract although unforeseen circumstances have arisen which make it unjust to enforce it against him. If he protests and says "I could not have foreseen it," the law replies: "It is your own fault. You ought to have put in a saving clause to protect yourself." This harsh ruling is not in accordance with the view of St. Thomas Aquinas who would hold him excused. If good faith is required in a person who gives a promise, so it should be in a person who takes the benefit of it. He should not enforce it in circumstances which it was never intended to cover.

Just as the law has over-reached itself with contracts, so it has also with the interpretation of statutes. If a situation arises which Parliament never intended, and a strict interpretation of the statute gives rise to injustice, nevertheless the law cannot, or will not, lift a finger to help. It is not for the judges to fill in the gaps in the Acts of Parliament.

"THE LETTER KILLETH"

I cannot help thinking that this literal interpretation of contracts or statutes is a departure from real truth. It makes words the masters of men instead of their servants. If you read your New Testament, you will find that there is nothing more condemned than the insistence on the letter. A good instance is the case about the Sabbath day. The fourth Commandment ordained that on it "thou shalt do no manner of work." It so happened that, on one Sabbath day, as the disciples went through the cornfields, they began to pluck the ears of corn. The Pharisees said to our Lord, "Why do they on the Sabbath day that which is not lawful?" He replied: "The Sabbath was made for man, and not man for the Sabbath."[6] And St. Paul put the principle succinctly when he said "the letter killeth but the spirit giveth life."[7] That precept was at one time remembered in our English law. In the days when the Bible was first put into English the judges laid down rules which were undoubtedly influenced by the Bible teaching. The statutes were to be interpreted, not only according to the language used, but also with regard to the mischief which Parliament sought to remedy, so as to give "force and life" to the intention of the legislature. Those words were clearly taken from the epistle "the spirit giveth life." But in the nineteenth century that broad view was supplanted by a rule which Baron Parke described as a golden rule. He said that statutes, and indeed all documents, were to be interpreted according to the grammatical and ordinary sense of the words. Even if the grammatical meaning gave rise to unjust results which Parliament never intended, nevertheless the grammatical meaning must prevail. This means I fear that the judges are too often inclined to fold their hands and blame the legislature, when really they ought to set to work and give the words a reasonable meaning, even if this does involve a departure from the letter of them. By so doing they are more likely to find the truth.

"LOVE THY NEIGHBOUR"

Let us now turn from truth to justice. No one here doubts, I hope, that it is his duty to be just and fair in

[6] St. Mark ii, 23–28.
[7] II Corinthians 3, 6.

all his dealings. But our conception of justice is only the Christian teaching of love. Such at least was the view of William Temple, Archbishop of Canterbury, one of the greatest thinkers of the present century. "It is axiomatic," he said, "that love should be the predominant Christian impulse and that the primary form of love in social organisation is justice." The Christian standpoint is summed up in the gospel when a certain lawyer asked our Lord, "Master, what shall I do to inherit eternal life?" He said unto him "What is written in the law? How readest thou?" And he answering said "Thou shalt love the Lord thy God with all thy heart, and with all thy soul and with all thy mind, and thy neighbour as thyself." And he said unto him "Thou hast answered right: this do and thou shalt live." This precept—love towards God and love towards your neighbour—is a precept of religion, but nevertheless in many affairs of life, love can only find expression through justice. William Temple gave this illustration: "Imagine a Trade Union Committee negotiating with an Employers' Federation in an industrial crisis on the verge of a strike. This Committee is to be actuated by love. Oh, yes, by all means, but towards whom? Are they to love the workers or the employers? Of course—both. But then that will not help them much to determine what terms ought to be either proposed or accepted. . . . Love, in fact, finds its primary expression through justice which, in the field of industrial disputes, means in practice that each side should state its case as strongly as it can before the most impartial tribunal available, with determination to accept the award of that tribunal. At least that puts the two parties on a level, and is to that extent in accordance with the command 'Thou shalt love thy neighbour as thyself.'"[8]

[8] Temple: *Christianity and the Social Order.*

THE JUDGE'S ANSWER

Such being the view of the theologian, let me now turn to the judge, whose task it is to be the tribunal. He must do justice between the parties. But how is he to know what is justice? Let me tell you how one great judge answered it. It arose in a case where a manufacturer of ginger beer had made it so carelessly that he left a snail in one of the bottles. He sold it as part of a consignment to a shopkeeper, who in turn sold a bottle to a man whose wife drank it and was injured. At one time the law held that the manufacturer was not liable to pay any compensation because he had made no contract with the ultimate purchaser or his wife. But in 1932 the House of Lords held that the manufacturer was liable. In a judgment of great importance in the law, Lord Atkin took the Christian precept as the underlying basis of the decision in these words: "The rule that you are to love your neighbour becomes in law you must not injure your neighbour: and the lawyer's question 'Who is my neighbour?' receives a restricted reply. You must take reasonable care to avoid acts or omissions which you can reasonably foresee would be likely to injure your neighbour. Who then in law is my neighbour? The answer seems to be—persons who are so closely and directly affected by my act that I ought reasonably to have them in contemplation as being so affected when I am directing my mind to the acts or omissions which are called in question."[9]

It is, I suggest to you, a most significant thing that a great judge should draw his principles of law, or rather his principles of justice, from the Christian commandment of love. I do not know where else he is to find them. Some people speak of natural justice as though

[9] *Donoghue* v. *Stevenson* [1932] A.C. 562, 580.

it was a thing well recognisable by anyone, whatever his training and upbringing. But I am quite sure that our conception of it is due entirely to our habits of thought through many generations. The common law of England has been moulded for centuries by judges who have been brought up in the Christian faith. The precepts of religion, consciously or unconsciously, have been their guide in the administration of justice.

BASIS OF CIVIL WRONGS

Perhaps the best illustration of this is the law of this country about civil wrongs. At one time the ruling principle (derived from Roman law) was that a person was not liable to pay damages unless he had been guilty of some fault, such as some negligence, some invasion on another's property, or the like. The underlying justification for this rule was that damages were a deterrent. If he was made to pay damages, he was not so likely to commit the same fault again. But those who put forward this view always had great difficulty in explaining why a master should be liable to pay damages for his servant's fault. Nowadays (save for rare exceptions), damages are not regarded as a deterrent or a punishment, but rather as compensation for harm done. The law proceeds, I suggest, on the Christian principle: If you love your neighbour, you will take care not to injure him. And if perchance you should by your negligence (or even by the negligence of your servants) do him some damage, you will wish to compensate him. If you do not do so, the law will require you to do what you ought to have done willingly, but it will not go further and punish you. It will not exact anything in the nature of vengeance or retribution. If proof of this were needed, it is to be found in the fact that you can insure yourself against any damages you have to pay. This means that the law does not insist on the compensation coming from your own pocket. It is sufficient if your insurance company pays. It is obvious that, when you have covered your liability by insurance, the award of damages has no punitive or deterrent effect on you. It is a compensation for the injured party and nothing else. Once this is appreciated, you can understand why a master should pay compensation for his servant's fault. The servant is doing the master's business and the master should be answerable for the servant's act as if it were his own. A noteworthy illustration of the modern approach is to be found in the case of a guest of a Brighton hotel who got annoyed with the manager and made a brutal assault on him. He was taken before the criminal courts and found to be insane. He could not therefore be said to be at fault but nevertheless he was ordered by a civil court to pay compensation to the injured manager.

PUNISHMENT FOR CRIME

Whilst civil wrongs are thus redressed by compensation, nevertheless there still remain all the criminal wrongs which must be met by punishment. The command that you are to love your neighbour does not mean that those who do wrong should not be punished. In the Epistle of St. Peter it is said that governors are sent by God "for the punishment of evil-doers." What then is the right way to punish them? What is to be done with people who are enemies of society, men who prey upon it by theft and fraud, men who assault innocent women and children, men who are murderers? At one time the law held that they should be exterminated. Nearly all serious offences were punishable by death. But under the influence of a more humane jurisprudence, or rather

I would say of a more Christian outlook, capital punishment has been abolished in all cases except murder or treason: and there are many who would abolish it even in those cases. The principal object of punishment is now generally accepted to be the reformation of the criminal: and the Criminal Justice Act, 1948 is a notable step to this end.

In any discussion of punishment it is important to recognise, as Christianity does, that society itself is responsible for the conditions which makes men criminals. It is a commonplace that broken homes produce juvenile delinquents. The child who has lost his sense of security feels that he must fight for his interests in a hostile world. He becomes anti-social and finally criminal. The broken home from which he comes is only too often a reflection on society itself, a society which has failed to respect the sanctity of marriage, a society which has failed to maintain its standards of morality, a society which has lost its religion. When we try to reform the criminal, we are only treating the symptoms of the disease. We are not tackling the cause of it. The best way to deal with it is to reform society itself: and in this regard, I need hardly say that the leaders of society have an especial responsibility. It is disturbing to find how many broken homes, how many matrimonial offences, exist among those in high positions.

INDIVIDUAL RESPONSIBILITY

Nevertheless, although society itself is largely responsible, neither religion nor the law excuses the criminal himself. Christianity has always stressed the responsibility of each individual for his own wrong-doing. It does not say to him "Poor thing, you couldn't help it, could you? You came from a broken home and nothing else could be expected." That would lead him to believe that he is more sinned against than sinning and implies that strenuous moral effort on his part is unnecessary or futile. The Christian approach is different. It allows no easy excuse but demands of everyone that he must repent and reform. You will remember the opening verse of the Book of Common Prayer: "When the wicked man turneth away from his wickedness that he hath committed, and doeth that which is lawful and right, he shall save his soul alive": and as it is said in the Gospel of St. Luke "There is joy in the presence of God over one sinner that repenteth."

THE GUILTY MIND

In order to hold a person individually responsible for his crime, so as to be liable to punishment, it is obviously necessary that he should have a guilty mind. This requirement is first found in St. Augustine's sermons where it is said that you are not guilty of perjury unless you have a guilty mind. Thence it found its place in the laws of Henry I when it was laid down as law that *reum non facit nisi mens rea*, that is, there is no guilt unless there is a guilty mind. That has been the rule of English law from that time to this. In order that an act should be punishable, it must be morally blameworthy. It must be a sin.

INSANITY AND CRIME

When you speak of a guilty mind, however, the question immediately arises, How are you to deal with those who are not of sound mind? At first sight the law seems clear enough. If a man is insane when he commits a crime, he cannot be punished, because he cannot be said to have a guilty mind. If he becomes insane after he has committed a crime, he cannot be hanged because he must not be deprived of the opportunity of repenting. But the difficulty arises when you ask, What is insanity? Time and time again it happens that a jury find a man guilty of wilful murder whilst of sound mind, but nevertheless he is afterwards reprieved on the ground that he has since been found to be insane. It is the accepted practice, authorised by statute, for the Home Secretary to appoint two doctors to examine him. If the doctors find him to be insane, he is reprieved. In theory the finding of the doctors does not contradict the verdict of the jury. The jury are only concerned with his state of mind when he committed the crime : whereas the doctors are concerned with it at the time they examined him. If he is insane at that time, he must not be hanged. As matter of common sense the findings of the jury and the doctors ought usually to coincide. One realises, of course, that they may differ. A man may be so mentally affected by his trial and sentence that he becomes insane afterwards : but that is a rare thing. His state of mind is usually the same throughout. The reason why the Home Office doctors so often find him to be insane is that they adopt a different test of insanity from that which the jury have to apply. Let me tell you about these tests because they can both be traced to the Christian conception of individual responsibility, but each regarding it in a different light.

THE MCNAGHTEN RULES

The test applied by the jury in judging insanity is the test laid down by the judges in 1843 in the McNaghten Rules. These lay the emphasis on the man's knowledge, not on his will-power. If he was so mad that he did not know what he was doing at all, any more than a sleep-walker does, then he is excused; or if he did not know

D. 6

that what he was doing was wrong, as if he was under a delusion that he was being attacked in war by the enemy, then also he is excused. But if he knew what he was doing and that it was wrong, then he is not excused. It may be that he was driven on by some blind impulse; nevertheless if he knew it was wrong, he is not excused in law.

The test applied by the doctors in judging insanity denies the distinction between a man's knowledge and his will-power. If the man is what they call a psychopathic personality, driven on by some morbid urge which he has not the will-power to resist, then the doctors hold that he should be excused, even though he knows perfectly well that he is doing wrong.

THE STRAFFEN CASE

The difference of approach is well illustrated by two recent cases of which you will all have read in the newspapers. A young man called Straffen strangled two small girls. He was arrested, but when brought up for trial the doctors said he was unfit to plead, and accordingly he was detained as a lunatic in the Broadmoor Asylum. He behaved himself well in the asylum, but one day he escaped for a few hours and strangled another small girl. He was again arrested and brought up for trial. This time the doctors said he was fit to plead. The defence of insanity was raised, but the jury rejected it and found him guilty of wilful murder. Later he was reprieved on the ground, no doubt, that the Home Office doctors found him to be insane.

I expect that the jury reasoned something like this: "This man is better out of the way. He is subject to such dreadful impulses that it is better for the community that he should be put to death rather than there should be any risk of another escape. This should be done, not so much to punish him as to protect the community." Whereas the view of the doctors presumably was: "This man is not responsible for his actions. He is subject to impulses which he cannot resist. He should be regarded as insane and should not be punished."

In contrast to the Straffen case, you must notice the case of Miles Giffard, a young man who murdered both his father and his mother and pushed the bodies in a wheelbarrow over the edge of a cliff. He did it because they wouldn't let him have the use of a car or some other quite inadequate reason. There was a history of mental instability in him and in the family. The defence of insanity was raised but the jury found him guilty. This time the Home Secretary did not grant a reprieve and Giffard was hanged. This case seems to show that there are some crimes which shock the public conscience so much that ordinary members of the public say that the murderer is better out of the way, even though he was mentally unstable. It is not so much a matter of punishing him. It is rather the community defending itself. It is said that Giffard went to his death repentant for his sins and, it may be hoped, at peace with his Maker.

A PROBLEM OF ETHICS

It is worth pausing for a moment at this point, because those two cases illustrate one of the most difficult problems of Christian ethics of our time. It is this: Is it permissible for society to exterminate those who have an irresistible impulse to murder? A similar problem arises about sterilisation. If a man is subject to mad sexual impulses which causes him to inflict grave injury on innocent women, is it permissible to sterilise him? or alternatively to keep him in prison indefinitely until he is past the age when he will do such things? In Denmark they have now a law whereby a sexual offender is sentenced to prison for as long as the State thinks fit to keep him there, but he can obtain his freedom by submitting to sterilisation. In England we have never gone so far. We do not permit sterilisation of the unfit. I expect this has its origin in the sanctity which Christianity attaches to human life. Just as life itself is sacred, so are the means of producing it: and it is not to be taken away except by Him who is the Creator of it. The danger is, of course, that once authority is given to society to exterminate, to sterilise or to intern indefinitely some of its members, you may find that those who are in authority in the State may use it, as the Nazis did, against those whom they dislike. I offer no solution except to suggest that true Christianity should try to strike a correct balance between the individual and the society of which he forms part.

MAN AND THE STATE

I have now told you all I wish of Truth and Justice : but these lead me on to consider the relations between man and the State. Truth and Justice do not exist in a vacuum. They exist in a society of human beings, in short, in a State : and a State can be so organised that Truth and Justice can disappear, or at any rate be stifled. What does Christianity say about this? Let me take for an answer again the words of William Temple : " The primary principle of Christian ethics and Christian politics must be respect for every person simply as a person. If each man and woman is a child of God, whom God loves and for whom Christ died, then there is in each a work absolutely independent of all usefulness to society. The person is primary, not the society; the

State exists for the citizen, not the citizen for the State."

The Christian Church has always insisted that the State has no ultimate and omnipotent authority of its own but derives its authority from God. St. Paul in his epistle to the Romans (xiii, 1) made this clear. "There is no power but of God: the powers that be are ordained by God." This has been the shield under which our forefathers resisted oppression. To quote St. Paul again—the Ruler of the State was the "Minister of God for good," and so long as he fulfilled his high trust it was not right to resist him; but if he forsook it and sought absolute power, then resistance was justified.

THE CASE OF JAMES I

A celebrated instance occurred when James I claimed the right to rule in England as an absolute sovereign. He claimed that he could judge whatever cause he pleased in his own person, free from all risks of prohibition or appeal. He called in aid the authority of Archbishop Bancroft, who declared that it was clear in divinity that he could try cases himself. Such power, said the Archbishop, doubtless belongs to the King by the word of God in the scriptures. But there was a great Lord Chief Justice in those days, Lord Coke, who made it a rule of his life to spend one-fourth of each day in prayer; though I must say I do not know how he managed it, considering the vast amount of other things that he did. Lord Coke told the King that he had no power to try cases himself, and that all cases ought to be determined in a Court of Justice. King James replied: "I always thought and I have often heard the boast that your English law is founded upon reason. If that be so, why have not I and others reason as well as you the judges?" The Lord Chief Justice replied: "True it is, please your Majesty, that God has endowed your Majesty with excellent science as well as great gifts of nature: but your Majesty will allow me to say, with all reverence, that you are not learned in the laws of this your Realm of England . . . which is an art which requires long study and experience before a man can attain to the cognizance of it. The law is the golden met-wand and measure to try the causes of your Majesty's subjects, and it is by that law that your Majesty is protected in safety and peace." King James, in a great rage, said, "Then I am to be under the law—which it is treason to affirm." The Chief Justice replied, "Thus wrote Bracton, 'The King is under no man, save under God and the law.'"

Those words of Bracton quoted by Coke, "The King is under God and the law" epitomise in one sentence the great contribution made by the common lawyers to the Constitution of England. They insisted that the executive power in the land was under the law. In insisting upon this they were really insisting on the Christian principles. If we forget these principles, where shall we finish? You have only to look to the totalitarian systems of government to see what happens. The society is primary, not the person. The citizen exists for the State, not the State for the citizen. The rulers are not under God and the law. They are a law unto themselves. All law, all courts are simply part of the State machine. The freedom of the individual, as we know it, no longer exists. It is against that terrible despotism, that overwhelming domination of human life, that Christianity has protested with all the energy at its command.

THE PERILS OF INDIVIDUALISM

In noticing, however, the evils of the totalitarian system, let us also remember that individualism has its perils.

The Puritans, who insisted that the King was under God and the law, carried their individualism too far, or, at any rate, some of their successors did. On the one hand they had a great sense of the supreme importance of the individual soul and a vital instinct for setting bounds to the State; but on the other hand they held that there was a natural law which gave every man a right of property in all that he could acquire by his own labour, and once having acquired it, he could amass it, increase it and dispose of it as he willed, without any obligation to account to anybody for his stewardship. The great exponent of this individualism was our own philosopher John Locke, who has had more influence on American thought even than he had on ours. The Constitution of the United States shows one side of the Puritan outlook. It imposes strict limits on the action of those who wield power in the land. The extreme importance attached to the ownership of property in the United States shows another side of Puritanism.

No one doubts now that it is wrong to treat rights of property as sacred. As Sir Ernest Barker has well said, the individualism of the Puritans "based on religion was made to trail clouds of ingloriousness." There have been many people who, having amassed or inherited property, have only too often forgotten that it is only through society that they have acquired it. They have failed to realise that they are under a duty to use it for the benefit of society as a whole and not for their own material advantage. When rights of property are carried to these lengths they are contrary to all Christian teaching. They disregard the high duty of unselfishness. As it is said in the Epistle of St. John, "Whoso hath this world's goods and seeth his brother have need, and shutteth up his compassion from him, how dwelleth the love of God in him?"

THE INFLUENCE OF CHRISTIANITY

This brings me to the latest and most important influence of Christianity on our law. The preaching of many divines and notably of William Temple brought home the evils of the excessive accumulation of wealth and opportunity in few hands. This has played a considerable part in great changes in the law. The most important, no doubt, have been made by Parliament, which has turned us into a Welfare State which recognises that the State has a duty to secure for every citizen so far as possible full freedom and opportunity for the development of his talents, unhampered by poverty or ill-health. And this action by Parliament has been reflected in decisions of the judges, notably in cases relating to employers and workmen. The courts have repeatedly emphasised the responsibility of employers to provide safe conditions of work for their workmen, and in case of accident to compensate them for their injuries.

But this new state of society has its dangers. It has brought in its train a great increase in the powers of the central government and a lessening in the authority of Parliament and of the courts, so much so that there are fears that the initiative and enterprise of the individual have been hampered too much. We must hope that this danger can be overcome; but it can, I suggest, only be done if we recognise that Christianity is not only a personal religion but also that it has much to teach society itself.

FAMILY LIFE

There is one more subject I must mention, and in some ways it is the most important of all. It is the institution of marriage. The Christian Church has always maintained that marriage is a life-long union, for better or for worse, so long as both shall live. Divorce was never allowed so as to give the right to remarry. This principle was in marked contrast to other legal systems such as the Jewish laws or the Roman law, which always permitted divorce to a greater or less extent. The principle of the indissolubility of marriage was in England for centuries not only the law of the Church but also the law of the land. It has had a profound influence on the social life of the country. The family is the primary social unit. The well-being of the whole community requires that children should, so far as possible, be brought up by their own parents as members of one family, with all the give and take that family life demands, and also with the security that it affords. The institution of marriage is the legal foundation of this family life. The principle of indissolubility was the binding force which cemented it. During the last 96 years the State has abandoned the principle. Divorce has been allowed for grave causes prescribed by law, but the consequences that were foreseen by the Church, and of which its leaders gave warning, have followed. Undeserving cases have slipped through. Collusion has not been detected. The result is that people have come to regard divorce as a matter which can be arranged between the parties. In so doing, they only too often disregard the interests of their children and pursue their own selfish ends. Every thinking person is profoundly disturbed by this state of affairs. It has a grave effect on the family unity and on the national character. It is almost impossible for the State to retrace its steps so as to make the divorce law more difficult. The only real remedy is the growth of a strong public opinion condemning divorce, and, I would add, condemning infidelity. It should not be regarded, as it now is, as the private concern of the parties with which no one else has anything to do. It is the concern of everyone who has the welfare of the country at heart.

CONCLUSION

This brings me to the end. And what does it all come to? Surely this, that if we seek truth and justice, we cannot find it by argument and debate, nor by reading and thinking, but only by the maintenance of true religion and virtue. Religion concerns the spirit in man whereby he is able to recognise what is truth and what is justice; whereas law is only the application, however imperfectly, of truth and justice in our everyday affairs. If religion perishes in the land, truth and justice will also. We have already strayed too far from the faith of our fathers. Let us return to it, for it is the only thing that can save us.

APPENDIX

François Wendel [D. en Droit, D. Théol., Doyen de la Faculté de Théologie Protestante, Strasbourg], previously unpublished lectures (delivered in 1964-1965) on Luther's approach to the relationship between natural law and Christian theology.

Jacques Ellul [Prof. of Law, Bordeaux], "Christianisme et droit. Recherches américaines" [American investigations in the field of Christianity and law], 5 *Archives de Philosophie du Droit* 27.

H I S T O I R E   D E S   D O G M E S

LOI NATURELLE ET

THEOLOGIE CHRETIENNE

Cours de Monsieur le Doyen F. WENDEL. Strasbourg, 1964-1965.

CHAPITRE V. LA REFORME:LUTHER,MELANCHTON ET CALVIN

I. Luther

Il ne faut pas s'attendre à trouver chez Luther une doctrine systématisée du droit naturel, analogue à celle que nous avons rencontrée dans la Somme Théologique de s.Thomas d'Aquin. Bien qu'il fût fort averti des grandes constructions classiques de la théologie catholique, rien ne répugnait davantage au génie du réformateur que d'en entreprendre à son tour.Son esprit impulsif ne pouvait s'accommoder des lents cheminements de la dialectique scolastique, ni de sa méthode d'argumentation impitoyablement logique, mais dépourvue de tout élément imprévu.Mais, à défaut d'un traité savamment é aboré sur le droit naturel,Luther nous a laissé dans ses travaux éxégétiques notamment de nombreuses remarques qui nous permettront d'esquisser ses conceptions à ce sujet. Toutefois le caractère même de ces passages de son oeuvre leur donne un aspect fragmentaire qui n'autorise pas toujours le commentateur moderne à reconstruire une doctrine sans lacunes.Comme il arrive souvent, lorsqu'on essaie de dégager la pensée de Luther sur un point précis de théologie ou de philosophie, des affirmations en apparence contradictoires viennent compliquer encore la tache de l'éxégète. Il en est tellement ainsi en ce qui concerne la question qui nous occupe ici, que les auteurs ont abouti à des conclusions non seulement divergentes, mais parfois diamétralement opposées. Si la plupart d'entre eux ont cru pouvoir aboutir à des reconstitutions plus ou moins harmonieuses, il en est d'autres, par exemple LOOFS , qui n'ont pas réussi à réduire à l'unité des déclarations qui leur paraissaient inconciliables. D'autres encore, ont délibérément faussé leur exposé de la pensée luthérienne en ne retenant de ses déclarations que ce qui cadrait avec leur conception générale à priori de la théologie du réfirmateur. C'est ainsi que l'un des interprètes les plus avisés de Luther, Karl HOLL, a par deux fois (dans "Der Neubau des Sittlichkeit" et dans sa conférence sur la "Kulturbedeutung der Reformation") soutenu à l'encontre de Troeltsch que Luther n'avait en aucune façon admis l'existence d'un droit naturel. Or il s'est avéré que les explications de Troeltsch pèchent par une simplification excessive et par parti pris, la réponse de Holl ne tient pas compte non plus de tout un aspect de la pensée luthérienne.

Plutôt que d'examiner tour à tour les différentes explications qui ont été proposées depuis une cinquantaine d'années, il conviendra d'étudier les textes de Luther et de nous efforcer d les replacer dans le cadre de sa théologie. Nous aurons ainsi le plus de chance de ne point nous égarer en un domaine aussi difficile et embrouillé.

Le premier de ces textes, au point de vue chronologique, se trouve dans le fameux commentaire de l'épitre aux Romains de 1515 et va rejoindre directement St.Augustin. Il s'agit de l'exégèse de Romains 2/14-16. L'importance de ce passage pour le problème du droit naturel nous est apparu dès le début de ce cours. De même qu'il nous a permis de préciser l'attitude de s.Augustin, il nous donnera dès le début des indications précieuses sur la position adoptée par Luther.

Après avoir cité Romains 2/14, Luther écrit: "s.Augustin entend cela de deux manières.D'abord, il entend par paiens les croyants issus du paganisme qui sont justifiés par la grace de Christ, grâce que, selon son opinion, l'apotre oppose aux juifs incroyants et se targuant orgueilleusement de la loi et de la justice. Ainsi explique-t-il le terme "naturellement" c'est à dire: en vertu d'une nature restaurée par l'esprit de la grace du Christ après avoir été viciée par le péché; non pas que la grace soit niée par la nature, mais la nature est restaurée par la grace. Il penche lui-même vers cette interprétation. En second lieu, (St.Augustin) dit qu'on peut entendre aussi cette parole de ceux qui ,bien que menant une vie impie et n'honorant pas Dieu comme il se doit et vraiment, accomplissant pourtant tel ou tel bien, de sorte qu'on peut en dire équitablement qu'ils font quelque chose de ce que la loi exige ou qu'ils en comprennent quelque chose. Alors il faut entendre par "les pensées qui les excusent réciproquement" celles par lesquelles ils essayent de s'excuser, afin de recevoir un chatiment plus doux. Car, de même que quelques péchés véniels, qu'on ne peut éviter en cette vie, n'excluent pas un juste de la vie éternelle, inversement qelques bonnes oeuvres ne sont d'aucune utilité à l'impie pour le salut éternel.C'est à peine si la vie d'un homme même entièrement dévoyé n'offre pas quelques bonnes oeuvres de ce genre. Mais à cette conception s'oppose la parole qu'ils font par nature ce qu'exige la loi; mais ceux qui accomplissent la loi sont justes. Il ne semble donc pas que St.Paul veuille parler des impies de ce genre,mais pas non plus de ceux qui croient en Christ.Car cette interprétation du terme "naturellement" est forcée.Je ne crois pas non plus que l'apotre se serait servi tout juste de cette expression,à moins qu'il n'ait voulu cacher au lecteur la véritable opoinion, car ailleurs il ne s'exprime pas ainsi."

Il aut nous arrêter ici un instant, pour constater que Luther commence, au début du texte que je viens de citer, par analyser très correctement d'ailleurs, les deux hypothèses avancées par s.Augustin dans le De spiritu et littera: ou bien, et c'est la solution que s.Augustin préfère, les gentils de Romains 2/14 sont des pagano-chrétiens, ou bien il faut y voir des paiens qui peuvent bien à l'occasion faire une action moralement bonne, mais à qui cette action ne peut servir qu'à diminuer le chatiment qu'ils ont encouru. Luther rejette comme forcée l'interprétation de s.Augustin, qui jouant sur le mot naturellement l'applique à la nature régénérée par la grâce. Il n'accepte pas non plus sans discrimination la seconde hypothèse, qui, suggère-t-il, ne tient pas compte de la parole de s. Paul selon laquelle les gentils en question font par nature ce qu'exige la loi et qui doivent donc être assimilée à des justes. Dans la suite du texte, il s'efforce au contraire, de trouver une solution moyenne:" C'est pourquoi, continue Luther, je me tiens ici à mi chemin des paiens impies et des croyants qui ont mérité dans la mesure où ils le pouvaient, en vertu de leur force naturelle, par quelque action pieuse et bénie de Dieu, la grace qui a ensuite continué à les guider. Non pas en ce sens que la grace leur aurait été donnée en raison d'un tel mérite, car alors ce n'aurait plus été une grace; mais parce que, en ce monde, ils se sont préparés à recevoir la grace comme un pur don." Luther admet donc la possibilité d'existence d'une catégorie de paiens intermédiaires entre les pagano-chrétiens et les paiens entièrement corrompus et voués à la damnation. Il s'agirait de paiens, qui, par leurs actions conformes à la loi inscrite dans leur coeur, se seraient préparés à recevoir le christianisme. Je me hate d'ajouter que cette position concevable à un moment où le réformateur n'avait pas encore dégagé entièrement les conséquences d sa doctrine de la grace, fut radicalement abandonnée par la suite; car ce sera une des thèses fondamentales de Luther que l'homme est incapable, par ses propres forces, non seulement d mériter la grace, comme il le dit ici, mais même de s'y acheminer. D'ailleurs cette interprétation n'a pas du satisfaire beaucoup Luther, dès l'époque où il composait son commentaire. Car il poursuit immédiatement: " On peut aussi admettre qu'il faille interpréter restrictivement la phrase: par nature ils accomplissent le contenu de la loi (c'est à dire une partie de la loi).Alors, en effet, ce passage devient clair, et l'opinion de s.AUgustin, en ce qui concerne la deuxième hypothèse envisagée par lui est parfaitement justifiée. Car alors l'apotre fait allusion aux gentils, parce qu'ils ont observé la loi, tout aussi peu que les juifs. Sans doute ont-ils accompli telle ou telle bonne oeuvre presccite par la loi, grace à laquelle ils essayeront de se soustraire à un chatiment plus sévère au jour du jugement. Ils n'en ont pas moins besoin ainsi que le démontre l'apotre à leur sujet, de la grace et de la miséricorde du Christ d'autant plus que l'observance extérieure de la loi ne servira de rien aux juifs non plus. Les uns et les autres sont donc sons la loi du péché quelque soit le bien qu'ils puissent avoir accompli: Les juifs selon l'homme intérieur, parce qu'ils n'ont pas compris la loi que selon la lettre; les paiens a un double titre, parce qu'ils n'ont accompli la loi que partiellement et non totalement et en esprit. J'adopte cette interprétation, car tout l'exposé de ce chapitre n'a pas d'autre but que de montrer que tous les hommes, les juifs et les paiens, sont pécheurs et ont besoin de la grace divine; c'est ce que Paul dit lui-même en Romains 3:9 : Car nous avons prouvé que les juifs et les paiens sont sous l'empire du péché".

Ce passage fait apparaitre en pleine lumière la véritable pensée de Luther; tout comme s.Augustin, il donne deux interprétations possibles de Romains 2:14, mais il ne tient pour fondée qu'une seule. En admettant la possibilité d'interpréter d'une manière restrictive l'expression: le contenu de la loi, c'est à dire en y voyant l'indication qu'il s'agit d'une partie seulement des exigences de la loi, Luther arrive à donner de tout le passage une explication conforme à la deuxième hypothèse proposée par s.Augustin, et , ce qui est mieux, conforme aussi au sens général de toute l'argumentation de s.Paul. Nous avons vu qu'il ne s'agit point pour celui-ci de mettre enévidence les oeuvres moralement bonnes qu'il peut arriver aux paiens d'accomplir, mais bien de placer sur une même ligne juifs et paiens, et de montrer que les uns comme les autres étaient placés sous l'empire de la loi, afin de pouvoir d'autant mieux souligner leur commune défaillance. Dès lors nous sommes en préssence de l'un des thèmes centraux de la pensée luthérienne, aussi bien que paulinienne: quoiqu'il fasse, l'homme n'est rien devant Dieu, tant qu'il na pas reçu la grace.

Mais ce n'est pas tout. Ay moyen d'une distinction qui au premier abord peut paraitre une subtilité scolastique, mais qui repose effectivement sur une conception très profonde, Luther essaie de préciser le sens de la phrase: l'oeuvre de la loi est écrite dans leur coeur. Rendons lui la parole : " Comment concilier avec cela et maintenir la parole de l'apotre que l'oeuvre de la loi est écrite dans leur coeur, alors que le prophète (Ezéchiel 11:19) dit pourtant que seul le peuple croyant obtiendrai à l'avenir que Dieu n'écrirait pas sa loi sur des tables de pierre, mais dans leur coeur ? Sauf meilleur avis, je crois qu'il faut faire une distinction entre la parole :"que l'oeuvre de la loi soit écrite dans leur coeur" et cette autre parole "que la loi soit écrite dans leur coeur". Car l'apotre n'a point voulu dire en cet endroit, l'eut-il su et pu dire, que les gentils possèdent la loi, mais que l"oeuvre de la loi est inscrite dans leur coeur. C'est pourquoi j'estime que la phrase: "que la loi soit écrite dans leur coeur" signifie autant que "l'amour est infusé au coeur par le s.Esprit (Romains 5:5). L'amour est au vrai sens du terme la loi du crhist et l'accomplissement de la loi de Moise. Il est une loi sans loi, sans mesure, sans but ni limites et qui dépasse tout ce qu'une loi ordonne ou peut ordonner.Mais "que l'oeuvre de la loi soit inscrite" cela signifie: "que la connaissance de cette oeuvre soit inscrite, c'est à dire la loi écrite concernant l'oeuvre à accomplir, mais non la grace nécessaire à l'accomplissement de l'oeuvre. C'est pourquoi il a fallu évidemment que demeurent confinés dans la lettre qui tue ceux qui ne possédaient pas plus que l'oeuvre de la loi inscrite dans leur coeur."

La simple lecture de cespassages démontre que, dans le commentaire sur l'épitre aux Romains, Luther avait pris une orientation telle que sa position à l'égard de la loi naturelle ne pouvait faire de doute. En dépi de certaines hésitations et d'une certaine imprécision dans la manière de s'exprimer, il avait acquis la conviction que l'homme naturel ne pouvait rien devant Dieu et que la loi naturelle, la loi inscrite dans son coeur avait p our fonction de mettre en évidence sa culpabilité au jour du jugement. L'homme naturel he possède, selon Luther, que la lettre de la loi et encore n'arrive-t-il pas à s'y conformer entièrement. Il ne dépasse pas la stade de la connaissance du bien et du mal et d'un accomplissement fragmentaire et servile des prescriptions qu'il parvient à dégeger de cette connaissance Dépourvu de la charité, il ne peut prétendre posséder la loi selon l'esprit, ni par conséquent être justifié devant Dieu.

Mais après avoir pris connaissance de ce texte tiré du commentaire de 1515, il nous faut maintenant essayer de dégager l'attitude définitive du réformateur, telle qu'elle s'inscrit dans ses oeuvres ultérieures et plus spécialement dans ses oeuvres d'exégèse et dans ses sermons.

Ainsi que Luther l'avait déjà fortement souligné, dans le commentaire dur l'épitre aux Romains, l'homme naturel, c'est à dire l'homme sans Dieu et donc sans foi, se confond avec le pécheur voué à la damnation. Chez lui, les effets de la chute se manifestent dans toute leur horreur. Le descendant d'Adam et d'Eve est chargé de la malédiction qui a frappé ses premiers parents. Il n'est rien devant Dieu et l'on peut ajouter que jusque dans l'ordre naturel lui-même ses facultés sont diminuées et affaiblies. Même si on pouvait lui en supposer le désir, il ne pourrait rien par ses propres forces, pour sortir de cet état de misère et de réprobation. Mais cel ne veut pas dire que Luther ait voulu affirmer que l'homme naturel soit pur néant, du moins lorsqu'on le considère dans sa sphère naturelle. Le souvenir de s.Augustin et, à son défaut, l'expérience courante, auraient au besoin enseignés à Luther l'absolue nécessité de reconnaitre qu'il subsiste un certain bien dans l'homme naturel dans le cadre de l'ordre de la création. Certes, ce bien, il faut le répéter, est obscurci et amoindri du fait de la chute; mais celle-ci av beau pu avoir pour conséquence de rejeter la créature humaine du domaine surnaturel et de limiter ses capacités naturelles, elle ne l'a pourtant pas ravalé au rang de la bête. La raison, bien qu'imparfaite ou troublée, continue à être au service de l'homme déchu. Il peut donc agir et bien agir, dans les limites de ce qui est rationnel. Bien plus, Luther admet en plusieurs endroits la survivance dans l'homme naturel d'une certaine connaissance naturelle de Dieu, voire d'une certaine tendance ou inclination à l'honorer, ainsi que des tendances parallèles vers le bien. C'est ainsi qu'il en arrive à parler dans son cours sur la Genèse de 1535 de l'existence, chez l'homme naturel, d'une sagesse qui provient "ex luminae rationnis divinitus insito" .Gardons-nous pour autant de nous hater d'accuser Luther d'inconséquence ou de penser qu'il ne s'agit là que d'un emprunt maginal à la terminologie de s.Augustin et des scolastiques, bien que la parenté entre sa conception et la leur soit évidente. Avant de conclure, il faut s'efforcer de préciser d'avantage. Luther lui-même nous en fournit l'occasion dans un texte important qui se trouve dans son commentaire de 1535 sur l'épitre aux Galates. S'agissant du passage 2:2o Luther écrit:

"Versus: Ultra posse viri non vult (deus ulla requiri).Wer fein,si in loco.Si sum in regno rationis,adifico domum,custodio vaccas. Ibi facio, quantum possum; ibi excusatus.Da ghorts hin dictum: quantum; debet facere, - in politico et oeconomico non sic in regno spirituali. Homo hic nihil facere potest,quia est servus peccati. In oeconomia non est servus vaccae.Non debent politica dicta trahi in ecclesiam"

(L'adage: "Dieu ne veut rien exiger qui soit audessus des forces de l'homme" serait bon s'il etait ici à sa place.Etant dans le domaine de la raison,je batis ma maison,je garde mes vaches j'y fais ce que je peux; j'y trouve mon excuse. C'est à ce domaine qu'appartient l'adage: il doit faire ce qu'il peut,à savoir dans le domaine politique et économique; mais il n'en est pas de même dans le royaume spirituel.Ici l'homme ne peut rien entreprendre,parce qu'il est l'esclave du péché.En matière économique,il n'est pas l'esclave de la vache.Il ne faut pas trainer dans l'église les règles de la politique").

Il existe donc deux domaines distincts qu'il ne faut pas confondre: l'un qui est spirituel et où l'homme naturel est impuissant en raison de son peché; l'autre; le domaine politique et économique, ce dernier terme étant entendu au sens du 16°S.; qui est sous l'empire de la raison et où la chute n'empêche pas l'homme d'agir.Luther revient, toutjours dans le même passage sur cette distinction, à laquelle il faut donc admettre qu'il attribuait de l'importance:

" Distinguo naturalia contra spiritualia,Spiritualia sunt extincta in homine impio et diobolo; ibi nihil, quia voluntas adversaria, inimica Dei. Naturalia sunt integra,concedo;homo in impietate mersus et servus biaboli habet potestatem edificandi domum,gerendi magistratum ,quae sunt homini subiecta,Gen I.

Ista generalia non adempta (homini), quia oeconomia et politia" (Je distingue les choses naturelles et spirituelles. Les spirituelles sont éteintes dans l'homme impie et dans le diable; il ne s'y trouve rien, parce que la volonté est opposée et hostile à Dieu. Les naturelles demeurent entières, je le concède (remarquons en passant que c'est une concession de pure forme, et, en tout les cas, très limitée quant à l'objet en cause) l'homme plongé dans l'impiété et serviteur du diable a le pouvoir de batir sa maison, de remplir les fonctions politiques, car ces choses sont soumises à l'homme. Ses affaires générales ne lui ont pas été enlevées, car elles ressortissent à l'économique et au politique).

La séparation est donc bien tranchée entre le domaine naturel et le domaine spirituel. C'est pour ne l'avoir pas bien compris que des auteurs tel que Holl se sont mépris sur la pensée de Luther. Ou, plus exactement, c'est parce qu'ils se sont faits du domaine rationnel une donception purement morale et qu'ils n'ont admis qu'une morale unique, la morale surnaturelle du chrétien. Or, s'il ext exact que pour Luther, comme pour s. Augustin, l'acte véritablement moral se situe sur le plan surnaturel et n'est accessible qu'à l'homme pourvu de la grace, il est exact aussi, et nous en trouverons encore plusieurs témoignages, que sa conception du droit naturel et partant du domaine rationel n'est pas cantonnée dans les euls actes de la vie matérielle et dans les formes élémentaires de la vie sociale, comme pourrait le faire croire l'affirmation que nous venons de lire. Quoiqué il en soit, la conclusion qu'il donne à ce passage souligne encore la séparation des domaines naturel et spirituel et place le principa de cette séparation dans la volonté mauvaise et dans l'intellect vicié de l'homme naturel: "quicquid in voluntate nostra est malum; in intellectu nostro est error. In rebus divinis nihil homo habet quam tenebras er errores, malicias et perversitates" (Tout ce qui se trouve dans notre volonté est mal; tout ce qui se trouve dans notre intellect est erreur. En ce qui concerne les choses divines, l'homme n'a rien que ténébres et erreurs, malices et perversité.)

Il est donc bien établit que pour Luther l'homme naturel peut accomplir toute une série d'actes qui dépendent de sa seule raison, et que ces actes il les accomplira bien, en dépit de son péché. Seulement, ces actes ne peuvent en aucun cas prétendre à la qualification d'actes moraux. Ou, pour reprndre le langage du commentaire sur l'épitre aux Romains, ils ne sont pas donformes à l'esprit de la loi, mais s'efforcent d'en accomplir la lettre. Rejetant résolumment, la notion d'une morale purement naturelle qui viendrait doubler et comme préparer la morale surnaturelle, notion qui avait, on le sait, été mise en avant par les théologiens du M yen-Age, Luther rejoint une fois de plus s. Augustin. Pour lui aussi, les vertus des paiens ne sont au fond que des vices cahhés. Un autre passage de l'épitre aux Galates lui fournit d'ailleurs l'occasion de s'expliquer avec quelques détails sur ce problème qui n'est que l'application pratique du principe que seule la grace peut permettre d'accomplit le bien véritable. Commentant Galates 3/28, Luther écrivit dans ce même commentaire de 1535 :

"Parmi les gentils il y eut en effet des hommes grands et remarquables, tel que Xenophon, Témistocle, Marcus Fabius, Attilius Regulus, Cicéron, Pomponius Atticus et beaucoup d'autres qui, doués de vertus insignes et vraiment héroiques, administrèrent fort bien l'état, accomplirent avec un grand éclat bien des choses pour le salut de la République. Et cependant, tousces hommes, avec leur sagesse, leur puissance, leurs actes très honnètes, leurs vertus insignes, leurs lois, leur justice, leur culte, et leur religion (car nous ne devons pas imaginer que les gentils aient méprisés l'honnetété et la religion, mais tous les gentils dispersés dans le monde ont eu leurs lois,leurs cultes et leurs religions, sans lesquelles il est impossible de gouverner les hommes) tous ces hommes dis-je, avec toute leurs qualités ne sont rien devant Dieu."

En vertu de la seule raison naturelle les hommes peuvent donc se montrer honnètes,drouts,religieux même sans que, pour autant ils satisfassent aux exigences spirituelles de la loi divine. Sans doute, dira-t-on, mais c'est parce que ces paiens ont soit simulés les vertus qui viennent d'être énumérées,soit accomplis les actes qui en découlaient d'une manière purement extérieure. Est-il donc impossible d'admettre qu'un paien se comporte vraiement de façon vertueuse ? Luther renchérit aussitôt et du même coup il montre tout l(abime qui sépare, selon lui, le paien, même honnête et religieux, du chrétien qui bénéficie de la grace:

"Ainsi, écrit-il, que le serviteur remplisse son offuce avec la plus grande diligence, que le héros serve avec obéissance et fidélité, que l'homme libre préside et gouverne la république ou ses affaires privées d'une manière digné d'éloges; de même tout ce que fera l'homme en tant qu'homme, en se mariant, en administrant bien ses affaires domestiques, en obéissan aux autorités,en se conduisany honnêtement et décemment à l'égard de tout le monde si la femme de son côté, vit chastement,si elle obéit à son mari, si elle prend grand soin de sa maison,si elle élève bien ses enfants (et ce sont là certes des dons et des oeuvres magnifiques et excelletntes) - pourtant,tout cela n'est rien quant à la justice devant Dieu. En résumé, tout ce qu'il peut y avoir dans le mo,de en fait de lois, de cérémonies,de cultes,de justices et d'oeuvres, y compris celles de Juifs qui eurent les premiers une royauté et un sacerdoce divinement institués et ordonnés par Dieu, avec leurs lois leur religion et leur culte, pourtant toutes ces choses n'enlèvent pas les péchés, ni le libèrent de la mort, ni ne procurent le salut."

Les examples donnés dans ce texte part Luther permettent de se faire une notion très nette de l'etendue du domaine naturel que le réformateur entend séparer du domaine spirituel. Mais on peut toujours rétorquer qu'il ne s'agit là que de choses purement terrestres, que là même où il est question de religion, il ne s'agit que d'une religion fausse qui n'a rien de commun avec la vraie spiritualité chrétienne. D'autres textes viennent ici préciser en profondeur la portée exacte que Luther donne à la loi naturelle. Tout comme les théologiens de l'antiquité et du moyen-age, Luther affirme volontiers que le principe des lois promulguées par Moise se retrouve dans la loi naturelle et qu'il en est ainsi notamment du premier commandement qui prescrit d'honorer Dieu. Ces lois fondamentales qui sont inscrites au coeur de tous les hommes ne contiennent donc pas seulement, comme on aurait pu croire, une vague orientation vers la divinité, une sorte de sentiment religieux diffus. Elles contiennent aussi les principes de la morale et du droit, tels qu'ils sont exprimes dans le Décalogue: "les dix commandements écrit Luther, sont écrits dans le coeur de tous les hommes'" Mais c'est surtout dans ses sermons de 1527 sur la Genèse que le réformateur a developpé son point de vue, Faisant allusion aux anabaptistes qui préconisaient un retour à la législation mosaique, Luther déclare :" Quand viennent les sectaires et qu'ils disent:Moïse l'a ordonné ainsi; laisse Moïse de coté et réponds:Je ne m'occupe pas de ce qu'a ordonné Moise.Pourtant, disent-ils, il a ordonné d'avoir un seul Dieu,de lui faire confiance et de croire en lui, de ne pas prêter serment en son nom, d'honorer père et mère, de ne pas tuer,ni dérober,ni commettre d'adultère, ni porter de faux témoignages, ni convoiter la femme d'autrui.Ne devons-nous pas observer tout cela ? Réponds ainsi: La nature a aussi ces mêmes lois. La nature nous dit d'invoquer Dieu, c'est ce que montrent aussi les paiens; car il n'y a jamais eu nul paien qui n'ait invoqué ses faux dieux, bien que le vrai Dieu leur ait fait défaut, comme aussi aux juifs.Car les Juifs aussi sont tombés dans l'idolatrie, comme les paiens, sauf qu'ils ont reçu la loi.Mais les paiens ont la loi écrite dans leur coeur,et il n'y a point de différence,ainsi que l'indique aussi S.Paul aux Romains:Les paiens qui n'ont pas la loi ont la loi écrite dans leur coeur.Mais de même que les juifs transgressent la loi, de même la transgressent aussi les paiens.Et c'est pourquoi il est naturel d'honorer Dieu,de ne pas dérober,de ne pas commettre d'adultère,de ne pas porter de faux témoignage,de ne pas tuer,et ce que Moïse ordonne n'est pas nouveau.En effet, ce que Dieu a donné aux Juifs du haut du ciel par l'intermédiaire de Moise, il l'a écrit aussi dans le coeur de tous les hommes, à la fois des juifs et des paiens, avec cette seule différence qu'il l'a fait écrire au surplus à l'intention des juifs qui sont son propre peuple élu, à l'aide d'une voix et d'une écriture corporelle[86].

Luther se rattache ici à la tradition augustinienne et scolastique sur l'identité du contenu de la loi naturelle et du Décalogue.C'est là une question quil nous faudra reprendre à un autre point de vue un peu plus tard. Pour l'instant il convient de souligner fortement ce fait que Luther, loin de nier l'existence ou la portée de la loi naturelle, l'affirme au contraire avec autant de force qu'un s.Augustin ou un s.Thomas. Mais il ne s'est pas borné à suivre ses modèles; il insiste plus fortement encore que ne l'avait fait s.Augustin sur la nécessité de la grace pour l'accomplissement de tout acte vraiment bon. Tandis que s.Thomas concevait la coexistence comme la superposition d'une morale naturelle et d'une morale surnaturelle et qu'il admettait que, dans l'ordre naturel, tout ce qui était fait sous l'impulsion de la raison et en vue du but naturel de l'homme était bon, Luther réserve expressément le bien à l ordre sunaturel et n'accorde aucune valeur autre que celle d'une conformité avec la création aux vertus dont peuvent témoigner les paiens et les juifs.Il n'y a pas pour lui plus de vertu dans un acte raisonnable accompli par un paien qu'il n'y en a dans une opération arithmétique correctement menée. Sous cette réserve fondamentale, on peut dire que Luther a été le continuateur des théoriciens scolastiques du droit naturel. Comme eux,il en fait, par exemple dans ses sermons sur lè Exode de 1524/1527, la source et la mesure qui permettent de juger dt d'appliquer comme il faut les lois positives. La raison naturelle, toute corrompue qu'elle soit par la chute, suffit à donner à l'homme une certaine sagesse qui le rend capable, ainsi que nous l'avons vu, de règler le culte,d'organiser l'état et de diriger sa famille.En vertu de cette raison naturelle encore, il peut donner des lois positives une application conforme à l'équité,à cette fameuse 'epiiciaē que Luther place très haut, au-dessus de la science juridique, attachée à la lettre de la loi positive, telle qu'elle prévalait de son temps, sous l'influence du droit romain nouvellement introduit en Allemagne.

On peut donc essayer dès maintenant de déterminer ce que Luther entendait au fond par droit naturel. Le premier élément qu'il y trouve, c'est une disposition naturelle à l'homme à se conformer à certaines aspirations religieuses et morales. Pourtant, dans son commentaire de 1519 sur le Psuatier, Luther refuse, à propos du Ps. 4/7 à l'homme ce qu'il appelle les "prima principia in moralibus per se nota" Ces premiers principes moraux, dit-il ne peuvent être communiqués à l'homme que par la foi. Alors, et alors seulement, l'homme est rendu capable en vertu de ses dispositions naturelles de donner son adhésion pleine et entière à ces premiers principes. Tant qu'il n'a pas reçu la foi, ces dispositions naturelles le mettent seulement en mesure d'organiser sa vie matérielle et de créer à cet effet les règlements de droit positif. Mais il lui est complètement interdit d'atteindre et même de concevoir la charité qui est le fondement de tout acte vraiment moral et qui ne peut être acquise que par un don de Dieu agissant par la foi, ainsi que Luther le souligne à maintes reprises et notamment dans son commentaire de 1535 sur l'épitre aux Galates.

J'ai réservé jusqu'à maintenant un passage du cours de 1535-1545 sur la Genèse. Luther y expose en termes qui me paraissent particulièrement heureux et précis, la position que j'ai essayé de définir jusqu'à présent. Il commence par imaginer les objections qui lui sont faites par les partisans d'une morale naturelle ou rationnelle :

"Mais on oppose l'affirmation d'Aristote: La raison aspire aux biens su-prêmes; et cette opinion, on essaie de la confirmer par certains passages de l'Ecriture. De même par ce point de vue que soutiennent les philosophes: que la droite raison est la cause de toutes les vertus. Je me garde bien de nier la vérité. de ces affirmations, à condition de ne les faire porter que sur les choses qui sont soumises à la raison, telles que la garde des bestiaux, la construction des misons ou l'encemensement des champs. Mais dans les choses supérieures, ces opinions ne sont pas vraies. Comment en effet la raison peut-elle être qualifiée de droite, quand elle hait Dieu ? Comment la volonté peut-elle être dite droite, quand elle résiste à la volonté de Dieu et refuse d'obéir à Dieu ? Si donc on te dit: La raison aspire aux biens suprêmes, tu répondras: Aux biens suprêmes en ce qui concerne l'organisation de la Cité, càd, aux choses dont peut juger la raison. Dans ce domaine, elle gouverne et conduit à ce qui est honnête et utile, corporellement ou charnellement. Du reste, lorsque la raison est emplie d'ignorance de Dieu et d'aversion à l'égard de sa volonté, comment peut-elle être dite bonne à ce point ? Mais il est connu que, quand on prêche la connaissance de Dieu et qu'il s'agit de restaurer la raison, ceux qui sont les meilleurs et qui ont, pour m'exprimer ainsi, une meilleure raison et une meilleure volonté, sont ceux-là même qui ont d'autant plus violemment haï l'Evangile."

(note: le tapiste a négligé de vous communiquer le texte original latin).

Et pourtant, nous avons constaté que Luther en arrive à qualifier le Décalogue de 'loi naturelle', et il fait d'ailleurs de même pour le Sermon sur la Montagne. C'est qu'il s'agit pour lui d'une objectivation, d'une actualisatiin des préceptes dont le germe se trouve dans la nature humaine, mais n'y est plus développé depuis la chute. Les principes qui forment la base et le contenu de la loi naturelle se sont perdus du fait du péché. Pour les rétablir dans leur ancien éclat il est nécessaire qu'intervienne la révélation. Ainsi se trouve parachevé la nature humaine dont Luther ne nie naturellement pas la bonté originelle, mais dont, plus qu'un autre, il souligne la corruption présente. C'est donc la même volonté divine qui se manifeste d'une part dans la nature et d'autre part dans la révélation. Luther reprend ici à son compte certains développements chers aux scolastiques au sujet de la diversité historique, mais de l unité profonde des manifestations de la potentia ordinata. Mais le réformateur insiste d'avantage que n'avaient fait les théologiens du moyen-âge sur l'opposition qui existe entre la loi divine et la loi naturelle. Tandis que le passage de la seconde à la première s'opérait avec aisance dans la pensée des scolastiques et que la loi divine leur apparaissait comme un simple complément ou une correction de la loi naturelle, Luther met en relief que le péché a privé celle-ci de ses principes moraux; Il ne lui reste donc plus d'autre domaine que le domaine des activités purement naturelles et de l'ordre matériel de la vie, à l'exclusion de toute activité vraiment morale. Et il en est ainsi, selon Luther, tant que l'Esprit Saint n'a pas opéré en l'homme la rupture avec le péché et la conversion à la vie nouvelle.

Nous pouvons approfondir cette conception luthérienne de la loi naturelle en la mettant en rapport avec sa notion de la conscience. Il est arrivé à Luther, comme à ses devanciers, de confondre loi naturelle et conscience. Parfois, il emploie même ce terme dans son sens purement intellectuel de perception d'une connaissance. Mais le plus souvent il entend par conscience la faculté qui permet à l'homme de prononcer des jugements d'ordre moral, ce que nous nommons, en langage courant, le tribunal de la conscience. Il distingue avec soin cette 'virtus iudicandi' des 'virtutes operandi' qui nous permettent d'agir conformémént à tel précepte donné ou à telle inclination de la volonté. La conscience a pour mission de nous accuser, de nous condamner ou de nous absoudre nsmêmes, lorsque nous considérons notre conduite. Elle est, pour employer la formule qui se trouve dans la "Postille latine" 'suum iudicium de seipso'. Or quel est le résultat de cette intervention de la conscience dans notre vie morale ? Luther n'a cessé d'afirmer hautement que cette critique de soi-même à la-quelle se livre le pécheur le conduit nécessairement à la misère intérieure et au désespoir. En effet, le pécheur est obligé de se condamner, pour peu qu'il juge son activité à la lumière de la loi naturelle ou de la loi divine, et il en sera encore ainsi lors du jugement dernier, comme l'a laissé entendre saint Paul dans l'épître aux Romains. Seulement, ne croyons pas que cette conscience naturelle propre à tous les hommes du seul fait de laur humanité ait été laissée indemne par la chute. Elle aussi a été faussée, du moins en ce qui concerne les jugements à porter sur les 'bona optima'. Réduite à ses propres forces, la conscience naturelle n'est plus qu'une faculté affaiblie, souvent faussée, et qui ne peut atteindre la moralité vraie, qui seule compte devant Dieu. On comprend dès lors que Luther ait pu considérer comme coupable celui-là même qui ne croyait rien avoir à se reprocher, en se fondant sur le jugement de sa conscience naturelle. Sans doute nous fait-elle entrevoir le bien et le mal, mais déformés et comme à travers un voile. L'homme naturel aurait donc les meilleures intentions du monde et il aurait accompli toutes les exigences de sa conscience, qu'il n'en serait pour autant justifié, ni même certain d'avoir bien agi. A plus forte raison devra-t-il se condamner, lorsque l'expérience lui prouvera, comme elle fait en réalité, qu'il n'a même pas su atteindre le but que lui proposait sa conscience.

Il existe à ce propos un texte important de Luther dans sa "Postille allemande" de 1522 où il précise son point de vue par rapport à saint Augustin:

> "Que personne écrit-il, ne me fasse grief que, sur ce point j'aie une autre opinion que saint Augustin, qui estimait qu'il était question de la lumière naturelle dans Jn 1/4. Je ne rejette pas cette interprétation, car je sais très bien que toute lumière de la raison est allumée à la lumière divine, et, de même que j'ai dit au sujet de la vie naturelle qu'elle est une partie et le commencement de la vie véritable, lorsqu'elle parvient à une droite connaissance, de même j'estime que la lumière de la raison est aussi une partie et un commencement de la lumière véritable, lorsqu'elle reconnait et honore Celui qui l'a allumée. Mais elle ne le fait pas d'elle-même, mais reste repliée sur elle-même et est faussée et fausse du même coup toute chose. C'est pourquoi elle s'éteindra et sombrera; mais la lumière de la grâce n'engloutit point la lunmière naturelle: c'est ainsi qu'il est clair selon la lumière naturelle que trois et deux font cinq et il est clair aussi qu'il faut faire le bien et éviter le mal; et la lumière de la grâce n'éteint pas cela. Mais la lumière naturelle n'atteint pas au point de pouvoir dire ce qui est bien et ce qui est mal. Il en va d'elle comme de celui qui devait aller à Rome et qui se mit à marcher sur un faux chemin; car cet homme savait bien qu'il fallait prendre le bon chemin pour se rendre à Rome; mais il ignorait quel était ce droit chemin. Ainsi fait aussi la lumière naturelle; elle ne prend pas le bon chemin, celui qui mène à Dieu, et elle ne le connait pas non plus, bien qu'elle sache fort bien qu'il faut prendre ce bon chemin. C'est

pourquoi la raison confond tout le temps le bien et le mal, et elle ne prendrait pas le mal pour le bien, si elle ne savait pas clairement qu'il convient de choisir le bien seul...

Et, du moment que l'occasion s'en présente, nous voulons dénoncer plus amplement cette fausse lumière naturelle qui provoque toute misère et tout malheur. Il en est de la lumière naturelle comme de toutes les autres forces et facultés de l'homme. Qui mettrait en doute que l'homme ait été créé par la parole éternelle de Dieu avec toutes ses forces, de même que toutes les autres choses et qu'il soit une créature de Dieu ? Mais cependant il n'y a nul bien en lui, càd comme le dit Moïse Gen 6: toutes ses pensées et ses intentions avec toutes ses forces sont uniquement orientées vers le mal. C'est pourquoi, la chair a beau être vraiment une créature de Dieu, elle n'en est pas moins encline à l'impudicité et non point à la chasteté. Bien que le coeur soit vraiment une créature de Dieu, il n'en est pas moins enclin non pas à l'humilité et à l'amour du prochain, mais à l'orgueil et à l'amour de soi; et il agit aussi selon cette inclination, à moins qu'on ne l'en empêche de force. De même en est-il de la lumière naturelle. Bien qu'elle soit par nature assez claire pour savoir qu'il ne faut faire que le bien; elle est pourtant faussée au point de ne jamais savoir au juste ce qui est bon; mais elle appelle bon ce qui lui plait; elle s'y fixe et en conclut que le bien qu'elle a choisi doit être accompli. ainsi elle poursuit sa course et suit toujours le mal, comme s'il s'agissait toujours du bien."

Il en résulte que l'homme naturel possède bien la faculté qui lui permet de savoir qu'il faut faire le bien et éviter le mal, faculté qui était aux yeux de st Thomas d'Aquin le principe unique d'où dérive toute la loi naturelle. Mais Luther n'en dégage pas, comme avait fait l'auteur de la Somme Théologique, la conclusion que l'homme naturel est en mesure de faire dériver de ce premier principe les préceptes genéraux et particuliers qui règleront sa conduite. Du fait de la chute, la raison naturelle est trop obscurcie et faussée pour ne pas l'induire désormais et de manière presque convaincante en erreur, chaque fois qu'il s'agit de déterminer ce qui est bien et ce qui est mal. Une fois de plus apparait ici la séparation absolue introduite par Luther entre le domaine de l'activité matérielle et terrestre et le domaine de l'activité morale. En admettant que l'homme naturel était capable d'accomplir des actes bons sur le plan de la morale naturelle, st Thomas avait trouvé une solution qui lui parut résoudre le problème. Luther, en revanche, n'en veut pas entendre parler: il rejette toute idée d'une morale naturelle et développe pleinement les conséquences de la chute qui ont privé la nature humaine de toute possibilité d'action sur le plan spirituel et moral, ou, plus exactement, de toute possibilité d'appliquer en fait les enseignements de la loi morale.

Tout autre est la situation du chrétien. Alors que le paien ne pouvait en venir qu'à se condamner sans rémission au jugement de sa conscience, le chrétien a acquis, en même temps que la rédemption, la rémission des péchés et la "bona vel laeta conscientia". Non pas qu'il n'ait plus conscience d'être pêcheur. On sait tout au contraire, combien Luther a insisté sur le fait que le chrétien se sait pécheur aussi longtemps qu'il vit ici-bas. Il ne s'agit donc nullement d'une justice active sur laquelle il prétendrait fonder sa bonne conscience, càd d'une justice qu'il s'imputerait à lui-même. Il s'agit de ce que Luther qualifie de "iustitia passiva" et qu'il identifie à la rémission des péchés, càd de cette justice que Dieu nous impute par un libre mouvement de sa grâce. Il en faut conclure nécéssairement que la bonne et joyeuse conscience du chrétien ne dérive en rien de la lumière de la raison naturelle qui conduit presque surement au mal, en dépit de sa tendance générale au bien. Ce n'est que par la foi et l'espérance que l'homme converti parviendra à la bonne conscience. Celle-ci sera d'autant plus assurée que sera libre de toute hésitation la foi du chrétien. Si donc la foi au Christ est ébranlée par le doute ou le péché, du même coup la conscience perdra sa certitude.

L'historien R. Seeberg a fait remarquer, avec sa perspicacité habituelle dans son analyse de la pensée de Luther, la cohésion systématique qui unit entre elles, dans ce domaine particulier, les diverses notions défendues par le réformateur. Sa conception de la conscience correspond exactement à sa notion de l'homme naturel, et l'une et l'autre présupposent la double opération de la 'potentia ordinata' de Dieu, à la fois dans la loi naturelle liée à la création et dans la loi scripturaire liée à la révélation. Luther ne se borne pas, en effet, à releguer Dieu, en dehors de la révélation bien entendu, dans le rôle de cause première, comme avaient fait les scolastiques. Il admet, au contraire, son intervention permanente au sein de toute la création. A ce point de vue, les effets de l'action divine dans le monde actuel naturel ne peuvent évidemment être dénués de toute valeur positive. La providence et le gouvernement du monde agissent tout aussi bien chez les paiens que chez les chrétiens. Bien plus, Luther affirme que, du moins chez certains hommes prédestinés, la raison naturelle reconnait, lorsqu'elle est mise en sa présence, la morale chrétienne comme la seule vraie et comme l'accomplissement de ses propres tendances innées. D'avantage encore, il déclare avec toute la clarté désirable, que, si elle ne trouvait pas dans l'homme naturel un point de contact, la prédication de l'Evangile resterait sans effet:

> "Sans nul doute, dit-il dans ses sermons sur l'Exode, la Loi nous serait prêchée en vain pendant cent ans, comme à un âne insensible, si elle n'était pas inscrite dans nos coeurs, de sorte que, avertis par elle, nous disions: Cela est vrai".

Il faut donc se demander, s'il existe entre l'action de Dieu au sein de la nature et son action par la révélation une relation directe. Dans ce cas, les préceptes que la raison et la conscience de l'homme naturel parviennent à dégager devraient être considérés comme un acheminement vers la morale chrétienne qui n'en serait que le parachèvement. Mais dans ce cas aussi, Luther prendrait, en dépit de tout ce que nous avons cru pouvoir constater, la suite de la scolastique. Il se serait déjugé lui-même, et ceux-là auraient raison qui s'avouent incapables d'harmoniser ses différentes affirmations concernant la loi naturelle. D'une part, en effet il aurait déclaré infranchissable l'abîme entre la vie naturelle et la vie chrétienne et sans rapports la loi naturelle et la loi de la morale; d'autre part, il accepterait de faire de la loi naturelle un premier degré de la loi morale, une sorte de disposition innée, qui préparerait l'homme à la vie chrétienne. Les nombreux passages où Luther a proclamé la valeur positive, non seulement naturelle, mais religieuse, de l'organisation politique semblent confirmer encore cette interprétation. De plus, n'a-t-il pas également affirmé que l'homme naturel possède une tendance, une orientation innée vers la vie morale et vers Dieu. Et comment d'un point de vue plus élevé et plus général, ne pas admettre à priori que l'action de Dieu sur le plan naturel de la création ne peut contredire son action sur le plan surnaturel de la révélation.?

L'objection qu'on en peut tirer contre l'interprétation que j'ai proposée jusqu'à présent en me fondant sur d'autres passages non moins importants du réformateur, cette objection n'est pas sans valeur, et l'on ne peut la rejeter sans plus. Et pourtant, on n'a pas de peine à s'apercevoir qu'elle est en contradiction avec toute la pensée de Luther et que cette pensée présente en réalité une unité profonde. Il suffit, en effet, de constater que les deux modes d'action de la 'potentia ordinata' de Dieu (son action dans la nature et son action dans la révélation) sont évidemment orientées dans le même sens; mais que depuis la chute, elles ne s'exercent plus avec la même efficacité. Tandis que l'action divine qui opère par la révélation et par la grâce n'a pas été affectée par la chute, l'action de Dieu qui se conforme à l'ordre de la nature s'est vue opposer la résistance de la volonté viciée de l'homme. La puissance du péché, -et il ne faut pas hésiter à employer le mot: la puissance du diable- fait constamment obstacle à la réalisation du plan divin naturel. L'ordre de la création tout entière a été troublé par le péché. Il en résulte que les rapports qui unissaient initialement les deux modes de l'action divine ont été troublés eux aussi. Sans doute, la volonté de Dieu continue à déterminer le cours du monde dans son ensemble, mais elle doit tenir compte, depuis la chute, du non-vouloir que lui oppose le cours naturel des choses. En d'autres termes, Dieu a incorporé le mal au plan de la création, depuis que l'homme a résisté par sa révolte au plan initialement prévu. Dieu ne s'impose pas à sa créature en anéantissant le mal; il veut que la créature réponde librement à son appel, ou du moins le veut-il, pour celles d'entre ses créatures qu'il a prédestinées au salut.

Luther y voit l'explication de ce fait que, pour se tourner vers l'appel divin, la créature doit abandonner sa volonté naturelle. C'est la négation de cette volonté naturelle ou sa transformation, qui permet la conversion de l'homme, conversion qui ne peut se faire sans une nouvelle intervention de Dieu par le moyen de la grâce. Cont irement aux scolastiques qui s'étaient efforcés de ménager des transitions entre le échour et le chrétien, Luther n'a jamais cessé d'insister sur le caractère infranchissable de l'abîme qui sépare le vieil homme de l'homme régenéré, le péché de la grâce, et l'action du Créateur de l'action nécessairement faussée de la création déchue. Certes, il a reconnu, comme nous l'avons vu, que les facultés naturelles qui subsistent dans l'homme déchu tirent, elles aussi, leur origine de la sagesse divine, dont elles présentent encore comme un pâle reflet plus ou moins déformé; mais à côté de cette trace souillée de la lumière divine, il proclame l'existence d'une autre lumière réservée aux élus et qui leur ouvre les yeux à la vérité de la révélation. C'est ainsi qu'il a pu écrire dans ses sermons de 1537 sur les deux premiers chapîtres de l'Evangile selon st Jean:

> "indépendamment de la lumière qui est commune à tous les hommes, aux pieux comme aux méchants, il existe encore une lumière particulière que Dieu donne aux siens, afin que son Verbe se révèle à ses élus par l'Esprit Saint et par la prédication orale."

En résumé Luther a donc affirmé deux propositions qui ne sont contradictoires qu'en apparence, et dont je pense avoir montré la conciliation possible.

D'une part il souligne que l'homme naturel comme tel est absolument incapable de reconnaitre la vérité de la révélation et même de se disposer à la recevoir. Le péché a rendu l'homme totalement étranger à Dieu et l'a confiné dans des activités et des préoccupations purement terrestres ou si étroitement liées à celles-ci, qu'elles ne participent en rien au caractère spirituel qu'il leur arrive de simuler. Ce n'est que par la grâce que l'homme peut être arraché à ce plan naturel. D'autre part, Luther a reconnu que l'homme naturel ne cesse d'être une créature de Dieu et qu'il se trouve placé par conséquent dans l'ordre de la création tel que

Dieu l'a déterminé. Au sein même de sa vie terrestre, il arrive même au pécheur de tendre vers la vérité et vers le bien. Mais il est incapable d'y atteindre. Si néanmoins cette tendance est telle chez certains hommes qu'elle leur permet, le moment venu, d'accueillir la prédication du salut, c'est que ces hommes étaient prédestinés à compter un jour parmi les élus.

Cette conception implique l'affirmation que tous les hommes ne possèdent pas au même degré la loi naturelle. Elle implique aussi que la loi naturelle est un privilège propre à l'homme. Luther a insisté sur ce point dans un fragment de ses propos de table, daté de l'automne 1533:

> "Les jurisconsultes, y est-il dit, ne définissent pas convenablement le droit naturel, en le déclarant commun aux hommes et aux bètes; il est en effet nécessaire de distinguer dans le droit naturel l'homme en tant que seigneur des autres bètes et de lui attribuer un rôle supérieur. Ils parleraient donc plus correctement, s'ils disaient qu'il y a un droit naturel brutal et un autre rationnel. En second lieu, on ne peut parler de droit à propos de la bète, mais seulement à propos de l'homme, donc le droit naturel n'est pas nommé normalement de façon convenable. Car le droit est ce qui doit être fait. Cinq et trois ne doivent pas être huit, mais font huit. De même dit-on improprement qu'il y a un droit naturel dans la bète parce qu'elle se défend; la défense est en effet une réaction spontanée et se confond avec la nature. Il ya donc une chose dans la bète et non pas un droit qui n'existe que dans l'homme. Engendrer et nourrir sont des faits, des choses, et non des droits. Dans tout droit doit être le "debet". Il n'est pas nécessaire de dire [illegible] truie qu'elle mange, elle le fait d'elle-même. Les jurisconsultes n'ont donc pas une notion convenable du droit naturel, mais seulement du droit des gens qui dérive de la raison humaine. Le droit n'est pas ce qui sera fait. Le pommier porte des fruits, [illegible] scris rien. Mais dans la théologie le droit naturel est non ce qui est fait mais ce qui doit être fait."

Dans tout ce passage, d'une allure presque scolastique, Luther fait donc résider l'originalité du droit, et par conséquent aussi du droit naturel, dans l'obligation. Mais il n'a pas, à ma connaissance, essayé d'approfondir son analyse, en scrutant les raisons de cette obligation et en en décomposant le mécanisme psychologique, comme avait tenté de le faire un saint Thomas d'Aquin.

Quant au contenu de ce droit naturel, Luther le conçoit de deux manières différentes. Dans les textes que nous avons examinés jusqu'à présent, les diverses manifestations de la loi naturelle peuvent toutes être comprises sous la rubrique générale du gouvernement divin dans la nature, tel qu'il se réalise et se révèle dans l'organisation de la création et dans ses lois immuables. De ce point de vue, Elert a pu dire avec raison dans la "Morphologie des Luthertums" que 'la loi naturelle chez Luther n'est rien d'autre que l'ordre de la création". Mais on peut se borner à n'y voir que cela. Toujours est-il que cet aspect de la notion luthérienne devait avoir d'importantes conséquences pratiques, analogues, sur plus d'un point, à celles que les thomistes avaient fait dériver de leur définition du droit naturel. Comme eux, Luther conclut en effet à l'origine divine et partant à la valeur durable de l'ordre politique et social. Loin de partager l'attitude critique d'un Ockham qui faisait de la loi naturelle le critère selon lequel devaient être jugées et au besoin rejetées les institutions existantes, Luther les a justifiées, du moins dans l'ordre purement politique et civil. En dépit de ses injustices ou de ses incohérences, le régime temporel a toujours trouvé un défenseur tantot convaincu, tantot résigné, dans le réformateur. On sait combien ont été graves les conséquences d'un tel point de vue? Et il n'est pas impossible que Luther s'en soit rendu compte. Mais il n'a jamais pu se résoudre à abandonner son attitude conservatrice, surtout après la guerre des paysans, ni diminuer en quoique ce fût la puissance qu'il attribuait à l'autorité civile, puissance qui reposait à ses yeux sur le droit naturel lui-même. Il a deplus été confirmé dans cette attitude par cette idée qui lui était chère, à savoir qu'une législation positive fondée sur le droit naturel était indispensable pour empêcher le péché de se répandre en brutale sauvagerie. Et, ici encore, Luther se rattache de près aux conceptions médiévales.

Mais, je le répète, ce n'était point là le seul domaine du droit naturel pour Luther. Il y voyait encore le fondement de cette équité selon laquelle il voulait que fussent appliquées les lois positives aux relations entre les hommes. L'enseignement de la loi naturelle vient ici rejoindre dans une certaine mesure les inspirations de la charité chrétienne. "La nature enseigne, écrit Luther dans son 'traité de l'autorité civile',

> tout comme fait la charité, que je dois faire ce que je voudrais qu'on me fit. Mais si tu perds de vue le droit de la charité et de la nature, tu ne parviendras pas à agir d'une façon qui soit agréable à Dieu, même si tu avais dévoré tous les livres de droit et tous les juristes."

Cela signifie naturellement pas qu'il faille mettre sur le même plan le droit naturel et la charité, ni même que leur contenu ait jamais été conçu comme interchangeable. Il n'en reste pas moins que le droit naturel présente comme une exigence de la raison cela même que la charité accomplit spontanément dans le domaine particulier de l'interprétation des lois positives, à savoir l'équité. Cette interprétation de la loi positive à la lumière de la loi naturelle repose elle-même sur le postulat souvent répété par Luther que la raison est la source de tout droit. La tendance pareillement orientée du droit naturel et de la charité explique d'autre part que, aux yeux de Luther, l'ordre juridique institué et appliqué par l'Etat puisse jusqu'à un certain point satisfaire les exigences de la morale chrétienne. Seeberg a donc pu écrire finement que: "Luther a réalisé avec la plus grande énergie la différenciation théorique entre l'autorité temporelle et le gouvernement de l'Eglise, mais qu'en inculcant aux autorités et aux princes le devoir d'appliquer le droit temporel selon la raison ou selon la règle naturelle de l'équité, il a ouvert la voie à une influence de la morale chrétienne sur le gouvernement civil." Sans doute cette influence n'est-elle pas comme chez Calvin directement produite par l'adoption de la loi divine comme source du droit; mais bien qu'indirecte et bien que n'agissant pas par le détour de l'équité, elle n'en est pas moins réelle, et il est possible de la déceler historiquement dans les Etats qui ont pris au sérieux la doctrine luthérienne.

Avant d'en finir avec ce point particulier, il n'est pas sans intéret de préciser ce que Luther entendait au juste par équité. Selon la définition qu'il en donne dans un de ses propos de table, il voyait dans l'équité non point une modération ou une mansuétude arbitraire, de la part du juge chargé d'appliquer la loi. Il s'agit au contraire d'une application rationnelle qui tiendrait compte des circonstances particulières de chaque cas concret, tout en se gardant,de transgresser la loi naturelle ou la loi divine. Luther avait en horreur le littéralisme légal avec le quel était interprèté dans l'Allemagne de son temps le droit romain nouvellement réintroduit. Il aurait souscrit à l'adage qui veut que la loi est faite pour l'homme et non l'homme pour la loi. Celle-ci doit être utile pour la société et appliquée de manière à ne pas exclure la charité. On conçoit sans peine que les principes qu'il énonçait en ce qui concerne l'application de la loi positive étaient d'un maniement fort délicat dans la pratique. Jusqu'à quel point était-il li ite de faire céder la lettre de la loi, garantie suprême de l'ordre établi, devant la loi naturelle? Comment savoir exactement aussi, quelles étaient les exigences précises de l'équité dans tel ou tel cas ? Théoriquement, la question ne ' pose guère de difficulté lorsqu'on admet, comme le firent l'antiquité et la scolastique, que tous les hommes ont reçu en partage la loi naturelle. Il doit donc être à la portée de tous d'en dégager les applications pratiques. Mais nous avons vu que st Thomas d'Aquin déjà avait hésité à tirer ces conclusions simplistes, et qu'il distinguait avec soin entre les principes de la raison pratique et les conclusions qu'il en faut tirer, pour n'affirmer en définitive la généralité et l'universalité que des seuls principes. Luther, instruit par l'expérience et notamment par les excès révolutionnaires des paysans et des sectaires qui se prévalaient du droit naturel, Luther est allé beaucoup plus loin dans cette voie indiquée par st Thomas. Un passage tiré de l'explication du Psaume lol de 1534/5 en fournira la preuve:

> " On se met à vanter de nos jours, y écrit-il, le droit naturel et la raison naturelle comme l'origine et la source de tout droit écrit. Et cela est bien vrai et la louange n'est pas vaine. Mais l'erreur réside en ceci, que chacun s'imagine avoir dans sa tête le droit naturel...

Si le droit et la raison naturels se trouvaient dans toutes les têtes qui ressemblent à des têtes humaines, les fous, les enfants et les femmes pourraient aussi bien gouverner et guerroyer que David, Auguste ou Hannibal, et les Phormions (càd les gens qui parlent de ce qu'ils ignorent) seraient aussi bons que les Hannibal. Bien plus, tous les hommes seraient égaux et nul n'aurait le droit d'en gouverner un autre. Quelle sédition et quelle confusion n'en sortiraient-elles pas ? Or voici que Dieu a voulu que les hommes soient inégaux, que l'un gouverne l'autre, que l'un obéisse à l'autre ... C'est pourquoi il se trouve aussi, que, parmi ceux qui se targuent et se vantent de leur raison naturelle ou de leur droit naturel, se trouvent beaucoup de grands fous naturels. Car le précieux joyau que l'on appelle droit ou raison naturels, est chose rare parmi les enfants des hommes."

Nous avions déjà constaté que Luther admettait une répartition inégale de la raison naturelle chez les hommes selon qu'ils étaient ou non prédestinés au salut. Mais cette inégalité affecte même ceux qui sont étrangers au christianisme. Les uns ont un reflet plus fort, les autres en ont un moidre de la lumière naturelle. Selon leur aptitude personnelle, ils sauront donc appliquer plus ou moins bien la loi naturelle et ses préceptes d'équité. De même que tous les hommes sont doués de raison en général, mais que certains ont une raison théorique plus développée ou plus affinée que d'autres, de même la raison pratique est-elle plus inégalement distribuée entre eux.

Nous en sommes arrivés ainsi à circonscrire, au moins dans ses grandes lignes, la conception que Luther se fait de la loi naturelle et de son rôle. Mais il est un problème que nous n'avons fait que toucher en passant, et qu'il convient d'éclairer d'avantage, si nous voulons bien comprendre la place que Luther a réservée à la loi naturelle dans la vie du chrétien. A cet effet il nous faut partir de la célèbre opposition entre l'Evangile et la loi ce qui nous permettra du même coup de préciser la question des rapports entre le droit naturel et la Loi divine.

On ne fait sans doute pas erreur, en admettant que les idées de Luther sur cet ensemble de problèmes ont été déterminées, pour une large part, par différentes circonstances historiques, et notamment par ses querelles avec les anabaptistes et avec les antinomistes, et par les exigences de la pratique ecclésiastique. A l'encontre des anabaptistes qui rêvaient d'une restauration de la legislation mosaïque, Luther en est arrivé à rejeter toute loi pour le chrétien. C'est ainsi qu'il a pu écrire dans son commentaire sur l'Epître aux Galates,

> " aut enim Christus stabit et lex peribit, aut lex stabit et Christus peribit; ubi dominatur iustitia legis, ibi non potest dominari iustitia gratiae et vicissim; opportet alteram cedere altéri."

Est-ce à dire qu'il ait rejeté toute appréciation positive de la loi ? c'est à dire de la loi mosaïque , C'est ici que l'on peut faire intervenir la distinction, dont nous avons déjà eu à nous occuper, entre la loi mosaïque comme telle et les parties qui y correspondent à la loi naturelle innée. Tandisque tout le reste n'avait d'importance que pour le peuple juif, ces parties conformes à la loi naturelle ont eu une valeur permanente, du fait même qu'elles reproduisent la loi naturelle. Enfin, il ne faut pas perdre de vue que les efforts concrets tentés par Luther pour organiser l'Eglise Evangélique en Saxe lui ont ouvert les yeux sur la nécessité de la loi, même à l'égard de populations qui se prétendent chrétiennes. Il a été fortement frappé par le fait que la régénérattion n'allait pas nécessairement de pair avec l'imputation de la justice et que, tout justifié qu'il puisse être, le chrétien n'en restait pas moins pécheur et enclin à céder aux tentations.

Si nous essayons maintenant de préciser ce que Luther entendait au juste en employant le terme de Loi ou de Loi de Moïse, nous constatons qu'il est synonyme à ses yeux avec le Décalogue. Soit que la Décalogue apparaisse comme la norme d'où le reste de la législation de l'Ancien Testament aurait été dérivé, soit qu'il se présente comme la fraction de cette législation la plus aisément applicable aux chrétiens, parce que la plus réductible à la loi naturelle, toujours est-il que Luther emploie presque indifféremment les termes de Décalogue et de Loi mosaïque. Luther voit dans le Décalogue une série de préceptes englobant toute la piété et la morale chrétiennes. Prenant à la lettre l'expression de "sommaire de la loi", il fait des différents commandements une rédaction explicite des deux préceptes fondamentaux du Christ: l'amour de Dieu et l'amour du prochain. Le contenu de la loi ne peut donc différer du contenu de l'Evangile et leur opposition ne repose donc pas là dessus. Elle réside bien plutot, extérieurement, dans la différence de leur transmission, intérieurement, dans la différence de leur finalité et de leur efficacité. Luther exprime cela avec toute la clarté désirable dans sa Postille allemande de 1522, lorsqu'il ecrit:

> " Le nouveau Testament n'est pas plus qu'une révélation de l'ancien, comme quand quelqu'un possède d'abord une lettre close, qu'il ouvre ensuite."

Mais il y a plus. Dans son cours sur le Deutéronome de 1525, Luther affirme:

> "Dieu nous ayant promis la grâce a donné tant de lois aux Juifs, afin qu'ils devinssent plus aptes à recevoir la grâce (capaciores gratiae), afin que par le moyen de la loi ils fussent amenés à la connaissance de Dieu et à avoir soif de la grâce. "

La loi apparait ici comme une étappe dans l'économie du salut. Certes Luther ne renie pas pour autant ce qu'il a pu dire ou écrire, afin de démontrer que la loi ne conduisait pas à la grâce et quétaient perdus ceux qui vivaient sous la loi sans avoir reçu la grâce. Néanmoins, il constate que, historiquement, l'humanité a été comme préparée à recevoir la grâce en recevant préalablement la loi, qui lui a rappelé et lui a renforcé son orientation naturelle vers Dieu et qui a éveillé en elle le désir du salut. Nous verrons d'ailleurs, que c'est ici qu'intervient la distinction admise par Luther entre le rôle de la loi naturelle et le rôle de la l , divine, dont pourtant le contenu est semblable.

Le réformateur a mainte fois souligné que la loi et l'Evangile sont et demeurent tous les deux des expressions de la volonté de Dieu, qu'ils sont l'un et l'autre, au sens strict du terme, Parole de Dieu. Mais pas de la même façon. La loi enseigne à l'homme le bien, mais elle exige son intervention active, qui setraduit par des oeuvres positives ou par des abstentions. L'Evangile ne demende rien de tel à l'homme; il lui enseigne qu'il doit se soumettre à la grâce divine, et que c'est Christ qui alors agira en lui. Le christianisme, aimsi que Luther s'est efforcé de l'inculquer à ses contemporains, le christianisme n'est pas une religion légale, il ne consiste donc pas à accomplir un certain nombre de prescriptions révélées. C'est dans ce sens qu'il faut entendre la liberté chrétienne; le chrétien est libéré de la Loi, parce que, en vertu de la grâce qui lui est conférée, il fait spontanément ce qui plait à Dieu, sans avoir besoin d'y être poussé par une obligation, et, encore moins, par l'espérance d'une récompense. La bonté d'un acte humain réside dans cette spontanéité (1), qui est leseul fondement de la moralité. Luther a pu écrire:

> "Lorsque tu demandes à un homme chaste pourquoi il est chaste, il doit te répondre: ce n'est pas pour l'amour du ciel ou de l'enfer, ni pour l'honneur ou la honte, mais uniquement parce que cela me semble bien et me plait de tout coeur, même si ce n'est pas prescrit."

Ici se place le point de séparation de la Loi et de l'Evangile, et aussi, on le comprend, l'un des points d'attaque de Luther contre le catholicisme.

> "Distinguer exactement la Loi de l'Evangile, dit Luther dans un sermon de 1532, c'est l'art suprême dans la chrétienté. Cet art nous devons le connaitre, et si tu ne t'y entends pas, tu ne peux savoir exactement distinguer un chrétien d'un paien ou d'un Juif, car c'est dans cette distinction que réside tout."

Mais alors, si la loi ou une partie de la loi ne doit pas représenter seulement une forme abolie ou périmée de la volonté divine, c'est que la fonction de cette loi sera d'instruire l'homme de ce qu'il doit faire et de ce qu'il n'a pas fait. Le propre de la loi est, en effet, de stature des exigences qui dépassent les forces de l'homme. Elle en est donc réduite au rôle d'une norme permettant à l'homme d'évaluer toute la distance qui le sépare de l'accomplissement. Cela est vrai de la loi na-

---

N'oublions pas que Monsieur Wendel a bien voulu nous donner ses notes pour nous permettre de polycopier ce cours!

turelle, aussi bien que de la loi divine exprimée dans le décalogue. Nous avons vu que, dès 1515, Luther mettait sur le même rang paiens et Juifs, quant à leur commune incapacité de satisfaire à la loi, et par conséquent quant à leur commune culpabilité. Mais, pour employer une expression de Luther, la Loi se borne à mettre en évidence cette culpabilité, parce qu"elle est comme un poteau indicateur qui ne montre que le chemin, mais qu'elle ne peut se comparer à la force qui animeles jambes. La Loi manifeste donc à l'homme sa faiblesse et son humiliation. D'ailleurs, la loi naturelle innée à l'homme confirme les exigences divines et le jugement de la conscience corrobore la condamnation de l'homme. Et de nouveau la question se pose, de savoir ce qui différencie loi divine et loi naturelle. Elle peut maintenant trouver sa solution. sans doute, l'homme, qu'il soit Juif ou paien, possède la loi et c'est une même LOi que Dieu a donnée aux Juifs et qu'il a inscrite dans le coeur de tout homme. Mais à la loi juive est intimement liée la promesse qui, elle, fait défaut à la loi naturelle. C'est par cette promesse divine par conséquent, que la loi mosaique se distingue de la loi naturelle, et l'on comprend maintenant aussi, que, parlant de la loi divine, Luther ait pu, grâce à l'existence de la promesse, la considérer comme une étappe préalable avant l'avènement de l'Evangile et de la grâce.

En revanche, les deux lois, la divine et la naturelle, ont en commun leur exigence religieuse fondamentale, que Luther résume dans la crainte, l'amour et la confiance à l'egard de Dieu (perfectum timorem, dilectionem, fiduciam Dei). Luther y a insisté notamment dans les explications du Décalogue qu'il a insérées dans ses catéchismes: "nous devons craindre et aimer Dieu, afin de..." Or, cette exigence fondamentale de la loi divine, se rencontre également dans la loi naturelle. Mais, qu'il s'agisse de l'une ou de l'autre, les hommes qui leur sont assujettis ne peuvent, en raison de leur péché, parvenir à cette crainte, ni, à plus forte raison, à cet amour de Dieu. Car il s'agit ici -et Luther l'a souligné plusieurs fois- de la crainte filiale, intimement unie à l'amour, et non point de la crainte servile.

Cette dernière en effet, qu'inspire la peur du chatiement et de la colère divine, est le propre du pécheur. Seul le chrétien à qui la grâce a été accordée atteindra du même coup la possibilité de craindre et d'aimer Dieu au sens de la Loi.

Mais quelle reste l'autorité de cette Loi en ce qui concerne le chrétien ? Nous avons déjà vérifié que, pour Luther, la loi juive comme telle ne lie plus le chrétien, que c'est une loi particulière donnée à un dertain peuple pour un certain temps. Toutefois, cette loi juive a, comme toute autre législation, pour base le droit naturel. Dans la mesure où elle lui correspond, et dans cette mesure seulement, elle garde sa valeur. Ce qui importe dit Luther dans ses sermons sur l'Exode, c'est

> "que ses exigences soient naturellement implantées en moi et que Moïse concorde avec la nature".

Ou encore, dans les propos de table:

> "Le Décalogue et les autres lois issues des patriarches ne sont pas propres à Moïse... Il est bon de s'en tenir à Moïse, là où il nous plait; mais qu'il soit notre maitre, cela nous le refusons, car ce que Moïse enseigne, la nature l'enseigne aussi, mais il s'était mieux exprimé que les paiens, qui cependant enseignaient la même chose."

A quoi l'on peut ajouter un autre passage encore, que j'emprunte aux sermons de 1527 sur la Genèse:

> "Les commandements donnés au peuple d'Israel et concernant les choses extérieures, je les abandonne, ils ne me contraignent ni ne m'obligent; ces lois sont mortes et abolies, sauf pour ce que j'adopte librement de Moïse. C'est comme si je disais: ainsi a gouverné Moïse, cela me semble bien; je veux le suivre sur tel ou tel point. Je voudrais volontiers que les seigneurs gouvernassent selon l'exemple de Moïse, et si j'étais empereur, je le prendrais pour modèle de mes lois, non pas que Moïse dût m'obliger, mais que je fusse libre de l'imiter et de gouverner comme lui."

Et, un peu plus loin, Luther ajoute:

> "Les commandements de Moïse qui ne sont pas implantés dans tous les hommes par la nature, les paiens ne les observent pas, et ils ne les concernent pas. D'autre part, je trouve en Moïse une chose que la nature ne me donne point; ce sont les promesses de Dieu au sujet du Christ. Et c'est de loin ce qu'il y a de mieux en Moïse, à savoir ce qui n'est pas naturellement inscrit dans le coeur des hommes, mais qui leur vient du haut du Ciel; par exemple que Dieu a promis que son Fils

naitrait dans la chair, cela nous annonce l'Evangile. Et c'est là le plus important dans Moïse, qui nous appartient à nous autres paiens aussi."

La Loi se différencie donc de la loi naturelle par les promesses évangéliques. Pour le reste, elle contient des éléments identiques au droit naturel et d'autres qui sont propres au peuple Juif et qui n'ont aucune valeur pour nous. Quant à savoir pourquoi Dieu a jugé bon de répéter les prescriptions du droit naturel dans sa loi divine, Luther répond à cette question, comme l'avait fait toute la tradition. Il a fallu que ces préceptes fussent renouvelés et remis en lumière, parce qu'ils avaient été obscurcis par le péché. Au reste, Moïse leur a donné, par la même occasion, une expression particulièrement remarquable et adéquate.

Luther rejoint également l'attitude traditionnelle en rejetant comme spécifiquement juives les lois écrites dites cérémonielles, comme surajoutées à la loi naturelle. On peut noter en passant qu'il a compris dans les lois cérémonielles l'observation du sabbat, telle qu'elle est enoncée dans le Décalogue; il y a là une entorse occasionnelle au principe, selon lequel les dix commandements représentent la loi naturelle. Ajoutons que cela n'a pas empêché le réformateur de maintenir le troisième commandement (le 4ème pour Calvin) en le transférant au dimanche chrétien. La polémique contre les sectaires et contre les anabaptistes a donné de fréquentes occasions à Luther d'insister sur notre liberté à l'égard des loi juives. Dans ses sermons sur l'Exode il a énoncé à ce propos le principe que toute loi, y compris la loi divine, n'a de valeur qu'à l'égard de celui pour qui elle a été édictée. La loi mosaïque ne peut donc avoir plus de valeur pour ses auditeurs allemands, que n'en ont les lois promulguées par le roi de France.

En résumé, la loi apparait donc chez Luther comme l'expression des exigences que Dieu formule à légard de l'homme pécheur. Dans la mesure où il n'y satisfait point, il se trouve exposé à la colère divine. Il en est ainsi de toute loi, aussi bien de la loi positive mosaïque ou édictée par queque autre pouvoir temporel, que de la loi naturelle écrite dans la conscience humaine. Au surplus, c'est cette dernière qui constitue la base de toute loi, celle-ci ne demeurant en vigueur que dans la mesure où elle peut être considérée comme l'expression du droit naturel.

(suivraiant en principe les théories philippistes et réformées de la loi naturelle, surtout l'exposé de la conception de Mélanchton et de Calvin, mais que les necéssités du temps ne nous permettent plus d'aborder cette année)

++++++++++

ARCHIVES
DE
PHILOSOPHIE DU DROIT

N° 5

LA THÉOLOGIE CHRÉTIENNE ET LE DROIT

Publié avec le concours du C. N. R. S.

SIREY

22, Rue Soufflot, PARIS 5e

1960

Christianisme et droit. Recherches américaines

par JACQUES ELLUL
Professeur à la Faculté de droit de Bordeaux.

Depuis quelques années a commencé aux U.S.A. un mouvement d'études sur la relation entre le christianisme et le droit. Bien entendu, les positions traditionnelles étaient assez voisines des positions européennes avec une dominante du Droit naturel. La minorité catholique l'affirmait fortement. La majorité protestante, assez incertaine, s'y était laissé gagner en partant des positions de Calvin (qui est, avec des réserves, favorable au Droit naturel) et en y ajoutant une notion libérale et semi-romantique. Car l'adhésion à cette doctrine était le fait des idéalistes, et toute la conception du Droit aux U.S.A. était idéaliste, même chez les non-chrétiens (cf. Learned Hand, *l'Esprit de liberté*). Or, précisément l'on vient d'entreprendre une sorte de « révision » de ces positions acquises. Bien entendu, ce cercle d'études est encore restreint mais il est très significatif et les travaux de ses derniers congrès (1957, 1959) sont assez intéressants. Il semble que ce mouvement résulte de plusieurs causes, comme l'a analysé un de ses membres (Lehmann-*Law as a function of forgiveness*). D'une part, de l'intérieur du christianisme, il y a la critique de la position catholique traditionnelle par les catholiques eux-mêmes dans la recherche d'une nouvelle éthique, et la critique de la position protestante à partir de la « nouvelle théologie » (issue de Karl Barth). D'autre part, il y a le progrès d'un certain positivisme qui semble se développer rapidement depuis vingt ans, et l'influence de l'existentialisme qui modifie les perspectives du droit. Enfin il y a la situation de fait : on ne peut maintenir l'idéalisme juridique en présence de l'inapplication, l'inefficacité de la loi, le peuple commence à ne plus « croire » à la loi en soi, il est désillusionné et le fossé entre la réalité et la loi s'agrandit. L'on prend alors conscience à la fois de la nécessité d'un ré-examen des positions traditionnelles et des impasses dans lesquelles on se trouve : contradiction entre la loi naturelle et la loi positive, entre l'immutabilité d'une valeur du droit et le changement rapide des conditions d'application, entre la foi chrétienne qui est le fait d'une faible minorité et son expression dans un droit fait pour tous. A la fois tentés et troublés par le positivisme juridique et par le relativisme, les chrétiens essaient de trouver un fondement du droit commun à tous et sentent en même temps que ceci est impossible à cause de la spécificité du christianisme.

Tout ceci n'a rien de bien nouveau, et nous pouvons dire qu'il y a longtemps que nous connaissons ces problèmes. Il est déjà significatif qu'ils se posent maintenant dans une société qui se veut chrétienne. Mais ce qui est intéressant c'est l'attitude prise en face de cette situation. Un premier élément curieux : qui est inquiet de ces questions ? les théologiens ? les philosophes ? point. Ce sont les juristes et les juristes praticiens (*attorney, counselors*, etc.) qui s'en inquiètent d'abord, considérant qu'il est essentiel pour la pratique du droit d'en connaître le fondement et la valeur. Et lorsqu'ils posent le problème, ce n'est pas d'une façon académique, ce n'est pas un débat de philosophie, c'est une question de conscience en vue de l'exercice du droit. Ainsi le praticien estime qu'il ne peut valablement exercer sa fonction et servir la loi que si les problèmes fondamentaux ont reçu une réponse. Et ceci va à la fois dicter la méthode et les orientations de recherche.

La méthode : elle réside essentiellement en un dialogue entre le juriste et le théologien : sur un même point un juriste et un théologien apportent chacun leur étude, confrontent leurs positions, font éclater les contradictions. Il n'y a donc à aucun moment une construction globale, théorique, dogmatique, mais un enseignement réciproque, le théologien ramené à des problèmes concrets, obligé de tirer des conséquences de ses positions dogmatiques, le praticien obligé de passer sa pratique au crible éthique et théologique. Cette méthode est extrêmement féconde et correspond bien au souci américain de référence à la réalité. Mais, bien entendu le dialogue est difficile à établir effectivement. Dans ces travaux deux difficultés paraissent nettement —, l'une qui provient des juristes : d'une part en tant que juristes, d'autre part en tant qu'Américains, ils sont tentés de tout ramener tout le temps à des *casus* : dans tel cas que faut-il faire ? et l'on pose le problème juridique non plus sous l'aspect de la signification de la loi mais sous l'aspect de la recherche d'une solution dans un problème particulier de pratique. Or, à ce point, le théologien est souvent impuissant, il ne connaît pas les conditions juridiques du problème, et de toutes façons si cela, en tant que contre-épreuve, peut amener à considérer les conséquences de telle interprétation philosophique du droit, réciproquement cela ne peut guère servir à faire avancer l'étude des fondements du droit, de son autorité, de sa signification. L'autre difficulté tient aux théologiens : les travaux de ces congrès montrent que les théologiens sont sans cesse amenés à confondre la loi morale et la loi juridique (par exemple *Markus Barth — Christ and Law*) et s'appuient alors constamment sur ce qui, dans la Bible, concerne la loi morale pour l'appliquer au droit ; ou encore prennent à partir de là une vision purement abstraite et théorique de la loi. Il est difficile pour un juriste de souscrire à des affirmations aussi générales et tranchées par exemple que celle de Markus Barth : « Dieu a donné la loi à l'homme ». L'on conçoit que dans ces conditions le dialogue soit particulièrement difficile, et ce sont les théologiens qui manifestent le plus d'attachement aux positions traditionnelles.

En ce qui concerne les orientations de recherche, elles sont multiples : Il y a pour les uns recherche d'une philosophie chrétienne du droit, ou d'un critère chrétien de discrimination entre les diverses philosophies du droit. Il y a la recherche de « standards » éthiques pour procéder à la critique des lois particulières, ou pour une compréhension chrétienne de la critique envers la loi ; il y a la recherche plus fondamentale d'une signification chrétienne du droit païen ; et celle d'une éthique du juriste comme serviteur du droit. Il ne s'agit donc nullement d'un dialogue entre une science théologique et une science juridique, deux disciplines anciennes ayant leurs méthodes et leurs critères spécifiques, établis depuis des siècles, mais d'une recherche « existentielle », qui n'a pas pour but d'établir une doctrine satisfaisante intellectuellement de la vérité du droit, une axiologie chrétienne du droit comme s'il s'agissait de deux entités, mais au contraire l'établissement de points de départs et de points de référence par rapport auxquels une insertion du chrétien dans le monde du droit puisse avoir lieu en le plaçant devant sa responsabilité et en faisant appel à son initiative. Mais on est très loin d'être arrivé à un accord. L'on peut dire en schématisant un peu qu'il y a dans ce mouvement trois tendances, l'une cherchant à rénover l'idée de droit naturel, la seconde qui se rattache indirectement à la théologie de Niebuhr, la troisième qui exprime directement la théologie de K. Barth. Nous en indiquerons sommairement les principales caractéristiques.

***

L'on se rend aisément compte que l'on ne peut plus s'en tenir simplement à la conception du Droit naturel de Saint-Thomas ou de Calvin : mais n'est-il pas possible de la rénover, en usant des critiques et des doctrines du positivisme. Il s'agit alors moins de formuler une doctrine opposée à une autre, que de dépasser le débat « Droit naturel — Positivisme », qui débouche sur une impasse et qui peut-être avait été mal posé. Le professeur Stumpf (Prof. Philo. du Droit — Vanderbilt University) indique ainsi que la science du droit déforme nécessairement le sens du droit parce qu'elle ne pose pas la question « Quelle est la pleine *nature* du droit », mais au contraire, « avec quels aspects du phénomène juridique peut-on utiliser une méthode dite scientifique » ? La méthode scientifique saisit certains éléments mais non pas l'ensemble. « Un concept du droit adéquat doit être assez large pour saisir tous les *faits* relatifs au phénomène du droit, en y comprenant le fait de la valeur. Et c'est précisément parce qu'il est nécessaire d'élargir le contexte dans lequel le droit doit être étudié, que la théologie est directement concernée par la formulation du droit ». C'est dans cette ligne que le professeur Stumpf pose le problème de la Source, de la Nature et du but du Droit : et dans chaque cas, il s'efforce à la fois de montrer que la question est parfaitement concrète, comporte des effets pour le droit positif, mais aussi que l'on ne peut répondre à cette question que d'un point de vue théologique, et il procède à la critique des autres réponses. Il insiste contre les théories positivistes sur la capacité de l'homme à prendre une certaine distance par rapport au droit existant et à procéder à la critique de ce droit, qui alors en tant que tel n'est pas une expression totale de la société dont l'homme ne serait que le reflet... L'homme prend un point de référence pour sa critique du droit à l'extérieur de celui-ci et à l'extérieur de la société, il assume une responsabilité plus élevée que celle qui est exprimée dans la loi, et ce faisant, il témoigne de ce que le droit est appelé à exprimer autre chose que la simple normalité concrète. Ainsi la référence à un droit naturel (lié à la nature de l'homme et à sa place dans l'ordre naturel) ne peut pas donner naissance à une doctrine fermée du droit, établie, éternelle, et moins encore à formuler un contenu préétabli du droit, mais à une conception « créativiste », dynamique du droit, qui avance par le moyen de l'affirmation et de sa critique. Le Droit doit être vu comme une extension du pouvoir créateur de Dieu, car il a pour effet de façonner l'homme en ordonnant sa conduite. La création et le droit sont tous deux des moyens par lesquel la puissance donne une forme en se manifestant. Et ceci à la fois légitime la puissance créatrice du droit, et lui interdit tout arbitraire.

Mais en outre quand on parle de nature de l'homme, il faut s'entendre. Cette nature ne peut plus être conçue essentiellement comme raisonnable ainsi que des écoles théologiques anciennes l'admettaient, mais cette nature est d'abord liberté et amour (qui sera l'expression chrétienne de la nécessité d'une relation vraie avec autrui), l'homme exprimera alors sa liberté par la création de la loi, mais celle-ci doit être ordonnée à l'expression de la nature de l'homme qui est amour, relation, sociabilité, fraternité. La fraternité n'est pas seulement le besoin essentiel de l'homme mais sa raison d'être. Or, la loi est là pour donner une forme à cette nécessité, et l'amour, tel qu'il est révélé dans la pensée chrétienne, est le seul « modèle » satisfaisant (*pattern*) de cette loi. Le droit apparaît donc rattaché à cette nature de l'homme. Et en même temps, le but dernier qui doit « informer » la loi positive est fourni par l'Evangile. Le droit est en réalité finaliste, et c'est l'Evangile qui lui donne une vraie finalité. Le modèle de l'amour chrétien, quand il est exprimé dans sa pleine nature fournit une base pour les fins les plus spécifiques du droit.

Les critiques qui l'on peut faire à ce système sont qu'en définitive un droit ainsi conçu présuppose une société « christianisée », la nature de l'homme dont on parle c'est en réalité la nature de l'homme occidental formé par des siècles d'éducation chrétienne, et par conséquent ceci ne rend pas compte de l'ensemble du phénomène juridique. L'on est d'ailleurs amené à admettre qu'il y a des droits positifs qui sont des « Non-Droits » ainsi Pr. Stumpf estime que le droit hitlérien ou le droit communiste sont des « Non-Droits », mais ceci est toujours très dangereux : car on est bien obligé d'admettre que des hommes les tiennent pour le droit. On a d'ailleurs en même temps pu objecter à cette conception qu'elle assimilait le droit chrétien avec celui de la démocratie libérale moderne, ce qui est manifestement dit par certains de ces juristes. Enfin l'on doit aussi considérer que l'effort de repenser le droit naturel dans une perspective existentielle comporte une certaine contradiction en soi, car l'existentialisme ne reconnait précisément pas une nature de l'homme, une donnée préalable. Cette tentative reste donc très ambiguë.

***

Un second ensemble de recherches est dominé par la théologie de Niebuhr. L'on sait que celui-ci reste assurément le plus grand théologien protestant des U.S.A. Dans le domaine qui nous intéresse, il a procédé à la critique du droit naturel et a refusé de rechercher un lieu commun à des chrétiens et des non-chrétiens sur lequel ils pourraient s'entendre et construire en commun un système juridique. Il admet pleinement qu'il existe des systèmes juridiques, créés par des non-chrétiens, et que ce fait juridique doit être pris en considération en tant que tel, sans essayer de le voiler ou de lui imposer une christianisation artificielle. Il conçoit donc déjà la notion du dialogue entre une réalité du droit et une vérité du christianisme. Et pour lui, l'essentiel du christianisme se ramène à l'amour (selon les commandements donnés par J.-C.). Mais il n'étend pas cette notion à toute fraternité, sociabilité, etc. il reste très précis sur le sens de l'Agapè. Le problème qui se pose est alors celui de la relation entre l'amour et le droit. Et à un second degré, des possibilités de l'expression juridique de l'amour chrétien. Car c'est seulement quand le droit réussit à donner une forme concrète, valable pour un groupe, à cet amour qu'il accomplit pleinement sa vocation qui lui est assignée par Dieu. Il rejoint alors ici la position de Tillich (*Love, Power and Justice*) : « L'amour est la dynamique d'une justice créatrice » — « L'amour dans sa faculté d'écouter l'Autre, de lui accorder des possibilités de s'exprimer, de lui pardonner, accomplit ce que la justice demande ». Et Niebuhr avait par exemple étudié les conséquences concrètes pour un système juridique de l'expression de l'amour dans la non-violence (*An interpretation of christian ethics*). A partir de là se développent certaines recherches dans les Congrès de 1957-1958. Ainsi le professeur Lehmann étudie le droit comme ayant une fonction de pardon. Il se refuse à séparer les concepts de justice et d'amour, l'un qui serait relatif au droit, le second à la religion, — l'un relatif aux relations sociales, abstraites, entre un grand nombre de personnes, l'autre relatif aux relations de prochain à prochain selon la théorie de Brunner (*Justice and the social order*). De même qu'il y a une relation rigoureuse et indissoluble théologiquement entre l'amour et la justice, de même cette relation doit être maintenue dans le monde du droit. La justice seule n'est pas en réalité la justice, elle n'est qu'une contrefaçon, un légalisme, elle ne trouve sa signification et sa plénitude que par l'amour, et de ce fait le droit n'est jamais valable quand il cherche à exprimer la seule justice. Dans cette perspective, le droit n'a plus pour but la réalisation de la justice, mais la réconciliation des hommes par le pardon. « L'amour chrétien en vue de la justice est authentiquement exprimé dans l'usage de la loi comme moyen de pardon ». — « La justice correctement comprise est l'agent d'application de l'amour dans le pardon concret, et la transformation de la loi en instrument de réconciliation ». — « L'amour doit s'exprimer en effet dans le pardon, et la loi est l'instrument grâce auquel la justice devient l'occasion et le contexte de la réconciliation ». — « Lorsque la loi est ainsi fonction du pardon, la justice est située dans une relation valable avec l'amour ». Ces citations montrent bien l'orientaion de cette recherche. Cela suppose aussi d'ailleurs que, dans cette orientation, l'on se préoccupe beaucoup moins de la valeur du droit tel qu'il existe réellement dans les sociétés, ou de sa nature, ou de son fondement, que des possibilités de l'influencer, de le transformer concrètement de façon à ce qu'il remplisse bien cette finalité. Mais, justement, à ce point, on comprend bien que ces principes soient très difficiles à exprimer concrètement et que les juristes se trouvent un peu réticents. Bien entendu, il y a des cas très simples où l'on aperçoit l'application : droit criminel, droit de la famille... Mais ce sont là les domaines du droit, toujours les mêmes, évoqués par les théologiens et les moralistes parce qu'ils posent des questions de morale en définitive. Il est relativement aisé pour le droit matrimonial ou pour la peine de mort de dire que ce droit doit être fondé sur l'amour et exprimer le pardon. Spontanément le théologien pense à cela quand il pense « droit ». Mais il est bien évident que ce sont au contraire les immenses domaines du contrat, du droit administratif, etc. qui doivent être l'objet de la réflexion. Et là, il semble bien que ces orientations ne rendent guère compte de la réalité du droit. D'autre part nous pourrions formuler une autre critique : invinciblement, les auteurs américains raisonnent dans l'hypothèse d'une société christianisée, où l'échelle des valeurs reste pour tous, chrétiens et non-chrétiens, une échelle des valeurs chrétiennes, où tous ont reçu une éducation chrétienne, où les autorités respectent et avouent officiellement le christianisme. C'est là, et là seulement, que l'on peut proposer une telle signification du droit. Mais cela ne rend pas compte de la réalité générale, globale du phénomène juridique, dans les autres sociétés.

***

Nous arrivons à la troisième tendance, plus difficile, mais à la fois peut-être plus concrète et exprimant plus fidèlement une attitude chrétienne. Considérant que le christianisme n'est pas un système intellectuel ni un ensemble de principes ni une explication du monde mais uniquement une vie humaine vécue en Christ (ἐν χρίστω) les auteurs qui s'attachent à une stricte pensée biblique récusent toute possibilité d'une philosophie chrétienne du droit. Il ne peut déjà pas, à leurs yeux, y avoir une philosophie chrétienne, car toute réflexion systématique sera ou bien théologique c'est-à-dire explicitant la révélation et débouchant dans l'action, ou bien ne sera pas chrétienne, prenant d'autres points de départ et s'attachant à tout autre chose qu'à déterminer une vie chrétienne selon la volonté de Dieu. Bien moins encore y aura-t-il une philosophie du droit qui se dirait chrétienne, car l'on serait en présence d'une explication intellectuelle à partir de principes dits chrétiens, d'un phénomène de la société. Mais ces principes n'ont aucune valeur détachés de la personne actuelle et vivante de Jésus-Christ. Le seul problème pourrait être alors celui de la relation hic et nunc entre *ce* droit et Jésus-Christ, dans sa Seigneurie actuelle sur le monde. Le christianisme, dès lors, en tant que théorie du monde, de l'homme, de la société, de l'Etat, du droit, est une trahison de Jésus-Christ. D'autre part, le christianisme ne peut fournir aucune norme éthique utilisable en vérité par le droit, car ce serait élaborer un droit en fonction d'une éthique qui ne peut être vécue que dans la foi. Or, le droit est fait pour les chrétiens et pour les non-chrétiens vivant ensemble, dans une même société. Mais quelle valeur une éthique chrétienne peut-elle avoir pour un non-chrétien ? Elle ne pourrait qu'avoir une valeur de *raison*, or ceci serait la négation même du qualificatif de chrétien, car en tant qu'éthique elle ne peut être l'expression *que* de la foi. Et si les chrétiens ont le pouvoir, ils n'ont pas le droit d'élaborer un système juridique s'imposant à des non-chrétiens et qui supposerait une conduite chrétienne des individus. Dès lors le christianisme n'a pas à essayer d'inspirer des lois qui seraient dites chrétiennes, pas davantage, en tant que tel, le christianisme n'offre de «'standards » pour une critique *rationnelle* du droit. Il reste en dehors du problème de la discriminsation des lois bonnes et mauvaises. La pensée chrétienne n'a pas à séparer deux corps de lois suivant qu'elles sont plus ou moins conformes à un « idéal chrétien ». Il faut considérer le droit tel qu'il est, dans sa réalité, sans porter de jugement sur lui, et admettre que tout ce que les hommes appellent « droit » en est bien, que le droit nazi ou le droit communiste est bien du droit. Car l'ensemble du droit fait partic de ce que Jésus-Christ appelle le Monde. Et dans cette mesure l'Evangile est opposé à *tout* le droit (car il est parole de Dieu, et n'appartient pas au monde) que celui-ci soit à nos yeux bon ou mauvais. Le vrai problème est alors que le christianisme adresse vocation à des hommes pour le service de Dieu et pour le témoignage de la foi qui peuvent être vécus dans l'exercice du droit, et auxquels le droit peut en définitive servir. Nous sommes donc en présence d'une attitude active à l'égard du droit, et non pas systématique.

D'autre part l'on considère l'histoire du christianisme et l'on se rend aisément compte que non seulement à l'égard du droit dans son ensemble, l'Eglise a eu des interprétations très diverses selon les époques (la théorie du droit naturel par exemple que l'on considère comme l'expression traditionnelle et quasi-unanime du christianisme n'est pas du tout aussi permanente qu'on veut le dire !) mais encore à l'égard de tel ou tel problème réglé par le droit, l'Eglise a eu des positions très variables selon les lieux et les moments ; suivant les époques et les sociétés, les chrétiens ont eu des « approches » du droit bien différentes. Est-ce à dire qu'à tel moment l'Eglise se trompait ? ou que le christianisme est neutre envers la loi ? ou qu'il y a, derrière ces variations, une attitude purement relativiste ? Non, mais seulement que l'Eglise, dans sa fonction exclusive de service de Dieu, a eu à assumer suivant les époques, des tâches différentes en relation avec le droit. Dès lors le chrétien peut adopter des théories de la loi, diverses, en tant qu'explication actuelle de la relation entre le droit et la politique, ou l'Etat, ou la justice, mais sans que la vérité chrétienne soit jamais liée à l'une d'elles. Il peut être positiviste, réaliste, historiciste, ou s'attacher au droit naturel, mais il ne peut jamais dire que cette théorie est l'expression éternelle du christianisme pour le droit, il ne peut jamais attacher une valeur éternelle à aucune de ces théories. Mais à chaque moment, il est possible pour le chrétien d'utiliser telle disposition du droit, d'entrer dans telle orientation juridique en vue de la gloire de Dieu : car à toute époque le droit offre un certain nombre de possibilités de cette œuvre spécifiquement chrétienne. Même la désobéissance à telle loi, le refus de telle loi peut-être un acte juridique positif, dans la mesure même où cette contestation (qui n'est pas intellectuelle mais vivante) est un témoignage hic et nunc de la volonté de Dieu. Il y a donc une « jurisprudence » chrétienne envers la loi qui n'est pas une théorie abstraite, une philosophie du droit, mais une « approche » fonctionnelle et toujours renouvelée du droit. Le droit est alors considéré comme un ensemble de moyens de création de relations et de situations dans lesquelles pourra, ou ne pourra pas, se manifester le témoignage de l'amour de Dieu, car la tension entre la grâce et la loi n'est pas résolue en traduisant la grâce dans des termes légaux, moraux, etc. : la grâce n'est pas une norme, et ne peut pas le devenir. Et si l'essence même de la Révélation est que Dieu fait grâce, il ne saurait être question d'en tirer une législation. La grâce est un acte, et comme telle s'adresse à une personne, forcément dans une situation *actuelle.* L'Evangile n'est pas une loi, il est un Don. Mais qu'il n'y ait pas de conciliation ou d'élaboration d'un contenu chrétien de la loi n'implique absolument pas que le chrétien se désintéresse du droit. Il considère seulement ce droit pour ce qu'il est : la loi et la justice sont des moyens grâce auxquels les hommes se comportent et se maintiennent dans le cours de l'histoire (Stringfellow -- *The christian lawyer as a churchman*). Le droit est une condition nécessaire de l'existence historique, et appartient par conséquent au monde de la chute. Ce droit, auquel le chrétien est soumis, ne discrimine jamais un bien et un mal selon Dieu mais des conduites relatives, et utiles. Il a son origine dans une situation de péché et ne peut surmonter le pouvoir du mal. Mais le chrétien vit sous l'autorité de ce droit et avec lui. Et c'est dans la mesure même où il sait que le droit n'a pas de pouvoir d'expression de la Justice de Dieu, de la Vérité, du Bien, qu'il entreprend ce qui peut être le plus fécond pour le droit : l'établissement d'une tension, d'un dialogue, d'un mouvement dialectique entre le droit et l'Evangile, entre la loi et la Grâce. Cette tension est la seule situation de vérité pour le droit qui n'est pas chargé de formuler une vérité permanente mais seulement d'accepter ce dialogue : il constitue le pôle le plus élaboré de la réalité, face à l'expression de la vérité absolue. Il est nécessaire que ce droit soit à la fois technique et cohérent à la société, et le plus juste possible selon les normes de la société, pour soutenir la dialectique dans laquelle la Justice de Dieu l'engage. Il y a une confrontation décisive, et toujours renouvelée (mais qui disparaît lorsque le droit se prétend chrétien : et alors commence le mensonge) qui est celle même de Dieu et de sa création déchue. Or, une fois encore, cette confrontation ne peut se résoudre dans une doctrine, elle est une réalité vivante et toujours recommencée. Et elle ne peut être portée dans et par des personnes, elle doit être incarnée et non pas objectivée. Dès lors ce qui fera l'objet de l'attention constante, dans ces études, c'est la situation du juriste chrétien (Ellis — *The christian lawyer as a Public Servant.* — Stringfellow — *The christian lawyer as a churchman*). Il se trouve, en effet, dans une situation de conflit non pas pris « entre » deux devoirs, avec un choix à faire entre les deux, mais situé au point de tension entre une réalité (celle du droit) et une vérité (celle de la Révélation) qui doivent toutes deux être maintenues, et qui ne peuvent l'être que dans la contradiction : il n'est question ni de fusion, ni de choix entre les deux, — et le problème n'est pas une simple question de conscience, une affaire purement intérieure : cela détermine un certain comportement envers le droit, un certain usage juridique, qui ne sont jamais fixés une fois pour toutes, qui ne peuvent s'exprimer un règles objectivables (mais qui pourraient contribuer à influencer une création coutumière du droit...). L'on a pu dire par exemple que le juriste chrétien a une personnalité « vicaire » dans la société. Il est appelé à représenter tous les types d'intérêts, il est un carrefour de rencontres, il peut être ouvert à toutes les réponses, à toutes les exigences, et c'est dans son comportement que peut se manifester la relation vraie entre la Révélation et le Droit, qui est une relation de vie, et non pas une relation abstraite (Stringfellow — *Poverty, christianity and law*).

***

Telles sont les principales lignes de recherche de ce mouvement, dont on voit aisément les incertitudes, la diversité des inspirations, mais qui manifeste un sérieux dans la considération du phénomène juridique, un effort de renouvellement de la pensée sur le droit, en temps même qu'il porte un témoignage sur une crise indiscutable de la société américaine, car lorsque ces questions évoquées ici sont soulevées, c'est une preuve que le droit traverse une crise de conscience, qui n'est que le reflet de celle de la société elle-même.